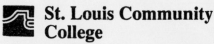

Running with the Devil

MUSIC / CULTURE

A series from Wesleyan University Press

Edited by George Lipsitz, Susan McClary, and Robert Walser

Published titles

My Music by Susan D. Crafts, Daniel Cavicchi, Charles Keil,
and the Music in Daily Life Project

*Running with the Devil: Power, Gender, and Madness in
Heavy Metal Music* by Robert Walser

Subcultural Sounds: Micromusics of the West by Mark Slobin

ROBERT WALSER

Running with the Devil

POWER, GENDER,

AND MADNESS IN HEAVY

METAL MUSIC

WESLEYAN UNIVERSITY PRESS

Published by University Press of New England

Hanover & London

WESLEYAN UNIVERSITY PRESS
Published by University Press of New England, Hanover, NH 03755
© 1993 by Robert Walser
All rights reserved
Printed in the United States of America 5 4 3 2 1
CIP data appear at the end of the book

Acknowledgments for song lyrics quoted:

"Electric Eye": Words and music by Glenn Tipton, Rob Halford, and K. K. Downing, © 1982 EMI APRIL MUSIC, INC. / CREWGLEN LTD. / EBONYTREE LTD. / GEARGATE LTD. All rights controlled and administered by EMI APRIL MUSIC, INC. International copyright secured. All rights reserved. Used by permission.

"Suicide Solution": Words and music by John Osbourne, Robert Daisley, and Randy Rhoads, TRO—© Copyright 1981 Essex Music International, Inc. and Kord Music Publishers, New York, N.Y. Used by permission.

Contents

5. Can I Play with Madness? Mysticism, Horror, and Postmodern Politics 137

Photographs follow page 107

Acknowledgments

*

I am grateful for the generosity of the nearly two hundred heavy metal fans who discussed their music and their lives with me, through interviews, casual conversations, and questionnaires; their assistance was invaluable in helping me to understand heavy metal. In contrast to the common stereotype of metal fans as sullen and inarticulate, I was surprised by the friendliness and enthusiasm I found among fans and musicians alike. Most fans were pleased to find someone taking their music seriously; they were eager to fill out the questionnaires I circulated at concerts, and far from having to persuade people to let me interview them, I received many more requests to do interviews than I could accomodate. In particular, I thank Peter Del Valle for helping me to set up my first interview with a group of fans.

I have learned from conversations about heavy metal and popular culture with many other people, particularly Chris Kachian, Csaba Toth, and Metal Mark of GMS. I thank Gary Thomas and the members of his Gay Studies class for an evening spent discussing heavy metal videos and gender construction. My work has benefited from the ideas and criticisms of my students at the University of Michigan, the University of Minnesota, and Dartmouth College, especially those in my Contemporary Popular Music Studies course at Michigan. Thanks also to my metal guitar teacher, Jeff Loven, and to the many other rock musicians I have performed with and learned from, especially Gene Retka, Steve Cekalla, James Capra, Dave Michel, John Helgen, and Gregg Ramseth.

William Shurk at Bowling Green State University is the knowledgeable curator of an enormous archive of popular music, including heavy metal recordings and fan magazines (many confiscated from fans by parents or police). I thank him for his assistance and for granting me access to materials that I found useful. For travel funds that enabled me to carry out that research and to present papers on heavy metal at a number of academic conferences, I thank the University of Minnesota, especially Vern Sutton and the School of Music, as well as the School of Music at the University of Michigan, and Dartmouth College. And I am pleased to have an opportunity to acknowledge the influence of Bruce Lincoln, who introduced me to cultural criticism and changed my life nearly fifteen years ago.

Several non-metal-fan friends were brave enough to overcome strong misgivings and accompany me to heavy metal concerts; I thank Bruce Holsinger, Chris Kachian, George Lipsitz, Susan McClary, and John Mowitt for the pleasure of their company and for their insights concerning what they saw and heard. It is regrettable that the only violence I ever witnessed at a heavy metal concert was committed by one of these people.

For their helpful comments on drafts and portions of this book, I thank Andrew Goodwin, Wendy Kozol, Carolyn Krasnow, Richard Leppert, John Mowitt, and Christopher Small. I am particularly grateful to those who read the entire book and provided much-needed corrections, provocations, and encouragement: Simon Frith, Dave Marsh, Terry Cochran, Charles Hamm, and Ross Chambers.

Finally, I owe my largest intellectual debt to Susan McClary and George Lipsitz. To put it simply, Susan taught me how to think about music, and George taught me how to think about popular culture. I feel proud and fortunate to have been their student and friend, and it is to them that I dedicate *Running with the Devil.*

November 1992   R.W.

Introduction

In the catacombs of a nineteenth-century warehouse, hulking in a run-down riverfront district, passageways wind through rough stonework to connect small rooms, each fronted by a sturdy iron door. Behind these doors musicians compose and rehearse through all hours of the day and night. Wandering the crooked hallways, I hear waves of sound clashing and coalescing: powerful drums and bass, menacing and ecstatic vocals, the heavy crunch of distorted electric guitars. In some rooms, lone guitarists practice scales, arpeggios, heavy metal riffs, and Bach transcriptions. Occasionally, I pass an open door, and musicians who are taking a break consider my presence with cool curiosity.

I am struck by the resemblance of these underground rehearsal spaces to the practice rooms of a conservatory. The decor is different, but the people are similar: musicians in their late teens and early twenties, assembled for long hours of rigorous practice. There is a parallel sense of isolation for the sake of musical craft and creativity, a kindred pursuit of technical development and group precision. And like conservatory students, many of these heavy metal musicians take private lessons, study music theory, and practice scales and exercises for hours every day. They also share the precarious economic future faced by classical musicians; in both cases, few will ever make enough money performing to compensate them for the thousands of hours they have practiced and rehearsed.

There are important differences from the conservatory environment, too, not the least of which is the grungy setting itself, which underlines the fact that this music does not enjoy institutional prestige or receive governmental subsidy. The musicians must pool their funds to pay for rental of the rooms, and the long hair that marks them as members of a heavy metal subculture also ensures that they are not likely to have access to jobs that pay well. On the other hand, many of these people are actually working as musicians, at least part-time. Unlike most of their peers in the academy, they know a great deal about the commercial channels to which they hope to gain access. Some talk of not compromising their art for popular success, but there is little evidence of the music academy's pretense that art can be pursued apart from commerce. This is in part because they are more closely connected with their potential audiences, through their own fan activities and those of their friends, while relatively few aspiring classical musicians actually belong to the moneyed class that underwrites the performance of classical music. Heavy metal musicians are, in fact, strongly influenced by the practices of the musical academy, but their activities also retain the priorities of collective creation and orality derived from traditions of popular music making.

The noisy vaults of that warehouse and the musicians who haunt them evoke images and raise issues that will be central to my discussions of heavy metal. If metal could be said to have gotten started in any single place, it would be Birmingham, England, the industrial city whose working class spawned Ozzy Osbourne, Black Sabbath, and Judas Priest in the late 1960s and early 1970s. That heavy metal bands now labor in spaces abandoned by industry is particularly appropriate for a music that has flourished during the period of American deindustrialization. And just as the labor of industrial production is invisible in mass media representations of consumer products, the musical labor that sustains and reinvents mass-mediated popular music often takes place in such marginal locations. Heavy metal is perhaps the single most successful and enduring musical genre of the past thirty years; yet it is in such dank cellars that many of its future stars serve their apprenticeships. This noisy basement is a good analogy for the position heavy metal occupies in the edifice of cultural prestige.

When I began writing about heavy metal in 1986, it seemed a strange thing for a cultural critic—let alone a musicologist—to do. Metal has been ignored or reviled, not only by academics of all stripes but even by most rock critics. Yet in the United States and many other countries, heavy metal was arguably the most important and influential musical genre of the 1980s; throughout the decade, it became increasingly clear that, between them, hip hop and heavy metal were redefining American popular music. Moreover, the debates surrounding heavy metal and the people who make it—over meaning, character, behavior, values, censorship, violence, alienation, and community—mark metal as an important site of cultural contestation. This is most obvious when attacks come from groups with overt moral missions, such as the Parents' Music Resource Center, Christian fundamentalist groups, rock critics, or academics. But intense reactions to heavy metal are widespread: a recent marketing survey found that ten million people in the United States "like or strongly like" heavy metal—and that nineteen million strongly dislike it, the largest backlash of any music category.[1] People care deeply about heavy metal, one way or another, which suggests that it engages with some fundamental social values and tensions.

Such strong reactions, along with heavy metal's sheer popularity, might seem sufficient justification for the study of heavy metal, since the genre embraces such a significant portion of the musical activity of our time. However, I was initially drawn to writing about metal not because of such a sociological or political mandate. Rather, I became interested in exploring heavy metal because I found the music compelling. Already active as a professional musician on other instruments, I began playing guitar in the late 1970s. I moved among bands and musical styles for several years, learning on stage rather than in a practice room, from other musicians instead of from sheet music or recordings, and in 1980 I found myself playing heavy metal before I had actually listened to much of it. As a performer, metal granted me access to its power almost immediately—it doesn't take long to learn to play power chords—yet its musical subtleties and technical demands continued to inspire and challenge me a decade later.

I once heard a prominent sociologist of popular music tell an audience that he actually had no interest in the music he had been studying for years. The reason he gave for having become involved with studying popular music, rather than some other "product," was that all of the other industries were taken. He was not embarrassed by this admission; rather, he seemed to take it as a point of pride, perhaps because he thought such objectivity would enhance his scholarly rigor. It seemed appropriate to have no particular investment in the products of the industry he studied; he thought it no more important to discuss or discriminate among musical texts than it would be to analyze individual tires or refrigerators.

To be sure, scholars who interpret cultural texts should notice the commercial processes and power struggles that make those texts available to their attention, as well as the social structures and tensions that make them meaningful. But to analyze popular culture only in terms of the commercial structures that mediate it is to "imagine markets free of politics."[2] Economics becomes an autonomous abstraction from a conflicted society, and the hard-nosed study of institutions and monetary power is but a false veneer of political engagement, masking a refusal to confront the political dimension of economic choices. As Christopher

Small asks those who discuss popular culture only in terms of production and consumption,

How do you "consume" music, when (a) music isn't a thing and (b) it's still there after you've used it—or you think you've used it. Just because the industry markets it as commodity doesn't mean we have to accept their terms of reference. It's time people stopped talking about "consuming" art and culture and so on and started thinking of art as an activity, something you do. Even buying and playing records are activities; the record is only the medium through which the activity takes place.[3]

Just as important, most scholars of popular music assume that recent mass-mediated music is somehow more "compromised" than earlier music by its involvement with commercial structures and interests. This is simply not true. Music has always been "commercial," at least since the Renaissance; that is, music has always been supported by the interests and patronage of particular social groups and enmeshed in institutional politics, mechanisms of distribution, and strategies of promotion.[4] If it makes sense to study specific operas as sites of the exchange and contestation of social meanings, rather than as interchangeable epiphenomena of a patronage structure, it makes equal sense to treat more recent popular texts with similar specificity and care.

As a musician, I cannot help but think that individual texts, and the social experiences they represent, are important. My apprenticeships as a performer—conservatory student and orchestral musician, ethnic outsider learning to play Polish polkas, jazz trumpeter, pop singer, and heavy metal guitarist—were periods spent learning musical discourses. That is, I had to acquire the ability to recognize, distinguish, and deploy the musical possibilities organized in styles or genres by various communities. Each song marshals the options available in a different way, and each musical occasion inflects a song's social meanings. Becoming a musician in any of the styles I have mentioned is a process of learning to understand and manipulate the differences intrinsic to a style, which are manifested differently in each text and performance. Unlike many scholars, I think it is possible to analyze, historicize, and write about these processes.

Moreover, I find some songs powerfully meaningful and others not; so do all of the fans and musicians I know. Some of us are better than others at explaining why we care about this song and not that one, but for most people, music is intimately involved with crucial feelings of identity and notions of community. This is where sociological approaches to the study of popular music have so often failed. For while I do not suggest that either technical training or performing experience are necessary prerequisites for insightful writing about popular music, one must be able to experience—not just discern—differences among musical texts, in order to avoid imposing an interpretation of monotony and singularity of meaning that fans and musicians do not recognize.

Accordingly, I have integrated methods of musical analysis, ethnography, and cultural cricitism in this study. Following the example of scholars of popular culture such as Janice Radway and ethnomusicologists like Steven Feld, I have tried to find out what real listeners hear and how they think about their activities. Along with those working in cultural studies, like John Fiske and George Lipsitz, I want to situate the texts and practices I study within a forthrightly politicized context of cultural struggle over values, power, and legitimacy. And finally, I owe an important debt to the few musicologists, such as Susan McClary and Christopher Small, who have discussed musical structures as social texts imbued with political significance.[5]

My interest is less in explicating texts or defining the history of a style than in analyzing the musical activities that produce texts and styles and make them socially significant. I find Christopher Small's notion of "musicking" helpful. Small revives the idea of music as a verb rather than a noun in order to challenge our common practice of analyzing and understanding music in terms of objects, which encourages abstract stylistic description and effaces the social activity that produces musical texts and experiences.[6] "Musicking" embraces composition, performance, listening, dancing—all of the social practices of which musical scores and recordings are merely one-dimensional traces. To understand heavy metal as musicking, I studied it from many aspects. I attended concerts, studied recordings, interviewed fans and musicians, took heavy metal guitar lessons, and read fan magazines, industry reports, and denunciations.[7] My goal was to find answers through a kind of cultural triangulation, using ethnography as a check on textual interpretation and developing ethnographic strategies out of my own and others' cultural analyses.

I have chosen to focus on the most popular examples of heavy metal —the bands with multiplatinum record sales and arena-filling concert tours, the bands named as exemplary by fan magazines and by the fans I consulted through questionnaires and interviews: Ozzy Osbourne, Iron Maiden, Judas Priest, Poison, Van Halen, Megadeth, Guns N' Roses, etc. While much interesting work could be done on less popular, "underground" metal subcultures, this study concentrates on massively popular heavy metal because that focus enables engagement with important contemporary debates over music, mass mediation, morality, and censorship. Like Stuart Hall, I see "the popular" as an important site of social contestation and formation, and I find unconvincing the common assumption that culture that exists either at the margins of society or among a prestigious elite is necessarily more important, interesting, complex, or profound than the culture of a popular mainstream.[8] Popular culture is important because that is where most people get their "entertainment" and information; it's where they find dominant definitions of themselves as well as alternatives, options to try on for size.

I have elected to concentrate primarily on music of the 1980s, since that is the music both my informants and I know best, and because that is the decade of heavy metal's greatest popularity and influence. I have not tried to write a full history of heavy metal, nor have I attempted a comprehensive study of its most important artists or works. Neither have I pursued a more tightly focused study of a particular style or performer. Rather, I have tried to begin establishing an analytic context within which such work could be undertaken by examining several aspects of heavy metal that I feel are crucial to its success and meaningfulness—to its power.

Most important, perhaps, I have tried to pay particular attention to the *music* of heavy metal, in ways that are both textually specific and culturally grounded. For like most musicians and fans, I respond more intensely to music than to words or pictures. Before I knew any lyrics, before I had even seen any of the major performers, I was attracted to heavy metal by specifically musical factors. Within the context of the other kinds of music I knew, I found the "language" of heavy metal— the coherent body of musical signs and conventions that distinguished it as a genre—powerful and persuasive. Much of this book will be concerned with what has been conspicuously absent from discussions of popular music, whether academic, journalistic, or moralistic: analysis of the specific musical choices embodied in individual songs and organized by genres. Musicians take such conventions and details seriously, and fans respond to them; critics and scholars cannot justify continuing to ignore them.[9]

Chapter 2 prepares for such discussions by sketching the terms of heavy metal as a discursive practice, as a coherent, though always changing, universe of significant sonic options. I examine heavy metal music as a social signifying system rather than an autonomous set of stylistic traits, employing an approach to musical analysis that construes musical details as significant gestural and syntactical units, organized by narrative and other formal conventions, and constituting a system for the social production of meaning—a discourse. This chapter dissects and discusses heavy metal music as a discourse, with reference to an example that is in many ways paradigmatic for the genre. Both this and the following chapter are fairly "guitarocentric," since the point is to get "beyond the vocals," and guitarists have been the primary composers and soloists of heavy metal music.

Chapter 3 focuses on the intersection of heavy metal and classical music, an example of what I call "discursive fusion." Makers of popular culture have always thrived on borrowing, customizing, and reinterpreting other peoples' cultural property; yet this aspect of popular music has received little analytical attention, for many critics remain influenced by ideologies of authenticity that accord a higher place to supposedly pure popular creations (e.g., "folk music"). Heavy metal musicians have appropriated musical materials from eighteenth- and nineteenth-century concert music, reworking what is now the most prestigious of musical discourses to serve the interests of what is now the least prestigious of musical communities. Chapter 3 examines this appropriation of musical signs as a case study in cultural politics, comparing means and ends across the sacrosanct boundaries of classical/popular and high/low culture.

In comparing the techniques of heavy metal musicians to those of classical musicians, I am not simply making a bid for academic legitimacy on behalf of the former. The point of such comparisons is to pursue what Bakhtin called "interillumination," his method of "de-privileging languages," or what Marcus and Fischer characterize as "defamiliarization by cross-cultural juxtaposition," part of their plan for remaking "anthropology as cultural critique."[10] It is to contribute to demystifying classical music's aura of transcendent autonomy and to debunking sterotypical notions of heavy metal's musical crudity. Arguing for the worth of popular music in the terms of valuation used for more prestigious music is not without risk: jazz has gained a certain amount of academic respectibility through such toil by its defenders, but at the cost of erasing much of the music's historical significance, its politics, its basis in non-European modes of musical thinking and doing. (Indeed, this is precisely what has happened to the many different kinds of historical music making that have been collapsed into "classical music" by our century.) However strange it might seem to compare heavy metal and classical music, heavy metal musicians themselves have already accomplished this juxtaposition, and we must reach beyond accepted cultural categories to understand what they are doing. Such comparisons reveal much about both musics and challenge hegemonic assumptions about "trained" musicians and "serious" music.

Chapter 4 takes up issues of gender in heavy metal. Since the social contexts within which heavy metal circulates (primarily Western societies in the late twentieth century) are highly patriarchal, it is not surprising to find that an important concern of metal is to represent male power and female subordination. Music, lyrics, visual images, and behavior serve to construct gender identities, infusing them with power and implying that they are natural and desirable. These representations primarily serve the interests of the male musicians who dominate heavy metal performance and the male fans who until recently were their primary constituency. Through discussion of heavy metal songs and videos, I trace four strategies for dealing with the "threat" women embody to patriarchy. But as a genre that now boasts a gender-balanced audience, heavy metal depictions of gender identities and relationships must offer credible positions for women. In small part this is accomplished by female metal musicians, who search for a style that will articulate their contradictory position as women and performers. But women are more often offered heavy metal empowerment through adaptations of the ideology of romance, the ambiguous implications of androgyny, and their increasing ability to identify with constructions of power that had previously been understood as inherently male. This chapter, more than the others, explicitly analyzes music videos because of the connections that exist in contemporary Western cultures among music, gender, and spectacularity.[11]

Chapter 5 assesses the significance of violence and mysticism in heavy metal. I begin with recent critiques, controversies, and court cases involving heavy metal, including debates over suicide and censorship. Through discussions of selected songs, I argue that while it is clear that some heavy metal music does articulate struggle, madness, violence, and disorientation, metal does not invent or inject these affective states; instead, it mediates social tensions, working to provide its fans with a sense of spiritual depth and social integration. Many people who condemn heavy metal accept historically contingent formations of youth, socialization, and deviance as absolutes: "Heavy metal's subject matter is simple and virtually universal. It celebrates teenagers' newfound feelings of rebellion and sexuality. The bulk of the music is stylized and formulaic."[12] But such characterizations essentialize the category of youth, removing it from history and depoliticizing it. Heavy metal fans do tend to be young, and this is surely relevant to any explanation of its appeal; but youth itself must be understood within a larger social framework, as a category constructed by ideological labor. And the rebellious or transgressive aspects of heavy metal, its exploration of the dark side of social life, also reflect its engagement with the pressures of a historical moment.

For rebellion and escapism are always movements away from something, toward something else. Rebellion is critique; whether apparently effectual or not, it is politics. But even more important, what seems like rejection, alienation, or nihilism is usually better seen as an attempt to create an alternative identity that is grounded in a vision or the actual experience of an alternative community. Heavy metal's fascination with the dark side of life gives evidence of both dissatisfaction with dominant identities and institutions and an intense yearning for reconciliation with something more credible.[13] To explain this side of metal as the pathological imprint of malicious musicians or as adolescent socialization gone awry (as is often done) is to dehistoricize the specific forms and practices of heavy metal.

For I simply don't find persuasive arguments that explain heavy metal in terms of deviance. The context for this study is the United States during the 1970s and 1980s, a period that saw a series of damaging economic crises, unprecedented revelations of corrupt political leadership, erosion of public confidence in governmental and corporate benevolence, cruel retrenchment of social programs along with policies that favored the wealthy, and tempestuous contestation of social institutions and representations, involving formations that had been thought to be stable, such as gender roles and the family. This social climate, besides shaping lyrical concerns and distributive networks, provided the context within which heavy metal became meaningful for millions of people. Heavy metal is intimately embedded in the social system of values and practices that its critics defend.

Chapter 1, then, situates heavy metal as a cultural practice that is historically constituted and socially contested; it examines how "heavy metal" means different things to the variety of people who are involved with it—fans, musicians, historians, critics, academics, censors. I trace the history of heavy metal as it has been assembled by critics, fans, and musicians and then discuss ongoing disputes over the boundaries of the genre, emphasizing the divergent interests of fans, musicians, critics, fan magazines, and other commercial mediators. A summary of the characteristics, activities, and beliefs of heavy metal fans is followed by discussion of the very different interpretations of those activities provided by academics and rock critics.

I have intersected the texts and debates of metal fans and musicians with analytical and historical perspectives that are sometimes foreign to that experience but find common ground in my arguments for the cultural coherence of that experience. This study is organized around the issues that fans and musicians, through their activities and statements and the music itself, have indicated are central to the power and meaning of heavy metal. But it also reflects my own position as an academic and cultural critic, and it engages with ongoing arguments about music and culture that not all readers will find interesting or important. In some circles, for example, it is still necessary to argue that music can be analyzed as having social meaning; readers who are willing to grant this point may wish to skip over parts of chapter 2.

In my attempts to make sense of heavy metal, I have learned from and taken issue with the arguments of sociologists, musicologists, rock critics, and cultural theorists because I have found such interdisciplinary inquiry the only adequate approach to the study of something as complex as popular music. While heavy metal appears as the object of study of my cultural and musicological investigation, I have tried through my engagement with heavy metal to raise larger questions about the politics of culture, recent American history, "classical" music, and the nature of musical discourses, experience, and analysis.

The specific sites of metal activity—concert arenas, clubs, record stores, warehouse rehearsal rooms, fans' bedrooms and cars—may be distant and unfamiliar to many people. Similarly, the musical discourses of metal are grounded in semiotic codes that are widely shared but often drawn upon by metal musicians precisely to articulate alienating noise and exclusivity. *Running with the Devil* attempts to resituate heavy metal within contemporary debates over music and cultural politics without muting that noise. It offers some explanations of how heavy metal works and why people care about it.

Running with the Devil

CHAPTER ONE

Metallurgies

Genre, History, and the Construction of Heavy Metal

I have been invited to try my hand at explaining heavy-metal music.
First, heavy metal is power. . . .   —Rob Halford of Judas Priest[1]

The Oxford English Dictionary traces "heavy metal" back through nearly
two hundred years. In the late twentieth century, the term has two
primary meanings: for chemists and metallurgists, it labels a group of
elements and toxic compounds; for the rest of us, it refers to a kind
of music. But these meanings are not unrelated. Even in the nineteenth century, "heavy metal" was both a technical term and a figurative,
social one:

1828   Webster s.v., *Heavy metal*, in military affairs, signifies large guns, carrying
balls of a large size, or it is applied to the balls themselves.

1882   Ogilvie s.v., *Heavy metal*, guns or shot of large size; hence, *fig.* ability,
mental or bodily; power, influence; as, he is a man of heavy metal; also, a person
or persons of great ability or power, mental or bodily; used generally of one
who is or is to be another's opponent in any contest; as, we had to do with heavy
metal. (Colloq.)[2]

"Heavy metal," in each of its parts and as a compound, evoked power
and potency. A "man of heavy metal" was powerful and daunting, and
the *OED* vividly confirms a long-standing social conflation of power
and patriarchal order. The long history of "heavy metal" in the English
language resonates with modern usage, even as contemporary musicians converse with the musical past in their work. "Heavy metal" is
not simply a recently invented genre label; its meaning is indebted to
the historical circulation of images, qualities, and metaphors, and it was
applied to particular musical practices because it made social sense to
do so.

"Heavy metal" now denotes a variety of musical discourses, social practices, and cultural meanings, all of which revolve around concepts, images, and experiences of power. The loudness and intensity of heavy metal music visibly empower fans, whose shouting and headbanging testify to the circulation of energy at concerts.[3] Metal energizes the body, transforming space and social relations. The visual language of metal album covers and the spectacular stage shows offer larger-than-life images tied to fantasies of social power, just as in the more prestigious musical spectacles of opera. The clothing and hairstyles of metal fans, as much as the music itself, mark social spaces from concert halls to bedrooms to streets, claiming them in the name of a heavy metal community. And all of these aspects of power provoke strong reactions from those outside heavy metal, including fear and censorship.

The names chosen by heavy metal bands evoke power and intensity in many different ways. Bands align themselves with electrical and mechanical power (Tesla, AC/DC, Mötorhead), dangerous or unpleasant animals (Ratt, Scorpions), dangerous or unpleasant people (Twisted Sister, Mötley Crüe, Quiet Riot), or dangerous and unpleasant objects (Iron Maiden). They can invoke the auratic power of blasphemy or mysticism (Judas Priest, Black Sabbath, Blue Öyster Cult) or the terror of death itself (Anthrax, Poison, Megadeth, Slayer). Heavy metal can even claim power by being self-referential (Metallica) or by transgressing convention with an antipower name (Cinderella, Kiss). Some bands add umlauts (Motörhead, Mötley Crüe, Queensrÿche) to mark their names as archaic or gothic.[4]

If there is one feature that underpins the coherence of heavy metal as a genre, it is the power chord. Produced by playing the musical interval of a perfect fourth or fifth on a heavily amplified and distorted electric guitar, the power chord is used by all of the bands that are ever called heavy metal and, until heavy metal's enormous influence on other musical genres in the late 1980s, by comparatively few musicians outside the genre. The power chord can be percussive and rhythmic or indefinitely sustained; it is used both to articulate and to suspend time. It is a complex sound, made up of resultant tones and overtones, constantly renewed and energized by feedback. It is at once the musical basis of heavy metal and an apt metaphor for it, for musical articulation of power is the most important single factor in the experience of heavy metal. The power chord seems simple and crude, but it is dependent upon sophisticated technology, precise tuning, and skillful control. Its overdriven sound evokes excess and transgression but also stability, permanence, and harmony.

But what is the nature of this power? Where does it come from, how is it generated, mobilized, circulated? How can heavy metal music articulate claims to power, and what social tensions are addressed or mediated by it? These are the issues that animate this book. In chapter 2, I will take up the problem of defining heavy metal structurally, as a musical discourse comprising a coherent system of signs such as power chords. In this one, I will be concerned with a more functional view of heavy metal as a genre, with the processes of definition and contestation that go on among those concerned with the music. In other words, I will be focusing here on how heavy metal gets construed—by fans, historians, academics, and critics.[5] The essential characteristics of heavy metal not only vary according to these different perspectives, but the very existence of something called heavy metal depends upon the ongoing arguments of those involved. Heavy metal is, like all culture, a site of struggle over definitions, dreams, behaviors, and resources.

Genre and Commercial Mediation

Discursive practices are characterized by the delimitation of a field of objects, the definition of a legitimate perspective for the agent of knowledge, and the fixing of norms for the elaboration of concepts and theories. Thus, each discursive practice implies a play of prescriptions that designate its exclusions and choices. —Michel Foucault[6]

I hate that term "heavy metal." —Angus Young, AC/DC

Heavy metal began to attain stylistic identity in the late 1960s as a "harder" sort of hard rock, and a relatively small but fiercely loyal subculture formed around it during the 1970s. Because heavy metal threatened to antagonize demographically targeted audiences, metal bands received virtually no radio airplay, and they had to support their album releases by constant touring, playing to an audience that was mostly young, white, male, and working class.[7] The 1980s was the decade of heavy metal's emergence as a massively popular musical style, as it burgeoned in both commercial success and stylistic variety. The heavy metal audience became increasingly gender-balanced and middle-class, and its age range expanded to include significant numbers of preteens and people in their late twenties. By 1989, heavy metal accounted for as much as 40 percent of all sound recordings sold in the United States, and *Rolling Stone* announced that heavy metal now constituted "the mainstream of rock and roll."[8] By then, metal had diversified into a number of styles and influenced other musical discourses. The term "heavy metal" itself became an open site of contestation, as fans, musicians, and historians struggled with the prestige—and notoriety—of a genre name that seemed no longer able to contain disparate musical styles and agendas.

Thus, heavy metal is not monolithic; it embraces many different musical and visual styles, many kinds of lyrics and behaviors. "Heavy metal" is a term that is constantly debated and contested, primarily among fans but also in dialogue with musicians, commercial marketing strategists, and outside critics and censors. Debates over which bands, songs, sounds, and sights get to count as heavy metal provide occasions for contesting musical and social prestige. "That's not heavy metal" is the most damning music criticism a fan can inflict, for that genre name has great prestige among fans. But genre boundaries are not solid or clear; they are conceptual sites of struggles over the meanings and prestige of social signs.

Fans care, often passionately, about difference; they find certain bands and songs meaningful and relevant to their lives, while others leave them indifferent or repulsed. But there are institutional pressures for a kind of generic coherence that effaces such distinctions. Fan magazines try to apply "heavy metal" very broadly, to attract as many readers as possible. But their editors must negotiate discursive boundaries cautiously. Magazines that define themselves as wholly or primarily about heavy metal strive to appear as inclusive as possible, in part to advise fans on new bands or even to market those new bands for the sake of record company sponsors, but also because every fan wants to read about (and look at pictures of) his or her favorites in every issue. On the other hand, to include bands that fans do not accept as metal would weaken the magazine's credibility and the fans' enjoyment of the heavy metal "world" portrayed.[9]

Record clubs ("Grab Ten Headbanging Hits for 1¢!") and fan merchandisers work to produce a notion of heavy metal that is inclusive and indiscriminate, just as in classical music, where orchestra advertising, music appreciation books, and record promoters campaign to erase historical specificity in order to stimulate consumption. And just as the promoters of classical music offer encounters with unspecified "greatness," those who market heavy metal present it vaguely, as participation in generalized rebellion and intensity.[10] But in both cases the coherence of the genre and the prestige of its history are crucial concerns of the music industry. An executive for Polygram Records describes the company's success in mobilizing a sense of heavy metal history as a marketing tool: "We used an in-store campaign for Deep Purple that emphasized peer pressure. Many of the potential buyers of DP records are too young to remember the band in its previous incarnation. So we had to instill in these young metal fans that they were not really hip, not dedicated headbangers until they knew about Deep Purple. The campaign was very successful."[11]

Rigid genre boundaries are more useful to the music industry than to fans, and the commercial strategy of hyping cultural genres while striving to obliterate the differences that make individual choices meaningful often works very effectively to mobilize efficient consumption (nowhere more so than in classical music). But not always. The consequences of such a coarse view of heavy metal can be seen in the failure of the biggest metal concert tour of 1988. Touted as the heavy metal event of the decade, the Monsters of Rock tour during the summer of 1988 was a mammoth disappointment for fans and promoters alike. At the moment of heavy metal's greatest popularity ever, several of the world's most successful heavy metal bands were assembled for a U.S. tour: Van Halen, Scorpions, Metallica, Dokken, and Kingdom Come. These were some of the biggest names in metal, yet attendance throughout the tour was surprisingly light, and it became clear that the promoters who had assembled the tour suffered substantial losses because they had misunderstood the genre of heavy metal: they saw it as monolithic, failing to realize that heavy metal and its audience are not homogeneous, that fans' allegiances are complex and specific. Many fans came to the Monsters of Rock concerts just to hear one or two bands; many Metallica fans, for example, despise bands like Scorpions and Kingdom Come. Waves of partisan arrivals and departures at the concert helped defuse the excitement normally generated in full arenas, and the fans' selective attendance undercut the concession and souvenir sales that are so important to underwriting tour expenses and profits.[12]

The crude assumptions about genre that sank the Monsters of Rock tour are also endemic in writings about metal, from the rectitudinous denunciations of would-be censors to sociologists' "objective" explanations—nearly everywhere, in fact, but in the magazines read by the fans themselves, where such totalizing errors could never be taken seriously. Outsiders' representations of heavy metal as monolithic stand in stark contrast to the fans' views, which prize difference and specificity. Because the magazines present heavy metal as exciting and prestigious at the same time that they apply the term more broadly than most fans can accept, the magazine itself becomes a site for contestation of the term. Writers of record reviews and articles gain credibility with their readers by arguing for distinctions that may contradict the inclusive stance of the magazine itself. But fans also contribute their perspectives directly through the letters columns that begin each issue. For example, one fan wrote to offer his canon of the best metal bands; his letter is emphatic about the importance of genre, and he sees "heavy metal" as a distinction of great value, something that can be attained and then lost:

Some other good groups are Accept, from Germany, and Exciter, Heaven, Twisted Sister, Girls School, Wild Dogs and so many others. Van Halen was once Heavy Metal but they got stuck on themselves. Van Halen is now what we refer to as "Bubblegum" hard rock. Loverboy, ZZ Top and Zebra are all hard rock. There is a difference between hard rock and Heavy Metal. Heavy Metal is actually a "New Wave" music for the 80s.[13]

Another fan addressed the controversial split between glam and speed metal, rebutting the many hostile letters that disparage one side or the other. She takes a liberal stance that retains the label "heavy metal" for her favorite band but acknowledges the merit of its incompatible cousins: "Poison and Metallica shouldn't even be compared really. Poison is heavy metal. Metallica is speed metal. Poison is good at what they do, and Metallica is good at what they do."[14] The letters columns of magazines like *RIP* or *Hit Parader* also serve as forums for other kinds of debates, including discussions of sexism, homophobia, and racism. Fans often write in to critique the representations of gender and race they find in heavy metal lyrics, interviews with musicians, and journalism.[15]

Musicians who are considered heavy metal by their fans may vary greatly in their allegiance to the genre. Judas Priest's goal has been "to achieve the *definition* of heavy metal," while members of AC/DC and Def Leppard claim to hate the term, even though all three bands are mainstay subjects of heavy metal fandom.[16] Many writers and fans consider Led Zeppelin the fount of heavy metal: "Quite simply, Led Zeppelin is, was, and will always be the ultimate heavy metal masters."[17] But Zeppelin's lead singer, Robert Plant, rejects that characterization, saying, for example, of the band's first album, "That was not heavy metal. There was nothing heavy about that at all. . . . It was ethereal."[18]

There are many reasons for bands to position themselves carefully with respect to a genre label. Their account of their relationship to heavy metal can imply or deny historical and discursive connections to other music. But more important, it situates them with respect to audiences, interpretative norms, and institutional channels. Guitarist Yngwie Malmsteen denies any connection with metal out of contempt for a genre that he views as technically and aesthetically inferior to his own music. Malmsteen hopes to gain greater prestige as an artist than is normally granted to metal musicians, but he is also bidding for the radio play that is often denied them.[19] Iron Maiden has always depended on selling tickets and albums to hard-core metal fans; they have no other audience. Yet the group's singer, Bruce Dickenson, affects nonchalance when discussing the genre and their place in it: "What is your viewpoint? I wouldn't call UFO a heavy metal band, but if you happen to be a fan of Human League, they probably are. And if you're a fan of

Motorhead, UFO aren't heavy metal. If we said we are heavy metal, it wouldn't matter much in the way we sound. It's a category."[20] Many artists bridle at genre categories because they see them as restrictive stereotypes, implying formulaic composition. Dickenson resists being pigeonholed by pointing to the relative, rather than absolute, nature of genre distinctions. But he must feign indifference to the meaningfulness of genre to fans and institutions in order to claim this appearance of artistic freedom.

The music of Rush meets the criteria of the definition of heavy metal held by most outsiders but fails the standards of most metal fans. Geddy Lee, the band's singer and bass player, muses on the problematic status of his band: "It's funny. When you talk to metal people about Rush, eight out of ten will tell you that we're not a metal band. But if you talk to anyone outside of metal, eight out of ten will tell you we *are* a metal band. *Metal* is a very broad term."[21] There is, of course, a great deal of coherence in the genre of heavy metal; there are many bands that would be considered metal by virtually all fans. But genres are defined not only through internal features of the artists or the texts but also through commercial strategies and the conflicting valorizations of audiences. These debates over heavy metal are grounded in historical formations of meaning and prestige. To understand the priorities and values of heavy metal musicians and fans, we will need to examine their history.

Casting Heavy Metal

The term "heavy metal" has been applied to popular music since the late 1960s, when it began to appear in the rock press as an adjective; in the early 1970s it became a noun and thus a genre. The spectacular increase in the popularity of heavy metal during the 1980s prompted many critics and scholars of popular music to begin to write metal's history. In histories of rock and of American music, in encyclopedias of popular music, in books and periodicals aimed at the dedicated metal fan or the quizzical outsider, writers began to construct a history of the genre. These historians have all understood their task similarly: they have attempted to define the boundaries of a musical genre and to produce a narrative of the formation and development of that genre, usually in the context of the history of rock music. The best of these histories, such as Philip Bashe's *Heavy Metal Thunder* or Wolf Marshall's articles in *Guitar for the Practicing Musician*, are insightful and lucid, written by journalists with intimate knowledge of the bands and their fans.[22]

Histories typically begin with a problem most writers regard as essential: the question of the origin of the term "heavy metal." The first appearance of "heavy metal" in a song lyric is generally agreed to be in Steppenwolf's "Born to Be Wild," a hit motorcycle anthem of 1968, celebrating the "heavy metal thunder" of life in the fast lane. But the term "heavy metal," we are usually told, had burst into popular consciousness in 1962, with the U.S. publication of William S. Burroughs's novel *Naked Lunch*, a beat junkie's fantasies and confessions of drugs, sleaze, and violent sex. Burroughs is often credited with inventing the term and sometimes even with inspiring the genre. Some sources claim that Steppenwolf lifted the phrase directly from Burroughs's book, although no one has provided any evidence for that link.

This story of the origin of "heavy metal" appears in nearly every recounting of metal's history.[23] It is, however, not only simplistic but wrong, since the phrase "heavy metal" does not actually appear anywhere in *Naked Lunch* (although a later novel by Burroughs, *Nova Express* (1964), introduces as characters "The Heavy Metal Kid" and the "Heavy Metal People of Uranus"). At some point this notion of origin got planted in rock journalism, and the appeal of a clear point of origin led others to perpetuate the error.[24] But as we are reminded by *The Oxford English Dictionary*, "heavy metal" enjoyed centuries of relevant usage as a term for ordnance and poisonous compounds. The longstanding use of the phrase as a technical term in chemistry, metallurgy, and discussions of pollution suggests that the term did not spring full-blown into public awareness from an avant-garde source. "Heavy metal poisoning" is a diagnosis that has long had greater cultural currency than Burroughs's book has had, and the scientific and medical uses of the term "heavy metal" are even cognate, since they infuse the music with values of danger and weight, desirable characteristics in the eyes of late 1960s rock musicians. The evidence suggests that the term circulated long before Steppenwolf or even Burroughs and that its meaning is rich and associative rather than an arbitrary label invented at some moment. Eventually, "heavy metal" began to be used to refer specifically to popular music in the early 1970s, in the writings of Lester Bangs and Dave Marsh at *Creem*.

A heavy metal genealogy ought to trace the music back to African-American blues, but this is seldom done. Just as histories of North America begin with the European invasion, the histories of musical genres such as rock and heavy metal commonly begin at the point of white dominance. But to emphasize Black Sabbath's contribution of occult concerns to rock is to forget Robert Johnson's struggles with the Devil and Howlin' Wolf's meditations on the problem of evil. To trace heavy metal vocal style to Led Zeppelin's Robert Plant is to forget James Brown's "Cold Sweat." To deify white rock guitarists like Eric Clapton or Jimmy Page is to forget the black American musicians they were trying to copy; to dwell on the prowess of these guitarists is to relegate Jimi Hendrix, the most virtuosic rock guitarist of the 1960s, to the fringes of music history. The debt of heavy metal to African-American music making has vanished from most accounts of the genre, just as black history as been suppressed in every other field.

Rock historians usually begin the history of heavy metal with the white (usually British) musicians who were copying urban blues styles. Mid-1960s groups like the Yardbirds, Cream, and the Jeff Beck Group combined the rock and roll style of Chuck Berry with the earthy blues of Muddy Waters and Howlin' Wolf. Along with Jimi Hendrix, these British blues bands developed the sounds that would define metal: heavy drums and bass, virtuosic distorted guitar, and a powerful vocal style that used screams and growls as signs of transgression and transcendence. The Kinks released the first hit song built around power chords in 1964, "You Really Got Me." Some credit Jimi Hendrix with the first real heavy metal hit, the heavily distorted, virtuosic "Purple Haze" of 1967. Blue Cheer, a San Francisco psychedelic band, extended the frontiers of loudness, distortion, and feedback (but not virtuosity) with their defiantly crude cover version of "Summertime Blues," a hit single in 1968, the same year Steppenwolf released "Born to Be Wild."

We had a place in forming that heavy-metal sound. Although I'm not saying we knew what we were doing, 'cause we didn't. All we knew was we wanted more power. And if that's not a heavy-metal attitude, I don't know what is.
    —Dick Peterson, singer/bass player with Blue Cheer[25]

These groups of the late 1960s, now identified as early heavy metal bands, favored lyrics that evoked excess and transgression. Some, such as MC5 and Steppenwolf, linked their noisiness to explicit political critique in their lyrics; others, like Blue Cheer, identified with the San Francisco–based psychedelic bands, for whom volume and heaviness aided an often drug-assisted search for alternative formations of identity and community. Inspired by the guitar virtuosity and volume of Jimi Hendrix and Eric Clapton, late 1960s rock bands developed a musical language that used distortion, heavy beats, and sheer loudness to create music that sounded more powerful than any other.[26] Groups like Iron Butterfly and Vanilla Fudge added organ to the musical mix; like the electric guitar, the organ is capable of sustained, powerful sounds as well as virtuosic soloing, and the combination of both resulted in an aural wall of heavy sound. Iron Butterfly's *In-A-Gadda-Da-Vida* (1969), featuring the seventeen-minute title tune with its interminable drum solo, became the biggest-selling album Atlantic Records had ever had. Drummers of the late 1960s hit their drums very hard, resulting in a sound that was not only louder but heavier, more emphatic. Their drum sets grew ever larger and more complicated, along with the expansion of concert amplification and guitar distortion devices.

The sound that would become known as heavy metal was definitively codified in 1970 with the release of *Led Zeppelin II*, Black Sabbath's *Paranoid*, and *Deep Purple in Rock*. Joe Elliot, now lead vocalist for Def Leppard, recalls this moment, which he lived as a young fan: "In 1971, there were only three bands that mattered. Led Zeppelin, Black Sabbath, and Deep Purple."[27] Led Zeppelin's sound was marked by speed and power, unusual rhythmic patterns, contrasting terraced dynamics, singer Robert Plant's wailing vocals, and guitarist Jimmy Page's heavily distorted crunch. Their songs were often built around thematic hooks called riffs, a practice derived from urban blues music and extended by British imitators such as Eric Clapton (e.g., "Sunshine of Your Love").[28] In their lyrics and music, Led Zeppelin added mysticism to hard rock through evocations of the occult, the supernatural, Celtic legend, and Eastern modality. Deep Purple's sound was similar but with organ added and with greater stress on classical influences; Baroque figuration abounds in the solos of guitarist Ritchie Blackmore and keyboardist Jon Lord.[29] Black Sabbath took the emphasis on the occult even further, using dissonance, heavy riffs, and the mysterious whine of vocalist Ozzy Osbourne to evoke overtones of gothic horror.

A "second generation of heavy metal," the first to claim the name unambiguously, was also active throughout the 1970s: Kiss, AC/DC, Aerosmith, Judas Priest, Ted Nugent, Rush, Motörhead, Rainbow, Blue Öyster Cult. Scorpions, from Germany, became the first heavy metal band from a non-English-speaking country to achieve international success. Heavy metal shows became increasingly spectacular as musicians performed in front of elaborate stage sets to the accompaniment of light shows, pyrotechnics, and other special effects. Incessant touring of these impressive shows built the metal audience in the 1970s. Kiss, between 1974 and 1984, made nineteen albums, seventeen of which went gold (thirteen went platinum) with virtually no radio airplay.[30] Many of the most successful performers of heavy metal, like Judas Priest and Iron Maiden, have never had a Top 40 single.

The rise of heavy metal was simultaneous with the rise of professional rock criticism, but their relationship was not cordial. Flushed with enthusiasm for the artistic importance of rock music, critics were deeply suspicious of commercially successful music, which smacked of "sell-out" because it appealed to too many people. Many critics were also hostile toward visual spectacle, which they saw as commercial artifice, compromising rock music's "authenticity." With the exception of some writers at *Creem*, they abhorred the face paint and fantastic costumes of Kiss, the macabre theatricality of Alice Cooper, and the fireworks, smoke, and unearthly props of everyone else in heavy metal. The pronouncements of the critics had little effect on the loyalties of heavy metal fans, for whom the concert experience remained primary: Led Zeppelin's 1973 tour of the United States set new concert attendance records, breaking the previous records held by the Beatles. However, critics contributed to the establishment of heavy metal as a genre, since such labels were useful to them, as they were to the music industry, then in a phase of commercial growth and diversification (including increasingly specialized radio formats).

Heavy metal record sales slumped severely during the second half of the 1970s, as attention shifted to disco, punk, and mainstream rock bands like Fleetwood Mac. Writing for posterity in 1977, Lester Bangs summarized: "As the Seventies drew to a close, it appeared that heavy metal had had it." Bangs described metal's obsolescence: "What little flair and freshness remained in heavy metal has been stolen by punk rockers like the Ramones and Sex Pistols, who stripped it down, sped it up and provided some lyric content beyond the customary macho breast-beatings, by now not only offensive but old-fashioned."[31] Bangs's description of that moment was a fair one, but the 1980s saw the growth of heavy metal on a scale none had imagined.

Heavy Metal in the 1980s

During the 1980s, heavy metal was transformed from the moribund music of a fading subculture into the dominant genre of American music. Eddie Van Halen had revolutionized metal guitar technique with the release of Van Halen's debut album in 1978, fueling a renaissance in electric guitar study and experimentation unmatched since thousands of fans were inspired to learn to play by Eric Clapton's apotheosis in the late 1960s and Jimi Hendrix's death in 1970. But the real boom occurred with what became known as the "new wave of British heavy metal," around the turn of the decade. The United States was overrun by another "British invasion," as important for metal as the Beatles and Rolling Stones had been fifteen years earlier for pop music. Singer Joe Elliot recalls: "As years went on, hard rock did feel a certain loss of popularity with record audiences. But around 1979 or '80, it came back again. Suddenly, there was us [Def Leppard], Iron Maiden and Saxon doing really well."[32] Bands like Iron Maiden and Motörhead exported very different styles of music, but they all were experienced as a wave of renewal for the genre of heavy metal. For the most part, the new wave of metal featured shorter, catchier songs, more sophisticated production techniques, and higher technical standards. All of these characteristics helped pave the way toward greater popular success.

The next wave of metal came out of Los Angeles around 1983–84. Mötley Crüe and Ratt spearheaded a revival of "glam" metal androgyny, and other L.A. bands, like Quiet Riot, Dokken, and W.A.S.P., gained international attention. Southern California emerged as the center of heavy metal music for the 1980s, and bands from other parts of the country, among them Poison and Guns N' Roses, flocked to Los Angeles in hopes of getting signed to a major label contract. In 1983, Def Leppard released *Pyromania*, the album that brought them stardom, leading the metal boom of the following year. In 1983, heavy metal records accounted for only 8 percent of all recordings sold in the United States; one year later, that share had increased phenomenally, to 20 percent.[33] Dokken, Iron Maiden, Mötley Crüe, Ratt, Twisted Sister, and Scorpions rode the crest of this new success.

The following year, bands from around the world joined in the metal boom: Japan's Loudness, Sweden's Europe, and Germany's Scorpions all achieved widespread acceptance, not only in their homelands but also among English-speaking fans. Swedish guitar virtuoso Yngwie Malmsteen had comparatively less commercial success with his albums of 1984–88, but his extension of metal's neoclassical tendencies greatly influenced other heavy metal guitarists. Malmsteen's fusion of heavy metal with Baroque musical rhetoric upped the ante for technical prowess and inspired legions of young imitators.[34] Heavy metal fan magazines proliferated in France (*Hard Force*, *Hard Rock*), Italy (*HM*, *Heavy Metal*, *Rockstar*, *Flash*), and Germany (*Rock Hard*, *Horror Infernal*, *Metalstar*, *Breakout*, *Metal Hammer*), just as new magazines appeared in the United States and Britain (*RIP* and many others), and already established rock and pop magazines began focusing exclusively on metal (*Hit Parader*, *Circus*).

The popularity of heavy metal continued to increase throughout the decade. *Billboard* attributed this trend in the economy of American popular music to a shift in the subcultural support of metal: "Metal has broadened its audience base. Metal music is no longer the exclusive domain of male teenagers. The metal audience has become older (college-aged), younger (pre-teen), and more female."[35] The release of Bon Jovi's third album, *Slippery When Wet*, in 1986 was an important moment in this transformation of the metal audience, for Bon Jovi fused the intensity and heaviness of metal with the romantic sincerity of pop and the "authenticity" of rock, helping to create a huge new gender-balanced audience for heavy metal.[36] Bon Jovi's success not only reshaped metal's musical discourse and sparked imitations and extensions, but it also gained metal substantial radio airplay for the first time. A *Billboard* writer summarized: "Many credit the mass-appeal success of Bon Jovi's 'You Give Love a Bad Name' last summer with opening programmers' ears to the merits of metal. Others give a nod to Motley Crue's "Smokin' in the Boys Room" for dispelling the notion that top 40 and hard rock don't mix. Metal and hard rock have fallen between the programming cracks because of their predominantly teen appeal."[37]

In December 1986, MTV significantly increased the amount of heavy metal it programmed, initiating a special program called "Headbangers' Ball" and putting more metal videos into their regular rotation. The response was tremendous; "Headbangers' Ball" became MTV's most popular show, with 1.3 million viewers each week.[38] Heavy metal's spectacular live shows made it a natural for television, where its important visual dimension could be exploited and presented virtually unchanged. Once heavy metal achieved access to the airwaves, its popularity and influence increased sharply. In June 1987, the number-one album on the *Billboard* charts was by U2, but the next five places were held by metal bands: Whitesnake, Bon Jovi, Poison, Mötley Crüe, and Ozzy Osbourne/Randy Rhoads. For the rest of the decade, metal usually accounted for at least half of the top twenty albums on the charts.[39]

The expansion of the metal scene during the 1980s, however, was accompanied by its fragmentation. Genres proliferated: magazine writers and record marketers began referring to thrash metal, commercial metal, lite metal, power metal, American metal, black (satanic) metal, white (Christian) metal, death metal, speed metal, glam metal—each of which bears a particular relationship to that older, vaguer, more prestigious term "heavy metal."[40] Just as one of the major musical debates of nineteenth-century Europe was over who should be considered Beethoven's musical heir (Wagner versus Brahms), metal bands and fans continually position the music they care about with respect to a lineage dating back to the late 1960s founders: Led Zeppelin, Black Sabbath, and Deep Purple. Though allegiances were often complex and genre boundaries blurred, two main camps formed during the 1980s.

On the one hand, there was the metal of the broad new audience forged during the mid-1980s by bands like Mötley Crüe and Bon Jovi. This was the heavy metal on the sales charts, with radio play, the metal seen on MTV and at huge arena concerts. On the other hand, a different camp disparaged the newfound popularity of what they call lite metal or the music of "posers." These fans and bands attempted to sustain the marginal status metal enjoyed during the 1970s; they shunned the broad popularity that they saw as necessarily linked to musical vapidity and subcultural dispersion. The "underground" metal scene was, until the late 1980s, based in clubs rather than arenas, in subcultural activity rather than mass-mediated identity. Its literature often took the form of local, self-published fanzines instead of slick, full-color, national publications like *Hit Parader* or *Circus*. Sometimes lumped together as "speed metal" or "thrash," these underground styles of metal tended to be more deliberately transgressive, violent, and noisy.

The thrash metal style coalesced in the San Francisco Bay area and Los Angeles in the early 1980s, with groups like Metallica, Slayer, Testament, Exodus, Megadeth, and Possessed. The musicians who created thrash were influenced by both heavy metal and punk; Motörhead, an important pioneer of speed metal, has played for both punk and metal audiences since the 1970s. The punk influence shows up in the music's fast tempos and frenetic aggressiveness and in critical or sarcastic lyrics delivered in a menacing growl. From heavy metal, thrash musicians took an emphasis on guitar virtuosity, which is usually applied more generally to the whole band. Thrash bands negotiate fast tempos, meter changes, and complicated arrangements with precise ensemble coordination. Speed metal was in part a reaction against the spectacular dimension of other metal styles; thrash bands appealed to "a new generation for whom Zeppelin and Sabbath were granddads but Quiet Riot and Mötley Crüe were too glam."[41] However, though it is often compared to punk rock because of its speed, noise, and violence, thrash metal contrasts with punk's simplicity and nihilism, both lyrically and musically. The Ramones and the Sex Pistols placed musical amateurism at the aesthetic core of punk rock; but to be considered metal, bands must demonstrate some amount of virtuosity and control.

Bubbling underground since the mid-1970s, thrash or speed metal broke through to the surface of popular music in the late 1980s, with successful major-label releases by Metallica, Megadeth, Anthrax, and Slayer, at that time the Big Four of thrash metal.[42] The breakthrough came in 1986, when Metallica's *Master of Puppets*, their first album on a major record label, began to receive the acclaim that would make it thrash metal's first platinum album. Metallica's success sparked increased interest in speed metal among the major record companies, who developed promotional tactics to help bring underground bands to mainstream attention. Until then, speed metal bands had recorded on independent labels like Combat, Megaforce, and Metal Blade, relying on a loyal underground of fans to spread the word. In 1989, MTV sponsored their "Headbanger's Ball Tour," which gained wide exposure for Anthrax, Exodus, and Helloween.

By the end of the decade, thrash metal had successfully challenged the mainstream of metal and redefined it. Metallica and a few other bands were able to headline arena concerts and appear regularly on MTV, although radio play remained incommensurate with their popularity. Other styles of metal coexisted, despite a slump in heavy metal record and ticket sales in 1990, which was explained by music industry figures as the result of the economic recession and overexploitation of the metal market—too many bands signed, too many records released, too many concert tours—as the industry scrambled to cash in on the boom of the late 1980s.[43]

Throughout the 1980s, the influence of heavy metal on other kinds of popular music was pervasive and substantial. On what became the best-selling record of all time, Michael Jackson (or his producer Quincy Jones) brought in guitarist Eddie Van Halen for a cameo heavy metal solo on the song "Beat It" (1982). Just as Jackson and Jones used Vincent Price's voice on "Thriller," on the same album, to invoke the scary thrills of horror films, Van Halen's noisy, virtuosic solo fit well in a song about danger and transgression. As the 1980s went on, heavy metal guitar sounds became well enough known to be used in all sorts of contexts, to evoke danger, intensity, and excitement. Rappers Run-D.M.C. brought metal guitar into hip hop in 1986 with their remake of Aerosmith's "Walk This Way," and Tōne Lōc had a huge hit in 1989 with "Wild Thing," a rap song built around guitar and drum licks digitally sampled from a song on Van Halen's first album. Pop stars frequently used metal guitar sounds to construct affective intensity and control, as in Robert Palmer's "Simply Irresistible." By the middle of the decade, metal sounds had begun appearing often in advertising jingles. Even ads for the U.S. Army ("Be All That You Can Be") featured metal guitar in a kind of subliminal seduction: military service was semiotically presented as an exciting, oppositional, youth-oriented adventure. Rebel, escape, become powerful: join the army!

Like the boundaries of the genre, the history of heavy metal is widely contested. In October 1988, MTV conducted a survey of its viewers, asking the question "What was the first metal band?" The bands most often named were Led Zeppelin, Kiss, Alice Cooper, Black Sabbath, and Metallica. The first of these is not a surprising choice; the others perhaps are. But Kiss and Alice Cooper did found that type of heavy metal that is heavily dependent on spectacle, while Black Sabbath initiated dark metal, oriented toward the occult. Even the choice of Metallica can be understood, as it was that band that brought speed metal to the attention of a wide audience.

The ancestors chosen by fans and musicians reflect the characteristics of metal they valorize. Some want to connect metal closely to the history of rock music, while others emphasize that metal is something new and original. Heavy metal vocalist Dee Snider stresses connections to rock's roots and an "authenticity" grounded in protest: "Heavy metal is the only form of music that still retains the rebellious qualities of '50s rock and roll."[44] Responding to the common perception of technological mediation as artifice and commercial mediation as ideological compromise, critics sometimes minimize metal's musical and technical complexity:

While modern musical technology continued to gather praise from the elite caught up in its spell, a special breed of musicians remained true to "the roots." Instead of layering their sound with electronics, they chose to TURN IT UP! Rock and Roll, they said, was raw and gritty; a means of escape; an uncomplicated element whose purpose was to entertain. Those groups, the survivors, upheld "the roots" in their original form, delivered at blistering volume, filled with urgency and fury. They earned the title Heavy Metal.[45]

Here metal fans are hailed as hardheaded realists, members of a grassroots community unswayed by the false hype that has lured "the elite" away from the clear purpose and simple means of early rock. Yet such explanations obscure aspects of metal that are equally important and collapse tensions that are mediated by metal, for much heavy metal places a great premium on virtuosity and innovation, on spectacle, on effects that can be created only with the help of very sophisticated technology. Heavy metal history, its genre distinctions, and the interpretation of its texts and practices all depend upon the ways in which metal is used and made meaningful by fans.

Headbangers

I Metallari di Salerno Salutano i Metallari di Firenze —Graffito scrawled
on the Uffizi Museum in Florence, July 1989.[46]

Who is the audience for heavy metal? As recently as 1985, *Billboard* asserted that heavy metal fans were still most concentrated in "the blue-collar industrial cities of the continental U.S."[47] A different marketing study, conducted at about the same time, concluded that the metal audience lived in "upscale family suburbs."[48] Probably both are correct; class background correlates, to some extent, with preferences for different kinds of metal, but heavy metal in the 1980s claimed a huge audience that overruns these categories. And they are an active audience; the fans I surveyed claimed, on the average, to buy a new metal recording every week, even though many of them have little money.[49] Heavy metal fans are loyal concertgoers, too; many metal bands, long denied radio airplay, have built their audiences through touring, and according to *Billboard*, metal "attracts a greater proportion of live audiences than any other contemporary music form."[50]

Fans of heavy metal are also, overwhelmingly, white. Neither the lyrics nor the fans are noticeably more racist than is normal in the United States; in fact, the enthusiasm of many fans for black or racially mixed bands, like Living Colour and King's X, and their reverence for Jimi Hendrix suggest the opposite. If few African-Americans have been attracted to heavy metal, it is probably due in part to the genre's history. For heavy metal began as a white remake of urban blues that often ripped off black artists and their songs shamelessly. If the motive for much white music making has been the imperative of reproducing black culture without the black people in it, no comparable reason exists to draw black musicians and fans into traditionally white genres. Heavy metal has remained a white-dominated discourse, apparently offering little to those who have been comfortable with African-American musical traditions. Moreover, it has been transformed into something quite different from its blues origins. Metal's relatively rigid sense of the body and concern with dominance reflect European-American transformation of African-American musical materials and cultural values. At the end of the 1980s, though, musical interactions among metal, rap, rock, and funk became increasingly popular, perhaps presaging at least a partial breakdown of the racial lines that often separate music audiences (hip hop has already accomplished this to a considerable extent).

To begin assembling some information about metal fans and to make contacts for later interviews, I distributed questionnaires to fans at several concerts and through a record store.[51] The fans I surveyed ranged in age from eleven to thirty-one years, with an average age of nineteen. This reflects the specific demographics of concert audiences, rather than magazine readers or record buyers, for example; a survey done in 1984 found that two thirds of heavy metal fans were between the ages of sixteen and twenty-four; one fifth were under fifteen.[52] My sample, like the actual crowds I saw, was almost evenly balanced in gender. Their occupations ranged from car wash attendant to law school student, from computer programmer to construction worker. Their parents' occupations covered the whole gamut of working- and middle-class jobs, with the exception of one sample, collected in a bar in Detroit, which was entirely industrial working class.

The questionnaire began with items intended to pique the curiosity of the fans, such as queries about how long they have listened to heavy metal and how many hours each day, on the average, they hear metal. Further questions concerned subcultural activities, such as watching MTV's "Headbanger's Ball" or reading fan magazines. Eventually, I asked more personal questions about age, occupation, gender, and parents' occupations. At the very end of the form, most fans indicated that they were willing to be interviewed and provided their names and phone numbers.

I am making no claims for the statistical precision of my sample— I used it as a source of guidance and contacts with fans—but I will summarize the responses I found clear and useful. Nearly all of the fans said that most of their friends were also metal fans, an indication of the centrality of heavy metal to fans' social lives. More listen to metal from recordings than from radio programming, confirming the importance of the fan activities of owning, collecting, and being knowledgeable about the music (and the paucity of metal programming on the radio). Nearly all fans sing along with heavy metal lyrics, suggesting that, however unintelligible they may sound to outsiders, lyrics are comprehended by fans. Although this contradicts some academic studies, it agrees with Iron Maiden guitarist Steve Harris's observation that in the United States, "about 90% of the fans know the words to every song."[53]

There were substantial differences among the audiences I surveyed. Compared to the fans at a Poison concert, for example, Judas Priest fans were somewhat older and more likely to be male. While quite a few of the Poison crowd indicated that they play musical instruments, a clear majority of the Judas Priest sample played instruments and owned musical equipment. The Poison fans called "Top 40" their second favorite style of music, while Priest's fans chose classical music as the runner-up to metal. One section of the questionnaire (which many fans told me was their favorite part) invited fans to indicate whether or not they considered various bands to be "heavy metal." Judas Priest fans clustered around other hard metal bands, like Iron Maiden and Metallica, while Poison's fans extended the genre label to Bon Jovi and Mötley Crüe as well.

There was much overall agreement about why heavy metal was important. To avoid asking fans to compose brief explanations of complex feelings at the drop of a hat, I developed a list of plausible statements about metal from my study of fans, magazines, and music. I included a wide range of possibilities, including some that were mutually contradictory; fans were asked to check those with which they most agreed:

——It's the most powerful kind of music; it makes me feel powerful.
——It's intense; it helps me work off my frustrations.
——The guitar solos are amazing; it takes a great musician to play metal.
——I can relate to the lyrics.
——It's music for people like me; I fit in with a heavy metal crowd.
——It's pissed-off music, and I'm pissed off.
——It deals with things nobody else will talk about.
——It's imaginative music; I would never have thought of some of those things.
——It's true to life; it's music about real important issues.
——It's not true to life; it's fantasy, better than life.

There was solid concurrence that the intensity and power of the music, its impressive guitar solos, the relevance of its lyrics, and its truth value were crucial. Surprisingly, fans overwhelmingly rejected the categories of the pissed-off and the fantastic. The most common grounds for dismissal of heavy metal—that it embodies nothing more than adolescent rebellion and escapism—were the qualities least often chosen by fans as representative of their feelings.[54] Megadeth's video for "Peace Sells . . . But Who's Buying?" makes this point explicitly. A young headbanger is watching metal videos when his father interrupts: "What is this garbage you're watching? I want to watch the news." The dad brusquely changes the channel but his son switches it back, explaining: "This *is* the news."

While the responses to my questionnaire cannot be taken as transparent explanations of heavy metal's social functions, they are revealing of the ways in which fans make sense of their own responses, as are the collective understandings developed by fans through their involvement with magazines, friendships, and fan clubs. Besides the separate fan clubs surrounding each band (which are usually not clubs as much as marketing lists) there exist social clubs for particular groups of metal fans, from the Gay Metal Society in Chicago to the Headbanger Special Interest Group of American Mensa. Clubs usually publish their own newsletters (GMA puts out *The Headbanger*, and the Mensa group calls theirs *Vox Metallum*); they also sponsor social events and promote discussion of metal and related issues. Such internal analyses of heavy metal culture contrast sharply with most discussions by outsiders.

"Nasty, Brutish, and Short"? Rock Critics and Academics Evaluate Metal

Heavy metal: pimply, prole, putrid, unchic, unsophisticated, antiintellectual
(but impossibly pretentious), dismal, abysmal, terrible, horrible, and
stupid music, barely music at all. . . . music made *by* slack-jawed, alpaca-haired,
bulbous-inseamed imbeciles in jackboots and leather and chrome *for* slack-
jawed, alpaca-haired, downy-mustachioed imbeciles in cheap, too-large
T-shirts with pictures of comic-book Armageddon ironed on the front. . . .
Heavy metal, mon amour, where do I start?   —Robert Duncan [55]

Heavy metal has rarely been taken seriously, either as music or as cultural activity of any complexity or importance. At best it is controversial;
the enthusiasm of metal fan magazines is paralleled by the hysterical denunciation of the mainstream press and smug dismissals of most rock
journalism. And like country music, metal is a genre that rarely inspires
uncertainty in its critics; though few commentators lay claim to much
knowledge or understanding of the music or its fans, such ignorance
is seldom allowed to hinder confident judgment of both as simple and
brutal. Even critics and academics who are scrupulous in distinguishing
among the details of other genres display unabashed prejudice when it
comes to heavy metal.

For example, the only reference to metal in a recent book on the rock
music industry is this casual summation: "Today's 'hot' rock is heavy
metal, this generation's disco, an apolitical sound more concerned with
the conquest of women than the triumph of the spirit." [56] Another new
book on rock music offers nothing but heavy metal's bottom line, apparently so obvious as to require neither evidence nor even argument:
"This is not a music of hope, and in no way is it a music of real freedom,
because it firmly rejects the possibility of actual change. . . . the rules
of the form have been established . . . they cannot be violated." Moreover, the author assumes that the credibility of this judgment will be
unaffected by his nonchalant admission: "I don't know anything about
heavy metal." [57] Articles on heavy metal in news magazines, like the infamous *Newsweek* conflation of metal and rap as "the culture of attitude,"
usually replicate the same combination of derogatory stereotypes and
blithe ignorance. In an advertisement for their special issue on teenagers,
Newsweek located them in "the age of AIDS, crack, and heavy metal." [58]

Those rock critics who actually do know the music have rarely written
anything about it that its enemies haven't already said. Robert Duncan's vivid description of heavy metal, quoted above, defiantly celebrates
an outsider's fearful view of metal. But his defense is superficial, never
really taking the metal seriously as music or politics; he ends up mutter-

ing about "draining of hope," "deadening of passion," metal as "anaes-
thetic."[59] Chuck Eddy's guide to the five hundred best metal albums is
filled with virtuosic style analysis; ultimately, though, Eddy seems envi-
ous of a nihilism he thinks he sees in heavy metal but that he could never
quite dare to embrace.[60] Charles M. Young says fondly: "Heavy metal is
transitional music, infusing dirtbags and worthless puds with the courage to grow up and be a dickhead."[61] Young makes some good comments about how metal creates feelings of equality and worth, but lacking analysis of musical and social tensions, his article is much better at
asking questions than answering them. Other than Philip Bashe's useful
history and some fine analytical and historical articles in guitar players'
magazines, rock journalists have published relatively few insights about
heavy metal.[62]

Academics have achieved much less. The academic study of popular
music is in transition; scholarship of recent popular music has until recently been dominated by sociological approaches that totally neglect
the music of popular music, reducing the meaning of a song to the literal meaning of its lyrics. This is called "content" analysis, and it assumes
that an outside reader will interpret lyrics just as an insider would; it
also assumes a linear communication model, where artists encode meanings that are transmitted to listeners, who then decipher them, rather
than a dialectical environment in which meanings are multiple, fluid,
and negotiated. Parallel to this, it presumes a Parsonian view of society, wherein social systems tend toward a natural equilibrium, instead
of seeing society in permanent flux, as various groups strive for equality
or dominance. Most writing about popular music also suffers from a
lack of history; with little sense of how music has functioned in other
times and places, writers often mistake transformations of ongoing features of popular music for unprecedented signs of innovation or decay.
Also, most sociological studies offer no integration of ethnographic and
textual analytic strategies. Mass mediation is typically assumed to be a
barrier, standing between artist and audience with the power to corrupt both. But while it is crucial to acknowledge that mass mediation
functions to disrupt a sense of history and community, it is just as important to see how it can make available the resources with which new
communities are built.[63]

Quite a few "content analyses" of heavy metal lyrics have been published. Usually, the researchers who conduct such studies evince an
obliviousness to power relationships, which they regard as "objectivity."
They may interview fans at school, with no thought to the constraints on
articulation that are already in place in that setting. Students have little

motivation to admit to knowledge of lyrics of which their teachers or parents would not approve, and researchers are too willing to see teenagers as inarticulate. For example, Prinsky and Rosenbaum concluded that recent efforts at censorship of rock lyrics are misguided because fans are too dumb to know what the lyrics mean.[64] Their study not only ignored the constraints imposed by the classroom environment and the estrangement caused by the researchers' own "objectivity"; it also implicitly assumed that adults would do better, without considering that classical music audiences, for example, would probably be even less likely to be able to summarize song texts to their satisfaction. Many opera fans prefer not to know what the lyrics are, and the hermeneutic framework promoted by schools and concert halls emphasizes appreciation of sensuous beauty over understanding of meanings.

In another study, Hansen and Hansen assumed that the "themes" of heavy metal (sex, suicide, violence, and the occult, as they saw them) were obvious at the beginning of the experiment. Thus they chose songs they thought fit each category and had four undergraduate research assistants grade heavy metal fans' understanding of the lyrics. For example, after reading two lines from Ozzy Osbourne's "Suicide Solution"—"Evil thoughts and evil doings / Cold, alone you hang in ruins"—fans were asked "What does 'hang in ruins' mean?" The correct answer was "His life is a mess; every aspect of his world is in shambles." Thus Hansen and Hansen reduced a haunting image to a platitude, made it sexist by inserting a male pronoun, and went on to generate an astonishing array of tables of data. Their study is framed by the assumptions that the music of heavy metal is irrelevant (they refer to "distractive influences produced by the music itself"); that images can be reduced to singular, literal meanings; that such meanings exist apart from the contexts of their reception; that sociologists and college students understand heavy metal better than metal fans do; that "correct comprehension" of lyrics is a measure of the seriousness and worth of a musical genre or a cultural activity. Hansen and Hansen were arrogantly "objective"; their study tells us nothing about heavy metal because their premises produced their results.[65]

The growing impact of British cultural studies and new approaches to musicology has so far had disappointingly little effect on the study of rock music, despite the appearance of several pieces on heavy metal that claim that influence. In one of the earliest academic articles about heavy metal, Will Straw argued in 1984 that metal fans do not comprise a subculture because fans don't engage in subcultural activities, such as record collecting and magazine reading, and because there are no intermediate strata between fans and stars, which indicated little chance for participation. All of these assertions are contradicted by my research, although it is possible that Straw's assessment may have been partially true of heavy metal at an earlier moment. It is difficult to know how much credence to give to his arguments, however, since Straw gives no evidence of ever having read a fan magazine, talked with a fan, attended a concert, or even listened to a record. The first published version of his paper "explained" heavy metal as an epiphenomenon of record industry shifts, thus removing politics and agency from the activities of everyone except record industry executives.[66]

Marcus Breen has offered an explanation of heavy metal that combines the worst characteristics of postmodern theorizing. For Breen, metal celebrates numbness and oblivion; it is "a joyride into the spirit of post-industrial alienation."[67] Such conclusions are possible because Breen's analysis is equally unhampered by musical analysis and ethnography. In an amazing flight of fancy, he imagines that when Axl Rose sang, "I want to see you bleed" (in "Welcome to the Jungle"), he might have been referring to menstruation. Lacking any understanding of how heavy metal could be a vehicle for meaning, he concludes that its popularity is due to the "modern marketing and selling methods" of a show business cabal.

Late in 1991, the first book-length academic study of heavy metal was published, Deena Weinstein's *Heavy Metal*.[68] Weinstein is a sociologist, and her book has all of the virtues and faults of most strictly sociological studies of popular culture. It carefully summarizes the details of concert behavior, describing the icons and activities of metal fans and musicians. But Weinstein has nothing useful to say about the music of heavy metal, and her perspective is a familiar Parsonian one, grounded in "taste publics" and structural positions. "Music is the master emblem of the heavy metal subculture," she asserts, a tribute that makes the latter static and trivializes the former. In fact, Weinstein regards the music as but a distraction from analysis; when she teaches about heavy metal, she no longer makes tapes available, giving her students only lyrics to work with.[69]

Though her book is nothing if not an impassioned defense of heavy metal, Weinstein, as a sociologist, must aspire to "objectivity," and she even disingenuously claims not to be joining in debates over whether metal is good or bad.[70] Weinstein's attempt to efface her own participation in heavy metal (she has long been a fan) results in a particularly strange gap in the book's coverage, for she virtually ignores women's responses to heavy metal. Moreover, her objectivity fosters a peculiar sort of arrogance: she brags of having browbeaten one fan into admitting that his understanding of some metal lyrics was inadequate.[71] Her stance hampers her social analysis seriously, for she rarely moves beyond descriptions of the pleasures of metal—musical ecstasy, pride in subcultural allegiance, male bonding—toward placing the activities of fans in the political contexts that make such pleasures possible.

It is not suprising that academics have ignored or misconstrued heavy metal, although it seems curious that few professional rock critics have found anything interesting to say about what was, in the 1980s, the most popular genre of rock music. For many academics, denigration of metal is a necessary part of the defense of "high" culture, while for rock critics it is as an easy route to hipness: their scorn is displayed as a badge of their superiority to the musicians and audiences of heavy metal. All see metal as a travesty of various dearly held myths: about authenticity, beauty, and culture, on the one hand, and authenticity, rebellion, and political critique on the other. If neither academics nor rock critics have had much impact on metal's popularity with its fans, they have helped to shape the dominant stereotype of heavy metal as brutishly simple, debilitatingly negative and violent, and artistically monotonous and impoverished. Thus it is necessary to examine their views criticially in order to clear space for a different sort of account of heavy metal.

For both careless condemnations and flip celebrations can have serious effects: especially since the mid-1980s, heavy metal has been at the center of debates over censorship. Rock critics and academics have the power to sway public opinion on issues of real consequence, for their access to effective and prestigious channels of mass mediation makes their opinions more influential than the writings of fans and musicians. It is clear from the ongoing public furor that attends metal that this music matters: around it coalesce cultural crises in authority, threats of breakdowns in the reproduction of social relations and identities.[72] Besides the sociological significance of heavy metal as a phenomenon that absorbs the time, energy, thoughts, and cash of millions of people, it is a site of explicit social contestation that can tell us much about contemporary American society. As with country music, such critical dismissals as I have cited are the product of a prejudicial view of metal as something monolithic and crude; many casual condemnations of heavy metal depend upon misunderstanding its complex status as a genre. But the significance of heavy metal, including the opportunities it creates for important debates over social values and policies, makes it imperative to sort out the social and commercial tensions negotiated by heavy metal musicians and fans.

Several recent attacks on heavy metal have made the import of these issues very clear; they will be discussed in greater detail in chapter 5, where I critique several influential denunciations of heavy metal—by Tipper Gore, Joe Stuessy, and others—and propose what I consider more sophisticated explanations of the violent aspects of some metal. My task throughout this book has been to work toward such explanations, and my method is to examine carefully the sounds and images of heavy metal, take seriously fans' statements and activities, and situate metal as an integral part of a social context that is complex, conflicted, and inequitable. This chapter has explored the interests and tensions that have defined "heavy metal" as a genre with a history. In it, I have taken a functional approach to the study of metal, stressing the ways that genres are constituted through social contestation and transformation. The following chapter takes a more structural tack, investigating the specific musical characteristics that underpin heavy metal as a discourse.

CHAPTER TWO

Beyond the Vocals

Toward the Analysis of Popular Musical Discourses

> Beyond the vocals, it's the way a guitar makes you feel when
> someone hits a particular chord, the way a snare drum is cracked.
> —Rob Halford of Judas Priest.[1]

When asked if he thought his mother would approve of his band's lyrics, guitarist Eddie Van Halen replied that he had no idea of what the lyrics were.[2] Many people talk about the "meaning" of a song when what they are really discussing is only the song's lyrics. But verbal meanings are only a fraction of whatever it is that makes musicians and fans respond to and care about popular music. This chapter is a prelude to the musical aspects of the chapters that follow, where heavy metal songs will be analyzed within the context of social practices and ideologies. It is also meant as a contribution to an underdeveloped strain in academic work on popular culture: analysis of the *music* of popular music, in which discussion is grounded in the history and significance of actual musical details and structures, "beyond the vocals." Specifically, it sketches a view of metal as a discourse by analyzing the signifying practices that constitute heavy metal music. But first a more general argument must be advanced: that musical details can be evaluated in relation to interlocked systems of changing practices and that shifting codes constitute the musical discourses that underpin genres.

This chapter has three parts: It begins with discussion of some theoretical bases for the analysis of musical meaning in popular music; then it proceeds to analyze certain generic features of heavy metal and related musical styles, with reference to a single example, a song by Van Halen; finally, a more integrated analysis of that same piece of music appears, as a way of connecting musical details with generically organized social experience.

Genre and Discourse

Nowhere are genre boundaries more fluid than in popular music. Just as it is impossible to point to a perfectly exemplary Haydn symphony, one that fulfills the "norms" in every respect, pieces within a popular genre rarely correspond slavishly to generic criteria. Moreover, musicians are ceaselessly creating new fusions and extensions of popular genres. Yet musical structures and experiences are intelligible only with respect to these historically developing discursive systems. As Fredric Jameson argues,

> *pure* textual exemplifications of a single genre do not exist; and this, not merely because pure manifestations of anything are rare, but . . . because texts always come into being at the intersection of several genres and emerge from the tensions in the latter's multiple force fields. This discovery does not, however, mean the collapse of genre criticism but rather its renewal: we need the specification of the individual "genres" today more than ever, not in order to drop specimens into the box bearing those labels, but rather to map our coordinates on the basis of those fixed stars and to triangulate this specific given textual moment.[3]

Jameson reminds us that genre categories are fluid and that individual texts are never static fulfillments of conventional norms but rather are understood with reference to other texts.

Yet Jameson's concept of genre seems to operate only at the level of texts. We can profitably add to his model Bakhtin's idea of genre as a "horizon of expectations" brought to bear on texts by historically situated readers. Genres are never sui generis; they are developed, sustained, and reformed by people, who bring a variety of histories and interests to their encounters with generic texts. The texts themselves, as they are produced by such historically specific individuals, come to reflect the multiplicities of social existence: in Bakhtin's view, language is irreducibly "heteroglot," and dialogue takes place not only between genres, as Jameson points out, but also within them. Bakhtin contrasts formalistic genre categories with what he calls "speech genres," relatively stable types of utterance. "Each utterance is filled with echoes and reverberations of other utterances to which it is related by the communality of the sphere of speech communication."[4] Thus, we might say that a C major chord has no intrinsic meaning; rather, it can signify in different ways in different discourses, where it is contextualized by other signifiers, its own history as a signifier, and the social activities in which the discourse participates.

Simon Frith has recently called for renewed genre analysis of popular music, at the same time that he has asserted that "we still do not know nearly enough about the musical language of pop and rock: rock critics still avoid technical analysis, while sympathetic musicologists, like Wilfrid Mellers, use tools that can only cope with pop's nonintentional (and thus least significant) qualities."[5] These two needs are connected, for delineating musical parameters may be the best way to distinguish genres, and genre conventions, in turn, can help us to place the significance of musical details. The challenge is to analyze signification dialectically, working between the levels of specific details and generic categories toward social meanings.

Heavy metal seems particularly appropriate terrain for such methods. As it has gained in popularity, metal has grown in stylistic innovation and pluralism. The term "heavy metal" is now used to designate a great variety of musical practices and ideological stances. Moreover, metal has contributed to the development of many discursive "fusions": metal-influenced pop, rock, rap, funk, and so on. But as Jameson argues, the proliferation of styles within a genre and the concomitant lessened capacity of the norms to explain divergent practices do not mean that genre is no longer a fruitful analytical category. On the contrary, the recent expansion and diversification of heavy metal musical practices and their audiences make it all the more imperative to map the norms that make such fusions and transformations intelligible.[6]

The analytical notion of discourse enables us to pursue an integrated investigation of musical and social aspects of popular music.[7] By approaching musical genres as discourses, it is possible to specify not only certain formal characteristics of genres but also a range of understandings shared among musicians and fans concerning the interpretation of those characteristics. The concept of discourse enables us to theorize beyond the artificial division of "material reality" and consciousness. Discourses are constituted by conventions of practice and interpretation, and, as John Fiske puts it, "Conventions are the structural elements of genre that are shared between producers and audiences. They embody the crucial ideological concerns of the time in which they are popular and are central to the pleasures a genre offers its audience." Genre, then, is "a means of constructing both the audience and the reading subject: its work in the economic domain is paralleled by its work in the domain of culture; that is, its work in influencing which meanings . . . are preferred by, or proffered to, which audiences."[8]

Traditionally, only language has been thought to be discursive. But recent usage has opened up the concept of discourse to refer to any socially produced way of thinking or communicating. The literary critic Tzvetan Todorov has analyzed the relationship of genre and discourse in a way that helps clarify the relevance of these terms to music.[9] Building on Bakhtin's theory of speech genres, Todorov argues that discourses are made up not of sentences but of utterances. That is, they are constituted not of abstract rules or patterns but of the concrete deployment of such abstractions in real social contexts. Sentences are transformed into utterances by being articulated among themselves in a given sociocultural context. For music, this implies that any formal or syntactical patterns an analyst may recognize must be interpreted as abstractions from utterances or speech acts that can only be said to have meaning in particular, socially grounded ways.

Genres, according to Todorov, arise from metadiscursive discourse. The discussion in chapter 1 of the competing definitions and understandings of heavy metal promoted by fans, business interests, critics, and others was meant to demonstrate precisely this point. It is from the discourse about discourses that concepts of genre are formed, transformed, and defended. Genres then come to function as horizons of expectation for readers (or listeners) and as models of composition for authors (or musicians). Most important, Todorov argues that genres exist because societies collectively choose and codify the acts that correspond most closely to their ideologies. A society's discourses depend upon its linguistic (or musical) raw materials and upon its historically circumscribed ideologies. Discourses are formed, maintained, and transformed through dialogue; speakers learn from and respond to others, and the meanings of their utterances are never permanently fixed, cannot be found in a dictionary. Thus, the details of a genre and its very presence or absence among various social groups can reveal much about the constitutive features of a society.

Like genres and discourses, musical meanings are contingent but never arbitrary. There is never any *essential* correspondence between particular musical signs or processes and specific social meanings, yet such signs and processes would never circulate if they did not produce such meanings. Musical meanings are always grounded socially and historically, and they operate on an ideological field of conflicting interests, institutions, and memories. If this makes them extremely difficult to analyze, it does so by forcing analysis to confront the complexity and antagonism of culture. This is a poststructural view of music in that it sees all signification as provisional, and it seeks for no essential truths inherent in structures, regarding all meanings as produced through the interaction of texts and readers. It goes further in suggesting that subjectivity is constituted not only through language, as Lacan and others have argued, but through musical discourses as well. Musical details and structures are intelligible only as traces, provocations, and enactments of power relationships. They articulate meanings in their dialogue with other discourses past and present and in their engagement with the hopes, fears, values, and memories of social groups and individuals. Musical analysis is itself the representation of one discourse in terms of another, the point being to illuminate the social contexts in which both circulate.

Many critics and historians of rock music have been dismissive of any sort of musical analysis. Peter Wicke, for example, claims: "Rock songs are not art songs, whose hidden meaning should be sought in their form and structure."[10] Wicke is right to be dubious of the sort of reductive musicological analysis that simply abstracts and labels technical features, but he is wrong to assume that the specific details of rock music are insignificant. He accepts uncritically a highly problematic dichotomy when he argues, "Rock is not received through the critical apparatus of contemplation, of consideration by visual and aural means; its reception is an active process, connected in a practical way with everyday life."[11] To argue that critical scrutiny of the details of rock music is inappropriate because people don't hear that way is like arguing that we can't analyze the syntax of language because people don't know that they're using gerunds and participles. But more important, reception of *all* music is "connected in a practical way with everyday life," however hard some people may work to hide the social meanings of their music. The danger of musical analysis is always that social meanings and power struggles become the forest that is lost for the trees of notes and chords. The necessity of musical analysis is that those notes and chords represent the differences that make some songs seem highly meaningful and powerful and others boring, inept, or irrelevant.[12]

The split between academic contemplation and popular understanding is not a function of repertoires but rather of interpretive ideologies. As recent musicological colonizations of jazz and even rock have shown, any cultural text can be made over into a monument of neutralized order. But too many analysts of popular music are unaware of the extent to which this process has already remade what is now "classical" music. They assume that traditional musicological methods are simply appropriate for the traditional musicological repertoire and that popular musics do not warrant such analysis. Yet much recent work in musicology has been directed toward undoing the formalist depoliticization of classical music. The problem is not with musical analysis per se but with the implicit or explicit ideological context within which such analysis is conducted. Rock songs, like all discourse, do have meanings that can be discovered through analysis of their form and structure, but such analysis is useful only if it is grounded culturally and historically and if it acknowledges its interests forthrightly.

This is where I differ from most semioticians of music. Jean-Jacques Nattiez, for example, might agree with much of what I have asserted thus far, but there are two important divergences.[13] First, his concern is primarily metadiscursive; he seems more interested in debating definitions and concepts than in analyzing actual music and musical activities. Second, while Nattiez recognizes the conventional basis of semiological meanings, he seems to want to retain some sort of absolute notion of truth, against which interpretations can be measured. That is, he stops short of recognizing the conventional basis of semiology itself; he is unwilling to acknowledge the ultimate grounding of analytical credibility in nothing more absolute or less complex than social contestation, institutional prestige, and power. But there can be no meaningful semiology apart from ethnographic inquiry, historical analysis, and argumentation about culture. There is no way to decide what something means without making a political statement. Underpinning all semiotic analysis is, recognized or not, a set of assumptions about cultural practice, for ultimately music doesn't have meanings; people do. There is no essential, foundational way to ground musical meaning beyond the flux of social existence. Ultimately, musical analysis can be considered credible only if it helps explain the significance of musical activities in particular social contexts.

Some semioticians and philosophers of language, such as David Lidov and Mark Johnson, have worked to ground discursive meanings somatically, in terms of (socially constructed) bodily gestures, tensions, and postures.[14] In *The Body in the Mind*, philosopher Mark Johnson argues that meanings of all sorts, even the ones that seem most abstract and mental, are grounded in bodily experience. While Johnson's own analyses of artworks are rather simplistic, his epistemological challenge to the Western mind/body split is important. Human experiences of meaningfulness, Johnson argues, are grounded at the level of prelinguistic structures which organize our experience and comprehension, which he calls "image schemata." These schemata are not concepts; they are patterns of *activity*, fundamental mechanisms of meaning production that inform the more abstract operations of language and conceptual thinking. Johnson argues that metaphor links these bodily image schemata to language. Metaphor, in this view, occupies a central place in the production of human meaning. It is not merely a kind of poetic expression or a literary figure of speech; rather, metaphor is a crucial process for generating meaning, whereby we come to understand one area of experience in terms of another.[15] It is by means of metaphor that image-schematic structures are extended, transformed, and elaborated into domains of meaning that may seem less directly tied to the body, including language, abstract reasoning, and, I would argue, music.

Attempts to explain "music as metaphor" have appeared with some regularity, but metaphorical interpretations appear to many scholars to be arbitrary: the images you describe in response to a piece of music may be wholly unlike those I would use, and a positivistic orientation would then declare meaning, in this sense, subjective and out of bounds. In rebuttal to what he calls the Objectivist rejection of metaphor, Johnson stresses that meanings at the level of image schemata and metaphor are grounded in physical and social experience that is *shared*. He argues that image schemata "*can have a public, objective* character . . . , because they are recurring structures of embodied human understanding."[16] Johnson presents his theory of image schemata and metaphoric links as a solution to what he sees as the false dichotomy between objectivist absolutism and "anything goes" relativism. That is, meanings are neither objectively inherent nor subjectively arbitrary; they arise out of human experiences of social interaction with a material world.

As Johnson acknowledges, experiences of the body differ with place, time, and culture; musical meaning can be situated in bodily experience not in any essentialist way, then, but as a reciprocal element in a "web of culture" in which real human bodies are ensnared and supported. Yet even such theorizing cannot ground meaning "below" the level of discourse, for the body and the physical world cannot be experienced or thought outside of discourse. If musical gestures are experienced as physical or emotional gestures, these experiences are dependent on the discursive operation of the concepts and metaphors that make all of these terms meaningful.

In an important intervention in the field of the cognitive psychology of music, John A. Sloboda argues that while some responses to music seem to be consistent across cultures—fast and loud is perceived as arousing, slow and soft as soothing—listeners within a culture can generally agree upon finer readings of the "emotional character" even of pieces they have never heard before. Thus, musical meanings are neither a matter of "conditioning" through nonmusical associations nor of aggregative perception of atomized sound events—both influential formulations in the field. Rather, Sloboda's arguments point toward the utility of discourse as a way of conceiving of the musical production of meaning.[17]

Even while they try to map the terms of a discourse, analysts must keep in mind that a variety of interpretations of musical texts is always possible, for popularity among various audiences arises both from the polysemy of texts and conventions—their potential to mean different things to different people—and from what Bakhtin calls their heteroglossia: their reproduction of multiple discourses and social voices. That is, signs are always susceptible to various interpretations because meanings can never be absolutely fixed. But because the social world is not monolithic, discourses inevitably structure in plural and contradictory meanings; many meanings are contained within any text. And the more popular a text is, the more likely it is to be found relevant in different ways. As Dee Snider of Twisted Sister says of the song "We're Not Gonna Take It," "It's very general—we weren't specific about just what it is we aren't taking—work, school, whatever—so you can apply it to anything you want."[18] And in fact the song has found unexpected utility as the theme song of several workers' strikes.[19]

However, the fact that ideas can be fairly consistently communicated, regardless of the nuances of individual response, is what points to the importance of musical discourses as coherent systems of signification. The range of possible interpretations may be theoretically infinite, but in fact certain preferred meanings tend to be supported by those involved with a genre, and related variant meanings are commonly negotiated. As Fiske says, the text "establishes the boundaries of the arena within which the struggle for meaning can occur."[20] So while meanings are negotiated, discourse constructs the terms of the negotiation. Genres such as heavy metal are sites where seemingly stable discourses temporarily organize the exchange of meanings. In practice, subcultural and other social alignments play a large role in channeling the reception of popular music. For music is not just a symbolic register for what really happens elsewhere; it is itself a material, social practice, wherein subject positions are constructed and negotiated, social relations are enacted and transgressed, and ideologies are developed and interrogated.[21]

Musical discourses constantly cross national boundaries and revise cultural boundaries, but they signify variously in different contexts. For example, a friend gave me a tape of Pokolgep, a Hungarian heavy metal band, and I discovered that their music is very different from that of the bands that are popular in the United States. It sounds oppressive, lacking what I've called the heavy metal dialectic; the guitar solos, which are fewer than is normal in U.S. and British metal, offer no escape, no transcendence. The guitars don't contribute transgressive fills (harmonics, bent notes, etc.), and the mood is very controlled and mechanical. No harmonic momentum is ever built up; progressions are heavily grounded by dominant chords, which are rare in Western metal. The lyrics, which my friend translated for me, are poignant and desperate, speaking eloquently of a state of alienation where there is no future, no past, no freedom, no security, and also no hope, no fantastic transcendence, no dreams of anything better. The lyrics recount youthful and historical pain but, along with the music, suggest no youthful exuberance, no energetic defiance. I don't know the context well enough to assert that the implications of this reading are correct; what seems clear is that the international conventions of heavy metal have been strongly inflected by the particular ideological needs of a local community.

Musical meaning, then, has more or less broad social bases and constituencies upon which interpretation is dependent, as well as its associated political economies, the commercial contexts that organize all stages of production and consumption. The latter field has been extensively analyzed by scholars of popular music;[22] what has been relatively neglected is the problem of just how popular musical texts produce meaning and how such meanings operate not only within the contexts of political economies but also within social history and lived experience. Specific musical analysis is important because music is social practice. Music and society are not just related phenomena; music is a type of social activity and a register of such experience. John Blacking remarked that it has long been a commonplace of ethnomusicological analysis that, while music is socially grounded, it cannot articulate any new meanings, express anything not already in the mind of the listener.[23] But music can enact relationships and narratives that have not previously been imagined or valued. Its potential to create new meanings for listeners is particularly great in mass media cultures, where music is mobile, sometimes the only means of contact among different ways of life. Thus, musical analysis of popular music can help us make sense of the seemingly fragmented modern world; it can help us understand the thoughts and desires of many whose only politics are cultural politics.

Musicological Analysis

In this section, I want to discuss a few select approaches to musical analysis in order to situate more clearly my own methods and goals. This is in no way a comprehensive or balanced survey; its purpose is illustrative.[24] One of the central issues concerns the disabling methodological split between aesthetic and sociological analysis. The continuing prestige and influence of eighteenth- and nineteenth-century European aesthetics, which relied upon claims of disinterestedness to mask the ideological agendas of its culture, have obscured the fact that this is not typical of how most people have understood the operation of culture throughout history.[25]

In the twentieth century, Theodor W. Adorno has been the foremost musicologist to challenge the Kantian orthodoxy that has ruled musicology.[26] Adorno's musical analysis posited a homological relationship between dynamic processes in music and those most central to society at the time. For him, musical and social structures were metaphorically linked, and musical and social criticism were thus inseparable. Adorno's work has been of major importance for cultural criticism and mass media scholarship, but more as obstacle than inspiration. Although Adorno did attempt to analyze popular music as well as art music, he did so only in order to prove the former's depravity and to underscore its role in perpetuating what he saw as modern capitalism's fascistic control of the masses. Adorno neglected to admit that his illuminating analyses of the German canon were dependent on his encyclopedic knowledge of and ideological commitment to that repertoire. His few analyses of popular music are so vague, vitriolic, and transparently racist that one wishes he had limited the scope of his analytical attentions even more than he did. So for those working in the area of popular music, the need to recoup that music from Adorno's damning criticism has taken precedence over the possibilities of adapting his methods to other ends.[27] This imperative has obscured the potential value of Adorno's methods as a model for analysts who want to understand musical details as socially significant. But Adorno's analyses of classical music ought to be counted important precedents for any project of musical-cultural criticism.

Other approaches pertinent to socially grounded analysis of popular music have emerged from the field of ethnomusicology. One of the most impressive collections of data was developed by Alan Lomax. After an exhaustive, computerized comparison of the "folk songs" of the whole world, Lomax felt able to specify some correlations between the social organization of communities and the musical characteristics of their songs. "In general, a culture's song performance style seemed to represent generalized aspects of its social and communications systems."[28] Lomax described not only homological links within sociomusical systems, but he also posited broader parallels across cultures; for example, he noted correlations between restrictive sexual mores and vocal tension. The range of observed manners of musical organization (e.g., choral singing vs. solo singing, homophony vs. polyphony) was matched with observed social organization, with results that suggest that some sort of connection exists among these practices. Lomax tried to avoid implying anything about the nature of that link; he simply insisted that it was there.

Lomax's refusal to theorize this link greatly reduces the value of his work for cultural studies and for ethnomusicology as well. Lomax and his research team produced a triumph for the positivistic analysis of human behavior: Lomax tried to give the impression that his work proceeded in total objectivity, without *any* informing theoretical bent. But in the end, the data Lomax collected imply that music is simply determined by social structure. In his refusal of theory, he arrived at one of the most unsophisticated of cultural models: he was unwittingly a "vulgar Marxist," for whom base simply determines superstructure. In applying social science methods across cultures and by not questioning the romantic assumption that cultures are naturally pure until corrupted by outsiders, Lomax was drawn into a refusal to supplement "objective" observation with any of the many methods anthropologists have used to make sense of what they see and to learn how others make sense of what they do.[29] By ignoring the ideological basis of meaning, Lomax diluted the richness and complexity of cultural interaction. Lomax discerned a variety of provocative correlations between music and society, but his implicit theoretical model is too simplistic to be of much use in understanding them.

This "scientific" approach to the study of culture continues to have great influence on ethnomusicology and on popular music study as well. The 1970s were the heyday of ethnomusicology's involvement with linguistics. Adopting the Saussurean assumption that symbols are arbitrary, musical scholars reasoned that (as Bruno Nettl summarized this position) "If all music is a system of symbols, one ought to be able to analyze it in a way similar to or derived from the accepted analysis of the intellectual grandfather of symbol systems, human language."[30] Spurred especially by interdisciplinary acclaim for Levi-Strauss's structuralist anthropology, musicologists and ethnomusicologists leapt at analytical models from linguistics and semiotics, adapting them for the study of musical structures, musical grammars, and musics as symbolic systems. The results, for the most part, included disappointingly few useful insights, in spite of a great many breathtakingly intricate charts and thrilling, cryptic abbreviations. As Steven Feld pointed out in 1974, during the midst of the linguistics craze, there was little real theorizing going on as to the *relevance* of linguistic models for the study of music.[31]

Scholars were attracted by the promise and appearance of scientific rigor and precision, but they gave little thought to the price they paid, which was the customary one for formalist prestige—abstraction; that is, abstraction of musical structures out of the richness and social complexity of musical practices. Feld, himself trained in linguistics, asserted that most of this work was little more than trendy dabbling, yielding only fancy new ways to describe musical sound, not explain it. Despite the later development of structuralist thought in anthropology, then, this work seemed to run counter to ethnomusicology's fundamental commitment to an anthropological interest in musical culture, to studying musical activities as well as musical structures.

But ethnomusicology has also fostered a number of sophisticated, sensitive analyses of musical meaning in social contexts; among the best are those by John Blacking and John Miller Chernoff. The latter sometimes presents conclusions very like those Lomax produced; for instance, he argues that "African affinity for polymetric musical forms indicates that, in the most fundamental sense, the African sensibility is pluralistic."[32] But Chernoff's insights are not distanced, "objective" correlations; they result from an extensive and intense engagement with African music and social life. Similarly, Blacking's fieldwork leads him to conclude: "It is not enough to identify a characteristic musical style in its own terms and view it in relation to its society. . . . We must recognize that no musical style has 'its own terms:' its terms are the terms of its society and culture, and of the bodies of the human beings who listen to it, and create and perform it."[33]

Some more recent ethnomusicological work, such as Feld's study of Kaluli aesthetics, further explores homological and complex metaphorical relationships among musical and other cultural practices.[34] And Judith and Alton Becker have written about Javanese music in a way that supports the idea that musical discourses are systems of coherence that differ among cultures and change over time. "We call iconicity the nonarbitrariness of any metaphor. Metaphors gain power—and even cease being taken as metaphors—as they gain iconicity or 'naturalness.'"[35] Becker and Becker argue that scholars must discover what makes a music powerful and relate its iconicity to epistemology, to the understandings and desires that make that music meaningful to a particular group of people. In the Javanese gamelon music they study, for example, cyclicity and coincidence establish the coherence that organizes meaning, in contrast to the way that tonality organizes the production of meaning in Western classical music. This suggests that heavy metal, too, should have its own mechanisms and metaphors, its own terms of discourse. Although few ethnomusicologists have produced studies of popular music, their field provides important models for such work.

The discipline of musicology, with its long history of positivism and ideological commitment to a canon of European "classical" music, has much less to offer scholars of popular music. Many musicologists remain unconvinced that any music outside their canon could be worth studying, and, as Simon Frith complains, the few who have addressed popular music have largely missed the point. More promising is the fact that a few musicologists, influenced by anthropology, feminism, and literary theory and building on the syntactical and affective insights of Theodor Adorno, Leonard Meyer, and others, have begun to produce detailed analyses of the Western musical canon in its social and political contexts.[36] Such sophisticated engagements with classical music are of great value for the study of popular music, both for the deconstructive, demystifying task they perform, which allows the investigation of popular music to proceed without an inferiority complex, and for their specific contributions to our understanding of musical texts and their cultural operation.

A singular exception to the predominant tendency to ignore music itself when studying popular music is found in the work of Philip Tagg.[37] Yet Tagg's work has had much less impact on the study of popular music than such distinction would seem to merit because of what many see as the excessive complexity and artificiality of his analyses. Tagg has created an elaborate taxonomy of the analytical process, built up through interrelationships of acronymic abstractions reminiscent of structuralist linguistics or of the formalist music analysis Tagg himself rejects. Tagg admits that his methodology is "cumbersome," but he sees no alternatives, for if "sterile formalism" is unproductive, "unbridled application" of hermeneutics is no better.[38] Tagg's results command a certain amount of respect: he is almost alone in having produced compelling explanations of the meanings of musical details in popular music. Moreover, Tagg's analysis of the historical factors that have led to musicology's denial of semiotic meaning are acute, and his rigor and caution are understandable given this context. As he well knows, to try to make the case that a particular musical configuration sounds mournful (something that may be obvious to virtually all listeners), in the face of dominant ideological commitments to formalism and the ineffability of artistic meaning, is to have to invent a philosophical argument for meaning in music and to try to reconstruct long-forgotten or suppressed codes.

Tagg's skill at unpacking the significance of musical gestures and structures is impressive, but he too often ignores or marginalizes both the political economy of popular music and its actual operations in social contestation. The features of his method that provoke resistance among scholars of popular music are mostly the product of methodological assumptions Tagg accepts from formalist musical and linguistic analysis. For example, the scientific rigor for which he assumes it is necessary to strive and the objectivity that is supposed to guarantee accurate delineation of meaning actually inhibit the kind of social explanations Tagg seeks. The problem is that there are no people in Tagg's analytical world save anonymous "respondents" who help the researcher establish "a bank of IOCM" (interobjective comparison material). There are no voices but Tagg's own; musicians and fans are dehumanized into "Emitters" and "Receivers," perpetuating the flawed model of art as a pipeline for delivering meaning, rather than as a social field for constructing, negotiating, and contesting it.[39] Tagg accepts too many of the premises of the people with whom he is arguing: you have the problem of connecting art and society only if you accept the assumptions that separate them; if you don't, then you work at explaining how meanings and relationships are created through artistic activities. Ultimately, Tagg is able to pay little attention to how popular music circulates socially, how it functions in articulating complex senses of identity, why people care about it.

Writing about Music

As Rob Halford and Eddie Van Halen remind us, musicians and fans alike tend to respond primarily and most strongly to musical meanings.[40] Analysts and critics, on the other hand, are trained in ways that privilege literate over oral modes of communication. A fundamental problem in accounting for musical meaning has always been the conflicting modalities of print and sound. Both music and language are meaningful to us, but they seem to be fundamentally different sorts of discourse. We can use language to describe musical processes or effects, but we usually find that propositional statements about music are clumsy compared to the efficiency of the music itself, and the feeling persists that much remains unaccounted for, no matter how lengthy the explanation. It seems to me that the uneasy fit of musical practices and linguistic theory is the result of epistemological tensions: on the one hand, the often very satisfying intuitions we gain from ethnography, listening to music, and performing it; and on the other, the understanding of all meaning as abstract and propositional that we inherit from the dominant philosophical tradition of the West. When we talk about music, we must use propositional language, but our mode of description is not the same as what we describe. Moreover, as Mark Johnson argues, propositional meaning in language, as well as musical meaning, is itself dependent on nonpropositional experience. Propositional statements cannot account fully for any kind of meaning.

The problem is not only that of representing musical experiences in words but more fundamentally one of analyzing musical meaning in terms of literate conceptions. Fiske and Hartley compare oral and literate modes of communication by means of a list of differences:[41]

Oral Modes	Literate Modes
dramatic	narrative
episodic	sequential
mosaic	linear
dynamic	static
active	artifact
concrete	abstract
ephemeral	permanent
social	individual
metaphorical	metonymic
rhetorical	logical
dialectical	univocal/"consistent"

The correspondence of music as discursive sound to the first column, and music's lyrics, scores, and criticism to the second is striking. Music enacts through patterns and gestures of sound a dramatic, episodic, dynamic experience, at once concrete and ephemeral. It is a social practice, rhetorically powerful and dialectically active. Writing about music, on the other hand, tends to treat music as an artifact, as it attempts to pin down the concrete realities of sound into static, abstract words in a logical, linear order. Musical scores and song lyrics, as literate modes of communication, are both closer in character to writing about music than to music itself. This discursive affinity is itself in part responsible for the historical neglect of musical meaning in popular music, in favor of concentration on either lyrics or static score-based musicological analysis.[42]

The argument is not that true meaning resides in the music, that popular music should be analyzed only in terms of sounds, removed from their distracting visual and verbal contexts. But lyrics have been granted disproportionate significance. Class and race prejudices have long inhibited the study of popular music by musicologists, and a long tradition of literate-mode analysis—of lyrics, interviews, etc.—has disguised the fact that we don't know nearly enough about how popular music constructs meanings musically. But I would argue that musical codes are the primary bearers of meaning; lyrics, like costumes and performers' physical motions, help direct and inflect the interpretation of the meanings that are most powerfully delivered, those suggested by the music. The most pressing task for the study of popular music is to begin to analyze the musical production of meaning within a discursive framework that is sensitive to many kinds of social experience even as it focuses on specifically musical practices.

I will turn now to a series of discursive parameters, discussing each in turn as it relates specifically to the musical practices of heavy metal. After introducing each parameter and tracing its operation in the case of metal rather generally, I will discuss its bearing on the song I have chosen to serve as an illustrative example. That song is "Runnin' with the Devil," written and recorded by Van Halen and released in 1978 as the first cut on their debut album, *Van Halen*. "Runnin' with the Devil" helped to propel the group to both popular success and critical acclaim, and it is still rated by critics and fans as among the best heavy metal songs ever recorded.[43] As we will see, this song is not paradigmatic in every respect; arguably, no text ever is perfectly representative of a genre. But its popularity and influence qualify it as an approximation of a "fixed star," as Jameson calls the hypothetical texts that help define genres. And the ways in which "Runnin' with the Devil" fails to exemplify the norms of heavy metal also are significant. But the main purpose of this section is to outline the qualities that are important in heavy metal and to describe how they signify. The first question is: what makes heavy metal heavy?

Metal as Discourse

TIMBRE: GUITAR DISTORTION

Of all musical parameters, timbre is least often analyzed, but its significance can hardly be overstated. Scan across radio stations, and a fraction of a second will be sufficient time to identify the musical genre of each. Before any lyrics can be comprehended, before harmonic or rhythmic patterns are established, timbre instantly signals genre and affect. Imagine this text being done by AC/DC, with raucous screaming and pounding: "I hear footsteps and there's no one there; I smell blossoms and the trees are bare." Now compare Frank Sinatra crooning it, backed by strings. The musical cues create very different effects: one is the frantic agony of paranoia; the other is the delicious disorientation of bourgeois love.

The most important aural sign of heavy metal is the sound of an extremely distorted electric guitar. Anytime this sound is musically dominant, the song is arguably either metal or hard rock; any performance that lacks it cannot be included in the genre. For people who use any sort of audio equipment, the relationship of distortion to power is familiar:

a small radio turned on full blast, a portable cassette player booming cacophonously, a malfunctioning stereo system. This electronic distortion results when components are overdriven—required to amplify or reproduce a signal beyond their capacity to do so "cleanly." Historically, such distortion has been regarded as undesirable, and generations of audio engineers have joined in the quest for perfect audio fidelity, laboring to eliminate all types of distortion while increasing power-handling capabilities. To the horror of these engineers, in the 1960s they began to receive requests from guitar players to produce devices that would deliberately add electronic distortion (in the late 1950s, guitar players had experimented with distortion by slashing their speaker cones). For despite its previous status as noise, at this historical moment such distortion was becoming a desirable sign in an emerging musical discourse.

Not only electronic circuitry, but also the human body produces aural distortion through excessive power. Human screams and shouts are usually accompanied by vocal distortion, as the capacities of the vocal chords are exceeded. Thus, distortion functions as a sign of extreme power and intense expression by overflowing its channels and materializing the exceptional effort that produces it. This is not to say that distortion always and everywhere functions this way; guitar distortion has become a conventional sign that is open to transformation and multiple meanings. Heavy metal distortion is linked semiotically with other experiences of distortion, but it is only at a particular historical moment that distortion begins to be perceived in terms of power rather than failure, intentional transgression rather than accidental overload—as music rather than noise.

Overdriving an amplifier actually creates two main effects: harmonic distortion and signal compression. The latter translates aurally as sustain; while a note played on an acoustic guitar or a nonoverdriven electric guitar decays quickly, a heavily distorted guitar signal is compressed and fed back so that the note, once struck, can be held indefinitely, with no loss of energy or volume. Since sustaining anything requires effort, the distorted guitar sound signals power, not only through its distorted timbre but also through this temporal display of unflagging capacity for emission. As one successful heavy metal producer puts it, "Distortion gives that feeling of ultimate power. The more distortion you get, the more satisfying it is. There's something slightly superhuman, psychologically speaking, about the sustain, the nearly endless notes."[44]

In Western musical history, the only other instrument capable of indefinite, unarticulated sustain is the organ (and its contemporary descendant, the synthesizer), which shares one other singular attribute with the electric guitar: the capacity to produce power chords. Power chords result from distortion of the chord voicings most often used in metal and hard rock, an open fifth or fourth played on the lower strings. Power chords are manifestly more than these two notes, however, because they produce resultant tones. An effect of both distortion and volume, resultant tones are created by the acoustic combination of two notes.[45] They are most audible at high volume levels, and they are intensified by the type of harmonic distortion used in metal guitar playing. Such resultant tones are also produced by pipe organs, where high volumes and open voicings on very low notes are sometimes employed to similar effect: to display and enact overwhelming power—usually, in that context, for the greater glory of God.

The strongest resultant tone is produced at the frequency that is the difference between the frequencies of the main tones. If, for example, the open A string on the guitar (which vibrates at a frequency of 110 cycles per second, or 110 Hz) and the E above it (165 Hz) are played as a power chord, then the A an octave lower ($165 - 110 = 55$ Hz) will sound very prominently as a resultant tone. If the A is played with a fourth above instead of a fifth, D (147 Hz), the D two octaves lower (37 Hz) will be produced. These resultant tones are often at frequencies lower than the instrument itself can normally produce; both of these examples result in the production of pitches far below the actual range of the guitar.

Distortion also results in a timbral change toward brightness, toward a more complex waveform, since distorting a signal increases the energy of its higher harmonics. Power chords, on the other hand, produce powerful signals *below* the actual pitches being sent to the amplifier. Thus, the distorted guitar signal is expanded in both directions: the higher harmonics produced by distortion add brilliance and edge (and what guitarists sometimes call "presence") to the sound, and the resultant tones produced by the interval combinations of power chords create additional low frequencies, adding weight to the sound. The power of power chords, the weight of heavy metal, the hardness of hard rock are all constructed and maintained discursively by factors besides timbre, but the sustain, distortion, and resultant tones discussed above are absolutely crucial.

The guitar sound in "Runnin' with the Devil" is famous among guitarists and often celebrated as paradigmatically "hot." Guitarist Eddie Van Halen produced this sound by means of a risky but effective innovation: using a voltage controller to increase the power source to the guitar amplifier from normal wall voltage (110–120 volts) to 140, 160, or more volts. The stronger power source overdrives the amplifier, creating an extremely energized sound, with maximum sustain and distortion (along with frequent destruction of amplifiers through burnout and the risk of electrocution). Van Halen's method was unusual, but it is symptomatic of the fanatical attention to "sound"—qualities of timbre and distortion—that is typical of all metal guitarists.

The quality of heavy metal distortion depends mainly on the amplifier and the pickups of the guitar. The Marshall amps Van Halen uses are overwhelmingly the heavy metal amp of choice, but many companies compete to offer the player the crucial "sound." Their advertisements are useful documents because they establish links between sound quality and the music's desired effects. For example, this description accompanies a picture of an explosion inside a vacuum tube:

One Word. Tube. Musicians call it *The Sound*. It's what matters in your music; It cannot be measured by watts or metered distortion, only by ear. Yours. The Classic Tube Sound. Overlord has harnessed the sound by using a genuine vacuum tube. It will give your music the power and mystery, color and range of the classic tube sound. Fire over to your music store and hear the sound in your soul. But beware, for Overlord takes no prisoners.[46]

The ad copy employs short, blunt sentences and a menacing tone to evoke a mysterious, powerful aura for what is, actually, a little metal box. Compare this ad for guitar pickups, which relies on the reputation of virtuoso guitarist Yngwie Malmsteen:

Yngwie's brand of drop dead playing is loaded with darkly mythic themes, classically-inspired solo riffs played at hypersonic speed and brutally precise technique—all executed with the Devil-may-care defiance of a true rock warrior. DiMarzio delivers all the power, tone and deadly accurate performance Yngwie demands. He uses two HS-3 ™ vertical humbuckers in the neck and bridge because he likes their fat, "single-coil" tone, and they give him the smooth sound he needs for playing at blistering volume with no hum or screechiness.[47]

Musicians themselves also testify to the importance of sound in interviews. Judas Priest's Glenn Tipton emphasizes: "If you've got a bad sound or very little sustain, where your guitar is not singing, it's very difficult to play a lead break. . . . If you've got a sound that you're struggling with then you'll never play a lead break properly or with the right amount of feel."[48] Such comments and advertisements are valuable corroboration of the discursive significance of timbre as a means of articulating power and affect.

VOLUME

Timbre is in part dependent on volume, and heavy metal is necessarily loud. The complete electronic control of sound reproduction that characterizes modern music allows metal to be reproduced, theoretically, at any dynamic level. However, the nature of metal and the needs and pleasures it addresses demand that it always be heard loud. Even when it is heard from a distance, or even softly sung to oneself, metal is imagined as loud, for volume is an important contributor to the heaviness of heavy metal. Robert Duncan writes of the "loudestness" of heavy metal, its perceived status as the most sonically powerful of musical discourses.[49]

Heavy metal relies heavily on technology for its effects, not least for this sheer volume of sound, impossible until recent decades. But reverb and echo units, as well as sophisticated overdubbing techniques, have also become important to metal performance and recording. Such processing can expand aural space, making the music's power seem to extend infinitely. This spatiality complements the intense physicality of what is aptly called "heavy metal," a materiality paradoxically created by sound, but sound so loud and compelling as to conflate inner and outer realities for the audience. Both extreme volume and artificially produced aural indicators of space allow the music to transform the actual location of the listener; music affects the experience of space as well as time. Loudness mediates between the power enacted by the music and the listener's experience of power. Intense volume abolishes the boundaries between oneself and such representations; the music is felt within as much as without, and the body is seemingly hailed directly, subjectivity responding to the empowerment of the body rather than the other way around.

VOCAL TIMBRE

The vocal sounds of heavy metal are similar, in some ways, to the guitar sounds. Quite often, vocalists deliberately distort their voices, for many of the same reasons that guitar players distort theirs. Heavy metal vocalists project brightness and power by overdriving their voices (or by seeming to), and they also sing long sustained notes to suggest intensity and power; sometimes heavy vibrato is used for further intensification (Rob Halford of Judas Priest is a prominent example).[50] The tough solo voice, the norm of vocal delivery, is occasionally supplemented by a chorus of backup voices, most often during the chorus section of the song. These additional voices serve to enlarge the statements of the solo vocalist, enacting the approval or participation of the larger social world, or at least a segment of it.

David Lee Roth's vocals on "Runnin' with the Devil" are typically raucous and flamboyant. His lyrics are punctuated by screams and other sounds of physical and emotional intensity. Singing alone on the verses,

Roth is joined by a chorus on the chorus, where the title hook, "Runnin' with the Devil," is confirmed by other voices. Processed to give a sense of great space, these chorus vocals virtually demand that the listener feel included in the collective affirmation of what is presented as an exciting image.

MODE AND HARMONY

A basic component of any song's affect is the set of pitch relationships it establishes, which is often referred to as a musical mode. Scholars seldom examine the operation of mode in popular music, but discussions of mode are common in professional and semiprofessional guitarists' magazines like *Guitar for the Practicing Musician*, *Guitar Player*, and *Guitar World*.[51] Academics usually think of mode as but a technical, descriptive category, while rock journalists are likely to regard any discussion of mode as academic obfuscation. The guitarist/theorists who write for other guitarists, on the other hand, often explicitly discuss the affective meanings of specific modes: "The patented quasi-classical, Gothic sound of the Aeolian mode (natural minor) is found in numerous familiar applications. . . . Another modal sound closely associated with modern metal is the more exotic Phrygian mode."[52]

Mode is, in fact, widely acknowledged by heavy metal musicians as a crucial part of the musical production of meaning; they know their audiences respond differently to each mode, and they find it useful to think and teach in terms of modal theory.[53] On my first day of heavy metal guitar lessons, my teacher, Jeff Loven, gave me a mimeographed handout he had devised called "Those Crazy Modes." It spelled out the seven medieval modes and, more important, gave examples of specific songs and typical chord progressions for each mode.

The terminology for these modes is borrowed from medieval and Renaissance music theory, which had already borrowed from an ancient Greek theoretical system, where scales were named after the musical practices of various ancient ethnic groups: the Dorians, the Aeolians, the Phrygians, and others. While the particular associations that were once attached to each mode vanished long ago, modes continue to produce powerful and specific affective charges. In fact, mode is one of the primary constituents of genre in popular music. Most heavy metal is either Aeolian or Dorian, for example, although speed metal is usually Phrygian or Locrian; most pop songs are either major (Ionian) or Mixolydian.

To say that a piece is in a particular mode is to suggest quite a bit about how that piece works, for a mode is a scale that also implies a set of functional syntactical relationships and affective potentials. The differences are quite easy to hear: imagine (or play) the beginning riff of Deep Purple's "Smoke on the Water" in its original blues-Aeolian form (G–B♭–C, G–B♭–D♭–C); now play it in major/Ionian (G–B–C, G–B–D–C)—it sounds like a Pat Boone cover; give it a Phrygian twist (G–A♭–D, G–A♭–E♭–D), and it sounds like Megadeth.[54] Modes are not merely abstruse theoretical categories; they can serve as a shorthand for referring to sets of meaningful elements of musical discourses.

The pitch relations established by modes provide the framework within which harmonic progressions operate. Wolf Marshall, a prominent teacher of metal guitar theory and technique, summarizes the basics: "By building triads or power chords on root, 7th, and 6th: i, VII, and VI—Am, G, F—the characteristic Aeolian chord progression, absolutely indigenous to modern rock/metal, is generated." Marshall continues with the Phrygian mode, which "produces an immediately recognizable chord sequence by building chords on root, 2nd, and 7th—i, II, and VII—Am, B♭, G."[55] Affectively, the Phrygian mode is distinctive: only this mode has a second degree only a half step away from the tonic instead of a whole step. Phenomenologically, this closeness means that the second degree hangs precariously over the tonic, making the mode seem claustrophobic and unstable. Hedged in by its upper neighbor, even the tonic, normally the point of rest, acquires an uncomfortable inflection in this mode.

Many academics who write about popular music have continued to assume that rock harmony is simple, even "primitive." There are two problems with this view. First, calling something simple does not explain its function, and second, all rock harmony is *not* simple, especially in the 1980s. Consider this excerpt from the "Performance Notes" for a published transcription of a heavy metal guitar solo by Joe Satriani, on his song, "Surfing with the Alien":

"Surfing" . . . literally explodes (using an overdubbed jet plane sample) into the opening rhythm figure based on the G Dorian mode. The melody enters eight bars later and by alternating between phrases using both the major and minor 3rd (B and B♭) a combined modality of Dorian and Mixolydian modes is achieved using a "Pitch Axis" of G. . . . After another jet plane break, we hit hard into the first guitar solo on the "and" of beat 4, launching into a series of trilled sextuplets based on the C♯ Phrygian-Dominant mode (the fifth mode of F♯ harmonic minor).[56]

Not only is heavy metal harmony often quite complex, but the analytical discourse used by teachers and players is often very sophisticated (see chap. 3). Cultural critics can make use of the analytical categories provided by modal theory, and used by many popular musicians themselves, to produce more detailed explanations of musical effects.

"Runnin' with the Devil" makes its Aeolian basis clear immediately. Over a pulsing pedal E in the bass, guitar chords move from C to a suspended D, then finally resolve to the tonic E. This is the ♭VI–♭VII–I harmonic progression discussed by Wolf Marshall; its affective character is discursively coded as aggressive and defiant (in part because of its difference from the tonal syntactical norms that underlie other popular music). But the modal basis of this song is unusually active; it is transformed at the end of every two-measure rhythmic phrase. The opening chords are all power chords, without thirds, and thus the minor implication of the E chord is established by the G in the C power chord. But the resolution from the suspended D to the tonic E is accomplished through a passing full A chord, which resolves to a full E chord with a G♯. I will return to the significance of this modal shift (from Aeolian to Mixolydian) when I discuss the song in a more integrated way later on.

RHYTHM

Rhythm has been particularly neglected in Western theories of musical meaning. This is usually explained in terms of the difficulty of generalizing rhythmic concepts except on the simple metric level. But it is also because it is in rhythm that the relationship of bodily experience to musical gesture is most apparent. Music theorists who are concerned with addressing rhythm have either ignored the body completely or argued that physical involvement with music is perverse or primitive:

Of course one often does hear exciting interpretations that build up so much energy that the overflow is imparted to the audience, which has to respond by immediate clapping; but I wonder whether these performances are not, for that very reason, a bit meretricious. Leo Stein has suggested that music requiring bodily motion on the part of the listener for its complete enjoyment, like much popular dance music, is by that token artistically imperfect.[57]

Denial of the body, related to the common fear of music's "feminizing" effects, is a recurrent anxiety of Western music criticism (and Western culture more generally). It is connected with suspicion of the sensual subversion of reason, and it is often invoked in the context of the reactionary projection of innovative threats onto the most immediate—and therefore dangerous—of others: women.[58] The fact that non-Western and popular cultures have not evinced the same commitment to denying physical meaning and pleasure has historically been construed, circularly, as evidence of their inferiority. In situations where the radical splits of Western culture—mind/body, art/life, individual/social—are not epistemological givens, quite different accounts of the role of the body in making and enjoying music are told.

Although rhythm is generally understood to be an important parameter of musical meaning in popular music, and the importance of the body's physical response is more openly acknowledged there than in "art" music, rhythm remains an elusive aspect to theorize and explain. One study of rhythm in popular music implicitly assumes that rhythmic complexity is equivalent to artistic merit and compares the simple rhythms of much rock with the military march: "The relentless drumbeat of the military band helps to mobilize soldiers for mindless war games, while the oppressive 4/4 beat that characterizes so much commercial rock captures and concentrates young people's energies on less harmful, but equally mindless, activity."[59] But the author misses the point of military marches, which is not to inculcate mindlessness but rather *single*-mindedness. He assumes that rhythmic complexity corresponds to artistic value; but both marches and metal sometimes rely upon an impression of simplicity for their social effectiveness, an impression that in fact may be made possible only by considerable skill and technical mediation and that may serve to help articulate complex social meanings.

Rhythm in heavy metal often seems very simple; it appears only to rouse physical energy and cue collective participation in heavy metal's version of dancing, headbanging. But a dialectic of freedom and control, which I will later trace in terms of ensemble and solo sections, is also inscribed rhythmically. Accents and rhythmic deviations, whether performed by the vocalist, the guitar soloist, or the whole band, are all the more significant for being played against the solid pulse that characterizes metal. Although most metal is in 4/4 time, the rhythmic framework is organized more basically around a pulse than a meter. Ensemble punches and solo or vocal syncopations alike strain against the beat more than the barline. Larger metrical patterns, usually two measures or four, function like harmonic progressions in indicating short-term goals.

The simple rhythmic pulse of "Runnin' with the Devil" is a major contributor to its affective power. Introduced by the bass alone at the beginning, a monolithic, inexorable pulse underlies most of the rest of the song. There is no interplay of polyrhythms, such as John Chernoff relates to the complex social networks articulated through African rhythmic polyphony. Instead, the pulse utterly dominates the rhythmic dimension of the piece; its function is in part to articulate control of time and energy. The control it represents is unitary, not multiple, and insofar as power is strongly gender-coded, it could be called phallic (see chap. 4). Rhythmically, "Runnin' with the Devil" celebrates power and offers to the listener an experience of that power; the pulse lets us feel what we might imagine extreme power feels like. The guitar chords pull away from that control and return to alignment with it, as do the vocals, in order to offer the pleasures of escape and reintegration.

MELODY

Melody is relatively less important in metal than in many other kinds of music, just as timbre is much more significant; discourses implicitly prioritize musical parameters differently. Two typical characteristics of metal melody stand out: first, melodic patterns in heavy metal frequently include long notes at the ends of phrases; these notes are either held out to signify power and intensity, like sustained notes on the guitar, or they are rasped, shrieked, or moaned, to contribute noise and extremity. Second, some singers tend to use a great deal of syncopation in their melodic lines. This can function as a solution to the problems of intelligibility in the face of metal's high instrumental volumes, as the singer places syllables between the beats, or it can have the effect of signifying resistance with respect to the context constructed by the instruments.

The former problem is not present in "Runnin' with the Devil," since it is the guitar that syncopates and since the accompanying instruments reduce their volume during the verses. And vocal syncopation as resistance is inappropriate here because the singer's rebellion is supported by the music rather than opposed to it. Closer attention to melody in "Runnin' with the Devil" would be repaid to some extent. For example, the opening vocal phrase is distinguished by an upward leap from the tonic A to the seventh degree of the mode, which then functions in a 4–3 suspension over the D chord. In the context of the song, the leap contributes to the sense of willfulness and excess that the lead singer projects, and the fact that he leaps to a suspension adds striving to the gesture.

GUITAR SOLOS

The electric guitar is the most important virtuoso instrument of the past three decades. Virtually every heavy metal song features at least one guitar solo; few contain solos by any other instrument (drum solos are special set pieces, often performed once during a concert but almost never recorded, at least in the 1980s). The sustain of the distorted electric guitar, besides being important for the production of power chords, increases its potential as a virtuoso solo instrument.[60]

Eddie Van Halen revolutionized electric guitar playing, as had Jimi Hendrix before him, in the direction of greater virtuosity. Van Halen's solos, featured on nearly every song his band recorded, along with his sensitive, imaginative "comping" behind the singer, inspired a whole generation of young guitar players toward greater technical facility and theoretical sophistication. It is therefore surprising and significant that no real guitar solo appears in "Runnin' with the Devil." Several guitar solos will be analyzed in the next chapter, but to explain their absence in "Runnin' with the Devil" requires a more integrated reading of that song.

"Runnin' with the Devil"

Simultaneous with the release of Van Halen's first album came the release of the band's image. Although all four members of the band were reputed to be wild and party-prone, perhaps the most important gossip concerned David Lee Roth, the lead singer, for the lead singer of a rock band usually "fronts" the band not only on stage but in interviews and in rumor. Roth's notoriety and success grew when it was revealed that he had purchased insurance against paternity suits from Lloyd's of London. Lewd and athletic on stage, Roth also affected exaggeratedly sexy costumes, such as tight leather pants with most of the buttocks cut out.

The cover of the first Van Halen album featured motion-blurred photos of the four band members, each figure accented with colored light against a deep black background. The musicians appear in an abstracted performance scene, and all four are caught in poses that suggest physical intensity: bodies bent and taut, mouths open as though screaming. Roth displays his naked chest and holds his microphone so that it juts from his crotch. The Van Halen logo, bright and metallic, connects the four musicians. On the inner sleeve another set of pictures portrays the band members as though they have just finished playing: exhausted, dripping with sweat, drained yet satisfied. In a live performance, a tremendous apparatus of promotion and production comes into play to help define the event, as well as lighting, special effects, musicians' behavior and banter, and the crowd's own contribution to the dynamic of the performance. But even when a listener encounters only the album, much of the same framing is presented, as the packaging of the album is designed to evoke the excitement of live performance.

The lyrics emphasize that running with the Devil is a trope for having freedom; the music glorifies that image by implying power as well.

I live my life like there's no tomorrow
And all I've got, I had to steal

. . . .

I've got no love, no love you'd call real
Ain't got nobody waiting at home

Runnin' with the Devil . . .

Freedom is presented as a lack of social ties: no love, no law, no responsibility, no delayed gratification. One might feel lonely, but that loneliness can also be a source of pride. Running with the Devil means living in the present, and the music helps us experience the pleasure of the moment. The fantasy is one of escape from all social conventions; it is based on a quite bourgeois concept of the individual, who supposedly has some sort of essence that can be freed from social constrictions. In fact, though, the social boundaries that are felt to contain are also the structure within which these very fantasies are produced.[61]

The verses and choruses are presented from very different perspectives. The verses relate an individual experience; the singer is reflective and confessional as he describes his life-style. Indeed, during the verses, which are presented musically in a different key, the lyrics are inflected with awareness of doubt and guilt. The fantasy is even questioned: the singer admits that running with the Devil is not exactly as he thought it would be, that it has its drawbacks. But the choruses sweep those doubts away in a collective affirmation of the fantasy. It is the backing chorus that is so sure of the fantasy's validity, not the singer, who punctuates the chorus lines with pained/ecstatic screams. This is fundamentally a social fantasy, one believed in much more completely by those who feel constrained than by the lonely individual on the road, who is able to see its contradictions.

That the fantasy is so powerfully articulated, though, is due to the music of the chorus. In particular, the chords move from a typically metallic Aeolian ♭VI–♭VII motion through a surprise transformation to the tonic major. The main gesture is a syncopated suspension of a power chord on ♭VII (D) over the pulsing bass tonic (E); the E serves as a pedal point that clashes with the D, creating desire for resolution while guaranteeing it. But the resolution is simultaneous with a modal shift that occurs every two measures and constructs an affective transcendence. Every two bars we are lifted out of the familiar negative Aeolian terrain into the perfect resolution of the major mode's tonic.

Immediately thereafter, we are plunged again into Aeolian gloom and then carried up out of it once more. This description may seem fanciful in words, but the affective meaning is unmistakably coded discursively.[62]

This two-measure pattern of tension and release, negativity and transcendence, is the most important signifying feature of the song. This modal shift is the song's "hook," and the formal/narrative structure of the song is built around it. After each statement of a verse, there is a tremendous affective charge in moving into this chorus material. In part, this is a switch from an individual, prominently verbal section into a section of collective participation, backed by higher musical energy. Audiences respond to narrative patterns such as this by increasing their physical response and engagement at the beginning of the chorus.

The move into the chorus is propelled not only by shifts in key and mode but also by dynamic, timbral, and rhythmic changes. The verses are quieter, accompanied by syncopated, descending chords (not power chords) in the guitar. All of this is blown away with each entry of the chorus, with its power chords and inexorably pulsing bass. The rhythms of the chorus are not static, though; the two-measure units of the chorus's harmonic progression are also articulated rhythmically. The ♭VII power chord suspension begins on the upbeat of beat 1, is held through the bar, and is resolved on the upbeat of beat 2 of the next measure. The attack of the suspension feels jarring, but its resolution anticipates rather than follows a strong beat (beat 3). Thus, the harmonic resolution (and modal shift) precedes the rhythmic resolution, stretching out the moment of transcendence.

"Runnin' with the Devil" has one other formal section that has not yet been discussed: the four-measure guitar solo that comes after the chorus following the second verse (and again when the second verse is repeated). The guitar is featured alone, with its own melodic material, but these four bars are actually very little like most heavy metal guitar solos: too short, too simple, and since the same statement is repeated later in the song, the necessary impression of spontaneity and improvisation is lacking. Most recorded solos are, in fact, composed and practiced ahead of time, but a sense of immediacy is crucial, for metal guitar solos typically take the form of rhetorical outbursts, characterized by fast licks and soaring, amazing virtuosity that can create a sense of perfect freedom and omnipotence; they model escape from social constraints, extravagant individuality (see chap. 3).

Heavy metal revolves around identification with power, intensity of experience, freedom, and community. Musically, a dialectic is often set up between the potentially oppressive power of bass, drums, and rhythm guitar, and the liberating, empowering vehicle of the guitar solo or the resistance of the voice. The feeling of freedom created by the freedom of motion of the guitar solos and fills can be at various times supported, defended, or threatened by the physical power of the bass and the violence of the drums. The latter rigidly organize and control time; the guitar escapes with flashy runs and other arrhythmic gestures. The solo positions the listener: he or she can identify with the controlling power without feeling threatened because the solo can transcend anything.

Why, then, is there no true heavy metal guitar solo in "Runnin' with the Devil," which many have argued is exemplary metal? It is certainly no accident; not only are solos virtually required by the conventions of the genre, but Van Halen's success was largely owing to the phenomenal virtuosity of Eddie Van Halen's guitar playing. The "song" that follows "Runnin' with the Devil" on the album is simply an extended guitar solo, an unaccompanied cadenza called "Eruption." Every other song on the record boasts at least one real guitar solo; why not this one?

"Runnin' with the Devil" is an exception to the norms of the genre because it conflates control and freedom, two core concerns of the genre, in a way that is unusual in metal. The brief guitar fills allow some display of the guitar without the disruption that a real solo would cause. But the transcendent moment usually provided by a guitar solo can be omitted since it is already constructed every two measures through a harmonic/modal shift. The chorus of the song is at once powerfully controlled—stable, regular phrases; an immutable bass pedal point, pulsing absolutely reliably—and free, constantly transcending its modal premises. This is not to say that the guitar solo *had to be* left out but rather to explain how the song could deviate from generic norms and still be effective.[63]

Because the verses and guitar fills are presented in a different key, the modulation back to the chorus reestablishes order (the proper, original key). But since the chorus section begins with a *suspension* in that key, it is not legitimated by any harmonic logic, and the reestablishment of the tonic key is heard at the same time as an arbitrary leap. The usual dialectical tension between the rhythm section's control and the soloist's freedom has been obviated by this unusual fusing of both impulses within the same musical phrase. Much of the pleasure of "Runnin' with the Devil" is a result of this ingenious, compelling reconciliation of these two fundamental desires for freedom and security—ideologically crucial concerns in the world of heavy metal.

Negotiation and Pleasure

Early in this chapter, I asserted that it was important to analyze musical texts in ways that kept them open to the kinds of negotiated receptions they get in real life. Yet my analysis of "Runnin' with the Devil" has, so far, been quite monovocal; I have specified meanings that I identified as discursively produced, as though all metal fans had the same understanding of all metal songs. In fact, my interviews with heavy metal fans and musicians tell me that this is not the case. Both groups come to heavy metal with a wide range of personal histories and needs; they all not only take selectively from the genre but contribute to it. Their conversations with each other—at concerts, through magazine letters columns, and among friends—as well as their consumption choices themselves, constitute a dialogue with the shifting structures and meanings of the genre.[64]

However, the word *negotiations* reminds us that discourses do have the power to organize the exchange of meanings; deviations are resistant or creative. For example, the Christian heavy metal band Stryper demonstrates that the specific musical gestures of heavy metal operate within a code to communicate experiences of power and transcendent freedom because their attempt to appropriate the codes of metal is posited on the suitability of precisely such experiences for evangelism. The power is God's; the transcendent freedom represents the rewards of Christianity; the intensity is that of religious experience. Stryper appropriates and reinterprets the codes of heavy metal, using metal's means to produce different meanings. Metal's noisiness might seem incompatible with a Christian agenda, but Stryper exploits just that subversive aura to make more appealing what would otherwise seem a wholly institutional message. Stryper presents Christianity as an exciting, youth-oriented alternative; they offer their fans a chance to enjoy the pleasures of heavy metal and feel virtuous at the same time.

It is easy to forget that culture exerts the influence it does because it provides us with pleasure. Many analyses of musical works give no hint at all that music is experienced, that it has impact because it is enjoyed. In part this is a result of a long Western tradition of rationalist suspicion of sensuality. Yet in modern times, this problem is in part one that chronically plagues those scholars who are interested in taking popular culture seriously: a desire to find explicit political agendas and intellectual complexity in at least some popular art, and a distrust of those dimensions of art that appeal to the senses, to physical pleasure. But pleasure frequently *is* the politics of music—both the pleasure of affirmation and the pleasure of interference, the pleasure of marginalized people which has evaded channelization.

In the case of popular music, this pleasure is largely experienced in response to the discursively organized signification of the music itself—beyond the vocals. The analytical perspectives and techniques developed in this chapter are meant to be both provocative and enabling of further discussions of musical meaning in popular music. And the readings given here are not intended to be essential or definitive; while these interpretive arguments are grounded in ethnography as well as musical and social history, at a more general level this chapter simply points out that there is ample evidence that music is meaningful, notes that musical meanings are almost never dealt with, and insists that this is an important task for scholars, for it seems the only way to account for the power and pleasure of popular music. Beyond this are the questions to be addressed in the following chapters: Whose pleasure? To what ends? In the service of what interests is pleasure offered and experienced?

At the end of an Iron Maiden concert I attended in 1988, light, happy, Muzak-style music came through the house PA system to accompany the crowd's exit. I didn't recognize the tune, but it was very close to "It's a Small World," the mindlessly cute, cloyingly smug song around which an entire ride was built at Disneyland. This vapid music, so incongruous after Iron Maiden's powerful show, was clearly intended to disperse the energy of the concert, promoting orderly exit and calm reintegration with the world outside. It succeeded remarkably: fifteen thousand screaming, sweating, straining heavy metal fans were transformed into a group as sedate as any homeward-bound symphony orchestra fans. This impressive feat can be credited to the invisible, intangible, affective power of music that seemed quite incidental to the concert experience. The orderliness and affirmativity of the exit music had calming effects that no conceivable verbal utterance could have accomplished. It was effective precisely because it, like much of the concert itself, seemed to come from everywhere and no one, from beyond the vocals.

CHAPTER THREE

Eruptions
Heavy Metal Appropriations
of Classical Virtuosity

> We have now heard him, the strange wonder, whom the superstition
> of past ages, possessed by the delusion that such things could never
> be done without the help of the Evil One, would undoubtedly have condemned
> to the stake—we have heard him, and seen him too, which, of course,
> makes a part of the affair. Just look at the pale, slender youth in his
> clothes that signal the nonconformist; the long, sleek, drooping hair . . .
> those features so strongly stamped and full of meaning, in this respect
> reminding one of Paganini, who, indeed, has been his model of
> hitherto undreampt-of virtuosity and technical brilliance from the
> very first moment he heard him and was swept away.[1]

In the liner notes for his 1988 album *Odyssey*, heavy metal guitar-ist Yngwie J. Malmsteen claimed a musical genealogy that confounds the stability of conventional categorizations of music into classical and popular spheres. In his list of acknowledgments, along with the usual cast of agents and producers, suppliers of musical equipment, and rela-tives and friends, Malmsteen expressed gratitude to J. S. Bach, Nicolo Paganini, Antonio Vivaldi, Ludwig van Beethoven, Jimi Hendrix, and Ritchie Blackmore.[2] From the very beginnings of heavy metal in the late 1960s, guitar players had experimented with the musical materials of eighteenth- and nineteenth-century European composers. But the trend came to full fruition around the time of Malmsteen's debut in the early 1980s; a writer for the leading professional guitar magazine said flatly that the single most important development in rock guitar in the 1980s was "the turn to classical music for inspiration and form."[3]

Heavy metal, like all forms of rock and soul, owes its biggest debt to African-American blues.[4] The harmonic progressions, vocal lines, and guitar improvisations of metal all rely heavily on the pentatonic scales derived from blues music. The moans and screams of metal guitar playing, now performed with whammy bars and overdriven amplifiers, derive from the bottleneck playing of the Delta blues musicians and ultimately from earlier African-American vocal styles. Angus Young, guitarist with AC/DC, recalls, "I started out listening to a lot of early blues people, like B. B. King, Buddy Guy, and Muddy Waters."[5] Such statements are not uncommon, and heavy metal guitarists who did not study the blues directly learned secondhand, from the British cover versions of Eric Clapton and Jimmy Page or from the most conspicuous link between heavy metal and blues and r&b, Jimi Hendrix.

But from the very beginning of heavy metal there has been another important influence: that assemblage of disparate musical styles known in the twentieth century as "classical music." Throughout metal's twenty-year history, its most influential musicians have been guitar players who have also studied classical music. Their appropriation and adaptation of classical models sparked the development of a new kind of guitar virtuosity, changes in the harmonic and melodic language of heavy metal, and new modes of musical pedagogy and analysis.

Classical Prestige and Popular Meanings

The classical influence on heavy metal marks a merger of what are generally regarded as the most and least prestigious musical discourses of our time. This influence thus seems an unlikely one, and we must wonder why metal musicians and fans have found such a discursive fusion useful and compelling. Musicologists have frequently characterized adaptive encounters among musical practices as natural expansions of musical resources, as musicians find in foreign musics new means with which to assert their innovative creativity. Yet such explanations merely reiterate, covertly, a characteristically Western interest in progress, expansion, and colonization. They do little to account for the appearance of specific fusions at particular historical moments or to probe the power relations implicit in all such encounters. We will need more cogent explanations than those with which musicology has traditionally explained classical exoticism, fusions of national styles, and elite dabblings in jazz.

I should emphasize that my discussion of the relationship of heavy metal and classical music is not simply a bid to elevate the former's cultural prestige. Attempts to legitimate popular culture by applying the standards of "high" culture are not uncommon, and they are rightly condemned as wrongheaded and counterproductive by those who see such friends of "low" culture as too willing to cede the high ground.

That is, the assumptions that underpin cultural value judgments are left untouched, and the dice remain loaded against popular culture. An attempt to legitimate heavy metal in terms of the criteria of classical music, like prior treatments of the Beatles' and other rock music, could easily miss the point, for heavy metal is in many ways antithetical to today's classical music. Such a project would disperse the differences between metal and other musics, accomplishing a kind of musicological colonization that musicians, fans, and cultural historians alike would find alienating and pointless.[6]

But in the case of heavy metal, the relationship to classical modes of thought and music making is not merely in the eye of the beholder. To compare it with culturally more prestigious music is entirely appropriate, for the musicians who compose, perform, and teach this music have tapped the modern classical canon for musical techniques and procedures that they have then fused with their blues-based rock sensibility. Their instrumental virtuosity, theoretical self-consciousness, and studious devotion to the works of the classical canon means that their work could be valorized in the more "legitimate" terms of classical excellence. But more important, metal guitarists' appropriations of classical music provide a vital opportunity for examining musical signification in contexts of popular creativity and cultural contestation.

The history of American popular music is replete with examples of appropriation "from below"—popular adaptations of classical music. As I discuss examples drawn from heavy metal, I will be describing a number of ways in which classical music is being used, all of which have antecedents in other twentieth-century popular music. The sorts of value popular appropriators find in classical music might be grouped around these topics: semiotics, virtuosity, theory, and prestige. I will explore each of these aspects in turn as I discuss the work of several of the most influential and successful heavy metal guitarists. But before examining the classical influence upon metal, I must clarify my understanding of the term "classical music," particularly my attribution to it of prestige and semiotic significance.

The prestige of classical music encompasses both its constructed aura of transcendent profundity and its affiliation with powerful social groups. Although the potency of its aura and the usefulness of its class status depend upon the widespread assumption that classical music is somehow timeless and universal, we know that "classical music" is a relatively recent cultural construct. The canon of the music now known as "the great works of the classical tradition" began to form early in the nineteenth century, with revivals of "ancient" music (Bach and Mozart) and series publications of composers' collected works. Lawrence W. Levine has carefully detailed the process of elevation and "sacralization," begun midway through the nineteenth century, whereby European concert music was wrenched away from a variety of popular contexts and made to serve the social agenda of a powerful minority of Americans. Along with the popular plays of Shakespeare, German music was elevated, as an elite attempted to impose a monolithic "moral order," repudiating the plurality of cultural life.[7] By the twentieth century, institutional and interpretive structures came to shape musical reception so completely that what we know today as "classical music" is less a useful label for a historical tradition than a genre of twentieth-century music.

Perhaps the most forceful critique of the institution of modern concert music is that of Christopher Small, who argues that this process of sacralization has almost completely effaced original social and political meanings.[8] Musical works that were created for courts, churches, public concerts, and salons of connoisseurs, and that had modeled and enacted the social relationships important to those specific audiences, have become a set of interchangeable great pieces. All of the vast range of meanings produced by these disparate musics are reduced to singularity in the present. That single meaning, Small maintains, is one of defense—specifically, defense of the social relationships and ideologies that underpin the status quo. Cultural hierarchy is used to legitimate social hierarchy and to marginalize the voices of all musicians who stand outside the canon, representing those who stand at the margins of social power. Small's critique is important because it is essential to realize that classical music is not just "great" music; it is a constructed category that reflects the priorities of a historical moment and that serves certain social interests at the expense of others. Classical music is the sort of thing Eric Hobsbawm calls an "invented tradition," whereby present interests construct a cohesive past to establish or legitimate present-day institutions or social relations.[9] The hodgepodge of the classical canon—aristocratic and bourgeois music; academic, sacred, and secular; music for public concerts, private soirees, and dancing—has one thing in common: its function as the most prestigious culture of the twentieth century.

Once established, though, classical music can be negotiated; it has been both a bulwark of class privilege and a means whereby other social barriers could be overcome. African-American performers and composers have long worked to defeat racist essentialism by proving their ability to write and perform European concert music. The chamber jazz of the Modern Jazz Quartet, with its cool fusions of swing and classical forms, was also a statement of black pride, however conservative it seemed amid the turmoil of the 1960s. Duke Ellington was a crucial figure in the struggle to achieve widespread respect for African-American music, in large measure because his skills as composer, orchestrator, and leader made him, of all jazz musicians, most closely match the prestigious model of the classical composer.

Rock fusions with classical styles are most often associated with the "progressive rock" or "art rock" of the late 1960s. With *Sgt. Pepper's Lonely Hearts Club Band*, the Beatles kicked off an era of self-conscious experimentation with the instrumentation and stylistic features of classical music. Producer George Martin's training as a classical oboist exposed him to many of the peculiarities that appeared on the Beatles' recordings: piccolo trumpet (a modern instrument now associated with Baroque music), classical string quartets, odd metric patterns perhaps inspired by Stravinsky or Bartók (or more directly by the non-Western music that had inspired *them*). The Moody Blues collaborated with the London Festival Orchestra for *Days of Future Passed* in 1968, and groups as different as The Who, Yes, The Kinks, and Emerson, Lake, and Palmer composed classically influenced rock songs, rock concertos, and rock operas. Deep Purple, eventually recognized as one of the founding bands of heavy metal, began to develop in that direction only after guitarist Ritchie Blackmore grew dissatisfied with fusions such as keyboardist Jon Lord's ambitious *Concerto for Group and Orchestra* (1969) and reoriented the band: "I felt that the whole orchestra thing was a bit tame. I mean, you're playing in the Royal Albert Hall, and the audience sits there with folded arms, and you're standing there playing next to a violinist who holds his ears everytime you take a solo. It doesn't make you feel particularly inspired." [10] Blackmore realized that the institutions and audience expectations that frame classical music would always control the reception of any music performed within that context; while he was attracted to classical musical resources, he found that he would have to work with them on his own turf.

Discussions of art rock rarely move beyond sketching influences to address the question of *why* classical music was used by these groups. [11] Certainly one of the most important reasons is prestige. Rock critics' own preoccupation with art rock reflects their acceptance of the premises of the classical model. Performers who haven't composed their own material—"girl groups," Motown, soul singers—have rarely won critical respect comparable to that granted artists who better fit the model of the auteur, the solitary composing genius. Sometimes performers stake their claims to classical prestige explicitly. Emerson, Lake, and Palmer's neoclassical extravaganzas, such as their rendering of Mussorgsky's *Pic-*

tures at an Exhibition (1972), were intended as elevations of public taste and expressions of advanced musicianship. Keith Emerson's attraction to classical resources was unabashedly elitist; he considered ordinary popular music degraded and took on the mission of raising the artistic level of rock. In such art rock, classical references and quotations were intended to be recognized as such; their function was, in large measure, to invoke classical music and to confer some of its prestigious status and seriousness.

Other popular musicians have been attracted to classical resources for reasons of signification beyond prestige. At least since the late 1920s, when classical string sections began to appear on recordings of Tin Pan Alley music, classical means have been used to expand the rhetorical palette—and social meanings—of popular music. In Bing Crosby's Depression-era hit, "Brother, Can You Spare a Dime?" (1932), the strings function to underscore the sincerity of Crosby's voice and magnify the poignancy of his character's plight. The recorders on Led Zeppelin's "Stairway to Heaven" (1971) similarly contribute to the song's musical semiotics. They sound archaic and bittersweet; their tranquil contrapuntal motion is at once soothing and mysterious.

Of all of the stylistic or historical subdivisions of classical music, rock music has borrowed most from the Baroque. Richard Middleton has tried to account for this by arguing that there is a "relatively high syntactic correlation" between Baroque and rock musical codes. Like rock music, Baroque music "generally uses conventional harmonic progressions, melodic patterns and structural frameworks, and operates through imaginative combinations, elaborations and variations of these, rather than developing extended, through-composed forms. It also tends to have a regular, strongly marked beat; indeed, its continuo section could be regarded as analogous to the rhythm section of jazz and rock."[12] Middleton suggests, for example, that Procul Harum's "A Whiter Shade of Pale" (1967), by fusing harmonic and melodic material taken from a Bach cantata with the soul ballad vocal style of Ray Charles and Sam Cooke, presented the counterculture with an image of itself as "sensuously spiritual" and "immanently oppositional."[13]

Here the usefulness of Baroque materials depends on both their aura as "classical" and their present semiotic value, to the extent that these meanings are separable. For although this music was composed long ago, it is still circulating, producing meanings in contemporary culture. Metal musicians generally acquire their knowledge of classical music through intense study, but they owe their initial exposure to the music and their audiences' ability to decode it not to the pickled rituals of the concert hall, but to the pervasive recycling of all available musical discourses by the composers of television and movie music. Classical musics are alive and omnipresent in mass culture, despite the best efforts of proponents of cultural apartheid and in part due to their missionary efforts. Mass mediation ensures that there can be no absolute separation of "high" and "low" culture in the modern world; classically trained composers write film scores that draw upon their conservatory studies but succeed or fail on their intelligibility and meaningfulness for mass audiences. Classical music surely no longer signifies as it did originally, but neither are its meanings ahistorical or arbitrary. It is available to culturally competitive groups who claim and use its history, its prestige, and its signifying powers in different ways.

Heavy metal appropriations of classical music are, in fact, very specific and consistent: Bach, not Mozart; Paganini rather than Liszt; Vivaldi and Albinoni instead of Telemann or Monteverdi. This selectivity is remarkable at a time when the historical and semiotic specificity of classical music, on its own turf, has all but vanished, when the classical canon is defined and marketed as a reliable set of equally great and ineffable collectibles. By finding new uses for old music, recycling the rhetoric of Bach and Vivaldi for their own purposes, metal musicians have reopened issues of signification in classical music. Their appropriation suggests that despite the homogenization of that music in the literatures of "music appreciation" and commercial promotion, many listeners perceive and respond to differences, to the musical specificity that reflects historical and social specificity. Thus, the reasons behind heavy metal's classical turn can reveal a great deal, not only about heavy metal but also about classical music. We must ask: if we don't understand his influence on the music of Ozzy Osbourne or Bon Jovi, do we really understand *Bach* as well as we thought we did?

Ritchie Blackmore and the Classical Roots of Metal

That many rock guitarists of the late 1960s experimented with classical influences in their playing can be seen as part of a widespread interest in musical exploration—itself part of the search for social and conceptual options that characterized the decade. Jimmy Page listened to a great range of music to acquire the means to create the varied moods of Led Zeppelin, which ranged from heavy blues to ethereal ballads, Celtic mysticism, Orientalist fantasies, and folkish ballads. Mountain's Leslie West inflected his heavy blues sensibility with classical and jazz licks, and many other early examples could be cited. But the most important musician of the emerging metal/classical fusion was Ritchie Blackmore. As lead guitarist for Deep Purple, Blackmore was one of the most influential guitarists of the late 1960s and early 1970s. Though he was not the first hard rock guitarist to employ classical features, Blackmore greatly affected other players; for many of them, Blackmore's was the first really impressive, compelling fusion of rock and classical music.

Born in 1945, Ritchie Blackmore began playing at age eleven; six years later he was working as a studio session guitarist in London. Blackmore became impressed by Jimi Hendrix's guitar sound, and like Hendrix, he became a pioneer of flashy virtuosity.[14] While young, Blackmore took classical guitar lessons for a year, which affected his fingering technique: unlike most rock guitarists of his generation, he made full use of the little finger on his left hand. But the classical influence shows up most, Blackmore himself maintained, in the music he wrote: "For example, the chord progression in the 'Highway Star' solo on *Machine Head* . . . is a Bach progression." And the solo is "just arpeggios based on Bach."[15] Recorded in 1971 (released in 1972), *Machine Head* contained not only the hits "Highway Star" and "Space Truckin'" but also the heavy metal anthem "Smoke on the Water." The album came to be regarded by fans as one of the classic albums of heavy metal, and it helped generate great enthusiasm for classical/rock fusions.

"Highway Star" is a relatively long and complex song; it winds its way among several different keys, and both Blackmore and the keyboard player, Jon Lord, take extended solos. The organ solo begins over a descending chromatic bass line, reminiscent of the ground bass patterns favored by seventeenth-century composers such as Henry Purcell. Much of the soloing is made up of series of arpeggios, in the style of Vivaldi (or Bach, after he absorbed Vivaldi's influence). The members of Deep Purple abstracted and adapted a particular set of classical features: repetitious melodic patterns (such as arpeggios), square phrase structures, virtuosic soloing, and characteristic harmonic progressions, such as descending through a tetrachord by half steps or cycling through the circle of fifths. The harmonic progressions, as Blackmore asserted, are typically Baroque, as are the rapid, flashy sixteenth-note patterns organized symmetrically through repetition and balanced phrases. In Deep Purple, guitarist and organist alike drew upon these materials to construct a new and effective style of rock virtuosity.

In his "Highway Star" solo, Blackmore begins with blues-derived licks and brings in the Baroque materials climactically at the end, where he overdubs a matching harmony part in thirds, with figuration that recalls Vivaldi's energetic articulation of harmonic progressions in his

Example 1. Deep Purple (1972), "Highway Star," excerpt from Ritchie Blackmore's solo (author's transcription).

Example 2. Antonio Vivaldi, Violin Concerto in D Minor (F. 1, No. 21 in the *Collected Works*, ed. Malipiero, Edizioni Ricordi, 1949), first movement, mm. 87–97.

violin concerti (see examples 1 and 2). As in Vivaldi, a regular and predictable (though dynamic) harmonic sequence provides the backdrop for exhilarating figuration. The harmonic cycles set up rational articulation of time and direction, enabling us to predict what will come next, and the guitar solo energizes these patterns with virtuosic exhibitionism. As in the concerto grosso, the soloist provides the dynamic individual element, in contrast to the stable collectivity of the rhythm section.[16] Vivaldi's social model transfers well to the context of the guitar hero.

Throughout the 1970s, guitarists continued their experimentation with fusions of rock and classical music. Just as jazz musicians had done in the late 1940s, some rock guitarists turned to classical music theory for new musical resources. The *Thesaurus of Scales and Melodic Patterns* by musicologist Nicolas Slonimsky introduced both jazz and rock musicians to harmonic and melodic possibilities such as harmonic minor scales, modal scales, and diminished arpeggios.[17] Ulrich Roth of the German band Scorpions advanced virtuosic standards with his fast scales and dramatic diminished chords. Jazz/rock fusion guitarist Al DiMeola had an important influence on some rock guitarists; his music was by no means heavy metal, but he used a similar distorted, highly sustained guitar tone, and his melodic and harmonic language was close enough to that of metal that his modal explorations influenced heavy metal musicians.

Other major metal guitarists of this period did not pursue the classical influence directly. Michael Schenker, who was perhaps the most influential metal guitarist of continental Europe during the 1970s, had no formal training and no exposure to academic music theory. He taught himself to play, learning Beatles songs and Clapton solos by ear, and his virtuosity has always been primarily blues-based, grounded in the pentatonicism and timbral nuance of the blues guitar. The musical roots of Angus and Malcolm Young of AC/DC are in early rock and roll and r&b, and they have stuck doggedly to them. Glenn Tipton and K. K. Downing, the guitar players of Judas Priest, also had little formal training, and it was only in the late 1980s that the classical influence became pronounced in their playing. But in spite of these exceptions, appropriations of classical music were increasingly important throughout the history of heavy metal and even helped define the genre.

After leaving Deep Purple to pursue a solo career, Ritchie Blackmore continued his study and adaptation of classical music. The liner notes for his first album with his new band, Rainbow (1975), include the acknowledgment: "Inspiration: J. S. Bach." A few years later Blackmore even took up study of the cello, and Rainbow's 1981 release featured a very direct use of classical music in its title cut, "Difficult to Cure," an instrumental built around the "Ode to Joy" from the last movement of Beethoven's Ninth Symphony. Blackmore begins with a distorted version of Beethoven's instrumental recitative, which he transforms into a sitar-like modal flurry over a pedal; the band then moves into the theme of the "Ode" itself. Initially, Blackmore simply repeats the melody without developing or embellishing it, while the band modulates to different keys to freshen the repetitions. The musicians eventually alter the progression for the solos, which are a blend of a boogie blues rhythmic feel with the Orientalist modality of the beginning. In "Difficult to Cure," classical material is quoted literally so that it is sure to be recognized; in fact, the song is self-consciously parodic. The classical model is spoofed by a bouncy 12/8 beat, an incongruous introduction, and the finishing touch: as the song ends, we hear candid laughter in the recording studio. If Blackmore had drawn on Bach for inspiration, Beethoven was merely quoted, with a funny accent. The major mode of Beethoven's tune is rarely used in heavy metal, and when it is combined with a similarly inappropriate bouncy rhythm, Blackmore's distorted guitar and heavy drums end up sounding frivolous and silly. "Difficult to Cure" is a comic anomaly; it reminds us that heavy metal musicians are in fact very selective in their appropriations of the various styles that are usually lumped together as "classical music," and that fusions signify quite precisely.

In an interview published in 1985, Blackmore was asked about his current musical tastes: "I still listen to a great deal of classical music. . . . That's the type of music that moves me because I find it very dramatic. Singers, violinists and organists are generally the musicians I enjoy listening to most of all. I can't stand guitarists!"[18] Twelve years earlier, Blackmore had recommended to the readers of *Guitar Player* that, above all, they study guitarists. He had complained: "Jimmy Page says he listens to piano solos. But I don't see how that helps, because a pianist can play about ten times the speed of a guitarist."[19] In 1973, such technical limitations had been accepted; Blackmore's change of heart may reflect the fact that in 1978 Edward Van Halen redefined virtuosity on the electric guitar.

Edward Van Halen and the New Virtuosity

Alex and Edward Van Halen were born in the Netherlands (Alex in 1955, Edward in 1957) but moved with their family to California while still in grade school. Their father was a professional musician (saxophone and clarinet) whose gigging included live radio shows; he was "constantly practicing, working and going on the road," according to Alex.[20] Jan Van Halen encouraged his sons to become classical musicians, and both boys started piano lessons while very young, dutifully practicing Mozart until their interests in guitar and drums prevailed. After a brief period during which Edward played drums and Alex guitar, they switched instruments and grew increasingly serious about music, playing in a series of bands that would culminate in their tremendous success with Van Halen. Throughout his teens, Eddie was completely absorbed in the guitar, practicing "all day, every day. I used to cut school to come home and play, I was so into it."[21]

Like most rock guitarists, Van Halen was heavily influenced by the dialogic "question-and-answer" of the blues, which he knew mainly by way of the guitar playing of Eric Clapton. "I started out playing blues,"

Van Halen recalls: "I can play real good blues—that's the feeling I was after. But actually I've turned it into a much more aggressive thing. Blues is a real tasty, feel type of thing; so I copped that in the beginning. But then when I started to use a wang [vibrato] bar, I still used that feeling, but rowdier, more aggressive, more attack. But still, I end a lot of phrasing with a bluesy feeling."[22] But along with the influence of the blues, Van Halen's classical piano training taught him music theory that would later prove useful, and his continuing exposure to classical repertoires helped him to transform the electric guitar and forge a new virtuosity for it. Even after he became a rock star, Van Halen still played piano and violin and continued to listen to classical music, especially Bach and Debussy.

Edward Van Halen's impact on rock guitar playing was enormous. The readership of *Guitar Player* elected him Best New Talent in a 1978 poll, and Van Halen went on to win Best Rock Guitarist for an unprecedented five straight years, 1979–83. Yngwie Malmsteen, who himself won Best New Talent in 1984 and Best Rock Guitarist in 1985, credits Van Halen with revolutionizing rock guitar: "When I heard the first Van Halen album, I couldn't believe how great the guitar playing was. . . . I mean, he totally changed the whole guitar field." And even a decade after Van Halen's debut, Billy Gibbons of ZZ Top asserted that "if you had a guitar poll, I'd put Edward Van Halen in the first five slots and then the next five slots would start opening up."[23]

The solo that transformed rock guitar was called, appropriately enough, "Eruption." Released in 1978 on Van Halen's first album, "Eruption" is one minute and twenty-seven seconds of exuberant and playful virtuosity, a violinist's precise and showy technique inflected by the vocal rhetoric of the blues and rock and roll irreverence. Here and elsewhere, Van Halen's guitar playing displays an unprecedented fluidity, due to his skillful use of string bending, two-handed tapping, and his deft touch on the vibrato (or "whammy") bar.

Van Halen's fluid style and innovative technique depend upon the capabilities of amplification equipment that can produce very high electronic gain and indefinite sustain. The electrification of the guitar, begun in the 1920s, and subsequent developments in equipment and playing techniques, particularly the production of sophisticated distortion circuitry in the 1970s, helped make it possible for Baroque music to be newly relevant to guitar players. The electric guitar acquired the capabilities of the premier virtuosic instruments of the seventeenth and eighteenth centuries: the power and speed of the organ, the flexibility and nuance of the violin. Technological increases in sustain and volume made possible the conceptual and technical shifts that led players to explore Baroque models. Of course, the attraction of guitar players to those models helped spur particular technological developments, as when puzzled engineers reluctantly produced distortion-inducing devices for the first time in the mid 1960s, in response to guitarists' demands. Van Halen himself helped develop the sounds upon which his techniques depend by experimenting with a Variac voltage control that made his amps sound "hotter."[24] Van Halen also built some of his guitars himself, and this knowledge of guitar construction and modification affected his performing, just as his musical imagination drove the technological experiments.

In "Eruption," an initial power chord establishes A as tonal point of departure (see example 3). Van Halen moves the first section from blues-based pentatonic licks in A, through a couple of flashy patterns of less clear provenance, to collapse finally back to a low A, which he "wows" with the whammy bar. The opening sounds startlingly effortless, the easy flow of hammer-ons and pull-offs (articulation with the fretting fingers alone, without picking) interrupted by a few confident pauses and precisely picked harmonics. Three power chords introduce the next phrase, ostensibly moving the tonal center to D, although what follows is still mostly based in the A blues mode. Van Halen quickly moves through some Chuck Berry–inspired bends to an exuberant series of bends and wows in a swung rhythm. This section moves directly into a quotation of the best-known cliché of violin pedagogy, an etude by Rodolphe Kreutzer (see examples 4 and 5).[25] Rather than simply playing it straight, though, Van Halen picks each note three or four times in a tremolo style. He is toying with this primer of classical technique, and after two repetitions he spins down and out of it in the same style, pointedly introducing an F natural—which transforms the mode from Kreutzer's major to a darker Phrygian—on his way to the song's midway resting point.

After a second's silence, the piece is reattacked with a flurry of fast picking and hammering. The initial phrase is repeated, first centered on A, then on E; it is rhythmically very complex but rhetorically clear, the accented interruptions of a line of repeated notes suggesting both resolution and mobility.[26] Each time this motive is played, a disorienting scramble with harmonically remote pitches (deftly played by pulling off to open strings) ends up on a trill of the fifth scale degree, which conventionally requires resolution, thus setting up the repeat. A series of fast trills follows a recapitulation of the entrance on A, leading into the most celebrated section of this solo, the lengthy tapping section with which it culminates.

The audacious virtuosity of the rest of the solo was certainly impressive, but it was the tapping that astonished guitarists and fans. Reaching over to strike against the frets with his right hand, Van Halen hammers and pulls with his left, relying on the enhanced gain of his amplifier to sustain a stream of notes. Although a few other guitarists had used tapping to a limited extent, nothing like this had ever been heard before, and "Eruption" spurred guitarists to hyperbole: "Edward Van Halen practically reinvented the art of electric guitar with his incendiary "Eruption" solo."[27] Rock guitarists hailed tapping as not merely a fad or gimmick but a genuine expansion of the instrument's capabilities, the most important technical innovation since Jimi Hendrix. Their enthusiasm for the potentials of the tapping technique increased throughout the 1980s; since 1988 *Guitar for the Practicing Musician* has published a monthly column by Jennifer Batten, "On Tap," solely devoted to exploring this technique.[28] Edward Van Halen's development of two-handed techniques for the guitar is comparable to J. S. Bach's innovations in keyboard fingering. C. P. E. Bach recalled of his father: "He had devised for himself so convenient a system of fingering that it was not hard for him to conquer the greatest difficulties with the most flowing facility. Before him, the most famous clavier players in Germany and other lands had used the thumb but little."[29] Tapping similarly enabled Van Halen and the players who came after him to deploy more fingers and conquer great difficulties, and it particularly encouraged a "flowing facility."

The final section of "Eruption" is wholly tapped. Here the pitches are formed into arpeggios outlining triads. Van Halen's rhythmic torrent of sextuplets energizes a relatively slow rate of harmonic change, a strategy learned from Vivaldi (see example 6; compare example 3). In "Eruption," C# minor is changed to A major by moving one finger up one fret; a diminished triad then pushes through B major to land on E, which is made to feel like a point of arrival. This sense is quickly dispersed, though, when a subtle adjustment transforms the chord to C major. With the help of a couple of passing tones, C moves through D back up to E, in the familiar heavy metal progression of ♭VI–♭VII–I. Chromatic slides confirm E but then sink to establish D and then C in the same way. An abrupt move to B confirms E minor as the new tonic, and increasingly frantic alternation between them (reminiscent of Beethoven's use of similar patterns to increase tension before a final

Example 3. Van Halen (1978), "Eruption" (Music by Edward Van Halen, Alex Van Halen, Michael Anthony and David Lee Roth, Copyright © 1978 Van Halen Music. International Copyright Secured. All Rights Reserved. Reprinted by Permission of Cherry Lane Music Co., Inc. Transcription by Andy Aledort).

Example 4. Rodolphe Kreutzer, "Caprice Study No. #2" for violin, mm. 1–2.

Example 5. Van Halen (1978), "Eruption," excerpt showing transformation of Kreutzer motive.

Example 6. Antonio Vivaldi, Violin Concerto in A Minor, Op. 3, No. 6, third movement, solo violin, mm. 75–91.

cadence; see the end of his Ninth Symphony) leads to a noisy breakdown on E.

Tapping directs musical interest toward harmony, the succession of chords through time. It produces an utterly regular rhythmic pattern to articulate the motion, just as in, for example, J. S. Bach's famous Prelude in C Major, from the *Well Tempered Clavier* (see example 7). As in Bach's prelude and so much of Vivaldi's music, the harmonic progressions of "Eruption" lead the listener along an aural adventure. Van Halen continually sets up implied harmonic goals and then achieves, modifies, extends, or subverts them. At the end of the solo, he increases the harmonic tension to the breaking point with frenetic alternation of tonic and dominant. Finally, he abandons purposeful motion; the piece undergoes a meltdown. It comes to rest finally on the tonic, but echo effects, ringing harmonics, and a gradual fade make this an ambiguous closure. Engaging the listener with the conventions of tonal progress and then willfully manipulating his audience's expectations, Van Halen reiterates Vivaldi's celebration of the rhetoric of the virtuoso.

Though it certainly exists elsewhere, this kind of individual virtuosity is a conceptual model of musical excellence derived from classical music making. The word *virtuoso* is derived from the Italian *virtù*, an important term in the aristocratic courts of northern Italy in the fifteenth and sixteenth centuries. *Virtù* designated a type of individual excellence; as used by Machiavelli, it can denote "talented will," ingenuity, skill, efficacy, strength, power, or virtue. As applied to art, it reflected the relationship of art to power, as larger-than-life images and performances celebrated the wealth and power of an elite.[30] Though it existed earlier in European music, virtuosity came to be especially celebrated in the Renaissance. By the middle of the sixteenth century, a well-developed virtuosic solo repertoire existed, particularly for lutenists. Francesco da Milano, on the lute, and the three ladies of Ferrara, as vocalists, are reported to have astonished and transported listeners with their extraordinary technique and the expressiveness it enabled. Virtuosity attained broader social relevance in the nineteenth century, along with the popularity of public concerts for middle-class audiences. Franz Liszt invented the solo recital in 1839, and the piano—"newly reinforced by metal parts; newly responsive to every impulse of hand, foot, and brain— became music's central vehicle for heroic individualism."[31]

Example 7. J. S. Bach, "Prelude in C Major," from the *Well Tempered Clavier*, Book I, mm. 1–7 (© 1983 by Dover Publications, Inc.).

Virtuosity—ultimately derived from the Latin root *vir* (man)—has always been concerned with demonstrating and enacting a particular kind of power and freedom that might be called "potency." Both words carry gendered meanings, of course; heavy metal shares with most other Western music a patriarchal context wherein power itself is construed as essentially male. At least until the mid-1980s, heavy metal was made almost exclusively by male musicians for male fans, and "Eruption" is a metaphorical ejaculation—a demonstration of physical and rhetorical potency. But it can also signify a more general sort of social capability. It is for this reason that some women are able to identify with even the most macho culture (Judas Priest, Beethoven), mapping its experiences of transcendence and empowerment onto their own social positions and needs. Like all musical techniques, virtuosity functions socially. Some might find virtuosity inherently distancing or elitist, since it is a sensational display of exceptional individual power. But for many others, virtuosi are the most effective articulators of a variety of social fantasies and musical pleasures.

Classical music certainly does not provide the only model for virtuosity, but the prestige of that repertoire has made its particular model very influential. The virtuoso not only possesses unusual technical facility but through music is able to command extraordinary, almost supernatural rhetorical powers. Robert Schumann reported this of a performance by Liszt:

The demon began to flex his muscles. He first played along with them [the audience], as if to feel them out, and then gave them a taste of something more substantial until, with his magic, he had ensnared each and every one and could move them this way or that as he chose. It is unlikely that any other artist, excepting only Paganini, has the power to lift, carry and deposit an audience in such high degree. . . . In listening to Liszt are we overwhelmed by an onslaught of sounds and sensations. In a matter of seconds we have been exposed to tenderness, daring, fragrance and madness. . . It simply has to be heard—and seen. If Liszt were to play behind the scenes a considerable portion of the poetry would be lost.[32]

Schumann's account points to the importance of spectacle in virtuosic music and to the mystery that surrounds virtuosic performers. Compare Jay Jay French's account of his experiences performing with the heavy metal band Twisted Sister:

You walk on stage some nights and you feel more muscular, you just all of a sudden feel like the power is pouring out of you, the tune is just ripping itself through your body, out of the speakers, out of the PA, blowing people away, and you haven't even broken a sweat yet. The night's just beginning and they're already going crazy, and you're just cruisin' in first gear. Then you move it up a notch. . . . And you lay it out, and then put it into third, and then it's one of those nights, and the audience goes even crazier, and you're just blowing away, and you're just lookin' at yourself and you go "Gee, I am God!" And then you kick it into fourth, and the whole night's amazing.[33]

The first truly virtuosic hard rock guitarist was Jimi Hendrix; Pete Townshend of The Who is usually credited with being the first to exploit power chords and feedback for musical purposes, but it was Hendrix more than anyone else who made these techniques—along with whammy bar dives, pick slides, and a bag of other tricks—part of a virtuoso's vocabulary of extravagance and transgression. As Billy Gibbons, ZZ Top's guitarist, said, Hendrix "took the guitar into Martianland."[34] Virtuosity can signify in many different ways, though. Charles Shaar Murray writes of Jimi Hendrix's famous version of "The Star Spangled Banner":

Hendrix's "out" playing was not necessarily always an expression of pain, rage or grief: the brief exercise in pure crash-and-burn pyrotechnica with which he opened up "Wild Thing" at the climax of his Monterey Pop Festival US début was Hendrix *playing* in the most literal sense of the word. It was playful, mischievous, exuberant, euphoric, extrovert; an ex-underdog's high-spirited slapstick display of hey-look-what-I-can-do. But as the mood of the times darkened, so did Hendrix's music; when he moved into his trick-bag, it was increasingly to express that which simply could not be communicated in any other way.[35]

Murray's explication of Hendrix is illuminating; it highlights the fact that virtuosity can have many different sorts of social meanings. Throughout his book, though, Murray indulges in the sort of gratuitous and unsupported bashing of heavy metal that is fashionable among rock critics: "Eddie Van Halen, by far the most influential hard and heavy guitarist of the eighties, has borrowed the Hendrix vocabulary—tremolo tricks and all—in order to say very little."[36] What Van Halen "said" had much in common with the exuberance and struggle of Hendrix's playing; but he became the most influential player of his generation by achieving a kind of rational control over all of these risky, noisy techniques. The oral virtuosity of the blues, nuanced and dialogic, had become in Hendrix a psychedelic wail of transgression and transcendence. With Van Halen, this virtuosity is differently managed; his precision and consistency became new benchmarks for a rock guitar virtuosity more closely tied to classical ideals. For (as I will discuss below) metal guitarists absorbed not only licks and harmonic progressions but ways of making and valuing music derived from classical music.

Many heavy metal musicians link themselves with the classical model of virtuosity quite explicitly. Wolf Marshall, in an article titled "The Classical Influence" in the leading professional guitarists' magazine (*Guitar for the Practicing Musician*), compares today's metal guitarists to

Liszt and Paganini in their virtuosity, bravura manner, mystique, attractiveness to women, and experimentation with flashy, crowd-pleasing tricks.[37] These parallels seem very apt when we recall that women swooned and threw flowers to Liszt during his performances, that fans followed Frescobaldi's tours through Italy, congregating in crowds as large as thirty thousand for the chance to hear him sing or improvise toccatas on the organ.[38] The contemporary description of Franz Liszt with which I began this chapter could just as well refer to Ritchie Blackmore or Eddie Van Halen ("the strange wonder . . . the pale slender youth in his clothes that signal the nonconformist; the long, sleek, drooping hair . . . undreampt-of virtuosity and technical brilliance.").

As I have suggested, the classical influence on heavy metal is due in part to the early training of many guitarists. Moreover, this concept of virtuosity is easy to reinvent in a culture that glorifies competitive individualism in so many other ways. But beginning in the early 1980s, metal musicians turned increasingly to direct study and emulation of modern and historical classical performers. Not only the musical discourse of metal but its conceptions of musicianship and pedagogy were transformed by increasingly vigorous pursuit of classical models. One of the leading players of this moment, hero to thousands of budding metal neoclassicists, was Randy Rhoads.

Randy Rhoads: Metal Gets Serious

Like Edward Van Halen, Randy Rhoads grew up in a musical household. The son of two music teachers, Rhoads was born in 1956, in Santa Monica, California. He enrolled as a student at his mother's music school at age six, studying guitar, piano, and music theory, and a few years later began classical guitar lessons, which he would continue throughout his career. During the late 1970s, Rhoads built a regional reputation playing with Quiet Riot, but his big break came in 1980, when he landed the guitar chair in a new band fronted by ex–Black Sabbath vocalist Ozzy Osbourne, perhaps the single most durable and successful performer in heavy metal. During his brief tenure with Osbourne's band (ending with his death at age twenty-five in a plane crash), Rhoads became famous as the first guitar player of the 1980s to expand the classical influence, further adapting and integrating a harmonic and melodic vocabulary derived from classical music.

Among his early musical influences, Rhoads cited the dark moods and drama of Alice Cooper, Ritchie Blackmore's fusion of rock and classical music, Van Halen's tapping technique, and his favorite classical composers, Vivaldi and Pachelbel.[39] His musical experiences were unusual in their close focus on hard rock and classical music because Rhoads supported himself, until he joined Osbourne, by teaching rather than playing. Unlike many guitar players, Rhoads wasn't out hustling gigs indiscriminately in order to pay the rent. Instead of playing blues, disco, r&b, country, or any of the multitude of styles with which most working musicians must cope, Rhoads concentrated on his chosen interests and learned by teaching: "The way I started to get a style was by teaching. . . . I taught eight hours a day, six days a week, every half hour a different student. I had little kids, teenagers, and even some older people. . . . When you sit there and play all day long, you're going to develop a lot of speed. . . . I started combining what they wanted to learn with a bit of technique. Every day with every student I'd learn something."[40] Rhoads had a lifelong attraction to the technical challenges, the theoretical rigor, and the dramatic syntax of classical music. According to his friend and collaborator Ozzy Osbourne, "Randy's heart was in the classics, to be honest; he wanted to be a classical guitar player. In fact, with the first record royalties he received, he went out and bought himself a very, very expensive classical guitar. He sat there for days and nights working on his music theories. . . . On days off I'd get in the bar. He wouldn't: he'd practice all day, every day."[41]

The classical influence is pervasive in the music Rhoads recorded with Osbourne. Rhoads adapted the harmonic progression of the famous Pachelbel canon for "Goodbye to Romance" (on *Blizzard of Ozz*, 1981), and many songs rely on the gothic overtones evoked by much Baroque music in the twentieth century. The best example of this, J. S. Bach's Toccata in D Minor for organ (1705), has been recycled in movies, television, and advertising as a highly effective aural signifier of mystery, doom, and gloom. A bit of this toccata was used to introduce Bon Jovi's tremendously successful *Slippery When Wet* album (1987); the power and sustain of the organ are matched only by the electric guitar, and Bach's virtuosic style and rhetorical flair is perfectly suited to heavy metal. On Bon Jovi's recording, reverberation is added to evoke the auratic space of a cathedral, imputing similar mystery and weight to the album that follows. Baroque music is most often employed to these ends by metal musicians, but Osbourne also used the artificial archaism of Carl Orff's *Carmina Burana* to open the show on his 1986 concert tour.

Rhoads and Osbourne's "Mr. Crowley" (1981) also begins with synthesized organ, playing a cyclical harmonic progression modeled on Vivaldi. The minor mode, the ominous organ, and the fateful cyclicism, culminating in a suspension, set up an affect of mystery and doom. The sung verses and first guitar solo of "Mister Crowley" are supported by a metal-inflected Baroque harmonic progression: Dm | B♭ | C | Dm | B♭ | Em7♭5 | Asus4 | A. The move from B♭ back up through C (♭VI–♭VII–I) is uncharacteristic of Baroque music (where ♭VI usually resolves to V), but it frequently occurs in metal, where it normally functions in an aggressive and dark Aeolian mood. The progression that underpins Rhoads's "outro" solo at the end of the song is similar, but it is a more straightforward Vivaldian circle of fifths progression: Dm | Gm7 | C | F | B♭ | Em7♭5 | Asus4 | A. Until classically influenced heavy metal, such cyclical progressions were unusual in rock music, which had been fundamentally blues-based. The classical influence contributed to a greater reliance on the power of harmonic progression to organize desire and narrative. The circle of fifths progression was picked up by metal because it sounds archaic, directional, and thus fateful. Rhoads's first solo in "Mr. Crowley" is a frantic scramble against the inevitability of the harmonic pattern. The second rides the wave of harmonic teleology with more virtuosic aplomb (see example 8); Rhoads uses arpeggios, tremolo picking, trills, and fast scales to keep up with the drive of the progression.

Rhoads displays similar techniques on a live recording of "Suicide Solution" (1987) during the course of a lengthy virtuosic cadenza. The crowd's reactions are clearly audible as counterpoint to Rhoads's phrases, confirming that the purpose of virtuosic technique is to facilitate fantastic rhetoric; the virtuoso strives to manipulate the audience by means of skillfull deployment of shared musical codes of signification. In the seventeenth and early eighteenth centuries, music was theorized in these terms very openly in treatises on the *Affektenlehre*, before the rise of aesthetics led to circumlocutions and mystifications of music's power.[42] Moreover, contemporary accounts show that until late in the nineteenth century the behavior of concert audiences was far from today's "classical" norms of silence and passivity. Musical audiences were tamed around the turn of this century, as part of the cultural segregation of private emotions and public behavior so well analyzed by Lawrence W. Levine. Until the twentieth century, it seems that large audiences for opera and public concerts behaved very much like today's audiences for heavy metal and other popular music. Listeners reacted to musical rhetoric with "spontaneous expressions of pleasure of and disapproval in the form of cheers, yells, gesticulations, hisses, boos, stamping of feet, whistling, crying for encores, and applause."[43]

In the studio recording of "Suicide Solution," which appeared on *Blizzard of Ozz* (1981), there is no guitar solo at all, an unusual departure from the formal norms of heavy metal but an appropriate one, given the song's musical delineation of powerlessness.[44] But in concert, Osbourne used "Suicide Solution" as an opportunity for Rhoads to display his prowess as a soloist. Where the song would normally end, it is suspended inconclusively instead, and Rhoads begins a virtuosic cadenza made up of carefully paced statements and flourishes, divided by charged gaps that seem to demand replies from the audience (see example 9). Rhoads uses speedy patterns and fast runs to build excitement, and he manages the rhythmic impulses of his lines so as to create and then suspend metric expectations. Tried and true harmonic devices, such as diminished arpeggios and chromatic "meltdowns," are borrowed from the semiotic trick bag of classical music to manipulate desire by suggesting, deflecting, achieving, or making ambiguous a variety of tonal goals.

Rhetorically, Rhoads's cadenza follows Baroque models. Susan McClary has written about the narrative organization of desire in J. S. Bach's extraordinary harpsichord cadenza for the first movement of his Brandenburg Concerto No. 5. McClary contrasts the manipulative strategies of this unusually lengthy solo with the pressure of generic norms toward closure (see example 10).

Most cadenzas at the time would have been a very few measures long—a slightly elaborate prolongation and preparation before capitulation to the ritornello and the final resolution. . . . Thus in order to maintain necessary energy the harpsichord part must resort to increasingly deviant strategies—chromatic inflections, faster and faster note values—resulting in what sounds like a willful, flamboyant seventeenth-century toccata: in its opposition to the ensemble's order, it unleashes elements of chaos, irrationality, and noise until finally it blurs almost entirely the sense of key, meter, and form upon which eighteenth-century style depends.[45]

Like Bach's cadenza, Rhoads's invokes the toccata, a virtuoso solo instrumental genre of the late sixteenth through mid eighteenth centuries, mainly performed on fretted and keyboard instruments (guitar, lute, organ, harpsichord). Heavy metal guitarists rely on precisely those musical tactics that characterized the toccata: "quasi-improvisatory disjunct harmonies, sweeping scales, broken-chord figuration, and roulades that often range over the entire instrument. . . . [N]othing is more inappropriate than order and constraint."[46]

The formal plan of Rhoads's cadenza is similar, in some respects, to that of Bach's. In both, an impressive array of virtuosic figuration is explored, until a disorienting harmonic meltdown leads to a long drive toward cadence. In Rhoads's solo, the harmonic confusion precedes a lengthly tapped section, which itself melts down. Initially, the tapped arpeggios circumscribe, with only some ambiguity, the closely related

Example 8. Ozzy Osbourne (1981), "Mr. Crowley," solo by Randy Rhoads (Words and Music by Ozzy Osbourne, Randy Rhoads, and Bob Daisley, Copyright © 1981 Blizzard Music Limited, 12 Thayer Street, London W1M 5LD, England. International Copyright Secured. All Rights Reserved. Reprinted by Permission of Cherry Lane Music Co., Inc. Transcription by Wolf Marshall).

harmonic areas of E minor and A minor. But a succession of more dis-
tant chords—G | Am | F | Faug. | A | C♯m—leads to a com-
plete breakdown, embellished by whammy bar wows and a wailing high
harmonic. After pausing to let the audience voice its approval of his
transgressions, Rhoads begins again with a fast-picked figure, which he
slides chromatically up the neck with increasing frenzy. This sequence
winds up with another high wail and some low growls; at this point, he
allows the framing "ritornello" to return, and the band joins in a short
reprise of "Suicide Solution."[47]

Not only the classical materials in his music but also Rhoads's study
of academic music theory influenced many guitarists in the 1980s.
Throughout the decade, years after his death, Rhoads's picture continued to appear on the covers of guitar magazines, advertising articles
that discussed his practicing and teaching methods and analyzed his
music. The inner sleeve of the *Tribute* album (1987) reproduces a few
pages from Rhoads's personal guitar notebook. One sheet is titled "Key
of C♯"; on it, for each of the seven modes based on C♯ (Ionian, Dorian,
Phrygian, etc.), Rhoads wrote out the diatonic chords for each scale degree, followed by secondary and substitute seventh chords. On another
page, he composed exercises based on arpeggiated seventh and ninth
chords. Rhoads's interest in music theory was symptomatic of the increasing classical influence on heavy metal, but his success also helped
promote classical study among metal guitarists. Winner of *Guitar Player*'s
Best New Talent award in 1981, Rhoads brought to heavy metal guitar
a new level of discipline and consistency, derived from classical models.
Besides his classical allusions and his methods of study and teaching,
Rhoads's skill at double-tracking solos (recording them exactly the same
way more than once so that they could be layered on the record to add
a sense of depth and space) was extremely influential on subsequent
production techniques.[48] Rhoads's accomplishments also contributed to
the growing tendency among guitarists to regard their virtuosic solos in
terms of a division of labor long accepted in classical music, as opportunities for thoughtful composition and skillful execution rather than
spontaneous improvisation.

Classically influenced players such as Van Halen and Rhoads helped
precipitate a shift among guitar players toward a new kind of profes-
sionalism, with theory, analysis, pedagogy, and technical rigor acquiring new importance. *Guitar for the Practicing Musician*, now the most
widely read guitarists' magazine, began publication in 1983, attracting
readers with transcriptions and analyses of guitar-based popular music.
Its professional guitarist-transcribers developed a sophisticated set of

Example 9. Ozzy Osbourne (1981), "Suicide Solution," cadenza by Randy Rhoads (Words and music by John Osbourne, Bob Daisley and Randy Rhoads, Copyright © 1981, 1986, 1987 Essex Music International and TRO Music. Transcription by Wolf Marshall).

*Flick pickup switch
in specified rhythm.

(noise)

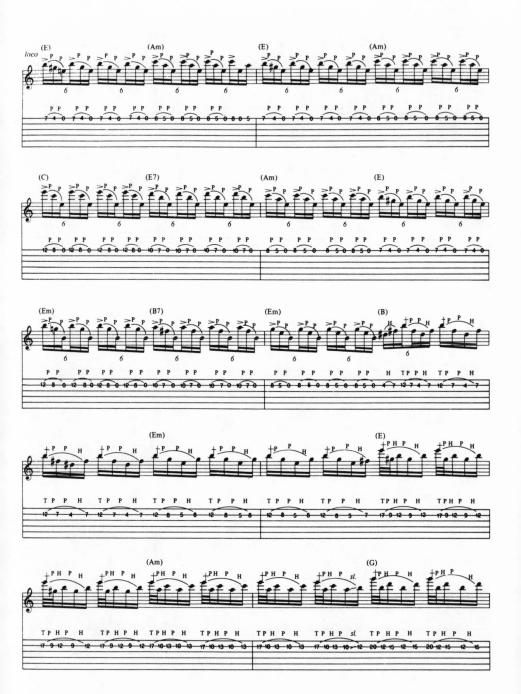

*Depress trem. bar one whole step
before striking note, then release.

Example 10. J. S. Bach, Brandenburg Concerto No. 5, first movement, mm. 199–201 (© Cambridge University Press).

special notations for representing the nuances of performance, rather like the elaborate ornament tables of Baroque music (see example 11). Their transcriptions are usually accompanied by analysis, both modal (e.g., "The next section alternates between the modalities of E♭ Lydian and F Mixolydian") and stylistic, relating new pieces to the history of discursive options available to guitar players.

Other guitar magazines increased their coverage of metal in time with the early 1980s metal boom, not only in order to keep up with musical trends, but also because many of their readers valued technique and heavy metal was the main site of technical innovation and expansion.[49] The magazines became increasingly informed by academic music theory, with columns on modes, harmony, and chord substitution, and analyses of classical music. The first installment of a new column called "Guitar in the 80s" was titled "The Bach Influence."[50] Guitar's columnist discussed two excerpts from J. S. Bach's music for unaccompanied violin, transcribed them into guitar tablature, and suggested playing techniques. The article argued that the point of studying such music is to rise to its technical challenge, to learn from its examples of clear voice-leading, and to understand its relevance to the music of Yngwie Malmsteen and other metal guitarists.

Institutional support for such technical study grew as well. Classical guitar teachers had begun to appear on college faculties around the

TABLATURE EXPLANATION

TABLATURE A six-line staff that graphically represents the guitar fingerboard. By placing a number on the appropriate line, the string and fret of any note can be indicated. For example:

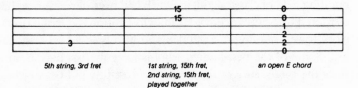

5th string, 3rd fret

1st string, 15th fret,
2nd string, 15th fret,
played together

an open E chord

Definitions for Special Guitar Notation (For both traditional and tablature guitar lines)

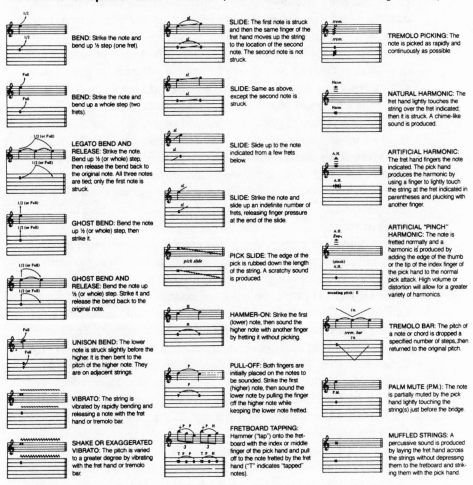

BEND: Strike the note and bend up ½ step (one fret).

BEND: Strike the note and bend up a whole step (two frets).

LEGATO BEND AND RELEASE: Strike the note. Bend up ½ (or whole) step, then release the bend back to the original note. All three notes are tied; only the first note is struck.

GHOST BEND: Bend the note up ½ (or whole) step, then strike it.

GHOST BEND AND RELEASE: Bend the note up ½ (or whole) step. Strike it and release the bend back to the original note.

UNISON BEND: The lower note is struck slightly before the higher. It is then bent to the pitch of the higher note. They are on adjacent strings.

VIBRATO: The string is vibrated by rapidly bending and releasing a note with the fret hand or tremolo bar.

SHAKE OR EXAGGERATED VIBRATO: The pitch is varied to a greater degree by vibrating with the fret hand or tremolo bar.

SLIDE: The first note is struck and then the same finger of the fret hand moves up the string to the location of the second note. The second note is not struck.

SLIDE: Same as above, except the second note is struck.

SLIDE: Slide up to the note indicated from a few frets below.

SLIDE: Strike the note and slide up an indefinite number of frets, releasing finger pressure at the end of the slide.

PICK SLIDE: The edge of the pick is rubbed down the length of the string. A scratchy sound is produced.

HAMMER-ON: Strike the first (lower) note, then sound the higher note with another finger by fretting it without picking.

PULL-OFF: Both fingers are initially placed on the notes to be sounded. Strike the first (higher) note, then sound the lower note by pulling the finger off the higher note while keeping the lower note fretted.

FRETBOARD TAPPING: Hammer ("tap") onto the fretboard with the index or middle finger of the pick hand and pull off to the note fretted by the fret hand ("T" indicates "tapped" notes).

TREMOLO PICKING: The note is picked as rapidly and continuously as possible.

NATURAL HARMONIC: The fret hand lightly touches the string over the fret indicated; then it is struck. A chime-like sound is produced.

ARTIFICIAL HARMONIC: The fret hand fingers the note indicated. The pick hand produces the harmonic by using a finger to lightly touch the string at the fret indicated in parentheses and plucking with another finger.

ARTIFICIAL "PINCH" HARMONIC: The note is fretted normally and a harmonic is produced by adding the edge of the thumb or the tip of the index finger of the pick hand to the normal pick attack. High volume or distortion will allow for a greater variety of harmonics.

TREMOLO BAR: The pitch of a note or chord is dropped a specified number of steps, then returned to the original pitch.

PALM MUTE (P.M.): The note is partially muted by the pick hand lightly touching the string(s) just before the bridge.

MUFFLED STRINGS: A percussive sound is produced by laying the fret hand across the strings without depressing them to the fretboard and striking them with the pick hand.

Example 11. "Tablature Explanation and Definitions for Special Guitar Notation" (From *Guitar for the Practicing Musician,* August 1990, p. 33. Copyright © 1992 Cherry Lane Music Co., Inc. International Copyright Secured. All Rights Reserved. Reprinted by Permission of Cherry Lane Music Co. Inc.).

time heavy metal emerged as a genre in the early 1970s. The classical influence owed something to the fact that virtually all of these teachers had started by playing some kind of popular music, turning later to the budding field of classical guitar, which had been almost single-handedly chartered by Andrés Segovia.[51] Other institutions flourished outside the ivory tower, offering their students a much broader professional training. Some of the best-known schools for guitarists have been around since the 1960s, such as the Musicians' Institute in Los Angeles, which incorporates the Guitar Institute of Technology. The recordings of Van Halen and Rhoads, among others, signaled a rise in the technical standards of rock guitar playing that prompted many new players to seek out organized musical study. Music Tech in Minneapolis, founded in 1985, was by 1990 a fully accredited music school with a faculty of 30 and a full-time student body of 195. Their professional programs in guitar, bass, drums, keyboard, and recording engineering include required courses in music theory, history, composition, performance practice, and improvisation in a variety of popular styles. Moreover, all rock guitarists are required to study classical guitar.[52] The success of schools such as GIT and Music Tech demonstrates the incomplete hegemony of classically oriented music schools; since colleges and university music departments have been very slow to broaden their focus to include the musics that matter most in contemporary culture, popular musicians have built their own institutions.

The fluidity of musical discourses enables guitarists to draw upon many influences, and even the guitar magazines cater simultaneously to very different groups of guitarists, contributing to the interchange of styles. Of Def Leppard's guitarists, for example, Steve Clark was classically trained; Clark's father had given him a guitar on the condition that he take lessons, so he learned Bach and Vivaldi along with Led Zeppelin and Thin Lizzy. Phil Collen, on the other hand, studied mostly jazz; Collen says that both influences show up in their music. Dave Mustaine of Megadeth claims as influences the Supremes, Marvin Gaye, and Pink Floyd. Dan Spitz of Anthrax took lessons in jazz while he privately studied the recordings of Iron Maiden, Black Sabbath, Judas Priest, Jimi Hendrix—and lately, rap music. Guitarist Vinnie Vincent was impressed by the speed of classical violinists and attempted to imitate their technical facility with scales and arpeggios, but he also integrated the steel-guitar style he heard his father using in country music.[53]

Guitarists do vary greatly in the degree to which they have adopted the classical model of rigorous practice and theoretical study. Danny Spitz of Anthrax practices guitar five hours each day, more than most

classical musicians. Izzy Stradlin' of Guns N' Roses doesn't really practice in the same sense at all; having no technical or theoretical knowledge
of music, he "screws around," playing with sounds. Eddie Van Halen
seldom practices guitar in any formal way, preferring instead to "play
when I feel like it. . . . Sometimes I play it for a minute, sometimes half an
hour, and sometimes all day. . . . But I am always thinking music. Some
people think I'm spacing off, but really I'm not. I am always thinking of
riffs and melodies."[54]

One of the most highly respected heavy metal guitarists of the late
1980s, George Lynch, learned to play entirely without reading music
or studying music theory: "What I mean when I refer to myself as
being non-technical is that I don't know what I'm doing. It's all up here
[points to head]. To be completely honest, I don't even know a major
scale. I don't know what one is, if you can believe that. But somehow
I get away with it. And sometimes I think I'm afraid to learn because I
might spoil a good thing."[55] Lynch is an extraordinary musician, with
impeccable technique and awesome rhetorical skills. He certainly does
know what he is doing, even if he lacks a technical vocabulary for describing it. Yet he feels keenly the contemporary pressure to theorize,
and his fame makes him turn to the new crop of mass mediated private
study aids to help him redress this lack: "It's hard to be in the position
I'm in and to walk somewhere to get a guitar lesson, so I learn from
tapes—home study courses, video tapes. . . . I don't know if I should be
admitting any of this."[56]

Such confessions point to the coexistence in heavy metal of completely different ways of understanding musicality and musical creation.
But the classical model, stressing rationalization and technical rigor, was
ascendant throughout the 1980s. The most influential metal guitarist
after Van Halen clarified the issues, expanding the classical influence
and also convincing many that the trend toward systemization did not
represent unambiguous progress.

Yngwie Malmsteen: Metal Augmented and Diminished

Swedish guitar virtuoso Yngwie J. Malmsteen continued many of the
trends explored by Blackmore, Van Halen, and Rhoads and took some
of them to unprecedented extremes. Born in 1963, Malmsteen was exposed to classical music from the age of five. But he says, "I played the
blues before I played anything."[57] In fact, he relates a pair of musical
epiphanies that, taken together, started him on the path to becoming
the most influential rock guitarist since Van Halen.

Malmsteen's mother gave him a guitar on his fifth birthday, but he expressed little interest in it at first. She wanted him to be a musician and made sure he received piano lessons, ballet lessons, vocal lessons, flute lessons, trumpet lessons—all in vain. None of it interested him, and he claims to have hated music until "on the 18th of September, 1970, I saw a show on television with Jimi Hendrix, and I said, 'Wow!' I took the guitar off the wall, and I haven't stopped since."[58] Malmsteen's first fruitful encounter with classical music—his exposure to the music of Paganini, the nineteenth-century violin virtuoso—also took place through the mediation of television: "I first heard his music when I was 13 years old. I saw a Russian violinist playing some Paganini stuff on TV, and freaked. . . . Paganini's intensity blew my socks off. He was so clean, dramatic and fast; his vibrato, broken chords and arpeggios were amazing. That's how I wanted to play guitar."[59]

Upon the release of his U.S. debut album in 1984, which won him *Guitar Player*'s Best New Talent award that year and Best Rock Guitarist in 1985, Malmsteen quickly gained a reputation as the foremost of metal's neoclassicists. Malmsteen adapted classical music with more thoroughness and intensity than had any previous guitarist, and he expanded the melodic and harmonic language of metal while setting even higher standards of virtuosic precision: "With the coronation of King Yngwie, there isn't one aspiring guitarist who isn't now familiar with diminished seventh chords, harmonic minor scales and phrygian and lydian modes. His advent has been accepted by guitar teachers as well, because he brought discipline into a world where study used to be considered sacreligious [sic]."[60] Not only do Malmsteen's solos recreate the rhetoric of his virtuosic heroes, Bach and Paganini, but he introduced further harmonic resources, advanced such techniques as sweep-picking, and achieved the best impression yet of the nuance and agility of a virtuoso violinist (see his solo on "Black Star," example 12).

Moreover, Malmsteen embraced the premises of classical music more openly than had anyone before him. His fetishization of instrumental technique complemented his move toward "absolute" music. Only two of the songs on his first album have vocals; in the other six, the norms of songwriting are completely subordinated to the imperative of virtuosic display. Melodies are presented by multilayered guitar tracks, interrupted by multiple guitar solos. Later albums, such as *Odyssey* (1988), include more vocals, but it seems clear that Malmsteen regards them as a capitulation to the requirements of commercial success. With titles evoking myth ("Icarus' Dream Suite," *Odyssey*), mysticism ("Crystal Ball," "Deja Vu," "Evil Eye," "As Above, So Below"), and power ("Riot in the

Dungeon," "Bite the Bullet," "Faster Than the Speed of Light," "Far Beyond the Sun"), Malmsteen signals the reliance of his music on the gothic aura of classical music previously exploited by musicians such as Ritchie Blackmore and Randy Rhoads. But these evocations are fleshed out not by means of lyrics so much as through Malmsteen's harmonic progressions and virtuosic rhetoric.

Guitar for the Practicing Musician published a detailed analysis of Malmsteen's "Black Star," from his first U.S. album, *Yngwie J. Malmsteen's Rising Force* (1984). Such analytical pieces are intended as guides to the music of important guitarists, facilitating the study and emulation practiced by the magazine's readers. The following excerpts from Wolf Marshall's commentary can serve both as a summary of some technical features of Malmsteen's music and as a sample of the critical discourse of the writers who theorize and analyze heavy metal in professional guitarists' magazines:

Black Star shows off the many facets of Yngwie's singular style. Whether he is playing subdued acoustic guitar or blazing pyrotechnics, he is unmistakably Yngwie—the newest and perhaps the most striking proponent of the Teutonic-Slavic *Weltsmerz* (as in Bach/Beethoven/Brahms Germanic brooding minor modality) School of Heavy Rock. . . . The opening guitar piece is a classical prelude (as one might expect) to the larger work. It is vaguely reminiscent of Bach's *Bourree* in Em, with its 3/4 rhythm and use of secondary dominant chords. . . . The passage at the close of the guitar's exposition is similar to the effect . . . [of the] spiccato ("bouncing bow") classical violin technique. It is the first of many references to classical violin mannerisms. . . . This is a diminished chord sequence, based on the classical relationship of C diminished: C D♭ F♭ A (chord) to B major in a Harmonic minor mode: E F♯ G A B C D♯. . . . The feeling of this is like some of Paganini's violin passages. . . . While these speedy arpeggio flurries are somewhat reminiscent of Blackmore's frenzied wide raking, they are actually quite measured and exact and require a tremendous amount of hand shifting and stretching as well as precision to accomplish. The concept is more related to virtuoso violin etudes than standard guitar vocabulary. . . . Notice the use of Harmonic minor (Mixolydian mode) in the B major sections and the Baroque Concerto Grosso (Handel/Bach/Vivaldi) style running bass line counterpoint as well.[61]

Marshall's analysis is quite musicological in tone and content; he deliberately compares Malmsteen's recorded performance to classical techniques, contextualizes it through style analysis, and translates certain features into the technical vocabulary of music theory. The style analysis situates "Black Star" with respect to two musical traditions: rock guitar (Blackmore) and classical music (Bach, Paganini, Beethoven, Vivaldi, etc.). Marshall simultaneously presents a detailed description of the music and links it to the classical tradition by employing the language of academic music theory: chords, modes, counterpoint, form.

Example 12. Yngwie Malmsteen's Rising Force (1988), "Black Star," end of exposition and solo by Malmsteen (Words and Music by Yngwie Malmsteen, Copyright © 1985 by Unichappell Music, Inc. and De Novo Music. All Rights Administered by Unichappell Music, Inc. International Copyright Secured. All Rights Reserved. Transcription by Wolf Marshall).

*slide tap finger
down 3rd stg. to
15 fr. before pull-off.

loco

Dive w/bar   gradual return

Solo
guitar

*Gtrs. I & II

*Gtr. I downstemmed; Gtr. II upstemmed in parentheses.

As rock guitarists have become increasingly interested in studying the history and theory of classical music, Marshall can safely assume that his audience is able to follow such analysis. In fact, in my experience, many heavy metal guitarists (most of whom, like Bach and Mozart, never attended college) have a much better grasp of harmonic theory and modal analysis than do most university graduate students in music.

Moreover, Marshall's analysis shows that metal guitarists and their pedagogues have not only adopted the trappings of academic discourse about music, but they have also internalized many of the values that underpin that discourse. Even as he carefully contextualizes Malmsteen's music, Marshall insists on its originality and uniqueness ("Yngwie's singular style," "unmistakably Yngwie"). The commentary emphasizes Malmsteen's precision of execution as well ("measured and exact," "tremendous . . . precision"). Most tellingly, Marshall implicitly accepts the categories and conceptions of academic music analysis, along with its terms.[62] For apart from the comment about "arpeggio flurries," Marshall deals exclusively with pitch and form, the traditional concerns of musicological analysis. And just as the discipline of musicology has drawn fire from within and without for ignoring or marginalizing musical rhythm, timbre, gesture, rhetoric, and other possible categories of analysis, metal guitarists' own theorists and pedagogues could be criticized for the same restricted analytical vision. If they are to become effective musicians, metal guitarists must, in fact, learn to maneuver within musical parameters beyond pitch and form, just as their counterparts within conservatories and music schools must learn much that is not written down. In the academy, such learning is referred to as "musicality," and it is often the focal point of a mystification that covers up classical music's reliance on oral traditions. In both classical music and heavy metal, virtually the same aspects of music are far less theorized, codified, and written; music students must learn by listening, emulating, and watching the rhythm and gesture of bodily motion. Theorists of metal seem no more able than their academic counterparts to deal with musical rhetoric and social meanings; one analysis of Van Halen's "Eruption" merely named the modes employed (E Phrygian, A and E Aeolian) and summed up with the blandness of a music appreciation text: "a well-balanced, thought-out guitar solo, which features a variety of techniques."[63]

Yngwie Malmsteen exemplifies the wholesale importation of classical music into heavy metal, the adoption of not only classical musical style and vocabulary, models of virtuosic rhetoric, and modes of practice, pedagogy, and analysis but also the social values that underpin these activities. These values are a modern mixture of those that accompanied music making of the seventeenth, eighteenth, and nineteenth centuries with more recent cultural imperatives. Along with the model of virtuosity I have described above, the reigning values of metal guitar include a valorization of balance, planning, and originality; a conservatory-style fetishization of technique; and occasionally even a kind of cultural conservatism. Malmsteen bemoans the lack of musicianship in today's popular music and looks back on the "good old days" of the seventeenth century, when, he imagines, standards were much higher.[64]

Malmsteen is particularly noted for his elitism, another value he derives from contemporary classical music and justifies by emphasizing his connections with its greater prestige. In interviews, he constantly insists on his own genius, his links to the geniuses of the classical past, and his distance from virtually all contemporary popular musicians, whose music he regards as simple, trite, and inept. He denounces the genre he is usually thought to inhabit, insisting, "I do NOT play heavy metal!"[65]

While he has been known to claim that, as a genius, he never had to practice, Malmsteen also presents himself as one who has suffered for his art. A joint interview with bassist Billy Sheehan preserves an account of his early devotion to music, and its costs:

YNGWIE: I was extremely self-critical. I was possessed. For many years I wouldn't do anything else but play the guitar.
BILLY: I missed a lot of my youth. I missed the whole girl trip. I didn't start driving until I was 25.
YNGWIE: I also sacrificed a lot of the social thing. I didn't care about my peers. To me, nothing else was even close in importance.[66]

Such statements undoubtedly reflect the tendency toward self-aggrandizement and self-pity that have made Malmsteen unloved by his peers in the guitar world. But they also further reflect his virtually total acceptance of the model of music making promulgated in classical music. Malmsteen, along with many other musicians, sees a need for music to evolve toward greater complexity and "sophistication." The pursuit of virtuosic technique usually requires many thousands of hours of patient, private repetition of exercises. To this end, many young players pursue a fanatical practice regimen, a pursuit of individual excellence that often leaves little room for communal experiences of music making, just as is the case in the training of classical musicians.[67]

Like most classical musicians, rock musicians usually acquire their skills through total dedication during their youth. Jeff Loven, a professional rock guitar player and teacher, explained how he learned to play: "I taught myself, actually. I sat in my room when other guys were playing baseball and stuff and I just sat and learned solos and songs, note for note: Hendrix songs, a lot of Van Halen, and then Ozzy came out with Randy Rhoads."[68] And one of the guitar magazines recently printed this letter from a young metal musician:

I am a 16 year old guitarist who's been playing since I was six years old. I switched from playing country to rock music when I was 10 and decided that one day I would be among the masters. I started pushing myself with eight hours a day, then slowly but steadily it increased. I now usually practice 16 hours daily, all day and sometimes all night. Recently, I was expelled from school due to my continuous absences when I was practicing. I have become a skilled player, but I am losing sleep and my social life is hurting. My philosophy is practice makes perfect, but my friends, my school, and my parents say I have blown my life out of proportion with it. I could cut my practicing down, but with the excellence among today's players, I fear I will not stay in the game.[69]

The extreme extension of this set of ideological values is the complete withdrawal of the musician from his or her public, in pursuit of complexity and private meanings. This strategy, which had earlier been championed by academic composers such as Milton Babbitt, can now be recognized in some virtuosic guitar players. Steve Vai boasts of his most recent album:

What I did with *Passion and Warfare* is the ultimate statement: I *locked* myself into a room and said, "To hell with everything—I'm doing this and it's a complete expression of what I am. I'm not concerned about singles, I'm not concerned about megaplatinum success, I'm not concerned about record companies." It was a real special time. All too often kids and musicians and artists just have to conform to make a living. I'm one of the lucky few and believe me, I don't take it for granted.[70]

Vai is trying to claim "authenticity" here, trying to prove his autonomy as an artist who is free of the corrupting influences of the very social context that makes his artistic statements possible and meaningful. When he goes on to describe his fasting, his visions, his bleeding on the guitar, he presents himself as an updated self-torturing Romantic artist, reaching beyond the known world for inspiration. When he details his compositional process of painstaking and technologically sophisticated multi-track recording, he updates this vision by celebrating modern means of simulating artistic autonomy. This individualism and self-centeredness unite classical music and heavy metal and stand in stark contrast to many other kinds of music. A bit later in the same issue of *Musician*, B. B. King says: "What I'm trying to get over to you is this: . . . when I'm on the stage, I am *trying* to entertain. I'm *not* just trying to amuse B. B. King. I'm trying to entertain the people that came to see me. . . . I think that's one of the things that's kind of kept me out here, trying to keep *pleasing* the audience. I think that's one of the mistakes that's happened in music as a whole: A lot of people forget that they got an audience."[71]

The success of the classical ideologies of complexity, virtuosity, and individuality is most obvious in the recent emergence of "guitar for guitarists" metal. Hypervirtuosic players like Vai, Joe Satriani, Tony MacAlpine, Paul Gilbert, Jason Becker, Greg Howe, The Great Kat, and Vinny Moore record their albums on specialty labels (such as Shrapnel Records) that sell mainly to the legions of semiprofessional and amateur metal guitarists. Their records tend to follow the template of Malmsteen's early work: few (if any) vocals, heavy classical influences, virtuosic speed and rhetoric, and song titles evocative of intensity and transgression. Most of these "mail order" guitarists rarely tour, and little of this music is known outside its devoted circle of fans, although a few players, notably Vai and Satriani, have achieved some amount of popular success. It is a kind of avant-garde, wherein originality, technique, and innovation are highly prized. MacAlpine and Moore, for example, draw upon nineteenth- and twentieth-century classical music for their metallic fusions: Chopin, Brahms, Liszt, Messiaen. Few find these fusions convincing; I would argue that these musical discourses are less compatible (rhetorically and ideologically) with metal than the seventeenth- and eighteenth-century music that comprises the bulk of the classical influence on heavy metal. But classical music, from any period, provides prestigious materials that can be reworked in a demonstration of musical creativity and sophistication. Paul Gilbert of Racer X (1986), for example, quoted Paganini's "Moto Perpetuo" literally and then went on to outdo it in speed and complexity. Gilbert's quotation is meant to be recognized, and it suggests a kind of seriousness, of meeting the technical standards of "high art," in contrast to Van Halen's more irreverent citations.[72]

Although some of these players have developed a virtuosic technique that is, in some respects, beyond the pioneering achievements of Eddie Van Halen, few are able to deploy their skills with comparable rhetorical success. As Van Halen himself remarked, when prodded to comment on the challenge of his imitators, "Maybe they cop the speed because they can't cop my feel. Maybe they shouldn't think so much."[73] Yngwie Malmsteen claims to be aware of the dangers of speedy, purposeless patterns—"You can do a diminished scale up and down till the fuckin' cows come home, but the cows won't come home"—yet it is for precisely this that he has drawn critical fire (and yawns).[74] Many metal guitarists and critics feel that if listening to one Malmsteen song is an amazing experience, listening to a whole album gets a bit tiresome, and each new album sounds like the last one, only more so. Malmsteen's work has convinced some that the classical influence is played out, even as it has been the leading inspiration for the eager experimentation of the avant-garde. He has helped turn many players to a fruitful engagement with the classical tradition, even as he has helped lead them toward the impoverishing regimens of practice and analysis that now dominate that tradition. And Malmsteen's abrasive elitism contrasts with his attempt to forge links with the musical past and reinvigorate reified discourses for mass audiences. His music brings to light contradictions that can add to our understanding of both heavy metal and classical music.

Popular Music as Cultural Dialogue

There are different ways to view the encounter of classical music and heavy metal, in part because there are, as I have suggested above, two different "classical musics": the twentieth-century genre of classical music, which comprises "great" pieces that are marketed and promoted (in part via "music appreciation") as largely interchangeable; and the collection of disparate historical practices—occupying vastly different social positions, employing incompatible musical discourses to varied cultural ends—that now are called by that name. On the one hand, heavy metal and classical music exist in the same social context: they are subject to similar structures of marketing and mediation, and they "belong to" and serve the needs of competing social groups whose power is linked to the prestige of their culture. The immense social and cultural distance that is normally assumed to separate classical music and heavy metal is in fact not a gap of musicality. Since heavy metal and classical music are markers of social difference and enactments of social experience, their intersection affects the complex relations among those who depend on these musics to legitimate their values. Their discursive fusion may well provoke insights about the social interests that are powerfully served by invisible patterns of sound.

On the other hand, there is a sense in which this sort of fusion marks an encounter among different cultures and affords an opportunity for cross-cultural critique. In their influential book, *Anthropology as Cultural Critique*, George E. Marcus and Michael M. J. Fischer called for new critical projects that would simultaneously explore multiple cultural moments. Besides the usual "objective" studies of individual cultural practices, ethnographic work, they argued, can become cultural criticism by reciprocally probing different "ways of knowing," by encouraging defamiliarization and the location of alternatives, and by breaking through patterns of thought that attempt to keep meanings singular and stable in the face of multiplicity and flux.[75] Marcus and Fischer were primarily concerned with encounters between Western and non-Western cultures; we can see an example of such comparison within one culture in the work of John Berger. Through analysis and juxtaposition of the multiple possibilities contained within a single cultural tradition, Berger's *Ways of Seeing* empowered thousands of scholars, students, and critics of culture by giving them a language for discussing the relationships of visual representation to social contestation.[76] But scholars are not the only ones who undertake such critical juxtapositions; heavy metal musicians, by engaging directly with seventeenth-, eighteenth-, and nineteenth-century composers and performers, by claiming them as heroes and forebears despite contemporary boundaries that would keep them separate, have already done something similar.

Historians and critics of popular music have so far failed to take seriously the musical accomplishments of heavy metal musicians. The prevailing stereotype portrays metal guitarists as primitive and noisy; virtuosity, if it is noticed at all, is usually dismissed as "pyrotechnics." One of the standard histories of rock grudgingly admitted that Edward Van Halen was an impressive guitarist but maintained doggedly that "the most popular 1980s heavy metal acts broke little new ground musically."[77] In the academy, heavy metal (along with rap) remains the dark "Other" of classical preserves of sweetness and light.[78]

Nor are metal's musical accomplishments acknowledged in the reports of the general press, where the performances of heavy metal musicians are invariably reduced to spectacle, their musical aspects represented as technically crude and devoid of musical interest. *Life*'s sensationalist dismissal of Judas Priest is typical: "The two lead guitarists do not so much play as attack their instruments."[79] Given the intensity and aggressiveness of Judas Priest's music, the characterization is not unfair; indeed, such a sentence, if printed in *Hit Parader* or *Metal Mania*, would be understood as a complimentary metaphor, praising the musicians' vigor. But in *Life* the image of attack takes the place of understanding; the magazine plays to class and generational prejudices by mocking the musical skills and imagination of the group.

In fact, heavy metal guitarists, like all other innovative musicians, create new sounds by drawing on the power of the old and by fusing together their semiotic resources into compelling new combinations. Heavy metal musicians recognize affinities between their work and the tonal sequences of Vivaldi, the melodic imagination of Bach, the virtuosity of Liszt and Paganini. Metal musicians have revitalized eighteenth- and nineteenth-century music for their mass audience in a striking demonstration of the ingenuity of popular culture. Although their audience's ability to decode such musical referents owes much to the effects of the ongoing appropriations of classical music by TV and movie composers, heavy metal musicians have accomplished their own adaptation of what has become the somber music of America's aristocracy, reworking it to speak for a different group's claims to power and artistry.

In one of his most incisive essays, Theodor Adorno criticized twentieth-century "devotees" of classical music for flattening out the specific signification of that music, making composers such as Bach into "neutralized cultural monuments."[80] In Adorno's view, the prestigious position of Bach in contemporary culture seems to demand that his music be tamed, that it be made to seem to affirm the inevitability of present social power relationships, at the top of which are the sources of the subsidies that sustain classical music. Metal musicians have appropriated the more prestigious discourses of classical music and reworked them into noisy articulations of pride, fear, longing, alienation, aggression, and community. Their adaptations of classical music, though they might be seen as travesties by modern devotees of that music, are close in spirit to the eclectic fusions of J. S. Bach and other idols of that tradition. While a few musicologists have tried to delineate strategies for performing and interpreting Bach's music that reclaim its cultural politics,[81] it may be that only heavy metal musicians have achieved this to a significant degree. To alter slightly the closing of Adorno's essay on Bach, "Perhaps the traditional Bach can indeed no longer be interpreted. If this is true, his heritage has passed on to [heavy metal] composition, which is loyal to him in being disloyal; it calls his music by name in producing it anew."[82]

For we should have learned long ago from Adorno that social relations and struggles are enacted within music itself. This is especially visible when musical discourses that belong to one group, whose history has been told according to that group's interests, are made to serve other social interests. Metal appropriations are rarely parody or pastiche; they are usually a reanimation, a reclamation of signs that can be turned to new uses. Unlike art rock, the point is typically not to refer to a prestigious discourse and thus to bask in reflected glory. Rather, metal musicians adapt classical signs for their own purposes, to signify to their audience, to have real meanings in the present. This is the sort of process to which V. N. Vološinov referred when he wrote that the sign can become an arena of class struggle. Vološinov and the rest of the Bakhtin circle were interested in how signs not only reflect the interests of the social groups that use them but are also "refracted" when the same signs are used by different groups to different ends. Thus, heavy metal musicians and "legitimate" musicians use Bach in drastically different ways. As Vološinov wrote:

Class does not coincide with the sign community, i.e., with the community which is the totality of users of the same set of signs for ideological communication. Thus various different classes will use one and the same language. As a result, differently oriented accents intersect in every ideological sign. Sign becomes an arena of the class struggle.

This social *multiaccentuality* of the ideological sign is a very crucial aspect. By and large, it is thanks to this intersecting of accents that a sign maintains its vitality and dynamism and the capacity for further development. A sign that has been withdrawn from the pressures of the social struggle—which, so to speak, crosses beyond the pale of the class struggle—inevitably loses force, degenerating into allegory and becoming the object not of live social intellibility but of philological comprehension. The historical memory of mankind is full of such worn out ideological signs incapable of serving as arenas for the clash of live social accents. However, inasmuch as they are remembered by the philologist and the historian, they may be said to retain the last glimmers of life.[83]

The discourse of signs that make up "Baroque music" certainly survives in the present; since its revival in the middle of the nineteenth century, Bach's music has occupied an important place in the concert and Protestant liturgical repertoires. Moreover, as with all classical music, Baroque signs appear in the music of television and film, where visual cues depend upon and reinvest the music with its affective power. While the music of the precanonic Dufay or Philippe de Vitry may have become largely the concern of musicological "philologists," mass mediation has made the musical discourses of all times and places available to contemporary composers, and the semiotic vocabulary and rhetoric of the European classical canon still forms the backbone of Hollywood's prodigious musical output.

Heavy metal musicians, too, draw upon the resources of the past that have been made available to them through mass mediation and their own historical study. But it is precisely such predations that the musical academy is supposed to prevent. Bach's contemporary meanings are produced in tandem by musicologists and the marketing departments of record companies and symphony orchestras, and the interpretation of Bach they construct has little to do with the dramatic, noisy meanings found by metal musicians and fans and everything to do with aesthetics, order, and cultural hegemony. The classical music world polices contemporary readings of the "masterworks"; the adaptations of Randy Rhoads and Bon Jovi are ignored while the acceptability of Stokowski's orchestral transcriptions is debated. Malmsteen's performances fall outside the permissible ideological boundaries that manage to contain Maurice André and Glenn Gould. The drive to enforce preferred ideological meanings is, as Vološinov put it, "nondialogic." It is oppressive, authoritative, and absolute. "The very same thing that makes the ideological sign vital and mutable is also, however, that which makes it a refracting and distorting medium. The ruling class strives to impart a supraclass, eternal character to the ideological sign, to extinguish or drive inward the struggle between social value judgements which occurs in it, to make the sign uniaccentual."[84]

But since the world of language (or music) preexists its inhabitants, and since cultural hegemony is never absolute, such appropriations constantly appear on the field of social contestation we call "popular culture."[85] Such disruptions are rarely even acknowledged by academics. In the histories they write and the syllabi they teach, most musicologists continue to define "music" implicitly in terms of the European concert tradition, ignoring non-Western and popular musics and treating contemporary academic composers such as Milton Babbitt as the heirs to the canon of great classical "masters." But Babbitt's claim to inherit the mantle of Bach is perhaps more tenuous than that of Randy Rhoads, and not only because the latter two utilize, to some extent, a common musical vocabulary. The institutional environment within which Babbitt works (and which he has vigorously championed) rewards abstract complexity and often regards listeners and their reactions with indifference or hostility, whereas both Bach and Rhoads composed and performed for particular audiences, gauging their success by their rhetorical effectiveness. Babbitt's music demonstrates his braininess; Bach's and Rhoads's offer powerful, nuanced experiences of transcendence and communality.

Many heavy metal musicians are acutely aware of their complicated relationship to the prestigious music of the classical past. Theorists like Wolf Marshall necessarily refer to that canon in their efforts to account for the musical choices displayed in particular pieces, and other musicians recurringly articulate the similarities they perceive in the values and practices of these two musics, which are usually assumed to be worlds apart. Vocalist Rob Halford earnestly emphasizes the discipline and skill needed to succeed in either style:

This might sound like a bizarre statement, but I don't think playing heavy metal is that far removed from classical music. To do either, you have to spend many years developing your style and your art; whether you're a violinist or a guitarist, it still takes the same belief in your form of music to achieve and create. It is very much a matter of dedication. . . . You get narrow-minded critics reviewing the shows, and all they think about heavy metal is that it is just total ear-splitting, blood-curdling noise without any definition or point. This is a very, *very* professional style of music. It means a great deal to many millions of people. We treat heavy metal with respect.[86]

Metal musicians' appropriations have already profoundly changed not only their music but their modes of theorization, pedagogy, and conceptualization. Their fusions may even come to affect the reception and performance of classical music as well. We should welcome such re-vitalization: contrast today's pious, sterile reiterations of the "Pachelbel Canon" with Vinnie Moore's furious soloing over that piece in concert. Compare classical musicians' timid ornamentation of Italian sonatas with Yngwie Malmsteen's free and virtuosic improvisations over the chord progressions of Albinoni, more faithful to the practices of the early eighteenth century despite his nonclassical instrument.

Heavy metal musicians erupted across the Great Divide between "serious" and "popular" music, between "art" and "entertainment," and found that the gap was not as wide as we have been led to believe. As Christopher Small put it, "The barrier between classical and vernacular music is opaque only when viewed from the point of view of the dominant group; when viewed from the other side it is often transparent, and to the vernacular musician there are not two musics but only one. . . . Bach and Beethoven and other 'great composers' are not dead heroes but colleagues, ancestor figures even, who are alive in the present."[87]

It should come as no surprise that such an eruption, propelled by the social desires and tensions of patriarchy and capitalism, reinscribes familiar constructions of masculinity and individuality, even as the new meritocracy of guitar technique opens doors to female and African-American musicians.[88] And we should not be dismayed to find that classically influenced heavy metal can reinterpret the past even as it is itself co-opted into the world of advertising and soundtracks. For that is how popular culture works: through ingenuity and contradiction toward revisions of meaning and prestige. Heavy metal musicians' appropriations from classical music have already changed popular music; they may yet change classical music and perhaps even our understanding of how the cultural labor of popular musicians can blur the distance between the two, defying the division that has been such a crucial determinant of musical life in the twentieth century.

Album cover art from heavy
metal recordings.

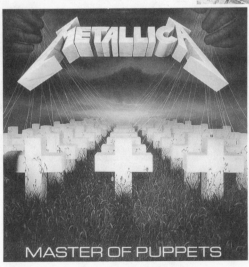

Ritchie Blackmore. © Justin Thomas/Relay Photos.

Eddie Van Halen. © Bill Thomas/Photofeatures International.

Randy Rhoads. © Relay Photos/Photofeatures International.

Yngwie Malmsteen. © Joe Giron/Photofeatures International.

Lita Ford. © Annamaria Di Santo/Photofeatures International.

Judas Priest. © Ray Palmer/Photofeatures International.

Poison. © Annamaria Di Santo/Photofeatures International.

Ozzy Osbourne. © Annamaria Di Santo/Photofeatures International.

Iron Maiden. © Photofeatures International.

Axl Rose. © Gene Ambo/Photofeatures International.

CHAPTER FOUR

Forging Masculinity
Heavy Metal Sounds and Images of Gender

The spectacle is not a collection of images, but a social relation
among people, mediated by images.   —Guy Debord[1]

Orpheus, the godlike musician of Greek mythology, was a natural figure
for opera plots, which must reconcile heroics and song; his legend-
ary rhetorical powers made him the most popular subject of early-
seventeenth-century dramatic music, with settings by Monteverdi, Peri,
Caccini, and many other composers. But his story contains a built-in
contradiction: Orpheus must sing in such a way as to demonstrate his
rhetorical mastery of the world, yet such elaborate vocal display threatens to undermine Orpheus's masculine identity. Flamboyant display
of his emotions is required as evidence of his manipulative powers,
but such excess makes him into an object of display himself and suggests a disturbing similarity to the disdained emotional outbursts of
women. Western constructions of masculinity often include conflicting imperatives regarding assertive, spectacular display, and rigid self-
control. Spectacles are problematic in the context of a patriarchal order
that is invested in the stability of signs and that seeks to maintain women
in the position of object of the male gaze.[2]

Today's heavy metal musicians must negotiate the same contradiction. Like the story of Orpheus, heavy metal often stages fantasies of
masculine virtuosity and control. Musically, heavy metal articulates a
dialectic of controlling power and transcendent freedom. Metal songs
usually include impressive technical and rhetorical feats on the electric
guitar, counterposed with an experience of power and control that is
built up through vocal extremes, guitar power chords, distortion, and

sheer volume of bass and drums. Visually, metal musicians typically appear as swaggering males, leaping and strutting about the stage, clad in spandex, scarves, leather, and other visually noisy clothing, punctuating their performances with phallic thrusts of guitars and microphone stands. The performers may use hypermasculinity or androgyny as visual enactments of spectacular transgression. Like opera, heavy metal draws upon many sources of power: mythology, violence, madness, the iconography of horror. But none of these surpasses gender in its potential to inspire anxiety and to ameliorate it.

Heavy metal is, inevitably, a discourse shaped by patriarchy. Circulating in the contexts of Western capitalist and patriarchal societies, for much of its history metal has been appreciated and supported primarily by a teenage male audience. But it is crucial to specify not only age and gender but the corresponding political position of this constituency: it is a group generally lacking in social, physical, and economic power but besieged by cultural messages promoting such forms of power, insisting on them as the vital attributes of an obligatory masculinity. As John Fiske concluded from his study of "masculine" TV shows such as "The A-Team," "our society denies most males adequate means of exercising the power upon which their masculinity apparently depends. Masculinity is thus socially and psychologically insecure; and its insecurity produces the need for its constant reachievement."[3] I would emphasize in Fiske's analysis the words *apparently* and *socially*, for I see sex roles as contradictory, mutable social constructions rather than as normative formations somehow grounded in biology or an ahistorical psychology. Moreover, it is not only masculinity that is insecure; no component of identity is stable or natural. Heavy metal, like all other culture, offers occasions for doing "identity work"—among other things, for "accomplishing gender."[4] That is, notions of gender circulate in the texts, sounds, images, and practices of heavy metal, and fans experience confirmation and alteration of their gendered identities through their involvement with it.

For Fiske, the contradictions built into male sex roles and the insecurity that men feel as a result help explain the episodic and generic aspects of male culture. Television shows such as "The A-Team" are structured as repeated enactments of paradigmatic narratives and representations because their function is to address anxieties that can never be resolved. Fiske's ideas are easily transferable to music and music video, where repetition and genre are also crucial phenomena. The purpose of a genre is to organize the reproduction of a particular ideology, and the generic cohesion of heavy metal until the mid-1980s depended upon the desire of young white male performers and fans to hear and believe in certain stories about the nature of masculinity. But metal's negotiations of the anxieties of gender and power are never conclusive; that is why, as Fiske says, these imaginary resolutions of real anxieties must be reenacted over and over again. That such representations can never be definitive or totally satisfying also means that they are always open to negotiation and transformation. But social circumstances may change so that particular forms of culture are no longer relevant for particular individuals: metal fans tend mostly to be young because much of metal deals with experiences of powerlessness that may be, to some extent, overcome. As they get older, fans may acquire some amount of economic power, or they may beget children who replace them at the bottom of the familial and social ladders, whose physical power and mobility are far less than theirs and who thus assuage some of their culturally produced anxieties.[5]

Such a theoretical perspective cannot be a comprehensive one for the study of gender in heavy metal, though, since there are many female metal fans, for whom such explanations are inadequate. Indeed, since around 1987, concert audiences for metal shows have been roughly gender-balanced. But metal is overwhelmingly concerned with presenting images and confronting anxieties that have been traditionally understood as peculiar to men, through musical means that have been conventionally coded as masculine. Since the language and traditions of heavy metal have been developed by and are still dominated by men, my discussion of gender in metal will initially be an investigation of masculinity; I will return later to issues of the reception of these male spectacles by female fans.

For two decades, heavy metal has offered a variety of compensatory experiences and opportunities for bearing or resolving the contradictions of masculinity as they have been constructed by societies that are aligned by patriarchy, capitalism, and mass mediation. Thus, one of the most important items on the heavy metal agenda has long been to deal with what patriarchy perennially perceives as the "threat" of women. I will be framing my discussion of heavy metal songs and videos in terms of a loose list of strategies concerning gender and power: misogyny, exscription, androgyny, and romance. Heavy metal musicians and fans have developed tactics for modeling male power and control within the context of a patriarchal culture, and metal's enactions of masculinity include varieties of misogyny as well as "exscription" of the feminine—that is, total denial of gender anxieties through the articulation of fantastic worlds without women—supported by male, sometimes homoerotic, bonding. But heavy metal also participates in rock's tradition of rebellion, and some metal achieves much of its transgressiveness through androgynous spectacle. Until the mid 1980s, one of these three strategies—misogyny, exscription, androgyny—tended to dominate each heavy metal band's "aesthetic." A fourth approach, increasingly important in recent years, "softens" metal with songs about romance; this kind of music has drawn legions of female fans to metal.

In spite of the fact that this categorization of metal might look like a menu for sexual abuse, I intend neither to denounce utterly, nor to try to rescue wholesale, heavy metal's politics of gender. To do only the former would be to ignore the politics of critique, particularly the fact that criticism of popular culture never takes place apart from implicit comparisons with more prestigious culture. Like racism, sexism is sustained and naturalized across class lines. Writers who expose racism and sexism in popular culture must take care that their critique does not collude with those who want to identify such barbarisms with an economic and cultural underclass that can thus be more self-righteously condemned and oppressed. Critics of popular music must take care to acknowledge the politics of their work: while it is imperative to be critical, to avoid bland enthusiasm or dispassionate positivism, analyses of popular culture must also be empathetically drawn if they are to register accurately the contradictions and subtleties of popular practices. Otherwise, they too easily serve as mandates for elitist condemnation and oppression. It is beyond dispute that some of the images and ideologies of heavy metal are violent and irresponsible. But of course, the violence and irresponsibility of much so-called high culture and of the economic elite that underwrites its existence is also demonstrable. The politics of prestige work to position "high" culture beyond scrutiny and "low" culture beneath it; in either case the effect is to forestall critical understanding. It is less important simply to denounce or defend cultural representations of gender than to critique them in the context of an explanation of how they work, what social tensions they address, where they come from, and why they are credible to particular audiences.

Gender constructions in heavy metal music and videos are significant not only because they reproduce and inflect patriarchal assumptions and ideologies but, more importantly, because popular music may teach us more than any other cultural form about the conflicts, conversations, and bids for legitimacy and prestige that comprise cultural activity. Heavy metal is, as much as anything else, an arena of gender, where spectacular gladiators compete to register and affect ideas of masculinity, sexuality, and gender relations. The stakes are as high in metal as anywhere, and they are more explicitly acknowledged there, both in visual and musical tropes and in the verbal and written debates of fans. By taking the trouble to distinguish carefully among the varieties of representation within heavy metal, we can gain a better understanding of larger interrelationships of gender and power.

Behind the Screen: Listening to Gender

In her pathbreaking study of music video, *Rocking around the Clock*, E. Ann Kaplan makes two main points about metal videos: that their violence and rebelliousness place them in the "nihilistic" category of her typology of videos and that their reputation for blatant sexism is well deserved.[6] Neither of these might seem particularly bold assertions, but taken together, I think they are contradictory. Sexism is in fact a major ideological constituent of much heavy metal, but sexism is never nihilistic; the intensity and variety of modes of sexist discourse must be understood as indices of the urgency and influence of patriarchal ideals. To call such discourse nihilist is to obscure its real ideological functions.

Kaplan's readings of videos as texts embedded in the contexts of MTV and consumer culture are sometimes acute and illuminating. But two serious methodological shortcomings flaw her comments on heavy metal. First, beyond her observation that metal audiences are made up of "young males," Kaplan's comments appear to be uninformed by any ethnographic or personal contact with the heavy metal musicians and fans whose texts and lives she presumes to explain. While Kaplan's conclusions are based on her analysis of MTV as a spectacular reinforcement of universal decenteredness and passivity, the interviews and questionnaires I have received from heavy metal fans point to a wide range of activities connected to their involvement with the music. "Headbangers' Ball," the weekly three-hour MTV program devoted to heavy metal, is quite popular with the fans I surveyed, but it is hardly the most important aspect of their involvement with metal. Concerts, records, radio, fan magazines, and quite often playing an instrument figure as primary components of metal fans' lives. A significant number of fans (especially male) watch MTV seldom or never, and for many (especially female) the glossy photographs of rampant musicians to be found in the copious fan literature are more important sources of visual pleasure than videos. This is not to argue that metal videos are unimportant but rather to say that they do not operate in a social vacuum: their analysis must be inflected by knowledge of the lives and cultural investments of the viewers.

Second, certainly the most serious shortcoming of Kaplan's book is the almost total neglect of the *music* of music video. Kaplan's few comments addressing musical details of heavy metal songs are hardly helpful: she characterizes heavy metal as "loud and unmelodious," filled with "relatively meaningless screaming sounds."[7] Though musical discourses are invisible, they are nonetheless susceptible to analysis, and musical analysis is crucial for music video analysis because aural texts are indisputably primary: they exist prior to videos and independently of them, and fans' comments make it clear that it is the music of music video that carries the primary affective charge. That is, it is the music that is mostly responsible for invoking the libidinal and corporeal investment that intensifies belief, action, commitment, and experience. The challenge of analyzing music videos is that of interpreting and accounting for *both* musical and visual discourses, simultaneous but differently articulated and assuming a variety of relations.

If the cinema, as Laura Mulvey asserts, "has structures of fascination strong enough to allow temporary loss of ego while simultaneously reinforcing the ego," the same was surely true of music long before cinema was invented.[8] Musical constructions, in metal or elsewhere, are powerful in part because they are made to seem so natural and unconstructed. We experience music's rhetorical pull apart from language, seemingly apart from all social referents, in what is usually thought a pure, personal, subjective way. Yet that impression of naturalness depends on our responding unself-consciously to complex discursive systems that have developed as historically and socially specific practices. It is not only lyrics or visual imagery but the music itself that constructs gendered experiences.[9] The musicians I will discuss have used musical codes to articulate visions of the world that are filled with the pleasures of energy, freedom, power, and a sense of community. Discursively, specific details of rhythm, pitch, and timbre *signify*—some of them through the conventions of heavy metal proper, some as part of a complex, mutable tradition of musical semiotics that stretches back centuries. Such signification always occurs in social contexts structured through political categories such as gender, class, and race; musical meanings are thus inseparable from these fundamental constituents of social reality.

Only with its complex sonic texts and ethnographic contexts disregarded, as in analyses such as Kaplan's, can heavy metal be casually characterized as both sexist and nihilistic or as a monolithic, adolescent deviance. For "heavy metal" is a genre label that, by the late 1980s, included a substantial and growing female audience, a number of distinctive and sophisticated musical discourses, and many different solutions to complex problems of gender relations. As I discuss several heavy metal songs and their videos, I hope to delineate their musical and ideological strategies more precisely than is accomplished by such vague but pervasive terms of dismissal. As I work through the various gender strategies I have identified in heavy metal, I will be arguing, on the one hand, that music videos cannot reasonably be analyzed without the musical component of such texts being examined; and on the other hand, that it is crucial for the cultural critic to develop an understanding of the interests and activities of the communities that find meaning in their encounters with these texts.

No Girls Allowed: Exscription in Heavy Metal

The most distinctive feature of heavy metal videos is that they typically present the spectacle of live performance; bands are shown on stage, performing in synch with the song. Other kinds of pop music videos also frequently feature "live" synched performances, but pop songs are less often "performed" on a stage than mimed in front of fantastic or arty backgrounds or in unlikely locations; often only vocals are synched, as only the singer is visible. In the typical metal video, however, actual concert footage is often used, and when it is not, sets, backdrops, and musicians' posturings usually imitate the spectacle of an arena concert. Bands as different in their styles and constituencies as Guns N' Roses, Poison, and Metallica all rely on scenes of "live" performance for most of their videos. Heavy metal has long had the most loyal touring support of any popular musical genre, and the arena concert experience of collectivity and participation remain the ideal that many videos seek to evoke.

Besides the videos of metal singles to be seen on programs like MTV's "Headbangers' Ball," full-length heavy metal concerts are popular rentals at video stores. Since a favorite performer might come through town once a year at best, and since many younger fans are not allowed by their parents to attend concerts, heavy metal videos make more widely available the singular events that are most highly valued by fans. The video in a concert setting, with or without fans, presents the performers in all their glory, as larger-than-life figures whose presence is validated by feelings of community and power, and evoked by venue and music.

Many such performance videos offer for the pleasure of young males a fantasy not unlike that constructed by "The A-Team," as John Fiske describes it: a world of action, excess, transgression but little real violence, one in which men are the only actors, and in which male bonding among the members of a "hero-team" is the only important social relationship. As Barbara Ehrenreich has pointed out, for young men maturing in a patriarchal world where men dominate the "real" world while women raise kids, growing up means growing away from women.[10] Fiske's analysis of the television show stresses the value of male bonding for creating close social ties while excluding the threat of the feminine: "Feminine intimacy centers on the relationship itself and produces a dependence on the other that threatens masculine independence. . . . Male bonding, on the other hand, allows an interpersonal dependency that is goal-centered, not relationship-centered, and thus serves masculine performance instead of threatening it."[11] Even in many nonperformance metal videos, where narratives and images are placed not on a stage but elsewhere, the point is the same: to represent and reproduce spectacles that depend for their appeal on the exscription of women.

Even exceptions to the metal concert video format emphasize the performative. In Judas Priest's "Heading Out to the Highway," a song from 1981 that was still popular as a video in 1988 and 1989, performance is not literally represented. The band's two guitar players drag race on an empty highway in the middle of nowhere, flagged on by the singer, whose macho stances, gestures, and singing are the only elements of the real performance retained in the fantastic setting. The song and the images are about freedom and adventure, and we don't even need the initial "Hit 'em, boys" to know that we're talking about a specifically male kind of freedom. There are no women to be seen in this video, and what is there to be seen—the cars, the road, the leather, the poses— have long been coded as symbols of male freedom, linked as signs of aggressiveness and refusal to be bound by limits.

The performance enacts this in musical terms as well. The vocals and guitars constantly anticipate the downbeats, punching in ahead of the beat defined by the bass and drums throughout the song. Rob Halford's rough, powerful voice finds support in harmony vocals that sound as menacing as a gang's chant. He sustains triumphant high notes at the end of each chorus, in a display of power that has counterparts in the guitars' solo section and the bass pedal under the verse. Not only his voice but the singer's writhing and posing provide a spectacle of male potency for a male audience, including both the band on-screen and the presumed male viewer of the video.[12]

But images of masculine display are available to be construed in a variety of ways. Gay heavy metal fans sometimes celebrate forthrightly the homoeroticism that is latent in such displays of exclusive masculine bonding. This can be seen, for example, in the activities of the Gay Metal Society, a social club of over one hundred members, based in

Chicago. In addition to sponsoring and organizing parties and nights out on the town for its members, GMS publishes a monthly newsletter that contains commentary on the history, criticism, and discography of heavy metal. The GMS *Headbanger* also functions as a forum for debate of issues involving sexuality and music. Gay fans celebrate metal musicians whom they believe are gay, such as Judas Priest's Rob Halford, and confirm and contest each other's "negotiated" readings of popular texts. They may see metal videos as erotic fantasies, while straight fans resist the homoerotic implications and insist on identification with the power and freedom depicted.[13] Of course, straight fans must negotiate their readings, too. Some of Accept's lyrics are explicitly homosexual if studied closely; despite this, the band is quite popular among heterosexual, often homophobic, men. As with classical music, heterosexual and even homophobic audiences can negotiate their reception and find the constructions of gay composers powerfully meaningful.

Male bonding itself becomes crucial to the reception of metal that depends on masculine display, for it helps produce and sustain consensus about meaning. Exscripting texts do occasionally refer to sexuality, but typically as just another arena for enactments of male power. Mutual erotic pleasure rarely appears in the lyrics of heavy metal, just as it is seldom discussed by men in any other context. Metal shields men from the danger of pleasure—loss of control—but also enables display, sometimes evoking images of armored, metalized male bodies that resemble the Freikorps fantasies analyzed by Klaus Theweleit.[14] The historical context and social location of these fantasies marks them as very different from heavy metal, but the writings and drawings of the German soldiers Theweleit studied evince a similar exscription of women and a concomitant hardening and metallic sheathing of the male body as a defense against culturally produced gender anxieties. Such images from heavy metal lyrics and album cover art could be cited by the hundreds, in a tradition that goes back to one of the founding texts of heavy metal, Black Sabbath's *Paranoid* (1970), which included the song "Iron Man."[15]

The seductive women who sometimes intrude into otherwise exscripting videos signify in several ways. First, these shots function just as they do in advertising: to trigger desire and credit it to the appeal of the main image. But the sexual excitement also serves as a reminder of why exscription is necessary: the greater the seductiveness of the female image, the greater its threat to masculine control. Moreover, the presence of women as sex objects stabilizes the potentially troubling homoeroticism suggested by the male display. I will have more to say about the anxieties produced by homoerotic display in my discussion of androgyny below. There are, however, many videos that attempt to manage gender anxieties more overtly, through direct representations of women.

The Kiss of Death: Misogyny and the Male Victim

Blatant abuse of women is uncommon in metal videos. There are unequivocal exceptions, such as the brutal stage shows of W.A.S.P. or the forthrightly misogynistic lyrics in some of the music of Guns N' Roses and Mötley Crüe. But despite heavy metal's notorious reputation among outsiders, few heavy metal videos have ever approached the degree of narcissistic misogyny routinely displayed by pop star Michael Jackson (e.g., his videos for "Dirty Diana" or "The Way You Make Me Feel"). If the exscripting music of Judas Priest or AC/DC conflates power and eroticism, making pleasure contingent upon dominance, many of heavy metal's critics have similarly confused the issue. Tipper Gore, for example, makes it clear that she considers rape and masturbation equal threats to "morality." And William Graebner has offered an analysis of "the erotic and destructive" in rock music that too often fails to distinguish between the two themes.[16] But articulations of gender relations in contemporary patriarchy are complex, and if constructions of sexuality in popular music are to be understood, their relationship to structures of power and dominance must be delineated, not crudely presumed.

Like heavy metal, sexually explicit films have an undeserved reputation for physical violence, according to a recent historical study of hard-core pornographic films. Building on the observation that sex is more shocking than violence in the United States, Joseph W. Slade explains the rampant violence in "legit" films as a result of prohibitions of representations of eroticism. Violence is often used as a metaphor for passion, Slade maintains, in discourses where explicit depiction of sexual activity is banned. In X-rated films, on the other hand, where representation of sex is not only permissible but primary, power relations are articulated through sexual relations rather than violence. The central purpose of pornography, Slade summarizes, has been "to assuage male anxieties about the sexuality of females."[17] Male authority is characteristically made secure through porn because that authority is represented as being founded in love: women are seen to submit themselves voluntarily and gladly, and force is unnecessary.

While nonviolent fantasies of dominance might be, for some, no less repugnant than blatant misogyny, it is important to recognize that they are different. As is typical of hegemonic constructions, overt force is not only unnecessary in most pornography, but it would be disruptive of a representation that depends on presenting itself as natural and un-coerced. Heavy metal too relies much less on physical violence against women than on a number of more hegemonic representations. Because metal has developed discourses of male victimization, exscription, and androgyny, its power to reproduce or adapt patriarchy is often contingent on the absence of overt violence. Although some of these discourses embody challenges to or transformations of hegemonic ideology, some reproduce rather directly the hegemonic strategies of control and repression of women that permeate Western culture.

For example, there is the strategy of confronting the "threat" head-on: one of the more successful representations of women in metal is the femme fatale. Such images are quite popular, from Mötley Crüe's "Looks That Kill" to Whitesnake's "Still of the Night," but the metal band Dokken could be said to have specialized in such constructions, embedded in narratives of male victimization. Many of their best-known songs enact the same basic story of the male entrapped, betrayed, or destroyed by the female: "Heaven Sent," "Prisoner (Chained by Love)," "Just Got Lucky," "Into the Fire," and "Kiss of Death."[18] Dokken's success with this formula was enabled by two of the band's particular assets: singer Don Dokken's voice and face are clean and soulful, the perfect complement to his tragic, self-pitying lyrics; and guitarist George Lynch is a powerful rhetorician whose solos and fills demonstrate a perhaps unmatched command of the semiotics of frantic but futile struggle.

Dokken's "Heaven Sent" (1987) is reminiscent of nineteenth-century operatic constructions such as Salome and Carmen in the way it locates women at a nexus of pleasure and dread.[19] Dokken sings of a woman who is simultaneously angel and witch, temptress and terror. A slim young woman in the video appears inexplicably, metamorphosed from a much heavier and older woman. She never speaks but walks alone through the night—sometimes in black miniskirt and leather, sometimes in a flowing white gown—holding a candelabra; she is followed by a rushing, tipping camera until she mysteriously dissolves. Jump cuts and shifts in point of view fragment the video, but the decentering and transformations are precisely the point: the boys in the band, first seen playing chess in a bar (in an unlikely portrait of innocence), wind up doing their onstage posturing in a graveyard, to the tune of their own victimization. Of course, the woman in the video never actually does anything threatening; it is enough that she exists. Women are presented as essentially mysterious and dangerous; they harm simply by being, for their attractiveness threatens to disrupt both male self-control and the collective strength of male bonding.

Musically, "Heaven Sent" constructs this victimization through images of constraint and struggle. The song opens with the repetition of a pair of open fifths, a whole step apart. But the fifths are not the usual power chords; they lack sufficient sustain and distortion. Instead, they sound haunting and ominous, and their syncopation and sparseness gives them an anticipatory air, in contrast to the rhythmic control and driving energy of the rest of the song (and of most other metal songs). Once the song gets under way, the rhythm is inexorable and precise, in that articulation of power and control that is one of the primary musical characteristics of heavy metal. In tension with the rhythmic stability, though, are the sudden and unexpected harmonic shifts that articulate "Heaven Sent" formally. Like the jump cuts in the video, these key changes are initially disorienting; but since the song stays in its gloomy Aeolian/Dorian mode throughout, each new section is affectively felt as the same scene, however distant harmonically—just as the various manifestations of "woman" in the video are linked by an aura of mystery and dread.

The guitar solo, often the site of virtuosic transcendence of a metal song's constructions of power and control, is, in "Heaven Sent," a veritable catalog of the musical semiotics of doom. As with "ground bass" patterns in seventeenth-century opera, the harmonic pattern uses cyclicism to suggest fatefulness; as in certain of Bach's keyboard pieces, the virtuoso responds to the threat of breakdown with irrational, frenzied chromatic patterns.[20] The guitar solo is an articulation of frantic terror, made all the more effective by its technical impressiveness and its imitations of vocal sounds such as screams and moans. After the solo, the song's chorus intensifies these images through ellision: seven measures long instead of the normal, balanced eight, the pattern cycles fatalistically, without rest or resolution.

Visual images, narrative, and the music itself combine in this video to represent women as threats to male control and even male survival. The mysteriousness of women confirms them as a dangerous Other, and their allure is an index of the threat.[21] Female fans, who now make up half of the audience for heavy metal (though only a very small fraction of metal musicians are women), are invited to identify with the powerful position that is thus constructed for them. It is a familiar one, since women are encouraged by a variety of cultural means to think of appearance as their natural route to empowerment. Men, on the other hand, are reassured by such representations that patriarchal control is justified and necessary. Such constructions are by no means to be found only in heavy metal, of course; not only do they belong to a long and esteemed tradition of Western cultural history, but their success in the 1980s has been widespread in a political context marked by reactionary governmental policies and a significant backlash against feminism. It is crucial to recognize that heavy metal is not the aberrant Other that many conservatives would have it be. But neither is it simply patriarchal. The sexual politics of heavy metal are, as we will see, a conflicted mixture of confirmation and contradiction of dominant myths about gender.

Living on a Prayer: Romance

Heavy metal changed a great deal in the last half of the 1980s, and one particular album of 1986 is a good register of the shift, as well as a major factor in precipitating it. With *Slippery When Wet*, one of the biggest-selling hard rock albums of all time (over 13 million copies), Bon Jovi managed to combine the power and freedom offered by metal with the constructed "authenticity" of rock, and, most important, the romantic sincerity of a long tradition of pop. Though Bon Jovi offered typical experiences of the heavy metal dialectic of absolute control and transcendent freedom in a performative context of male bonding, lead singer Jon Bon Jovi also projected a kind of sincerity and romantic vulnerability that had enormous appeal for female fans. It is this discursive fusion that enabled the band's mainstream success and helped spark the unprecedented entry of much heavy metal and metal-influenced music into the Top 40 of the late 1980s.

Bon Jovi was certainly not the first to achieve this fusion; bands like Van Halen, Boston, Journey, Foreigner, Loverboy, and others were engaged in similar projects some time before. But Bon Jovi's music was a phenomenal success, and it helped transform what had long been a mostly male subcultural genre into a much more popular style with a gender-balanced audience. The fusion was developed and managed very deliberately: once a standard leather/chains/eyeliner heavy metal band, with lots of tragic, macho songs about running, shooting, and falling down, the band sought to capture a wider audience for *Slippery When Wet*. The most obvious change was in the lyrics: abandoning heavy metal gloom, doom, and creepy mysticism, they began cultivating a positive, upbeat outlook, where the only mystical element was bourgeois love. Writing songs about romantic love and personal relationships, they tempered their heavy metal sound and image and pitched their product to appeal as well to a new, female market.

There is still a lot of metal in Bon Jovi's music, although the question of his inclusion in the genre is vigorously contested among various factions of metal fans. Features of heavy metal are evident in the timbres and phrasing of both instruments and vocals; the emphasis on sustain, intensity, and power; the fascination with the dark side of the daylit respectable world. But by not wearing makeup anymore and by wearing jeans, not leather or spandex, Bon Jovi abandoned much of heavy metal's fantastic dimension in favor of signs of rock "authenticity." Moreover, from pop music the band got its constructed sincerity, just the right degree of prettiness, and a conscious appeal to a female audience. The sustained and intense sounds of heavy metal are channeled behind the romantic sincerity of pop, while smooth, sometimes poignant synthesizer sounds mediate the raw crunch of distorted guitars.

The biggest hit song from *Slippery When Wet* was "Livin' on a Prayer," which invites us to sympathize and identify with Tommy and Gina, a young couple who are good-hearted but down on their luck. Tommy, now out of work, is a union man, working-class tough—but also tender, caring, and musical. He used to make music, that is, until he had to hock his guitar; Tommy's loss of his capacity to make music is a sign of the couple's desperate circumstances. The lyrics of the song fall into three groups, each with a different sort of text and musical affect: the verses of the song tell the story of Tommy and Gina's troubles; the prechoruses are resolutions not to give up, the pair's exhortations to each other about the power of love; and the choruses are Tommy's affirmation that such hope and faith in love is justified, that love really can transcend material problems.[22]

The source of the song's main pleasures is its musical construction of romantic transcendence. As with most pop songs, the transcendent moment is the place in the chorus where the title hook is presented, where the affective charge is highest: it is there, if ever, that we are convinced that Tommy and Gina *will* make it, that love *must* triumph over adverse social conditions, that bourgeois myths *can* survive even the despair of joblessness. Such affirmative stories have led to critical dismissal of Bon Jovi as fatuous rock "perfect for the Reagan era."[23] But such disparagements typically ignore gender as a site of political formation, and critical sneering does little to help us understand the tensions that are mediated by such a vastly popular song.

There are at least three ways of understanding how this sense of transcendence is constructed musically. First, and simplest, it is at this moment that the piece moves out of its minor key and into its relative major. Such a key change accomplishes a tremendous affective change, moving from what is conventionally perceived as the negativity or oppression of the minor key to the release and affirmation of the major.

Experientially, we escape the murk that has contained us since the beginning of the song. Second, this moment in the chorus offers an escape from the C–D–E pattern that has been the only chord progression the song has used until this point and thus has seemed natural and inevitable, however cheerless.[24] "Livin' on a Prayer" breaks out of its gloomy treadmill at this point of transcendence, moving from C to D to G, not E. By breaking free of its oppressive minor tonality, and by doing so through a brand-new progression, the song leaps into an exciting new tonal area and constructs a transcended context for Tommy and Gina, and for the song's audience. To clinch it, a background group of voices joins in here to support Tommy's tough solo voice; the rest of the social world seems to join in this affirmation.

Finally, this new progression, C–D–G, has discursive significance. This pattern has been one of the most important formulas for establishing resolution and closure in Western music, from Monteverdi to the "Monster Mash"; it is not, however, a common progression in heavy metal. The C–D–E progression upon which most of "Livin' on a Prayer" is built, on the other hand, is strongly associated with metal. Thus, when "Livin' on a Prayer" reaches its moment of transcendence, the shift in affect is marked by the use of a different harmonic discourse. The transcendence is in part an escape from heavy metal itself, with all of its evocation of gloominess, paranoia, and rebellion. "Livin' on a Prayer" breaks away from the musical discourse of heavy metal at the point where it offers its bottom line: transcendence through romantic love. To offer such a payoff, it *must* break away from metal.

The success of the song depends on the contrast of and tension between two affective states: the Aeolian grunge of the beginning, which sets up the story of Tommy and Gina's hardship, and the transcendent change to G major in the chorus, which symbolically and phenomenologically resolves it. For most of the song, the grunge frames and contains the chorus. It seems more realistic, since it returns as though inevitable whenever Bon Jovi's fervent vocalizing stops. The utopian promise is thus made contingent on the singer's efforts. Only at the end of the song, where the chorus endlessly repeats through the fade-out, does it seem that the transcendence might be maintained—and then only if the singer never ceases. At the same time that the magical power of romantic love, transcending material conditions, is being touted as the solution to what are in fact social problems, the Horatio Alger solution of individual hard work is also suggested. In the end the utopian moment wins out, keeping the realistic grunge at bay and even suggesting that transcendence is more real. But all of this is possible only because Bon Jovi has created these realities: a bleak, resonant social landscape, the power of romantic love to offer transcendence, and a tough but sensitive male to make it work. The patriarchal premises of Bon Jovi's fusion are clear.

Toward the end of the song the transcendent moment is kept fresh through a key change, up a half step. Not only does the pitch rise, creating an overall affective elevation, but it also forces Bon Jovi's voice higher, charging it with even more effortful sincerity and, since he meets the challenge successfully, utopian promise. Moreover, the key change is made to coincide with a dropped beat, so the music jumps forward suddenly, unexpectedly, onto this new, higher harmonic plateau. In the concert footage used in the video of "Livin' on a Prayer," Jon Bon Jovi sails out over the audience on a wire at precisely this moment, tripling the transcendent effect.

The rest of the video seems to have little to do with the song. It consists mostly of grainy black-and-white footage of Jon and the band backstage and in rehearsal, without any visual connection to the song's romantic narrative. Neither is it a typical performance video, like the ones I discussed above, since more camera time is devoted to backstage and rehearsal scenes than to actual or even faked (synched) performance. Yet the video is closely connected to the music; the biggest visual gesture is the sudden switch to color film and a live concert audience, which occurs two thirds of the way through the song, precisely at the climactic moment of transcendence indicated by the song's chorus. The video marginalizes the literal narrative of the lyrics, in accordance with the way that typical heavy metal videos cater to fans' enjoyment of live concerts. The transcendence constructed by the music, originally mapped onto the story of Tommy and Gina, has now become the transcendence available through Bon Jovi: the music, the concert, and even the grainy black-and-white footage that purports to let the fan in on the behind-the-scenes lives of the musicians. What was framed by the lyrics as a moment of transcendence for a romantic, heterosexual couple, made possible by the male narrator, is now a celebration of the band members as objects of desire and of the concert as an experience of collective pleasure. The "Livin' on a Prayer" video is less a romantic story than a spectacle of masculine posturing, and the musically constructed transcendence of the song is linked to patriarchy through both narrative and visual pleasure.

It has been argued that the cinema has only recently begun to present the masculine as spectacle, in something like the way that women have been so presented. This is in contrast to theorizations of earlier cinematographic practice, where women were typically presented as erotic objects of the male gaze, but representations of men functioned as embodiments of a powerful, ideal ego.[25] Such a development is of great interest because the contradictions historically coded into representations of gender result in an almost androgynous glamour being attached to male objects of desire. Bon Jovi's image has been carefully managed so as to simultaneously maintain two different kinds of appeal to male and female fans. For example, the release order of singles from *Slippery When Wet* was carefully balanced between romantic and tougher songs, to sustain interest in the band from both genders.[26] But we will see more serious problems of managing desire in the face of gender blurring in a subgenre of heavy metal distinguished by blatant visual androgyny.

Nothing but a Good Time? Androgyny as a Political Party

Androgyny in heavy metal is the adoption by male performers of the elements of appearance that have been associated with women's function as objects of the male gaze—the visual styles that connote, as Laura Mulvey put it, "to-be-looked-at-ness."[27] The members of bands like Poison or Mötley Crüe wear garish makeup, jewelry, and stereotypically sexy clothes, including fishnet stockings and scarves, and sport long, elaborate, "feminine" hairstyles. Though they are normally included within the genre of heavy metal, such "glam" bands are considered by most fans to be less "heavy" than the mainstream. This is due less to musical differences than to their visual style, which is more flamboyant and androgynous than that of heavier metal.[28]

Androgyny has a long history in music; I have already mentioned problems of gender and representation in Baroque opera. (And one could also mention the seventeenth-century castrati, perhaps the most dedicated androgynes in history.) Recent examples of male androgyny outside heavy metal range from Liberace to Little Richard to Lou Reed, not to mention the androgynous glamour of many country-western stars.[29] Some of this history has faded through supercession: some thought the Beatles' hair, for example, threateningly androgynous in 1964. But in glam metal, androgyny has found popular success to a degree unique in the rock era. And it's a particular sort of androgyny; unlike the 1970s' great androgyne, David Bowie, heavy metal usually lacks ironic distance. It is this absence of irony more than anything else that leads rock critics to scorn glam metal, for the ridiculous seriousness of metal's gender constructions is at odds with the patriarchal premises undergirding the ideologies and institutions of rock.

Poison is a good example of a successful glam metal band: one that boasts millions of fans and no critical approval. "Nothin' but a Good Time," from Poison's multiplatinum album *Open Up and Say . . . Ahh!* (1988), is shot almost entirely as a performance video, one that presents the band as though actually performing the song we hear. It includes, however, two framing scenes, which I will describe and discuss briefly before focusing on Poison's androgyny. The opening scene shows us a young man, with a metal fan's long hair, washing dishes in the back of a restaurant. He is swamped with work, surrounded by dirty plates and hot steam, and he is alone except for a small radio, which is playing a song by Kiss, the founders of spectacular metal. Next we meet his boss, loud and rude, who has stomped back to apply a verbal whip; he threatens and insults the dishwasher, flipping off the radio as he leaves. Disgusted and exhausted, the kid sullenly turns the radio back on as soon as the boss leaves. Then he kicks open a nearby door, as though to grab a bit of air before returning to the grind. When the door opens, we are instantly plunged into a Poison performance, taking place just outside. "Nothin' but a Good Time" begins with that door-opening kick, and while it lasts, the framing narrative is suspended; we don't see the dishes, the washer, or the boss until the song is over. Afterward, we are returned to the same scene as at the beginning. Having heard the music, the boss storms back into the frame to lash again at the kid; he suddenly notices, however (at the same time that we notice it), that all of the dishes, miraculously, are clean. Confounded, he sputters and withdraws, as the dishwasher relaxes and smiles.

The framing scenes of this video call to mind culture critics' debates about class and resistance in popular culture. The issue is whether or not popular narratives such as that presented by this song and video contain any oppositional potential or critical perspective, whether they offer viewers anything more than an experience of rebellion that is ultimately illusory and inconsequential. We must be wary of simply dismissing such "unreal" resolutions of real social antagonisms; as Fredric Jameson has argued, although mass culture has conservative functions, though it commonly arouses utopian hopes but perpetuates their containment within hegemonic social forms, the very representation of social fantasies is risky, and maintenance of dominant ideologies is never complete.[30] However, the overt political lesson of the video's framing narrative may be far less important than the implications of the band's visual and musical styles for notions of authenticity and gender. "Nothin' but a Good Time" can serve as an example of those subcultural challenges to hegemony which, as Dick Hebdige has argued, are not issued directly but rather are "expressed obliquely, in style."[31]

In the "Nothin' but a Good Time" video, the song itself is framed as a fantastic experience. Reality is the world of the frame, the world of work, steam, sweat, and abuse; as in *The Wizard of Oz*, the real world is shot with its colors muted so as to enable the fantasy to seem more real. When the dishwasher kicks open the door, Poison explodes in color and musical sound and the real world, the one that supposedly includes the fantasy, vanishes; the fantasy takes over as a more real reality. Even the dishwasher himself disappears for the duration of the song, in a kind of dissolution of the ego in the flux of musical pleasure. This fantasy is credited with magical agency as well: at the end of the song, we are returned to gray reality to find the dishes done, the impossible task fulfilled. The boss's torrent of abuse is plugged; something has been put over on him, though he can't say what or how.

When combined with the song's lyrics, the video's message seems fairly simple self-promotion: the good time being sung about is something that can be accessed through Poison's music, no matter what the "real" conditions. As with many TV advertisements, Poison's fantasy is represented as more real than mundane reality, and the fantasy is to be enjoyed through involvement with a commercial product. Such an appeal, though, must evoke our desires for community and for greater freedom and intensity of experience than are commonly available in the real world. Poison, like Pepsi, uses narrative and image to arouse these longings and to present us with a particular kind of consumption as the means of satisfying them.

But it would be a mistake to exaggerate the importance of the narrative framing of the song; however obvious the "political" message of the framing narrative may seem, it may be less important than the gender politics of the song and its performance. Debates over the liberatory possibilites of mass culture all too often proceed in terms that neglect the gendered character of all social experience. Yet popular music's politics are most effective in the realm of gender and sexuality, where pleasure, dance, the body, romance, power, and subjectivity all meet with an affective charge. The significance of the musical section of the video may be overlooked because it seems to be simply a representation of a live performance, whereas the frame is more arbitrary and thus presumably more meaningful. But it is the band's performance that is privileged visually, through color, free movement, and spectacle—and through the transgressive energies of male display and flamboyance. Most tellingly, it is the performance rather than the framing narrative that benefits from the affective invigoration of the music. If the framing scenes address labor relations, they do so in a rather flat, pedantic way. It is the video of the song itself that deals with the issues of greatest importance to metal fans: the power, freedom, transcendence, and transgression that are articulated through fantastic, androgynous display. The young man we meet in the frame finds his release from drudgery in Poison's spectacular androgyny.

Significantly, the video's "live" performance of "Nothin' but a Good Time" is neither live nor a real performance, but a constructed fantasy itself. The musicians undergo impossibly frequent and sudden changes of costume, without narrative explanation, through the invisible, extradiegetic powers of editing. Along with similar metamorphoses of the guitar player's instrument, which is a different model and color each time we see it, these unreal transformations contribute to the fantastic aura of the performance by offering an experience of freedom and plenitude. Moreover, there is no audience; the band "performs" in an abstract space, a contextless setting for pure spectacle. Such a location can serve as a "free space" for Poison's play of real and unreal, authenticity and desire, and the ambiguous subversiveness of androgyny, supported by the energy of the music.

The lyrics of the song are fairly simple: they combine a lament about overwork with a celebration of partying. The music is similarly straightforward, built around a vigorous rock beat and standard power chords on the scale degrees I, ♭VII, and IV. The musical mode is Mixolydian, quite commonly used in pop-oriented hard rock or metal, as it combines the positive affect of the major third with the "hard" semiotic value of the minor seventh. "Nothin' but a Good Time" derives much of its celebratory energy from the repeated suspension of the fourth scale degree over this major third, and the conventional move to ♭VII adds to the song's rebellious or aggressive tone. The visual narrative and the musically coded meanings are roughly parallel; the lyrics are supported by music that is energetic, rebellious, and flamboyant.

But in "Nothin' but a Good Time" we can also detect the association of androgynous visual styles with a particular set of musical characteristics. The song features compelling rhythmic patterns, it contains the requisite guitar solo, it utilizes the distorted timbres one would expect in the electric guitar and vocals of a metal song; in short, the song meets generic criteria in every way. It is, of course, successful music, exploiting discursive potentials with skill and effectiveness. However, one would be hard-pressed to find it very distinctive in any way; this is not especially innovative or imaginative music. Androgynous metal usually includes less emphasis on complexity and virtuosity than do other styles of metal, and many arguments among fans are provoked by the collision of visual spectacle and transgression with metal's dominant aesthetic valorization of sonic power, freedom, and originality. This alignment of androgynous spectacle with a musical discourse relatively lacking in sonic figurations of masculinity is crucial, for it signals the extent to which a linkage of "feminine" semiotic instability with monolithic, phallic power is deemed impossible.

To be sure, if the music of glam metal were separated from its visual context, it would still sound like hard rock. Compared to other kinds of popular music, glam rock is replete with constructions of masculine power. But within the context of heavy metal, glam metal's relative lack of virtuosity, complexity, and originality are aural contributors to androgyny. Fans link visual signs of androgyny with an abdication of metal's usual virtuosic prowess. "It seems like if you have the makeup you're thought of as less than a musician," complains Poison's guitarist C. C. Deville. "It seems because of the image we can't get past that hurdle. Now we try to stay away from the glam thing. When we first came out we were a little extreme." [32]

Indeed, when I attended a Poison concert I discovered that their drummer, Rikki Rockett, was actually an excellent musician, whose featured solo was marked by sophisticated polyrhythms and rhetorical intelligence. I was surprised by this because his playing on Poison's recordings had always been extremely simple, however accurate and appropriate. But Poison's simplicity is constructed, like that of much American popular music throughout its history. From Stephen Foster to Madonna (not to mention Aaron Copland), many musicians have used great skill to craft musical texts that communicate great simplicity. The musical construction of simplicity plays an important part in many kinds of ideological representations, from the depiction of pastoral refuges from modernity to constructions of race and gender. Poison succeeded in a genre dominated by virtuosity because their musical simplicity complemented their androgynous visual style and helped them forge a constituency. As Deville's comment indicates, the band now yearns to be respected musically as well, and though they have yet to make much progress toward this goal, they have drastically reduced the amount of makeup they wear, in pursuit of it.

"Real Men Don't Wear Makeup"

In the case of bands such as Poison, we might understand androgyny as yet another tactic for dealing with the anxieties of masculinity. Androgynous musicians and fans appropriate the visual signs of feminine identity in order to claim the powers of spectacularity for themselves. But while it is certainly important to understand heavy metal androgyny as patriarchal, metal takes part in a rock and roll tradition of Oedipal rebellion as well: the musical and visual codes of heavy metal may function to relieve anxieties about male power, but they are incompatible with the styles previous generations of men developed for doing the same thing. Teenage boys and young men chafe under patriarchal control even as women do, and boys often develop innovative ways of expressing control over women as simultaneous proof of their achievement of manhood and their rebellion against dominant men. This internal tension is never entirely manageable or predictable, and heavy metal transgresses against patriarchal control in ways that sometimes undermine, sometimes affirm its tenets.

Musicians themselves may notice how the ambiguities of androgyny provoke compensatory strategies. Aerosmith's hit song and video "Dude Looks like a Lady" (1987) confronts the gender anxieties aroused by androgyny, airing the problem with a tone of mock hysteria. And singer David Lee Roth self-reflexively connects his enthusiasm for bodybuilding and martial arts training to his "feminized" image on stage: "A lot of what I do can be construed as feminine. My face, or the way I dance, or the way I dress myself for stage. . . . But to prove it to myself, to establish this [his masculinity], I had to build myself physically. I had to learn to fight."[33] Roth's private regimen allows him to go on being androgynous in public. His personal anxieties about masculinity are shaped by conventional patriarchy, yet the attraction of androgynous transgression is also strong. Among the most leering of rock's lyricists, Roth seems neither personally nor artistically to have resisted sexist objectification of women, as is attested by his notorious paternity insurance policy and the video for his swaggering remake of the Beach Boys' "California Girls." Yet Roth has also publicly criticized the sexism of a society that discourages women from becoming professional musicians: "What if a little girl picked up a guitar and said 'I wanna be a rock star.' Nine times out of ten her parents would never allow her to do it. We don't have so many lead guitar women, not because women don't have the ability to play the instrument, but because they're kept locked up, taught to be something else. I don't appreciate that."[34] Roth's ideal of personal freedom is in conflict with the limitations of conventional gender definitions, though he doesn't grapple with the problem of how patriarchal power relations might be further strengthened by transgressions that rely on objectified representations of women.

In the journalism of heavy metal, the most heated debates are over "authenticity," which often implicitly revolves around issues of gender and sexuality. Fans frequently write to the letters columns of metal magazines to denounce or defend glam metal bands. Attackers label such musicians "poseurs," implying either that the band is all image with no musical substance or that they find androgyny fundamentally offensive, a perversion. As one female fan complained in a letter to a fan magazine, "real men don't wear makeup."[35] On the other side, defenders of glam metal are quick to respond, though they rarely defend androgyny per se: "This is to Kim of Cathedral City . . . who said that real men don't wear makeup. I have just one question: Do you actually listen to the music, or just spend hours staring at album covers? True, Metallica and Slayer kick f?!kin' ass and Megadeth rules—but Poison, Motley Crue and Hanoi Rocks f?!kin' jam too."[36] Unwilling to discuss gender constructions directly or lacking cultural precedents for doing so, fans usually defend the musical abilities of the band's members or argue for the intensity of experience provided by the group. But they may also respect the courage that is required of those who disrupt the symbolic order through androgyny, those who claim social space by having "the guts to be glam."[37]

Male fans of "harder" styles of heavy metal are often frantic in their denunciations of androgyny, seeing in it a subversion of male heterosexual privilege and linking it to the threat of homosexuality. On the cover of an album by MX Machine (*Manic Panic*, 1988), a picture of a grimacing boy with his fist in the air is accompanied by a sticker proclaiming "No Glam Fags! All Metal! No Makeup!" Both homosexuality and symbolic crossing of gender boundaries threaten patriarchal control, and they are thus conflated in the service of a rhetoric that strives to maintain difference and power. Musicians who wear makeup often compensate in private for their transgressions with homophobic banter, insulting each other in order to call masculinity into question and provide an opportunity for collective affirmation of heterosexuality.[38] An interview with Charlie Benante, drummer in the thrash metal band Anthrax, confirms that even instruments themselves are conventionally gender-coded, and that the use of a feminine-coded instrument in the context of heavy metal evokes the specter of homosexuality. When an interviewer asked, "Would you ever consider using keyboards as a major part of the song?" Benante replied, "That is gay. The only band that ever used keyboards that was good was UFO. This is a guitar band."[39]

However, since many "glam" metal performers appeal in particular to young women, an analysis of heavy metal that understands it only as a reproduction of male hegemony runs the risk of duplicating the exscription it describes. Heavy metal androgyny presents, from the point of view of women, a fusion of the signs specific to current notions of femininity with musically and theatrically produced power and freedom that are conventionally male. Colorful makeup; elaborate, ostentatious clothes; hair that is unhandily long and laboriously styled—these are the excessive signs of one gender's role as spectacle. But onstage in a metal show, these signs are invested with the power and glory normally reserved to patriarchy. As usual, women are offered male subject positions as a condition of their participation in empowerment, but the men with whom they are to identify have been transformed by their appropriations of women's signs. In their bid for greater transgression and spectacularity, the men onstage elevate important components of many women's sense of gendered identity, fusing cultural representations of male power and female erotic surface.[40] At the symbolic level, prestige—male presence, gesture, musical power—is conferred upon "female" signs, which, because they mark gender difference and are used to attract and manipulate, men pretend are trivial but take very seriously.

Feminist scholars have long been concerned with investigating the gendered aspects of the relationship of symbolic and political orders, and the long-standing linkage of women with ephemeral spectacle is highly relevant to metal videos. Kaja Silverman has pointed out that the instability of female fashion has historically marked women as unstable, while male sartorial conservatism represents the stable and timeless alignment of men with the symbolic and social orders.[41] Heavy metal androgyny challenges this "natural" alignment, drawing on the power of musical and visual pleasures. It is true that there is no inherent link between subversive textual practices and subversive politics, but the relationships I have delineated among the lyrics, music, images, fans, musicians, and ideologies of heavy metal, particularly with respect to gender, are intended to make the case for a conventional link.[42] Glam metal has prompted a great deal of thought and discussion about gender by demonstrating, even celebrating, the mutability of gender, by revealing the potential instability of the semiotic or symbolic realms that support current gender configurations. In some ways, heavy metal reflects the impact of what Jane Flax has called the greatest achievement of feminist theory, the problematization of gender.[43]

Metal replicates the dominant sexism of contemporary society, but it also allows a kind of free space to be opened up by and for certain women, performers and fans alike. Female fans identify with a kind of power that is usually understood in our culture as male—because physical power, dominance, rebellion, and flirting with the dark side of life are all culturally designated as male prerogatives. Yet women are able to access this power because it is channeled through a medium, music, that is intangible and difficult to police. Female performers of heavy metal can become enabled to produce and control very powerful sounds, if they meet other genre requirements and acquiesce in the physical display that is so sexist and widespread in society generally but may in fact seem less so in metal, where men similarly display themselves.[44] Thus, when metal guitarist and singer Lita Ford brags, "I wear my balls on my chest," she combines her seemingly inevitable status as an object of sexual spectacle with her metallic stature as a subject embodying the spectacle of power.[45]

Women's reception of these spectacles is complex, and female performers of heavy metal may be advancing provocative arguments about the nature and limits of female claims to power. I have observed and interviewed female fans who dress, act, and interpret just like male fans, for example, particularly at concerts of bands like Metallica—bands that avoid references to gender in their lyrics, dealing instead with experiences of alienation, fear, and empowerment that may cut across gender lines. Elements of rock music that had been coded as masculine, such as heavy beats, are negotiable, insofar as female fans are willing to step outside traditional constrictions of gender identity.[46] It may well be, then, that the participation of female metal fans reflects the influence that feminism has had in naturalizing, to a great extent, the empowerment of women. Even in the 1970s, fewer women would have been comfortable identifying with power, when power was more rigidly coded as male. The choice was between being powerful and being a woman, a dichotomy that has since eroded somewhat.

But female fans also maintain their own distinctive modes of engagement with heavy metal, including practices that are often too quickly dismissed as degrading adoration. Sue Wise has argued that the young women who screamed and swooned over Elvis were not so much worshiping him, as so many male rock critics have assumed, as *using* him. Instead of a subject who caused his helpless fans to go into frenzies, Elvis was for many women an object by means of which they explored their own desires and formed friendships.[47] Similarly, many female heavy metal fans take great pleasure in collecting, owning, and looking at pictures of male heavy metal musicians. Predictably, male fans tend to be scornful of the pin-up magazines and their devotees.[48] But the enthusiasm of young women for glam styles of heavy metal is not simply an example of masochistic submission to male idols. Such spectacle also infuses with power the signs of women's hegemonically constructed gender identity, offers visual pleasures seldom available to women, and provides them with opportunities to form their own subsets of the fan community.

The channeling of so much masculine prestige through feminine forms thus represents a risky sexual politics, one that is open to several interpretations. Heavy metal's androgyny can be very disturbing, not only because the conventional signs of female passivity and objectification are made dynamic, assertive, and transgressive, but also because hegemonic gender boundaries are blurred and the "natural" exclusiveness of heterosexual male power comes into question.[49] For all of its male rhetoric of supremacy—phallic imagery, macho posturing, the musical semiotics of male power—metal's rebellion and fantastic play offer its fans, both male and female, opportunities to make common cause against certain kinds of oppression, even as the same text may enable each gender to resolve particular anxieties in very different ways. The level of discussion of gender among heavy metal fans is impressive, in statements that reflect their awareness of the mutability of gender roles and other cultural constructions. Practically every issue of the fan magazine *RIP* in 1989 contained letters from fans protesting sexism, racism, and even homophobia.[50] Glam metal fostered greater perception of the conventionality of gender roles, and thus helped lead to greater participation in metal by women and to debates over gender stereotypes, masculinity, behavior, and access to power.

Androgyny offers male performers (and vicariously, male fans) the chance to play with color, movement, flamboyance, and artifice, which can be a tremendous relief from the rigidity expected of them as men. Philip Gordon argues that singer Dee Snider "grew his hair and wore women's clothes and make-up, not merely to assert a difference between himself and his parents (as if any sign of difference would be equally effective), but as a carefully constructed style signifying attractiveness, energy and opposition to authoritative restrictions on particular pleasures."[51]

Critics have not generally understood glam metal in this way. E. Ann Kaplan denies any significance to heavy metal's gender politics: "Unlike the genuine Bakhtinian carnival, the protest remains superficial: mere play with oppositional signifiers rather than a protest that emerges from a powerful class and community base."[52] But Kaplan can make such a statement only because she made no efforts to discover anything about the "class and community base" of heavy metal. There is nothing superficial about such play; fans and musicians do their most important "identity work" when they participate in the formations of gender and power that constitute heavy metal. Metal is a fantastic genre, but it is one in which real social needs and desires are addressed and temporarily resolved in unreal ways. These unreal solutions are attractive and effective precisely because they seem to step outside the normal social categories that construct the conflicts in the first place.

Like many other social groups, metal musicians and fans play off different possibilities available to them from mainstream culture, at the same time that they may draw upon the facts of a social situation that is not mainstream. Androgynous metal's bricolage of male power and female spectacle and its play of real and unreal are complex responses to crucial social contradictions that its fans have inherited. Heavy metal's fantastic representations clash with the visions of many other social groups in the cultural competition to define social reality, and like the tensions to which they are a response, metal's fantasies are themselves richly conflicted. If male heavy metal fans and musicians sometimes assert masculinity by co-opting femininity, what they achieve is not necessarily the same kind of masculinity that they sought, as the conflicting demands of masculinity and rebellion are mediated through new models and the free play of androgynous fantasy shakes up the underlying categories that structure social experience.

However, androgyny is by no means a purely utopian sign. Capitalism, after all, feeds on novelty as a spur to consumption, and mass culture may colonize existing tensions and ambiguities for consumer purposes rather than to prefigure new realities. As Fred Pfeil points out, mass audiences are increasingly offered "scandalously ambivalent pleasure," and the same "de-Oedipalization" of American middle-class life that makes androgyny possible, attractive, and thrilling can also block further development toward new collective social forms, beyond fragmentation.[53] Moreover, postmodern cultural "decentering" can serve capitalism by playing to sensual gratification in ways that deflect people from making the connections that might enable critique.

But postmodern disruptions also open up new possibilities and enable new connections and formulations to be made by delegitimating conceptual obstacles; androgynous metal's defamiliarization of social categories that are still thought normative by many must be given its due. Poison's music and images reflect a concern with shifting boundaries of gender and reality that cannot simply be disregarded as no more than inauthentic or commodified fantasies, for such fantasies are exercises in semiotic power, offering challenges at the level of both what representations are made and who gets to make them. Dismissing fantasy and escapism "avoids the vital questions of *what* is escaped from, *why* escape is necessary, and *what* is escaped to."[54]

Simon Frith and Angela McRobbie ended their early theorization of rock and sexuality with what they saw as a "nagging" question: "Can rock be nonsexist?"[55] The obvious answer would seem to be no, for there is no way to step outside the history of a discourse, and Frith and McRobbie's question begs for a kind of music that is recognizably— that is, discursively—rock, but that does not participate in the sexism that rock has articulated. Rock can never be gender-neutral because rock music is intelligible only in its historical and discursive contexts. Rock can, however, be antisexist; instead of dreaming of a kind of music that might be both "rock" and "nonsexist," we can spot many extant examples of rock music that use the powerful codings of gender available in order to engage with, challenge, disrupt, or transform not only rock's representations of gender but also the beliefs and material practices with which those representations engage. The point of criticism should not be to decide whether rock music is oppositional or co-optive, with respect to gender, class, or any other social category, but rather to analyze how it arbitrates tensions between opposition and co-optation at particular historical moments.[56]

I have ranged widely within heavy metal in this chapter, turning to a number of very different bands and to various visual and musical strategies for dealing with the contradictions inherent in gender roles in the 1980s. The range of examples is necessary, I think, to demonstrate that heavy metal as a genre includes a great variety of gender constructions, contradictory negotiations with dominant ideologies of gender that are invisible if one is persuaded by metal's critics that the whole enterprise is a monolithic symptom of adolescent maladjustment. In fact, it is those most responsible for the very conditions with which metal musicians and fans struggle—the contradictory demands of subordination and socialization, of "masculine" aggressiveness and communal harmony, the possibilites of transcendent pleasure and street pain—who insist on reading this music as impoverished and debased "entertainment."

Heavy metal, like virtually all cultural practices, is continually in flux, driven by its own constitutive contradictions. Patriarchy and capitalism form the crucible, but human experience can never be wholly contained within such a vessel: there are aspects of social life that escape the organization of one or the other; there are also aspects organized in contradictory ways by the pair. Culture cannot transcend its material context, but culture very often transcends hegemonic definitions of its context: heavy metal perpetuates some of the worst images and ideals of patriarchy at the same time that it stands as an example of the kinds of imaginative transformations and rebuttals people produce from within such oppressive systems. Masculinity is forged whenever it is hammered out anew through the negotiations of men and women with the contradictory positions available to them in such contexts. It is also forged because masculinity is passed like a bad check, as a promise that is never kept. Masculinity will always be forged because it is a social construction, not a set of abstract qualities but something defined through the actions and power relations of men and women—because, with or without makeup, there are no "real men."

CHAPTER FIVE

Can I Play with Madness?

Mysticism, Horror, and Postmodern Politics

> Cradled in evil, that Thrice-Great Magician,
> The Devil, rocks our souls, that can't resist;
> And the rich metal of our own volition
> Is vaporized by that sage alchemist. —Baudelaire [1]

In his course on rhetoric, the Roman orator Quintilian included a ficti-
tious legal exercise in the politics of music and madness. He presented
the case of a musician who is accused of manslaughter because he played
in the wrong musical mode during a sacrifice; by playing in the Phrygian
mode, a piper allegedly caused the officiating priest to go mad and fling
himself over a cliff.[2] Quintilian used this story to support his argument
that musical training is essential for the development of oratorical skills,
but the problem of the musician's liability is also of interest because it
raises questions about the nature and power of music, about social mis-
trust of those whose rhetorical abilities find their outlet through musical
discourse. As the popularity of heavy metal grew in the late 1980s, it
came increasingly under fire from critics who accused its musicians of
"playing in the wrong mode," causing madness and death. In this chapter I will criticize a number of influential condemnations of heavy metal
and propose alternative explanations of the significance of mysticism,
horror, and violence in heavy metal.

Professing Censorship: The PMRC and its Academic Allies Attack

The single most influential critic of heavy metal in the 1980s was
Tipper Gore, whose status as the wife of U.S. Senator Albert Gore, Jr.,

provided her with access to media attention and political muscle to support her cause. In 1985, Gore, along with several other wives of powerful government figures (among them Susan Baker, wife of then treasury secretary James A. Baker) established the Parents' Music Resource Center (PMRC). The PMRC has been quite successful in articulating a reactionary cultural agenda and accomplishing its political goals. Since its founding, the group has pressured record companies into placing warning stickers on recordings with "adult" lyrics and has underwritten partially successful campaigns to persuade state legislatures to censor certain types of music, chiefly rap and heavy metal. Through its conjugal connections with Capitol Hill, the PMRC was able to provoke congressional hearings, in September 1985, on the subject of what they called "porn rock." Though the PMRC and Congress described the hearings as neutral "fact-finding," others saw them as terrorism, since congressional interrogation of musicians and leaders of the music industry suggested implicit (and illegal) threats of legislation if the moralistic demands of the PMRC for "voluntary" censorship were not met.

Although the PMRC has been accused of not really being a "resource center" because its publications display little familiarity with the scholarly literature on popular music, it is unmistakably "parental."[3] The fullest articulation of the PMRC brief is Tipper Gore's *Raising PG Kids in an X-Rated Society*, published in 1987. In it, Gore takes care to establish her authority as a social and cultural critic by emphasizing that she is a parent; she dwells on the numbers and genders of the children of PMRC leaders, while neglecting to mention that her main opponents at the Senate hearings, musicians Frank Zappa and Dee Snider, are also concerned parents.[4] Her references to twenty-year-old "boys" mark her concern to represent heavy metal as a threat to youth, enabling her to mobilize parental hysteria while avoiding the adult word *censorship*. Objecting to eroticism and "lesbian undertones" in popular music, along with sadism and brutality, she conflates sex and violence, which have in common their threat to parental control.

It is clear from Gore's book that heavy metal participates in a crisis in the reproduction of values, that it is a threat because it celebrates and legitimates sources of identity and community that do not derive from parental models. For the PMRC, assuming the universality of "the American Family," an institution of mythic stature but scant abundance, provides an absolute norm that can be righteously defended. Gore attempts to naturalize her perspective by appealing to "common sense" universals, such as the "shared moral values" that underpin "our" society. She combines such grand claims with disingenuousness about her own political clout, as when she refers to "our friends (some of whom happen to hold public office)." Like so many recent appeals to "common sense" and "morality," Gore's book is a call for the imposition of official values and the elimination of cultural difference.[5]

To bolster her attack on heavy metal, Gore relies heavily on a pamphlet by a professor of music, "The Heavy Metal User's Manual" by Joe Stuessy.[6] Not only is Stuessy often cited in Gore's book; he was also called upon as an expert witness for the Senate hearings in 1985. In both his testimony and his pamphlet, Stuessy argued that heavy metal lyrics are violent and deviant and that metal music is artistically impoverished. "Most of the successful heavy metal," he testified, "projects one or more of the following basic themes: extreme rebellion, extreme violence, substance abuse, sexual promiscuity/perversion (including homosexuality, bisexuality, sadomasochism, necrophilia, etc.), Satanism."[7] In fact, heavy metal lyrics dealing with these topics are uncommon. For example, examination of eighty-eight song lyrics reprinted by *Hit Parader* reveals relatively little concern with violence, drug use, or suicide. Reduced to the crudest terms, the songs could be grouped thematically so:[8]

> Assertion of or longing for intensity: 27
> Lust: 17
> Loneliness, victimization, self-pity: 17
> Love: 14 (affirmation, 8; regret or longing, 6)
> Anger, rebellion, madness: 8
> Didactic or critical (antidrug, anti-Devil, anti–TV evangelism,
>   critique of the subversion of justice by wealth): 5

Moreover, when such transgressive lyrics do appear, it is in contexts where they often function in ways that are more complex and sophisticated than Stuessy recognizes, as we will see below.

Connections between heavy metal and drug use have certainly existed throughout the music's history, beginning perhaps with the success of Blue Cheer among San Francisco speed freaks in the late 1960s.[9] But drugs cannot explain a style of music, since the music, lyrics, and images of even heavily drug-influenced music cross the boundaries of subcultural scenes and make sense to people who are using different drugs or even no drugs at all. And because both music and drugs are involved in strategies for coping with particular social circumstances, criticism of one cannot depend on denunciation of the other; both must be located in the real world of material and cultural tensions.[10] Moreover, critics have failed to notice that as heavy metal became both individually and collectively more virtuosic during the 1980s, musicians increasingly confided that they could no longer afford to indulge in drugs and alcohol because their music would suffer too much.[11]

Finally, criticism of rock music because of drug use often implicitly relies upon an absurdly sanitized version of musical history. Many now-canonic nineteenth-century artists "confidently engaged in 'mad' behavior—debauchery, drinking, drug use, irrational thinking—hoping thus to stimulate their creativity. . . . the viewpoint prevailed that genius and madness are inseparable."[12] Berlioz made no bones about his use of opium; his program for the *Symphonie fantastique* explicitly connects opium use with the rhetorical splendor of his music. Abuse of alcohol is well documented for composers such as Schumann, Schubert, and Mussorgsky, and much more information about drugs and canonic composers would no doubt be available were it not for the musicological whitewashing of the lives of these musicians, which has retroactively enforced compulsory sobriety, heterosexuality, and Christianity. Berlioz's *Symphonie fantastique* is, of course, more than the random outcome of an opium dream that it pretends to be; it is a powerful metaphorical articulation, grounded in contemporary social currents and musical discourses. Contemporary popular music is made to seem especially vulnerable to certain kinds of critique because so much has been purged from our hagiological histories of music and so much is hidden by the assumptions about cultural hierarchy we take for granted.

Throughout his book, Stuessy pursues the simplistic argument that healthy minds don't think negative thoughts, and he alleges that heavy metal is socially unique in its glorification of violence, which network news shows, for example, merely report. But Steussy, like Gore, is being disingenuous, because struggles for power are hardly unique to youth culture or popular culture. From the Super Bowl to Monster Truck races, from Capitol Hill to corporate boardrooms (where handbooks of advice have titles like *Swim with the Sharks* and *Leadership Secrets of Atilla the Hun*), adult Americans (especially men) display their seemingly insatiable fascination with power and violence, a way of thinking that is continually affirmed by the brutality of American capitalism and government policy. From President Johnson's War on Poverty to President Bush's War on Drugs, American politicians have found military metaphors the most effective means of selling programs that might have been described in communal and compassionate terms. In this light, Stuessy's concluding recommendations for action against metal are patently hypocritical: "I think the attack on heavy metal must be waged on all fronts using every weapon at our disposal. . . . Warning labels and ratings might be helpful, but that is not the final solution. Printed lyrics would be helpful, but that is not the ultimate weapon."[13] Glorification of violence in American society is hardly deviant, as we see from Stuessy's own plan for a "final solution" to the problem of heavy metal.

— Stuessy's status as a professor of music makes him a useful ally to those who would strip heavy metal of First Amendment protections as free artistic expression, for he is able to offer an aggressive twist on the usual mystification that elevates classical music and protects it from ideological critique, leaving popular musics more vulnerable to attack. Stuessy assures us that the process of artistic creation remains "shrouded in mystery," and the inspiration of composers like Beethoven was "mysterious and quite possibly divine"; but heavy metal, he argues, is merely cranked out according to a formula, which disqualifies it from protection under freedom of expression, making it instead subject to "consumer protection" regulation like other manufactured products.[14]

At the same time, the aesthetic tradition has been so successful in effacing the social meanings of culture that Stuessy found it necessary to argue at length that music can in fact affect us. He adopts, and Gore accepts from him, a "hypodermic model" of musical effects; music's meanings are "pounded" or "dumped" into listeners, who are helpless to resist. Young people in particular are thought to be more vulnerable, especially when repetitive listening and headphone use help create "a direct, unfettered freeway straight into the mind."[15] Stuessy's problem is to define music so that heavy metal can be held responsible for harming listeners without calling into question the violence in Beethoven's *Eroica*, for example, or the glorification of drugs, violence, and Satanism in the *Symphony fantastique*.[16] The solution is simply to assume that the meanings of classical music are essentially benign because they are art, whereas heavy metal ought to arouse our suspicions because it is popular and commercially successful. Those who embrace such a position seem undaunted by the elitism that is required to underpin it, or by the fact that what we now call "classical music" is and always has been "commercial."[17]

Another academic, this one a professor of religious studies at the University of Denver, has recently launched a full-scale attack on heavy metal. Like several earlier book-length denunciations of rock music, Carl A. Raschke's *Painted Black: From Drug Killings to Heavy Metal— the Alarming True Story of How Satanism Is Terrorizing Our Communities* is explicitly concerned with defending "the values of Christian civilization," which he presumes are shared by all right-thinking citizens.[18] The book "reveals" a national epidemic of Satanism, manifest in ritual crimes and supported by heavy metal music. Unlike Tipper Gore's book, which maintains a rather calm tone and clear documentation, Raschke's is a potboiler, filled with sensational claims backed by shoddy scholarship. On the one hand, he uses unsubstantiated and marginally coherent similes to suggest that heavy metal is a terrible threat: "The end result [of heavy metal] is to erode the nervous system with noise, as drugs destroy the cerebrum"; "A national epidemic of 'satanist-related' crime was growing faster than AIDS"; and, most puzzling: "Heavy metal belongs to a so-called avant-garde art form that has stayed veiled from the eyes of mass audiences, the style known as aesthetic terrorism."[19]

On the other hand, Raschke also pretends to have objective, scientific justification for his hysteria:

In 1985, the *Wall Street Journal* reported that a fat sheaf of neuro-psychological research has shown remarkable, and complex, relationships between music listening and brain organization. Roger Shepard, a professor at Stanford University, believes that certain kinds of music "mesh effectively with the deep cognitive structures of the mind." Heavy metal seems to mesh with the limbic brain, the most primitive and potentially violent stratum of cerebral processing.[20]

But the last, damning sentence of this passage is a deliberate fabrication, for heavy metal was never mentioned by Shepard. Raschke has tacked onto his summary of a quite uncontroversial report his own condemnation of heavy metal, carefully couched in scientific language ("limbic brain," "cerebral processing") so as to suggest that it is justified by the findings of Shepard's research. He misleads his readers in an attempt to whip up a repressive frenzy directed against metal musicians and fans. Raschke invokes science as part of his effort to essentialize what are in fact social tensions: "Heavy metal does more than dissolve the inherent inhibitions against violence. It actively fosters, configures, anneals, reinforces, and purifies the most vicious and depraved tendencies within the human organism."[21] When he describes both "inhibitions against violence" *and* "depraved tendencies" as inherent qualities rather than socially negotiated ones, Raschke wants to have it both ways: heavy metal dissolves the fragile bonds of repression that make civilization possible, *and* it unnaturally corrupts human nature itself.

The terrorism of Raschke and similar critics depends upon two tactics: anecdote and insinuation. Raschke himself cites a group of sociologists of religion who determined that there was "not a shred of evidence" that Satanism is a problem in America, directly contradicting the thesis of Raschke's book. The "evidence disintegrates as close examination occurs" whenever Satanism and crime are linked, according to J. Gordon Melton, director of the Institute for the Study of American Religion in Santa Barbara.[22] Raschke replies by recounting, in sickening detail, a few instances of crimes involving satanic symbols, without addressing the question of how significant this sort of crime is—how it compares statistically with, for example, crimes committed by clergy or suicides related to plant closings.[23] In Stuessy's book, in Raschke's, and in a lecture I heard by a touring campus crusader against rock music, I found the same handful of stories repeated rapidly and balefully so as to suggest that they stood as select examples of widespread trends rather than the bizarre and anomalous events they were. In the end Raschke waffles and hedges: "And if no one can blame rock music directly for the 300 percent rise in adolescent suicides or the 7 percent increase in teenage pregnancies, it *may surely* be more than a negligible factor." [24] With the word *may*, Raschke admits that no link can be made; with the word *surely*, he attempts to cover up that admission. Moreover, if we assume that rock music is to blame for that rise in suicides, do we then credit rap and heavy metal with causing the dramatic decrease in drug use among high school students in the 1980s, the decade during which those styles came to dominate musical culture? [25]

In fact, none of these critics is able to connect heavy metal directly with suicide, Satanism, or crime. Tipper Gore does provide information on Dungeons and Dragons, a fantasy role-playing game that has been attacked for the same reasons. According to her, over eight million sets of D&D have been sold in the United States; yet even the game's harshest critics can link it with fewer than fifty people involved in suicides or homicides.[26] As with metal, one might reasonably infer from such statistics that D&D is to be applauded as a stabilizing factor in many adolescent lives. If I have dwelt on these critiques longer than seems necessary, it is because they have in fact been extremely influential. The flimsiness of these arguments seems to escape readers who are predisposed to accept heavy metal as a convenient scapegoat; Raschke was given a complimentary "Portrait," for example, in *The Chronicle of Higher Education.*[27]

Gore and other critics also point to actual violence at heavy metal concerts as more proof of the music's malignancy. But such violence is greatly exaggerated by metal's critics; mayhem is no more common at metal concerts than at sports events—or at the opera in nineteenth-century Paris or performances of Shakespeare in nineteenth-century New York.[28] In fact, concert security guards report that crowds at country music concerts are far more difficult to manage than heavy metal crowds.[29] Culture is valued because it mobilizes meanings with respect to the most deeply held social values and the most profound tensions. Only by effacing cultural history can heavy metal be portrayed as singularly violent in thought or deed. But insinuations of metal's violent effects are also contradicted by a recent study that finds no correlations between teenagers' preferences in music and their likelihood of having "behavioral problems" at school.[30]

To be sure, Tipper Gore raises legitimate concerns about sexual violence in the lyrics and visual representations of metal shows. But she labors to portray such violence as an aberration of youth and commercial exploitation, scapegoating heavy metal musicians and fans for problems that are undeniably extant but for which she holds entirely blameless the dominant social systems, institutions, and moral values she defends. Calls for censorship serve to divert attention from the real social causes of violence and misogyny.

All of these critics share the notion that heavy metal is bad because it is perverse deviance in the midst of a successfully functioning society. They ascribe much too much importance to a transhistorical notion of "adolescence," which allows them to overlook the specific forms that culture takes in particular circumstances of power and pain. They believe that insisting that "healthy minds don't think negative thoughts" will make people overlook the devastation caused by deindustrialization and disastrous social policies. They imagine that fans are passive, unable to resist the pernicious messages of heavy metal, and thus they themselves commit the sort of dehumanization they ascribe to popular culture. They make fans into dupes without agency or subjectivity, without social experiences and perceptions that might inform their interactions with mass-mediated texts.[31] And they portray heavy metal musicians as "outside agitators," just as social authorities tried to blame civil rights violence on Communist troublemaking, as though poverty, joblessness, and police brutality weren't sufficient explanation. But heavy metal exists not in a world that would be fine if it were not marred by degraded culture, but in a world disjointed by inequity and injustice.

In his 1987 movie, *The Hidden*, director Jack Sholder satirized such portrayals of the horrific effects of heavy metal. The back of the videocassette release summarizes the plot: "a demonic extraterrestrial creature is invading the bodies of innocent victims—and transforming them into inhuman killers with an unearthly fondness for heavy metal music, red Ferraris and unspeakable violence."[32] *The Hidden* replicates precisely the understanding of heavy metal promoted by its harshest critics, linking metal with violence, and depicting it as a threat coming from elsewhere, with no connection to this world, working its evil on helpless, innocent victims. The arguments of critics like Gore, Stuessy, and Raschke depend upon denying fans subjectivity or social agency so that they can be cast as victims who can be protected through censorship. By depicting fans as "youth," an ideological category that lifts them out of society and history, these critiques manage to avoid having to provide any explanation of why fans are attracted to the specific sounds, images, and lyrics of heavy metal.

Suicide Solutions

The most celebrated public controversy over heavy metal to date revolved around a lawsuit against Judas Priest, tried in 1990. Five years earlier, two young men from Reno, Nevada—Ray Belknap, eighteen, and Jay Vance, twenty—had consummated a suicide pact by taking turns with a shotgun. Belknap was killed instantly; Vance survived to undergo three years of reconstructive surgery before dying of a drug overdose in 1988. Both men had been avid Judas Priest fans, and the suit alleged that subliminal messages embedded in the band's 1978 release, *Stained Class*, had created a compulsion that led to their deaths. According to the plaintiffs, one song contained commands of "do it" that were audible only subconsciously, and other songs, when played backward, exhorted "try suicide," "suicide is in," and "sing my evil spirit."[33] As with previous accusations of "backward masking" in rock music, the suit depended on the premise that such hidden messages can be decoded without conscious awareness and on the idea that they affect listeners more powerfully than overt communication.

The strategy of the defense was simple: they argued that the lives of Vance and Belknap had been such that no mysterious compulsion was required to account for their suicides. During the two years preceding the suicide pact, for example, Vance had run away from home thirteen times; his mother admitted beating him "too often" when he was young.[34] His father beat him, too, especially after he lost his job (when a GM plant closed in 1979) and began drinking heavily. Vance's violent behavior long predated his involvement with heavy metal; a school psychiatrist had expressed concern about his self-destructive behavior when Vance was in second grade, and his mother testified that he had tried to strangle her and hit her with a hammer while he was still in grade school.[35] He had even been institutionalized for attempted suicide in 1976, at age eleven.

Ray Belknap's background was just as bad. At the time of his suicide attempt, he had just decided to quit his job with a local contractor, after his boss had won his week's wages in a pool game. His mother, a born-again Christian whose religious beliefs increased the tension at home, had just separated from her fourth husband, "a reportedly violent man who had once been arrested for menacing Ray's mother with a gun" and who sometimes locked Ray in the garage and beat him with a belt.[36] Defense lawyers argued that in such circumstances, there was little need to postulate secret musical compulsions in order to account for suicidal thoughts. The prosecution replied that many people have bad home lives yet do not kill themselves—a risky line of reasoning, one would think, since their case depended on overlooking the millions of people who listen to heavy metal yet do not kill themselves.

The Judas Priest case hinged, though, on the question of the impact of subliminal commands, allegedly masked but made no less effective by being placed on the album backward. As part of the substantial media attention given the case, "Newsline New York" interviewed an "expert," Wilson Bryan Key, who claimed that such messages in heavy metal music lead to violence. (The host of the show neglected to mention that Key has in the past claimed to have found satanic or sexual messages on Ritz crackers, $5 bills, and Howard Johnson's placemats.)[37] Yet studies by psychologists have repeatedly shown that while intelligible messages can be found in virtually anything played backward, there is no evidence that listeners perceive or are affected by backward messages. "Even when messages are there, all they do is add a little noise to the music," says one researcher. "There is absolutely no effect from content."[38]

Lead singer Rob Halford may have tipped the scales of justice when he appeared for the last day of testimony with a tape containing backward messages *he* had found on the *Stained Class* album. Reversing the fragment "strategic force / they will not" from "Invader" yielded an intelligible, if cryptic, "It's so fishy, personally I'll owe it." Halford reversed "They won't take our love away," from the same song, and had the courtroom howling when they heard "Hey look, Ma, my chair's broken." Finally, he played his last discovery: "Stand by for exciter / Salvation is his task" came out backward as "I-I-I as-asked her for a peppermint-t-t / I-I-I asked for her to get one."[39]

The trial ended with Judas Priest cleared of all charges, for the judge remained unconvinced that the "subliminal" messages on the album were intentionally placed there or were necessary to explain the conduct of Vance and Belknap. There seemed no credible motive for the subliminal crimes of which the band was accused; as their lawyer put it, "In order to find for the plaintiffs here, you'd have to assume that there is at work out there an Evil Empire of the media and the artist who want to damage the people who are buying their works. You hafta be nuts to think that if Judas Priest had the capability to insert a subliminal message they would tell the fans who've been buying all their albums, 'Go kill yourselves.' "[40]

In the face of such evidence, why is it that accusations of subliminal compulsions persist? Those who condemn heavy metal often posit conspiracies in order to scapegoat musicians and fans, avoiding questions of social responsibility for the destructive behavior of people such as Vance and Belknap. But charges of secret messages may persist because we as a society have afforded ourselves no other ways of explaining music's power to affect us. Subliminal manipulation substitutes for a conception of music as a social discourse; since we are trained not to think of music, or any other art, as symbolic discourse, drawing its power from socially grounded desires and contestations, we fall back on a kind of mysticism to explain the effects that music undeniably produces. Such effects may be acceptable when they are created by dead "great" composers, but they are perceived as dangerously manipulative when produced by others, such as heavy metal musicians.

Another reason the Priest suit hinged on subliminal messages was that an important precedent had already been set in 1985, when a judge decided that overt lyrics about suicide were protected speech under the First Amendment. This earlier case was a suit against Ozzy Osbourne, whose song "Suicide Solution" (1981) was alleged to have promoted suicide in its lyrics and to have compelled nineteen-year-old John McCullom to shoot himself.[41] Osbourne's claim that the lyrics were inspired by the alchohol-related suicide of a friend and that the song is in fact antisuicide and antidrug in sentiment was dismissed as sham social conscience, feigned after the fact. Although this suit too was eventually dismissed, the case became a cause célèbre, for it was timely. The PMRC was in the midst of a campaign against Osbourne and other musicians that had just culminated in widespread discussion of regulation of the record industry and the infamous Senate hearings, and they were quick to use the McCullom suicide as yet another example of the evil effects of heavy metal.

But despite his reputation for transgression—he once bit the head off a live bat (which he thought was rubber) tossed onstage by a fan— Ozzy Osbourne's lyrics tend to be quite moralistic. His *Blizzard of Ozz* album (1981), which contains "Suicide Solution," also includes an antiporn song, "No Bone Movies," which deplores the degradation caused by obsessive lust. "Revelation (Mother Earth)" is a plea for environmental responsibility, and "Crazy Train" attributes its craziness to the modern pressures faced by the "heirs of a cold war." "Steal Away (The

Night)" celebrates love; "Goodbye to Romance" mourns its loss. And in "Mr. Crowley," Osbourne's lyrics refer to the infamous English Satanist Aleister Crowley (1875–1947); but far from celebrating occult practices, the song taunts Crowley, displaying an ironic tone often used by Osbourne (and never noticed by his literal-minded critics). Osbourne evokes the fascination with the supernatural that Crowley represents— "Uncovering things that were sacred / manifest on this earth"—at the same time that he tweaks Crowley's nose:

> Mister Charming, did you think you were pure?
> Mister Alarming, in nocturnal rapport
> . . . .
> Mister Crowley, won't you ride my white horse?
> Mister Crowley, it's symbolic, of course.

Osbourne plays with signs of the supernatural because they evoke a power and mystery that is highly attractive to many fans, but his song offers an experience of those qualities and even a critique, not a literal endorsement of magical practices.

In chapter 3, I discussed in more detail how "Mr. Crowley" uses signs taken from Baroque music to evoke gloom and fatefulness. It is also musical semiotics, I would argue, that has led virtually everyone to reject Osbourne's defense of the lyrics of "Suicide Solution" as an antisuicide statement. The lyrics by themselves are perhaps ambiguous:

> Wine is fine but whiskey's quicker
> Suicide is slow with liquor
> Take a bottle, drown your sorrows
> Then it floods away tomorrows
> . . . .
> Where to hide, Suicide is the only way out
> Don't you know what it's really about?

But musically, "Suicide Solution" is very carefully crafted to produce an affect of despair and futility. The song is built around a syncopated power chord riff, played at a morose, plodding tempo. Pulsing bass notes propel each square phrase inexorably into the next, while Osbourne's whiny voice, double-tracked to blur its pitch, repeats sneering, descending lines. Other chords slide inevitably back to a power chord on A; in spite of their syncopated energy, they can never escape.

In the bridge section of the song, brutal, unexpected punches form an irrational, disorienting pattern, accompanying the lines " 'Cause you feel life's unreal and you're living a lie" in the first bridge and "Breaking laws, knocking doors, but there's no one at home" the second time. The harmonic motion of the guitar chords again is a struggle up away from the tonic pedal which is always defeated. Chords are suspended against the pedal, generating great tension, particularly during the section where the vocal sounds are panning back and forth. But the chords are always forced back to the tonic, accompanied by screams and moans. Throughout, the bass remains immutable, implacable, relentlessly pounding tonic downbeats.

The fact that there are no guitar solos in "Suicide Solution" represents a significant exception to the rule, for heavy metal songs almost invariably have them. Often a dialectic is set up between the potentially oppressive power of bass, drums, and rhythm guitar, and the liberating, empowering vehicle of the guitar's solo flights. The feeling of freedom created by the virtuosic guitar solos and fills can be at various times supported, defended, or threatened by the physical power of the bass and the temporal control of the drums. The latter rigidly organize and control time; the guitar escapes with flashy runs and other arrhythmic gestures. The solo allows the listener to identify with the controlling power without feeling threatened, because the solo can transcend anything. "Suicide Solution," however, gains in impact by frustrating this norm; there is power and intensity of existence but no freedom. The song depicts a situation (which the text attributes to alcoholism) of frustration, of intense need balked by no options for action save suicide.

"Suicide Solution" also ends unusually; indeed, I do not know of another song with a comparable ending. Heavy metal songs, in line with their concern with control, typically achieve complete, unambiguous closure; they end with a punch that is withheld slightly, to create desire, but always given. Fade-outs are less often used by metal bands; a fade-out is indeterminate, a way of suggesting that the music continues forever. In "Suicide Solution," guitar cries fade into the "distance" (reverb helps create an engineered sense of space) over a monotonously pulsing, static bass, which also slowly fades but not completely; the song does end with the obligatory punch but at reduced volume. Near the end, the bass line finally changes, moving to a heartbeat pattern. The guitar's activities are reduced to demented noise, crazed sounds from all over sonic space. A cry from the guitar is stifled at the very end. The ending suggests neither continuing forever through a standard fade-out nor assertive closure, the metal norm; it ends uncomfortably, snuffing itself.

Throughout the song, the timbre of Osbourne's voice is ironic, mocking. His vocals are sometimes quickly panned across the stereo field, from left to right and back again, a scary, disorienting effect, especially on headphones. Other metal songs, and other kinds of music, too, have made such use of space to construct a paranoid's experience of persecution.[42] All of these other details support the affect of the opening riff, as the guitar chords struggle up a couple of steps and then sink back down, all over a constant, unyielding bass note; they resonate with a particular experience of life—life with no social support, no ethical core, no future.

But to construct such an affect is not to condone or compel suicide. To talk about something is not the same as promoting it; metal has a critical conscience many of its critics lack.[43] Many young people are frustrated at the hypocrisy they perceive around them, at the lack of history and genuine politics in their educations and in their lives. Many fans value heavy metal because it deals with issues that are of great importance but that are too often swept under the rug. "Metal is the only thing that says how the world really *is*," said one fan who attended the Judas Priest trial. "They want us to say that the grass is green and the air is clean and everything is beautiful."[44] Judas Priest guitarist K. K. Downing reflected after the trial: "I do feel haunted when I hear about their lives, 'cause they were the same as mine. . . . These kids just didn't get to live long enough to put all that past them. . . . I do feel angry, though, when they play all that backward surf music and talk about the *harm* our music did these kids, 'cause I think it was the best thing they had."[45]

Suicide is a serious problem (some estimates report six thousand teenage suicides per year in the United States),[46] and that is why popular artists address it. But music does not simply inflict its meanings upon helpless fans; texts become popular when people find them meaningful in the contexts of their own lives. That is why a wide range of responses is possible; indeed, the evidence suggests that only a tiny minority of fans found "Suicide Solution" depressing rather than sobering and thought-provoking. One fan wrote to Metallica to thank them because he had decided *not* to kill himself after hearing their song about suicide, "Fade to Black."[47] The lead singer of Dark Angel described a song from their album *Leave Scars* (1989): "There's a song called 'The Promise of Agony' that covers the depression and anxiety of being an adolescent. Hopefully there will be kids who pick up the new album and realize from reading the lyrics that even in their darkest despair they really aren't alone."[48]

A study of patients hospitalized for contemplating suicide indicates that a feeling of helplessness is the strongest predictor of which of them would actually go on to kill themselves.[49] Nobody listens to heavy metal because it makes them feel helpless. Sociologists distinguish between fatalistic suicide, caused by overregulation, and anomic suicide, attributable to nonintegration. Donna Gaines points out that many young people are doubly vulnerable, since they feel both overregulated by adults and alienated from them.[50] It is possible that texts can resonate with such attitudes; Goethe's *The Sorrows of Young Werther* seems to have helped make suicide a Continental fad of the late 1770s. But although its explicit treatments of violence might make suicide seem more familiar, metal is attractive precisely because it offers a way of overcoming those feelings of loneliness and helplessness. Even when it models musical despair, heavy metal confronts issues that cannot simply be dismissed or repressed, and it positions listeners as members of a community of fans, making them feel that they belong to a group that does not regulate them.

The vast majority of heavy metal fans don't worship Satan and don't commit suicide; yet many fans enjoy that fraction of heavy metal songs that deals with such things. Heavy metal's critics have provided no credible explanations for this, for they deny fans the agency that is necessary for attraction to exist, preferring to believe that such images are inflicted rather than sought. To find this unsatisfactory is to open up the problem of explaining the attractiveness of mysticism and horror.

Mysticism and Postmodernism in Heavy Metal

"The occult" is the remaining thread of critics' condemnations of heavy metal that has not yet been addressed. Tipper Gore, Carl Raschke, and others condemn heavy metal muscians for even mentioning the Devil, as though there were something deviant about such mysticism. Yet a 1990 Gallup Poll found that 55 percent of the American public believes in the Devil, up from 39 percent in 1978; half believe that demonic possession sometimes takes place.[51] In light of these statistics, it is perhaps surprising that comparatively little heavy metal touches on satanic topics. But as with other transgressive icons, the Devil is used to signify and evoke in particular social contexts; he is not simply conjured up to be worshipped. Even King Diamond, heavy metal's most infamous "Satanist," is scornful of his critics' literal-mindedness: "Satan, for me, is not like the guy with two horns and a long tail. I don't believe in hell as being a place where you burn for eternity. That's not what Satan is all about. Satan stands for the powers of the unknown, and that's what I'm writing about."[52] Heavy metal engagements with occult symbols and legends are more complex than the flat hermeneutics of the PMRC would have it.

Iron Maiden is among the most mystical and philosophical of heavy metal bands; many of their lyrics, taking inspiration from the Bible, Romantic poetry, and various other mythologies, explore the meaning of life, the contingency of existence, and the mysteries of fate and death. Critics often label them a "satanic" group, citing lines such as these, from "The Number of the Beast":

> The ritual has begun, Satan's work is done
> 666 the number of the beast
> Sacrifice is going on tonight

But the lines that immediately follow (less often quoted) complicate the simple endorsement read by critics:

> This can't go on, I must inform the law
> Can this still be real, or some crazy dream?
> But I feel drawn towards the evil chanting hordes

The lyrics are less concerned with celebrating satanic rituals than with exploring tensions between reality and dream, evil and power. As one fan told me, adults tend to take everything too literally, not understanding more sophisticated allegorical or figurative meanings.[53] Just as important, criticisms of metal often emanate from those who strive to eliminate difference and ambiguity in order to enforce their own brand of morality.

Iron Maiden draws upon a variety of religious and philosophical traditions in order to explore and interrogate moralities. Sometimes their lyrics present explicit critique; for example, "Run for the Hills" evokes the horror of the genocide of Native Americans, and "Flight of Icarus" retells the Greek legend with a paranoid twist: the boy's father has encouraged him to fly high, deliberately setting him up for disaster.[54] More often, though, Iron Maiden's lyrics ponder the meaning and nature of existence, frequently by investigating the attractions of mysticism. Many songs also consider the contradictory significance of battle, which they usually portray as exciting because of its intensity but ultimately futile— both glamorous and horrible.[55]

Iron Maiden's *Seventh Son of a Seventh Son* (1988) is a song cycle. That is, as with nineteenth-century song cycles by composers such as Schubert and Schumann, the songs on this album constitute a literary and musical unit, related by poetic theme and drawn together by musical means such as related keys and thematic materials. The song cycle structure binds together a great variety of musical styles and moods within a narrative frame, and *Seventh Son of a Seventh Son* contains some very gentle, ethereal music, as well as power chords and heavy beats. Given metal's reputation among outsiders as a monolithic genre, violent and unimaginative, the variety and affective range of Iron Maiden's music is worth stressing. But all of the songs are concerned with the related topics of fate, clairvoyance, visions, and philosophical speculation. To address these subjects, Iron Maiden mobilizes a fantastic array of musical, literary, and visual allusions, combined in ways that might usefully be considered postmodern.

To begin with visual images, Iron Maiden has for many years featured at its concerts and on its albums and T-shirts a mascot named Eddie. Eddie's appearance has varied over the years, but he has rather consistently retained many of the horrible qualities of an animated corpse. Skinless but sinewy, sometimes part machine, corporeally incomplete but still functioning, both damaged and threatening, Eddie is an oxymoron of disintegration and power. He has appeared in a number of different contexts, from the *Live after Death* album, where he is emerging from a grave, to *Powerslave*, where he appears as an Egyptian pharaoh, to *Seventh Son of a Seventh Son*, where on the front cover he floats, incomplete, in a surreal, icy solid/liquid nowhere; on the inner sleeve he is an ominous seer.[56] During Iron Maiden's 1988 tour, the concert stage featured, besides Eddie, two pieces of Egyptian statuary (references to the band's past tropes) and a miscellany of mystical symbols painted on all available surfaces.[57]

The cover and liner art of *Seventh Son of a Seventh Son* also contains visual references to a variety of mythologies, religions, and alchemies. A crystal ball floats between candlesticks fashioned after an angel and a demon, enacting a suspension between dualities characteristic of many mystical traditions. And Iron Maiden's lyrics reflect a similar hodgepodge of referents. Many songs draw upon the Book of Revelation for images of heaven and hell, Babylon, seven seals, seven deadly sins, fallen angels, and whatnot. But biblical references rub up against the parareligious objects of astrology, alchemy, and witchcraft: crystal balls, Gemini, the undead, and mandrake roots. Old books and quill pens further suggest secret knowledge, obscure meanings of unspecified lineage.

How are we to make sense of these seemingly arbitrary juxtapositions, unconnected and unexplained? Many theorists of contemporary culture would seize on such practices as evidence of what Fredric Jameson has called "pastiche" or "blank parody," a primary feature of postmodern art, according to his very influential formulation.[58] Jameson argued that such postmodern assemblages are neutral mimicry, ultimately signifying nothing. Since Iron Maiden borrows only superficially from various historical traditions and doesn't attempt to articulate any logical reconciliation of these incongruities, their bricolage would be seen by many theorists of the postmodern as meaningless imitation of a past that is no longer understood.

Yet these are not arbitrary choices of referents. On the contrary, Iron Maiden's symbolic borrowings all have certain fundamental characteristics in common, not in terms of their "real" history, but rather in terms of their present significance. Christianity, alchemy, myth, astrology, the mystique of vanished Egyptian dynasties: all are available in the modern world as sources of power and mystery. Such eclectic constructions of power, which might usefully be called postmodern, are possible *only because* they are not perceived as tied to strict historical contexts. All can be consulted, appropriated, and combined, used to frame questions and answers about life and death. If religion functions both to explain the world—providing models for how to live, tenets of faith and empowerment, and comfort for when they don't work—and to offer a sense of contact with something greater than oneself, then heavy metal surely qualifies as a religious phenomenon. But mystical metal draws upon the power of religious traditions without obeisance to any. One sociologist, observing teenagers' use of metal to carve out social space and experience communion there, referred to Led Zeppelin as "liberation theology in vinyl."[59]

Significantly, all of the mystical traditions drawn upon by Iron Maiden offer resources that seem to exist outside hegemonic notions of economic and material power. The situation we call "youth" is in large measure constructed by the contradictory demands of subordination and culturation. Young people are bombarded with messages promoting material power, but their lives, typically, are carefully regulated to deny them opportunities for acquiring much of it. If many of the bands on MTV seem to celebrate consumption and thus fit well with the channel's primary mission of delivering a demographic to advertisers, mystical metal bands like Iron Maiden often draw upon the mystique of precapitalist cultures to construct their spectacles of empowerment. And despite their reliance on transgressive and horrific images such as Eddie, Iron Maiden's songs and concerts put relatively little emphasis on violence and excess. Instead of violence or acquisition as antidotes to powerlessness, Iron Maiden offers experiences of community and feelings of contact with mystical meaningfulness. Fans at a concert participate in an empowerment that is largely musically constructed, but which is intensified by ritualistic images that sanctify the experience with historical and mystical depth. The solitary listener to records, likewise, is in fact almost never solitary, since metal fans tend to have other metal fans as friends, and they build much of their lives and identities around various social forms of involvement with heavy metal. In concerts or with recordings, Iron Maiden fans can experience a utopia of empowerment, freedom, and metaphysical depth, constructed in part out of ideas that have been excluded from the utilitarian world of work and school.

The lyrics of "Seventh Son of a Seventh Son" ostensibly relate the legend of the magical healing powers possessed by a seventh son of a seventh son:

> Here the birth from an unbroken line
> Born the healer the seventh, his time
> Unknowingly blessed, and as his life unfolds
> Slowly unveiling the power he holds
>
> . . . .
>
> Then they watch the progress he makes
> The Good and the Evil, which path will he take?
> Both of them trying to manipulate
> The use of his powers before it's too late

But these lyrics have relatively little to do, I would argue, with promoting pagan mysticism, as the PMRC might have it. Rather, they engage with socially produced anxieties and fantasies about power, history, and morality. Similarly, the title song of this album is less about literal madness than about madness as a trope for unconventional thought:

> Give me the sense to wonder
> To wonder if I'm free
> Give me a sense of wonder
> To know if I can be me
> Give me the strength to hold my head up
> Spit back in their face
> Don't need no key to unlock this door
> Gonna break down the walls
> Break out of this bad place
>
> Can I play with madness?

As medical historian Roy Porter has argued, the writings of the truly mad preserve important historical insights and perceptive critiques:

The mad highlight the hypocrisies, double standards and sheer callous obliviousness of sane society. The writings of the mad challenge the discourse of the normal, challenge its right to be the objective mouthpiece of the times. The assumption that there exist definitive and unitary standards of truth and falsehood, reality and delusion, is put to the test. . . . Mad people's writings often stake counter-claims, to shore up that sense of personhood and identity which they feel is eroded by society and psychiatry.

Such a form of critical madness can be a powerful model for those who feel alienated from dominant social logic, who feel decentered by the pressures of modernity.[60]

Musically, "Seventh Son of a Seventh Son" begins with a series of dramatic flourishes that sound decidedly nonmetallic. They are annunciatory, preparatory; although the harmonic progression C–D–E (♭VI–♭VII–I again) is common in heavy metal, this introduction only gradually acquires the regular heavy beat that typically undergirds rock songs. The mood is dark and ominous, largely due to the use of the Aeolian mode. There is also a vaguely angelic choir hovering overhead, in the form of a synthesizer, adding to the gravity and mystical air of this opening. After an introduction sufficiently portentous for the subject at hand, the music settles into an absolutely steady, relentless rhythmic groove. It is the galloping, repeated eighth-and-two-sixteenths figure that Iron Maiden often uses, with heavily distorted guitars muted with the picking hand to make them more percussive.[61] The harmony is static, holding on E while the vocalist begins his declamation. The verses and choruses alike are built around this rhythm and these same chords and mode, so the first part of the song seems grimly consistent and fateful. The singer has a powerful voice, and he uses heavy vibrato to add to the impression of urgency and gravity. After some of the stanzas, he interjects a long, drawn-out "Ooooh," which is especially effective when the harmony changes underneath the sustained note, redefining it from the stable fifth degree to the mournful minor third as he holds it. This first part of the song, then, is quite unified; it exploits a number of musical parameters in ways that quite consistently articulate an affect of power, dread, and awe.

After all of the lyrics have been delivered, the song moves into a lengthy series of instrumental sections. At the end of the last chorus, while the voice hangs onto its final syllable (another drawn-out "Ooohh"), one of the guitars jumps to a different, faster tempo, playing a Baroque figuration that the other guitar soon joins in harmony. Another abrupt cut follows, to a fast tempo set by the drums, with acoustic guitar outlining poignant sustained chords. Spiked by one guitar's distant (lots of reverb), crying fills, this section combines slow harmonic change with a frantic drumbeat, articulating decenteredness, lack of progress, and urgency all at once. The singer then delivers a dramatic recitation over this conflicted aural landscape.

Finally, the song returns to what sounds like a recapitulation of the beginning, pompous and stable. But a guitar solo suddenly bursts in, shifting to a completely new key, a driving rhythmic pattern, and a fast tempo. Perhaps most important, the musical mode shifts from Aeolian to Phrygian, which carries with it a more frantic, claustrophobic affect. After the short guitar solo, the music moves through a period of what sounds like utter breakdown. The tritone, Western music's most ambiguous interval, is emphasized, throwing tonal grounding up in the air, and with it any sense of experiential stability. The drumming becomes complex and uneven, and the structure of time similarly seems to come unglued. A second guitar solo leads to another change of tempo and beat, and so on. A series of variations over a short harmonic cycle, another Baroque derivation, leads to a truncated, tense version of the opening flourish, which decisively closes the song.

A kind of postmodern logic applies to Iron Maiden's music as well as to their use of mystical images and phrases. Affective stabilities and narrative implications are constantly being defused and subverted by sudden shifts into new keys and tempos within their songs. The organic unities one can usually assume in pop song forms are often calculatedly undermined. But it is important to avoid confusing constructions of disintegration with artistic anarchy. Iron Maiden, in order to accomplish such disruptive shifts, in order to articulate decenteredness, must be much more precise and coordinated than most bands. Their seemingly chaotic ruptures require extreme precision of conception and execution, like the coordination of lighting and choreography at their concerts that relies on rigorous timing to create the impression of casual, free movement.

Iron Maiden's songs are bound together by regular phrases and precise execution, no matter how disjunct they are formally, in the same way that their pastiche of mystical referents is ideologically consistent, no matter how anachronous its elements may seem. Moreover, the musicians' precision contributes crucially to the experience of their music. For at the same time that their ruptures evoke what we might call postmodern decenteredness and anxiety, the musicians' musical successes offer an experience of coping and control in the face of those difficulties. Iron Maiden articulates decenteredness but simultaneously enacts resistance to it. The precision of the ensemble evokes the complexity and overwhelming force of the threat, and at the same time offers the only hope of surviving it.

Thrash metal bands like Metallica and Megadeth have developed a musical discourse based on a similar agenda. Their songs are formally even more complex, filled with abrupt changes of meter and tempo that model a complex, disjointed world and displaying a formidable ensemble precision that enacts collective survival. Thrash guitar is even more distorted than in other kinds of heavy metal, and sonic energy is further shifted to high and low frequencies, yielding a crunchy, percussive sound. While usually less mystical than Iron Maiden, thrash bands very often address violence, death, and madness in their lyrics. Frequent use of the Phrygian mode; faster, sometimes frantic tempos; and a vocal style that is rough, percussive, and nonvirtuosic make thrash metal darker than other metal—angrier, more critical and apocalyptic. Megadeth's album release of 1990 includes these lines, which have been quoted by moralistic critics as evidence of Satanism: "Satan rears his ugly head, to spit into the wind; I spread disease like a dog." But the song from which they are excerpted is called "Rust in Peace . . . Polaris," an evocation of the horror of nuclear holocaust; the "I" that speaks is the weapon of "defense" itself. Megadeth uses the supernatural figure of Satan to strengthen their condemnation of horrors that are entirely real. If their imagery is horrible, it is intended—and understood by fans—as an honest reflection and critique of a brutal world.

The mystical fusions of Iron Maiden continue a long tradition in heavy metal, dating back to such founding documents as Led Zeppelin's "Stairway to Heaven." Musically, "Stairway" fuses powerful "authentici- ties," which are really ideologies. On the one hand, a folk/pastoral/mys- tical sensibility; on the other, desire/aggression/physicality. The song begins with the gentle sound and reassuringly square phrases of an acoustic guitar, complemented by the archaic hooting of recorders, sug- gesting a preindustrial refuge in the folk. Soon, Jimmy Page trades in his acoustic for the twangy punch of an electric guitar and, eventually, the raucous roar of heavy distortion. After a Hendrix-like guitar solo (blues- based, mildly psychedelic), Robert Plant's voice rises an octave, wailing over countless repetitions of a two-measure pattern, propelled by the band's frantic syncopations. The apotheosis/apocalypse breaks off sud- denly, and the song ends with Plant's unaccompanied voice, a return to the solitary poignancy of the beginning. This narrative juxtaposition of the sensitive (acoustic guitar, etc.) and the aggressive (distorted elec- tric guitar, etc.) has continued to show up in heavy metal, from Ozzy Osbourne to Metallica. It combines contradictory sensibilities without reconciling them, as do Led Zeppelin's lyrics and cover art, as much as Iron Maiden's.

The cover of the album containing "Stairway to Heaven" juxtaposes a photograph of a laboring peasant with a view of a modern city, com- plete with both high rises and crumbling tenements. The photo seems very old, but it is colorized and thus strangely displaced in time. Inside, a mysterious sage looks down on a slumbering town from his mountain- top; a bell-bottomed seeker of wisdom scales the rocks toward him. The runes that give the album its nickname ("ZOSO") appear on the liner, along with the enigmatic lyrics of "Stairway to Heaven." These images seem not to have any historical coherence, but they are all available in the present as sources of power and mystery; it is how they are used that makes them coherent.

We might better understand the associative powers of the famously enigmatic lyrics by breaking them up into categories. We encounter a number of mysterious figures: a lady, the piper, the May Queen. Images of nature abound: a brook, a songbird, rings of smoke, trees, forests, a hedgerow, wind. We find a set of concepts (pretty much summing up the central concerns of philosophy): signs, words, meanings, thoughts, feelings, spirit, reason, wonder, soul, the idea that "all are one and one is all." We find a set of vaguely but powerfully evocative symbols: gold, the West, the tune, white light, shadows, paths, a road, and the stairway to heaven itself. At the very end, we find some paradoxical self-referentiality: "to be a rock and not to roll."

These lyrics provide a very open text; like those of Don McLean's "American Pie" (also released in 1971), they invite endless interpretation.[62] Yet they are resonant, requiring no rigorous study to become meaningful. Like the music, they engage with the fantasies and anxieties of our time; they offer contact with social and metaphysical depth in a world of commodities and mass communication. "Stairway to Heaven," no less than canonized works of artistic postmodernism, addresses "decentered subjects" who are striving to find credible experiences of depth and community. It strains at mystery and promises utopia: "A new day will dawn," and "If you listen very hard / The tune will come to you at last."

Film historian Dana Polan has warned that postmodern art can "work in support of dominant power by encouraging a serialized sense of the social totality as something one can never understand and that always eludes one's grasp."[63] Yet art that ignores the complexities, the decentering forces of contemporary capitalism, remains unconvincing, especially to those who have grown up knowing nothing else. For example, one young Twisted Sister fan told me that she starts feeling paranoid when she hears the "easy listening" music favored by her mother, because it so obviously seems to lie to her about the world. The heavy metal of Iron Maiden and Megadeth, on the other hand, articulates the anxieties and discontinuities of the postmodern world, but not in a way that concedes to such experiences. In their free appropriation of symbols of power, and in their material enactments of control, of hanging on in the face of frightening complexity, such heavy metal bands suggest to many that survival in the modern world is possible, that disruptions, no matter how unsettling, can be ridden out and endured.

It is not surprising, then, that many of Iron Maiden's fans study the band's sources, actually buy and read the books referred to in the song lyrics: the Bible, Coleridge's "Rime of the Ancient Mariner," a bevy of histories of various times and places.[64] For the idea that school prepares adolescents for adulthood is increasingly perceived as an obsolete fantasy; too often, adolescence is but a "psychic holding pen for superfluous young people, stuck in economic and social limbo."[65] Leaping beyond what they might see as the boring reverence of their school curriculum and the shallow expediency of the working world, metal musicians and fans draw on the power of centuries' worth of imaginative writing to make sense of their own social experiences and to imagine other possibilities.

The loss of historical specificity we see in the bricolage of Iron Maiden is surely not something to celebrate in itself, but it is important to see that the loss of monovocal, hegemonic history enables other constructions and connections to be formed. Moreover, the reasons for this loss of history deserve examination, and they may be found, I will argue, in the operation of the very bourgeois ideals that are supposedly being resisted. After discussing horror more specifically, I will be shifting theoretical ground, from the notions of postmodernism evoked above to Marshall Berman's broader vision of a modernism that spans the nineteenth and twentieth centuries. For unlike most postmodern theory, Berman's formulation calls upon us to make enabling connections to past experiences of disruption and dislocation.

Horror and History

The tale of the irrational is the sanest way I know of expressing the world in which I live. These tales have served me as instruments of both metaphor and morality; they continue to offer the best window I know on the question of how we perceive things and the corollary question of how we do or do not behave on the basis of our perceptions.   —Stephen King[66]

Horror, manifest primarily in literature and film, has been one of the most popular artistic themes of the past two centuries. Horror originated with the Enlightenment, in late eighteenth-century tales and novels; in 1756, Edmund Burke published his theorization of the aesthetic category of the Sublime—which included horror, astonishment, pain, danger, and terror—thus legitimating the gothic. A variety of psychological explanations have been offered to explain the success of horror: it enables us to overcome safely the objects of our fears, it is the return of the repressed, it represents rites of passage to adulthood or reproductive sexuality.[67] But we must seek for more specific treatment of the social situations within which horrific texts are meaningful. For example, historians have noted that horror films have tended to resurge in popularity in cycles of ten or twenty years, coinciding with periods of social strain or disorder: the Expressionist horror films at a time of crisis in the Weimar Republic, the classical Hollywood monster films that first appeared during the Depression, their revival in the 1950s as metaphors for the Red Threat and other internal enemies, and their greatest popularity ever in the 1970s, another time of crisis of legitimacy for dominant institutions and the economy.[68]

The development of heavy metal in the late 1960s and its continuing popularity through the 1970s and 1980s coincides exactly with the period of the greatest popularity horror films and books have ever known. Founding films of modern horror, such as *Rosemary's Baby* in 1968 and *The Exorcist* in 1973, mark a transitional moment in American history: the end of the Pax Americana; new economic crises; corrupt leadership; powerful social movements challenging dominant policies on race, gender, ecology, and consumer rights; new challenges to the stability of social institutions such as the family; and redefinitions of political themes like freedom. Not surprisingly, historians have noted that horror films are very specific in the threats they evoke: most center on the family, children, political leadership, and sexuality.

As Michael Ryan and Doug Kellner argue, the horror film functions to restore "the sense of security undermined by the dysfunctions of capitalism and the crises of political confidence that corrupt leadership in an underdeveloped democratic context provokes. It is less an irrational phenomenon than a way of dealing with the irrationality of the American social system."[69] Both heavy metal and the horror film address the insecurities of this tumultuous era. Both provide ways of producing meaning in an irrational society; both explore explanations for seemingly incomprehensible phenomena.

The heavy metal audience is part of the first American generation that will be worse off economically than its parents. Many young people have accepted relative affluence as normative, yet society has no real role for its young, and their chances of attaining affluence in the future are fading. Due to factors that include deindustrialization, the decline of union jobs, and the rise of low-paid service jobs, the earnings of young white men dropped 18 percent between 1973 and 1986; those of male high school dropouts, 42 percent.[70] A congressional study indicates that 97 percent of the new jobs filled by white males in the 1980s paid less than $7,000 a year.[71] And while some of its citizens still take pride in its unmatched military strength, the United States now ranks nineteenth worldwide in quality of life, according to a United Nations survey measuring literacy, life expectancy, social services, and average income.[72] Much of the blame is rightly placed on the disastrous social policies of Reaganism, but the 1960s had already seen the greatest wave of mergers, conglomeration, and transnationalization ever, and the first effects of the domination of the economy by large corporations were felt in the 1970s. From their peak in 1973, overall real wages had fallen more than 16 percent by 1990.[73] The 1980s were the first time that "a middle-level income no longer guaranteed what we have come to think of as a middle-class lifestyle."[74]

Heavy metal is, among other things, a way of articulating and sustaining individual and communal identities that can survive such strains. Critics and outsiders like *U.S. News and World Report* continue to prattle that the "primary theme" of metal is nihilism, but heavy metal is rarely nihilistic.[75] Nihilism is frightening because it undermines the myths that sustain social order and struggle alike; it may serve to invite or justify authoritarian repression by making the world seem irrational. Heavy metal, on the contrary, is nearly always concerned with making sense of the world. If it offers opportunities for expressing individual rage, it is largely devoted to creating communal bonds that will help fans weather the strains of modernity. Fans rely on an alignment with that which is "other" but powerful as a way of making sense of their own situation and of compensating for it. Heavy metal explores the "other," everything that hegemonic society does not want to acknowledge, the dark side of the daylit, enlightened adult world. By doing so it finds distinction in scandalous transgression and appropriates sources of communal empowerment. Heavy metal cannot be simply dismissed as alien and aberrant; the meaningfulness of images of horror, madness, and violence in heavy metal is intimately related to the fundamental contradictions of its historical moment.

Historian Marty Jezer traces recent violence in youth culture back to the 1950s, locating its sources not in deviance but in the fundamental contradictions of mainstream ideology: "A rising rate of juvenile delinquency, along with a growing cult of violence, was the first indication that the socialization of young people was not going well. Or, put another way, it was going *too* well, and the young were learning the underlying values of postwar society while ignoring the glossy suburban image that supposedly represented the real thing."[76] John Fiske makes the same point about violence on television, pointing out that not all violence is popular, that popular violence is tightly organized in terms of prevalent social tensions:

Represented violence is popular (in a way that social violence is not) because it offers points of relevance to people living in societies where the power and resources are inequitably distributed and structured around lines of conflicting interests. . . . Violence . . . is popular because of its metaphorical relationship to class or social conflict. Popular representations of the relationships between the socially central or dominant and the deviant are violent because the social experience of the subordinate is one of conflict of interests, not of a liberal pluralist or ritualistic consensus. So it is no surprise to find that the United States, where the difference between the haves and the have-nots is extreme, has the most violent popular television, whereas Britian and Australia, whose welfare and taxation systems mitigate *some* of the socioeconomic differences, have fewer acts of violence per hour on their screens."[77]

The dark side of heavy metal is intimately related to the dark side of the modern capitalist security state: war, greed, patriarchy, surveillance, and control. The lyrics of many heavy metal bands articulate a variety of fantasies of empowerment in this context, but some of the songs of Judas Priest address these issues quite specifically.

"Electric Eye" appeared on Judas Priest's first platinum album, *Screaming for Vengeance* (1982), and it has remained a staple of their concert programs. In it, lead singer Rob Halford adopts the point of view of a spy satellite, a perfect metal governmental agent, omniscient and detached. The eye's persona is split: the first stanza is official and public, marked by Halford with measured, middle-range singing and by added chorus and reverb that suggest spatial power and social legitimacy:

> Up here in space
> I'm looking down on you
> My lasers trace
> Everything you do

These lyrics begin just after a sudden shift from the tonic established by the introduction, E, to the fourth degree, A; they are made to feel temporarily suspended above the tonic, adding to the sense of space.

But then, with an emphatic shift to reconfirm E, a different voice appears: high, thin, sneering, slightly crazed, lacking the support and resonance of studio effects. Now the eye openly taunts those below; it is intoxicated with pride in its metallic perfection and inescapable gaze.

> I take a pride in probing all your secret moves
> My tearless retina takes pictures that can prove

Driven by frenetic but precisely controlled music, the song evokes the paranoia of state surveillance and control, at the same time that the narrator's position as the electric eye offers the seductive experience of omniscience and near omnipotence, the pride of metallic, technological perfection.

I'm made of metal
My circuits gleam
I am perpetual
I keep the country clean

I'm elected electric spy
I'm protected electric eye

With a decisive, galloping beat and Aeolian power chords, "Electric Eye" semiotically calls up power and danger and offers identification with both sides: both the threat and the thrill of concentrated power. The guitar solo scrambles, seeming barely to keep up with the demands of the progression. The choruses are filled with syncopations, pushing against the solid metric organization and resetting with each line of text. The song ends with feedback and echo, like a science fiction movie soundtrack accompanying a view of space—vast, mysterious, and ineffable. With "Electric Eye," Judas Priest evokes a modern technological environment of high-tech energy and conflict; in their live concerts, computer-controlled laser beams flash around the stage with scary precision. The split address of the lyrics keeps intact the unresolvable tensions of fear and envy that such an environment can create. And the power of the music energizes both the representation of that danger and the fans who must survive it.

Many of Judas Priest's songs engage with similar tensions and fantasies. The title song from *Painkiller* (1990) offers a more mythical embodiment of power flying through the skies. The Painkiller is a "metal monster," "half man and half machine," again addressing anxieties about the collision of human beings and technology. "Metal Meltdown," from the same album, portrays the seduction and spectacularity of modern technological power while simultaneously stressing its tremendous dangers. "The Sentinel," from Judas Priest's *Defenders of the Faith* (1984) presents a knife-throwing hero as an epic figure; though his battlefield is urban, he is as awesomely capable at killing as Achilles, a more respectable culture hero. But like Arnold Schwarzenegger's popular Terminator character, he is impassive, unconflicted, supremely rational. The Sentinel's violence is justified; he is "sworn to avenge" (thus he is not the aggressor) and he never doubts that setting things right requires overwhelming power and violence.

Such a fantasy is nothing less than the logical result of the radical individualism demanded by contemporary capitalism, confounded by widespread disillusionment with the proper channels offered for individual success: corrupt government and a rhetoric of freedom and equality undermined by the obviously systematic maintenance of inequity.[78] More overtly "political" bands, such as Queensrÿche, whose lyrics call for educating the masses and overthrowing the control of the rich, are usually less popular than bands that avoid didacticism and find indirect ways to stage fundamental social contestations and alternatives. But if violence in heavy metal is not the nihilism decried by its foes, neither is it the Dionysian creativity claimed by some of its defenders, discussed below, for both of these interpretations lift metal out of history.

Guns N' Roses N' Marx N' Engels

The fullest attempt to explain heavy metal in terms of Dionysian revel is Danny Sugerman's *Appetite for Destruction: The Days of Guns N' Roses*.[79] In contrast to critics such as Gore, Stuessy, and Raschke, Sugerman has read widely and knows the music intimately. Most important, Sugerman is genuinely interested in understanding the appeal and power of heavy metal—although he is careful not to call it that because he wants to position Guns N' Roses at the center of the rock tradition. His analysis remains circumscribed, however, by a reluctance to historicize; both Sugerman and Guns N' Roses celebrate the central bourgeois values of individuality and dynamism as essential human traits.

Sugerman's explanation of the phenomenal success of Guns N' Roses —their debut album, *Appetite for Destruction* (1987), sold over ten million copies and remained in the *Billboard* Top Ten for over a year—is that the band taps into timeless and universal sources of power. Lead singer Axl Rose is a shaman, reviving the mad frenzy of Dionysus, Shiva, and the Romantic poets. The response of his audience is "instinctual," a function of their underlying "animal nature."[80] At a Guns N' Roses show, "ancient customs and rituals are being reenacted and the inherent powers still exist."[81] Sugerman rightly points to large-scale sources of alienation, such as the mind/body split or the loss for many people of meaningful ritual or credible myth. But his account essentializes and mystifies, stopping short of explanation of the specific sounds and sights of heavy metal as the activities of particular people at a certain historical moment. In their rhetoric, both Sugerman and Guns N' Roses reveal their fidelity to certain narratives about modernity that have been most successfully analyzed and critiqued by Karl Marx and Marshall Berman.[82]

Marxist criticism of popular music has usually focused on the music's mediation, the ways in which it is marketed and circulated. Less often, scholars have tried to analyze the meanings of popular music in societies shaped by the ideologies of capitalism, but even then the approach is usually marked by assumptions of class essentialism. That is, critics too often look only for articulations of a particular class position, which may then undergo interference and vitiation through the processes of mass mediation. But Marx himself was less interested in the culture of classes than in the culture of environments shaped by the dominance of particular classes. This is why the fact that heavy metal attracts fans from varied class positions does not confound Marxist analysis of that music. On the contrary, Marx's diagnosis of the strains of the era of bourgeois capitalism, particularly as Marshall Berman has extended it through a number of cultural moments, enables much fuller accounts of certain aspects of heavy metal's value to its audiences.

Marx's attitude toward the bourgeoisie was complex: he genuinely admired their accomplishments while criticizing unflinchingly the personal and social devastation they wrought; he endorsed their notion of individual and collective development at the same time that he hoped that the bourgeois project would self-destruct and be transcended. Berman summarizes the dialectical tension that has inspired so much modern art and thought:

In the first part of the *Manifesto*, Marx lays out the polarities that will shape and animate the culture of modernism in the century to come: the theme of insatiable desires and drives, permanent revolution, infinite development, perpetual creation and renewal in every sphere of life; and its radical antithesis, the theme of nihilism, insatiable destruction, the shattering and swallowing up of life, the heart of darkness, the horror. Marx shows how both these human possibilities are infused into the life of every modern man by the drives and pressures of the bourgeois economy.[83]

What Berman calls bourgeois society's "insatiable drive for destruction and development" Axl Rose calls the "Appetite for Destruction."[84] Both are awed by it, both are aware of the damage it does; but in some ways, what Berman finds in Marx is very much like what millions of fans have found in heavy metal:

Marx plunges us into the depths of this life process, so that we feel ourselves charged with a vital energy that magnifies our whole being—and are simultaneously seized by shocks and convulsions that threaten at every instant to annihilate us. Then, by the power of his language and thought, he tries to entice us to trust his vision, to let ourselves be swept along with him toward a climax that lies just ahead.[85]

As one of the most dynamic of contemporary performers, Axl Rose, too, plunges us into a maelstrom of energy and turbulence, offering the strength of his performance and the power of the music as the only guarantees of survival.

"Welcome to the Jungle" is Guns N' Roses' indictment of the environment in which they had to operate when they landed in Los Angeles with hopes of becoming stars. As Marx could have warned them, they found a world where there is "no other nexus between man and man than naked self-interest, than callous 'cash payment.'"[86]

> We are the people that can find
> Whatever you may need
> If you got the money honey
> We got your disease
> . . . .
> You can taste the bright lights
> But you won't get them for free
> . . . .
> You can have anything you want
> But you better not take it from me

The jungle of L.A. is not just a commercial environment; it is mercenary, hyped, cutthroat, and cynical. The song's sinuous, chromatic guitar and bass lines suggest instability and deception; sudden key shifts and pounding drums disorient the jungle's newest victims. Worst of all, the jungle remakes the inhabitants in its own cruel image. Axl Rose gloats at the plight of the newcomer: "You're in the jungle baby, you're gonna die. . . . I wanna watch you bleed." The only relief is through brief intoxication: at one point an undistorted guitar gently resolves 4–3 suspensions while Rose sings, "And when you're high you never, ever want to come down." But the rest of the music is either chaotic, brutal, or both, using headlong chromatic descents, forceful $\flat VI$–$\flat VII$–I progressions, and heavy distortion to charge the air with menace.

Sugerman offers an explanation of Rose's success in this environment: "He refuses to compromise, insists on a divine right to be himself. . . . He not only survived, he did it on his terms."[87] But where did "his terms" come from, and why do communities form around such expressions of individual autonomy? By calling the principle of individualism "divine," Sugerman obscures its origins and places it beyond critique. What Berman points out about Marx is equally true of Axl Rose: for all of their invective against bourgeois society, both Marx and Rose embrace the ideals and personality structure that arise from the priorities of bourgeois economic development. "Our goal is to break down as many barriers as we can," says Axl Rose. "I mean not just musical, I mean we want to break down the barriers in people's minds, too."[88]

Sugerman rightly points out, as have others, that there are certain direct links between rock and Romanticism: Jim Morrison read Nietzsche, for example, and influenced many other rock musicians in turn. But if an attitude of rebellion can be said to link artists across time, there is still the question of what precisely is being rebelled against at each moment, and, just as important, what sort of vision is being offered in its place. The dynamism and individuality celebrated in so much rock music are not derived from nineteenth-century Romanticism, as some critics have argued.[89] Rather, both of these cultural moments engage in dialogue with strains of modernity they have in common; rock's response contains an admixture from African-American music and reflects a different emphasis on bodily pleasure and communality.

"Paradise City," another hit single from *Appetite for Destruction*, is a good example. In its verse sections, the song uses guitar and bass lines that are low, chromatic, repetitive, and menacing, reminiscent of "Welcome to the Jungle." The verses sketch an urban environment just as bleak and chaotic, and Axl Rose has called the song "just some more lyrics about the jungle."[90]

> Just a' urchin livin' under the street
> I'm a hard case that's tough to beat
> . . . .
> Ragz to richez or so they say
> Ya gotta-keep pushin' for the fortune and fame
> . . . .
> Strapped in the chair of the city's gas chamber
> Why I'm here I can't quite remember
> . . . .
> Captain America's been torn apart
> Now he's a court jester with a broken heart
> He said—
> Turn me around and take me back to the start
> I must be losin' my mind—"Are you blind?"
> I've seen it all a million times

But the song's chorus offers an escape from the jungle that had seemed impossible in the other song, a kind of transcendence reached through the gospel music of the black church. A choir of voices sings the chorus, representing the sort of communal participation in music making that can submerge individual alienation in what is literally social harmony. Above this group, Rose soars like the ecstatic sopranos of many gospel choirs, transcending even this collective transcendence. His delivery of the text is smoother, but no less passionate, than the jagged hysteria of the verses. The lyrics of the chorus are simple:

> Take me down
> To the paradise city
> Where the grass is green
> And the girls are pretty
> Take me home

If only the lyrics are considered, this vision of Paradise City is hardly a vivid one. Rose gives us few details; the important parts are the invocation of desire to be transported ("take me down") and the characterization of Paradise City as "home." Even these barely sketch the fantasy; only the music endows this vision of an ideal (male) social space with power and credibility. The gospel qualities are borrowed to energize this vision as they have so many others.[91] During the chorus, the note G rings out over the G–C–F–C–G progression like a guarantee of homecoming. At the end of the song the tempo doubles, and a guitar solo scrambles euphorically over countless repetitions of the chorus progression. As with many gospel performances, there seems to be too much energy to stop; Paradise City exists only as long as it is supported by collective effort, especially by the straining of Axl Rose's voice toward transcendence.

Appetite for Destruction's other hit single offers a different refuge from the jungle:

> Her hair reminds me of a warm safe place
> Where as a child I'd hide
> And pray for the thunder
> And the rain
> To quietly pass me by.

"Sweet Child o' Mine" is startlingly tender, with acoustic guitar blended with chorused electric and a haunting opening riff based on poignant 4–3 suspensions. As in nineteenth-century notions of the separate sphere of the "Angel in the House," women are understood as salve for the wounded man recuperating from the brutality of industry and commerce.

What is so remarkable, what calls us to reexamine the dichotomies of modern and postmodern, of elite and popular, of politics and culture, is that Berman's discussion of the "voice" of modernity applies just as well to Axl Rose as to the nineteenth-century philosophers and literati he is describing:

What is distinctive and remarkable about the voice that Marx and Nietzsche share is not only its breathless pace, its vibrant energy, its imaginative richness, but also its fast and drastic shifts in tone and inflection, its readiness to turn on itself, to question and negate all it has said, to transform itself into a great range of harmonic or dissonant voices, and to stretch itself beyond its capacities into an endlessly wider range, to express and grasp a world where everything is pregnant with its contrary and all that is solid melts into air. This voice resounds at once with self-discovery and self-mocking, with self-delight and self-doubt. It is a voice that knows pain and dread, but believes in its power to come through. Grave danger is everywhere, and may strike at any moment, but not even the deepest wounds can stop the flow and overflow of its energy. It is ironic and contradictory, polyphonic and dialectical, denouncing modern life in the name of values that modernity itself has created, hoping—often against hope—that the modernities of tomorrow and the day after tomorrow will heal the wounds that wreck the modern men and women of today.[92]

Certainly, Marx and Rose have lived in very different worlds, and I have argued throughout this chapter that heavy metal must be understood within the specific context of recent history. But critics of heavy metal have striven to suggest that artistic treatment of violence and madness is unique to today's popular culture and that it reflects a breakdown of values. Such critics depend upon the notion that horror is abnormal, is outside the system, in order to scapegoat heavy metal as deviant and threatening. Instead, I have tried to show how heavy metal can be understood as immanently social and historical, as action engaged with the deepest of contemporary desires and tensions. And such formations have roots; they do not belong to our moment alone.

Moreover, criticism of metal as deviance depends upon historical amnesia, for much of the respected culture of the past made use of similarly transgressive imagery, however much its present context of reception hobbles our recognition of its original force. For example, musicologist Richard Taruskin wrote recently of the "vast sanitizing project" that "has for nearly two centuries been keeping the essential Bach at bay." He cites examples such as Bach's text for Cantata 179, which includes images worthy of any thrash metal band: "My sins sicken me like pus in my bones; help me, Jesus, Lamb of God, for I am sinking in deepest slime."[93] Taruskin concludes:

Anyone exposed to Bach's full range . . . knows that the hearty, genial, lyrical Bach of the concert hall is not the essential Bach. The essential Bach was an avatar of a pre-Enlightened—and when push came to shove, a violently anti-Enlightened—temper. His music was a medium of truth, not beauty. And the truth he served was bitter. His works persuade us—no, *reveal* to us—that the world is filth and horror, that humans are helpless, that life is pain, that reason is a snare.[94]

Like Bach, but at the other end of the Enlightenment, heavy metal musicians explore images of horror and madness in order to comprehend and critique the world as they see it. Although they are continually stereotyped and dismissed as apathetic nihilists, metal fans and musicians build on the sedimented content of musical forms and cultural icons to create for themselves a social world of greater depth and intensity. They appropriate materials for their music and lyrics from the myriad sources made available to them by mass mediation, selecting those they can fuse into a cultural alloy that is strong and conductive.

They develop new kinds of music and new models of identity, new articulations of community, alienation, affirmation, protest, rage, and transcendence by "Running with the Devil."

Not all of heavy metal's formulations point toward a society that is more just and peaceful, though some do. If in some ways heavy metal replicates the ruthless individualism and violence that capitalism and government policy have naturalized, it also creates communal attachments, enacts collective empowerment, and works to assuage entirely reasonable anxieties. Heavy metal, like all culture, can be read as an index of attempts to survive the present and imagine something better for the future; it is one among many coherent but richly conflicted records of people's struggles to make sense of the contradictions they have inherited, the tensions that drive and limit their lives.

Heavy Metal Canons

✳

Hit Parader's *Top 100 Metal Albums* (Spring 1989; release dates added)

1. Led Zeppelin, *ZOSO [IV]*, 1971
2. Def Leppard, *Pyromania*, 1983
3. AC/DC, *Back in Black*, 1980
4. Mötley Crüe, *Theatre of Pain*, 1985
5. Van Halen, *Van Halen*, 1978
6. Judas Priest, *Screaming for Vengeance*, 1982
7. Kiss, *Destroyer*, 1976
8. Metallica, *. . . And Justice for All*, 1988
9. Deep Purple, *Machine Head*, 1972
10. Ozzy Osbourne, *Blizzard of Ozz*, 1981
11. Iron Maiden, *Powerslave*, 1985
12. Bon Jovi, *Slippery When Wet*, 1987
13. Aerosmith, *Rocks*, 1976
14. Black Sabbath, *Paranoid*, 1971
15. Led Zeppelin, *II*, 1970
16. Guns N' Roses, *Appetite for Destruction*, 1987
17. Kiss, *Alive*, 1975
18. Judas Priest, *British Steel*, 1980
19. AC/DC, *Highway to Hell*, 1979
20. Poison, *Open Up and Say . . . Ahh*, 1988
21. Alice Cooper, *Love It to Death*, 1971
22. Megadeth, *So Far So Good . . . So What!*, 1988
23. Ratt, *Out of the Cellar*, 1984
24. Ozzy Osbourne, *The Ultimate Sin*, 1986
25. Mötley Crüe, *Shout at the Devil*, 1984
26. Whitesnake, *Whitesnake*, 1987
27. Scorpions, *Love at First Sting*, 1984
28. Cinderella, *Long Cold Winter*, 1988
29. Rainbow, *Ritchie Blackmore's Rainbow*, 1975
30. Dokken, *Back for the Attack*, 1988
31. Quiet Riot, *Metal Health*, 1983
32. Def Leppard, *Hysteria*, 1987
33. Aerosmith, *Permanent Vacation*, 1987
34. Black Sabbath, *Heaven and Hell*, 1980
35. The Jimi Hendrix Experience, *Are You Experienced?*, 1967
36. Cinderella, *Night Songs*, 1986
37. Van Halen, *1984*, 1983
38. Slayer, *South of Heaven*, 1988
39. Iron Maiden, *Number of the Beast*, 1984
40. Europe, *The Final Countdown*, 1986
41. Saxon, *Wheels of Steel*, 1980
42. Anthrax, *State of Euphoria*, 1988
43. Bad Company, *Bad Company*, 1974
44. Dio, *The Last in Line*, 1984
45. Van Halen, *II*, 1979
46. Kiss, *Animalize*, 1984
47. Poison, *Look What the Cat Dragged In*, 1986
48. Scorpions, *In Trance*, 1976
49. Accept, *Restless and Wild*, 1982
50. Deep Purple, *Made in Japan*, 1972

51. Lita Ford, *Lita*, 1988
52. Mötley Crüe, *Girls, Girls, Girls,* 1987
53. Queensrÿche, *Operation: Mindcrime*, 1988
54. Dokken, *Tooth and Nail*, 1984
55. Metallica, *Master of Puppets*, 1986
56. Led Zeppelin, *Led Zeppelin*, 1969
57. Y&T, *Black Tiger*, 1982
58. UFO, *Lights Out*, 1977
59. Twisted Sister, *Stay Hungry*, 1984
60. Whitesnake, *Slide It In*, 1983
61. Rush, *2112*, 1976
62. Ted Nugent, *Ted Nugent*, 1975
63. Led Zeppelin, *Physical Graffiti*, 1975
64. Stryper, *In God We Trust*, 1988
65. Thin Lizzy, *Jailbreak*, 1976
66. Bon Jovi, *7800° Fahrenheit*, 1985
67. Angel, *Helluva Band*, 1976
68. White Lion, *Pride*, 1988
69. Metallica, *Ride the Lightning*, 1984
70. Great White, *Once Bitten*, 1987
71. Yngwie Malmsteen, *Odyssey*, 1988
72. Grand Funk Railroad, *Survival*, 1971
73. Uriah Heep, *The Magician's Birthday*, 1972
74. Iron Butterfly, *In-A-Gadda-Da-Vida*, 1968
75. Krokus, *Headhunters*, 1983
76. Aerosmith, *Aerosmith*, 1973
77. Montrose, *Montrose*, 1974
78. Tesla, *Mechanical Resonance*, 1987
79. Megadeth, *Peace Sells . . . But Who's Buying?*, 1986
80. Blue Öyster Cult, *Agents of Fortune*, 1976
81. Cream, *Disraeli Gears*, 1967
82. Starz, *Violation*, 1977
83. Blue Cheer, *Vincebus Eruptum*, 1968
84. Ted Nugent, *Cat Scratch Fever*, 1976
85. Mountain, *Climbing*, 1969
86. Motörhead, *Ace of Spades*, 1980
87. W.A.S.P., *Inside the Electric Circus*, 1986
88. Manowar, *Battle Hymns*, 1982
89. Kingdom Come, *Kingdom Come*, 1988
90. L. A. Guns, *L. A. Guns*, 1988
91. David Lee Roth, *Eat 'Em and Smile*, 1986
92. Stryper, *To Hell with the Devil*, 1986
93. Deep Purple, *In Rock*, 1971
94. Triumph, *Allied Forces*, 1981
95. Savatage, *Hall of the Mountain King*, 1987
96. Loudness, *Thunder in the East*, 1985
97. The Michael Schenker Group, *MSG*, 1981
98. Death Angel, *Frolic in the Park*, 1988
99. Warlock, *True as Steel*, 1986
100. Kix, *Midnite Dynamite*, 1986

"Heavy Metal: The Hall of Fame" (*Hit Parader*, December 1982)

AC/DC, *Back in Black*, 1980
Aerosmith, *Rocks*, 1976
Black Sabbath, *Paranoid*, 1971
Black Sabbath, *Master of Reality*, 1971
Blue Cheer, *Vincebus Eruptum*, 1968
Blue Öyster Cult, *Blue Öyster Cult,* 1972
Alice Cooper, *Love It to Death*, 1971
Cream, *Disraeli Gears*, 1968
Deep Purple, *In Rock*, 1971
Deep Purple, *Machine Head*, 1973
Grand Funk Railroad, *Survival*, 1970
The Jimi Hendrix Experience, *Are You Experienced?*, 1967

Judas Priest, *Hell Bent for Leather,* 1979
Kiss, *Destroyer*, 1976
Led Zeppelin, *Led Zeppelin*, 1968
Led Zeppelin, *II*, 1969
Led Zeppelin, *ZOSO [IV]*, 1972
Motörhead, *Ace of Spades*, 1980
Ted Nugent, *Cat Scratch Fever*, 1977
Queen, *Queen*, 1973
Rush, *Rush*, 1974
Scorpions, *In Trance*, 1976
UFO, *Lights Out*, 1977
Van Halen, *Van Halen*, 1978
Van Halen, *II*, 1979

Heavy Metal Questionnaire

Heavy Metal Questionaire

These questions are being asked for a book on Heavy Metal, being written by a guitar player/musicologist/metal fan. If you listen to heavy metal, your help would be appreciated.

How long have you been listening to heavy metal? _____ years

How many hours do you listen to metal each day? [circle one]
0 1 2 3 4 5 6 7 8+

How many hours do you listen to other music each day?
0 1 2 3 4 5 6 7 8+

What are your *three* favorite bands? _____ _____ _____

How many metal recordings did you buy last month?
0 1 2 3 4 5 6 7 8 9 10+

What do you usually buy?
A. albums   B. cassettes   C. compact discs

What other kinds of music do you like (if any)? _____

Are most of your friends into metal too?   yes   no

Do you know people who used to listen to metal but don't anymore?
yes   no

If yes, what do they listen to now instead of metal? _____

Which do you listen to more, radio or recordings?
A. radio more than records   B. both about the same
C. records more than radio

Do you play any musical instruments?   yes   no   If yes, what? _____

Do you own any musical equipment?   yes   no   If yes, what? _____

Do you sing along with metal songs?   yes   no

How important are these elements of metal?

	not important				very important
guitar solos	1	2	3	4	5
lyrics	1	2	3	4	5
powerful drums & bass	1	2	3	4	5
lead singer	1	2	3	4	5
special effects	1	2	3	4	5

How many hours do you watch TV each day, on the average?

0   1   2   3   4   5   6   7   8+

How much do you watch music videos?

A. none   B. 1–3 hr/week   C. 1 hr/day   D. 2–3 hr/day
E. 4–6 hr/day   F. more

Do you watch "Headbangers' Ball" on MTV?

A. no   B. once a month   C. twice a month   D. every week

What do you like about metal compared to other music? Check the ones you strongly agree with.

— It's the most powerful kind of music; it makes me feel powerful.
— It's intense; it helps me work off my frustrations.
— The guitar solos are amazing; it takes a great musician to play metal.
— I can relate to the lyrics.
— It's music for people like me; I fit in with a heavy metal crowd.
— It's pissed-off music, and I'm pissed off.
— It deals with things nobody else will talk about.
— It's imaginative music; I would never have thought of some of those things.
— It's true to life; it's music about real important issues.
— It's not true to life; it's fantasy, better than life.

What is heavy metal? *Circle* a few of the bands you think best define "Heavy Metal." *Cross out* the bands you think are not metal at all.

AC/DC	Aerosmith	Bon Jovi
Boston	Lita Ford	Heart
Hüsker Dü	Iron Maiden	Judas Priest
Kiss	Led Zeppelin	Yngwie Malmsteen
Megadeth	Metallica	Mötley Crüe
Ozzy Osbourne	Poison	Rush
Stryper	Twisted Sister	Van Halen
The Who	Frank Zappa	ZZ Top

Do you ever read heavy metal fan magazines?

A. never   B. occasionally   C. often   Which ones? _____

What is your age? _____   You are (circle one):   Male   Female

Education completed:
A. some high school   B. high school diploma   C. some college
D. college degree

Present employment:
A. unemployed   B. part-time   C. full-time   Occupation: _____

Your parents' employment:

Father: A. unemployed B. part-time C. full-time

Occupation: _____

Mother: A. unemployed B. part-time C. full-time

Occupation: _____

Would you be willing to be interviewed about metal? yes no

If yes, leave your name and phone number: _____

𝕿𝖍𝖆𝖓𝖐𝖘 𝖋𝖔𝖗 𝖞𝖔𝖚𝖗 𝖍𝖊𝖑𝖕   RAW 8/31/90

Notes

Introduction (Notes to Pages ix–xviii)

1. Blayne Cutler, "For What It's Worth," *American Demographics*, August 1989, pp. 42–45, 61–62.

2. Richard Parker, "Some with a Fountain Pen," *The Nation*, 24 December 1990, p. 820.

3. Christopher Small, private communication, 21 February 1991.

4. For an example of recent musicological work that vividly illustrates this point, see Ellen Rosand, *Opera in Seventeenth-Century Venice: The Creation of a Genre* (Berkeley: University of California Press, 1991). For a collection of documents that helps restore such erased aspects of musical history, see Piero Weiss and Richard Taruskin, eds., *Music in the Western World: A History in Documents* (New York: Schirmer Books, 1984).

5. Janice Radway, *Reading the Romance: Women, Patriarchy, and Popular Literature* (Chapel Hill: University of North Carolina Press, 1984); Steven Feld, *Sound and Sentiment: Birds, Weeping, Poetics, and Song in Kaluli Expression*, 2d ed. (Philadelphia: University of Pennsylvania Press, 1990); John Fiske, *Understanding Popular Culture* (Boston: Unwin Hyman, 1989), and *Television Culture* (New York: Methuen, 1987); George Lipsitz, *Time Passages: Collective Memory and American Popular Culture* (Minneapolis: University of Minnesota Press, 1990); Susan McClary, *Feminine Endings: Music, Gender, Sexuality* (Minneapolis: University of Minnesota Press, 1991); Christopher Small, *Music of the Common Tongue: Survival and Celebration in Afro-American Music* (New York: Riverrun, 1987).

6. See Christopher Small, *Music of the Common Tongue*, p. 50. Small is a maverick, and although his work belongs to a tradition of ethnomusicological study of music in culture (and music as culture), his is the strongest statement of this perspective because he doesn't shy away from developing his critique along political and philosophical lines.

7. Concerts are crucial to heavy metal, and they were my main avenue of contact with fans. I attended mostly arena concerts, by groups such as Ozzy Osbourne, Blue Öyster Cult, Iron Maiden, Megadeth, Def Leppard, Tesla, Dokken, Metallica, Scorpions, Van Halen, Living Colour, Poison, Fates Warning, Slave Raider, Judas Priest, and Lynch Mob.

8. See Stuart Hall, "Notes on Deconstructing 'the Popular,'" in *People's History and Socialist Theory*, ed. Raphael Samuel (London: Routledge and Kegan Paul, 1981), pp. 227–40.

9. See Susan McClary and Robert Walser, "Start Making Sense: Musicology Wrestles with Rock," in *On Record: Rock, Pop, and the Written Word*, ed. Simon Frith and Andrew Goodwin (New York: Pantheon, 1990), pp. 277–92.

10. M. M. Bakhtin, *The Dialogic Imagination*, ed. Michael Holmquist (Austin: University of Texas Press, 1981); George E. Marcus and Michael M. J. Fischer, *Anthropology as Cultural Critique: An Experimental Moment in the Human Sciences* (Chicago: University of Chicago Press, 1986).

11. See Kaja Silverman, "Fragments of a Fashionable Discourse," in *Studies in Entertainment: Critical Approaches to Mass Culture*, ed. Tania Modleski (Bloomington: Indiana University Press, 1986), pp. 139–52.

12. Jon Pareles, "Metallica Defies Heavy Metal Stereotypes," *Minneapolis Star Tribune*, 13 July 1988, p. 12 Ew.

13. Dave Marsh has argued that too much attention to the categories of youth and rebellion has skewed rock history and criticism in general; see *The Heart of Rock & Soul: The 1001 Greatest Singles Ever Made* (New York: New American Library, 1989), pp. xxiii–xxv.

Chapter 1. Metallurgies (Notes to Pages 1–25)

1. Philip Bashe, *Heavy Metal Thunder: The Music, Its History, Its Heroes* (Garden City, N.Y.: Doubleday, 1985), p. viii.

2. *The Oxford English Dictionary*, 2d ed., s.v. "heavy."

3. Headbanging is vigorous nodding to the beat of the music. Usually only a fraction of a concert audience headbangs, but heavy metal fans often refer to themselves as headbangers.

4. Compare the discussion of punk band names in Dave Laing, *One Chord Wonders: Power and Meaning in Punk Rock* (Philadelphia: Open University Press, 1985), pp. 42, 48–49.

5. Musicians' attitudes are discussed in chapter 3. On structural and functional perspectives on genres, see Tzvetan Todorov, *Genres in Discourse* (Cambridge: Cambridge University Press, 1990), pp. 9–19.

6. Michel Foucault, "History of Systems of Thought," in *Language, Counter-Memory, Practice: Selected Essays and Interviews*, ed. Donald F. Bouchard (Ithaca, N.Y.: Cornell University Press, 1977), p. 199.

7. The class origins of heavy metal have become obscured by its tremendous popularity, but many of the leading musicians of early metal were from working-class backgrounds, and the music has always retained a core audience of working-class youth. Judas Priest came out of the English industrial center of Birmingham, and Ozzy Osbourne, heavy metal's most enduring performer, was the son of a steelworker and a factory worker in the same city.

8. Anthony DeCurtis, "The Year in Music," *Rolling Stone*, December 15–29, 1988, p. 14. In 1989, heavy metal became "the largest revenue-grossing musical genre in the world . . . , generating more than 40 percent of all money made from record sales, concerts and promotions" (*Spin*, August 1990, p. 47). Estimates vary a great deal. In 1985, *Billboard* reported that heavy metal accounted for 10–30 percent of retail volume at record stores (Moira McCormick, "Metal Boom Levels Off at Retail As Indies Again Take Torch," *Billboard*, 27 April 1985, pp. HM-6, HM-18). In her book on metal, Deena Weinstein accepts figures reported in *Rolling Stone*, claiming that metal comprised 15–20 percent of the music industry's revenues in 1988 (*Heavy Metal: A Cultural Sociology* [New York: Lexington Books, 1991], p. 189). In *The Clustering of America* (New York: Harper & Row, 1988), Michael J. Weiss claimed that during the late 1980s, 5.62 percent of Americans (about 15 million) were buyers of heavy metal recordings

(p. 130). This last figure seems rather high, but it provides no way of distinguishing the occasional purchaser of a metal record from the serious fan.

9. See Appendix 1 for some canons of metal music, published in major fan magazines.

10. For example, an advertisement for the Columbia Record and Tape Club hypes: "Make Way For More Metal: Take 12 Heavy Metal Hits For A Penny! If you're heavy into heavy metal, this offer will blow you away with hard rockin' metal mania." The ad lists nearly one hundred albums by thirty-five bands, plus a section called "The Roots of Metal" (Led Zeppelin, Hendrix, Woodstock, Deep Purple, Mountain, Clapton) and a more general selection of rock (*Creem*, March 1988, pp. 10–11).
Compare:

If you're willing to be enchanted, enraptured, bedazzled, bewitched and spellbound by some of the most fantastically beautiful music ever recorded, then we'd like to send you a state-of-the-art compact disc, cassette or LP that is sheer musical euphoria! . . . To demonstrate the seductive power of music and to induce you to acquint yourself with the Society's mesmerizing musical fare, its outstanding recordings and its unique recording program, we'd like to send you, for just $1.00 post-paid, classical masterpieces by Mozart performed by The Academy of St. Martin-in-the-Fields, conducted by Neville Marriner and available only to new members of Musical Heritage Society, that will have you in a heady state of ecstasy within moments! . . . Each year Musical Heritage issues about 200 new recordings of the music of such great masters as Albinoni, the Bachs, Beethoven, Berlioz, Buxtehude. . . . Its recordings traverse all musical periods in great depth" (Musical Heritage Society advertisement, c. 1980).

11. Greg Ptacek, "Majors Return to Nuts and Bolts of Pre-MTV Metal Marketing Days," *Billboard*, 27 April 1985, p. HM-3.

12. There is a lot at stake here; metal merchandise outsells that of any other genre (although highest per capita sales are generated by bands appealling to preteens, such as New Kids on the Block). See Ethlie Ann Vare, "Heavy Metal: Pounding It Out," *Billboard*, 27 April 1985, p. HM-16.

13. Dan Zarpentine, Spencerport, N.Y., "Letters," *Guitar for the Practicing Musician*, January 1984, p. 5.

14. Co-Co, "Chain Mail," *Metal Mania*, July 1989, p. 23.

15. For example, a female metal musician decries sexism in *RIP*, May 1989, p. 5; the letters column in *RIP*, June 1989 (pp. 5–6) includes letters advising safe sex, admonishing sexist musicians and fans, and attacking the racism of the latest Guns N' Roses album, *G N' R Lies* (1988). The August 1989 issue features as its "Letter of the Month" (p. 5) the complaint of a gay metal fan about the homophobia of musicians like Axl Rose and Zakk Wylde. See chapter 4 for more discussion of such letters.

16. For Judas Priest's statement, see *Musician*, September 1984, p. 53; on Def Leppard, see David P. Szatmary, *Rockin' in Time: A Social History of Rock and Roll* (Englewood Cliffs, N.J.: Prentice-Hall, 1987), p. 205.

17. Andy Secher, "Heavy Metal: The Hall of Fame," *Hit Parader*, December 1982, p. 26.

18. *Musician*, September 1984, p. 53.

19. Fabio Testa, "Yngwie Malmsteen: In Search of a New Kingdom," *The Best of Metal Mania* #2, 1987, p. 35.

20. *Musician*, September 1984, p. 53.

21. Anne Leighton, "Rush: The Fine Art of Metal," *RIP*, June 1989, pp. 63, 97. Lee's perception was confirmed by the fans who filled out a questionnaire I

circulated at concerts. One section asked fans to circle the names of bands that best define "heavy metal" and to cross out the bands that are not metal. Many more fans rejected Rush as a possible metal band than accepted them.

22. The following sketch of the history of heavy metal draws upon Bashe, *Heavy Metal Thunder*; Wolf Marshall, ". . . And Justice for All," *Guitar for the Practicing Musician*, June 1989, pp. 81–86, 136–38; Nick Armington and Lars Lofas, "The Genesis of Metal," *Drums and Drumming*, August/September 1990, pp. 21–25, 62–64; Jas Obrecht, "The Rise of Heavy Metal," in *Masters of Heavy Metal*, ed. Jas Obrecht (New York: Quill, 1984), pp. 8–9; Ed Ward, Geoffrey Stokes, and Ken Tucker, *Rock of Ages: The Rolling Stone History of Rock & Roll* (New York: Rolling Stone Press, 1986); *Hit Parader's Metal of the 80's*, Spring 1990; and Elin Wilder, "Heavy Metal: A Fan's Perspective," *High Times*, August 1988, pp. 32–39.

23. See, for example, Bashe, *Heavy Metal Thunder*, p. 4; Donald Clarke, ed., *The Penguin Encyclopedia of Popular Music* (New York: Viking, 1989), p. 532; Ward et al., *Rock of Ages*, p. 399; Jon Pareles and Patricia Romanowski, eds., "Heavy Metal," in *The Rolling Stone Encyclopedia of Rock & Roll* (New York: Rolling Stone Press, 1983), p. 248; Jon Pareles, "Heavy Metal," in *The New Grove Dictionary of American Music*, ed. H. Wiley Hitchcock and Stanley Sadie (London: McMillan, 1986), vol. 2, pp. 358–59; Robert Duncan, *The Noise: Notes from a Rock 'n' Roll Era* (New York: Ticknor and Fields, 1984), p. 39. Thanks to Bruce Holsinger and Christopher Taylor for reading *Naked Lunch* to check me on this.

24. This error seems connected with rock criticism's fascination with authenticity. Of course, rock critics are not alone in mythologizing origins. As Foucault (quoting Nietzsche) reminds us: "The lofty origin is no more than 'a metaphorical extension which arises from the belief that things are most precious and essential at the moment of birth" (Michel Foucault, "Nietzsche, Genealogy, History," in *Language, Counter-Memory, Practice*, ed. Donald F. Bouchard, p. 143). Foucault's method, which I have found useful, is to look for beginnings rather than origins, shifts in discursive formation rather than generic birthdays.

25. David Fricke, "Metal Forefathers," *Musician*, September 1984, p. 56.

26. See chapter 2 for an extended discussion of musical constructions of power.

27. Szatmary, *Rockin' in Time*, p. 205. It is tempting to add other landmark albums of 1970, such as The Who's *Live in Leeds*, but metal musicians themselves consistently trace the genre back to these three founding bands.

28. The first Led Zeppelin album included two songs by Willie Dixon and one by Howlin' Wolf; only one of these was properly credited. On their second album, "The Lemon Song" is an uncredited cover of Howlin' Wolf's "Killing Floor," with a bit of Robert Johnson's "Traveling Riverside Blues" mixed in. That album's last cut is a grotesque mimicry of Sonny Boy Williamson's recording of Willie Dixon's "Bring It On Home." Plant and Page claimed songwriting credit (and royalties) without even bothering to change the title.

29. See chapter 3 for discussion of the classical influence on heavy metal.

30. See Vare, "Heavy Metal," p. HM-1. Gold albums have certified sales of five hundred thousand units; platinum status is awarded for one million sales.

31. Lester Bangs, "Heavy Metal," in *The Rolling Stone Illustrated History of Rock & Roll*, 2d ed., ed. Jim Miller (New York: Random House, 1980), p. 335.

32. Szatmary, *Rockin' in Time*, p. 205.

33. Ptacek, "Majors Return," p. HM-15.

34. See chapter 3.

35. Ptacek, "Majors Return," p. HM-15. As late as 1984, the heavy metal

audience was 80 percent male, according to a survey of record buyers cited in Charles M. Young, "Heavy Metal," *Musician*, September 1984, pp. 40–44.

36. See chapter 4 for further discussion of Bon Jovi's "fusion."

37. Kim Freeman, "Heavy Metal Bands Are Rocking Top 40 Playlists," *Billboard*, 20 June 1987, p. 1.

38. Tom Hunter, VP/Music Programming for MTV, in *RIP*, March 1989, p. 6.

39. See Paul Grein, "Metal Bands Dominate the Albums Chart," *Billboard* 13 June 1987, pp. 1, 12; Robert Edelstein, "The Last Heroes of Rock 'n' Roll," *Gallery*, April 1989, p. 42; and "Heavyosity," *Rolling Stone*, 15–29 December 1988, p. 124.

40. For brief metal typologies, see Kim Freeman, "Pioneering Indies Undaunted by Majors' Stripmining of Heroes and Profits," *Billboard*, 27 April 1985, pp. HM-3, HM-14; or Glenn Kenny, "Heavy Metal," *Genesis*, January 1986, pp. 42–43, 100–102.

41. David Fricke, "Heavy Metal Justice," *Rolling Stone*, 12 January 1989, p. 46.

42. *Metal Mania*, July 1989, p. 28.

43. See Elianne Halbersberg, "Heavy Metal and Hard Rock," *Billboard*, 25 May 1991, pp. HM-1, HM-8, HM-16, HM-18.

44. Elianne Halbersberg, *Heavy Metal* (Cresskill, N.J.: Sharon Publications, 1985), p. 41.

45. Halbersberg, *Heavy Metal*, p. 7. For a critique of rock's myths about technology and authenticity, see Simon Frith, "Art Versus Technology: The Strange Case of Popular Music," *Media, Culture, and Society* 8 (1986), pp. 263–79.

46. "The headbangers of Salerno salute the headbangers of Florence." See note 3, above.

47. Moira McCormick, "Metal Still Rock's Top Road Warrior As Street-Level Boom Fills Concerts," *Billboard*, 27 April 1985, p. HM-19.

48. Michael J. Weiss, *The Clustering of America*, p. 130. Weiss gathered his information from 1985 to 1987, relying in part on earlier census data.

49. One demographic study concluded that no one spends more money on music than a teenage metal fan in Atlanta. However, the author regretfully noted that most advertisers are unwilling to target this market segment because they don't want to be associated with the music; see Blayne Cutler, "For What It's Worth," *American Demographics*, August 1989, pp. 42–45, 61–62. That much is true, but advertisers also avoid contact with heavy metal because many of its fans don't buy nonmetal products, for which they lack means.

50. Malcolm Dome and Mick Wall, "World View: Metal Crusade in Global Gear," *Billboard*, 27 April 1985, p. HM-12.

51. See my questionnaire in Appendix 2. Nearly everyone I approached returned a fully completed questionnaire, and I collected 136.

52. Charles M. Young, "Heavy Metal," *Musician*, September 1984, pp. 40–44. The age range of metal fans has since expanded; I interviewed fans in their early teens whose parents were metal fans too.

53. Teri Saccone, "Somewhere on the Light Side of the Moon," *Rock Scene*, July 1987, p. 65. On the other hand, Harris says that only 30–40 percent of British fans know all of the lyrics. Dan Spitz of Anthrax claims that almost every one of their fans knows every word of their lyrics (Andy Aledort, "Devil's Advocates," *Guitar for the Practicing Musician*, April 1989, p. 80). I criticize some of these academic studies later in this chapter for ignoring the effects of their research methods on the answers collected.

54. I later discovered that my survey responses were consistently confirmed by the data collected by Jeffrey Arnett, in "Adolescents and Heavy Metal Music: From the Mouths of Metalheads," *Youth & Society* 23:1 (September 1991), pp. 76–98.

55. Robert Duncan, *The Noise: Notes from a Rock 'n' Roll Era* (New York: Ticknor and Fields, 1984), pp. 36–37.

56. Marc Eliot, *Rockonomics: The Money behind the Music* (New York: Franklin Watts, 1989), pp. 247–48.

57. Paul Williams, *The Map: Rediscovering Rock and Roll (a Journey)* (South Bend, Ind.: and books, 1988), p. 237. Williams makes the latter point twice, on pp. 17 and 239.

58. See Jerry Adler with Jennifer Foote and Ray Sawhill, "The Rap Attitude," *Newsweek*, 19 March 1990, pp. 56–59. Compare Guy Garcia, "Heavy Metal Goes Platinum," *Time*, 14 October 1991, p. 85 ("wah-wah guitars"?). The ad for the issue on teenagers appeared in *Newsweek*, 14 May 1990, p. 71.

59. Duncan, *The Noise*, pp. 45–47.

60. Chuck Eddy, *Stairway to Hell: The 500 Best Heavy Metal Albums in the Universe* (New York: Harmony Books, 1991).

61. Charles Young, "Heavy Metal," *Musician*, September 1984, p. 44.

62. Bashe, *Heavy Metal Thunder*; see the articles by Wolf Marshall in *Guitar for the Practicing Musician*, several of which are cited elsewhere in this book.

63. See George Lipsitz, *Time Passages: Collective Memory and American Popular Culture* (Minneapolis: University of Minnesota Press, 1990).

64. Lorraine E. Prinsky and Jill Leslie Rosenbaum, "'Leer-ics' or Lyrics: Teenage Impressions of Rock 'n' Roll," *Youth & Society* 18:4 (June 1987), pp. 384–97. On the complexity of conversations between the powerful and the subordinate, see James C. Scott, *Domination and the Arts of Resistance: Hidden Transcripts* (New Haven, Conn.: Yale University Press, 1990).

65. Christine Hall Hansen and Ranald D. Hansen, "Schematic Information Processing of Heavy Metal Lyrics," *Communication Research* 18:3 (June 1991), pp. 373–411. Dozens of similar studies have been published. For an attempt to reclaim a very different notion of "objectivity," see Donna J. Haraway, "Situated Knowledges: The Science Question in Feminism and the Privilege of Partial Perspective," in *Simians, Cyborgs, and Women: The Reinvention of Nature* (New York: Routledge, 1991), pp. 183–201.

66. See Will Straw, "Characterizing Rock Music Cultures: The Case of Heavy Metal," *Canadian University Music Review* 5 (1984), pp. 104–22. Revised as "Characterizing Rock Music Culture: The Case of Heavy Metal," in *On Record: Rock, Pop, and the Written Word*, ed. Simon Frith and Andrew Goodwin (New York: Pantheon, 1990), pp. 97-110.

67. Marcus Breen, "A Stairway to Heaven or a Highway to Hell?: Heavy Metal Rock Music in the 1990s," *Cultural Studies* 5:2 (May 1991), pp. 191–203.

68. Deena Weinstein, *Heavy Metal: A Cultural Sociology* (New York: Lexington Books, 1991).

69. Weinstein, *Heavy Metal*, p. 295.

70. Weinstein, *Heavy Metal*, p. 4.

71. Weinstein, *Heavy Metal*, p. 124.

72. See Stuart Hall, "Notes on Deconstructing 'the Popular,'" in *People's History and Socialist Theory*, ed. Raphael Samuel (London: Routledge and Kegan Paul, 1981), pp. 227–40.

1. J. D. Considine, "Purity and Power," *Musician*, September 1984, p. 49.

2. Edward Van Halen, interview in *Musician*, February 1987, pp. 94–95.

3. Fredric Jameson, "Towards a New Awareness of Genre," *Science Fiction Studies* 28 (1982), p. 322; quoted in Michael Denning, *Mechanic Accents: Dime Novels and Working-Class Culture in America* (London: Verso, 1987), p. 75.

4. M. M. Bakhtin, "The Problem of Speech Genres," in *Speech Genres and Other Late Essays*, ed. Caryl Emerson and Michael Holquist (Austin: University of Texas Press, 1986), p. 91. See also Horace M. Newcomb, "On the Dialogic Aspects of Mass Communication," *Critical Studies in Mass Communication* 1 (1984), pp. 34–50.

5. Simon Frith, "Towards an Aesthetic of Popular Music," in *Music and Society: The Politics of Composition, Performance, and Reception*, ed. Richard Leppert and Susan McClary (Cambridge: Cambridge University Press, 1987), p. 145. See Wilfred Mellers, "God, Modality, and Meaning in Some Recent Songs of Bob Dylan," *Popular Music* 1 (1981), pp. 142–57. I don't think the problem is primarily at the level of the types of musical qualities that are investigated by musicologists, though the discipline does bring to bear biases in favor of harmonic and melodic characteristics. Rather, the problem is the elitist, "apolitical" formalism that has plagued the musicological study of all repertoires. As I understand Frith, his real objection to musicological analysis is that it has, so far, been formalist; it hasn't really told us much about how any music produces meaning or why people care about it.

6. I have written elsewhere about how musical innovations often result in discursive fusions that can best be approached with respect to the previous genres upon which they draw; see Robert Walser, "Bon Jovi's Alloy: Discursive Fusion in Top 40 Pop Music," *OneTwoThreeFour* 7 (1989), pp. 7–19.

7. See Michel Foucault, "History of Systems of Thought," in *Language, Counter-memory, Practice*, ed. Donald F. Bouchard (Ithaca, N.Y.: Cornell University Press, 1977), pp. 199–201.

8. John Fiske, *Television Culture* (New York: Methuen, 1987), pp. 110, 114.

9. Tzvetan Todorov, *Genres in Discourse* (Cambridge: Cambridge University Press, 1990), especially pp. 9–19.

10. Peter Wicke, *Rock Music: Culture, Aesthetics, and Sociology* (Cambridge: Cambridge University Press, 1990), p. 24.

11. Wicke, *Rock Music*, p. 25.

12. To those who would question a detailed analysis of heavy metal music by asking, "Yes, but do heavy metal musicians *know* what they're doing?" I would answer that in those terms, some do and some don't. (See chap. 3 for discussion of the various ways heavy metal musicians theorize their practices.) But how musicians conceive of their activities is only part of what it is they are doing, and there are many different ways of "knowing."

13. See Jean-Jacques Nattiez, *Music and Discourse: Toward a Semiology of Music* (Princeton, N.J.: Princeton University Press, 1990).

14. David Lidov, "Mind and Body in Music," *Semiotica* 66–1/3 (1987), pp. 69–87; Mark Johnson, *The Body in the Mind: The Bodily Basis of Meaning, Imagination, and Reason* (Chicago: University of Chicago Press, 1987); George Lakoff and Mark Johnson, *Metaphors We Live By* (Chicago: University of Chicago Press, 1980). See also Robert Walser, "The Body in the Music: Epistemology and Musical Semiotics," *College Music Symposium* 31:1 (forthcoming).

15. This argument is, of course, not Johnson's alone; many scholars have

contributed to an expanded view of metaphor. See Johnson's own bibliography and citations in *The Body in the Mind.*

16. Johnson, 196.

17. John A. Sloboda, *The Musical Mind: The Cognitive Psychology of Music* (Oxford: Clarendon Press, 1985), pp. 1–2. Unfortunately, Sloboda limits musical meaning to "emotions."

18. Elianne Halbersberg, *Heavy Metal* (Cresskill, N.J.: Sharon Publications, 1985), p. 41.

19. The Editors of *Rock & Roll Confidential, You've Got a Right to Rock* ([Los Angeles]: Duke and Duchess Ventures, 1989), p. 5.

20. Fiske, *Television Culture,* p. 85. This approach derives from the work of various sorts of literary reader-response critics (Barthes, Eco, Fish, Holland, Iser, Jauss, et al.). See Susan R. Suleiman and Inge Crosman, *The Reader in the Text: Essays on Audience and Interpretation* (Princeton, N.J.: Princeton University Press, 1980), particularly Suleiman's Introduction, for a lucid introduction to and typology of this work. I would argue that musical analysis in terms of discourse should not be counterposed to reception-oriented approaches. On the contrary, it actually helps us understand problems such as what has been called "distracted listening." If we recognize the power of music to communicate very specific affective experiences, we can see how varying degress of incomplete verbal reception should not lead us to underestimate either the music or its audience.

21. Mounting a similar argument in a different discipline, Norman Bryson emphasizes that visual art is not simply *affected* by social economics (patronage systems, etc.) but is itself constituted through social discourse. Signs are activated through social labor; combinations of signifiers must make contact with discursive formations actually operative in society in order to be generally intelligible. See Norman Bryson, *Vision and Pointing: The Logic of the Gaze* (New Haven, Conn.: Yale University Press, 1983). Bryson argues that painter and viewer do not "communicate": "they are *agents* operating *through labor* on the *materiality* of the visual sign" (p. 150, original emphasis). By this he means to stress the inherently social nature of artistic production and reception; the artistic work, though guided by discursive channels, is unavoidably subject to the variety of readings produced by the various social experiences of its viewers (or auditors).

22. For good examples of this sort of work, see Steve Chapple and Reebee Garofalo, *Rock 'n' Roll Is Here to Pay* (Chicago: Nelson-Hall, 1977); and Reebee Garofalo, ed., *Rockin' the Boat: Mass Music and Mass Movements,* Boston: South End Press, 1992. But such approaches frequently degenerate into studies that ignore the social exchange of meanings that underpins the exchange of musical commodities.

23. John Blacking, *How Musical Is Man?* (Seattle: University of Washington Press, 1973), pp. 45, 54, 107. Blacking accepted this truism even as he bravely challenged many others.

24. For fuller critical surveys of approaches to musical analysis that have particular relevance for popular music, see Richard Middleton, *Studying Popular Music* (Philadelphia: Open University Press, 1990); John Shepherd, *Music as Social Text* (Cambridge: Polity Press, 1991); and Bruno Nettl, *The Study of Ethnomusicology: Twenty-Nine Issues and Concepts* (Urbana: University of Illinois Press, 1983).

25. See Terry Eagleton, *The Ideology of the Aesthetic* (Cambridge, Mass.: Basil Blackwell, 1990).

26. See, for example, Theodor W. Adorno, *Prisms* (Cambridge, Mass.: MIT

Press, 1981), *Introduction to the Sociology of Music* (New York: Continuum, 1988), and *Philosophy of Modern Music* (New York: Continuum, 1985).

27. See, for example, Bernard Gendron, "Theodor Adorno Meets the Cadillacs," in *Studies in Entertainment: Critical Approaches to Mass Culture*, ed. Tania Modleski (Bloomington: Indiana University Press, 1986), pp. 18–36; and Max Paddison, "The Critique Criticized: Adorno and Popular Music," *Popular Music* 2 (1982), pp. 201–18. To compare the best and worst of Adorno's musical analysis, see "Bach Defended against His Devotees" and "Jazz—Perennial Fashion," in his *Prisms*.

28. Alan Lomax, *Folk Song Style and Culture* (New Brunswick, N.J.: Transaction Books, 1968), p. ix.

29. Lomax's study displays many of the features of the anthropological tradition of "rescue" scholarship: the mission of saving folk cultures from their destruction at the hands of global mass culture, as though other cultures have never had history, have existed in timeless purity until their twentieth-century contamination. Thus, African-American blues are not included in his data; presumably their origin in cultural fusion marks them as abnormal, as though intercultural influence had never occurred before European colonizations. For a contrasting view, see Bruno Nettl, *The Western Impact on World Music: Change, Adaptation, and Survival* (New York: Schirmer Books, 1985).

30. Bruno Nettl, *The Study of Ethnomusicology* (Urbana, IL: University of Illinois Press, 1983), 212.

31. Steven Feld, "Linguistics and Ethnomusicology," *Ethnomusicology* 18:2 (1974), 197–217.

32. John Miller Chernoff, *African Rhythm and African Sensibility* (Chicago: University of Chicago Press, 1979), p. 155.

33. Blacking, *How Musical*, p. 25.

34. Steven Feld, *Sound and Sentiment: Birds, Weeping, Poetics, and Song in Kaluli Expression*, 2d ed. (Philadelphia: University of Pennsylvania Press, 1990).

35. Judith and Alton Becker, "A Musical Icon: Power and Meaning in Javanese Gamelan Music," in *The Sign in Music and Literature*, ed. Wendy Steiner (Austin: University of Texas Press, 1981), p. 203.

36. See, for example: Susan McClary, *Feminine Endings: Music, Gender, Sexuality* (Minneapolis: University of Minnesota Press, 1991); Lawrence Kramer, *Music as Cultural Practice, 1800–1900* (Berkeley: University of California Press, 1990); Rose Rosengard Subotnik, *Developing Variations: Style and Ideology in Western Music* (Minneapolis: University of Minnesota Press, 1991); and Richard Leppert and Susan McClary, eds., *Music and Society: The Politics of Composition, Performance, and Reception* (Cambridge: Cambridge University Press, 1987).

37. Philip Tagg, *Kojak—50 Seconds of Television Music* (Göteborg, Sweden: Musikvetenskapliga Institutionen, 1979); "Analysing Popular Music: Theory, Method, and Practice," *Popular Music* 2 (1982), pp. 37–67; "Musicology and the Semiotics of Popular Music," *Semiotica* 66–1/3 (1987), pp. 279–98.

38. Tagg, "Analysing Popular Music," pp. 43, 65.

39. See the discussion of this point in chapter 1, and Stuart Hall, "Notes on Deconstructing 'the Popular,'" in *People's History and Socialist Theory*, ed. Raphael Samuel (London: Routledge and Kegan Paul, 1981), pp. 227–40. See also John Fiske's discussions of these models in his *Introduction to Communication Studies*, 2d ed. (New York: Routledge, 1990).

40. This is confirmed not only by these musicians' statements and by the opinions of the fans I interviewed but also by a recent survey of metal fans, which reported that 48 percent said they pay attention mostly to the music; 41 percent, to both music and lyrics; and only 11 percent, primarily to the lyrics.

See Jeffrey Arnett, "Adolescents and Heavy Metal Music: From the Mouths of Metalheads," *Youth & Society* 23:1 (September 1991), p. 82.

41. John Fiske and John Hartley, *Reading Television* (New York: Methuen, 1978), p. 124–25.

42. Compare David Lidov's distinction between the alliance of language with exosomatic space and the endosomatic flux of bodily experience in "Mind and Body in Music," *Semiotica* 66–1/3 (1987), pp. 69–87. See also Shepherd, *Music as Social Text*, pp. 79–95.

43. For example, critic J. D. Considine includes "Runnin' with the Devil" in his list of the ten best metal songs of all time ("Good, Bad, and Ugly," *Musician*, September 1984, p. 53).

44. Mack, quoted in Chris Gill, "Dialing for Distortion: Sound Advice from 10 Top Producers," *Guitar Player*, October 1992, p. 86.

45. For a full explanation of resultant tones, see Arthur H. Benade, *Fundamentals of Musical Acoustics* (New York: Oxford University Press, 1976), pp. 273–74.

46. Advertisement for Dean Markley's Overlord effects pedal in *Guitar for the Practicing Musician*, February 1989, p. 102.

47. Advertisement for DiMarzio pickups in *Guitar for the Practicing Musician*, December 1988, p. 121.

48. John Stix, "Up to Par," *Guitar for the Practicing Musician*, January 1989, p. 70.

49. Robert Duncan, *The Noise: Notes from a Rock 'n' Roll Era* (New York: Ticknor and Fields, 1984), p. 47.

50. See the long and interesting discussion of vocal timbre in rock music in Shepherd, *Music as Social Text*, pp. 164–73.

51. See chapter 3.

52. Wolf Marshall, "Music Appreciation: Iron Maiden," *Guitar for the Practicing Musician*, January 1989, p. 113. See chapter 3 for further discussion of metal musicians' use of modal theory.

53. For a discussion of the relationship of music theory and popular music scholarship, see Susan McClary and Robert Walser, "Start Making Sense! Musicology Wrestles with Rock," in *On Record: Rock, Pop, and the Written Word*, ed. Simon Frith and Andrew Goodwin (New York: Pantheon, 1990), pp. 277–92.

54. Musicians often put tunes into foreign musical discourses for pedagogical reasons or just for the pleasure of such play. In an article called "Headbanger's Vocabulary," Wally Schnalle altered the basic metal drumbeat by changing the size of the snare drum, increasing the tempo, and exchanging the accompanying instruments and turned it into polka time (*Drums and Drumming*, August/September 1990, p. 52). *The Billboard Book of Rock Arranging*, by Mark Michaels with Jackson Braider (New York: Billboard Books, 1990), discusses the necessary ingredients of "the hard rock arrangement" by transforming "Silent Night," step by step, into "Sylint Nyyte" (pp. 147–50). The author deals well with timbre, rhythm, lyrics, idiomatic bass lines, etc., but he unfortunately neglects to adjust the mode, which would have improved his example enormously.

55. Marshall, "Iron Maiden," p. 113. For a lengthier discussion of the affective and functional characteristics of modes, see Susan McClary, "The Transition from Modal to Tonal Organization in the Works of Monteverdi" (Ph.D. diss., Harvard University, 1976).

56. Jesse Gress, "Performance Notes," in *Joe Satriani: Surfing with the Alien*, ed. Andy Aledort (Port Chester, N.Y.: Cherry Lane Music Company, 1988), p. 8. This is the sort of technical analysis that rock critics have always liked to ridicule when academics have produced it. Now that musicians themselves write

this way, it's harder to be so dismissive. In any case, musicologists are not the only ones to resort to arcane terminology in an attempt to describe musical affect and signification. Rock critic Chuck Eddy writes of Black Sabbath's *Paranoid*: "The rhythms compress circular zero-chops wah-wah wank over steady tomroll marches, with secondary beat-apparatus from powerchord pulverizations constructed into pseudosymphonic forceswing headbang progressions" (*Stairway to Hell: The 500 Best Heavy Metal Albums in the Universe* [New York: Harmony Books, 1991], p. 26).

57. Edward T. Cone, *Musical Form and Musical Performance* (New York: W. W. Norton, 1968), p. 17. For a very influential theory of rhythm that completely ignores the body, see Grosvenor Cooper and Leonard B. Meyer, *The Rhythmic Structure of Music* (Chicago: University of Chicago Press, 1960).

58. For a theoretical model dealing with the social projection of dread onto the female, the racial other, and the insane, see Sander L. Gilman, *Difference and Pathology: Stereotypes of Sexuality, Race, and Madness* (Ithaca, N.Y.: Cornell University Press, 1985). See also McClary, *Feminine Endings*.

59. James D. Graham, "Rhythms in Rock Music," *Popular Music and Society* 1:1 (1971), p. 37.

60. The virtuosity of guitar solos in heavy metal will be discussed more fully in chapter 3.

61. Compare Richard Dyer's argument that entertainment shows us how utopia *feels*, instead of describing it (as Plato, for example, did). Dyer emphasizes that the pleasures of entertainment are dispensed only with respect to historically determined sensibilities; see his "Entertainment and Utopia," in *Movies and Methods*, vol. 2, ed. Bill Nichols, pp. 220–32 (Berkeley: University of California Press, 1985).

62. The affective characters of the various modes are clear from the circumstances of their deployment, in connection with lyrics, images, and other musical factors. But more explicit explanations are available from metal guitar players themselves; see, for example, Wolf Marshall, "Music Appreciation."

63. In chapter 5, I analyze a similarly anomalous song, Ozzy Osbourne's "Suicide Solution." In brief, I maintain that "Suicide Solution" uses a variety of musical means to construct a trapped, claustrophobic affect that would be burst open by a transcendent guitar solo.

64. Chapter 4 compares the negotiated reception by men and women, straight and gay, of the same texts in different ways.

Chapter 3. Eruptions (Notes to Pages 57–107)

1. A contemporary description of Franz Liszt from the *Allgemeine musikalische Zeitung* of May 1838, quoted in Piero Weiss and Richard Taruskin, eds., *Music in the Western World: A History in Documents* (New York: Schirmer, 1984), p. 363.

2. Malmsteen's first U.S. album, *Yngwie J. Malmsteen's Rising Force* (1984), had offered "special thanks" to Bach and Paganini.

3. John Stix, "Yngwie Malmsteen and Billy Sheehan: Summit Meeting at Chops City," *Guitar for the Practicing Musician*, March 1986, p. 59.

4. "Rock and soul" is Dave Marsh's term; by eliding "rock 'n' roll" and "soul," he underscores the fundamental connectedness of these musics, which are normally kept separate by historians, who have too readily accepted the racist marketing categories of record companies. In particular, Marsh uses the term to insist on the enormous debt owed by white rockers to black r&b and gospel artists. My favorite moment in Marsh's polemic on this point is when he dryly

refers to "the British Invasion" of the 1960s (the Beatles, Gerry and the Pace-makers, the Rolling Stones, etc.) as "the Chuck Berry Revival" (Dave Marsh, *The Heart of Rock and Soul: The 1001 Greatest Singles Ever Made* [New York: Plume, 1989], p. 3).

5. David P. Szatmary, *Rockin' in Time: A Social History of Rock and Roll* (Englewood Cliffs, N.J.: Prentice-Hall, 1987), p. 154. Glenn Tipton, guitarist with Judas Priest, offers a demonstration of the blues origins of heavy metal licks in J. D. Considine, "Purity and Power," *Musician*, September 1984, pp. 46–50.

6. For a recent and flagrant example of such musicological colonization of popular music, see Peter Van der Merwe, *Origins of the Popular Style: The Ante-cedents of Twentieth-Century Popular Music* (Oxford: Oxford University Press, 1989). See also my review of his book: Robert Walser, "Review of *Origins of the Popular Style*, by Peter Van der Merwe," *Journal of Musicological Research* 12/1–2 (1992), pp. 123–32.

7. Lawrence W. Levine, *Highbrow/Lowbrow: The Emergence of Cultural Hier-archy in America* (Cambridge, Mass.: Harvard University Press, 1988).

8. Christopher Small, *Music–Society–Education* (London: John Calder, 1980), and *Music of the Common Tongue: Survival and Celebration in Afro-American Music* (New York: Riverrun, 1987). See also Susan McClary, *Feminine Endings: Music, Gender, Sexuality* (Minneapolis: University of Minnesota Press, 1991); McClary generally works to reconstruct the lost signification and politics of classical music, instead of directly critiquing modern institutions, as Small does. But for a pointed criticism of academic modernism, see her "Terminal Prestige: The Case of Avant-Garde Music Composition," *Cultural Critique* 12 (Spring 1989), pp. 57–81.

9. Eric Hobsbawm and Terence Ranger, eds., *The Invention of Tradition* (New York: Cambridge University Press, 1983).

10. Mordechai Kleidermacher, "Where There's Smoke . . . There's Fire!" *Guitar World*, February 1991, p. 62.

11. See, for example, John Rockwell, "Art Rock," in *The Rolling Stone Illus-trated History of Rock & Roll*, ed. Jim Miller (New York: Random House, 1980), pp. 347–52.

12. Richard Middleton, *Studying Popular Music* (Philadelphia: Open Uni-versity Press, 1990), p. 30.

13. Middleton, *Studying Popular Music*, p. 31.

14. See Wolf Marshall, "Ritchie Blackmore: A Musical Profile," *Guitar for the Practicing Musician*, March 1986, pp. 51–52.

15. Martin K. Webb, "Ritchie Blackmore with Deep Purple," in *Masters of Heavy Metal*, ed. Jas Obrecht (New York: Quill, 1984), p. 54; and Steve Rosen, "Blackmore's Rainbow," also in *Masters of Heavy Metal*, p. 62. Webb apparently misunderstood Blackmore's explanation, for what I have rendered as an ellip-sis he transcribed as "Bm to a D♭ to a C to a G," a harmonic progression that is neither characteristic of Bach nor to be found anywhere in "Highway Star." Blackmore was probably referring to the progression that underpins the latter part of his solo: Dm | G | C | A.

16. For a discussion of the social significance of Vivaldi's concerto grosso procedures, see Susan McClary, "The Blasphemy of Talking Politics during Bach Year," in *Music and Society: The Politics of Composition, Performance, and Reception*, ed. Richard Leppert and Susan McClary (Cambridge: Cambridge University Press, 1987), pp. 13–62.

17. Nicolas Slonimsky, *Thesaurus of Scales and Melodic Patterns* (New York:

Coleman-Ross, 1947). On Slonimsky's influence on metal guitarists, see Andy Aledort, "Performance Notes," *Guitar for the Practicing Musician*, February 1989, p. 33. Alex Skolnick, guitarist in Testament, has called Walter Piston's *Harmony* "brilliant." He also studied jazz improvisation books by Jerry Coker and Jamey Aebersold (Brad Tolinski, "When Worlds Collide," *Guitar World*, February 1991, p. 32).

18. Steve Gett, "Basic Blackmore," *Guitar for the Practicing Musician*, February 1985, p. 68.

19. Webb, "Ritchie Blackmore," p. 57.

20. Mary J. Edrei, ed., *The Van Halen Scrapbook* (Cresskill, N.J.: Starbooks, 1984), p. 27. Jan Van Halen plays a clarinet solo on "Big Bad Bill (Is Sweet William Now)" on Van Halen's *Diver Down* (1982). Edward Van Halen is usually called Eddie by journalists and fans and Ed by his bandmates, but he makes a point of using Edward on his album credits, and I'll generally follow that example here.

21. Jas Obrecht, "Van Halen Comes of Age," in *Masters of Heavy Metal*, (New York: Quill, 1984), pp. 148–49.

22. Obrecht, "Van Halen Comes of Age," p. 155. Eric Clapton, Jimmy Page, and Jeff Beck, all white and British, became the most influential guitarists of the 1960s (along with Hendrix) by playing cover versions of the music of African-American blues guitarists like Muddy Waters, Howlin' Wolf, Buddy Guy, Albert King, Robert Johnson, and Blind Willie Johnson.

23. *Guitar World*, July 1990, pp. 51, 74.

24. This is described in, among other places, Obrecht, "Van Halen Comes of Age," p. 156.

25. Rodolphe Kreutzer was a contemporary of Beethoven, slightly older than Paganini. He was best known as a violinist and pedagogue, although he composed forty-three operas and many other works. His *40 Études ou Caprices* has been published in countless editions.

26. I have made a similar argument for the semiotics of the main theme of J. S. Bach's *Jauchzet Gott in allen Landen*; see Robert Walser, "Musical Imagery and Performance Practice in J. S. Bach's Arias With Trumpet," *International Trumpet Guild Journal* 13:1 (September 1988), pp. 62–77.

27. Wolf Marshall, "The Classical Influence," *Guitar for the Practicing Musician*, March 1988, p. 102.

28. See also Andy Aledort's inaugural "Guitar in the 80s" column on tapping, "The Bach Influence," *Guitar for the Practicing Musician*, May 1985, 30–31.

29. Carl Philipp Emanuel Bach and Johann Friedrich Agricola, "Obituary of J. S. Bach," in Hans T. David and Arthur Mendel, *The Bach Reader*, rev. ed. (New York: W. W. Norton, 1966), p. 223.

30. See Peter Bondanella's "Introduction" to Niccolò Machiavelli, *The Prince*, edited and with an introduction by Peter Bondanella (Oxford: Oxford University Press, 1984), p. xviii. Compare also this excerpt from the letter of a patron to a sixteenth-century artist: "I recognize that in this magnificent work you have tried to express both the love which you cherish for me and your own excellence. These two things have enabled you to produce this incomparable figure" (Lauro Martines, *Power and Imagination: City-States in Renaissance Italy* [Baltimore: Johns Hopkins University Press, 1988], p. 228).

31. Joseph Horowitz, *The Ivory Trade: Music and the Business of Music at the Van Cliburn International Piano Competition* (New York: Summit Books, 1990), p. 61.

32. This quotation is taken from an article Schumann wrote in 1840 for his

Neue Zeitschrift für Musik; it was reprinted in Robert Schumann, *Schumann on Music*, ed. Henry Pleasants (New York: Dover, 1965), pp. 157–58. My thanks to Susan McClary for calling my attention to this passage.

33. Bruce Pollock, "Rock Climbing: Baseball," *Guitar for the Practicing Musician*, March 1989, p. 12.

34. *Guitar World*, July 1990, p. 74.

35. Charles Shaar Murray, *Crosstown Traffic: Jimi Hendrix and the Rock 'n' Roll Revolution* (New York: St. Martin's Press, 1989), p. 194.

36. Murray, *Crosstown Traffic*, p. 216.

37. Marshall, "The Classical Influence," p. 98.

38. On Liszt, see Weiss and Taruskin, *Music in the Western World*, pp. 363–67. On Frescobaldi, see Carol MacClintock, ed., *Readings in the History of Music in Performance* (Bloomington: Indiana University Press, 1979), pp. 132–36.

39. See Wolf Marshall, "Randy Rhoads: A Musical Appreciation," *Guitar for the Practicing Musician*, June 1985, p. 57.

40. Jas Obrecht, "Randy Rhoads," in *Masters of Heavy Metal* (New York: Quill, 1984), p. 174.

41. Obrecht, "Randy Rhoads," p. 182.

42. For an analysis of several pieces in terms of the performative articulation of affect, see Walser, "Musical Imagery and Performance Practice." See also Frederick Wessel, "The *Affektenlehre* in the Eighteenth Century (Ph.D. diss., Indiana University, 1955), and Robert Donington, *Baroque Music: Style and Performance* (New York: Norton, 1982) on Baroque affect; see Terry Eagleton, *The Ideology of the Aesthetic* (Cambridge, Mass.: Basil Blackwell, 1990) for a thorough critique of the concept of "the aesthetic."

43. Levine, *Highbrow/Lowbrow*, p. 192.

44. See chapter 5 for an interpretation of this omission.

45. McClary, "The Blasphemy of Talking Politics," pp. 32–36.

46. Don Michael Randel, ed., *The New Harvard Dictionary of Music* (Cambridge, Mass.: Harvard University Press, 1986), p. 859.

47. The first (interior) solo in this recording of "Suicide Solution" also plays with the semiotics of irrationality by violating the norms of tonal syntax: Rhoads uses feedback, pickup interruptions, an ascending sequence of tritones, a descending chromatic sequence, groans and wailing with the whammy bar.

48. See Wolf Marshall, "Randy Rhoads," *Guitar for the Practicing Musician*, April 1986, p. 51.

49. One fan told me that he respected heavy metal more than other kinds of music because it has the most "advanced" guitar playing. Scott, interview with author, 30 June 1989.

50. *Guitar for the Practicing Musician*, May 1985, pp. 30–31.

51. My thanks to Christopher Kachian, professor of guitar at the College of St. Thomas, for discussing these issues and metal recordings with me.

52. Doug Smith, educational director, Music Tech, Minneapolis, telephone interview with author, 12 December 1990.

53. On Clark, see David Fricke, "Steve Clark: 1960–1991," *Rolling Stone*, 21 February 1991, p. 14. On Collins, see Elianne Halbersberg, "Doing the Def Leppard Family Proud," *Faces*, May 1989, p. 21. On Spitz, see Andy Aledort, "Thrashing It Out," *Guitar for the Practicing Musician*, March 1988, p. 64. On Vincent, see FabioTesta, "Vinnie Vincent: Rockin' the Eighties," *The Best of Metal Mania #2*, 1987, p. 22.

54. On Spitz, see *Metal Mania*, July 1989, p. 40. On Stradlin', see John Stix, "In the Classic Way," *Guitar for the Practicing Musician*, September 1988, p. 76. On Van Halen, see Obrecht, "Van Halen Comes of Age," pp. 146, 154.

55. Matt Resnicoff, "George Lynch," *Guitar World*, July 1990, p. 92 (originally published in *Guitar World*, April 1988).

56. Resnicoff, "George Lynch," p. 92.

57. Joe Lalaina, "Yngwie, the One and Only," *Guitar School*, September 1989, p. 125.

58. Matt Resnicoff, "Flash of Two Worlds," *Musician*, September 1990, p. 76.

59. Lalaina, "Yngwie," p. 15.

60. FabioTesta, "Yngwie Malmsteen: In Search of a New Kingdom," *The Best of Metal Mania* #2, 1987, p. 33.

61. Wolf Marshall, "Performance Notes: Black Star," *Guitar for the Practicing Musician Collector's Yearbook*, Winter 1990, pp. 26–27. See example 12 (pp. 96–97).

62. Compare Janet Levy's cautious but valuable exposé of the values implicit in the writings of academic musicologists, in "Covert and Casual Values in Recent Writings about Music," *Journal of Musicology* 6:1 (Winter 1987), pp. 3–27.

63. Andy Aledort, "Performance Notes," *Guitar for the Practicing Musician Collector's Yearbook*, Winter 1990, p. 6.

64. John Stix, "Yngwie Malmsteen and Billy Sheehan: Summit Meeting at Chops City," *Guitar for the Practicing Musician*, March 1986, p. 59. On the other side of his lineage, Malmsteen cites early Deep Purple as another moment of high musicianship, adding, "I think what people are doing today is far worse than early heavy metal. If you consider today's music involves two or three chords and players in some bands do even less. They could just as well be plumbers" (p. 64).

65. FabioTesta, "Yngwie Malmsteen," p. 35.

66. Stix, "Yngwie Malmsteen and Billy Sheehan," p. 57. Heavy metal bass players have, for the most part, simply laid down a solid foundation for the music. Bassists had not attempted to transform their instrument into a vehicle for virtuosic soloing until the recent success of Sheehan, who has been hailed variously as the "Eddie Van Halen of the bass" and the "Jaco Pastorius of heavy metal." Like Malmsteen, Sheehan cites among his main influences Bach, Paganini, and Hendrix.

67. Guitar players who are members of bands, however, are usually the leading composers of their groups, and the collaborative experience of working out songs and arrangements in a rock band is a type of musical creativity seldom enjoyed by classical musicians.

68. Jeff Loven, interview with the author, 9 February 1989, Minneapolis, Minn.

69. *Guitar for the Practicing Musician*, February 1989, p. 162. This description may sound exaggerated to some, but as someone who has known young practice fanatics in both classical and popular styles, I find it quite credible.

70. Matt Resnicoff, "The Latest Temptation of Steve Vai," *Musician*, September 1990, p. 60. Compare Milton Babbitt's "Who Cares If You Listen?" *High Fidelity*, February 1958, pp. 38–40, 126–27.

71. *Musician*, September 1990, p. 112.

72. The opposite story is told by Mark Wood, the first heavy metal violinist, who recalls having to unlearn the rigidity fostered by his classical training before going on to modify his instrument, imitate blues singers and guitarists, and experiment with distortion and power chords (Pete Brown, "Mark Wood," *Guitar for the Practicing Musician*, September 1991, pp. 161–66).

73. *Guitar World*, July 1990, p. 51. As Chris Kachian pointed out to me, Van

Halen always keeps his virtuosity lyrical, while Malmsteen inserts lyricism parenthetically among the virtuosic licks. Some of the new speed demons dispense with lyricism entirely.

74. Resnicoff, "Flash of Two Worlds," p. 126.

75. George E. Marcus and Michael M. J. Fischer, *Anthropology as Cultural Critique: An Experimental Moment in the Human Sciences* (Chicago: University of Chicago Press, 1986). For an interesting early example of "musicology as cultural critique," see Sidney Finkelstein, *Jazz: A People's Music* (New York: International Publishers, 1988 [orig. pub. 1948]), especially chapter 2, "The Sound of Jazz," which includes a section called "What Jazz Teaches Us About the Classics."

76. John Berger, Sven Blomberg, Chris Fox, Michael Dibb, and Richard Hollis, *Ways of Seeing* (London: British Broadcasting Corporation, 1972).

77. Ed Ward, Geoffrey Stokes, and Ken Tucker, *Rock of Ages: The Rolling Stone History of Rock & Roll* (New York: Rolling Stone Press, 1986), p. 608. Other histories discuss heavy metal briefly and musical virtuosity not at all. See Szatmary, *Rockin' in Time*, pp. 204–5; and Robert G. Pielke, *You Say You Want a Revolution: Rock Music in American Culture* (Chicago: Nelson-Hall, 1986), p. 202. See also the relevant entries in Jon Pareles and Patricia Romanowski, eds., *The Rolling Stone Encyclopedia of Rock & Roll* (New York: Rolling Stone Press, 1983); or Donald Clarke, ed., *The Penguin Encyclopedia of Popular Music* (New York: Viking, 1989). Pareles's entry on "Heavy Metal" in the *New Grove Dictionary of American Music*, ed. H. Wiley Hitchcock and Stanley Sadie (London: McMillan, 1986), mentions only Edward Van Halen's virtuosity, and that in passing.

78. Within the academy, one hears occasional calls for reforms that will respond to modern cultural, demographic, and technological changes; perversely, these often turn out to be pleas to bolster sagging attention to "serious" music in order to combat the moral evils and musical crudities of heavy metal and other popular musics. The 1990 conference of the National Association of Schools of Music, held 15–20 November in Indianapolis, was one recent occasion where such calls to arms dominated.

79. Anne Fadiman, "Heavy Metal Mania," *Life*, December 1984, p. 106.

80. Theodor W. Adorno, "Bach Defended against His Devotees" [1950], in *Prisms* (Cambridge, Mass.: MIT Press, 1981), p. 136.

81. See, for example, McClary, "The Blasphemy of Talking Politics."

82. Adorno, "Bach Defended," p. 146.

83. V. N. Vološinov, *Marxism and the Philosophy of Language* (Cambridge, Mass.: Harvard University Press, 1986), p. 23. This aspect of the work of Bakhtin and Vološinov has been developed into a theory of "articulation" in cultural studies. For example, see Stuart Hall, "The Rediscovery of 'Ideology': Return of the Repressed in Media Studies," in Michael Gurevitch, Tony Bennett, James Curran, and Janet Woollacott, eds., *Culture, Society, and the Media* (New York: Methuen, 1982), pp. 56–90.

84. Vološinov, *Marxism*, p. 23.

85. See Stuart Hall, "Notes on Deconstructing 'the Popular,'" in *People's History and Socialist Theory*, ed. Raphael Samuel (London: Routledge and Kegan Paul, 1981), pp. 227–40.

86. J. D. Considine, "Purity and Power," *Musician*, September 1984, pp. 46, 48.

88. Small, *Music of the Common Tongue*, p. 126.

90. I refer to Jennifer Batten, guitarist (with Michael Jackson and others) and columnist for *Guitar for the Practicing Musician*, and to Vernon Reid of

Living Colour, who has been featured on the cover and in the analyses of the same magazine.

Chapter 4. Forging Masculinity (Notes to Pages 108–36)

1. Guy Debord, *Society of the Spectacle* (Detroit: Black and Red, 1983), §4.

2. See Susan McClary, "Constructions of Gender in Monteverdi's Dramatic Music," in *Feminine Endings: Music, Gender, Sexuality* (Minneapolis: University of Minnesota Press, 1991), pp. 35–52.

3. John Fiske, *Television Culture* (New York: Methuen, 1987), p. 202. See also Fiske, "British Cultural Studies and Television," in *Channels of Discourse*, ed. Robert C. Allen (Chapel Hill: University of North Carolina Press, 1987), pp. 254–89.

4. See Arthur Brittan, *Masculinity and Power* (New York: Basil Blackwell, 1989), especially pp. 36–41.

5. Deena Weinstein believes that heavy metal "celebrates the very qualities that boys must sacrifice in order to become adult members of society"; see her *Heavy Metal: A Cultural Sociology* (New York: Lexington Books, 1991), p. 105. I argue the opposite of this: that although behavior changes, the same patriarchal ideals are largely held in common by both "boys" and "adult members of society."

6. E. Ann Kaplan, *Rocking around the Clock: Music Television, Postmodernism, and Consumer Culture* (New York: Methuen, 1987).

7. Kaplan, *Rocking around the Clock*, p. 107.

8. Laura Mulvey, "Visual Pleasure and Narrative Cinema," in *Movies and Methods*, vol. 2, ed. Bill Nichols (Berkeley: University of California Press, 1985), p. 308.

9. For a full discussion of this point, see Susan McClary, "Introduction: A Material Girl in Bluebeard's Castle," in *Feminine Endings*, pp. 3–34.

10. See Barbara Ehrenreich, *The Worst Years of Our Lives* (New York: Pantheon, 1990), pp. 251–57. It is crucial to recognize that exscription is not subcultural deviance but a mainstream ideological convention. Daniel Patrick Moynihan once proposed that the "character defects" of young black men be solved by removing them to a "world without women" in the military (Adolph Reed, Jr., and Julian Bond, "Equality: Why We Can't Wait," *The Nation*, 9 December 1991, p. 733.

11. Fiske, "British Cultural Studies," p. 263. Fiske properly discusses the links between such a concept of masculinity and its context of patriarchal capitalism.

12. Of course, some women also find such images attractive, as I will discuss below. But the point is that "the social definition of men as holders of power is translated not only into mental body images and fantasies, but into muscle tensions, posture, the feel and texture of the body" (not to mention the music) (R. W. Connell, *Gender and Power: Society, the Person, and Sexual Politics* (Cambridge: Polity Press, 1987), p. 85.

13. When I first started studying metal, a friend and I discovered we were reading a Judas Priest concert film in these two very different ways. Occasionally, the threat of homoeroticism is addressed directly, as by metal star Ted Nugent, who remarked during a concert, "I like my boys in the band, as long as they don't fucking touch me." On the theory of "negotiated" readings of popular texts, see Horace M. Newcomb, "On the Dialogic Aspects of Mass Communication," *Critical Studies in Mass Communication* 1 (1984), pp. 34–50.

14. Klaus Theweleit, *Male Fantasies*, vol. 2 (Minneapolis: University of Minnesota Press, 1989).

15. For example, many Judas Priest songs, such as "Hard as Iron" and "Heavy Metal," from *Ram It Down*, and the album cover art from *Ram It Down*, *Screaming for Vengeance*, and *Defenders of the Faith*.

16. Tipper Gore, *Raising PG Kids in an X-Rated Society* (Nashville, Tenn.: Abingdon Press, 1987), pp. 17–18; William Graebner, "The Erotic and Destructive in 1980s Rock Music: A Theoretical and Historical Analysis," *Tracking: Popular Music Studies* 1:2 (1988), pp. 8–20.

17. Joseph W. Slade, "Violence in the Pornographic Film: A Historical Survey," *Journal of Communication* 34:3 (1984), p. 153. See also Linda Williams, *Hard Core: Power, Pleasure, and the "Frenzy of the Visible"* (Berkeley: University of California Press, 1989).

18. All from the album *Back for the Attack* (1987); further examples of this type of song can also be found on earlier Dokken albums, such as *Tooth and Nail* (1984). "Looks That Kill" is from Mötley Crüe's *Shout at the Devil* (1983); "Still of the Night" is on Whitesnake's *Whitesnake* (1987).

19. On this reading of the presentation of women in nineteenth-century opera, see Catherine Clément, *Opera, or the Undoing of Women* (Minneapolis: University of Minnesota Press, 1988). See also Susan McClary, *George Bizet: Carmen* (Cambridge: Cambridge University Press, 1992).

20. See, for example, the E Minor Partita. As I argued in chapter 3, such comparisons are neither arbitrary nor coincidental: album liner credits, published interviews with musicians, and the musical analyses in guitarists' trade journals all make explicit the relation of Baroque musical discourse to that of heavy metal, a relationship resulting from the continuing circulation of classical music in contemporary culture and metal guitarists' conscious and meticulous study.

21. In a stunning projection of violence onto the victim, the lyrics of "Midnight Maniac," by Krokus (*The Blitz*, 1984), warn of a female sex maniac creeping about at night, breaking in and killing; the singer evokes the terror of the presumably male victim.

22. I have written elsewhere about the musical organization of this song; see Robert Walser, "Bon Jovi's Alloy: Discursive Fusion in Top 40 Pop Music," *OneTwoThreeFour* 7 (1989), pp. 7–19.

23. Rob Tannenbaum, "Bon Voyage," *Rolling Stone*, 9 February 1989, pp. 52–58, 132–33.

24. This is the ♭VI–♭VII–I progression discussed in previous chapters.

25. See Steven Neale, "Masculinity as Spectacle: Reflections on Men and Mainstream Cinema," *Screen* 24:6 (November–December 1983): pp. 2–16; and Mulvey, "Visual Pleasure and Narrative Cinema."

26. Susan Orleans, "The Kids Are All Right," *Rolling Stone*, 21 May 1987, pp. 34–38, 108–111.

27. Mulvey, "Visual Pleasure and Narrative Cinema," p. 309.

28. See the album cover photos in Poison's *Open Up and Say . . . Ahh!* and the even more androgynous look on their first album, *Look What the Cat Dragged In*. See Mötley Crüe's photos on the albums *Shout at the Devil*, *Theatre of Pain*, and *Girls, Girls, Girls*. Such images fill the pages of metal fan magazines like *Hit Parader*, *Metal Mania*, *Faces*, *Metal Edge*, and *RIP*.

29. See Steven Simels, *Gender Chameleons: Androgyny in Rock 'n' Roll* (New York: Timbre Books, 1985). In 1987 the same costume designer was employed by both the metal band W.A.S.P. and Liberace (Anne M. Raso, "Video: Behind the Reel," *Rock Scene*, July 1987, p. 68).

30. Fredric Jameson, "Reification and Utopia in Mass Culture," *Social Text* 1:1 (1979), pp. 130–48.

31. Dick Hebdige, *Subculture: The Meaning of Style* (New York: Methuen, 1979), p. 17.

32. John Stix, "Ready or Not," *Guitar for the Practicing Musician*, March 1989, p. 56.

33. Roberta Smoodin, "Crazy like David Lee Roth," *Playgirl*, August 1986, p. 43.

34. Dave Marsh, ed., *The First Rock & Roll Confidential Report* (New York: Pantheon, 1985), p. 165.

35. Kim of Cathedral City, *RIP*, February 1989, p. 6.

36. Ray R., Winter Springs, Fl., *RIP*, May 1989, p. 6.

37. Scott, interview with author, 30 June 1989, St. Paul, Minn.

38. Besides observing this behavior among members of various bands, I discussed it openly with musicians during two interviews. Such behavior is equally widespread among orchestral musicians; indeed, it occurs whenever men transgress against hegemonic norms of masculinity by acting expressive, sensitive, or spectacular.

39. George Sulmers, "Anthrax: Metal's Most Diseased Band," *The Best of Metal Mania #2* (1987), p. 24.

40. Sheryl Garratt has argued that women identify with androgynous male musicians because they can dress like them and act like them. See Sue Steward and Sheryl Garratt, *Signed, Sealed, and Delivered: True Life Stories of Women in Pop* (Boston: South End Press, 1984), p. 144.

41. Kaja Silverman, "Fragments of a Fashionable Discourse," in *Studies in Entertainment*, ed., Tania Modleski (Bloomington: Indiana University Press, 1986), pp. 139–52.

42. For a critical view of this position, see Rita Felski, *Beyond Feminist Aesthetics: Feminist Literature and Social Change* (Cambridge, Mass.: Harvard University Press, 1989). Felski's criticism of avant-garde strategies of textual disruption as political action rests on her perception of a conflation of gender and class: avant-garde art is as elitist as anything it might challenge. It is worth noting that the same problem hardly exists with heavy metal.

43. See Jane Flax, "Postmodernism and Gender Relations in Feminist Theory," in *Feminism/Postmodernism*, ed. Linda J. Nicholson (New York: Routledge, Chapman, & Hall, 1990), pp. 39–62.

44. Pat Benatar discusses the difficulty of creating her own hard rock image: "I never considered the character [I play] to be a sex symbol. I just was looking for extreme strength and self-assuredness. . . . I listened to a lot of male-dominated groups like the Stones and Led Zeppelin. There weren't a lot of women around to emulate, no one female figure, so I took a shot in the dark and tried to figure out a way to do this without looking stupid and victimized" (Joe Smith, *Off the Record* (New York: Warner Books, 1988), pp. 406–407). See also Lisa A. Lewis, *Gender Politics and MTV: Voicing the Difference* (Philadelphia: Temple University Press, 1990), especially chapter five.

45. Laurel Fishman, "Lita Ford," *Metal*, May 1988, pp. 36–38. One fan told me that she was contemptuous of Ford and other female metal musicians because they are "stupid sex objects" but that she also saw some of the male musicians the same way (Rita, interview with author, 30 June 1989).

46. For writings that focus on female reception of heavy metal and hard rock, see Daniel J. Hadley, "'Girls on Top': Women and Heavy Metal," paper presented at the Feminist Theory and Music Conference, University of Minnesota, June 1991, and Lisa Lewis, *Gender Politics and MTV*, especially pp. 149–71.

Both Hadley and Lewis discuss the fanzine *Bitch*, wherein female heavy metal fans debated the meanings of their own involvement with metal.

47. Sue Wise, "Sexing Elvis," in *On Record: Rock, Pop, and the Written Word* ed. Simon Frith and Andrew Goodwin (New York: Pantheon, 1990), pp. 390–98.

48. This was debated at length during the author's interview with Lisa, Tammy, and Larry, 30 June 1989.

49. From her cross-cultural study of androgyny, Wendy Doniger O'Flaherty asserts that the androgyne expresses "conflict between one sex's need for and fear of the other, . . . primarily the male's need for and fear of the female." She concludes: "Dangling before us the sweet promise of equality and balance, symbiosis and mutuality, the androgyne, under closer analysis, often furnishes bitter testimony to conflict and aggression, tension and disequilibrium" (*Women, Androgynes, and Other Mythical Beasts* [Chicago: University of Chicago Press, 1980], pp. 331, 334).

50. See, for example, the letter from "Hard Rockin' and Homosexual, Boston, Massachusetts," in *RIP*, August 1989, p. 5; and a letter decrying sexism in metal by a female musician in *RIP*, May 1989, p. 5.

51. Philip Gordon, "Review of Tipper Gore's *Raising PG Kids in an X-Rated Society* and *Dee Snider's Teenage Survival Guide*," *Popular Music* 8:1 (January 1989), p. 122.

52. Kaplan, *Rocking around the Clock*, p. 72.

53. Fred Pfeil, "Postmodernism as a 'Structure of Feeling,'" in *Marxism and the Interpretation of Culture*, ed. Cary Nelson and Lawrence Grossberg (Urbana: University of Illinois Press, 1988), pp. 381–403.

54. Fiske, *Television Culture*, p. 317. Moreover, such explorations are not unique to capitalist societies, nor are they reducible to epiphenomena of commerciality. From his study of the music of the Venda people of South Africa, ethnomusicologist John Blacking learned that fantastic music is not an escape from reality; it is a creative exploration of reality, and of other possibilities (*How Musical Is Man?* [Seattle: University of Washington Press, 1973], p. 28).

55. Simon Frith and Angela McRobbie, "Rock and Sexuality," *Screen Education* 29 (1978–79), pp. 3–19.

56. See George Lipsitz, *Time Passages: Collective Memory and American Popular Culture* (Minneapolis: University of Minnesota Press, 1990), p. 102.

Chapter 5. Can I Play with Madness? (Notes to Pages 137–71)

1. Charles Baudelaire, "To the Reader," in *The Flowers of Evil: A Selection*, ed. Marthiel and Jackson Mathews (New York: New Directions, 1958), p. 3; this translation is by Roy Campbell.

2. See the excerpt from Quintilian's writings in Piero Weiss and Richard Taruskin, eds., *Music in the Western World: A History in Documents* (New York: Schirmer, 1984), pp. 12–15.

3. See James R. McDonald, "Censoring Rock Lyrics: A Historical Analysis of the Debate," *Youth and Society* 19:3 (March 1988); pp. 294–313.

4. Tipper Gore, *Raising PG Kids in an X-Rated Society* (Nashville, Tenn.: Abingdon Press, 1987). Snider, the lead singer for the heavy metal band Twisted Sister, has even written a book to help adolescents cope with their problems: Dee Snider and Philip Bashe, *Dee Snider's Teenage Survival Guide* (Garden City, N.Y.: Doubleday, 1987).

5. Gore, *Raising PG Kids*, p. 19. Subcultures and countercultures are often seen as marking a crisis in authority; a more useful formulation conceives of

such crises as breakdowns in the "reproduction of culture-class relations and identities." See John Clarke, Stuart Hall, Tony Jefferson, and Brian Roberts, "Sub Cultures, Cultures, and Class," in *Culture, Ideology and Social Process: A Reader*, ed. Tony Bennett, Graham Martin, Colin Mercer, and Janet Woollacott (London: B. T. Batsford, 1981), p. 73.

6. Joe Stuessy, "The Heavy Metal User's Manual," 18 pages, photocopied and privately circulated. Stuessy is professor of music at the University of Texas at San Antonio. I wish to thank him for sending me copies of his pamphlet and his notes for his Senate testimony.

7. Joe Stuessy, notes for testimony to U.S. Senate Commerce Committee, 19 September 1985, p. 6.

8. This sample includes all of the lyrics printed in *Hit Parader's Metal of the 80s*, Spring 1990, and *Hit Parader's Top 100 Metal Albums*, Spring 1989. Of course, lyrics about drugs can be at once moralistic and celebratory, which is why I offer this survey of lyrics only to make a limited point about the sorts of topics that are typically addressed in metal songs. *Interpretation* of songs must be much more complex. But critics' hysteria notwithstanding, as Jon Pareles says, "In all of rock, there are probably fewer songs about bestiality than about molecular biology" (*New York Times*, 11 February 1990, p. H30).

9. Harry Shapiro, *Waiting for the Man: The Story of Drugs and Popular Music* (New York: William Morrow, 1988), p. 121.

10. See Paul E. Willis, "The Cultural Meaning of Drug Use," in Stuart Hall and Tony Jefferson, eds., *Resistance Through Rituals: Youth Subcultures in Post-War Britain* (London: Hutchinson, 1976), pp. 106–18.

11. See, for example, the comments by Accept's Stefan Kaufmann in *The Best of Metal Mania* #2 (1987), p. 66, and by star drummer Tommy Aldridge in Andy Doerschuk, "The Big Heavy Picture," *Drums and Drumming*, August/ September 1990, p. 47.

12. Peter F. Ostwald, *Schumann: The Inner Voices of a Musical Genius* (Boston: Northeastern University Press, 1985), p. 191.

13. Stuessy, "User's Manual," p. 16.

14. Stuessy, "User's Manual," p. 6.

15. Stuessy, testimony, p. 8.

16. Berlioz ends his symphony with the triumphant frenzy of a witches' Sabbath.

17. The creation of "classical music" and its aesthetic ideology have been discussed in previous chapters.

18. Carl A. Raschke, *Painted Black: From Drug Killings to Heavy Metal—the Alarming True Story of How Satanism Is Terrorizing Our Communities* (San Francisco: Harper & Row, 1990), p. 170. Compare Dan Peters and Steve Peters, with Cher Merrill, *Why Knock Rock?* (Minneapolis: Bethany House, 1984); Steve Lawhead, *Rock of This Age: The Real and Imagined Dangers of Rock Music* (Downers Grove, Ill.: InterVarsity Press, 1987); Bob Larson, *Larson's Book of Rock* (Wheaton, Ill.: Tyndale House, 1987).

19. Raschke, *Painted Black*, pp. 56, 170, 244.

20. Raschke, *Painted Black*, p. 170. Raschke incorrectly cites the source of the article.

21. Raschke, *Painted Black*, p. 175.

22. Raschke, *Painted Black*, p. 246. Another study has charged that right-wing and religious groups have manufactured the Satanist threat; its authors claim that there are fewer than one thousand actual Satanists in the United States, that they are members of a religion protected by the First Amendment, and that none of them has been linked to any ritual crimes. See David Alexan-

der, "Giving the Devil More Than His Due," *The Humanist*, March/April 1990, pp. 5–14, 34.

23. For a real cause of statistically significant suicide, we might look to deindustrialization: "In the aftermath of the Federal Mogul Corporation closing of its roller-bearing plant in Detroit, eight of the nearly 2,000 affected workers took their own lives. This macabre statistic is unfortunately not unusual. In their study of displaced workers, Cobb and Kasl found a suicide rate 'thirty times the expected number'" (Barry Bluestone and Bennett Harrison, *The Deindustrialization of America: Plant Closings, Community Abandonment, and the Dismantling of Basic Industry* [New York: Basic Books, 1982], p. 65).

24. Raschke, *Painted Black*, p. 164. Ephasis added.

25. See *Rock and Roll Confidential*, September 1991, p. 2.

26. Gore, *Raising PG Kids*, p. 118.

27. "Portrait," *The Chronicle of Higher Education*, 9 January 1991, p. A3.

28. See Jane Fulcher, *The Nation's Image: French Grand Opera as Politics and Politicized Art* (Cambridge: Cambridge University Press, 1987), pp. 38, 88, 101–2; and Lawrence W. Levine, *Highbrow/Lowbrow: The Emergence of Cultural Hierarchy in America* (Cambridge, Mass.: Harvard University Press, 1988), pp. 61–65, 91.

29. Deena Weinstein, *Heavy Metal: A Cultural Sociology* (New York: Lexington Books, 1991), p. 181.

30. Jonathon S. Epstein, David J. Pratto, and James K. Skipper, Jr., "Teenagers, Behavioral Problems, and Preferences for Heavy Metal and Rap Music: A Case Study of a Southern Middle School," *Deviant Behavior* 11 (1990), pp. 381–94.

31. For a striking ethnographic refutation of this view, see the forthcoming collection of interviews with a variety of people about how they use music in their lives: *My Music*, edited by Susan D. Crafts, Daniel Cavicchi, and Charles Keil, to be published in 1993 by University Press of New England.

32. Jack Sholder (director), *The Hidden* (New Line Cinema and Heron Communications, 1987).

33. Ivan Solotaroff, "Subliminal Criminals: Judas Priest in the Promised Land," *Village Voice*, 4 September 1990, pp. 24–34.

34. The Editors of Rock & Roll Confidential, *You've Got a Right to Rock* (Duke & Duchess Ventures, 1990), p. 21.

35. *Minneapolis Star/Tribune*, 18 July 1990.

36. Dean Kuipers, "Executioner's Song," *Spin*, November 1990, p. 66.

37. Doug Ireland, "Press Clips," *Village Voice*, 20 March 1990, p. 9. Key was taken very seriously by many people; he also appeared on CNN's Larry King Live and in Jack Anderson's syndicated column.

38. John R. Vokey and J. B. Read, "Subliminal Messages: Between the Devil and the Media," *American Psychologist* 40:11 (1985), pp. 1231–39. See also S. B. Thorne and P. Himelstein, "The Role of Suggestion in the Reception of Satanic Messages in Rock and Roll Recordings," *Journal of Psychology* 116 (1984), pp. 245–48.

39. Solotaroff, "Subliminal Criminals," p. 34.

40. Kuipers, "Executioner's Song," p. 66.

41. See *Variety*, 6 November 1985, p. 2. Another suit concerning the same song was filed in 1989, but as in the Judas Priest case, the plaintiff alleged that subliminal messages were at fault rather than lyrics.

42. Including Heinrich Schütz, who used antiphonal choirs to achieve precisely that effect in his "Saul, Saul, was verfolgst du mich?" from his *Symphoniae Sacrae III* of 1650.

43. In a typical display of "Let's be nice and not talk about bad things" reactionary politics, *The Rock Rating Report*, endorsed by the PMRC, gave Phil Collins an extremely negative rating for opposing homelessness (The Editors of Rock & Roll Confidential, *You've Got a Right to Rock*, pp. 20–21).

44. Kuipers, "Executioner's Song," p. 66.

45. Solotaroff, "Subliminal Criminals," p. 34.

46. Patrick Goldstein, "Is Rock a Scapegoat for Teen Suicide?" *Los Angeles Times Calendar*, Sunday, 8 May 1988, p. 98.

47. David Fricke, "Heavy Metal Justice," *Rolling Stone*, 12 January 1989, p. 77. Another fan told me that "Fade to Black" made him realize how stupid suicide would be and helped get him motivated to make something of his life.

48. Gene Hoglan, quoted in Mike Gitter, "The Hellish Thrash of Dark Angel," *RIP*, June 1989, p. 94.

49. *New York Times*, 10 February 1985, p. A23.

50. Donna Gaines, *Teenage Wasteland: Suburbia's Dead End Kids* (New York: Pantheon, 1990), p. 253.

51. George H. Gallup, Jr., and Frank Newport, "Belief in Paranormal Phenomena among Adult Americans," *Sceptical Inquirer* 15:2 (Winter 1991), pp. 137–46. Catholics and members of some other denominations, of course, are required to believe in the Devil.

52. Mary Toledo, "Roll Over Lugosi," *The Best of Metal Mania #2* (1987), p. 84.

53. Rita, interview with author, 30 June 1989, Maplewood, Minn.

54. Both of these songs appear on *Live after Death* (1985).

55. For the former, see "No Prayer for the Dying" and "Fates Warning" on *No Prayer for the Dying* (1990). On the topics of violence and combat, see, for example, "Tailgunner," "Run Silent," and "Assassin," from *No Prayer for the Dying* (1990), and "Aces High," "Flash of the Blade," and "The Duellists," from *Powerslave* (1984).

56. As he appears on the cover of *Seventh Son of a Seventh Son*, Eddie is the best illustration I've seen of what Deleuze and Guattari call "the body without organs"—or in this case, the body with organs à la carte.

57. Eddie made his usual appearance at the concert I attended in 1988, garbed this time in a mummy's rags, but the band seems to be tiring of him, and his manifestation was perfunctory that night.

58. See Fredric Jameson, "Postmodernism and Consumer Society," in *The Anti-Aethetic: Essays on Postmodern Culture*, ed. Hal Foster (Port Townsend, Wash.: Bay Press, 1983), pp. 111–25. Jameson has since retreated somewhat from this position; see his revision of this essay in his *Postmodernism, or, The Cultural Logic of Late Capitalism* (Durham, N.C.: Duke University Press, 1991), pp. 1–54. Jameson's earlier formulation remains influential, however.

59. Gaines, *Teenage Wasteland*, p. 183.

60. Roy Porter, *A Social History of Madness: The World through the Eyes of the Insane* (New York: E. P. Dutton, 1989), pp. 3, 25. Artists have often cultivated madness or its signs, particularly in the nineteenth century. Porter describes Robert Schumann's engagement with artistic madness:

> What first drew attention to him as a musician was his astonishing gift of improvising at the piano, especially his capacity to conjure up music which perfectly captured someone's mood or character. This he called "fantasizing" or "mad improvising." He would often describe such elation as a form of madness. As such it was a hallmark of his genius. This was not merely an affectation, an adolescent self-indulgence. Rather it was a crucial milepost in the attempt to establish an identity which would advance his career, win

acceptance and recognition, and fulfill his "promise." . . . It was [also] a way of coming to terms with a deep unease towards the world." (p. 66)

61. Wolf Marshall discusses this characteristic rhythmic pattern in "Music Appreciation: Iron Maiden," *Guitar for the Practicing Musician*, January 1989, pp. 112–16.

62. Dave Marsh has tried to convince me that there is only one possible interpretation of McLean's lyrics, but surely many people have enjoyed this song while understanding it "incorrectly"—me, for instance.

63. Dana Polan, "Postmodernism and Cultural Analysis Today," in *Postmodernism and Its Discontents: Theories, Practices*, ed. E. Ann Kaplan (New York: Verso, 1988), p. 53.

64. Teri Saccone, "Somewhere on the Light Side of the Moon," *Rock Scene*, July 1987, p. 64.

65. Gaines, *Teenage Wasteland*, p. 254.

66. Stephen King, *Four Past Midnight* (New York: Penguin, 1990), p. 608.

67. See James B. Twitchell, *Dreadful Pleasures: An Anatomy of Modern Horror* (New York: Oxford University Press, 1985), and Noël Carroll, *The Philosophy of Horror, or, Paradoxes of the Heart* (New York: Routledge, 1990).

68. See Michael Ryan and Douglas Kellner, *Camera Politica: The Politics and Ideology of Contemporary Hollywood Film* (Bloomington: Indiana University Press, 1988), p. 170. Stephen King makes the same point in his analytical history of horror, *Stephen King's Danse Macabre* (New York: Berkeley Books, 1981), p. 28.

69. Ryan and Kellner, *Camera Politica*, p. 170.

70. Barbara Ehrenreich, "Marginal Men," in *The Worst Years of Our Lives* (New York: Pantheon, 1990), pp. 208–12.

71. *Rock & Roll Confidential*, January 1989, p. 8. That metal audiences have been gender-balanced since the mid-1980s may owe something to the fact that many women are finding such economic statistics more directly relevant to their lives than ever before.

72. Alexander Cockburn, "Beat the Devil," *The Nation*, 18 June 1990, p. 846.

73. Tim Wise, "Accounts Payable," *The Nation*, 18 June 1990, p. 845.

74. Barbara Ehrenreich, *Fear of Falling: The Inner Life of the Middle Class* (New York: HarperCollins, 1990), p. 205. Needless to say, economic security and social well-being in the United Kingdom, the most important source and site of heavy metal culture after the United States, also have dwindled.

75. John Podhoretz, "Metallic Rock That's Designed to Shock," *U.S. News and World Report*, 7 September 1987, p. 50. There are exceptions; during one interview I conducted, discussion turned to nuclear war, and one fan's comments reflected a nihilism born of helplessness and alienation from those who have the power to "vaporize us any minute." "Just get it over with," he said; "I've often wanted them to do that; felt like, all right, push the button right now; it'd be cool." But the other fans in the group disagreed emphatically. (Five metal fans, interview with the author, Spring Lake Park, Minn., 7 July 1988). All the same, nihilism is a complex concept: "The true nihilists are the ones who oppose nihilism with their more and more faded positivities, the ones who are thus conspiring with all extant malice, and eventually with the destructive principle itself. Thought honors itself by defending what is damned as nihilism" (Theodor W. Adorno, *Negative Dialectics* [New York: Continuum, 1973], p. 381). Nihilism is always political; James C. Scott relates: "Alice Walker began a speech at a nuclear disarmament rally with . . . an effort to explain why many blacks were not much interested in signing nuclear freeze petitions. Their 'hope for revenge' made them look on nuclear destruction brought about by a white-ruled world with equanimity if not malevolent pleasure. One has, she implies,

no right expecting civic spiritedness from those whose experience of community has mostly been that of victims" (James C. Scott, *Domination and the Arts of Resistance: Hidden Transcripts* [New Haven, Conn.: Yale University Press, 1990], p. 43).

76. Marty Jezer, *The Dark Ages: Life in the United States 1945–1960* (Boston: South End Press, 1982), p. 237.

77. John Fiske, *Understanding Popular Culture* (Boston: Unwin Hyman, 1989), pp. 134–35.

78. Compare Jeffrey Arnett's finding that metal fans are best categorized politically as libertarian, in "Adolescents and Heavy Metal Music: From the Mouths of Metalheads," *Youth & Society* 23:1 (September 1991), p. 90.

79. Danny Sugerman, *Appetite for Destruction: The Days of Guns N' Roses* (New York: St. Martin's Press, 1991).

80. Sugerman, *Appetite for Destruction*, pp. 92, 96.

81. Sugerman, *Appetite for Destruction*, p. 108. For similar interpretations of rock music, see also Jerry Hopkins and Daniel Sugerman, *No One Here Gets Out Alive* (New York: Warner Books, 1980), and Oliver Stone's film, *The Doors* (1991). Deena Weinstein also mystifies and depoliticizes heavy metal in just this way in her book *Heavy Metal*, especially pp. 35–43.

82. It should not be but probably is necessary to state that by discussing and quoting Marx I am not signaling my endorsement of any of the social plans that have been proposed or attacked in his name. Every social/economic system has its hazards, and Marx's critique of capitalism still offers insights into the pains and joys of contemporary culture.

83. Marshall Berman, *All That Is Solid Melts into Air: The Experience of Modernity* (New York: Simon and Schuster, 1982), p. 102.

84. Berman, *All That Is Solid*, p. 118. Of course, Rose and Berman have different projects and intentions; I am bracketing them to see what we can learn by taking them equally seriously, for strict divisions between "high" and "low" culture (which are constructed categories serving particular interests) conceal more than they reveal.

85. Berman, *All That Is Solid*, p. 102.

86. Karl Marx and Frederick Engels, *Manifesto of the Communist Party* (1848; reprint, Moscow: Progress Publishers, 1971) pp. 34–35. Along with the difficulties faced by struggling bands everywhere, there is "pay-for-play" in L.A.— bands often have to pay club owners as much as $800 in exchange for the exposure gained from being allowed to play a 45-minute set at an important venue. This figure is drawn from my interviews with a number of L.A. metal bands; see also Janiss Garcia, "Guns N' Roses," *Guitar for the Practicing Musician*, February 1989, pp. 81–90.

87. Sugerman, *Appetite for Destruction*, pp. 93, 85.

88. Quoted in Sugerman, *Appetite for Destruction*, p. 63.

89. Sugerman dwells on this idea throughout his book. An earlier book tried to explain rock music entirely in these terms: Robert Pattison, *The Triumph of Vulgarity: Rock Music in the Mirror of Romanticism* (New York: Oxford University Press, 1987).

90. Sugerman, *Appetite for Destruction*, p. 102.

91. Examples abound in recent popular music; two of the most effective are Dolly Parton's "9 to 5" (1980) and Madonna's "Like a Prayer" (1989).

92. Berman, *All That Is Solid*, p. 23.

93. Richard Taruskin, "Facing Up, Finally, to Bach's Dark Vision," *New York Times*, 25 January 1991, p. 28.

94. Taruskin, "Facing Up," p. 28. Here Taruskin follows in the footsteps

of Theodor Adorno and Susan McClary, both of whom have published essays that strive to reclaim the noise and politics of Bach's music. See Theodor W. Adorno, "Bach Defended against His Devotees," in *Prisms* (Cambridge, Mass.: MIT Press, 1981), pp. 133–46; and Susan McClary, "The Blasphemy of Talking Politics during Bach Year," in *Music and Society: The Politics of Composition, Performance, and Reception*, ed. Richard Leppert and Susan McClary (Cambridge: Cambridge University Press, 1987), pp. 13–62.

Select Discography

AC/DC. *High Voltage*. Atco, 1976.
——. *Highway to Hell*. Atlantic, 1979.
——. *Back in Black*. Atlantic, 1980.
——. *Dirty Deeds Done Dirt Cheap*. Atlantic, 1981.
——. *For Those About to Rock We Salute You*. Atlantic, 1981.
——. *Blow Up Your Video*. Atlantic, 1988.
——. *The Razors Edge*. Atco, 1990.
Accept. *Accept*. Passport, 1980.
——. *Balls to the Wall*. Portrait/ CBS, 1984.
——. *Russian Roulette*. Portrait/ CBS, 1986.
Aerosmith. *Rocks*. Columbia, 1976.
——. *Permanent Vacation*. Geffen, 1987.
Alice Cooper. *Love It to Death*. Warner Bros., 1971.
Anthrax. *State of Euphoria*. Megaforce/Island, 1988.
——. *Persistence of Time*. Megaforce/Island, 1990.
Black Sabbath. *Black Sabbath*. Warner Bros., 1970.
——. *Paranoid*. Warner Bros., 1970.
——. *Sabbath Bloody Sabbath*. Warner Bros., 1974.
——. *Never Say Die!* Warner Bros., 1978.
Blue Cheer. *Vincebus Eruptum*. Philips, 1968.
——. *Louder Than God*. Rhino, 1986.
Blue Öyster Cult. *Agents of Fortune*. Columbia, 1976.
Bon Jovi. *7800° Fahrenheit*. Mercury, 1985.
——. *Slippery When Wet*. Mercury, 1986.
——. *New Jersey*. Mercury, 1988.
Cacophony. *Speed Metal Symphony*. Shrapnel, 1987.
Celtic Frost. *"Into the Pandemonium."* Combat, 1987.
Cinderella. *Long Cold Winter*. Mercury, 1988.
Deep Purple. *Deep Purple in Rock*. Harvest, 1970.
——. *Machine Head*. Warner Bros., 1972.
——. *Perfect Strangers*. Polydor, 1984.
Def Leppard. *Pyromania*. Mercury, 1983.
——. *Hysteria*. Mercury, 1987.
Dio. *The Last in Line*. Warner Bros., 1984.
Dokken. *Tooth and Nail*. Elektra, 1984.
——. *Back for the Attack*. Elektra, 1987.
Ford, Lita. *Lita*. BMG, 1988.
Girlschool. *Screaming Blue Murder*. Mercury, 1982.
Guns N' Roses. *Appetite for Destruction*. Geffen, 1987.

——. *G N' R Lies*. Geffen, 1988.
Hendrix, Jimi. *The Essential Jimi Hendrix*. Reprise, 1989.
Impaler. *Rise of the Mutants*. Important, 1985.
Iron Butterfly. *In-A-Gadda-Da-Vida*. Atco, 1968.
Iron Maiden. *The Number of the Beast*. EMI, 1982.
——. *Powerslave*. Capitol, 1984.
——. *Live after Death*. Capitol, 1985.
——. *Seventh Son of a Seventh Son*. EMI, 1988.
——. *No Prayer for the Dying*. Epic, 1990.
The Jimi Hendrix Experience. *Are You Experienced?* Reprise, 1967.
Judas Priest. *Sin after Sin*. Columbia, 1977.
——. *Stained Class*. Columbia, 1978.
——. *Unleashed in the East*. Columbia, 1979.
——. *British Steel*. Columbia, 1980.
——. *Point of Entry*. Columbia, 1981.
——. *Screaming for Vengeance*. Columbia, 1982.
——. *Defenders of the Faith*. Columbia, 1984.
——. *Turbo*. Columbia, 1986.
——. *Ram It Down*. Columbia, 1988.
——. *Painkiller*. Columbia, 1990.
King Diamond. *Fatal Portrait*. Roadracer, 1986.
Kiss. *Alive*. Casablanca, 1975.
——. *Destroyer*. Casablanca, 1976.
Krokus. *One Vice at a Time*. Arista, 1982.
Led Zeppelin. *Led Zeppelin*. Atlantic, 1969.
——. *Led Zeppelin II*. Atlantic, 1969.
——. *Led Zeppelin III*. Atlantic, 1970.
——. *ZOSO [IV]*. Atlantic, 1971.
——. *Physical Graffiti*. Swan Song, 1975.
Living Colour. *Vivid*. Epic, 1988.
——. *Time's Up*. Epic, 1990.

Loudness. *Thunder in the East*. Atco, 1985.
Lynch Mob. *Wicked Sensation*. Elektra, 1990.
Megadeth. *Peace Sells . . . But Who's Buying?* Combat/EMI, 1986.
——. *so far, so good . . . so what!* Combat/Capitol, 1988.
——. *Rust in Peace*. Combat/Capitol, 1990.
Metallica. *Kill 'Em All*. Important, 1983.
——. *Ride the Lightning*. Megaforce/Elektra, 1984.
——. *Master of Puppets*. Elektra, 1986.
——. *. . . And Justice for All*. Elektra, 1988.
——. *Metallica*. Elektra, 1991.
Michael Schenker Group. *MSG*. Chrysalis, 1981.
Mötley Crüe. *Shout at the Devil*. Elektra, 1983.
——. *Theatre of Pain*. Elektra, 1985.
——. *Girls, Girls, Girls*. Elektra, 1987.
Motörhead. *Live: No Sleep 'til Hammersmith*. Mercury, 1981.
——. *No Sleep at All*. Enigma/GWR, 1988.
MX Machine. *Manic Panic*. Restless Records, 1988.
Nazareth. *2XS*. A&M, 1982.
Nugent, Ted. *Great Gonzos: The Best of Ted Nugent*. Epic, 1981.
——. *If You Can't Lick 'Em . . . Lick 'Em*. Atlantic, 1988.
Ozzy Osbourne. *Blizzard of Ozz*. Jet/CBS, 1981.
——. *Diary of a Madman*. Jet/CBS, 1981.
——. *The Ultimate Sin*. CBS, 1986.
——. *No Rest for the Wicked*. CBS, 1988.
——. *Just Say Ozzy*. CBS, 1990.
——. *No More Tears*. Epic Associated, 1991.
Ozzy Osbourne/Randy Rhoads. *Tribute*. CBS, 1987 [recorded in 1981].
Poison. *Look What the Cat Dragged In*. Enigma, 1986.

———. *Open Up and Say . . . Ahh!*
Enigma/Capitol, 1988.

Pokolgép. *Pokoli Szinjáték*. Start
(Hungary), 1987.

Possessed. *Beyond the Gates*. Combat, 1986.

Queensrÿche. *Operation: Mindcrime*.
EMI-Manhattan, 1988.

Quiet Riot. *Metal Health*. Pasha,
1983.

Racer X. *Street Lethal*. Shrapnel, 1986.

Rainbow. *Ritchie Blackmore's Rainbow*. Polydor, 1975.

———. *Difficult to Cure*. Polydor, 1981.

Ratt. *Out of the Cellar*. Atlantic, 1984.

Roth, David Lee. *Crazy from the Heat*. Warner Bros., 1985.

———. *Eat 'Em and Smile*. Warner
Bros., 1986.

———. *Skyscraper*. Warner Bros.,
1988.

———. *A Little Ain't Enough*. Warner
Bros., 1991.

Rush. *Moving Pictures*. Mercury, 1981.

Satriani, Joe. *Surfing with the Alien*.
Relativity, 1987.

———. *Flying in a Blue Dream*.
Relativity, 1989.

Scorpions. *In Trance*. RCA, 1976.

———. *Love at First Sting*. Mercury, 1984.

———. *Savage Amusement*. Mercury, 1988.

Slave Raider. *What Do You Know
about Rock 'n Roll?* BMG, 1988.

Slayer. *South of Heaven*. Def Jam,
1988.

———. *Seasons in the Abyss*. Def
American, 1990.

Steppenwolf. *Steppenwolf*. Stateside, 1968.

———. *16 Greatest Hits*. MCA, 1973.

Stryper. *To Hell with the Devil*.
Enigma, 1986.

Testament. *Souls of Black*. Megaforce/
Atlantic, 1990.

Twisted Sister. *Under the Blade*. Roadrunner, 1982.

———. *Stay Hungry*. Atlantic, 1984.

UFO. *Obsession*. Chrysalis, 1978.

Van Halen. *Van Halen*. Warner
Bros., 1978.

———. *Van Halen II*. Warner
Bros., 1979.

———. *Diver Down*. Warner Bros.,
1982.

———. *1984*. Warner Bros., 1983.

———. *5150*. Warner Bros., 1986.

———. *OU812*. Warner Bros., 1988.

Vinnie Vincent. *Invasion*.
Chrysalis, 1986.

Virus. *Pray for War*. Metalworks,
1987.

Voivod. *Dimension Hatröss*. Noise
International, 1988.

W.A.S.P. *Live . . . in the Raw*. Capitol, 1987.

———. *The Headless Children*. Capitol, 1989.

Warlock. *True as Steel*. Mercury, 1986.

Whitesnake. *Whitesnake*. Geffen,
1987.

———. *Slip of the Tongue*.
Geffen, 1989.

Y&T. *In Rock We Trust*. A&M, 1984.

Yngwie J. Malmsteen's Rising Force.
Yngwie J. Malmsteen's Rising Force.
Polydor, 1984.

———. *Odyssey*. Polydor, 1988.

Select Bibliography

✳

Adorno, Theodor W. *Prisms*. Cambridge, Mass.: MIT Press, 1981.

Aledort, Andy. "The Bach Influence." *Guitar for the Practicing Musician*, May 1985, pp. 30–31.

———. "Thrashing It Out." *Guitar for the Practicing Musician*, March 1988, pp. 62–64.

Armington, Nick, and Lars Lofas. "The Genesis of Metal." *Drums and Drumming*, August/September 1990, pp. 21–25, 27, 62–64.

Arnett, Jeffrey. "Adolescents and Heavy Metal Music: From the Mouths of Metalheads." *Youth & Society* 23:1 (September 1991), pp. 76–98.

Bakhtin, M. M. *The Dialogic Imagination*. Austin: University of Texas Press, 1981.

———. *Speech Genres and Other Late Essays*. Edited by Caryl Emerson and Michael Holquist. Austin: University of Texas Press, 1986.

Bangs, Lester. "Heavy Metal." In *The Rolling Stone Illustrated History of Rock & Roll*, 2d ed., edited by Jim Miller, pp. 332–35. New York: Random House, 1980.

Bashe, Philip. *Heavy Metal Thunder*. Garden City, N.Y.: Doubleday, 1985.

Berger, John, Sven Blomberg, Chris Fox, Michael Dibb, and Richard Hollis. *Ways of Seeing*. London: British Broadcasting Corporation, 1972.

Berman, Marshall. *All That Is Solid Melts Into Air: The Experience of Modernity*. New York: Simon and Schuster, 1982.

Blacking, John. *How Musical Is Man?* Seattle: University of Washington Press, 1973.

Blanchet, Philippe. *Heavy Metal Story*. Paris: Calmann-Levy, 1985.

Bluestone, Barry, and Bennett Harrison. *The Deindustrialization of America: Plant Closings, Community Abandonment, and the Dismantling of Basic Industry*. New York: Basic Books, 1982.

Breen, Marcus. "A Stairway to Heaven or a Highway to Hell?: Heavy Metal Rock Music in the 1990s." *Cultural Studies* 5:2 (May 1991), pp. 191–203.

Brittan, Arthur. *Masculinity and Power*. New York: Basil Blackwell, 1989.

Chapple, Steve, and Reebee Garofalo. *Rock 'n' Roll Is Here to Pay*. Chicago: Nelson-Hall, 1977.

Chernoff, John. *African Rhythm and African Sensibility*. Chicago: University of Chicago Press, 1979.

Clifford, James, and George E. Marcus, eds. *Writing Culture: The Poetics and Politics of Ethnography*. Berkeley: University of California Press, 1986.

Considine, J. D. "Purity and Power." *Musician*, September 1984, pp. 46–50.

Duncan, Robert. *The Noise: Notes from a Rock 'n' Roll Era*. New York: Ticknor and Fields, 1984.

Eagleton, Terry. *The Ideology of the Aesthetic*. Cambridge, Mass.: Basil Blackwell.

Edelstein, Robert. "The Last Heroes of Rock 'n' Roll." *Gallery*, April 1989, pp. 40–45, 73.

Eddy, Chuck. *Stairway to Hell: The 500 Best Heavy Metal Albums in the Universe*. New York: Harmony Books, 1991.

Ehrenreich, Barbara. *Fear of Falling: The Inner Life of the Middle Class*. New York: Harper Collins, 1989.

———. *The Worst Years of Our Lives: Irreverent Notes from a Decade of Greed*. New York: Pantheon, 1990.

Epstein, Jonathon S., David J. Pratto, and James K. Skipper, Jr. "Teenagers, Behavioral Problems, and Preferences for Heavy Metal and Rap Music: A Case Study of a Southern Middle School." *Deviant Behavior* 11 (1990): 381–94.

Feld, Steven. *Sound and Sentiment: Birds, Weeping, Poetics, and Song in Kaluli Expression*, 2d ed. Philadelphia: University of Pennsylvania Press, 1990.

Fiske, John. "British Cultural Studies and Television." In *Channels of Discourse: Television and Contemporary Criticism*, edited by Robert C. Allen, pp. 254–89. Chapel Hill: University of North Carolina Press, 1987.

———. *Television Culture*. New York: Methuen, 1987.

———. *Understanding Popular Culture*. Boston: Unwin Hyman, 1989.

Foster, Hal, ed. *The Anti-Aesthetic: Essays on Postmodern Culture*. Port Townsend, Wash.: Bay Press, 1983.

Foucault, Michel. *Language, Counter-memory, Practice*. Edited by Donald F. Bouchard. Ithaca, N.Y.: Cornell University Press, 1977.

Frith, Simon. "Art Versus Technology: The Strange Case of Popular Music." *Media, Culture, and Society* 8 (1986), pp. 263–79.

———. *Sound Effects: Youth, Leisure, and the Politics of Rock 'n' Roll*. New York: Pantheon, 1981.

———. "Towards an Aesthetic of Popular Music." In *Music and Society: The Politics of Composition, Performance, and Reception*, edited by Richard Leppert and Susan McClary, pp. 133–49. Cambridge: Cambridge University Press, 1987.

Frith, Simon, and Andrew Goodwin, eds. *On Record: Rock, Pop, and the Written Word*. New York: Pantheon, 1990.

Frith, Simon, and Angela McRobbie. "Rock and Sexuality." *Screen Education* 29 (1978–79). Reprinted in Frith and Goodwin, eds., *On Record*, pp. 371–89.

Gaines, Donna. *Teenage Wasteland: Suburbia's Dead End Kids*. New York: Pantheon, 1991.

Garofalo, Reebee. "How Autonomous Is Relative: Popular Music, the Social Formation and Cultural Struggle." *Popular Music* 6:1 (January 1987), pp. 77–92.

———, ed. *Rockin' the Boat: Mass Music and Mass Movements*. Boston: South End Press, 1992.

Gore, Tipper. *Raising PG Kids in an X-Rated Society*. Nashville, Tenn.: Abingdon Press, 1987.

Gramsci, Antonio. *Selections from the Prison Notebooks*. Edited by Quinton Hoare and Geoffrey Nowell Smith. New York: International Publishers, 1971.

Greenberg, Keith Elliot. *Heavy Metal*. Minneapolis, Minn.: Lerner Publications, 1986.

Hadley, Daniel J. "'Girls on Top': Women and Heavy Metal." Unpublished paper, Department of Communications, Concordia University, Montreal, 1991.

Halbersberg, Elianne. *Heavy Metal*. Cresskill, N.J.: Sharon Publications, 1985.

Halfin, Ross, and Pete Makowski. *Heavy Metal: The Power Age*. New York: Delilah Books, 1982.

Hall, Stuart. "Notes on Deconstructing 'The Popular.'" In *People's History and Socialist Theory*, edited by Raphael Samuel, pp. 227–40. London: Routledge and Kegan Paul, 1981.

Hamm, Charles. *Music in the New World*. New York: W. W. Norton, 1983.

Harrigan, Brian. *HM A-Z: The Definitive Encyclopedia of Heavy Metal from AC/DC through Led Zeppelin to ZZ Top*. London: Bobcat Books, 1981.

Harrigan, Brian, and Malcolm Dome. *Encyclopedia Metallica*. London: Omnibus Press, 1986.

The Heavy Metal Photo Book. London: Omnibus Press, 1983.

Hebdige, Dick. *Subculture: The Meaning of Style*. New York: Methuen, 1979.

Hit Parader's Top 100 Metal Albums, Spring 1989.

Hobsbawm, Eric, and Terence Ranger, eds. *The Invention of Tradition*. New York: Cambridge University Press, 1983.

Jameson, Fredric. "Reification and Utopia in Mass Culture." *Social Text* 1:1 (1979), pp. 130–48.

Jasper, Tony, and Derek Oliver. *The International Encyclopedia of Hard Rock and Heavy Metal*. New York: Facts on File, 1983.

Johnson, Mark. *The Body in the Mind: The Bodily Basis of Meaning, Imagination, and Reason*. Chicago: University of Chicago Press, 1987.

Kaplan, E. Ann. *Rocking Around the Clock: Music Television, Postmodernism, and Consumer Culture*. New York: Methuen, 1987.

King, Stephen. *Stephen King's Danse Macabre*. New York: Berkeley Books, 1981.

Laing, Dave. *One Chord Wonders: Power and Meaning in Punk Rock*. Philadelphia: Open University Press, 1985.

Leggett, Carol. *The Heavy Metal Bible*. New York: Pinnacle Books, 1985.

Leppert, Richard, and Susan McClary, eds. *Music and Society: The Politics of Composition, Performance, and Reception*. Cambridge: Cambridge University Press, 1987.

Levine, Lawrence W. *Highbrow/Lowbrow: The Emergence of Cultural Hierarchy in America*. Cambridge, Mass.: Harvard University Press, 1988.

Lewis, Lisa A. *Gender Politics and MTV: Voicing the Difference*. Philadelphia: Temple University Press, 1990.

Lipsitz, George. "'Ain't Nobody Here But Us Chickens': The Class Origins of Rock and Roll." In *Class and Culture in Cold War America: "A Rainbow at Midnight,"* pp. 195–225. South Hadley, Mass.: Bergin and Garvey, 1982.

———. *Time Passages: Collective Memory and American Popular Culture*. Minneapolis: University of Minnesota Press, 1990.

Lomax, Alan. *Folk Song Style and Culture*. New Brunswick, N.J.: Transaction Books, 1968.

Marcus, George E., and Michael M. J. Fischer. *Anthropology as Cultural Critique: An Experimental Moment in the Human Sciences*. Chicago: University of Chicago Press, 1986.

Marcus, Greil. *Mystery Train: Images of America in Rock 'n' Roll Music*, rev. ed. New York: E. P. Dutton, 1982.

Marsh, Dave. *The Heart of Rock and Soul: The 1001 Greatest Singles Ever Made*. New York: Plume, 1989.

———, ed. *The First Rock & Roll Confidential Report*. New York: Pantheon, 1985.

Marshall, Wolf. ". . . And Justice for All." *Guitar for the Practicing Musician*, June 1989, pp. 81–86, 136–38.

——. "The Classical Influence." *Guitar for the Practicing Musician*, March 1988, pp. 98–99, 102.

——. "Music Appreciation: Iron Maiden." *Guitar for the Practicing Musician*, January 1989, pp. 112–16.

Martin, Linda, and Kerry Segrave. *Anti-Rock: The Opposition to Rock 'n' Roll*. Hamden, Conn.: Archon Books, 1988.

Marx, Karl. *Capital*, vol. 1. New York: International Publishers, 1967.

Marx, Karl, and Frederick Engels. *Manifesto of the Communist Party*. Moscow: Progress Publishers, 1971.

McClary, Susan. "The Blasphemy of Talking Politics during Bach Year." In *Music and Society: The Politics of Composition, Performance, and Reception*, edited by Richard Leppert and Susan McClary, pp. 13–62. Cambridge: Cambridge University Press, 1987.

——. *Feminine Endings: Music, Gender, and Sexuality*. Minneapolis: University of Minnesota Press, 1991.

McClary, Susan, and Robert Walser. "Start Making Sense: Musicology Wrestles with Rock." In *On Record: Rock, Pop, and the Written Word*, edited by Simon Frith and Andrew Goodwin, pp. 277–92. New York: Pantheon, 1990.

Middleton, Richard. *Studying Popular Music*. Philadelphia: Open University Press, 1990.

Mulvey, Laura. "Visual Pleasure and Narrative Cinema." In *Movies and Methods*, vol. 2, edited by Bill Nichols, pp. 303–15. Berkeley: University of California Press, 1985.

Murray, Charles Shaar. *Crosstown Traffic: Jimi Hendrix and the Rock 'n' Roll Revolution*. New York: St. Martin's Press, 1989.

Nattiez, Jean-Jacques. *Music and Discourse: Toward a Semiology of Music*. Princeton, N.J.: Princeton University Press, 1990.

Newcomb, Horace M. "On the Dialogic Aspects of Mass Communication." *Critical Studies in Mass Communication* 1 (1984), pp. 34–50.

Obrecht, Jas, ed. *Masters of Heavy Metal*. New York: Quill, 1984.

Pfeil, Fred. "Postmodernism as a 'Structure of Feeling.'" In *Marxism and the Interpretation of Culture*, edited by Cary Nelson and Lawrence Grossberg, pp. 381–403. Urbana: University of Illinois Press, 1988.

Pielke, Robert G. *You Say You Want a Revolution: Rock Music in American Culture*. Chicago: Nelson-Hall, 1986.

Porter, Roy. *A Social History of Madness: The World through the Eyes of the Insane*. New York: E. P. Dutton, 1987.

Prinsky, Lorraine E., and Jill Leslie Rosenbaum. "'Leer-ics' or Lyrics: Teenage Impressions of Rock 'n' Roll." *Youth & Society* 18 : 4 (June 1987), pp. 384–97.

Radway, Janice A. *Reading the Romance: Women, Patriarchy, and Popular Literature*. Chapel Hill: University of North Carolina Press, 1984.

Raschke, Carl A. *Painted Black: From Drug Killings to Heavy Metal—the Alarming True Story of How Satanism Is Terrorizing Our Communities*. New York: Harper and Row, 1990.

Ryan, Michael, and Douglas Kellner. *Camera Politica: The Politics and Ideology of Contemporary Hollywood Film*. Bloomington: Indiana University Press, 1988.

Secher, Andy. "Heavy Metal: The Hall of Fame." *Hit Parader*, December 1982, pp. 25–27.

Shapiro, Harry. *Waiting for the Man: The Story of Drugs and Popular Music*. New York: William Morrow, 1988.

Shepherd, John. *Music as Social Text*. Cambridge: Polity Press, 1991.
Silverman, Kaja. "Fragments of a Fashionable Discourse." In *Studies in Entertainment: Critical Approaches to Mass Culture*, edited by Tania Modleski, pp. 139–52. Bloomington: Indiana University Press, 1986.
Simels, Steven. *Gender Chameleons: Androgyny in Rock 'n' Roll*. New York: Timbre Books, 1985.
Small, Christopher. *Music–Society–Education*. London: John Calder, 1980.
———. *Music of the Common Tongue: Survival and Celebration in Afro-American Music*. New York: Riverrun, 1987.
Straw, Will. "Characterizing Rock Music Cultures: The Case of Heavy Metal." *Canadian University Music Review* 5 (1984), pp. 104–22.
Street, John. *Rebel Rock: The Politics of Popular Music*. New York: Basil Blackwell, 1986.
Stuessy, Joe. "The Heavy Metal User's Manual." Photocopied typescript, privately circulated, San Antonio, Texas, 1985.
Sugerman, Danny. *Appetite for Destruction: The Days of Guns N' Roses*. New York: St. Martin's Press, 1991.
Szatmary, David P. *Rockin' in Time: A Social History of Rock and Roll*. Englewood Cliffs, N.J.: Prentice-Hall, 1987.
Tagg, Philip. "Analyzing Popular Music: Theory, Method, and Practice." *Popular Music* 2 (1982), pp. 37–67.
———. *Kojak—50 Seconds of Television Music*. Göteborg, Sweden: Musikvetenskapliga Institutionen, 1979.
———. "Musicology and the Semiotics of Popular Music." *Semiotica* 66–1/3 (1987), pp. 279–98.
Todorov, Tzvetan. *Genres in Discourse*. Cambridge: Cambridge University Press, 1990.
Tolinski, Brad. "Speed Kills: A Thinking Man's Guide to Thrash." *Guitar World*, October 1989, pp. 66–77, 128–29, 138.
Vološinov, V. N. *Marxism and the Philosophy of Language*. Cambridge, Mass.: Harvard University Press, 1986.
Walser, Robert. "The Body in the Music: Epistemology and Musical Semiotics," *College Music Symposium* 31:1 (forthcoming).
———. "Bon Jovi's Alloy: Discursive Fusion in Top 40 Pop Music." *OneTwoThreeFour* 7 (1989), pp. 7–19.
———. "Eruptions: Heavy Metal Appropriations of Classical Virtuosity." *Popular Music* 11:3 (1992), pp. 263–308.
———. "Musical Imagery and Performance Practice in J. S. Bach's Arias with Trumpet," *International Trumpet Guild Journal* 13:1 (September 1988), pp. 62–77.
———. "Out of Notes: Signification, Interpretation, and the Problem of Miles Davis." *Musical Quarterly* (forthcoming).
———. "The Polka Mass: Music of Postmodern Ethnicity." *American Music* 10:2 (Summer 1992), pp. 183–202.
———. "Review of *Origins of the Popular Style*, by Peter Van der Merwe." *Journal of Musicological Research* 12/1–2 (1992), pp. 123–32.
———. "What It Really, Really Means." *Esquire*, November 1991, pp. 130–32.
Ward, Ed, Geoffrey Stokes, and Ken Tucker. *Rock of Ages: The Rolling Stone History of Rock & Roll*. New York: Rolling Stone Press, 1986.
Weinstein, Deena. *Heavy Metal: A Cultural Sociology*. New York: Lexington Books, 1991.
Weiss, Piero, and Richard Taruskin, eds. *Music in the Western World: A History in Documents*. New York: Schirmer, 1984.

Wicke, Peter. *Rock Music: Culture, Aesthetics, and Sociology*. Cambridge: Cambridge University Press, 1990.

Wilder, Elin. "Heavy Metal: A Fan's Perspective." *High Times*, June 1988, pp. 32–39.

Young, Charles M. "Heavy Metal." *Musician*, September 1984, pp. 40–44.

Index

UNIVERSITY PRESS OF NEW ENGLAND publishes books under its own imprint and is the publisher for Brandeis University Press, Brown University Press, University of Connecticut, Dartmouth College, Middlebury College Press, University of New Hampshire, University of Rhode Island, Tufts University, University of Vermont, and Wesleyan University Press.

ROBERT WALSER is an Assistant Professor of Music at Dartmouth College. He holds doctoral degrees in musicology and musical performance from the University of Minnesota. He has long been active as a professional trumpet player, playing with jazz bands, polka bands, classical ensembles, and symphony orchestras, and as a guitar player, playing rock, country, world beat, and heavy metal.

Library of Congress Cataloging-in-Publication Data

Walser, Robert.
Running with the Devil : power, gender, and madness in heavy metal music / Robert Walser.
    p. cm.—(Music culture)
Includes bibliographical references, discography, and index.
ISBN 0–8195–5252–6 (cl).—ISBN 0–8195–6260–2
  1. Heavy metal (Music)—History and criticism.   I. Title.
II. Series.
ML3534.W29   1993
781.66—dc20   92–56911

and social skills in people with autism, uses a rich set of treatment procedures grounded in scientific principles, with current
research attesting to its efficacy. Indeed, if I had a child with

autism, I would definitely, with no question, select The Son-Rise Program to help him or her."

—Cynthia K. Thompson, Ph.D., distinguished professor
of communication sciences and neurology at
Northwestern University and world-renowned
researcher in the brain and language processing

"With *Autism Breakthrough*, Raun K. Kaufman has done what few else in the field of autism treatment today would dream of doing. He has empowered parents to take charge again, given them real hope for positive change, and armed them with specific tools and techniques to make those hopes a reality for their children. My own son fully recovered from autism to become the president of his sixth-grade class today (in a regular, mainstream school) thanks to my family's adoption of the very principles of The Son-Rise Program that Raun explains in *Autism Breakthrough*."

—Wendy Edwards, M.D.,
pediatrician, B. Sc. N., F.R.C. P. (C)

"Raun K. Kaufman's book, *Autism Breakthrough*, is an amazing resource to help you right here and right now to make a huge difference in your child's progress. His supereasy-to-digest guidance on using the techniques of The Son-Rise Program is a game changer. Given the program's record of success, the Autism Hope Alliance has funded families to take The Son-Rise Program courses at the Autism Treatment Center of America. My own son is the beneficiary of the principles explained in *Autism Breakthrough*. I gave birth to my son, but The Son-Rise Program gave him life." —Kristin Selby Gonzalez,
president, Autism Hope Alliance (AHA)

"Raun K. Kaufman has given humankind a roadmap for our journey to unravel the autism mystery. In my forty years in the field of disabilities, I have observed how well-intended behavior

Autism
Breakthrough

The groundbreaking method that has
helped families all over the world

RAUN K. KAUFMAN

Vermilion
LONDON

To my magnificent parents.
You believed in me when no one else did.
You helped me when no one else could.
You've been there for me like no one else has.
"Thank you" doesn't even scratch the surface.

To the wonderful staff of the
Autism Treatment Center of America.
My colleagues, my partners, my dear friends.
You've given such love and caring to so many families.
It's been my joy and privilege to walk this path with you.

To all the parents out there with special children.
You possess a depth and intensity of love for your children
that nobody else in the world can touch.
I hope that, by the end of this book, you will see that you are
the best thing that ever happened to your children.

To all you special kids still waiting for the people
around you to see and appreciate your specialness.
You're perfect exactly as you are.
And there's nothing you can't accomplish.

CONTENTS

Autism
Breakthrough

ONE

My Recovery from Autism and the Myth of False Hope

You LOVE YOUR child more than anything in the world.

In the early days of your child's life, long before any diagnosis was made, there may have been a hundred different hopes, dreams, and plans you had for your child. Maybe some were as simple as cuddling with your child or playing peek-a-boo. Perhaps some were as far-reaching as your child's high school graduation or wedding day.

But then your child was diagnosed with an autism spectrum disorder.

You may have felt that many doors were suddenly closed to the child you love because this diagnosis is often accompanied by a long list of dire predictions.

Your child will never talk.

Your child will never have friends.

Your child will never hold your hand.

Your child will never have a job or get married.

Perhaps even: your child will never love you.

You may have been told to discard many of those hopes and dreams and be "realistic" in the face of your child's diagnosis. Certainly, there are many, many parents who have heard the pronouncement: "Autism is a lifelong condition."

No one could fault you for feeling grief-stricken, scared, or even angry. You have just been told all of the things your child will never accomplish—as if it had been decided ahead of time. But before reading any further, it is crucial that you understand this: you don't have to accept the limits placed upon your child.

Your child has the capacity for learning and communicating, for experiencing real happiness, and developing warm, loving, and satisfying relationships. Your son or daughter can learn to enjoy affection, play a game, and laugh at something silly. He or she can learn to savor the experience of being hugged or held by you. That moment when your child spontaneously looks into your eyes with genuine joy and connection—that is something you can have, not just for a fleeting second but on a sustained basis. Do you ever imagine your child playing football, joining you on a bike ride, going on a skiing trip with you, playing with other kids at the park, or doing something in the future such as going to college? These events are possible. Children on the autism spectrum are capable of great change, including recovery.

Who am I to tell you this? I'm someone who's been there—not where *you* are, but where *your child* is.

I used to be autistic.

I know, I know. That one's a bit hard to digest. You don't often find "used to be" and "autistic" in the same sentence. This is truly unfortunate, because it points to the intense pessimism and utter hopelessness with which autism is viewed by the people doing the diagnosing. Do you know what my chances of recovery were, according to the specialists assessing me?

Zero percent.

That's right: 0%.

Here's what happened.

MY STORY

When I was a young boy, my parents (authors and teachers Barry Neil Kaufman and Samahria Lyte Kaufman) saw that I was developing very differently from my two older sisters. I cried incessantly and inconsolably. When I was picked up, I let my arms dangle loosely at my sides.

Before my first birthday, I suffered a severe ear and throat infection, compounded by a violent allergic reaction to the antibiotics prescribed. My life briefly hung in the balance. After a battery of hearing tests, my parents were told that I appeared deaf. As months passed, I seemed increasingly cut off, spiraling ever deeper into my own world.

I stopped responding to my name.

I ceased making eye contact.

I appeared alternately repulsed by and oblivious to the sights and sounds around me.

I appeared deaf to a loud noise right next to me and then mesmerized by an almost inaudible whisper in the next room.

I lost all interest in other people, but I would remain transfixed by inanimate objects, staring at a pen, a mark on the wall, even my own hands, for long periods of time.

I didn't want to be touched or held.

I spoke not a word (nor did I cry, yell, point, or do anything to communicate my wishes), displaying a total muteness that stood in sharp contrast to my earlier crying marathons.

And then something startling: I became fascinated with the simplest of repetitive activities, spinning plates on their edges for hours on the floor, rocking back and forth, flapping my hands in front of my face.

As my condition worsened, my parents raced from specialist to specialist, trying to find out what was wrong. Tests. Tapping pencils. Shaking heads. More tests. (Keep in mind that, in 1973, the year I was born, autism was much less common than it is now, affecting one out of every five thousand children. The latest study from the US Centers for Disease Control and Prevention (CDC) puts the incidence of autism at one out of every fifty children while in the UK the National Autistic Society gives a figure of one in one hundred children.) Soon I was diagnosed as severely autistic. My parents were informed that my IQ was less than 30.

What can feel like a devastating diagnosis is not really due to the autism diagnosis itself. The devastation comes primarily from the *prognosis*—all the things parents are told that their child will not do and cannot accomplish.

Like many parents today, my parents were told that the prognosis was certain. I would never speak or communicate in any meaningful way. I would never prefer people over objects. I would never emerge from my solitary world and be "normal." Moreover, I would never go to college, have a career, or play football. I would never fall in love, drive a car, or write a poem. I might, one day, be able to dress myself or eat with utensils, but that was the ceiling of my possibilities.

My parents, seeking solutions, were given only grim pronouncements. They searched for a light at the end of the tunnel and were given only dark predictions. Over and over again, it was drilled into my parents' heads: autism is a lifelong condition. The specialists explained that, when I got older, my parents would need to look into permanent institutionalization so that I could be properly looked after.

I am still astounded at what my mother and father chose to do in the face of such a damning verdict. They didn't believe what they were told. They didn't write me off. Instead, they turned their backs on all the dire prognoses. My parents looked at me and saw possibilities, not deficiencies. Instead of looking at me with fear, they viewed me with wonder.

And so they began an experiment. They began by seeking to create an environment where I felt truly safe. They didn't push me. They didn't try to change my behaviors. They sought first to understand me. Think about this for a moment. How often do we really do this—with *anyone*? People behave in ways we don't understand all the time. For most of us, our knee-jerk response is to try to get that person to change—whether that person is our partner, our friend, a shop assistant, an employee, our parent, or, indeed, our child. When do we ever *begin* our response by truly seeking to understand without pushing, to provide the other person with an experience of safety and caring without trying to get him or her to change? How amazing that my parents began from this most kind and useful place.

Having heard thousands of parents tell me about their experiences with their children's diagnosis and treatment, how they were given a laundry list of things "wrong" with their child, this description from the opening page of my father's book *Son-Rise: The Miracle Continues* touches me deeply:

> His little hands hold the plate delicately as his eyes survey its smooth perimeter. His mouth curls in delight. He is setting the stage. This is his moment, as was the last and each before. This is the beginning of his entry into the solitude that has become his world. Slowly, with a masterful hand, he places the edge of the plate on the floor, sets his body in a comfortable and balanced position, and snaps his wrist with great expertise. The plate begins to spin with dazzling perfection. It revolves on itself as if set in motion by some exacting machine. And it was.
>
> This is not an isolated act, not a mere aspect of some childhood fantasy. It is a conscious and delicately skilled activity performed by a very little boy for a very great and expectant audience—himself.
>
> As the plate moves swiftly, spinning hypnotically on its edge, the little boy bends over it and stares squarely into its motion. Homage to himself, to the plate. For a moment, the boy's body betrays a just perceptible movement similar to the plate's. For a moment, the little boy and his spinning creation become one. His eyes sparkle. He swoons in the playland that is himself. Alive. Alive.
>
> Raun Kahlil—a little man occupying the edge of the universe.
>
> Before this time, this every moment, we had always been in awe of Raun, our notably special child. We sometimes referred to him as "brain-blessed." He had always seemed to be riding the high of his own happiness. Highly evolved. Seldom did he cry or

utter tones of discomfort. In almost every way, his contentment and solitude seemed to suggest a profound inner peace. He was a seventeen-month-old Buddha contemplating another dimension.

A little boy set adrift on the circulation of his own system. Encapsulated behind an invisible but seemingly impenetrable wall. Soon he would be labeled. A tragedy. Unreachable. Bizarre. Statistically, he would fall into a category reserved for all those we see as hopeless . . . unapproachable . . . irreversible. For us the question: could we kiss the ground that others had cursed?

Coming from this reverential vantage point, my parents asked themselves what they could do to understand me and my world. The answer began with something that my mother did. She wanted to understand me—and also to show me that she accepted me as I was. That I didn't have to change to be loved.

So she began to join me in my repetitive, supposedly autistic behaviors. I would sit on the floor and rock . . . and she would rock with me. I would spin a plate on its edge . . . and she would spin her own plate next to mine. I would flap my hands in front of my face . . . and she would flap with me.

My parents so respected me that they focused totally on what *my* experience was—not on whether I looked strange or different to other people.

Hour after hour . . . day after day . . . month after month, my mother waited. Patiently, my parents waited.

Every once in a while, and only while "joining," as my parents came to call this true participation in my interests and activities, I glanced at my mother. I smiled at her. I grazed her with the tips of my fingers.

And as my parents began to truly understand my world, as they communicated in a thousand different ways, over and over again, that I was safe, that I was loved, that I was accepted, something astonishing happened. A connection began to form. Slowly, carefully, I began to peek out from behind the veil of my special world. Tentatively, I began to join them in theirs.

As my mother spent hour upon hour on the floor working with me, she made herself my friend in my world. In so doing, a bond of trust evolved. She cherished and celebrated every look, every smile, every moment of connection for which my parents had waited so long. She cheered me on with every small step.

As my relationship with my parents and the world of people strengthened, my mom and dad continued to build an entire program of therapy around me. They helped me to increase my social connection to them and to others, encouraging me to play with them, to look at them, to laugh with them, to take their hands. They constructed interactive games based upon my burgeoning interests, such as animals and airplanes. At every turn, they accomplished this with a deep caring, encouragement, and support—never pushing, always inviting.

Can you imagine it? They embarked on this experimental journey after hearing nothing but hopeless predictions for me. They continued to reach out to me when I gave them nothing in return.

And they persevered in the face of consistent criticism. Learned professionals told my parents that their "joining" would reinforce and increase my "inappropriate autistic behaviors." These professionals chastised my parents for doing the opposite of the behavior modification techniques they recommended—and for having "false hope," for putting their time into an unproven (and just created) approach that "had no hope of succeeding." Family members expressed grave doubts and concerns that my parents were "doing their own thing" and not leaving my treatment in the hands of professionals who "knew best."

Remember, too, that, in those days, the world of autism treatment was a barren wasteland. There were no nightly news stories waxing on about the latest treatments or detailing the lives of families with children on the spectrum. There was no Autism Awareness Month.

My parents witnessed children being jolted with electric shocks, tied to chairs, placed in dark prison-like rooms, held down—and were told that this was progress, the best modern medicine had to offer.

To help me, they had to walk in the opposite direction, alone. Without any support, they supported me. They worked and waited. They persisted and persevered. Not knowing what the future held, not requiring my reciprocation of their love, care, smiles, and cheers, they gave me every chance.

For three and a half years, they worked with me, painstakingly building a bridge from my world to theirs.

And it all paid off.

I recovered completely from my autism without any trace of my former condition. (Go to www.autismbreakthrough.com/chapter1 to see some childhood photos of me and my parents.) The years of work, the late nights, the persevering in the face of ongoing criticism, the love and dedication—it bore the kind of fruit it was never supposed to bear. It produced the outcome it was never supposed to produce. And I've lived the life I was never supposed to live.

THE CREATION OF THE AUTISM TREATMENT CENTER OF AMERICA

My parents developed this innovative, home-based, child-centered autism treatment program because of their very personal experiences entering my world. At the same time, the method they created was based upon what autism actually is—a difficulty connecting and bonding with others—rather than how autism is typically treated—as a problem of inappropriate behavior that must be extinguished, altered, and retrained.

They called their approach The Son-Rise Program.

There were several factors that made their approach unique. First, it was created by parents. That alone was a gigantic departure from the doctor/professional/lab-created norm. Second, my parents began with the premise that children on the autism spectrum are capable of limitless growth. Third, they started by joining me in my world rather than forcing me to conform to theirs. Fourth, they used motivation, rather than repetition, as the doorway to learning. Moreover, they focused on having a nonjudgmental and welcoming attitude with me, seeing that my responsiveness was largely dependent on the attitudes and emotions of the people working with me. And, finally, unlike every other treatment they saw, my parents prioritized human interaction over academics and tasks such as naming colors, adding numbers, and brushing teeth.

But until my recovery was complete, none of these concepts had spread beyond the walls of our house. Until my father wrote a book about it.

Shortly after my recovery in the late 1970s, my father wrote a best-selling book recounting our story entitled *Son-Rise*—now updated as *Son-Rise: The Miracle Continues.* (My father has written eleven other books as well.) Our story was then turned into an award-winning NBC television movie in 1979. As a result, people began to approach my parents for help.

In 1983, they founded the Autism Treatment Center of America (ATCA), part of a nonprofit, charitable organization. (As part of this not-for-profit organization, I've witnessed an incredible amount of generosity. So many sincerely giving people have donated money specifically to help families with children on the autism spectrum, allowing the ATCA to provide over $1.7 million in financial assistance last year alone.) The ATCA serves as the worldwide teaching center for The Son-Rise Program. It is situated on a gorgeous hundred-acre campus in Sheffield, Massachusetts. (I never appreciated how beautiful the campus was growing up. Only after living in Sweden, England, Ireland, Boston, southern California, and Portland, Oregon, did I realize the property's beauty.)

The Autism Treatment Center of America is a training facility for parents and professionals. (In the past, people have mistakenly concluded that the ATCA is a residential facility for children, which is not the case). It offers five-day programs during which parents learn how to use the techniques of The Son-Rise Program with their own children.

The beginning program, called The Son-Rise Program Start-Up, is important to remember because I will be making reference to it in many of the case studies we will be discussing. Parents and professionals attend the Start-Up program *without* their children in order to learn the fundamentals of The Son-Rise Program techniques. The course focuses on areas such as language, eye contact, facilitating interaction, teaching new skills, dealing with challenging behaviors, constructing an appropriate learning and sensory environment, creatively challenging your child, training others to work with your child, and sustaining an attitude of hope and optimism about your child. The course is very interactive, with lots of activities, video examples, question-and-answer sessions, and breakout "high-functioning" sessions for parents of children with Asperger's syndrome and similar diagnoses. So when I reference the Start-Up in case studies during later chapters, you will know what I'm talking about.

LIFE AFTER AUTISM

After my recovery from autism, I went to regular schools, and my friends and teachers had no idea about my history unless I told them. That was nice, because I was a minor celebrity on the ATCA campus, and that wasn't something I really savored as a teenager.

I was a very social kid and I had a wide circle of friends. Academically, things also went quite well. I went to my local public school growing up, but I spent my last three years of high school at an academically rigorous prep school.

Throughout this period of my life, I really didn't think that much about my history of autism. Sometimes, though, it would hit me.

At my high school prom, a couple of my buddies and I put on our tuxedos, picked up our dates, and pooled the money we had saved to rent a white stretch limousine with a giant sunroof. We thought we were pretty cool rolling into school standing on the seats with our heads and the top half of our bodies poking out from the top of the limo.

As the night was beginning, I remember feeling so happy, so excited, but also a little wistful. This was the final night of high school. I had two close friends in the car, with dates we cared for and a seriously fun night ahead. And I knew that I was experiencing the waning light of my childhood, my old friends, my high school experience. In the fall, I would be beginning college.

As I was drinking in the emotion of the whole evening, I had the sudden realization that none of this would have happened were it not for what my parents did to help me—not my prom or all the years before it, not my friends or the matches I played on the tennis team, not my classes or the many Sundays I had spent on day trips with my family, not my first kiss or my last exam. I had to catch my breath at the enormity of it. For a moment, I stood captivated by a deep sense of amazement at how different my life could have been.

And then my friends called to me, and I left my thoughts behind and tumbled back into my life, enjoying my prom, like millions of typical kids in typical towns across the nation.

Four years later, I graduated with a degree in biomedical ethics from Brown University. I spent my third year of college participating in an exchange program at Stockholm University in Sweden, and, after graduation, I got a work visa that allowed me to spend a year in London, England, and Cork, Ireland.

In Cork, I linked up with a family who had a little boy with autism and volunteered in their Son-Rise Program for a time.

This connection would prove to be especially important, as, seven years later, I was able to be of help to that little boy's mother when she was diagnosed with bone and lung cancer and given a 5 percent chance for survival. (That was ten years ago, and she's cancer-free and in excellent health—yet another example of how not buying into dire predictions can pay off.)

During my time at college and after graduating, I spent four summers working at, and then helping to manage, a summer program for teens on the campus of Wellesley College. Later on, I worked at an educational center for school-aged children in Boston and then opened and became the director of the same kind of educational center in southern California. These two jobs were seminal experiences for me, as I switched from a business focus to an education focus. I found the experience of working with kids to be so meaningful that it overwhelmed my interest in the business world, at least for a while.

I get asked by many parents about my love life. (And, yes, it can feel a bit strange to be asked for romantic details by someone you just met.) Though I don't think it's appropriate to go into detail about my former girlfriends, I will say that I feel very lucky in this regard. I have had the good fortune to be with some truly wonderful and caring women in my life. Although I am not yet married, I have found a very meaningful sense of intimacy and fulfillment in these relationships.

Because it is specifically relevant to this book—and because she specifically granted me her permission—I will, at various points, discuss one of my past girlfriends and her son (with names changed, of course). The reason for this is that she has a son with autism (we'll call him James), and while we were together, we co-ran her son's Son-Rise Program. I so loved and treasured my time with James, who was five and six during that time. I also had many different experiences with him that inform this book, over and above my professional experience working with parents and their children.

James's mom is an incredible woman on every level. She is an outstanding mother to James. She has a boundless energy and a sparkling intelligence that is so wonderful to be around. She's also pretty funny: when I asked her to choose the name that I would use for her in this book, she chose Charlotte because that is her favorite *Sex and the City* character. To me, she was a loving, tender, and devoted partner. Although our relationship did not ultimately work out, she remains one of my closest and dearest friends.

To answer a question I get asked a lot: no, I don't have any remnants of autism. I don't secretly crave a plate to spin, and I don't find social situations in any way difficult. I'm just a regular guy, living my life. Ironically, it is the interpersonal arenas that come most easily to me; I'm not so hot at the areas I should be good at, given my history—organization, routine, technical subjects. Go figure.

Since I get a lot of skeptical questions about autism recovery in general and mine in particular, let me go a bit further here. As a culture, we are still very much stuck in the "autism is a lifelong condition" paradigm. The problem here is that this mind-set cuts our children off at the knees and becomes a self-fulfilling prophecy.

I have spoken with parents who have been told—by people who have never met me—that I never recovered and am spending my life in an institution. On the rare occasions when I have met with people who made these claims and they see what a "typical guy" I am, they reverse their stance, instead saying that my autism was a misdiagnosis and that I must never have had autism in the first place.

Aside from the strangeness of them not noticing that they just switched positions, I find this claim interesting for the following reason. Remember the Son-Rise Program mom I was discussing earlier who recovered from cancer? (I know this seems like a left turn. Bear with me.) No one has ever approached her and said, "You know, since you don't have cancer now, you must never really have had it in the first place." Apparently we are willing to take one of the most deadly illnesses in the world and accept that people can recover, but when faced with a three-year-old child with autism, we are unable to accept anything other than a life sentence. This baffles me.

In the end, people can say what they will about my story because, although I may be the first, I am certainly not the last. For over a quarter of a century, parents from across the globe have been attending training programs at the Autism Treatment Center of America—putting in their time, energy, and love—and achieving remarkable results with their own children. Many children after me have made full recoveries. What are we going to do—say that *all* of them never had autism?

Of course, every child's journey is unique. I have seen so many children who, though they have not made full recoveries, have made astronomical progress. I've witnessed children with no language learn to speak. I've seen friendless children blossom into social kids with close friends. I watched as adults in their thirties left institutionalized environments to live on their own, with jobs, friends, and romantic partnerships. There are so many kinds of growth that our loved ones on the spectrum can achieve, and each one of these is a victory.

However, it is important that we acknowledge that recovery is possible so that each and every one of these children is given a chance. Though we can never predict where each child will end up, I know that my coworkers at the ATCA and I feel that the only ethical choice we have is to treat all of the children and adults that we work with as capable of recovery. That way, we aren't cutting children's chances off ahead of time, and we are ensuring that all children and adults get as far as they can go.

I can certainly tell you that, for me, working with all of these parents and seeing the depth of their love constantly renews my appreciation for my own parents' journey to help me. I am so grateful to have the opportunity, with the Autism Treatment Center of America's dedicated staff of over seventy, to enable parents to help their children in the same way.

THE EXPERIENCE BEHIND
THE TECHNIQUES

I wrote this book so that you can use my experience for your child's benefit. It is packed with what we could call autism intel: the inside scoop on what is going on with your child and what you can do to address the core issues of your child's disorder. This information isn't limited to my personal story of recovery or my experience with James. It encompasses my experience working with children and families throughout my life, and professionally since 1998, and the vast know-how contained in the decades of work done by the staff of the Autism Treatment Center of America.

In my case, I have spent over a thousand hours working individually with over two hundred children on the autism spectrum, worked with over a thousand families in-depth, and addressed more than fifteen thousand people in lectures and seminars. And now, after serving as CEO of the Autism Treatment Center of America from 2005 until 2010, I am its Director of Global Education.

Many of the other senior staff at the ATCA have considerably more experience. My parents have been teaching The Son-Rise Program for thirty-five years, and several of the other senior teachers are approaching or exceeding twenty years. They have all worked with families from a vast assortment of cultures who have children with widely varying diagnoses spanning the entire age spectrum from toddlers to mature adults. It would not be an exaggeration to say that there is no type of situation that they have not seen. The knowledge and experience of all these devoted individuals stands behind every principle, strategy, and technique you will read in this book.

For these people, their work with families isn't a nine-to-five job. It's their life. For example, my older sister Bryn and her husband William have been working at the ATCA for more than twenty years. But autism has also touched them in a very personal way—and I don't mean because Bryn had an autistic brother. When their daughter Jade was two years old, she began to exhibit a wide range of autistic behaviors. She would cry for hours. She had very little language. Her eye contact was rare, and her interest in people was fleeting. She was very sensitive to any sensory input (sights, sounds) and would scream when any sound became overwhelming or when too many people would look at her. She did not want to be touched. She spent much of her days engaged in repetitive "stims," repeatedly lining up toys or shaking a box filled with marbles, using the exact same motion over and over again.

Bryn and William set up a full-time Son-Rise Program for their daughter. I left my job running that educational center in southern California and moved back to Massachusetts to be a part of Jade's program, and to help out at the ATCA for what I thought, at the time, would be one year.

For me, working with Jade was one of the high points of my life. I truly cannot do justice to this experience with words (though I will do my best!).

Two aspects of my time with Jade made it very meaningful to me. The first is that, even with all of my personal and professional experience, I didn't fully grasp what the experience of having a special child and running a Son-Rise Program over time was like until I participated in Jade's program year after year. As I witnessed the intensive work, effort, creativity, and love that Bryn and William put into working with Jade, I developed a deeper, more profound understanding of exactly what my parents did for me. I have always been enormously grateful to them, but I just didn't get it on a visceral level until I had my time in Jade's program. (And, certainly, I internalized this understanding on yet another level during my later experience with Charlotte and James.)

The second facet of my experience that so moved me was Jade herself. I had such an amazing time with her! She was so precious, and I felt continually honored to step into her world over and over again. I found that, when I was with her, I was able to bring forth the most loving, caring, and creative parts of myself. This emotional connection has affected every moment I have worked with children since.

This is what I wrote back in 1999 about a pair of Son-Rise Program sessions I had with her, which took place one and two years into her program, respectively.

SEPTEMBER, 1998: The boat lists from side to side as it makes its way through the wavy ocean. Jostling around in my seat, barely able to keep myself from tumbling overboard, I look across the deck at Jade, who seems miraculously unaffected by the bounce and tip of the small, unstable boat. She sits in her self-constructed seat, staring intently at her stuffed animal (Ernie from *Sesame Street*), a small smile playing across her smooth, otherwise undisturbed features.

To the untrained eye, our boat might appear to be a purple blanket laid out across a white carpet, with pillows arranged at one end in a makeshift chair and a single scarf perched on the other end. As far I am concerned, however, we are sitting on a real sailboat making its way haphazardly across a rough sea—with our friends Ernie and Cookie Monster.

Earlier, Jade had made herself a plush chair with her pillows, and, when I asked her what I was to use for my chair, she casually deposited one of her scarves on my lap. And yet, despite the apparent disparity in the plushness of our chairs, I am incredibly excited. Not only am I greatly enjoying our time together, but I am now in the midst of a game that has gone on for almost 15 minutes! For Jade and I to be involved in a single interactive game for more than a few minutes is exceedingly rare, and I am savoring the experience.

Jade is weaving in and out of her connection with me at this point, sometimes looking at me and speaking, other times staring at and playing with Ernie as if I'm not in the room with her. Seeing that she is now playing with Ernie and less involved in our boat game, I take Cookie Monster and begin to look at and talk to it quietly but excitedly. Slowly, out of the corner of my eye, I notice Jade slowly raising her head. Her eyes lock onto me, and, for a moment, we both sit there, holding our stuffed animals and staring at one another. Then the (imaginary) boat rocks again, and I go tumbling overboard. Jade continues to eye me curiously, and so I reach up from where I'm lying on the carpet and ask her to help me climb back into the boat. She turns away from me and resumes her solitary play with Ernie.

AUGUST, 1999: The boat bounces around as it traverses the turbulent ocean. As I am being tossed from side to side by the motion of the boat, I glance across at Jade. She, too, is rocking around in the boat.

"This boat rocking around in water, Raun. Waves are coming in," Jade says.

"Here, Jadey, let's pull this sheet over us so that we don't get all wet." I say as I wipe some ocean water from my face.

She grabs her sheet and pulls it over her.

"You come in here, Raun. You come in close to me."

I scramble underneath the sheet next to her, and she slings an arm around me with great nonchalance.

"Thanks, Jade. You're a good friend," I say gratefully.

Jade smiles at me.

I can barely contain my excitement. Jade is being so sweet, so cuddly, so *interactive*. What's more, the two of us have been playing this particular game for over an hour!

Suddenly, another wave comes crashing into the boat, and I roll overboard.

"Hey, Jade! I'm in the water here. Can you help me out? Can

you help me back into the boat?" I reach up from the carpet, and . . . *she grabs onto me with both hands and hauls me back onto the boat!*

"Thanks for helping me, Jade-alicious! Whew!"

Jade looks at me quizzically. "Why you say 'whew'?"

Such a simple question, but, on this particular day, it got me thinking.

Jade helped me climb into her boat . . .

. . . we're helping her climb into our boat . . .

. . . as my parents helped me climb into their boat so many years ago.

So much distance traveled.

So many people lining the path.

Such a journey for one little girl.

How could I *not* say "Whew"?

Jade progressed more slowly than I had, but progress she did. Five years later, her program was finished. Now a social young adult with lots of friends and a great sense of humor, you would never guess her unique and special past.

Now, upon hearing this story, you couldn't be blamed for thinking that maybe Jade was predisposed to autism because she was related to me and that, furthermore, maybe she had a better shot at recovery for the same reason. However, you could only think this because you are missing a crucial element of the story: *Bryn and William adopted Jade when she was eight weeks old.* It was not until two years later that she began to show symptoms of autism. Isn't that incredible? (View a documentary of Jade's journey at www.autismbreakthrough.com/chapter1.)

So no matter what you have been told, please know that there is hope for your child. Of course, people who don't know your child will see what your child *does not* do, and they will speak as if they know what your child *cannot* do.

But you are the parent. You have love, a lifelong commitment, and an everyday experience with your child that no one else can match. You may sometimes feel dismissed or brushed aside, but nothing can change the fact that you aren't *in* the way, you *are* the way.

The only reason I can write to you today is because my parents believed in me when no one else on earth did. So you keep believing in your child—without apology. You have every right to have hope for your child, to see the potential within your child, and to want more for your child.

I am continually flabbergasted at some people's sincere and strenuous concern about parents of children on the autism spectrum being given "false hope." I continue to be befuddled as to what they think hope will do that is so harmful to our children. Who decided that a life sentence was better than an open heart and an outstretched hand?

The bottom line is this: hope leads to action. Without action, none of our children can be helped.

I hear people complaining about false hope, but I never hear anyone worrying about false pessimism. There is broad agreement that we don't want anyone promising a particular outcome for a particular child ahead of time. Why, then, do we abide people making promises about what a child will *never* do? Why is it that telling a parent all of the things that will not happen for his or her four-year-old or ten-year-old or fifteen-year-old over the next six decades is perfectly sensible, but giving every one of these kids a chance is deemed false hope?

Any of you reading this book right now knows that if there is one problem that families with children on the autism spectrum are *not* facing in our society, it is an epidemic of too much hope for their children. Of course, no one can know in advance what your child will accomplish. But let's not decide in advance what your child will *not* achieve. Let's give your child every chance.

Together, we'll spend the rest of these pages doing just that.

Joining: Entering Your Child's World

OKAY.

So.

Where to start?

Well, if you are reading this book, I'm going to go ahead and assume that:

1. You have a child on the autism spectrum.

2. You love your child.

3. You want to help your child.

Pretty obvious, I know. But what might be less obvious is just how much power you have to impact your child's growth and development.

This book will give you some very simple and clear techniques you can use to help your child progress. In some cases, these strategies may sound like the exact opposite of what you have been told to do. This is no accident. Many of them *are* the exact opposite.

That's okay. Nothing to get nervous about. In fact, quite the opposite: this may be the best news you've heard in quite a while. Why? Because if what you were doing was working, then you wouldn't be reading this book, would you? And if this book was just going to reiterate what you've already heard or thought of, it wouldn't be useful to you.

So that means that the first order of business is to fully

acknowledge the following: the path you have been on thus far hasn't got your child where you want her to be.

Let's head down a brand-new path.

WHAT AUTISM IS, REALLY

Most of what parents are told about autism is not accurate or, unfortunately, helpful. Sure, whoever diagnosed your child may have told you the symptoms of autism and how your child's behaviors matched those symptoms, but I'm not talking about symptoms. I'm talking about the central aspect of what autism *is*.

First, let's talk about what autism is *not*. It is not a behavioral disorder. This is important because, 99 percent of the time, that's exactly how it's treated. The methodologies used on our children tend to focus on behavior change. Practitioners ask: how can we stamp out or eliminate *this* behavior and train the child to do *that* behavior?

The problem is, autism is not a behavioral disorder; it is a *social-relational disorder*. Do our kids behave differently? Sure. But those behaviors are symptoms, not causes. If you saw someone scratching his arm and then set as your goal the elimination of the scratching behavior, there are a number of approaches you might try. You might tell the person to stop scratching. You might threaten him with an unpleasant consequence if he continues scratching. You might try to distract him by putting something he wants (an ice-cream cone, for instance) in the hand he is using to scratch. You might even tie his arm to his body so that he couldn't scratch.

Or you could actually look for the *reason* for his scratching and discover that he has a mosquito bite. Then, you could put some anti-itch cream on the bite. Violà! No more scratching! And instead of not addressing the real issue while at the same time totally alienating the person, you solve the *cause* of the scratching—and the person is grateful!

This analogy illustrates the difference between trying to stamp out your child's symptoms and addressing your child's core challenge. Every autistic behavior your child exhibits is a symptom. Trying to extinguish these behaviors does not address the actual autism and only serves to seriously disrupt the trust and relationship between you and your child.

This trust and relationship is your most important asset in helping your child progress!

Why? Because autism is a social-relational disorder.

What does this mean, exactly? Well, the primary challenge that your child has is a difficulty bonding and forming relationships with others. (I say "child" regardless of your child's age because she is *your* child, even as an adult.) There are a few different reasons for this, which we will go over later, but, for now, know this: almost every other issue your child faces stems from this one challenge.

This is why, if you take a five-year-old nonverbal child labeled "severely autistic" and a sixteen-year-old adolescent with Asperger's syndrome, you won't, in most cases, find a single behavior in common. These two people will look and act very, very differently from one another. And yet, they are both on the autism spectrum. What do they have in common, then?

They both have difficulty communicating, making eye contact, reading nonverbal cues, dealing with people and social situations, coping with high levels of sensory stimulation, and being flexible with changing circumstances and with other people's wishes and agendas. Also, they both have powerful interests (labeled by some as "obsessions") that they can engage in for long periods of time, often seeming oblivious to the interests of others.

Isn't that interesting? No behaviors in common, yet a whole array of underlying challenges in common. So, regardless of where your child is on the spectrum, he or she has the same key deficits. This is actually a good thing. You may not see it as a good thing right this second. That's okay. But, really, it is. It means that by addressing this one area, you are also tackling almost every other challenge that your child faces. It also means that everything in this book is designed to enable you to help your child grow and learn while going *with* instead of *against* your child, bonding more with your child instead of doing battle with him.

This leads us to a most important, paradoxically logical idea: *overcoming autism is not about getting your child to change his behaviors.* Really.

A TOTAL REVERSAL

First, we want to change the question we ask ourselves when seeking to help our child. Instead of asking, "What do I need to do in order to change my child's behavior?" we want to ask, "What do I need to do in order to create a relationship with my child?" Once we ask this question, everything changes. Our whole approach shifts.

You want to begin to focus on doing your very best to *see through your child's eyes*. I'm not asking you to be psychic here. I'm talking about imagining, with every single interaction you have with your child, what this might feel like for your child. When you stop your child from stimming, how might that feel for her? When you take him to a noisy park and he's covering his ears, how do you think that is for him? When your child seems engrossed in tearing paper into tiny strips, what do you think that experience is like for her? When your child talks incessantly about windmills, what is it that he loves so much about them?

We want everything we do with our children from now on to be in service to bonding and relationship building. This means that you want to make being part of our world extremely appealing to your child. You want interacting with others to feel totally nonthreatening, fun, exciting, and satisfying for your child. In fact, you want to *sell* human interaction. I mean really sell it. If you went up to your child and said, "Dude, I've got the best deal to offer you! It's called being part of our world, and it's really awesome. You know what the best part is? When you join us in our world, you get to stop doing all the stuff you *love*, and start doing all the stuff you *hate*! Doesn't that sound fantastic?" Now, no child or adult on earth is going to take that deal. And yet, that's the deal we usually offer.

It's time for a total reversal. Instead of focusing on your child conforming to your world, you want to become a student of your child's world. *Let your child be the teacher.*

Of course, you have many, many things you want to teach your child. A number of the upcoming chapters will help you with exactly that. But if you ever want to get to a place where your child is actually interested in what you and others have to offer, you must first build trust and form a bond on your child's own terms. You've got to build a bridge to your *child's* world first. Only then can you take your child's hand and guide her back across that bridge to *your* world. That is why The Son-Rise Program is guided by the following principle:

> The children show us the way in, and then we show them the way out.

Okay, so how do we do that?

Everybody loves the second half of this sentence. *Yes, I want to show my child the way out! I want to get my child to look at me, communicate, learn new things, be more neurotypical!*

However, it is right here that the first and primary mistake is usually made. With children on the autism spectrum, you can't just yank them out of their world and into ours. You can't *force* them to learn or grow or change. And you certainly cannot *make* them want to interact with other people.

JOINING

So, if we want to show our children the way out, then we must begin by focusing on the *first* half of that sentence. This means that, rather than forcing these children to conform to a world they do not understand, we begin by joining them in their world. In this way, we establish a mutual connection and relationship, which is the platform for all education and growth.

And this leads us to our first key technique: joining. What is joining? Well, you know all of those stimming behaviors that everyone is trying to get your child to stop doing? Not only do we not stop these behaviors, but we *join in with* and *participate* in those very same behaviors.

When your child performs his or her repetitive autistic-looking behaviors, you are going to do them, too. When your child lines up blocks, you will get some blocks of your own and line them up, too. When your child shakes a pen while making an "eeeee" sound, you will do the same. When your child is stimming, you are going to stim with him. (And, yes, children and adults with Asperger's syndrome *do* stim. They just do it differently, as we'll discuss in Chapter 15.)

I've often heard the concern, from people who have not yet tried this technique, that joining will "reinforce the very behaviors that we want the child to stop." The idea is that joining will supposedly teach your child that her repetitive behaviors are appropriate, leading to more of these behaviors.

However, once you have joined your child the way that we do it in The Son-Rise Program (which we'll get into shortly), you will see firsthand that the last thing on earth it leads to is more stimming.

At the Autism Treatment Center of America, we have been joining children and adults for decades—kids from Great Britain and Nigeria, from Germany and Japan, from Argentina and across the United States, two-year-olds and thirty-two-year-olds, kids labeled "severe" and kids deemed "mild." We have never, ever seen it make anyone more autistic. We've never seen it lead to increased stimming.

In fact, we see the opposite: the more we join a child, the less that child stims. Time and time again, we join children and then watch as these children look at us more, pay more attention to us, smile at us more, participate with us more, and become steadily less interested in the stimming behavior by which they previously seemed so captivated.

When my mother began joining me, she was told that this was unwise and would lead to more stimming. She was told to say "no," take the plate away, and redirect my behavior whenever I put a plate on the floor and spun it on its edge for hours at a time. To my eternal gratitude, she didn't listen. She wanted so much to peek into my world. She wanted so fervently to show me that she loved me—to connect with me. She got her own plate and spun with me. That was when I began looking at her, smiling at her, and becoming more interested in her.

AN ANALOGY

To illustrate why joining works, let me give you an analogy. I want you to imagine that you've had a hard, busy week, and you are totally out of steam. (I'm sure that won't be difficult for you.) Finally, Saturday arrives. Lo and behold, you have the day to yourself—a day off. (Okay, that might be harder for you to imagine, but go with me here.) Your spouse (or someone else if that doesn't apply) is covering the kids, and you can do what you wish.

So, you go to a nice local park, and you take your favorite book by your favorite author to read. You sit down on one of the benches, get out your book, and begin reading. It's a beautiful day out, and you're totally comfortable. As you read, you finally begin to decompress from your trying week. You start to relax. You become absorbed in your book, tuning out all of the events of the week and the formidable list of things you have to do when you get back home. You're at ease.

Then I approach you. "Hey, what's up?" I ask in a loud voice, "How ya doing? Listen, I've been watching you read, and you've been at it for quite a while. Ya know, this isn't the best way to spend your day, being kind of antisocial and not really doing anything. I'll tell you what. Let's forget about the book and go see a movie. There's a great flick playing just down the road. My treat. How about it?"

You look up at me, a little annoyed. "Um, look, I've had a very intense week, and I finally got a day to myself. I just want to hang out here and read. Thanks for the offer, though."

I stare at you, a bit dumbfounded. I'm making a great offer, and movies are fun. Why aren't you putting your book down and going with me? Maybe I just haven't adequately got your attention yet. So I stand right in front of where you are sitting and squat down so that my face is at eye level with yours. I take my hand and push your book aside so you can see me.

"Hi," I say, "Can you look at me? Over here." I snap my fingers in the direction you are looking and bring my hand back to my face. "Hi. I'm over here. Listen, the movie is starting in fifteen minutes. Come on, stand up. Let's go. We're going to the movies."

Now you're getting pretty peeved with me. You stand up and face me. "Hey, look, buddy. Back off. I've had a tough week, and I just want to read my book in peace. If I wanted to use my one day off to see a movie, that's probably what I'd be doing, okay? So just leave me alone. I just want to read my book in peace."

Suddenly, I have a realization. What was I thinking? How could I have missed this? I know what the problem is! The problem is: your book. It's clearly very distracting to you. I mean, you keep staring and staring at it. You're kind of obsessed with it. So, if I just take the book away from you, problem solved.

I snatch the book out of your hands. You try to grab it back, but I pull it back out of your reach.

"Ah-ah-ah," I tell you, "You'll get the book back *after* you go to the movies with me."

Okay.

It doesn't take a rocket scientist to figure out what's going to happen next. The very *last* thing that's going to happen is you deciding to come to the movies with me. In fact, next Saturday, if you see me approaching, you're going to grab your book and run the other way.

YOUR CHILD'S EXPERIENCE

Now, the important thing to understand here is that this problematic situation is not occurring because I'm trying to make your life difficult. Quite the opposite. I'm trying to *help* you! My intentions are good. I genuinely believe that it's not healthy for you to sit by yourself all day, and I'm endeavoring to get you to do something I think will be better for you. I have the very best of intentions.

The problem is, you're not a mind reader, so you don't know my reasons and intentions. All you know about me is two things:

1. I'm right up in your face.

2. I keep giving you the same message over and over. And that message is: *stop doing what you want—do what I want.*

Now let's take a moment and step behind your child's eyes. If your child has an autism spectrum disorder, two big things are happening. (I'm not saying that these are the *only* things going on with your child, but they are two of the biggies.)

The first is that your child has difficulty processing and making sense of sensory input. This means that he sees, hears, smells, tastes, and feels things very differently than you or I do. When your child hears something, for instance, it sounds louder, softer, or just plain different than what you hear.

If you take a moment right now and just listen in silence to any background noise, you may notice a lot of little sounds—cars, wind, the heater or air conditioner, a TV or a conversation in another room, etc. You probably didn't notice all of these noises until just now. That's as it should be.

The human ear is bombarded by a continuous cacophony of sounds. One of the brain's chief tasks is to filter out irrelevant sounds and filter in the important sound, such as your spouse/boyfriend/girlfriend talking. (Well, at least we'd call that sound important *most* of the time!)

With your child, all of those noises are coming in at the same volume! (It doesn't work in *exactly* this way, but this is the closest approximation to your child's experience that we can get into right now.) So when you tell your child to pay attention and listen, what, exactly, should he listen to? Which of the twenty-five sounds is your child supposed to pay attention to?

This is your child's experience day in and day out. You know how you feel after you've spent the day at an airport (tired, overwhelmed, like you just want to veg out)? Well, your child wakes up, has breakfast, lunch, dinner, then goes to sleep—in the middle of a busy airport. Even if it's just your living room, it's an airport to your child. This is why making a big effort to see things through your child's eyes is so important.

You may have a child who likes to take his clothes off and run around naked. He may step into the house and tear all of his clothes off. You may ask yourself, *Why is my child misbehaving? He knows that he's supposed to keep his clothes on!* The thing is, your child is not "misbehaving." His clothes probably feel like sandpaper, and he is taking them off just to get some relief!

When I was little, I used to see and hear things very differently. I would test deaf on hearing tests, even though the tests were monitoring *involuntary* responses from my eyelids and skin. At the same time, I would mimic a song that was playing on a television show being watched in a distant room. I can remember things being visually different to me at times, and this continued to occur from time to time for a couple of years after my recovery. For instance, sometimes, when I looked at a person's face, it would seem like I was looking through the wrong end of a pair of binoculars. The person's face would look like it was far away and down a tunnel. Sound strange to you? Welcome to your child's world.

The second big issue that your child faces is that she has difficulty recognizing patterns. This means that everyday occurrences that seem predictable and understandable to you and me seem random and haphazard to your child. That's why your child is constantly seeking familiarity and routine!

If I walk up to you, say "Hi," and stick out my right hand, you know, without even thinking about it, that I am greeting you and trying to shake your hand. You know how this works and you know what to do.

If I did that with your child (in most cases), I'm just some guy thrusting his hand out. Your child doesn't necessarily know what this is or what to do. (What's worse is that everyone thinks that she *should* know what to do and is annoyed or upset when she doesn't.) Your child is living in an unpredictable, confounding, and tumultuous world.

Any of us facing just the latter challenge would endeavor to cope in ways similar (though less extreme) to how our children behave. We've all been in situations, such as being in a foreign country, where we have encountered small versions of these challenges. The people don't speak our language. They have cultural traditions that seem unfathomable—yet we're expected to follow them. Even flushing the (strangely arranged) toilet can seem like an exercise in code breaking. Why can't everything just be understandable?! And why won't people get off my back and stop expecting me to obey rules I don't understand?! Often, in these situations, we become less social. We seek to wall ourselves in. And we seek familiarity and control. The same is true for many of us when we start a new job, move to a new area, or marry into a family that's very different from ours.

This is *exactly* what your child does. In fact, your child is so brilliant and so creative that he has come up with a way to handle both challenges at once: the stim.

How does the stim do that? First, it enables your child to focus intently on one thing so that he can most effectively tune out the sensory bombardment that he is experiencing every moment of every day. (Interestingly, this is the same reason why some people meditate.)

Second, by doing the same exact thing over and over in a way that he can control, your child is, in essence, creating an island of predictability in an ocean of randomness. So, you see, your child is actually addressing both neurological issues with one behavior! He is doing the best, smartest thing that he can possibly do to address what is going on for him. In reality, your child is not behaving abnormally. Your child is behaving extremely normally in the face of the abnormal situation that he is facing.

Isn't that amazing?

BACK TO THE ANALOGY

Let's return to our analogy for a few moments. Now suppose you are sitting on your bench in the park, reading your favorite book by your favorite author, just like before. This time I approach, sit down on the same bench, and begin reading a book I've brought with me. I don't say anything to you; I'm busy reading my book.

After a while, you glance over at me. And then you notice something startling. Holy frijoles! You can't believe it, but it appears that I am reading the very same book that you are! You try to go back to reading your book, but you keep thinking of how unbelievable it is that I am reading not just the same book as you, but your *favorite* book.

After glancing over at me for the tenth time, you can't resist; you have to at least ask me about it. So you tap me on the shoulder and ask me why I'm reading this book, do I like it, do I read many books by this author, etc. I enthusiastically answer you, and we fall into a discussion of our favorite books and why we love them.

Then, it's time for me to go. I say good-bye and leave.

The next Saturday, you are sitting on the bench reading, and along I come again (with my book). We read a bit, chat a bit, and then part ways. The same process happens again the following Saturday and the one after that.

Then, after several Saturdays of this, we're sitting and talking on the bench, and I say, "Hey, check this out. Next weekend, the movie version of this book we've been reading is coming out. Isn't that awesome? Listen, how about, next Saturday, instead of reading here, we meet at the cinema and watch that movie?"

Do you see what happened? Notice that, in both scenarios, I'm ultimately asking you to do *the exact same thing*. However, the *way* I got there is totally different. In the first scenario, it's all about *stop doing what you want—do what I want*. I have no interest in building a relationship with you, let alone trust. In the second scenario, I spend a lot of time building a meaningful relationship with you before I ask you for anything. What's more, we are building this relationship *around a common interest*.

This is important, because, although The Son-Rise Program

was unique in pioneering this idea with respect to autism, this is not at all new when it comes to how human beings relate to one another. Forming relationships based on a common interest, combined with reciprocity (the two-way street of "I go your way, then you go mine"), has been the way human beings have been creating relationships for thousands of years.

What is incredible is not that we would use this model, but that it is still controversial to use it with children whose main challenge is creating relationships! It seems almost too obvious to state that, if a child has a social-relational disorder, we would want to use bonding and relationship-building techniques with that child rather than techniques that do the opposite.

Moreover, there is a growing body of research suggesting that, for our children, stimming has all sorts of positive effects on the nervous system—calming, regulating, and relaxing it. (See Appendix 1.)

And what do we do when our children finally find something to calm themselves, self-regulate, and effectively cope with their environment? *Quiet hands. Don't do that. Put that down. Do this instead.*

To be clear, we do this to help our children. We do this because we love our children. But, through their eyes, it's not helpful and it's not loving.

At the Autism Treatment Center of America, we had a little girl named Keri in our Son-Rise Program Intensive (a program where we work directly with the child, which you'll hear more about later) who would flap her hands by the outside edges of her eyes near her temples. (I've changed Keri's name and the names of all the kids in this book.) Her parents—who loved their daughter very much—were constantly trying to stop her from flapping. "Quiet hands, honey," they would say, and then they would gently take her wrists and push her hands down to her sides.

We taught Keri's parents to use joining to help her, but that's not why I'm telling you about her. I'm telling you this because, later on, Keri was examined by an ophthalmologist who told her parents that the rods in her retinas were defective. (You have rods and cones in your retinas. Cones see colors and straight ahead, rods see in black and white, peripheral vision, and are involved in depth perception.) This doctor went on to explain that when Keri flapped her hands at the outside edge of her vision, she was stimulating the rods in her retinas, thereby helping herself to see better as she navigated around a room, a sidewalk, etc. So, this little girl was just trying to see, and everyone around her, trying, of course, to help her, was saying "Quiet hands" and pulling her hands away from her eyes.

A boy named Vincent would get on the floor, put a ball or pillow underneath his stomach, and roll back and forth for hours. As with Keri, his parents, teachers, and therapists all tried to discourage him from doing this. Later, Vincent's parents were told by a physician that he had severe chronic indigestion that was probably causing a great deal of stomach pain. So Vincent was just trying to give himself some relief!

If your child is doing something for hours on end every day, surely there is a purpose to what she is doing. She is not stimming (or doing anything else, for that matter) for no reason. There is always a reason and a purpose—otherwise, she wouldn't be doing it over and over.

You see, it's hard to see the purpose and usefulness of our children's behaviors when we're trying to stamp out the behaviors. This, in fact, is another benefit of joining: it enables us, often for the first time, to get a window into our child's world. It gives us the opportunity to see the *reasons* for our child's behaviors. It allows us to begin to answer the question: Why is my child doing this? What is he or she getting out of it?

MIRROR NEURONS

Neurologists have increasingly been studying (and getting excited about) mirror neurons. (The book *Mirrors in the Brain* charts their discovery.) These are a special class of neurons present in every person's brain. Among other things, mirror neurons enable us to identify with, learn from, and connect with other people.

Mirror neurons fire in our brains when we see—or sometimes even hear about—someone else taking an action or having an experience. For instance, when we are watching a basketball game and someone shoots a basket, the same pattern of neurons fires in our own brain that would fire *if we were actually shooting the basket.* What you may think of as empathy is a mirror neuron phenomenon. Mirror neurons allow us to walk in someone else's shoes.

When you see someone on TV bang his knee, and you wince, that's your mirror neurons firing. When you watch someone throw a ball, and you imagine throwing it yourself, that's your mirror neurons. When someone shows you a dance move, and then you try it, you're using your mirror neurons. When you cry during a sad movie scene, it is your mirror neurons that allow you to imagine yourself in the place of the movie character.

There is evidence that children and adults on the autism spectrum have difficulty firing their mirror neurons. If a person's mirror neurons aren't firing, then he or she would have difficulty identifying with and being interested in others, being motivated by social things, looking in other people's eyes, knowing what to look for in social situations, imitating and learning from others, and so on. Sound familiar?

Guess what? One of the key ways that mirror neurons begin to fire in the developing brain is when children are joined. In fact, even babies immediately become more interested in those who do what they do. (The book *Mirroring People* explains this phenomenon well and discusses much about how mirror neurons operate.) So if we want to help our children's mirror neurons to fire, we need look no further than the very first principle of The Son-Rise Program. It turns out that the simple act of stepping across the bridge from our world to that of our children may help to stimulate the exact part of their brains that seems to be having such difficulty.

WHEN TO JOIN

It's very important to know when to join because we don't join with everything.

THE ISM

In fact, you only join when your child is doing one very specific type of behavior: isms. *Only* isms.

What is an ism? The simplest way to think of an ism is to think of it as a stim. Of course, you might justifiably ask why we don't just go ahead and call it a stim, as everyone else does.

It is much more helpful to our children if we use a word that is easily definable—free from a history of negative connotations or any other baggage that might cause confusion about what we mean. After all, if we are only joining with isms, and we clearly define isms, then we will be absolutely clear on exactly what to join with.

If your child is doing an ism, your child is performing a behavior that has two main characteristics:

1. It is *repetitive*.

2. It is *exclusive*.

I don't think that the word "repetitive" really needs further explanation, but the word "exclusive" does. When we say "exclusive," we are talking about a behavior whereby your child is *excluding* other people. Exclusive means that the behavior is a one-person show. Your child isn't looking at anyone else, interested in others watching, inviting anyone else to join in, or allowing anyone else to participate. By definition, your child is doing something where there is only room for her. In most cases (but not all), your child, when doing these types of behaviors, will not be responsive to what you say or ask. You can call her name or invite her to do something different, but you'll get no real response

Think of it like this: your child is a member of a tiny little club with only herself as a member. The solution isn't to try to destroy the club. Rather, the solution is to do whatever it takes to get in!

When your child is doing a behavior that is both repetitive and exclusive, we call that an ism. When your child is doing an ism, *we always join.*

HOW TO JOIN

Joining isn't complicated. The technical aspect of entering your child's world by joining in with his isms is quite simple. However, there is one essential piece that cannot be overlooked. The attitude you have while joining your child is absolutely critical.

The goal here isn't to prove you can copy, mimic, or mirror your child. Anyone can do that. A machine can do that.

You, however, have a special role in your child's life and world. You're not just anyone. You're not a machine. You *love* your child. You *care about* your child. You are *invested* in your child.

You may sometimes wonder if your child really understands that you love her—and just how *much* you love her. Joining is how you will express your love in a way that your child can see it and *feel* it. This means that *you* need to focus on feeling it. You want to put all of your focus on loving your child and honoring her world. Not only will this help to make your joining a deep bond with your child, but, when your child *does* pause in her ism to look at you, she will be able to see—right in front of her eyes—that you love her.

I cannot overstate how much this matters.

How many times do people untouched by autism ask you how your son or daughter is doing, and then, when you answer, you watch as their eyes glaze over, and they nod uncomfortably—and you see that they aren't truly interested in your answer? After enough instances like this, you stop telling people about your child.

Your child is exquisitely intelligent and perceptive. He knows the difference in a heartbeat between you begrudgingly "copying" him and really joining. And you know, too. So now it's time to make the real thing happen.

If you want your child to be inclined to share her world with you, you need to be genuinely curious and interested. As best you can, endeavor to be fascinated by what you are doing. Now, you may be thinking, *How can I be fascinated with repetitive hand-flapping* (or block-stacking, or listing all capital cities, or whatever)?

Here's the thing: as long as you're asking yourself that question, you can't be fascinated. You can't be fascinated or interested when you're looking down on the behavior. And you certainly can't be fascinated when you're thinking about ways to stamp out the behavior. So you have to let all of this go.

It's not that you have to let go of wanting your child to learn and grow. It's just that you need to let go of the idea that pushing your child to change what he is doing is the way to get there. Remember, your child is doing what he is doing because that is the best way he knows how to help himself. Focus on finding out what your child loves about that behavior. Become an enthusiastic student of your child's world. Imagine that you are working with someone from another country, and your job is to learn all about that person's culture.

If, for instance, your child is flapping her hands, sit down near her (or stand if your child is standing) and flap your hands like there's no tomorrow. Amazingly, the more interested you are in your *own* hand-flapping, the more interested your child will be in *you*.

If your child is doing something more complex than hand-flapping, such as making an intricate tower with blocks, circuiting from toy to toy, repeating phrases from movies, or playing with toy figures in an elaborate but repetitive way, then you are still going to join in the same way. Look at what your child is doing. Get fascinated. Then dive in, and do the same activity yourself as best you can.

A note: if your child glances at you while you are joining, you can feel free to smile at him, thank him briefly, but then go right back to joining.

WHAT NOT TO DO

1. Don't stare at your child.
Once you begin, don't stare at your child or look at her every two seconds. Really get involved with what you are doing. Remember, you aren't trying to prove that you can mimic; you are getting involved with the activity that your child loves.

2. Don't get in your child's face.
That's part of the reason that your child is isming in the first place—to tune out everyone who's in his face! You want to give your child some space. If your child is sitting down, then, by all means, sit down, but don't sit down an inch from

where he's sitting. If your child is standing or pacing, then stand or pace, but not right up on top of him.

3. Don't take your child's stuff.

If your child is lining up small green cars, then, whatever you do, don't take her green cars and start lining them up. Yes, that's right, you've got to use the rejects. If your child likes to use the shiny green cars but shows no interest in the old, half-broken yellow cars, those yellow cars are all yours, baby! Use the same *type* of item that your child is using, but not the ones your child is actually using.

4. Most important: Don't try to change your child's behavior in any way.

This is the biggest mistake people make, and it's the mistake that is most detrimental to the whole point of joining. Your child is smart. If you try to use joining as a way to get your child to change, alter, or stop his behavior, your child will immediately see that, and you will have rendered the entire joining technique useless. This means no saying, "Hey, sweetie, look at me!" No trying to get your child to take his little car and race your little car. And no gimmicks to try to get his attention.

This last point deserves some more discussion. I could understand, for instance, if you were to ask, "I thought you said that joining will lead to my child becoming more interested in me and in others, my child looking and interacting more, and my child isming less. So why are you now saying *not* to use joining to try to change what he's doing?"

A totally fair question. The answer is that joining results in *child-initiated interaction* (which eventually replaces isming). A major characteristic of autism is the lack of social interaction *that is initiated and wanted by the child.*

One of the factors that makes The Son-Rise Program unique

is that it focuses on developing within each child the ability to *initiate* social interaction. We want to enter the child's world, wait for her to voluntarily initiate interaction, and then (and only then) use that interaction to invite her to stretch and communicate further.

We want our children on our side. The only way to achieve that is to join them in their world until they join us in ours. This simply cannot be forced.

Joining correctly means joining until your child stops isming of her own volition and looks at you or approaches you in some way. It does not mean that you set aside fifteen minutes for joining, after which your child must do as you say. *The length of the joining is determined by your child, not by you.* That is the key.

Interestingly, in the last several years, a number of autism treatment methods have sought to adopt aspects of The Son-Rise Program by doing what they *think* is joining as a way to create interaction. The problem is, these methodologies still end up missing the boat because they try to adopt joining without understanding it. (Ironically, they are trying to copy or mimic something without understanding it, which is the same mistake we make when we only seek to copy or mimic our kids.) I've seen programs where children are "joined" for a period of time—decided upon by the therapist. As the minutes progress, the therapist endeavors to guide the child into a more interactive activity. (By the way, this is the very best case scenario. With most treatment methods, no attempt is made at all to participate in the child's world.)

And this is where a true understanding of joining (and of autism) has real impact. Joining isn't a trick we use to sneak our child into a different activity or behavior. *Joining is the way we enable our child to form a bond with us.* We find that children become more interested in us, look at us more, and ism far less when we join. But these children do these things by choice—at their own initiation. *After* our children bond with us, trust us, and feel safe with us—which they show us by initiating interaction—then we can challenge them to do and learn new things, which is what the very next chapter addresses.

The Story of Reggie

Some time ago, a father came to our Start-Up program to help his son, Reggie. Now recall that the Start-Up course is a five-day introductory training course where parents and professionals learn the fundamentals of how to use The Son-Rise Program techniques with their children. Parents such as Reggie's dad attend without their children.

They learn strategies to increase language, eye contact, inter-action, and new skill acquisition. They learn to handle—and then reduce—challenging behaviors. They are taught how to put to-gether an appropriate learning and sensory environment, how to creatively challenge their children, how to train others to work with their children, and, of course, how to sustain an attitude of hope and optimism with regard to their children. The course is very inter-active, with lots of activities, video examples, question-and-answer sessions, and breakout "high-functioning" sessions for parents of children with Asperger's syndrome and similar diagnoses.

One of the first things we do in the Start-Up course is to teach parents how to join. When we began this with Reggie's father, he was pretty skeptical. He explained that his son would play with LEGOs for hours and hours on end. But Reggie didn't play with LEGOs the way a neurotypical child would. Every day, Reggie would do the exact same thing. He would grab his box of LEGOs, take out the exact same pieces, and build the exact same thing—a simple L-shaped structure. Then he would build another one so that he had two. Then he would take these two structures, hold them close together so that it looked like he was making a square, and walk around the room holding the square up to lights and windows while quickly bringing the two LEGO structures together and apart, together and apart.

Reggie's father explained to us that he couldn't imagine joining his son in this activity. As teachers, we find that one of the best ways to help people is first to seek to understand where they are coming from. What we do *not* do is to start arguing with them when they are struggling with the idea of implementing one of The Son-Rise Program techniques. By endeavoring to understand them, we are best equipped to help them.

So we began by asking this dad some questions. Why couldn't he imagine joining his son with the LEGOs? He answered that he really couldn't stand watching his son do that behavior. Again, we asked him why. He replied, this time becoming quite emotional. Every time he saw his son playing with the LEGOs, Reggie's father would see how "autistic" his son looked. And this provided a constant reminder to him that his son was different. He didn't like that his son was different. Moreover, he wondered whether it was somehow his fault. He saw his son's autism as the enemy, and, by God, he was not going to make friends with the enemy.

We asked him what he meant when he said his son's autism was the enemy, and this led to a powerful and in-depth discussion for the whole class. One of the key realizations that Reggie's dad came to that day was that by making autism the enemy, he was making a part of who his son was the enemy. He concluded that he wanted to love and embrace *all* of who his son was, including the part that was autistic. One crucial way that he could do this was to join his son. (This particular transformation is a pivotal component of the journey that many Son-Rise Program parents experience.)

At the end of his week, Reggie's father went back home excited to see his son through new eyes. Understand that before this, whenever Reggie's dad saw him playing with his LEGOs, he would try to stop him. He would say no, he would take the LEGOs away, he would try to get his son to do something else.

Also understand this: Reggie would not look at or acknowledge his father in any way.

Reggie's father had never tried joining before, and he wasn't totally sure about it, but he had agreed to totally commit to joining his son for a few weeks and see what happened. The next morning, Reggie pulled the box of LEGOs out first thing, not acknowledging his father. With some LEGOs, Reggie built his two L-shaped figures. As he always had, he began walking around the room, holding the two figures up to the lights, moving them closer together and farther apart.

This time, however, his dad was different. He made his own L-shaped structures and began strolling around the room, moving the structures closer together and farther apart. Every so often, he'd look at his son and really study what he was doing so that he could understand it and get it right.

As he did this, he realized something. He had always thought that his son had been simply looking through the square shape he had created with the two L-shaped figures. He was wrong. In fact, Reggie was looking sideways at the surface of each structure. And when his dad did the same thing, he noticed that, when he held the figures up to the light, he could see a reflection of his own face on the LEGOs themselves. And when he moved the two figures farther apart and then close together, the reflection of his face would get fatter and skinnier, as if he was looking at himself in a carnival mirror.

Yes! He was ecstatic! He finally understood what his son was doing, and it was actually pretty cool! Whoo-hoo! He glanced back over at his son, and Reggie had dropped his LEGOs and was staring in abject amazement at his father. His dad, looking back at him, couldn't believe it. He smiled at his son, enjoying the moment. Reggie smiled back. Then, on an inspiration, he waved to his son. Reggie waved back!

These two people, father and son, shared this beautiful moment, looking at each other, smiling at each other, waving to one another. It was a moment unlike any they had shared before. It was the first time Reggie ever really acknowledged and showed interest in his father—but it wasn't the last.

Reggie's father began to enthusiastically join his son every day. Finally, he had a way he could be with his son!

Before that first day of joining, Reggie had been isming with his LEGOs for upwards of five hours a day. Several weeks later, Reggie's time isming with the LEGOs had dwindled to just under an hour a day. And, of course, much of that time was replaced by Reggie doing things that were far more interactive—with his father and with others.

This story illustrates so many different aspects of why joining works, from giving us a window into why our children do what they do to creating a bonded relationship. But it also highlights something else. When you join, you may make a most amazing discovery: almost inevitably, joining will change you, too. It is rare, indeed, to connect with your child in this deep, abiding, and honoring way without it altering the way you see your child and the beauty of his unique world.

When you join your child fully, you can feel a level of closeness beyond anything previous. It's very hard to judge or feel scared by your child's behavior once you've truly joined him. And you develop a real sense of camaraderie with your child. A deeper understanding of his experience. A delight in his world.

And no one will ever be able to take this experience away from you.

JAMES BEFORE BED

Remember James, the son of my former girlfriend Charlotte? Well, one night years ago, I saw tears in Charlotte's eyes as she left James's room after putting him to bed. I asked her what was wrong, and she said that nothing was wrong—quite the opposite. And then, crying, smiling, she told me an extraordinary story.

James had been very connected all day. So when Charlotte went to put him to bed, she had the idea of reading James a bedtime story. This was something that she had looked forward to as a mom—her reading him a story and him listening and enjoying it. But every time she had attempted this previously, James hadn't shown any interest. Because James had been so interactive that day, Charlotte felt that maybe this was the night.

When she entered his room, though, she saw that he was sitting on his bed with one of his books, tapping on it with his fingers. Charlotte knew that this was one of James's isms, but she really had her heart set on reading him a bedtime story. So she interrupted him and said, "Hey, James, I'm going to read you a bedtime story!"

He ignored her and kept tapping.

"Hey, kiddo, let's put that book down. It's time for a fun story!"

He ignored her and kept tapping.

Then it hit her ("like a frying pan hitting me in the head" she told me). She was making her plan to read her son a bedtime story more important than bonding with him by joining him in his ism. She had known to join him but had been so focused on reading him a story that she had ignored all of the signs he was giving her.

Upon realizing this, she immediately ceased trying to get her son to stop. She had just had a wonderful day with him. She loved him. She just wanted to convey that to him. She just wanted to show him that she accepted him exactly where he was.

So she got out a book of her own, sat down, and began tapping her own book.

After doing this for some time, she stood up and began quietly making her way out of James's room so he could go to sleep. As she was leaving, he put his book down, looked up at her, and said, "I love you."

This was the first time he had ever said these words to her.

THE EXCEPTIONS TO JOINING

There are very few types of isms that you are not going to want to join in with. Most of them will be pretty obvious to you, and one of them may not.

First, if your child is doing anything that is dangerous or in any way putting his safety at risk (playing in traffic, opening a car door while moving, playing with a sharp object, standing on a high ledge), *stop your child immediately*. Safety always comes first. Don't join with anything dangerous.

Second, if your child is doing something such as touching her genitals or picking her nose, we are obviously not going to join with that, either. Importantly, this does not mean that you need to get uncomfortable and force your child to stop. This kind of behavior is very normal, it's just not something you would want to join in with. (As I said, very obvious points here.)

Third (not obvious), you don't want to join if your child is watching television (or a video). You can't really join in with watching TV. All you can do is just sit there, which is not joining with an activity, it's watching. So when it comes to television, either don't use that time to join or—better yet—turn off the TV and join whatever else your child does.

ACTIVITY TIME!

This is going to be super simple. Take a look at Table 1. All you are going to do is find five different behaviors—isms—that your child does that you haven't previously joined in with that you now will.

You don't have to fill out all five isms in one sitting. Take your time. You can fill out the first one or two that come to you, then come back to this table a day later, once you've noticed another ism.

The most important thing is to keep your eyes peeled for isms—and then to join your child in exactly the way we've discussed.

Ism	How you've been responding	What you will do now to join
1)		
2)		
3)		
4)		
5)		

Table 1

ONLINE RESOURCES

At the end of each chapter, the "Online Resources" section will point you to a special section of my website specifically oriented toward that chapter. There you will find a host of resources designed to help you more deeply understand and implement that chapter's principles and techniques, such as videos, webcasts, articles, and photos.

I want to very strongly encourage you to *use these resources.* They are completely free to you—to use as many times as you wish, as frequently as you wish.

For this chapter, please go to www.autismbreakthrough.com /chapter2. Enjoy!

STARTING POINT

When your child is isming, join him in what he is doing. Do it with delight! Get really involved in the activity. Remember to give your child some space and position yourself so that it is easy for him to glance at you.

THREE

Motivation: The Engine of Your Child's Growth

WANT TO LEARN the key to teaching your child new skills and facilitating learning?

I thought you might.

If joining is the right hand of The Son-Rise Program, motivation is the left hand. You need to join in order to get your child to a place where she is ready to learn and grow, and motivation is the lever you use to get the learning and growth to happen once she is ready.

Before we dive into the motivation principle and how to utilize it, it's important that we talk about the problems and pitfalls of the conventional way that children on the autism spectrum are taught.

THE TIMING PROBLEM

The biggest mistake we make is attempting to teach or challenge our kids when they are not in a state where they can take in new information. When your child is, for instance, isming, not giving you eye contact, not responding when you speak to him or call his name, he is giving you a red light. (We'll talk much more about red lights and green lights in Chapter 12.) When you try to teach, cajole, or enlist your child while he is giving you a red light, you are "running a red." When you're driving, and you run a red light, you might think you'll get to your destination more quickly, but, oftentimes, the result is quite different—maybe a

51

fender bender, maybe sitting on the side of the road getting a ticket. Likewise, when you're with your child, you might run a red, thinking that you'll get where you want to go with him faster. However, the result here is also the opposite.

It is crucial to wait until your child is ready and available before doing any teaching or challenging. We call these windows of availability green lights. (Again, this will be reintroduced later.) If your child is not isming and is looking at you and responsive, you probably have a green light. That is the time for teaching or asking for something from him. (You'll get more of these windows of availability if you join consistently, by the way.)

When we challenge our children at the correct times, the speed of learning and quality of interaction is drastically accelerated. You really will not believe how much it will pay off to follow your child's learning schedule rather than yours or anyone else's.

THE MOTIVATION MISMATCH

Motivation is the engine of growth. It is the single largest factor in your child's learning and progress. When a child is following his or her own intrinsic interests and motivations, learning comes fast and furious. Fortunately, very few people will fight you on this idea; there is widespread agreement on the importance of each child's motivation. Unfortunately, the motivation principle is rarely, if ever, put into practice with any consistency—*especially* with children on the autism spectrum.

Ninety-nine percent of the time, our children are taught in a way that works "against the grain" and slows down their learning. They are taught according to the schedule, curriculum, and dictates of the adults who are teaching them.

At home, the adults usually decide what activities will occur (bathtime, learning, eating, playtime) and how they will transpire (with what toys, food, silverware, games, books). In a school classroom, this system of adults choosing the what and the how is even more prevalent. Even the best, most dedicated, most talented teachers cannot possibly customize their teaching to every child's individual motivation when they face a roomful of students, each of whom has sharply divergent interests.

To add to the mismatch, children on the autism spectrum tend to have unusual and esoteric interests in the first place. What neurotypical children find motivating rarely interests children on the spectrum. Therefore, traditional modes of teaching will hardly ever be motivating to these children.

The end result is that the manner in which our kids are taught is not matched to what they find motivating and interesting. A child is asked to sit down at a table and fill out a worksheet. But it turns out that she likes Star Wars themes—and could be easily engaged in an activity involving Darth Vader or the Millennium Falcon. A child is told to say two new words in a certain order (for no reason that he can fathom). And yet, he might love to be chased—and might be happy to say "chase me" or "run fast" in the context of a chasing game.

A little girl is asked to count to five by counting black circles on a piece of paper. But she loves dinosaurs. Wouldn't she learn to count faster if we played a game with dinosaurs where she had to count out five dinosaurs that she wanted?

When we talk about the principle of using each child's intrinsic motivations, what we mean is this: customize the presentation of the curriculum (i.e., anything you are helping your child to do or learn) to match your child's highest areas of interest.

The books *The Brain That Changes Itself* and *The Art of Changing the Brain* point out that if you really want to change the brain—put the brain in a maximum growth state and foster the most learning—the key is to find and capitalize on the interests and motivations that a person already has, not to force-feed someone information or try to "make" someone motivated. When a child or adult is excited and motivated, neurotransmitters are secreted that act to turn on the brain, priming it for growth, change, and learning.

You want to introduce every skill you want your child to learn, every educational goal you have, every new activity you want your child to try within games or activities that are built around what your child already finds motivating and interesting.

PITFALLS OF THE REWARD PRINCIPLE

It is usually at this point that schoolteachers or therapists will say to me, "We're already using this technique—have been for years. We find something that each child likes—say, M&M's or a favorite toy—and we use these things as rewards to get the children to do something that we are trying to help them do or learn."

To be clear, using rewards is the exact opposite of the motivation principle, but we'll get to that in a bit.

For now, it is important to understand that the reward principle is the single most widely used teaching technique in the entire world when it comes to children with autism. (I am using the term "reward principle" here for clarity and simplicity. It is not an academic or technical term.) I'm sure, without even meeting you, that your child has been worked with using the reward principle. And there is nothing remotely strange about this.

Everybody looooves the reward principle. Hey, it's awesome! It gets our kids to do stuff! Why wouldn't we love it?

Without question, there is definitely a sizable number of our kids who will do something we want them to do when we offer them the right rewards. However, doing this comes with some pretty huge side effects.

Detrimental Desserts

Look, if you offer me chocolate, my first reaction is *chocolate: me likey.* And I'm not exaggerating when I say that I *really* like chocolate. I like things covered in chocolate. Things with chocolate in them. Things made out of chocolate. Did I mention chocolate?

I tell you this to make a larger point (and to plant the seeds now, in case you're thinking of buying me a gift). If you stick a plate of broccoli in front of me, I'm not going to beat down any doors to get at it. Don't get me wrong. I have a healthy respect for broccoli, and I do eat it, but it's not my favorite thing in the world. Truth is, I eat it purely out of some twisted sense of biological obligation.

Now, if you tell me that if I finish that plate of broccoli in front of me, you'll give me a bowl of double chocolate ice cream with hot fudge and chocolate-covered peanuts, then we're in business. I will probably finish the broccoli.

But what happens when you don't have any chocolate to offer me?

Did offering me that dessert magically transform me into a vegetable-loving health nut? Will I now scarf down any plate of broccoli that crosses my path?

Heck no! Unless you cover every plate of broccoli from here to eternity in a pound of chocolate, good luck! But let's take a closer look at why this is, because it goes to the heart of how all human beings—including our kids—operate.

When we set up the reward system, we are basically saying this: "Listen, if you do this awful, terrible thing that you can't stand, I'll give you this wonderful reward! In fact, the only reason to do what I'm asking is for the reward."

(Interestingly, a growing body of research—explained in books such as *Drive, The Medici Effect,* and *The Upside of Irrationality*—shows that, in business, offering people financial rewards such as a monetary bonus ahead of time for doing a task that requires thought and learning actually causes a *decrease* in performance!)

Think about it. We are a nation of people that love fattening, sugar-laden treats. But most of us grew up with loving parents who coaxed (or compelled) us to eat our vegetables. What the heck happened? Well, we grew up with the reward principle—at least in the food category. We were told that if we ate our vegetables, we would get to eat our delicious dessert. Sure, we ate our veggies when we had to, but, in most cases, we came to see the healthy stuff as the gross, obligatory food that we had to "get through" in order to get to the "good stuff," which was the fatty, sugary poison we call dessert.

In fact, the very idea of dessert conjures up notions of the good-tasting sweet reward following the meal. Why do we need the reward? Why isn't the meal enough? If we saw the meal as delicious and truly satisfying in its own right, it *would* be enough.

This is the exact scenario that children on the spectrum are presented with, except they are presented with it for *everything*. Nothing is too big or small to warrant a reward. And the less our children seem to want to do something, the bigger the reward they get for doing it.

The net result of all of this arrangement is that they grow to hate doing the very things we are endeavoring to get them to do on their own. Sure, they'll do it (some of the time), but now they're doing it *only* for the reward.

This is especially problematic for our special group of children because we are, in essence, telling them: "Let's get through this stinky human interaction crud, and then you can get the good stuff." But the thing is, *we want the human interaction to be the good stuff!* That's our children's only ticket out!

If you are the parent of a neurotypical teenaged girl, you don't have to offer her a reward to get her to talk on the phone with her friends. (You may have to reward her to get her *off* the phone.) Why? Because for her, talking on the phone with her friends (human interaction, socialization, and interpersonal relating) *is* the reward. It *is* the good stuff. *That's where we want our special kids to be!*

Robotic Behavior

One of the most common complaints I hear from parents with respect to the reward principle is that, yes, their children do perform some useful behaviors, but that they do so in a way usually described as "robotic." Their children may put the puzzle together or ask, "How are you today?" or shake a person's hand when prompted, but they do so in a programmed manner without any apparent joy or spontaneity.

In fact, many of these parents have been told that robotic behavior is a key symptom of autism. And, indeed, many children on the spectrum do appear this way. However, in our experience, robotic behavior, devoid of joy or spontaneity, is not a symptom of *autism*. Rather, it is a symptom of *the way we teach children with autism*. It is a symptom of the widespread and excessive use of the reward principle.

James, though he is still on the autism spectrum, does *not* have robotic behaviors. When my niece, Jade, was autistic, she did not have robotic behaviors. When I had autism, I did not exhibit robotic behaviors. At the Autism Treatment Center of America, we have worked with many children who did not display robotic behavior. Robotic behavior is not ubiquitous in Son-Rise Program children. The motivation principle is not a magic cure-all, but one thing it does *not* do is produce robotic behaviors.

Compliance-Centric

I was once shown a video (as an example of success) in which a little boy was repeatedly told "coat on" and then given an M&M when he complied. As soon as he finished putting his coat on, a facilitator would take the coat off again, offer the little boy his coat again, and say "coat on" again. This method was seen as a success because, by the end, the little boy was reliably putting on his coat when asked. (I am not trying to paint every therapy with one brush, and I know that not all therapists do what I saw on the video. However, some version of this—the reward may change, the activity may be less repetitive, etc.—is still the norm in autism treatment.)

I highlight this video for a very specific reason. As I watched it, what struck me—in addition to my concern about what this experience might have felt like for this boy—was that, in reality, this boy had not learned the skill the facilitators were aiming for. At the end of the day, this little boy learned one thing: compliance. Now, I'm not saying that compliance is a bad thing. But it is very different than learning the actual skill that the therapists were claiming to teach. The actual skill of putting one's coat on (to use this very simple example), entails the following: I walk outside, I realize that it's chilly out, I step back inside, I put on my coat, I go back outside.

What the little boy in the video learned was to put his coat on when someone said "coat on." As I said, this is by no means a bad thing for him to learn, but it means that someone has to follow him around and tell him to put his coat on, take it off, put his shoes on, take his shoes off, etc.

To be independent—and to feel successful, and to interact socially in a meaningful way—this little boy has to learn the real skill. He needs to learn not only the real coat-donning skill, but also, much more importantly, real social interaction skills—being interested in others, communicating, enjoying an interactive game or activity, etc. (rather than having someone next to him telling him what to do and say every minute).

The ability of a child or adult to take something that he has learned and apply it in different circumstances (home, school, etc.) is called generalization. For our children, being able to generalize what they learn is absolutely critical.

Truly learning something, and then being able to generalize it, comes from *enjoying* it. It comes from being *interested* in it. And it comes from being internally *motivated* to do it.

While repetitive teaching with rewards is not bad for getting a child to follow instructions, this method is utterly incapable of manufacturing motivation. It cannot enable that child to sincerely learn, generalize, enjoy, and be interested in what she is being taught. This is even more the case when it comes to social skills, which are the very abilities our children could most use help acquiring.

In short, these are the three main side effects of the reward principle:

1. Robotic behavior.

2. Your child will learn to hate what he is being asked to do or learn.

3. Your child will not really learn the actual skill (only to follow instructions), and thus will have great difficulty generalizing the skill to other situations where there is not a prompt → behavior → reward system in place.

James used to love games that involved us running. To be precise, he especially enjoyed watching *me* run. He would say "Waun, wun fast!" (his version of "Raun, run fast!") and then break out into peals of laughter when I did so. (I'm not sure whether to take this as a compliment or an insult.) I could get him to do almost anything if it involved me running. Charlotte once called me to tell me that, *in his sleep*, James was giggling and saying "Waun, wun fast." (He was apparently dreaming.) Could you imagine this happening with the reward principle?

USING THE MOTIVATION PRINCIPLE

If the motivation principle is not the reward principle, how is it different? This is another one of those Son-Rise Program techniques that isn't just different; it's the exact opposite. To use this technique, we must flip everything.

A good place to start is to change your focus as you are trying to teach or challenge your child. First, the starting point is no longer identifying what you want your child to do. Instead, think about what your child's areas of interests (motivations) are. Does your child like Disney characters? Airplanes? Physical play? Science fiction themes? Chasing games? You're going to focus on these first, and *then* think about what you want your child to do or learn.

You will want to write down some of your child's interests and motivations. You may be wondering how you know what these interests are. All you need to do is to observe your child. What does your child do? What does she gravitate toward? Is there anything that she really enjoys watching you do? If your child is verbal, what does she talk about when an adult isn't dictating the conversation?

You will also want to write down a short list of some educational goals—or, more simply, things that you want your child to do. Specificity is very important here. It is very difficult to effectively pursue a broad goal with your child. For example, you may be helping your child with verbal communication, but a goal of "using words" is too general. Rather, you'd want a goal such as "using the word 'chase'" or "saying 'I want chase,'" depending on your child's language level. Goals are by no means limited to language. They can involve eye contact, length of time he is willing to stay involved in a game, taking turns, a specific activity like going to the dentist, even self-care skills included in daily living, such as toilet training, taking a bath, eating a particular food that isn't his favorite, getting dressed, or tidying his room.

The Technique

At the core, it only takes three steps to implement the motivation principle:

1. Join your child until she is no longer isming, and she looks at you (more than just a one-second glance). Note: You can skip this step only if your child is already interacting with you and not isming at all.

2. Playfully invite your child to participate in an activity or game based upon something that she likes (as we've discussed).

3. **Beginner's version:** *If and only if* your child willingly gets involved in your game, keep that game going as long as possible. For example, if your child loves to be tickled or enjoys talking about the planets, simply participate in this activity (with great enthusiasm!) for as long as your child stays interested. Just having your child engage in that game for increasing amounts of time will stretch her interactive attention span—and thus her ability to interact with others.
   Advanced option: *If and only if* your child willingly gets involved in your game, add one thing. For example, if your child loves chase games, and you successfully get her to play chase with you, then try adding one thing, such as: you keep "running out of gas," and she has to keep saying "chase" to get you to chase her.

The Story of Pedro

Pedro's mother came to a Start-Up program exasperated and a bit desperate. She had been trying to toilet-train Pedro for six months. Not only was he not yet weeing in the toilet, but he had a greater aversion to anything toilet-related than he had six months prior. Pedro's mom brought this challenge up during one of the question-and-answer sessions of her Start-Up course, but she was not feeling optimistic about finding a solution.

We discussed the motivation principle, and we spent a few minutes coming up with an idea for her to use. First, we asked her what one of Pedro's motivations was. She hesitated, then said that her son loved stairs and anything (such as escalators or even stools) that had steps. She quickly added an apology, saying that she must not have chosen the right kind of motivation, since steps and stairs had nothing to do with weeing in the toilet.

We told her that this was exactly the right kind of motivation, as any of her son's interests would be. Sure, it was true that stairs and steps did not have anything intrinsically in common with using the toilet, but that was fine, as the whole principle is predicated on combining two things (a motivation and a goal) that don't necessarily relate together into one game or activity.

So, we helped her to come up with a game, and she returned home after the Start-Up, eager to try it with her son. Her first day back, she entered Pedro's room with a new three-step stool. Pedro walked over to it and climbed onto it, immediately interested. That first day, all Pedro's mom did was to play with him on this stool, in whatever way he liked.

The second day, she brought the stepping stool in again and invited Pedro to play on it once more. This time, however, the game involved her moving the stool to different locations around the room, and Pedro climbed on it only after his mom had moved it to its next "destination."

On the third day, they were playing this game again, and, at the height of Pedro's excitement and involvement, she pushed the stepping stool right up against the toilet and invited Pedro to walk up the three steps, stand on the stool, and wee into the toilet.

Pedro did it, and he did it happily and without a fight.

Now let's take a few minutes to uncover exactly why this worked. It would be reasonable for you to ask how it is possible that Pedro, a little boy who seemed unable to wee in the potty after six months of his mother trying, weed in the toilet for the first time in less than three days. (Furthermore, Pedro did not require rewards to continue to use the toilet. Over the next few days, his mom soon removed the stool, and Pedro was fine with using the toilet without it.) In fact, I used to be concerned that, when telling this story, the jump from six months to three days might seem too good to be true. But there is nothing mysterious about it. It's logic, not magic, that makes it work.

The motivation principle plays to your child's intelligence. It plays on the fact that your child has the intelligence to do many of the things that he isn't doing. Autism is not an intelligence problem. *Our job is not to make our children more intelligent; it is to unlock the intelligence that's already there.* Knowing this, we can say that Pedro's lack of toileting was not an intelligence problem; it was a motivation issue. Pedro did not lack the smarts to use the toilet. He lacked an interest, a trust, and a motivation.

And, in hindsight, this should not be at all surprising. First of all, he's getting his nappy changed every so often throughout the day. So, from his point of view, life is good—it's like living at a full-service petrol station! He wees, he poos, and—poof!—someone swoops in, takes the smelly nappy away, cleans him up, and provides him with a fresh new nappy. Sounds good to me!

Do any of us really think that Pedro is lying in his bed at night thinking: *You know, this nappy situation is pretty cool, but it would be so much more socially appropriate for me to go directly into the toilet?* Of course not! It's *us* who want our kids to go in the toilet (and many other things). And that's fine. We certainly don't have to apologize for that. But what we do need to do is to realize that since *we* are the ones who want these things for our children, it is *our* job to find a way to get *them* as interested as *we* are.

Second, as Pedro's mother was endeavoring to toilet-train him for the first six months before seeing us, she was doing what almost all parents and teachers do. She was pushing Pedro to use the toilet, even when he didn't want to. She was offering him rewards, which immediately sent the message that the toilet was something unpleasant that he had to do to get the reward. And she conveyed the message, in countless subtle ways, that there was a right way and a wrong way to go on the toilet. (For instance, weeing and missing the toilet is the "wrong" way.)

Pedro's thinking *Hey, I liked this better when I was getting my nappy changed. No one was pressuring me, and I couldn't get it "wrong"!* And, really, I can't blame him.

What Pedro's mom did so brilliantly with the motivation principle was use an interest Pedro already had; she didn't break trust by pushing him, and she made the toilet something that was fun and motivating to Pedro in its own right.

Important: This case study illustrates an example of using the motivation principle for a basic skill. Please don't take this to mean that this principle is only useful for teaching these types of skills. In fact, this strategy is incredibly powerful with more complex skills, such as social and conversational skills. We will be discussing a case study on exactly this area in Chapter 15.

ACTIVITY TIME!

Take a look at Table 2. You'll notice that it has two columns. In the left-hand column, write down five motivations or areas of interest that your child has. (Don't worry about the order.) In the right-hand column, write down five specific, short-term educational goals. These are things that you are trying to get your child to do or learn.

Now, draw a line from one of the motivations to one of the goals. How will you decide which two items to connect with a line? Look over your table, and think about which motivation might most easily go together in a game or activity with which goal.

This does not mean the motivation and the goal have to be similar or naturally "go together." Remember the example from this chapter, when Pedro's mom combined a stepping stool with peeing in the toilet? Those two things aren't at all similar. Another mom worked on her son's eye contact using his interest in airplanes. A dad worked on his daughter's language using her interest in Disney characters. So you are just going to do your best. Once you've connected one motivation with one goal, draw a line connecting a second motivation with a second goal. Then continue drawing lines until each motivation has one goal connected to it.

This will be your beginning blueprint for coming up with games and activities to help your child gain skills and achieve goals. You can use this blueprint to begin generating an idea or two of what kinds of games and activities you can do with your child to help him progress.

Motivation / Area of Interest	Educational Goal
1)	1)
2)	2)
3)	3)
4)	4)
5)	5)

Table 2

ONLINE RESOURCES

For more in-depth help with the principles and techniques of this chapter, please go to www.autismbreakthrough.com/chapter3. Have fun!

STARTING POINT

Remember the three-step technique we talked about earlier:

1. Join your child until she is no longer isming, and she looks at you (more than just a one-second glance). Note: You can skip this step only if your child is already interacting with you and not isming at all.

2. Playfully invite your child to participate in an activity or game based on something that she likes (as we've discussed).

3. **Beginner's version:** *If and only if* your child willingly gets involved in your game, keep that game going as long as possible. For example, if she loves to be tickled or enjoys talking about the planets, simply participate in this activity (with great enthusiasm!) for as long as your child stays interested. Just having your child engage in that game for increasing amounts of time will stretch your child's interactive attention span—and thus her ability to interact with others.

   Advanced option: *If and only if* your child willingly gets involved in your game, add one thing. For example, if your child loves chase games, and you successfully get her to play chase with you, then try adding one thing, such as: you keep "running out of gas," and she has to keep saying "chase" to get you to chase her.

FOUR

Creativity: How to Stay Fresh and Creative When Coming Up with Games and Activities for Your Child

ONE ASPECT OF The Son-Rise Program that makes it unique and fulfilling—but also scary for some people—is that it utilizes the creativity of the people working with your child (including you!). For this reason, it is important to spend some time really focusing on how to be (and stay) creative. Once you have the tools provided in this chapter, you can be a never-ending generator of ideas.

WHY COMING UP WITH GAMES AND ACTIVITIES CAN FEEL STRESSFUL

Okay, so before we go any further, we need to address the elephant in the room. We can talk about motivation all day, but none of it will matter if you don't use it. And you're not going to use it if you're nervous and stressed about using it. If you are like every other parent I've ever worked with, you may be saying to yourself: *This strategy sounds great on paper, and it may be great for creative types, but I'm just not creative like that. I can't just come up with ideas. And, even when I come up with something good, I quickly run out of ideas after that.*

The very first thing you need to know is that *having these thoughts is completely normal.* It means absolutely nothing about you as a parent. It doesn't mean that you're not creative, and it doesn't mean that you can't do this—or even that it will be hard for you. All it means is that you have an inaccurate idea of what creativity is and how to tap into it.

If you sit down right now and try to push out ten great game ideas for your child based upon his or her motivations, it's going to be rough sailing. The first reason for this is your attitude about yourself. Having a perspective that you aren't creative enough—or "whatever" enough—may be normal (as in "usual"), but it isn't natural (as in "a necessary part of the human condition").

STOP STEPPING ON YOUR CREATIVITY

Every time you start thinking that you aren't creative, you need to pause. Remind yourself that you are just telling yourself this based on an inaccurate idea of what creativity is. You are absolutely, without question, creative. I'm not telling you this as some rah-rah motivational speech. I'm saying this because every person is creative. I have not worked with a single parent who isn't. The human mind is inherently creative. Saying you're not is like saying you don't have a brain, and since you're alive and reading this, I'm going to go out on a limb and say that you do, in fact, have a brain.

Now, you may have met people whom you feel are much more creative than you. What you need to know is that these people aren't more creative than you; they just don't step on their creativity.

We step on our creativity in three key ways.

1. We tell ourselves that we aren't creative.
This kills any chance at creativity that we may have. Contrary to the cultural stereotype of the depressed or angry creative artist, you need your brain to be loose, relaxed, and upbeat to have a free flow of ideas. So you need to make a promise to yourself that you will cease the self-condemnation.

2. We censor our ideas.

Most of us wait for (and write down) only the "good" ideas. This will stifle your ability to generate ideas. You have to vomit up ideas. I'm serious! Come up with as many as you can, as fast as you can. You're going for quantity.

Have your list of your child's interests matched with goals, and then come up with as many games as possible that contain one from each. If that seems hard, slow down. Begin by looking at a list of your child's motivations. For each one, come up with as many games or activities as you can.

If you catch yourself starting to judge an idea, you want to tell yourself that your goal is to come up with lots of "bad" ideas. "Bad" ideas are terrific! Many of my best ideas began as ideas I could have originally called "bad."

For instance, I love coming up with titles and names for things. I often do this with respect to the courses we offer at the Autism Treatment Center of America. Several of the titles and subtitles of our courses have come from my idea-generation sessions. All I do is sit at my desk, relax, get myself revved up about the task at hand, and then just type out as many titles as I can think of as fast as I can. I have tried, in the past, only typing out the "good" ones. An hour later, I have one or two titles, and they aren't even that good. When I just spit out ideas, actively welcoming potential "bad" ones, I have a gigantic list after half an hour.

Whatever you do, don't censor your ideas. If you have a copious list of ideas, go back through your list, working through each of your ideas one at a time to flesh them out and add some details of your game or activity. If, at that point, some of your ideas seem totally unworkable to you, feel free to ditch them. But don't discard any of your ideas until *after* you've come up with a long list.

3. We insist on perfection.

We tell ourselves that our ideas *have to* work with our kids. We hobble our ideas ahead of time by coming up with all of the reasons why they might not work, why our children might not go with them. In addition, we crush countless ideas after we try them because our children weren't immediately interested.

Unless you are a mind reader, there is no way on earth that you will come up with and attempt only ideas that work the first time or immediately catch your child's interest. Some of your ideas will work brilliantly the very first time, but a whole bunch of others won't. Do you know how many times I've come up with a game, introduced it to a child I was working with, and promptly saw that game flop? Many, many times. When this happens, I just say to myself: *Well, that certainly didn't work. I'll try something different next time, and maybe I'll fiddle with this game some more and try it again next time, next month, etc.*

Take the notion that your idea has to be perfect and has to work, and chuck it out the window. You will feel so liberated, and, more importantly, you won't hamstring your creativity. You'll need that creativity to be maximally helpful to your child.

CREATIVITY TECHNIQUE: ADD ONE THING

We've talked about what *not* to do when creating games and activities that capitalize on your child's motivation. So what do you do?

First, let's talk about a straightforward game-creation technique that I actually learned from my older sister Bryn (Executive Director of the Autism Treatment Center of America).

Bryn often teaches parents a technique that can be summed up in these three words: add one thing.

Imagine that you are endeavoring to come up with a language-building game that involves chasing, since you know your child likes to chase or be chased. Rather than trying to think of all the ways that you could possibly change or expand chasing to help generate more language from your child, you simply add one thing. It could be that he must say the word "chase" every so often to keep you running. It could be that you suddenly freeze every so often, and he has to tag you or say "go" to get you going again. It could be that you chase in slow motion—or only by hopping on one foot. If your child has more sophisticated language, it could be that you freeze every so often, and he has to answer a question to get you going again.

When you begin trying this technique, make sure that you stick to adding just *one* thing—not two or three. Start with the absolute *simplest* thing you can think of. You can:

- Speed things up

- Slow things down

- Skip a turn

- Do something silly

- Use only high voices

- Add one additional step

- Skip a step

- Change one of the game's rules

- Add one request or challenge

The Story of Charles

The "add one thing" technique also works with much more complex games. I recently worked with a nine-year-old boy in England named Charles who was very verbal. He loved history, especially imagining different times (the 1920s, the 1800s) and how things were different then. I was at Charles's house, doing something called an outreach, which is when a Son-Rise Program teacher or child facilitator spends a couple of days in a family's house helping them implement their program. If a family has an outreach with a teacher, as was the case when Charles's family had me, the teacher observes the parents working with their child and gives them pointers and feedback. The teacher also gives feedback to others who work with the child—and helps the parents to most effectively train them. Of course, the teacher will also answer any questions and deal with any issues that come up. We have a host of staff who perform these outreaches, though my own schedule doesn't allow me to do them very often anymore. What I do really enjoy about doing outreaches is the segment of time I get to spend working directly with the child.

In Charles's case, I had planned a game based on his interest in historical times. In our game, we would use a time machine. We would enter the time machine, I would bounce him around a lot as we traveled through time, and then we would step out and have a short adventure in whatever time we were in. I had planned this out in advance, but something happened that I wasn't prepared for.

This was my very first time with Charles, so I had planned the game with the goals of building trust with him and getting him to interact with me as long as I could. However, our game succeeded beyond even what I had planned for. Charles completely engaged in every aspect of the game, showing no signs whatsoever of tiring of our interaction together. So I realized that I had some room to challenge Charles more.

I knew that Charles had no deficits in language; his main challenges were being flexible in his games and allowing them to
change based upon what another person wanted. Charles liked his
games and activities to go a particular way, and he was not usually
amenable to deviations instigated by others. This may sound trifling
to those of you who have children just learning to speak, but this
kind of difficulty with flexibility has far-reaching consequences for
any child's ability to make friends or get through the school day
successfully. (More on this in Chapter 9.)

I had only a few seconds to decide how I could challenge
Charles in this way, since we were right in the midst of our game. I
certainly did not have the time to sit down and come up with any
kind of intricate plan. So I fell back onto the idea of changing one
thing. Every time we reentered the time machine to go to a particular
year, I would ask Charles one question. The question was: What is
one activity that you like to do with your friends that we cannot do
in the year we're going to? (You will understand in the next chapter
why I chose a question about something he liked to do with others
as opposed to simply having him answer a factual question about
the year to which we were traveling.)

Keep in mind that I left everything else about the game the
same—I only changed this one aspect. At first, even this one change
proved challenging for Charles. He wanted to go to the next historical time immediately. Over time, as I stuck with this one change, he
got better and better at it, becoming more patient and more flexible.

Later that day, when one of his facilitators arrived, he ran up to
her, jumping up and down and saying excitedly, "Raun and I had a
great time! We built a time machine and traveled to the past and
the future!" And I probably had an even better time than he did.

CREATIVITY TECHNIQUE: ANYTHING CAN BE ANYTHING

The other creativity-boosting game or activity generation technique I find very helpful is this: anything can be anything. Sounds strange, but all it means is that any object in the room can be any object you want—any object that suits your purpose.

The BBC did a documentary following a family through The Son-Rise Program several years back. (Contact the Autism Treatment Center of America if you would like us to send you a DVD of this documentary. It is quite incredible and very moving.) There is one funny scene in which Bryn is working with the mom, helping her be more creative in coming up with games to play with her son. Bryn takes out a water bottle and says to the mom, "So, what could this be?" And the mom, with total sincerity says, "Something to drink out of?"

What makes this funny to watch is how this mom—at first—does what we are all trained to do, and that is to take the world exactly as it is. If someone tells you this is a water bottle, then, by gosh, that's what it is. But as the scene in the documentary continues, Bryn shows this mom how effortless it can be to think up scores of other objects that the bottle can be: a hairbrush, a trumpet, a rocket ship, an earring, a telescope, a telephone, etc. Soon this very sweet mom is creating with the best of them.

When you are coming up with a game or activity to do with your child, keep in mind the anything-can-be-anything idea. You may even want to practice with a few items ahead of time. For instance, take a water bottle, a pen, a ball, and a kitchen pot, and spend fifteen minutes thinking up ten other objects that each of these items could be.

One of the reasons that my parents were able to develop The Son-Rise Program and come up with ideas every day to help me was because they did nothing to hold themselves back from being creative and they did everything they could to foster their creativity. To this day, they remain among the most visibly creative people I know—not because they were born with creative brains, but rather because they have proactively chosen attitudes and perspectives that precipitate creativity. (We'll talk more about the importance of attitudes and perspectives in Chapter 17.)

In fact, they frequently practiced what most people might call "trial and error." When something didn't work, they didn't see it as a failure. Rather, they saw it as a fantastic opportunity to gather useful information about what did and did not work. So, really, it wasn't "trial and *error*." It was "trial and *info*."

ACTIVITY TIME!

Now is the perfect time to start flexing your creativity muscles—by using the anything-can-be-anything idea. Table 3 names four common household objects. Below each object, write down seven things that these objects might be in pretend play with your child. The only rule is that none of the seven things can relate to the original object. (For instance, you can't write down "canteen" under the object "water bottle" or "cooking utensil" under the object "frying pan.")

Frying Pan	Pillow	Ruler	Water Bottle
1)			
2)			
3)			
4)			
5)			
6)			
7)			

Table 3

ONLINE RESOURCES

For some assistance with the principles of this chapter, please go to www.autismbreakthrough.com/chapter4. Jump in, Dr. Creative!

STARTING POINT

Practice the anything-can-be-anything idea during an everyday activity with your child. Next time you are eating dinner with your child, take the spoon and make it an airplane. Take a frying pan and use it as a drum. Take your child's blanket, put it on the floor, and pretend it's a flying carpet.

Engaging in this practice will flex your creativity muscles and limber up your brain, which is crucial for developing effective motivation-based activities. On top of that, you will have more fun with your child!

FIVE

Socialization: The Son-Rise Program Developmental Model

MOST OF THE time, your child is being taught the *least* helpful things.

There is a national obsession (actually, it's worldwide) with teaching academic subjects to children on the autism spectrum. Teaching academics may sound like a good idea, but it really doesn't serve our children. Bear with me, and you'll see why.

The Story of Kwan

I sat in Kwan's house, observing his program. It was the first time I'd ever worked with his family, who had recently seen one of my lectures but had not yet been to the ATCA for a Start-Up course. They were running what would be considered by most to be an excellent in-home applied behavior analysis (ABA) program. (For those of you unfamiliar with ABA, see Appendix 2.)

Kwan was running back and forth in the kitchen when his lead ABA therapist arrived. Kwan ignored her and kept running back and forth. She stood in front of him (so that he had to stop momentarily) and put her hand a few inches in front of his face—and said "check schedule." In her hand was a Picture Exchange Communication System (PECS) card with a picture I couldn't make out.

Kwan immediately stopped running, walked over to his designated seat at his worktable, and sat down. His therapist sat down across from him and quickly pulled out some large flash cards. She turned to Kwan and said, "Show me you're ready."

He sat up and put his hands palms down on the table.

"Good boy," the therapist said approvingly.

She then flipped the cards over. Each card was a different color. There was a red, a green, and a blue card. "Kwan, point to the blue card."

He pointed to the blue card.

"Good boy, Kwan," she said, giving him a toy he liked. "Break time, Kwan. Two minutes."

Kwan played with his toy.

Two minutes later: "Okay, Kwan, show me you're ready."

Kwan sat up and put his hands palms down on the table.

The therapist showed Kwan three more cards, each with a different number. "Kwan, point to the number two."

Kwan pointed to the number two.

"Good boy, Kwan."

This continued for two hours.

This was among the most successful ABA sessions I had seen. I had, in the past, witnessed kids scream, hit, bite themselves, or completely tune out during these types of sessions. But Kwan had been completely trained into submission. And I could absolutely understand why these sessions—including their "successful" results—would be attractive to his parents and therapists. (At the same time, I knew his parents felt that something was missing; otherwise they wouldn't have attended my lecture, and they wouldn't have arranged for me to come to their home.)

Kwan was obedient, and he knew his numbers, colors, and the names of household objects.

Also:

Kwan had no friends.

Kwan could not play a game with another person.

Kwan displayed no interest in other people.

Kwan had very limited language.

Kwan had almost no eye contact.

Kwan did not engage in imaginative play.

Kwan did not laugh at jokes—or know what a joke was.

When left to his own devices, Kwan would ism for hours.

Kwan, like all children and adults with autism, had a social-relational disorder. His difficulties were social and interpersonal, not academic. And no matter how many colors he could name, no matter how far he progressed in maths, with his current set of skills Kwan was not going to become social or interact successfully.

Is it bad that Kwan learned his colors and his numbers? Of course not. It's just beside the point.

Kwan's parents wanted more for him, and they set up a Son-Rise Program to help him in the areas where he most needed help. His journey, filled with many changes and successes, really inspired me, especially when I returned a couple of years later (I had been there a couple of times in the interim) and saw Kwan.

As I approached his house, I heard him open a window and call out to me, "Hi, Raun, did you come to play with me?"

When I shouted out a yes in reply, he waited for me at the door, took my hand, and escorted me into his playroom to play.

THE PROBLEM WITH MATHS
(AND OTHER ACADEMIC SUBJECTS)

If Chapter 3 focused on *how* to teach, this chapter zeroes in on *what* to teach.

There are reasons schools and therapists are preoccupied with teaching academic subjects to children on the spectrum. First, academics are what schools are built to teach. Everything about a school is designed to teach maths, reading, science, etc. This is by no means a criticism of schools. This is what schools are *supposed* to do.

Also, for both schools and therapists, academic subjects are the low-hanging fruit. They are the easiest areas in which to generate (and measure) improvement. For a parent, being able to see (and easily explain to others) that their son or daughter with autism can name his or her colors, write his or her name, or count (or, on the other end, that their child with Asperger's syndrome can read Shakespeare or do calculus) provides a kind of tangible evidence that progress is being made.

So I truly, sincerely understand the appeal of teaching academic subjects.

But teaching academic subjects to children on the spectrum just isn't going to affect what really matters. Not yet.

Autism isn't a maths disorder. It isn't a color-naming disorder. And it isn't a reading disorder. It's a social, relational, interpersonal, interactional disorder. I know we've discussed this point at length, but it simply cannot be overemphasized.

When you are lying in bed awake at night, thinking and praying about your child's future, do you pray that one day your child will be at grade level in maths? Do you fervently look forward to the day when your child will be able to recite the periodic table of elements?

Or do you wish and pray that one day your child will have a best friend? That your daughter will say "I love you" and really mean it? That your son will have a romantic partner? That your child will grow up to live a happy, independent, and fulfilling life? Or even that he will argue with you about using your car to go out with his or her friends? (I had one mom say that she dreamed that one day her son would complain to her about his taxes.)

We need to seriously think about what is going to make our children's lives fulfilling, satisfying, rich, and meaningful to them. Academic subjects just aren't part of that equation. No matter how incredible your child gets at academic subjects, it will not give her the tools she needs to relate to people, laugh at a joke, make friends, and enjoy others.

Am I saying that academic subjects are pointless or useless? Absolutely not. They are valuable. But they are only valuable to someone who can function in the world, and only social enjoyment, connection, and participation can make that happen. In fact, social-relational skills are essential even to succeed at the overall experience of school. Your child needs to be able to relate to the teacher and to other students and have the ability to cope with all of the activities, noises, room switches, and changes of the school day. Excelling at academic subjects is, ironically, not nearly as important.

To be totally clear, I am in no way against academic subjects. My own academic life and attendance at an Ivy League university bears witness to the fact that I hugely value education and academics. But, with our children, focusing on academic subjects first is utterly irrelevant to their success until they can connect with other people and the world at large. It is putting the cart before the horse.

In The Son-Rise Program, we have taught an enormous number of children how to read, write, and do maths. But we have taught kids these subjects *after* we've got them to the point where they can interact and relate really well to people. When a child has crossed the bridge from his world to ours, then, by all means, let's work on academic subjects.

Instead of seeing me as simply a skill-deficient, behaviorally challenged little boy, my parents saw what was *really* going on. They understood, way back in 1974, that I wasn't just a child missing skills; I was a child missing *social* skills. In seeing this, they were not only decades ahead of their time, but they were the *only* people at that time to really "get" autism. And so, for three and a half years, my parents focused single-mindedly on my social development.

And ever since my recovery from autism, the social, interpersonal arena has come the most easily to me. It is also the arena in which I get the most satisfaction and feel the most fulfilled. In high school, I did about equally well in all subjects, ranging from maths to English, science to Spanish. So I could easily have chosen a profession in the sciences, mathematics, or computer sciences. I chose an extremely social and interpersonal profession because that is what I found most rewarding.

My parents, who founded and still teach extensively at the ATCA, are, to this day, very well-attuned to people's social and emotional states. People in our courses are often startled at the observations my parents make about them before they have even said anything.

You may wonder, if my parents worked so intensively with me on my social development, what happened academically when I entered school? Well, at first, in the very early days, I *was* missing academic skills. So my parents worked with me (post-autism) and caught me up. That was the easiest part of the process—the tutoring of a neurotypical child (me!) who was totally connected and completely integrated in their world.

If, years from now, your biggest complaint is that your child is now fully connected and social but is behind in maths, what a great problem to have!

The Story of Callum

Callum was a little boy from Ireland with autism who was nonverbal and deeply enveloped in his own world. He would not relate to or interact with people for more than a few minutes at a time. Two and half years after implementing their Son-Rise Program, Callum was successfully attending a mainstream school. He was sweet and affectionate. After seeing Callum's swift and remarkable progress, the government-appointed specialist who had initially told Callum's parents not to do The Son-Rise Program became an enthusiastic proponent, telling other parents that The Son-Rise Program was the only thing she had seen that actually worked.

One day, well into Callum's program, he and his parents were walking in a local park with a pond. He was having a terrific time, laughing, feeding the ducks in the pond, enjoying himself. His parents, too, were having a magnificent time because Callum seemed so at ease, so much like the totally engaged child they had hoped for him one day to become.

Then Callum noticed a group of kids at the other end of the park. His parents watched with anticipation and some nervousness as their son casually approached them. *How would he do? Would he connect easily with the other kids. Would they notice anything different about him?* After all, this was what they had worked so hard for. This very moment.

Callum joined the group of kids and began talking to them. They responded. He became part of the group. A simple occurrence that a parent of a neurotypical child might not even notice. A "normal" event. But, for this mother and father, it was as if the heavens had opened up. They had been assured that nothing like this could ever occur for their little boy. They had worked tirelessly in their Son-Rise Program to put their son on a different trajectory, and now they were seeing the spectacular fruits of their labor and their love. It was a day they would never forget.

No amount of maths, reading, or science would have led Callum to that day. Only social focus and human interaction can give your child a day like that.

OVERCOMING VERSUS COMPENSATING

Let's return to a point we touched on a few pages ago. Remember when I said that academic subjects were the low-hanging fruit? Why is this?

When we work with a child or adult on academic subjects, we are working on the nonautistic part of the brain—the part that is, essentially, working. (If it isn't working, that is often because the child is so enveloped in her world that her intelligence is not visible.)

The nonautistic part of the brain is also at work during tasks such as completing a puzzle, saying "thank you," learning the daily schedule, etc. All of these areas are attractive teaching opportunities for most parents and teachers because they are the easiest to teach, and they fulfill a basic goal that most of us have with our kids: compensation.

Compensation is the idea that since our children are so impaired in social and relational areas, we need to help them compensate for their deficits by teaching them to get really good at using the parts of their brains they *can* use. This is the same thinking, for instance, that goes into teaching someone who has lost an arm to get really good at using his one remaining arm. And, in the case of someone with one arm, this makes complete sense, since his arm will never grow back.

Unfortunately, this same thinking does *not* make sense with our kids, unless you are of the opinion (and many are) that our children have no possibility to ever grow and progress in the area of social and relational development. Focusing on helping our children to compensate causes us to miss the boat on the real key: overcoming.

Why not spend our time and energy helping our children to *overcome* their biggest deficits (socialization) instead of settling for helping them merely *compensate* by learning crutch skills? Why not shoot for the gold instead of forfeiting? This way, even if we fall far short of the gold, we have still helped our children to move forward in an area in which any progress at all will have immeasurable long-term benefits for them.

Helping our children to overcome their challenges will always yield more satisfying results than helping our kids to compensate for them.

THE IMPORTANCE OF WORKING THE WEAK MUSCLE

Suppose, for a moment, that I had been born with a condition that caused the weakening of the muscles in my legs, such that I could not walk. Suppose, also, that you had been hired as my physical therapist. How would you try to help me?

One strategy you could employ is to spend the next year working intensively with me on building my arm muscles. You could argue that, after all, my arms are perfectly healthy and capable of building muscle. You could point out all the benefits of having very strong arms—how it will help me get around, since I can't do much with my legs. Certainly, an argument can be made for this approach.

On the other hand, you might consider that, no matter how much time you spend building up my arms, no matter how strong you help my arms to get, I will never, ever walk. So you might choose a completely different approach, based upon this fact: the only way on earth that I will ever have a chance to walk is if you help me build up my leg muscles. There's simply no other way that walking is possible. No amount of arm strength will do it.

This analogy illustrates the principle of working the weak muscle. This strategy is a very powerful one, although it takes more work in the short term. In the long term, working the weak muscle pays off in a huge way. It is appealing to most people to work the strong muscle, and I understand why. We can already see what success looks like, and we can see immediate gain.

But when we work the strong muscle, we are always held back by the limits of the weak muscle. Strong arms will never lead to walking or running if our legs are weak.

When we work the *weak* muscles, it might feel challenging at first, but, in the long term, the sky is the limit. There is certainly no harm in working the strong muscles. But, until we work the weak muscle, its limitations will always constrain us.

How does this relate to your child? Your child's "weak muscle" is his socialization muscle. Your child's "strong muscles" (or potentially strong muscles) are his aptitude for memorizing movie lines, names of colors, how to introduce himself, words, daily schedules, directions, as well as possible talents in areas such as maths, mechanics, or drawing. In simpler form, these "strong muscles" may manifest as stacking blocks perfectly, balancing objects with precision, or lining up toys in exactly the same order over and over.

It is wonderful that your child has these strong muscles, and there is nothing wrong with your child eventually having the opportunity to pursue these areas (or even in your using one of these areas in a game as a motivation). It's just that, first, you're going to want to help your child to work her weak muscle.

Working the weak muscle opens the door to a satisfying, independent, and emotionally fulfilling life for your child. Also, even if your child ends up wanting to be a mathematician, without making that weak muscle stronger, it's going to be extremely difficult to get there. Even day-to-day family events, such has having dinner together, going to the shops or a park, playing a game, going to the doctor, or having an outing together all require basic socialization, coping, and flexibility. When it comes to our special and unique children, we never want to stop working the weak muscle.

SOCIAL GOALS *BEFORE* ACADEMIC GOALS

Not social goals *instead of* academic goals but social goals *before* academic goals. Waaaay before. Don't worry, I'm not going to argue this point again. What I *am* going to do is to give you some quick examples of what "social goals before academic goals" means in practice.

There are all sorts of times when you—or a teacher or

therapist—have opportunities to teach or work on something with your child. Sometimes it will be during a formal game or activity, and sometimes it will be during day-to-day events around the house. Most of us use these opportunities to challenge our children by, for instance, asking them questions such as:

- "How many are there?"
- "What's that called?"
- "What color is that?"
- "Tell him your name."
- "What do you say?"
- "Can you put that away for Mummy?"
- "What does that sign say?"
- "Can you tell her how old you are?"
- "What's the answer to that?"
- "Point to your nose."
- "Can you read that word for Daddy?"
- "What's that a picture of?"
- "What's his name?"
- "What animal is that?"
- "What sound does that animal make?"

None of these questions are bad or detrimental. They are just, as I mentioned before, beside the point. These aren't questions you need to avoid like the plague. But here is a list of questions or requests that are much more helpful to emphasize if you want your child to develop socially:

- "Which one do you want to show your friend Amy?"

- "Help me stand up so we can finish the fort!"

- "Grab the picture that shows all of your friends so we can write their names down for your birthday party."

- "What's your favorite . . . ?"

- "Which one does Daddy like?"

- "Who do you think . . . ?"

- "Which face should I make—serious or silly?"

- "When I make this face, do you think I feel happy or sad?"

- "I love when you look at me! Give me one more look, you silly goose!"

- "I love giving you this ride, but I'm so tired! Look at me so I can keep going!"

The above are all overtly social in nature. Instead of quizzing our kids on factual or academic questions, we can ask questions or make requests that challenge our children to think socially instead. All of the questions in the second list ask children to think about their friends (or therapists or family members), to look at you, to think about and help you, to think about other people's likes and desires, and to access their own personal opinions.

And thus we arrive at the perfect juncture to introduce a model for your child's development that is incredibly helpful and extraordinarily comprehensive.

THE SON-RISE PROGRAM DEVELOPMENTAL MODEL

There is no shortage in this world of developmental models upon which to measure your child. So we figured: *Well, there must be a simple social developmental model used in the area of autism that measures children's and adults' social functioning. We'll just use one of those models to measure our kids.*

We were wrong.

So we created our own. And it's pretty awesome.

This social developmental model was originally created by Bryn and William Hogan and then further developed by both of them plus Kate Wilde (Director of The Son-Rise Program), my parents, me, and, to some degree, our other staff members. It was developed over a period of years, based on decades of work with thousands of children and adults and the in-depth analysis of the development of people on the autism spectrum over long periods of time.

In the Start-Up program and our advanced courses, we delve into this model, discussing such areas as:

- How to pinpoint exactly what stage of development your child is at in four fundamental social areas

- How to track your child's social development over time

- Goal-setting

- What activities to use to reach these goals

- Perspectives to teach and model to your child

- The three to five components of each area of development

- How to tell whether a skill is not yet acquired, emerging, or acquired

It will seriously overload you if I even *try* to get into all of this here. If you really want to see the thirty-page layout of The Son-Rise Program Developmental Model, there is a link to it on this chapter's Web page. (but I still don't recommend downloading it yet).

Please, pretty please, believe me when I tell you: it will actually serve you and your child better if we start small and basic. Therefore, rather than laying out the entire model for you (which would really comprise a book in and of itself), I'm going to lay out just the vital areas for you to begin to focus on with your child.

THE FOUR FUNDAMENTALS OF SOCIALIZATION

There are four absolutely critical areas (each consisting of five stages of development) that you want to focus on if you are interested in your child's social development and progression through autism:

1. Eye contact and nonverbal communication

2. Verbal communication

3. Interactive attention span

4. Flexibility

Figure 1 shows where the four fundamentals fit into the overall blueprint of the model.

This diagram, and the ideas that underpin it, set up the framework of the next four chapters. We'll examine these fundamentals and explore techniques and strategies for helping your child move forward with each of them.

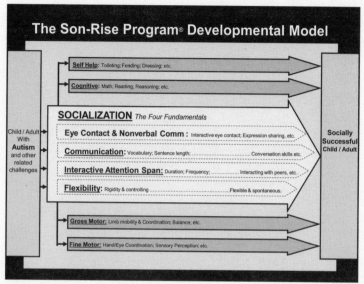

Figure 1

ONLINE RESOURCES

For more in-depth help with the principles and techniques of this chapter, please go to www.autismbreakthrough.com/chapter5. Enjoy delving into the model!

STARTING POINT

Guess what! There is no immediate action to take with your child from this chapter. Trust me: the next four chapters will keep you plenty busy! For now, just take a few moments and picture your child being more socially engaged and adept. What would that look like? What is one thing your child would be doing?

Now, let's make it happen.

SIX

Fundamental 1: Eye Contact and Nonverbal Communication

EYE CONTACT IS a very basic way that human beings connect with one another. It is also one of the most conspicuous traits missing in our children. Whether your child is a nonverbal three-year-old diagnosed with severe autism or a seventeen-year-old with Asperger's syndrome, eye contact is very likely something your son or daughter struggles with.

This makes total sense, given that autism is a social-relational disorder and eye contact is one of the most powerful ways to bond interpersonally. The largest concern with low eye contact is the correspondingly low social connection that goes with it. If you want your child to progress in the area of socialization, improving eye contact is a must.

However, the limited number of behavioral programs that work on eye contact tend to do so, not surprisingly, in a behavioral way. These approaches usually train children to give eye contact as a behavior. For example, "Look at me. Look at me. Look at me if you want to be allowed to play with the toy." Since the main point of eye contact is human connection, we want our children to look because they *want* to. This entails making eye contact fun, easy, and very celebrated.

"THE MORE THEY LOOK, THE MORE THEY LEARN"

This is a saying that I picked up from my sister Bryn. What it articulates is the direct correlation between how much our children look and how much they learn, take in, and develop. Looking helps our children to speak because they are looking at people's faces as they are speaking. It enables them to take in information because they are looking at the people talking to them. It improves their interactive attention span because they are looking at what we are doing and are thus "plugged in." It helps them to develop facial expression because they are looking at our faces. And it paves the way for learning to read others' facial and nonverbal expressions—one of the most socially limiting deficits our children face.

NONVERBAL COMMUNICATION IN GENERAL

While the first of the four fundamentals notes eye contact as a major priority, it also includes all other types of nonverbal communication: making gestures, reading the gestures of others, being more expressive facially, reading others' expressions, prosody—having inflection in one's voice and reading the voice inflections of others.

Nonverbal communication rarely gets sustained focus. Verbal communication tends to get the lion's share of attention. And while verbal communication is extremely important (it is, after all, the second fundamental), the vast majority of interpersonal communication takes place nonverbally.

Admittedly, nonverbal communication can be a bit more complex to notice and to work on with your child. The Son-Rise

Program Developmental Model tracks and measures nonverbal communication and includes goals and activities to develop this area. For now, though, it will be best for you to simply model nonverbal communication by exaggerating all of your own facial expressions, gestures, and voice inflections—while focusing your teaching efforts and goals around eye contact.

STRATEGIES

You want to take every opportunity to request eye contact. There are several strategies to do this.

1. **Ask for it directly**. Examples: "I love when you look at me! Give me one more look, you silly goose!" or "I love giving you this ride, but I'm so tired! Look at me so I can keep going!"

2. **Ask for it indirectly**. For instance, "Who are you talking to, sweetie? I'm not sure because you're not looking at me." Or, simply point to your eyes.

3. **Position for eye contact.** You want to make it as easy as possible for your child to look at you with the least amount of effort. This entails keeping your face at his eye level as much as possible (without being in his face). If your child is playing on the floor, you want to get down on the floor and sit or lie with your face as low as possible so he doesn't have to twist his head all the way up to look at you. You want him to be able to easily flick you a glance. If your child is staring at something off to his left, you can get your face down low next to what he is staring at. Again, you don't want to be right in your child's face. In fact, distance can often be more helpful

here. If you create a bit of physical distance between you and your child, it will actually be *easier* for him to look at you because he will have to move his head and eyes less.

4. When you offer something to your child that she wants, **hold it up next to your eyes.** This can apply to food, a toy, a ball, a bracelet—whatever. As you are doing this you can ask, "Is this what you want?" Or you can simply say, "Here's your ball!" You can even say nothing and simply hold the item up by your eyes with an excited expression on your face.

5. **Celebrate eye contact** whenever you get it from your child. This might feel funny at first, but it is very important. Every single time you get eye contact, thank your child or cheer for your child. (Of course, you will want to make this celebration appropriate to your child's age and maturity level, and you will want to be aware of not shouting if your child has sensitive hearing.) We will talk more about celebration overall in Chapter 11.

ACTIVITY TIME!

Pick a fifteen-minute block of time during the day or evening when you have one-on-one time with your child. This can be when you give her a bath, when you put her to bed, when you read her a story, during a meal, or simply when you are playing or hanging out with her.

Before you begin your session, note down in Table 4 how many times you think your child will look at you—right at your eyes or face—during this fifteen-minute period. *It does not matter in the least if you are right—or even if you are remotely close.* This is just so you can begin to see the difference between your guess and reality.

Just before you begin, make sure you have a pen and paper. During the fifteen-minute time, you are going to make a tick mark on your paper every time your child looks at your face or eyes. You don't have to be perfect. Don't stress about it. You are just trying to get a ballpark figure.

After the fifteen minutes are over, count up your tick marks, and write that number in the appropriate box in Table 4.

You can use this table as often as you like. It is designed to get you started so that you can begin to pay attention to roughly how much eye contact you're getting. (You may be surprised by how much less eye contact you are getting than you originally guessed.)

The good news: following the principles in this book can lead to exceptional gains in this area.

	Your Guess in Advance	The Actual Number
Number of Looks		

Table 4

ONLINE RESOURCES

For more in-depth help with the principles and techniques of this chapter, please go to www.autismbreakthrough.com/chapter6. Happy exploring!

STARTING POINT

Cheer and celebrate any eye contact that you get. This is the most important beginning principle for increasing voluntary eye contact. Have fun!

SEVEN

Fundamental 2: Verbal Communication

UNLESS YOUR CHILD is highly verbal, you are probably very aware of your child's speech deficits—and very motivated to help your child overcome them. Before we get into specific language-building strategies, though, it is vital to discuss the necessary precursor to all speech in children with autism.

BELIEVING THAT YOUR CHILD CAN SPEAK

I want to talk for a moment to those of you who have a child who has not spoken at all yet. A common trap that people fall into is to start believing—either because they've been told or because they've been waiting a long time to hear their child speak—that their child *can't* speak.

Your child's current lack of speech tells you absolutely *nothing* about his future speech. It tells you nothing about his potential to speak. It only tells you what is happening right *now*.

The perspective you want to hold is not: *My child can't speak.* Rather it is: *My child hasn't spoken yet.* And, furthermore: *My child can do this!*

As I said about creativity earlier, I'm not making these statements as part of some rah-rah motivational speech. Believing that your child can (or cannot) speak has a practical impact on two things: whether your child speaks and whether you hear your child speak when he does.

Let's discuss that last bit for a moment. We have a course

called The Son-Rise Program Intensive where parents come to the ATCA with their child. The family stays in their own private apartment, which includes a state-of-the-art autism-friendly playroom; there our child facilitators work one-on-one with each child for five days. At the same time, our teachers work one-on-one with the parents in an individualized program that is customized around each family's needs and concerns.

I'm telling you all of this because of something fascinating that we've seen multiple times in the Intensive program. We've had numerous instances where a child will speak for the very first time during this program. One of the walls of the child's playroom is made of one-way glass, on the other side of which is an observation room where parents can sit and observe what we are doing with their child whenever they like. (As a side note, I would counsel that you beware of any program or school where they don't permit you, as the parent, to observe what is happening with your child.)

Not surprisingly, when parents witness their child speak for the first time, they often have a huge emotional reaction. Some cry, some clap, some stand up and cheer, some turn around and hug one of us on staff if we are in the observation room with them. Participating in such an experience is indescribably beautiful.

However, in some cases, we see no reaction at all. This might sound strange to you. If your child has not yet spoken, you're probably thinking that you would sprout wings and fly if you heard your child speak, right? So why would any parent not react?

The answer is simple. Every parent reacts with joy, excitement, gratitude, and great emotion the first time their child speaks. *Unless they don't hear it.* You read that right. We have had parents with no hearing problems whatsoever who are sitting in the observation room watching their child speak for the very first time—and they neither see nor hear it.

When this occurs, it is because these parents have been told many, many times that their child cannot speak, and, eventually, they believed it. We have had scenarios where we have had to play back video footage of a child speaking seven or eight times before the parents watching could hear their child speaking.

Think about this: if you cannot hear when your child speaks, you cannot react to it and build upon it.

On top of that, we find that parents, therapists, and teachers don't persevere in endeavoring to get speech when they don't believe that the child is capable of speaking. And yet, it is precisely this perseverance that is necessary for many of our children to develop language!

It is of monumental importance that you believe that your child has the capability to speak—no matter what you've been told. Just remember: my parents were given a long list of items—including speech—that they were told I would never be capable of. Instead of believing in the predictions, they believed in me.

GIVING LANGUAGE MEANING

Sometimes, in our singular effort to get our child speaking, we can become overly focused on getting our child merely to repeat words. I see parents fall into this trap in one of two ways. The first is to point to an object, name it, and then try to get the child to repeat the word just spoken. The second is to say a sentence, leave the final word blank, and attempt to get the child to say the missing word. For example, a parent might say, "It's time to go to _____," then endeavor to get his or her child to say the word "sleep."

The problem with these strategies is that, even when you are successful at getting your child to say the word, there is no real communication being taught. Your child does not know what the word means and *has no independent interest in the word being taught.*

Many parents come to the Start-Up program seeking help

with their children's language. Indeed, we have specific parts of the course devoted to verbal communication. (During those segments, parents of highly verbal children are in a separate class more appropriate for their children.) Before Charlotte attended the Start-Up program, her son James was totally nonverbal. During the week following the conclusion of that course, he said his first three words: "Dipsy" (his favorite Teletubby), "red ball" (his favorite bouncy ball), and "Tiger" (his favorite stuffed animal).

I tell you this to highlight a particular point. All three of James's first words had intrinsic meaning to him. He didn't say them because Charlotte felt that they were the most important words for her son to learn first. He said them because they referred to items that were important to *him*.

When helping your child to use language, you always want to challenge her to use words that have meaning to her. You want the words to be linked to things that she already wants or cares about. If your child likes squash (as James does), you can begin with the word "squash"—but only when you have squash handy. Then you can take a piece of squash out, get excited about it, offer it to your child, and say "squash" right as your child takes it. Next, you can offer another piece, this time inviting your child to say "squash" for you to hand it to her. I have to tell you, when James would say, "I want quash please" (he wasn't big on the *s* sound yet), I felt like I was going to keel over from cuteness overdose. (As a side note, Charlotte and I never focused on teaching James to say "please"—we had bigger fish to fry. He simply picked it up from hearing his polite mom.)

Many children like having their feet squeezed. Here, you could do the same thing as with the squash. You might enthusiastically place your hands right above your child's feet and say "squeeze." Then you give his feet a big squeeze. Next, you could offer the squeeze again, this time inviting him to say the word—and immediately responding with a huge squeeze if he does. (When James would say this, he would drop the initial *s* and say

"Queeze my feet, please," which would lead me to yet another near-death cuteness overdose.)

The point is that you want your child to be learning words that are relevant to him, not just words for words' sake.

WORDS: MAKING THEM WORTH YOUR CHILD'S WHILE

It is crucial that your child see using words as worth her while. How you respond to your child's language or attempts at language will be the chief factor in making this happen. Since you might have a child who must work extra hard (for now) to produce language, your child needs to see an immediate and powerful connection between using words and getting what she wants.

Here are five key strategies to make using language far more appetizing for your child:

1. **Move fast.** When your child uses a word, such as "ball," *run* and get it. Don't stroll. Don't walk briskly. *Run*. If you are getting something on a shelf, get it *fast*—and with great excitement. Oftentimes, we meander over to get our children what they want when they use language. Other times, we are busy and tell them "later." From now on, unless something is on fire, you want to stop the presses and move heaven and earth to get your child what he wants when he uses words. Don't worry about "spoiling" your child. Right now we want language. (If your child is crying, pulling, or tantruming to get what he wants, that's a different story. We'll go over these types of situations in Chapter 14.)

2. **Celebrate any language you get.** We will talk more about celebration overall in Chapter 11, but we don't

want to forget about its importance here. It's easy to leave this out, especially as your child speaks more. Always, always celebrate language. Celebrate words. Celebrate parts of words. Celebrate sentences. Say something like, "Thank you so much for using your words! Here you go!" (Then hand your child what she is asking for.) You can vary this so that you are celebrating in a host of different manners.

3. **Request language.** This might seem obvious, but I watch many parents give their children items when their child points, pushes, cries, etc. Since you know your child so well, you may be able to discern what he wants with these kinds of signals, as opposed to actual words. I can totally understand if you feel tempted to read and respond to all of these nonverbal signals. Next time, when you get one of these signals, pause and ask for a word. ("Oh, I know you want something. Use your words, and I'll run and get it!" or "Say 'ball,' and I'll get it right down for you!") Note: only request language when your child clearly wants something. That's when you have his engagement—and, thus, leverage.

4. **Choose useful words.** When choosing which words to ask for, pick words that are either items your child wants (nouns such as "ball," "block," "food," "tiger," "drink," etc.) or actions *you* can do that are fun (verbs such as "squeeze," "tickle," "rub," "bounce," "ride," etc.). You want to choose words that are specific for objects you can immediately give or actions you can immediately do. (Don't choose items you can't or don't want to provide or do, such as "ice cream" or "drive.")

5. **Get progressively more clueless.** As your child improves her language, you want to keep shifting what you

understand so she has to expand the length of her sentences in order to be understood. If your child already says single words ("ball"), start to understand only two-word phrases ("want ball" or "red ball"). If she already uses two-word phrases, work on three-word phrases, and so on. ATCA's Programs Director, William Hogan, developed the concept of the Communication Ladder to outline this process.

THE COMMUNICATION LADDER

The steps of the Communication Ladder are:

1. From crying, screaming, tantruming, pushing, etc. to partial word sounds (i.e., "ba" for "ball").

2. From partial word sounds to single words.

3. From single words to multiple-word phrases.

4. From multiple-word phrases to sentences.

5. From sentences to single exchanges. (We call these "loops." One loop would be when you make a statement or ask a question, and your child responds—or vice versa.)

6. From single loops to multiple loops.

7. From multiple loops to conversations.

Let's look at the first three steps a little more closely for those of you whose child has little or no language. The first order of business is to make your home an environment where your child cannot simply get everything for himself. Most children that we work with live in homes where most of what they want is directly accessible to them. They can open the refrigerator and get food. They can retrieve any toy that they want to play with. The problem with this situation is that there is no reason for a child who has huge difficulties with language to try to produce words when he can simply get what he wants himself. You can ask for language all day, but if your child needs only to reach for what he wants, you have an uphill journey ahead of you.

If your child has little or no language, you must be the getter of all things. Everything must be out of reach so that your child has the chance to see that if he says something, you are going to get it for him. Language has force. Language has power. Language is useful. And *you* must be the vehicle to show this to your child.

Second, make sure that, in the early stages of your child speaking, you are very responsive to parts of words, such as "ba" or "ga." Do your absolute best to discern what these sounds mean, and respond according to the steps above. Let your child get used to seeing that these partial words work to communicate. Once he is using these sounds regularly, *then* you can move to the next step in the Communication Ladder by getting more "clueless" and asking for or responding to whole words.

Third, in these early stages of language development, you will have the most leverage to challenge your child to speak when he wants something. So make sure you use every one of these instances to ask for, respond to, and wildly celebrate language. At first, you may find that your child becomes a "wanting machine," using language mainly to ask for things and give people orders. That's okay. In fact, that's wonderful! He is learning the key fundamentals of verbal communication!

When your child gets proficient and consistent at asking for (or demanding) things that he wants, then we move to the next stage.

BEYOND "I WANT"

Verbal communication is not just about using words or about vocabulary size, although these things are certainly important.

Computers can use language. But they don't have friends. So, although vocabulary size is one of the aspects of communication that is tracked in The Son-Rise Program Developmental Model, it is not, by itself, the be-all and end-all of language.

Because most people tend to focus only on numbers of words in a child's vocabulary, one of the items that gets missed is what a child is using her words *for*. In The Son-Rise Program Developmental Model, we call this the *function* of verbal communication. This area is particularly relevant to children on the autism spectrum.

The first function—or purpose—of using language is to get needs and wants met. *I want food. I want my toy. I don't want a bath.* Indeed, helping your child to clearly see that using words is the most powerful way to get what she wants is essential. The good thing about this stage is that there is a very clear connection between talking and getting an immediate want met.

We don't want to stop here, though. Once your child can reliably articulate what she wants (or doesn't want), we want to build up to more overtly social kinds of language, such as:

- Speaking to start or continue an interaction or game

- Explaining or talking about a particular aspect of an interaction or game

- Sharing a story

- Telling someone how you feel or what you like

- Finding out more about someone (what they want to do next, what they like, how they feel, etc.)

- Eventually, discussing points of view, interests, hopes, and dreams

These are the functions of language that give verbal communication its richness. We can begin to build these parts of language by making them into goals. Some sample goals:

- Saying a word to indicate what is happening, such as exclaiming "running" when he or someone else is running

- Articulating her enjoyment of something, such as saying "feels good" when you are squeezing her feet

- Saying one feeling he has

- Explaining simple instructions of a game to you

- Sharing something that she likes to do before bed

- Telling a story of something that happened that day

- Asking you one question about yourself

- Asking you what you want

NOT TEACHING VERBAL COMMUNICATION IN A VACUUM

Often, parents, teachers, and therapists get verbal communication tunnel vision. They know the value of language, so it becomes the overriding priority. Without question, speech is very important. But, remember: autism is a social-relational disorder. Language is part of a much larger issue. If it weren't, you would have a child who looks at people, loves people, plays interactive games with people, is flexible, laughs at jokes, makes friends, and gestures emphatically and understandably to express his thoughts. In other words, you would have a non-autistic child who simply has a speech deficit.

When we teach verbal communication in a vacuum, it means that we don't teach it in the context of other types of communication. For instance, I've met children and adults on the spectrum who can speak fluently but have no eye contact, no voice inflection, no facial expression, no friends, and little interest in other people. It is not that this is bad or a failure in any way. It is wonderful that these people have come as far as they have. But they could be helped so much more if, in addition to language, someone were helping them with all of the components that go *with* language.

DON'T FORGET CLARITY

One area of language that is especially easy to overlook is clarity. Because you really know your child, you have a heightened ability to understand her. In many ways, this is a testament to your love and caring.

However, you might not realize if your child is not making herself understood to others. Being able to speak so that nonfamily members understand her is an important part of progressing through the five stages of verbal communication.

As you begin to address this challenge, I have two recommendations. The first one is to have one or two people come to your house (not at the same time) and see if they can understand what your child is saying. This will help give you a more objective picture.

The second recommendation is to "play dumb." If your child says something to you in a mumbling way, you can say something like, "Thank you, sweetie, for telling me what you want! I want to get it for you, but I couldn't understand you. Can you say it again slowly?" Then pause exactly where you are, and wait for her to try again.

There are additional ways to improve clarity, but for now the idea is to become much more aware of how clearly your child speaks (if your child speaks) and to keep encouraging more clarity.

We've talked a lot about what to do with regard to developing language. Let's highlight some very important things not to do.

TALKING TOO MUCH

One of the most common mistakes I see is for people to constantly narrate what is happening when they are with their child. "There you go bouncing the ball." "Wow, that's a big castle you're building." "I'm giving my doll a special hairdo." "Oh, look, there's a picture of two rabbits running across a field." "And there we go. I give one to you and take one for myself." There's nothing inherently wrong with any of these sentences by themselves. But I often hear parents and therapists conducting a nonstop string of these sentences. Sometimes I feel like I'm watching a narrated play.

What's the problem with narrating? When you do this, *you take up all of the verbal space*. When you take up the verbal space, *there is no room for your child to speak.*

Unless you have a fluently verbal child, it takes a lot of effort for your child to produce speech. And it takes a lot of time. You need to give your child that time. The more space (that is, silence) you give, the more opportunities your child will have to speak.

Along similar lines, don't constantly pepper your child with questions. This can also take up a lot of verbal space. In addition, it creates what your child will often perceive as pressure around language, which he may push against. (I'm not saying not to ask questions; I'm just saying not to produce a constant stream of questions.)

Fifteen years ago, when I began working with my niece Jade, I was Mr Talkative. I asked her lots of questions. I made lots of statements. I threw out lots of suggestions.

And Jade didn't say a word.

Bryn and William observed my first session, and they told me that I was taking up all of the verbal space with my own speaking. I took in what they said, but I was secretly thinking to myself, *Aw, I'm sure I didn't talk that much.* Then they played me back a video of my session. I was flabbergasted by the sheer quantity of my talking! I cringed as I watched, wanting to shout at myself, *Just shut up for a minute!*

The next time I worked with Jade, I focused on *listening* to her. It wasn't that I never ever spoke in that session, but since I was deeply focused on being attentive to her and to anything she might say, I found that I had a lot less to say.

In that session, Jade, who was in the early stages of speech, blurted out a word every few minutes. The difference in her quantity of speech in the two sessions was astounding.

So, make sure that you leave plenty of room for your child to speak. You can do this not by trying to stifle yourself but, rather, by having a strong and ongoing intention to *listen to your child.*

USING DIFFERENT TERMS FOR THE SAME THING AT DIFFERENT TIMES

Sometimes, when offering your child food, you might say "eat." Other times, you might say "food." When offering your child a Thomas the Tank Engine toy, you might call it "Thomas" one time and "train" the next. This can make things very confusing for your child.

It is very helpful to be totally consistent with the words you use. It doesn't matter what you decide to call the big purple ball with the pictures of Shrek on it, but whatever you decide, *call it the exact same thing every time.*

This does not apply, of course, to fluent, highly verbal children where language is not their challenge. With these children, you actually want to encourage more variation. But for children just learning to speak, using the same word for the same thing every time is key.

TEACHING "MORE" AND "AGAIN"

This one's a biggie. "More" and "again" are two easy words to teach, and your child will love to use them. Why? Because, once your child learns these two magic words, she doesn't need to learn much else! Your child can get 90 percent of what she wants with these two words (or with the sign language versions of them).

You know how we talked about it being worth your child's while to speak? Well, you don't want to create a situation where your child has no earthly reason to learn and use new words. You want to teach your child to use specific words for specific things. You want her to say "ride" (not "again") when she wants another ride on your back. You want her to say "grapefruit" (not "more") when she wants another grapefruit. This is how language is built.

USING COMMUNICATION AIDS

This one might be hard to hear. You've probably been extensively schooled in using either Picture Exchange Communication System (PECS), sign language, or some variation of both. You may have put a lot of time into these aids. And maybe your child has become quite good at communicating with them.

The thing is, what you really want is verbal communication. The only route to verbal communication is through spoken language. If you give your child a way to communicate and get all of his needs and wants met without speaking, why is he going to put in all of the hard work it requires to speak well? After all, your child now has a way around that.

I'm not saying that it is impossible for your child to speak when you use these communication aids. But there is a dramatically reduced necessity for him to do so. And there is certainly no rush. Remember: we want verbal communication to be worth your child's while.

In the short term, ditching these aids will make it harder for your child. The only way to effectively communicate will be to use words, and, if your child was using communication aids, then, by definition, using words is difficult for him. But if he gets better at verbal communication, and does so faster, then this will be a gigantic boon to him. Only a tiny population understands PECS or sign language. But *everyone* understands the spoken word! So, every time your child gets even a little better at speaking, an entire world opens up to him.

You might be thinking: *But what about those children who are truly unable to speak? Wouldn't we want to at least give those children some way to communicate?* That is a legitimate question. In fact, we have had a few children over the years (not many) who have severe bio-physiological obstacles that seem to prevent them from speaking. In those cases, yes, we *do* use PECS or sign language.

But the real issue is who we are going to put into that category. We require a very, very large amount of convincing before we are willing to say, "Let's forget speech for now and focus on these other ways of communicating." We need to have attempted to get speech, full-throttle, using Son-Rise Program principles, for *at least* a year before we will even consider going down this other road.

A VERY SPECIAL THANKSGIVING

It was Charlotte and James's first Thanksgiving with my family. My parents, my brothers and sisters and their families, and a couple of long-time family friends were all gathered at my parents' house for the day.

Throughout the day, members of my family took turns doing one-hour, one-on-one Son-Rise Program sessions with James in a bedroom set aside for this purpose. I have had many experiences of being thankful for my family, but few could compete with the emotional gratitude I felt at this incredibly sweet and meaningful expression of love.

I had my session early in the day, and Charlotte had hers last. At the end of Charlotte's session (it was early evening at this point), she came downstairs with her son. James was at a stage where he was very sensitive to environmental noise and commotion, and all of us, who had been engaged in an animated discussion in the living room, immediately hushed as Charlotte and James entered.

Charlotte was holding her son in her arms, and he was staring at us with a very serious expression on his face. My mother said hello to James sweetly. James paused for a moment, then said "Tan ups." At that time, he had trouble with the *s* sound if it was followed by a consonant, so he would drop it and move the *s* to the end of the word or phrase. So "tan ups" really meant "stand up." Often, if someone who was working with James would sit down, he would tell them to stand up. (I guess he wasn't a fan of idleness!)

In this case, the moment he told us to stand up, every single person in the room (there were a lot of us!), without any consultation with one another, wordlessly stood.

James stared, transfixed. It was as if he were thinking, *I said one little thing, and it got immediate and perfect results! I speak and the world moves!*

We waited silently, smiling at him.

"Sit down," he said.

Without a word, everyone sat.

James could not take his eyes off us.

"Tan ups," he said, asking us to stand again.

We all stood.

"Sit down," he said.

We all sat.

I looked at Charlotte, who had tears in her eyes. Never had she—or her son—been in a responsive, loving, and James-friendly environment!

Moreover, James, at that point in his life, would never speak—certainly not unsolicited—in the presence of a group. He might say those phrases in a one-on-one situation, but not with a host of people around, including many whom he barely knew.

James continued to order us to stand, then sit, then stand again for fifteen minutes. Then his mom took him to bed.

Brief though it was, Charlotte and I would never forget that event.

ACTIVITY TIME!

Table 5 is designed just to get you paying more attention to your child's language—and how you react to it. Spend fifteen minutes alone with your child, focusing on verbal communication. Your goal will be to remember one to three words or phrases that she said to you during your fifteen minutes. If your child isn't saying words yet, you will mark down speech-like sounds, such as "ba" or "ak."

Very important: For each word, phrase, or sound, you will write down *how you responded*. Did you clap? Did you cheer? Did you run and get your child something? Did you do nothing?

As with Table 4 in the previous chapter, keep the session to no longer than fifteen minutes for now. Getting an accurate reading of what your child is saying and how you responded is the most important thing at this stage.

Verbal Communication		
Word or Phrase	How You Responded	Did You Over-Talk or Narrate?
		(Yes/No)

Table 5

ONLINE RESOURCES

For more in-depth help with the principles and techniques of this chapter, please go to www.autismbreakthrough.com/chapter7. Cheering you on!

STARTING POINT

The next time your child wants something, enthusiastically request that he use words (one word, one sound, or multiple words, depending on where his language is right now). Resist the urge to act upon your child's other signals—reaching, moving your hand, looking at what he wants—and be persistent in your request for language. Believe in your child's ability to speak (or speak more)! Then, *make sure you pause and leave space for him to speak.*

Also, make sure that your child's immediate environment is arranged so that he cannot simply retrieve everything that he wants on his own. Remember, it has to be worth your child's while to speak!

EIGHT

Fundamental 3: Interactive Attention Span

LET'S ACKNOWLEDGE ONE thing: your child probably has an awesomely long attention span. After all, if your child isms for hours, that's some quality attention span! So, attention span is not the issue. *Interactive* attention span is.

What's the difference?

Ladies (those of you who have a male significant other), I'm sure many of you have noticed how your man seems to have a perfectly healthy attention span when he takes some reading on a bathroom excursion or when he's watching a game on TV, but when you want to tell him about your day, his attention span suddenly shrinks to about sixty seconds. You see how very different those two types of attention span feel to you?

Attention span simply measures how long your child can stay involved in an activity. *Interactive* attention span refers to how long your child can stay involved in an *interactive* activity with *another person* (before your child disconnects, isms, etc.). Your child's interactive attention span may be thirty seconds, two minutes, fifteen minutes, or possibly even an hour.

Here's the thing: if your child's interactive attention span is low (especially in the thirty seconds or two minutes category), she can never learn to participate in a bona fide social interaction. You can't have a real conversation or play a game in thirty seconds. But interactive attention span is a highly malleable skill. And as your child's interactive attention span increases, it will create a positive feedback loop whereby longer periods of participation lead to increased interest in what other people are doing, which, in turn, builds a longer and longer interactive attention span. Isn't that terrific?

You will want to become very aware of your child's interactive attention span. Start to keep track of how long your child spends engaged with you in any activity. Keep in mind that if your child is isming, he's not engaged. If your child is not responsive to you, he's not engaged. Your child must be interacting with you or someone else (playing, talking, chasing, looking) for it to count as "engaged time."

Suppose your child is isming and you are joining. Suddenly, your child interacts with you for a minute. Then, he goes right back to isming. You join again. Then he interacts with you for another minute. Then he resumes his ism.

That's an interactive attention span of one minute, not two. If a minute is the longest you get before the isming resumes, then that is what you are starting with. I want to emphasize that this is only what you are *starting* with; it tells us *nothing* about how much your child can improve or how much longer it will be in six months.

If your child's interactive attention span is low right now, then you can actually see that as a good thing. It means that your child's abilities and deficits only reflect what he is capable of *given his current interactive attention span*. Think of how much more is possible once we lengthen it!

STRATEGIES

Once again, the joining and motivation principles provide the building blocks here. The more you join, the shorter the isming periods and the longer the interactive periods. And when you focus the interactive activities around your child's areas of strong motivation and interest, you will always get longer periods of engagement than you will without utilizing your child's motivations. Here are some other key ways to begin increasing your child's interactive attention span:

1. Include plenty of "the good stuff."

Find the part of the game or conversation that your child likes, and include lots of it. If your child likes the part of the chase game where you catch and tickle her, do more of that. If your child enjoys watching you fall down, drop to the floor more often. If your child loves it when you swing her, swing her more. If your child likes the part of the "taking a trip" game where the (pretend) plane takes off, make that happen more often. If your child loves talking about Star Wars, ask her a Star Wars question when her interest in the conversation starts to wane.

2. Keep coming back to your game or activity.

Many parents are afraid of their child losing interest in an interactive game or activity once they've got their child's attention and interest. Maybe you feel this way. Check in with yourself. Have you ever seen your child disconnect and begin isming in the middle of a game or activity? (I bet you have!) Hopefully, you then joined him, right? (Right? Right? Say yes!) And then, possibly, he reconnected. So here's the key question: Have you ever, in this situation, decided not to attempt to engage your child in the previous game or activity because he appeared to "lose interest" last time? (If you have, don't sweat it—most parents have done exactly the same thing!) It is very beneficial to your child for you to endeavor to *continue the same activity where you left off.* When you have your child's willing attention again (after you've joined), you can say something like, "Hey, you know what? We still haven't finished our game! It's your turn!" or "I'm so glad you're back! We're almost up the mountain!" or "I'm so excited to hear your answer to the question I asked you before—what *is* your favorite animal?"

3. **Invite your child to come back to the game or
    activity—*once.***

Just as important as being willing to reintroduce an activity
is being willing to let it go. Have you ever found yourself so
excited to have your child engaged with you in a particular
activity that when your child disconnects, you miss your
child's signals—and keep trying to get your child to stay with
the activity? (If so, I promise you that I have yet to work with
a parent who has not done this, so you're in good company!)
In practice, though, this type of pushing breaks down the
rapport and trust that you have painstakingly built. So,
when you are in the middle of an activity with your child,
and you see her beginning to disconnect, invite her to continue. *Once.* Make sure you do this in a fun and easy way,
such as saying, "Oh! Oh! It's your turn! Let's finish your
turn!" or "You silly goose, you can't drive the truck from
over there! Come over here and take the wheel," or "Wait!
Wait! Stay for two more minutes so we can finish the game!
I'm having so much fun, and we're almost done!" Of paramount importance, though, is that you only do this once. *If
your child is not responsive, it is important to stop asking.* At
this point, bond with her by joining, being super user-friendly,
nondemanding, etc.

ACTIVITY TIME!

Table 6 tracks interactive attention span. Spend fifteen minutes
with your child. Do your best to spend that fifteen minutes playing some sort of interactive game. I would suggest keeping it
very simple. Pick something basic that you know he likes. Often,
it's easiest to pick a physical game, such as a chase game or wrestling. Remember, too, that you don't want to go in and deliberately pick a toy, object, or activity that your child does a lot of

isming with. (We're tracking *interactive* attention span, not regular attention span.)

You're going to use Table 6 to begin to keep track of the types of interactive games or activities that your child sticks with the longest (and the shortest). In the first column, write down a few words that sum up what the activity was, such as "chase game," "building a fort," or "draughts." In the second column, write down how long the activity went. In other words, how long did your child stay involved before he disengaged, started to ism, left to do something else, etc.?

Remember, you are not trying to be perfect by doing only games that will be wildly successful at engaging your child. The whole point here is to be a detective, try several different things, and start to notice what does and does not engage your child.

If your child does happen to remain engaged for the whole time, yippee! Next time, you can try for longer.

Interactive Attention Span	
Game/Activity	Length of Time

Table 6

ONLINE RESOURCES

For more in-depth help with the principles and techniques of this chapter, please go to www.autismbreakthrough.com/chapter8. Enjoy!

STARTING POINT

Pick one game or activity from Table 6 and introduce it once a day for a week. See if there is any change in whether your child engages and for how long.

Remember to introduce the activity in a fun but totally non-pushy way. If your child engages more with the activity by the end of the week, wonderful. If she doesn't, that's also great; now, through "trial and info," you know that this activity is not engaging yet for her. You can still try again in a month or two!

NINE

Fundamental 4: Flexibility

BEFORE WE DISCUSS this most crucial fundamental in detail, let me tell you about Arturo.

The Story of Arturo

Arturo's parents were very pleased to have got him into a school that used the Training and Education of Autistic and Related Communication-handicapped Children (TEACCH) model. They thought that this school would provide a great alternative to ABA, which they felt had been counterproductive for their son.

One of the aspects of the school that they really liked was that it claimed to respect the "culture of autism." With this model, the school felt that everything should be built around what children on the spectrum already had a knack for. One of the key tenets of the school was that "children on the autism spectrum need structure." (I'm sure you've heard that statement before.)

Everything was conducted according to a clearly defined schedule. The children were taught this schedule in-depth. They learned every single thing that happened at every single time throughout the day. They were shown pictures (PECS cards) for each aspect of the day and given as few transitions as possible (since "children on the autism spectrum have a hard time with transitions").

And in some ways this system really worked. Most of the children in Arturo's new school became very proficient at following the schedule, and there were fewer meltdowns than at most special schools.

So Arturo became adept at following schedules.

But what happened when the schedule changed?

Arturo's parents came to our Start-Up program chiefly because of a significant challenge that lay at the center of Arturo's autism: he was very rigid and inflexible and prone to meltdowns. If there was a deviation from the schedule at home, Arturo would have a screaming meltdown. If they took a different route to the park, Arturo had a meltdown. If his little sister was around him for more than a few minutes, Arturo would have a meltdown.

If anyone tried to get Arturo to play a different game than the one he wanted to play—or if anyone tried to change any aspect of a game he was playing—Arturo would refuse. He would play a small selection of regimented games with his parents, but the games had to be played the exact same way every time. His parents—and others—often described the experience of playing with Arturo as not really playing but rather as having to be a robot that Arturo controlled absolutely.

For example, whenever Arturo's parents would try to do a puzzle with him, he would snatch all of the larger pieces away from them. If they tried to use a larger piece, he would grab it or scream. They could put smaller pieces into the puzzle, but only beginning at the right-hand side of the puzzle; otherwise Arturo would grab those pieces or scream.

In the Start-Up program, we taught Arturo's parents how to build their son's flexibility by utilizing Arturo's motivation and by giving them some specific additional strategies.

When Arturo's parents returned home, they implemented what they learned, and they were elated to see the rapidity of the changes in their son. He hardly ever had meltdowns when the schedule changed or during transitions. He began to tolerate—and sometimes play with—his little sister. He became much more flexible within his games, allowing others to contribute and suggest changes. His repertoire of games and activities broadened considerably. Often, he would really play the games instead of having to simply repeat the exact same steps.

Most importantly, people who played with him actually had the experience of playing and interacting instead of feeling like controlled automatons.

One time, when Arturo's mom got his favorite puzzle out, he once again snatched up all of the larger pieces. Arturo's mom gently put out her hand and asked, "May I have one of your big pieces?"

Arturo stared at her. She smiled at him and continued to hold out her hand.

Arturo looked down at the puzzle pieces in his hand. He looked back up at his mother's outstretched hand. Then back to the pieces in his hand.

Then, with deliberate slowness, Arturo took his empty hand, plucked one of the big puzzle pieces from his hand, and held it out to his mom.

His parents found that Arturo would, more and more often, be flexible and have wonderful back-and-forth interactions, which allowed his parents to arrange and then witness something they had long been awaiting: Arturo's first playdate.

WHY FLEXIBILITY IS SO IMPORTANT

Flexibility is by far the most underappreciated of the four fundamentals. In fact, as in Arturo's story, most of us prize the opposite of flexibility: structure. Is it a bad thing for a child to know the day's schedule? Certainly not. But, as with maths, it is utterly beside the point. And, as with maths, it just helps our children to be better at being autistic. Remember: the rigid, structured part of your child's brain is just peachy. *You want to work the weak muscle.* You want to develop the part of your child's brain that's having difficulty. Then scores of doors open up for her.

Realities to consider:

- There will *always* be changes in the schedule (as well as routes, routines, the order in which things happen, the meals that are served, etc.).

- There will always be other people around your child, whether they be peers or adults, who want to have their say as to how a game is played, what activity to do, etc.

- A child who is different or who isms a little can absolutely succeed in school. A rigid child prone to frequent meltdowns cannot.

- Your life will be a thousand times easier if you can do things with your child and with the family without fights and meltdowns. So will your child's.

- *Every other area of your child's development* is profoundly affected by your child's level of flexibility.

Okay, let's take a few minutes to discuss that last point. The amazing thing about flexibility is that it doesn't just affect flexibility. For instance, let's say that your child is having difficulties with language. Now, certainly, there are cases where this is due purely to apraxia (difficulty using the muscles of the mouth to form words), and such a child will really need our help to build up the basic ability to form his mouth to make sounds.

However, we see so many cases where a child says a word or phrase with perfect clarity on Monday but seems unable to say it on Tuesday. How do we explain this? After all, if the child has, for instance, low oral muscle tone or is completely unable to use language, how did he use it yesterday?

This is where flexibility comes into play. Flexibility entails your child going your way. (Any time your child is being asked for anything, he is being asked to go your way.) For most of our kids, this is very, very challenging. It is a relinquishing of autonomy that can feel really tough for a child whose world feels out of control and unfathomable. Most of the time, when it comes to language (if your child is not already fluently verbal), someone is asking your child to speak. This may be overt ("Say 'water'") or more natural ("Which toy do you want?"). Either way, when it comes to the vast majority of instances, speaking requires your child to go someone else's way—in other words, it requires flexibility.

So, if your child lacks flexibility, then getting speech is going to be quite a challenge—*even if your child already has speech capability.* If, on the other hand, you address your child's flexibility issues, you remove a gigantic obstacle to language. And language is only one example. When you help your child to become more flexible, you remove an enormous obstacle to *everything.* Every other area of your child's development is freed to move forward.

STRATEGIES

I know I've said this many times with respect to the other fundamentals, but it bears repeating one more time: you don't want to attempt to work on your child's flexibility when your child is isming, not looking, not responding, etc. Work on flexibility when your child is engaged with you.

With that said, here are some flexibility-building strategies:

1. Start by being super user-friendly.
This means *you* being very flexible and responsive to your child. If she wants all of the toy cars to herself (and takes your toy cars from you), let her have them. If she says "Don't touch that," then don't touch it. If she wants you to stand on one foot, stand on one foot. This helps to set the stage because it helps to build trust and to relax your child.

2. Explain it in advance.

When there is a change or transition coming (dinner is later, we are changing rooms or activities, etc.), explain to your child what is going to happen in a nice, relaxed tone. Also briefly explain why. Example: "Hey, sweetie, in a half-hour, we are going to put our shoes on and get in the car. We have a dentist appointment." Do this again fifteen minutes before and again five minutes before.

3. Get it "wrong."

If your child usually requires a game or activity to go a certain way, make a "mistake" and do it "wrong." For instance, if the getting-ready-for-bed process typically begins with brushing teeth followed by getting into pajamas, get out the pajamas first. If the puzzle always gets put together in the same order, try beginning the puzzle in a different order. When your child calls you on it (whether he does this in a verbal or nonverbal way), say something like, "Ooops! I did it a different way!" You can add, "It's so fun to try things a different way!"

4. Role play.

In a fun way, play out a scenario in which your child would usually have difficulty, such as a transition. For example, if your child has difficulty transitioning out of the house, play a game inside where you two *pretend* to get ready to go outside. (Your child needs to be at a high enough stage in her overall development for you to be able to do this. For instance, if your child is totally nonverbal or only minimally interactive, you'll want to save this strategy for later.)

5. Be silly.

Normally, when something happens that is outside our children's comfort zone, we get uneasy and tighten up (because we "know what's coming"). This makes things worse. Instead, when your child seems to get a bit agitated over a change, transition, or someone wanting to do something a different way than he does, act silly and goofy about it. If dinner is served early, and your child is attached to having dinner at exactly six o'clock, you can say something like, "Holy moly, the wind is blowing me over to the dinner table!" or "I'm so weird! I'm eating before dinnertime!" You can also do things like bouncing over to the dinner table or falling down in slow motion as you go to the table.

QUESTIONS TO ASK, REQUESTS TO MAKE

It is surprising just how many opportunities we have (and often don't notice) to turn an activity that's already happening into one that challenges our children in the area of flexibility. It makes perfect sense that we tend to not notice these opportunities. No one ever tells us to pay any attention to our children's level of flexibility!

Here are some examples of questions we can ask and requests we can make (as long as your child is not isming) that will gently challenge your child to be more flexible during any activity:

- "That was fun watching you go the last few times. Now I want a turn!"

- "Oh my gosh! You have to try my game! It's so cool!"

- "I have an idea! Let's see what it's like to do it in a different order this time!"

- "Parking your car in that slot is cool! Let's try putting it in the other slot now!"

- "You're right—we usually have dinner at six. If we could have dinner at any time later than six, which time would you want it?"

- "Yeah, I know you like your piece to be the blue one. This time, let's try it a different way. What other color do you want to try instead?"

ACTIVITY TIME!

Table 7 is designed to be filled out over a three-day period. On day 1, choose something in your child's day that you will do differently—and invite her to enjoy it. For instance, change the time of one meal. Encourage your child to get dressed in a different order (pants, then shirt, instead of shirt, then pants). If there is a card game you usually play, change one rule, such as having each person get two turns in a row. On day 2, choose a different item to change. On day 3, choose another item to change. Remember to use the five strategies.

In each instance, use Table 7 to track what change you tried and how your child responded. In the first column, write the name of the game or activity. In the second column, simply circle "yes" or "no" according to whether your child agreed to the change or not. (She can refuse the change by saying no or simply by ignoring it.)

Reminder: don't get caught up in getting all yes answers. Even a no helps to stretch your child's flexibility.

Flexibility	
Item That You Endeavored To Change	Did Your Child Agree To The Change?
1)	YES / NO
2)	YES / NO
3)	YES / NO

Table 7

ONLINE RESOURCES

For some help with the principles of this chapter, please go to www.autismbreakthrough.com/chapter9. Have a great time!

STARTING POINT

Start practicing being silly in the face of change. Any time anything does not go the predicted way, respond in a fun, easy, silly manner. If Aunt Maria doesn't arrive when she says she will, you can jump around, exclaiming, "Whoo-hoo! Aunt Maria's not here yet! Now we have fifteen extra minutes to wrestle! [or draw, play, etc.]" If your child wants food that he cannot have, you can pretend to eat his arm—and maybe sneak in a tickle. There's no one perfect way to be silly, so give yourself permission to experiment!

Note: These past five chapters will powerfully jump-start your child's social and interpersonal development. However, these chapters are just the beginning of The Son-Rise Program Developmental Model, not the end. We spend much time in the Start-Up and advanced programs helping you to utilize the model step-by-step, including tracking exactly where your child is and implementing activities to bring your child to the next level. As noted in Chapter 5, you can download the full version of this model from my website. These Four Fundamentals of Socialization are trackable and understandable because of the insightful model that Bryn and William Hogan developed—and I thank them heartily!

TEN

How Giving Control Generates Breakthroughs

So we just finished talking extensively about setting and pursuing social goals for your child. And yet, paradoxically, the best way to enable your child to hit more goals is to *prioritize interaction with your child over any particular goal that you have*.

Remember: interaction is of primary importance when your child has a social-relational disorder such as autism. Building trust and increasing interaction doesn't just address trust and interaction. *It addresses everything.* Are specific goals important? Yes. Do we want to be persistent and consistent in pursuing them with our children? Absolutely.

You love your child and value your child's progress. That's wonderful and important. And I know that sometimes it's easy to get single-mindedly caught up in achieving a particular milestone with your child. In your pursuit of your child's progress, though, *it is essential to temporarily relinquish any goal as soon as it causes a control battle with your child*. In fact, control battles are one of the most disabling dealings you can have with your child. You want to avoid them whenever possible (except when safety is involved, of course).

THE PROBLEM WITH CONTROL BATTLES

Remember the analogy from Chapter 2 about reading on the park bench, when we talked about your child's experience of the world? I detailed two primary factors governing your child's experience: her sensory-processing challenges (how all sights, sounds, smells, and touches can be very challenging, overwhelming, or nonsensical to her) and your child's pattern-recognition problems (making her world feel unpredictable, haphazard, and out of control).

When people—not just people with autism but *all* people—are in the throes of an experience where they don't have control, don't have understanding, and have too much input to process, they react in very particular ways. They put everything they have into gaining a sense of control. They seek out situations where they can exert their own autonomy, rather than having their experience dictated to them. And they powerfully resist any efforts to impose control on them.

When people move to a totally new area, attend a brand-new school, go through a harrowing divorce, lose a longtime job, undergo a life-changing injury, or experience the loss of a loved one, they often become very controlling for a while. They may fall back on familiar routines, seek out only the most familiar people, seek time alone (where they can control everything), obsessively clean their house, watch familiar movies or TV shows, engage in very regimented or controlled eating habits. At the same time, they will often vehemently avoid new situations or people, push back hard if you try to alter their behavior, and push you away altogether if you persist.

As I mentioned in Chapter 2, when your child seems resistant, rigid, or routinized, he is not behaving abnormally; he is behaving normally, given the situation that he's facing. So it is not at all surprising that many of our children are highly controlling.

Most people's first response when dealing with a controlling child is to try to "break" the child of his controlling behavior by wresting control back from him. Some of you might think: *To function in the world, my child has to get used to doing things the right way, so I have to get him to do this particular thing the correct way* now.

For others of you, the situation may be more in-the-moment pragmatic. You might think: *I just have to get my child to brush his teeth* (for example), *and we'll be done. I know he's fighting me now, but soon it will be over, and it will be worth it because he'll have clean teeth.*

If either of these scenarios resonates with you, it's not only normal, it is totally understandable. You love your child, and you are trying to help him fit in with a world that will not necessarily understand or cater to his differences. On top of that, you have a million things you are juggling at once, and sometimes you may just be trying to get through the day.

The problem is that going down this road with your child will end up being highly counterproductive. Asserting control over someone who is controlling leads to that person becoming *more* controlling, not less. You see, when your child's control is challenged, he will feel compelled to dig his heels in and fight to reestablish that control and personal autonomy.

Think of a rope with a knot in it. I am holding fast to one end and you to the other. The harder you pull, the tighter the knot gets—'cause I ain't letting go. You can never release the knot by pulling harder. The only way to release the knot is to let the rope go so that there is enough slack in it for the knot to loosen.

The key to understand is this: if you want your child to be less controlling (and thus more flexible and able to learn more, grow more, and ultimately achieve more goals), *you have to give your child as much control as possible.*

Have you ever hugged your child when she didn't really want to be hugged (she was squirming or pulling away)? Have you ever physically moved items that your child was playing with, such as blocks, to show her the "right" way to play with them? Have you ever pressed your child to shake hands with someone—or to say "hello" or "thank you"? Have you ever held your child so that you could brush her hair, wash her face, etc. while she was trying to get away?

It's totally okay if you've done any or all of these things. I have rarely met any loving parent who *hasn't*. Most parents aren't aware of the cascade of unintended results that occur when these types of actions are taken with a child on the autism spectrum. You may address the issue in the moment (clean teeth, brushed hair, etc.) but you compromise interaction and learning long-term because you get a child who is not only more controlling but also *associates learning or doing something that you want with coercion and unpleasantness.*

The Story of Michael

Michael's mom felt that it was very important for him to have clean teeth. The problem was that Michael, a lanky seven-year-old with a little bit of language, didn't have the same enthusiasm for his oral hygiene. Not to worry. His mom came up with a solution.

Every night before bed, she would, as gently as she could, put Michael in a headlock and forcibly brush his teeth for him. She took no pleasure in this. In fact, she hated it. But she couldn't see any other way to get his teeth brushed. Was she supposed to let all of his teeth fall out?

This was one of the first issues we addressed when Michael and his mom came to the Autism Treatment Center of America for their Intensive program. Although tooth-brushing is rarely at the top of our agenda, it was with Michael because this nightly ritual had destroyed the interpersonal trust necessary for him to progress. (Early on, his mom said to us, "He's always running away from me. I don't understand it.")

To be clear, Michael's mom was a loving and caring mother who only wanted the best for her son. She simply hadn't been able to come up with a better solution, and she felt that abandoning the tooth-brushing altogether would make her a bad mom, so she felt like she was locked into this scenario.

We began a lengthy discussion with Michael's mother about her son's tooth-brushing situation. After hearing all of her reasons for doing what she was doing, we explained to her why forcing Michael to brush his teeth was so detrimental to him and to what she really wanted for him, which was his forward development. (We also highlighted the difficulty she would have attempting the tooth-brushing ritual when her son was fifteen.)

Then, our child facilitators, who were to work one-on-one with Michael all week, addressed tooth-brushing with him directly. To be sure, we didn't feel that Michael brushing his teeth was in and of itself his number one priority. However, we wanted to help Michael while, at the same time, showing his mom that, through The Son-Rise Program, we could enable her son to do things such as brush his teeth without using any force or coercion whatsoever (and without using any nonphysical pushing such as disapproval). Then *she* could do the same with Michael in the situations that she would encounter at home.

Our first child facilitator went into our playroom with Michael. In his back pocket, the child facilitator had two brand-new toothbrushes. After spending some time bonding with Michael and being very user-friendly (responding quickly to Michael, doing exactly what he wanted), our child facilitator said, "Hey! Guess what, buddy! I've got something fun for us to play with!"

With that, he enthusiastically pulled out the two toothbrushes. As soon as Michael saw them, he ran to the other side of the room, threw his hands up, and said, "No!" very loudly.

Without a moment's hesitation, our child facilitator put the toothbrushes down on a little table (which was low enough for Michael to easily see the toothbrushes).

"No problem, Michael," our child facilitator said, "we can play with them later. Thanks for telling me what you wanted!"

He then began to offer Michael rides on his back, which was something that Michael really enjoyed. After several minutes of giving rides (with Michael saying "ride" and giggling each time he wanted another), our child facilitator paused dramatically.

"Oh my gosh! Michael, do you know what I just remembered?" He leapt over to the table, picked up the two toothbrushes, and presented them to Michael with a flourish, "I got toothbrushes, buddy! They're so much fun!"

No sooner had the child facilitator finished his sentence than Michael again scampered to the other side of the room, saying "No!"

Our child facilitator didn't miss a beat. "Oh, okay. I thought you might be ready for some toothbrush fun. Not a problem. We're not going to do anything with the toothbrushes until *you* want to. Okay, Michael? Not until *you* want to."

He put the toothbrushes back on the table.

Then he smiled at Michael impishly. "I gotta tell you, though, Michael, those toothbrushes sure are fun!"

Once again, the two went back to playing the ride game. After several more minutes, our child facilitator, as if realizing that the toothbrushes are on the table for the very first time, grabbed them and introduced them again (with great enthusiasm!).

Michael responded the same away again.

The child facilitator again put them back on the table, explaining to Michael that he was going to keep trying because the toothbrushes are so fun—but also that they would not play with them until Michael wanted to. (We have a saying in The Son-Rise Program: "No means no . . . for the next five minutes. Then I get to ask again.")

This continued for over an hour, with our child facilitator offering the toothbrushes enthusiastically every five to seven minutes. Eventually, Michael began to see—and really believe—that our child facilitator was not going to use force with him.

The tenth or eleventh time that our child facilitator offered up the toothbrushes, Michael didn't back away, and he didn't say

"No." Instead, he just stood there, looking at the child facilitator—and at the toothbrushes.

Our child facilitator was ecstatic. Toothbrush liftoff! He cheered Michael fervently. Then, slowly, he offered Michael one of the toothbrushes. Carefully, Michael took it. The child facilitator jumped up and down, cheering, "You're doing it, buddy! You're holding the toothbrush! You are the man, Michael!"

Our child facilitator put his toothbrush in his mouth and began to brush his own teeth. As he was doing this, he spoke excitedly to Michael.

"Holy macaroli! This is awesome! This feels so good!" He continued brushing his teeth with huge enjoyment. "Michael, you gotta try this, man! Watch what I'm doing!"

He took the toothbrush out of his mouth, put it back in, and resumed brushing. "Oh, this feels terrific!"

Slowly, Michael brought his own toothbrush up to his lips.

"That's perfect, Michael!" the child facilitator said, "Now put it in your mouth like me! See?"

He showed Michael again.

Michael held the toothbrush an inch from his lips but made no further moves.

It was at this point that our child facilitator glanced at the time and realized that he had three more minutes to his session with Michael.

This is exactly the type of situation where most people might think, *three minutes left! We're so close! Why don't I just guide Michael's hand the rest of the way to his mouth.*

That would be the ultimate mistake because it would obliterate all of the trust that had just been built up. And here's the thing: it's not just about the tooth-brushing. After the tooth-brushing, we have a hundred other things we want to help Michael learn. If we violate trust now, each milestone becomes successively harder because Michael now sees each one as being accompanied by force and coercion.

What if, on the other hand, we were willing to take our time, build trust, and give control? Then the first milestone (say, tooth-brushing) might take longer, but everything else will be downhill from here because now we have trust. Now Michael associates learning with fun and with personal safety and control. Now he will work *with* us. Plus, we've preserved the cornerstone upon which all autism progress rests: interpersonal relationships and interaction.

The question you want to ask yourself, at every point where you feel the urge to push for something even though your child is resisting, is this: *Is it going to make any difference whatsoever in my child's life a year from now if he learns this skill on Thursday instead of Friday?*

I call this question the return-to-sanity question because asking—and answering—it will always wake you up and remind you what's really important as you endeavor to teach your child new things. You want your child to trust you and to enjoy human interaction. *And you want your child to come back for more.* That *will* make a difference in his life a year from now.

Of course, our child facilitator did not guide Michael's hand (and the toothbrush he was holding) to his mouth. He simply spent those last three minutes cheering Michael on and having fun with him, and they ended the session on a high note—but without hav-ing gotten Michael to actually brush his teeth.

As it turned out, it was the *next* child facilitator who got Michael to brush his teeth. She started a game called "Tickling Your Teeth," which inspired Michael to put the toothbrush in his mouth and brush his teeth.

From then on, Michael brushed his teeth nightly before bed—of his own volition and without having to be pushed, prodded, or put in a headlock.

So, remember: you want to be persistent and enthusiastic in pursuing goals with your child. But when your child says no or re-sists or you feel a control battle coming on, remember to *stop* what you're doing, put it aside and come back to it in an hour or a day or a week.

Your child needs to feel safe and in control before she can bond with you or anyone else. Once she *does* feel safe and in control, you will find that, in addition to being able to bond with you (the most important thing), she will become much less controlling, more flexible, and more willing and able to learn new things.

CONQUERING CAR WASHES

Just after my recovery from autism, when I was still getting used to the world, there were certain things that I found very scary. (This was actually a testament to my recovery because when I was autistic, I wasn't scared of—nor even aware of—much of anything. Once I had recovered, I was absorbing my environment fully for the very first time.)

One of the things I was afraid of was automatic car washes, and another was stopped-up toilets. Yes, I know that second one sounds strange, but I'll explain (after which, it will probably still sound strange).

Naturally, I did not know that I was scared of either of these two pieces of our everyday existence until I experienced them for the first time. I remember being in the car with my father, and him telling me I was about to go through a car wash, which would be really fun.

The car was on the tracks that take it through the car wash, and the car slowly began to move on its own, which I thought was pretty cool. Then, all of a sudden, these things started slamming against the car. (At least, that's how I perceived it.) I remember seeing these giant, monster-like arms crashing loudly against the windows.

Needless to say, I commenced screaming bloody murder.

My dad gently stroked my head. "I know this is new for you, Raun. It's going to be over in another two minutes."

I kept screaming.

My dad continued stroking my head, telling me that I was okay, letting me know when the wash was halfway done, then almost done, then finished.

And then it was over.

Now, there are two ways that parents tend to handle this kind of occurrence. One is to get really agitated when their child is agitated—and then promise him that they will never take him on that scary thing again. The other is to insist that there is nothing to be afraid of and keep trying to get their child into the car wash again so that he can "get over it."

My dad chose neither of these alternatives. First, once the wash was done and we got out of the car, he explained that it was okay if I didn't want to go in a car wash again (giving me control). So I immediately calmed down, knowing that I wasn't going to be pushed to do something that I felt was scary.

Second, he took me around to a big window where we could watch what was happening in the car wash, and he sent the car back through the car wash, this time with both of us watching what was happening to it from the outside. As this was happening, he explained to me exactly what was going on in the car wash.

As it turned out, I found it fascinating to watch from the outside—and to hear how it worked. My dad asked if I wanted to see it from the inside again, now that I'd seen what happened from the outside. I answered with an enthusiastic yes.

We got back in the car and took another ride through the car wash. This time, I really enjoyed it.

Funny as it sounds, this event was pivotal for me, and I actually became, henceforth, a kid who loved going through car washes!

SURMOUNTING STOPPED-UP TOILETS

As I mentioned earlier, one of my other fears was stopped-up toilets. Why, you ask? A valid question. Let me tell you in the context of a story.

I came running into the kitchen and wrapped my arms around my mom's leg. (Yes, I was that little.) She asked me what was wrong, and I explained that I had just flushed the toilet, and now it was stopped up (probably because I used too much toilet paper, a common rookie mistake). I told her that I was afraid to go near the bathroom.

She didn't get annoyed, she didn't say "Oh, poor baby," and she didn't try to make me go back into the bathroom (thus giving me control). In fact, the whole manner in which she helped me is an homage to the idea of giving control.

She asked me why I was afraid of stopped-up toilets. I replied that, when I saw the water rising in the toilet, I felt like it was going to keep overflowing, and I was going to drown. (In this case, the toilet wasn't actually overflowing. I was just afraid that it would.) She didn't laugh or do anything that communicated that what I had said was silly or not worthy of serious consideration.

Then she asked me to bring her some of my little people. (These were little toy people that I used to play with.) I brought three of them back to her. She put them in the empty kitchen sink and propped me up on the counter so that I could see into the sink. Then she told me to imagine that the sink was the bathroom and the drain was the toilet. Finally, she asked me to turn on the tap so that the water was coming out full force. (I could see the water coming out much harder than it had from the loo.)

We sat there, watching the sink slowly fill until the water reached the neck level of my little people. It took several minutes.

"See how long that took?" my mom said.

"Yeah," I said.

"Well, if you were one of those little people, what would you do during all those minutes while the bathroom was filling up?"

"I would just leave the bathroom," I said, realization dawning.

All of a sudden, I could see that even in an absolute, bathroom-filling worst-case scenario, I would have plenty of time to just walk out of the bathroom.

The conquering of this fear was so momentous for me that I became Mr Stopped-Up-Toilet Fixer in my house. Whenever the toilet got clogged for any reason, I was the person who would volunteer to plunge it!

As you can see, because my parents understood the importance of giving control, they were able to use this principle to help me overcome challenges even after my recovery from autism. You can use this principle to help your child today.

The stories in this chapter bring to light a core concept of The Son-Rise Program:

YOU ARE OUR WORLD'S AMBASSADOR

Have you ever met someone from a foreign country? Have you ever noticed that you attribute the characteristics of that person to the country from which he hails? If the person is pushy, you think. *People from that country are pushy.* If the person is loud, you think, *People from over there are loud.* If the person is respectful, you think, *That country has a very respectful culture.*

Every single second that you are with your child, you are, for better or worse, our world's ambassador. You represent the world of human interaction. Everything that you do tells your child what it's like to be a part of our world.

If you force or push, that tells your child that our world is one where she will be coerced. If you disapprove, that tells her that our world is a disapproving world. If you give control, that tells her that the interactive world is one in which she can feel secure and have autonomy. If you are approving, that tells your child that our world is an approving one.

You are asking your child to permanently join you in your world. For this reason, it is critical that you remain extremely aware of the messages you are sending about what that world is like.

REAL-WORLD RULES AND CONSTRAINTS

When I speak at autism conferences, I sometimes get asked how children who are given control will ever learn to deal with the "rules and constraints" of a world where they don't have all the control and can't say no to whatever they want.

I remind these questioners that they are not giving this control forever. Rather, they are giving control for the duration of their child's Son-Rise Program.

Our children cannot yet handle the sensory and social circumstances of the neurotypical world. Therefore, for now, we want to provide them with a situation that they *can* tolerate and then help them to stretch, bit by bit, in a welcoming atmosphere of trust and fun, toward being able to successfully handle greater and greater social connection.

When our children have crossed all or most of the bridge from their world to ours—they are interactive, enjoy relating to people, are flexible, can communicate effectively—then we can work on helping them with the rules of the "real world."

I can tell you from experience that, by and large, Son-Rise Program graduates are exquisitely sweet, easygoing kids who do really well with real-world constraints and don't expect everything to revolve around them. Quite the contrary: they tend to be extremely caring and attentive to other people. (For some outstanding videos of these kids that illustrate exactly what I am talking about, go to www.autismbreakthrough.com/recoveredkids.)

ACTIVITY TIME!

Take a look at Table 8. Think of five situations where you tend to have control battles with your child. You don't have to think of them all at once; you can fill out one or two and then come back later to do more.

Also, these don't have to be giant battles that you have with your child. For instance, maybe when you come home from work, you hug your child even though he is squirming a little to get out of the hug. Definitely not a battle, but still an area where you do something that takes control away from your child.

For each of the situations you come up with, write down what you might usually do, and then write down what you will do now.

Table 8 is designed to be simple; there is no hidden complexity here. Just keep it basic, and it will continue to be a guide and a reminder to you.

Control Battles	What you usually do	What you will do now
1)		
2)		
3)		
4)		
5)		

Table 8

ONLINE RESOURCES

For more in-depth help with the principles and techniques of this chapter, please go to www.autismbreakthrough.com/chapter10. Wishing you much delight!

STARTING POINT

Spend fifteen minutes doing whatever your child wants. (Of course, this does not include anything that might be unsafe or destructive.) Let your child be the boss. If she wants you to run around, run around. If she wants you to stand still, stand still. If she wants you to play a particular game or activity, do it. Don't do *anything* to influence what's happening. Just enjoy yourself and see what that feels like. And notice how your child responds.

ELEVEN

The Good-Tryer Principle: Turning Your Child into a Learning Powerhouse

MOST CHILDREN ON the autism spectrum are fairly poor tryers. What does that mean? For most of us, in most situations, it takes multiple attempts, or "tries," to master something new. This, I'm sure, comes as no shock to you. To be a good football player, you have to take thousands of shots at the goal, most of which don't go in. To become a good cook, you have to make hundreds of dishes, many of which end up tasting disgustilicious, at least in the beginning. Learning to weave entails doing it "wrong" first. Learning to read involves messing up lots of words first.

The point is, you have to try many times—and make many mistakes—before you can master almost anything.

WHAT THIS MEANS FOR YOUR CHILD

Your child is missing a whole host of skills that you would like to help him to master. The only way for this to happen is for him to make many, many attempts at every single thing that he is learning.

If your child remains unwilling to try things that seem difficult more than once or twice, there is no way for him to learn and master the skills he is missing—*especially* the social ones because those are the most challenging.

This is crucial to understand because most children on the spectrum are not good tryers, do not like trying, and thus hit various walls in their development. There are some very logical reasons for this, including our children's difficulties with flexibility and interactive attention span. However, the part of this equation that I want to address first is the most essential variable: you.

There are all sorts of little things that you may be doing unwittingly that exacerbate your child's trying problem. Let's discuss them one by one. (These aren't things you need to feel in any way bad about. If you do any of them, that just makes you a normal parent!)

BEING A POOR TRYER

Most of us like to succeed at the things we do. If we're not going to succeed, why do it, right? So we often go through life avoiding doing things that require several uncertain attempts where we are likely to make lots of mistakes.

It is impossible to operate this way without inadvertently communicating an anti-trying message to your child.

Maybe you don't believe me. Maybe you think that how you live has nothing to do with what you do with your child. Let me ask you this: Have you ever not tried a treatment with your child because you didn't want to "get your hopes up"? Have you ever cringed when your child keeps attempting something but seems unable to do it? In which situation do you show more excitement—when your child *attempts* something or when she does it successfully?

If any of these ring true for you, there is nothing to beat yourself up about. You're a human being. Most people, including some very confident parents, operate this way.

The important thing is to recognize any fears of trying that you have and focus on changing them so that you can be the most useful beacon for your child. One of the first steps I would recommend in starting down this road is to use any opportunity you get to practice trying. Deliberately attempt things when the likelihood is high that you will make mistakes. This applies even to the most minor circumstances, such as trying to fix something in the house that you don't know how to fix (if it's not dangerous, of course), attempting to cook something you have no experience with, learning a new skill (such as a language or a hobby), playing a game you've never played, etc.

Get so used to trying that it feels like the natural thing for you to do—so that you cease even noticing that you're "trying."

SABOTAGING YOUR CHILD'S TRYING

Because many of us feel bad about trying and "failing," we often don't like to see our children repeatedly trying without "success." Therefore, we do all kinds of subtle—and not so subtle—things to avoid or cut short such a situation.

When your child is repeatedly trying to say a word, you may find this difficult—and either finish the word for your child or give him what he is asking for. You might avoid playing a game that you know he finds challenging. You may make comments like, "It's okay, honey," when your child is struggling to do or say something, as if there were some reason why his attempts or "mistakes" were *not* okay.

It's so important that you not avoid, curtail, or "smooth over" your child's many attempts at whatever. Your child keeps trying and not getting it? Good! That's what you want because this is a muscle that he needs to work.

Just so there is no misunderstanding, I am not saying to deliberately make things more difficult for your child. I'm only talking about not taking away or undermining the trying that is already occurring.

THE IMPORTANCE OF CELEBRATION

Celebration plays a large role in any Son-Rise Program. Most children on the spectrum are highly undercelebrated, even when they do "get it right." We work with parents, grandparents, family members, volunteers, and professionals all the time who regularly miss literally hundreds of opportunities to celebrate. A child will look in someone's eyes. No celebration. A child will say a word or phrase. No celebration. A child will do something he is asked to do. Nothing.

One reason for this is that we are not taught to notice and be grateful for all of the things that our children are already doing well. We're taught, in countless direct and indirect ways, to look for what's wrong and what's missing. This not only deprives our children of being celebrated, but it also deprives *us* of the chance to see, appreciate, and build upon everything that our children are doing.

So the first order of business is to shift your focus. You want to actively seek out every little interaction or accomplishment that your child makes throughout the day—even if she has done it a thousand times before.

Your child looks at you the same way she has many other times. Celebrate her. Excitedly thank her for looking at you. Your child asks for water. Celebrate her, enthusiastically thanking her for telling you what she wants, even if she has done it hundreds of times previously.

Celebrating more will make you much more aware of—and grateful for—what your child is doing well. It will also have a profound effect on her. Whenever you want more of something, celebrating—giving a big reaction—will maximize the likelihood of your child repeating it. (In Chapter 14, we'll talk about the less convenient aspect of this phenomenon, but for now just think: big reaction—repeat action.) Celebrating shows your child that you are excited by what she did, it highlights it, it makes it fun, and it gives your child a sense of control by giving her a way to influence your reactions.

When you celebrate, it's important to make it sincere and big. I've seen many people celebrate as if they are going through the motions. "Nice job, Johnny," or "Nice look, Juanita" with barely a change in their voice.

When the staff at the ATCA say "celebrate," we mean: react as if you have just won the lottery. Celebrate as if something truly amazing has happened—because it has. "Holy cow! I love when you look at me!" or "Thank you so much for telling me what you want! Whoo-hoo!"

Doing this is not frivolous. Celebrating this way has an enormous impact on how responsive your child is.

CELEBRATING TRYING

You want your child to learn to do it the "right" way. Fair enough. There's no reason why you shouldn't want that. But many parents are told to praise their child *only* when he says the "right" word, does the "right" task, etc.

From now on, you'll want to take a different approach. The good-tryer principle says that you want to do everything you possibly can to encourage your child to be a good tryer—to be willing to make many attempts, even if he isn't getting it. This is a keystone for growth and change.

As we just discussed, you will want to celebrate much more than you do now—including when your child "gets it right." However, you want to add another component to your celebration: give big, bold celebration when your child *tries*. Celebrate every attempt, even if it's way off base.

If you ask your child to say "water" and he says "ba," go crazy with celebration. If you ask your child to touch his nose and he touches his belly, celebrate big. If you are working on toilet training, and your child goes to the toilet and wees—but totally misses the potty, cheer him for trying to wee in the potty.

I have heard some voice concern that learning to do a particular task or skill correctly is vital for our kids, so it might be unwise to treat everything a child does as the "right" answer. But that is why it is important to understand that *we are not talking about pretending your child's answer is correct when it isn't.*

In fact, the good-tryer principle is the best way I've seen to help every child get the "correct" answer. In The Son-Rise Program, when we ask a child to say "water" and he says "ba," we don't say "That's perfect! You said 'water'!"

On the other hand, we don't say, "No, that's not it. Say 'water,'" because this type of response is precisely the reason why many children don't like to try in the first place: they don't want the disapproval (even if mild), and they don't want the "no."

What we would say is, "That was close! Nice try! You are awesome! Now let's try again!" We enthusiastically celebrate the attempt while encouraging the child to try again. We are seeking to make it appetizing for your child to keep trying. We want to build a little bridge of encouragement from the first try to the second, from the second to the third, etc. We know that every additional try we can get from your child brings him one step closer to being a child that can learn anything.

Whenever your child has difficulty with something or gets something "wrong," don't feel bad, feel good! Think to yourself: *Yes! This is another opportunity to help my child be a good tryer. Getting it "right" won't help him with that. Only his striving plus my encouragement can make it happen!*

For your child, trying is actually a form of engagement with the outside world. You want to make *any* engagement as appetizing as possible for him. This leads to a concept that is central to The Son-Rise Program.

THE THREE Es: ENERGY, EXCITEMENT, AND ENTHUSIASM

Displaying energy, excitement, and enthusiasm isn't brain surgery, I know. But having the three Es is essential. We talk about it over and over in the Start-Up course and in all our advanced courses. If you look at circuses, Disney characters, *Sesame Street,* and *Teletubbies,* what do they have in common? They all appeal to children (with or without autism), and they all have the three Es.

Energy, excitement, and enthusiasm always have been and always will be compelling for children. Use this fact. Bring the three Es to every aspect of your interaction with your child

Bring it to your celebrations, yes. But also bring it to taking a walk with your child, giving her a bath, eating dinner, making a request of her, etc. Unless your child is isming (and you are joining) or she is tantruming (to be discussed in Chapter 14), you want to be using the three Es whenever you are with her.

This means making your face and voice super expressive. It also means moving your body more—jumping up and down when you're cheering your child, tiptoeing toward her with the sponge in an exaggerated manner during bath time, etc.

Why is this so important? Remember, you are the ambassador of your world. You want your child to be interested and compelled to be a part of that world. The most vital part of that world is *you.* You want your child to be excited to be with *you.*

The Story of Aeesha

Aeesha's mom attended the Start-Up program with great trepidation. She was worried that she might hear the same thing from us that she'd heard from her diagnosticians—that her daughter would not improve in any significant way and hoping for more was unhealthy for both of them.

Of course, we told her no such thing, but we weren't surprised when she told us that Aeesha would try something once, and if she didn't get it the first time, she was done. If her mom endeavored to get her to try again, Aeesha would "flip out" (her mom's words), screaming and sometimes hitting or scratching. Aeesha's mom had mostly stopped asking more than once.

As a result, Aeesha had, at this point, made very little progress, which also didn't surprise us, since it's very hard to learn anything new when you never try more than once. When we asked Aeesha's mother how she felt whenever she asked her daughter to try something (saying a word, for instance), she said that she felt uncomfortable and afraid. We asked her why.

Now you might think that her main reason for this was because of her daughter's reactions, but this wasn't the case. (That's why we always ask.) In fact, her discomfort *preceded* Aeesha's reactions.

The *actual* reason was that a part of her believed what the diagnosticians had told her about Aeesha. Because of this, she felt bad about asking Aeesha for more. She felt as if she was simply putting her daughter through more difficulty by challenging her further.

One of the biggest shifts that parents make in the Start-Up course—before they go home, and thus before their children change—is in the way they see their children. They see their children with new eyes and a new attitude. (We'll focus on the importance of our attitude in Chapter 17.)

Aeesha's mom made just such a change in her Start-Up

program. Over the course of the week, she began to shift her view of Aeesha. After being shown example after example of children just like Aeesha who made huge progress, she saw the possibilities for her daughter. As she connected with other parents in the same boat, facing the same fears, she found that she felt less alone, and thus less scared. After being armed with an arsenal of tools and techniques to help Aeesha, she started to feel competent. And as she learned that Aeesha's reactions were not a product of trying but rather a consequence of *not* being challenged to try, she no longer felt sorry for Aeesha and didn't see encouraging her as "putting her through more difficulty." By the end of the week, she saw her daughter as capable of sweeping growth and herself as capable of inspiring that growth.

Before her Start-Up, she had been working on Aeesha's language—without much success, since Aeesha wouldn't try a word more than once at a time. Aeesha's mother had heard her say parts of words but never whole words. However, armed with her new perspective on her daughter, she believed that more was possible.

Aeesha loved her Teletubbies, and her favorite one was Tinky Winky. (*Of course*, thought Aeesha's mom, *the Teletubby with the longest, hardest-to-say name.*) Aeesha's Teletubbies were on a shelf beyond her reach, so when she wanted one, she would start by pointing and making some sounds.

This time, Aeesha's mom said, "Oh! Thanks for pointing! I'm not sure which Teletubby you want, Aeesha. Can you tell me?"

Aeesha said, "Kee Kee," which was her way of saying Tinky Winky.

"Hey, thanks for telling me that!" her mom said, "That was a great try! Tell me again nice and slow so I can understand you."

Aeesha screamed and started walking away.

Aeesha's mom knew that this was her moment. Instead of feeling bad or giving up, she stepped it up a notch. "I can't believe it! You are so smart, Aeesha! I know you can say it! Say 'Tinky Winky.'"

Aeesha paused. Her mom had never done this before. "Ickee Ickee," Aeesha said.

Her mom jumped up and down some more, cheering her

daughter. "That was amazing, Aeesha! You're so close, girl! Let's try again. Say 'Tinky Winky.'"

Aeesha let out a short scream, circled the room, and then returned to her mom.

"Inky Inky," she said loudly.

Aeesha's mom decided to stick with it. "That's the best ever! We're almost there! One more time, honey. Say 'Tinky Winky.'"

Aeesha screamed again but stayed exactly where she was. A little smile had crept across her face. "Tinky Winky," she said.

Her mom immediately leapt up, grabbed Tinky Winky, and handed it to her daughter. "You did it, Aeesha! You did it! Your first whole word! I knew you could do it!"

Aeesha held fast to her Teletubby, but her eyes were riveted to her mom, who was still jumping up and down, celebrating her daughter.

ACTIVITY TIME!

For each column of Table 9, simply follow the instructions in the top box of each column. Have fun!

CELEBRATING	TRYING	THE 3 E'S
Something your child does that you can celebrate more (eye contact, language, etc.)	Something your child struggles with where you can celebrate his or her trying more	An activity you already do with your child (baths, meals, etc.) to which you can add the 3 E's

Table 9

ONLINE RESOURCES

For more in-depth help with the principles and techniques of this chapter, please go to www.autismbreakthrough.com/chapter11. Celebrating you!

STARTING POINT

Choose one activity that you already do with your child (from column 3 of Table 9), and really focus on bringing the three Es to this activity. Actively look for any opportunities to cheer your child on. For instance, if you are giving him a bath, be hugely excited about the bath. Cheer your child for getting in the bath (even if he does this every day). If your child picks up a flannel, celebrate that. You will be astounded at how much this transforms the entire experience—for both of you!

TWELVE

The Big Picture: The Son-Rise Program ABCs

IF YOU CAN'T SEE YOUR CHILD, YOU CAN'T HELP YOUR CHILD

What if I told you that there is an entire element of your child's existence that you have never seen? And what if I told you that I could give you a special pair of glasses that would instantly enable you to see what you've been missing?

If you aren't able to see what's truly going on with your child in a given moment, you can't make decisions about the best way to help her. Being able to see what is actually happening with a particular child from moment to moment is what's missing when most therapists work with a child on the autism spectrum. They see the child's skill deficits, but when they are working with a child from 2:00 to 3:00, they often don't see that the child they are working with at 2:00 is a different child from the one they are working with at 2:45.

At 2:15, the child may be completely encapsulated in her world, shutting out everything and everyone else, including the therapist. At 2:45, the child may be totally connected—participating, receptive, looking at the therapist, etc. But in most cases, the therapist's overall curriculum and methods continues unabated from 2:00 to 3:00. This is unfortunate, because the two modes described above require two completely different approaches.

Wouldn't it be great to be able to see clearly which mode your child was in so that you could use the approach that works best with her in each moment?

Now that you have the arsenal of principles, techniques, and approaches from the previous chapters, wouldn't it be terrific to be able to know exactly when a principle such as joining is optimal and when challenging your child using her motivations is ideal?

Get ready. Here come the glasses.

WHY TIMING IS EVERYTHING

Children—both with and without autism—are typically taught according to the schedule of the adult. We learn X from 9:00 to 10:00, Y from 10:00 to 11:00, etc. At home, it's no different. We do such-and-such activity in the morning, before bed, whatever. The point is, we (the adults) determine what happens when.

We can pull this off with neurotypical children. Sure, some of them might complain, but we have a guaranteed base level of interaction with them. They will, in general, respond to their name, follow instructions, and react to cajoling, threats of punishment, or promises of rewards.

We have no such luxury with our special children. Since they occupy a world all their own, free from the constraints of customary interpersonal dynamics, it is up to us to follow the ebbs and flows of *their* internal process. Of course, we can ignore this, as almost everyone does, but then we must live with the side effects: a constant push-pull with our children, damaged trust, a compromised relationship in which our children lack interest in our world, and a dramatically slowed pace of learning.

What ends up happening is that we push our children to learn, interact, or process incoming information during the times they are unavailable to do so. What we don't do is use this "unavailable" time to bond and relationship-build (by joining, for instance). On the other side of this same coin, we don't optimally utilize the small windows of connection, engagement, and availability that we *do* get to help our children to grow, stretch, communicate, and learn new things (by utilizing the motivation principle, for example).

The solution is to be able to see accurately when our children are in their own world, and thus unavailable for teaching or interacting, and when they are connected with us, and thus available to learn, interact, and go our way. Once we do this, we can then cater our interactions with our children to bond with them when bonding is most useful and to challenge them to grow when they are most ready to do so.

THE EXCLUSIVE-INTERACTIVE CONTINUUM

Every waking minute of every day, your child is somewhere on the exclusive-interactive continuum. Sometimes your child is isming, making no eye contact with you, and unresponsive when you call his name. In this instance, we would say that your child is all the way over on the exclusive end of the continuum. He is planted firmly in his own special world, which is "exclusive"—as in, he is excluding you and everyone else.

Other times, your child might play with you, look at you, laugh, talk to you, and you may notice that he is more flexible, more willing to go your way. In this instance, we would say that your child is all the way over on the interactive end of the continuum. He is participating in your world. He is "interactive"—as in willing and able to interact with you and others.

Of course, there are many times when your child isn't all one or the other. That's why we call it a continuum. Throughout the day, your child probably oscillates up and down the continuum. If you can see where he is on the continuum, then you will know exactly what to do to reach him. You will know precisely which Son-Rise Program technique to use and when to use it.

RED LIGHTS AND GREEN LIGHTS

A simple and easy-to-remember shortcut to these concepts is something we call red lights and green lights.

- Red lights = signals that your child is on the exclusive end of the continuum.

- Green lights = signals that your child is on the inter-active end of the continuum.

One other term I want to throw at you: micro-assessments. The word sounds more complicated than it is. When you take your child to be evaluated, they are given an assessment. The double flaw with these assessments is this.

- They only measure your child at one snapshot in time, even though long-term decisions about her are made from this one snapshot.

- The chances are high that your child will behave atypi-cally when confronted with a stranger making her do unfamiliar tasks.

With a micro-assessment, *you* take a moment to observe your child and make a quick assessment as to whether she is giving you a red light or a green light. So how can you tell whether your child is giving you a red light or a green light?

Red Light Signals

- My child is stimming.

- My child is excluding me from what she is doing.

- My child seems rigid and controlling.

- My child does not respond when I speak to her.

- My child moves away when I touch her.

- My child is making sure to move or turn away from me.

Green Light Signals

- My child is looking at me.

- My child responds when I call her name.

- My child seems flexible (i.e., willing to change or alter her activity).

- My child is being physically affectionate with me.

- My child is involving me in her activity.

- When I make a request, my child responds.

- My child is speaking to me.

Now, are you ready to put it all together?

THE SON-RISE PROGRAM ABCs

I developed the ABC model to make it easier for parents and professionals to make moment-by-moment decisions while working with their children. This model is outlined in Table 10.

"A" stands for Assess, which we've just discussed. It simply means that the first step in the model is to take a moment and do your best to gauge whether your child is giving you a red light or a green light, based upon the criteria above.

"B" stands for Bond. If you detect that your child is giving you a red light, you'll want to focus on bonding and relationship-building with him.

"C" stands for Challenge. This refers to the times when you get a green light from your child. These are the times to challenge your child—to teach, promote more interaction, introduce a new activity, etc. In this section of the model, you are asking your child for more.

Assess	Bond	Challenge
Is my child isming?	Join	
Is my child excluding me from what he or she is doing?	Give control	
	Be user-friendly	
Does my child seem rigid or controlling?	Celebrate	
	Don't ask for anything	
Is my child non-responsive if I speak to him or her?		
Does my child move away when I touch him or her?		
Is my child making sure to move or turn away from me?		

Table 10

Assess	Bond	Challenge
Is my child looking at me?		Use the Motivation Principle
Does my child respond when I call his or her name?		
Does my child seem flexible (i.e. willing to change or alter his or her activity)?		Play dumb
Is my child being physically affectionate with me?		Request something of your child
Is my child walking or moving over to me?		Use the 3 E's Encourage trying
Is my child involving me in his or her activity?		Focus on the 4 Fundamentals of Socialization
If I make a request, does my child respond?		
Is my child speaking to me?		

Table 10 continued

ACTIVITY TIME!

Spend five minutes with your child. However, instead of trying to do something with her (or getting her to do something with you), just *observe* your child. Using the assessment questions, see if you can figure out whether she is giving you a red light or a green light. Important: Once you've figured this out, *don't do anything!* Don't try to bond if you see a red light or challenge if you see a green light. This is about observing your child. As you are observing, fill out Table 11 by writing yes or no in answer to each question.

Assessment Question	Yes/No
Is my child isming?	
Is my child excluding me from what he or she is doing?	
Does my child seem rigid or controlling?	
Is my child non-responsive if I speak to him or her?	
Does my child move away when I touch him or her?	
Is my child making sure to move or turn away from me?	
Is my child looking at me?	
Does my child respond when I call his or her name?	
Does my child seem flexible (i.e. willing to change or alter his or her activity)?	
Is my child being physically affectionate with me?	
Is my child walking or moving over to me?	
Is my child involving me in his or her activity?	
If I make a request, does my child respond?	
Is my child speaking to me?	
Red Light?	
Green Light?	

Table 11

ONLINE RESOURCES

For more in-depth help with the principles and techniques of this chapter, please go to www.autismbreakthrough.com/chapter12. Happy assessing!

STARTING POINT

Spend five minutes with your child. Determine, as best you can (without using the chart above), whether he is giving you a red light or a green light. Repeat this throughout the day anytime you like. The whole point here is to practice and get used to looking for red lights and green lights whenever you are with your child. Eventually, you will see what signal he is giving you without having to pause and think about it. The "glasses" you're learning to wear will become permanent contact lenses! And, whenever you are with your child, you will have a feel for whether it's time to bond with or challenge him.

THIRTEEN

Sensory Overload: Optimizing Your Child's Environment

EARLIER IN THE book, we discussed what your child's daily experience is like. Let's return to a large component of that experience: your child's sensory-processing challenges. For simplicity's sake, allow me to reproduce a few paragraphs from Chapter 2.

Your child has difficulty processing and making sense of sensory input. This means that he sees, hears, smells, tastes, and feels things very differently than you or I do. When your child hears something, for instance, it sounds louder, softer, or just plain different than when you hear it.

If you take a moment right now and just listen in silence to any background noise, you may notice a lot of little sounds—cars, wind, the heater or air conditioner, a TV or conversation in another room, etc. You probably didn't notice all of these noises until just now. That's as it should be.

The human ear is bombarded by a continuous cacophony of sounds. One of the brain's chief tasks is to filter out irrelevant sounds and filter in the important sound, such as your spouse/boyfriend/girlfriend talking. (Well, at least we'd call that sound important *most* of the time!)

With your child, all of those noises are coming in at the same volume! (It doesn't work in *exactly* this way, but this is the closest approximation to your child's experience that we can get into right now.) So, when you tell your child to pay attention and listen, what, exactly should he listen to? Which of the twenty-five sounds is your child supposed to pay attention to?

This is your child's experience day in and day out. You know how you feel after you've spent the day at an airport (tired, overwhelmed, like you just want to veg out)? Well, your child wakes up, has breakfast, lunch, dinner, then goes to sleep—in the middle of a busy airport. Even if it's just your living room, it's an airport to your child.

For a deeper understanding of our children's sensory and self-regulation systems, read MarySue Williams and Sherry Shellenberger, the creators of the Alert Program® and authors of several books, including "How Does Your Engine Run?"® A Leader's Guide to the Alert Program®. They are very knowledgeable and competent when it comes to the ins and outs of sensory integration and self-regulation. I've attended one of their courses, and they have visited ours. They do wonderful work, and they also send parents our way because they understand both the significance of our children's sensory systems and the importance of trust and interpersonal relationships. They wrote an article for parents using The Son-Rise Program available under "Free Resources" at www.alterprogram.com. These two women are also deeply caring and magnificent people!

Because of your child's sensory-processing challenges, addressing your child's environment is essential. Often, an overstimulating environment (at school, at home, or elsewhere) can serve as a major obstacle to a child's progress and interaction. So you want to do everything you can to reduce overstimulation and make your child's immediate environment as conducive to successful sensory processing—and thus, to interaction and learning—as possible.

CREATING AN OPTIMIZED ENVIRONMENT

How do you do this? You set aside a room in the house to be a special playroom or focus room, where much of the momentous work with your child can occur. These are the characteristics of such a setting.

1. Distraction-free

Most rooms in which your child finds herself are riddled with low-level distractions—murals and pictures on the wall, items strewn across the floor, phones ringing, people talking, televisions blaring, people walking in and out, windows to look out of and let in blasts of light, etc. Even a single one of these distractions can be very overstimulating to someone with sensory challenges. Choose a totally enclosed room in the house with closable, lockable doors (you could use your child's bedroom if that works), and do whatever you can to eliminate from that room as many of the above distractions as possible. In fact, do your best to create a room that a neurotypical child might find boring. (It won't be boring to your special child.)

2. Free from control battles.

Remember our discussion in Chapter 10 about the importance of avoiding control battles? For this room to be a place where you can get extraordinary interaction and progress from your child, it needs to be a place where he feels totally safe and secure. Control battles obliterate that safety and security, to say nothing of how they compromise your child's trust and relationship with you. This means that you want to make this room a "yes" room. You want the room to be so safe that you don't have to say no to *anything*—for instance, "don't touch that," "don't climb on that," "don't do that"—unlike in the kitchen, for example, where you have to say no to many things—sharp knives, hot hobs, and so on.

3. Toys are on a shelf that your child cannot reach.

The goal here is not to make things difficult for your child. The idea is to foster communication. Your child can have anything on that shelf that she wants. But she will need *you* to get it. This arrangement sets you up as a partner and friend to your child (rather than an obstacle). Remember, this room is a "yes" room. This is a place where your child will have a huge sense of control and autonomy. However, she still cannot reach what she wants on the shelf without your help. And what a help you will be! You will be there, ready to move, ready to get her what she wants as soon as she asks for it.

4. No electronic toys, televisions, or computers.

I know that your first instinct might be to object to this guideline. I understand. I know that you may feel that your child enjoys these items—or that they serve as a short-term babysitter while you are making dinner. But it is essential to understand that *these items help your child to be autistic.* First, they are self-creating isms. (As we talked about in Chapter 2, there's nothing wrong with isms when your *child* creates them, but that doesn't mean *we* want to provide machinery that creates them.) Second, no matter how educational a video, toy, or computer program is, it can never teach your child to interact and be social. (In reality, these items make it easier for your child to be *less* interactive.) And, third, as long as these items are in the room, you will always be playing second fiddle to a machine. After all, you can't make multicolored lights come out of your eyes (or do anything else a machine does), and machines don't challenge your child to be social. So, in the short term, your child will always prefer these items to you. The bottom line is: less electronics, more interaction.

5. One-on-one.

For now (not forever), you want only one person at a time in the room with your child. This is to prevent overstimulation and promote interaction. You are trying to build a bridge from your child's world to yours. At first, this bridge needs to be from person to person—from your child to another individual. This is the simplest way to forge an interpersonal connection.

6. **If possible: a window of one-way glass or two to four mini-cameras.**

At the Autism Treatment Center of America, we have this in our playrooms, but of course our playrooms are set up to be perfect. Yours doesn't have to be, but you will want a way to see what is happening in your child's playroom or focus room. This is important both so you know how your child is doing and so you can tell how the person working with your child is doing.

WHY LOCKING THE DOOR CAN BE HELPFUL

I often get asked why Son-Rise Program parents often lock the door to their children's playrooms.

To be clear, we are not talking about locking your child in his room by himself. Remember, there is always an adult in the room.

With that said, it bears stating that I have never, in my life, heard anyone ask this question about the fact that front and back doors to houses are routinely locked (with the child and at least one adult inside). No one I know is advocating for an open-door house policy, where children with autism can simply leave the house when they please and go marching down the street.

I bring this up to highlight the fact that there is *always* an enclosed environment around every child. It's just a question of where that enclosure is. You cannot really work with a child that is running from room to room (*your* child may not do this, but many do).

And it's not about locking anyone up. It's about giving your child some relief—and providing him with a loving, nurturing, and helpful environment.

So, if you believe that it could be useful or important for

your child to have a one-on-one environment that is free from control battles and is not overstimulating, then being in a play-room or focus room where the door is not a revolving one might be what you choose. At the end of the day, it is, of course, your decision.

TAKING YOUR CHILD TO THE SUPERMARKET, PLAYGROUND, OR AMUSEMENT PARK

Many parents feel that it is very important to take their child to the playground or similar venue where their child can "be a regular kid." They feel that to skip this is to deprive their child of vital experiences.

It is essential to understand, though, that your child, right now, is not a "regular kid." Your child is different. Your child has special challenges. If having your child in a typical environment solved these challenges, you wouldn't be reading this book, and we wouldn't have an autism epidemic, because we could just take our kids to typical environments with neurotypical chil-dren, and—poof!—challenge solved.

You know better than anyone else that this isn't the way it works. I completely understand that you might sometimes *want* it to work this way. I really do. And I would never begrudge you wanting that. But I also know that you love and care about your child and would go to the ends of the earth to help her.

So, please, take this in: because of your child's sensory-processing challenges, she *can't* have a "regular" experience at the park—not right now. Your child can't experience success in these public arenas when she is overstimulated and cannot take the experience in.

However, wouldn't it wonderful to be able to reintroduce these types of experiences to your child later—when she *can*

process them and be successful? This is possible! It doesn't require perfection on your part. It just takes some investment now.
It takes some concentrated time now—time where you limit
excursions as much as possible—in order to get years of payoff
later.

I have heard parents adamantly exclaim that their child loves
being out of the house and in these public environments. I always respond with one of my favorite quotes from my sister
Bryn: "Heroin addicts really like heroin. That doesn't mean that
it's good for them." (This quote is so good, I'm going to bring it
back in Chapter 16, when we talk about diet.)

When children have sensory-processing challenges and
they enter an environment where their nervous system is overwhelmed, one of two things happens. Many children become
reactive and prone to meltdowns. Some, however, enjoy and
become addicted to the rush of adrenaline and cortisol that
courses through their fragile systems.

If your child is of the second variety, she will appear to love
being in overstimulating environments. That doesn't mean it's
good for her. It doesn't mean that her nervous system isn't compromised and that her ability to interact and learn is not severely
impaired by that environment.

Can I say for sure, without ever meeting your child, she cannot handle these public, highly stimulating environments that
she appears to enjoy? No. But I can tell you this: For 99 percent
of the children we see, these environments are detrimental to
learning and interaction. Unless your child is already highly interactive with other people, flexible, tolerant of all sounds and
lights, does not ism or have meltdowns on these excursions, and
does not ism or have meltdowns within two hours of returning
home from these excursions, your child is probably a member of
that 99 percent.

FROM THE PLAYROOM TO
THE "REAL WORLD"

The fact that the playroom or focus room is a "yes" room doesn't mean that your child will never be challenged. Quite the opposite. In that room, your child will be more directly and clearly challenged on the core aspects of his autism than anywhere else on earth.

When your child isn't trying to juggle a million other sensory inputs, he can actually move forward on the four fundamentals: eye contact and nonverbal communication, verbal communication, interactive attention span, and flexibility.

Once you eliminate overstimulation and get your child out of the fight-or-flight mode that accompanies that overstimulation, everything changes. I don't just mean that your child becomes more interactive, although this is certainly what we see. I also mean that children in focus rooms learn to adjust their sensory input systems. Slowly, they begin to tolerate more and more stimulation—*if* it is added piece by piece and not all at once.

If I tell you to lift two hundred pounds, you probably can't do it, even if I have you try all day (or all week). But if I start you off at thirty pounds, then build up to forty, then fifty, then sixty, eventually we can get to two hundred pounds.

Over time, we make the playroom more and more like the outside world until, eventually, there is no difference. Then your child doesn't need a special environment anymore. He can be successful in any environment.

I was in a playroom for three and a half straight years. Now I spend my days in crowded, crazy places in a host of countries worldwide. That distraction-free "yes" room that my parents set up way back in 1974 has proved to be a godsend to me now.

The Story of Jordan

Several years ago, a boy from the United Kingdom named Jordan came to the Autism Treatment Center of America. (I'm using his real name because his story was broadcast on TV internationally.) The BBC aired a documentary entitled "I Want My Little Boy Back," which followed Jordan and his parents as they traveled to the ATCA and then continued their Son-Rise Program at home. (Contact the ATCA if you would like a DVD of this documentary.)

Jordan's story is rather amazing; he changed quite radically. I'll let you see the documentary and experience it for yourself, but I wanted to highlight one part of Jordan's story because it so clearly applies here.

Before Jordan came to the ATCA, he was in perpetual sensory overload. He screamed and cried much of the time. He was overwhelmed. If someone was mowing the lawn near his house, he would cover his ears with his hands, screeching.

This was Jordan's parents' day-in, day-out experience. They often found it difficult just to get through the day.

After one week in our playroom environment, Jordan noticed one of our property maintenance workers mowing the lawn outside his window. He strolled to the window and calmly watched the lawn being mowed. He neither cried nor covered his ears.

Jordan's parents were shocked, but we weren't. We see the effect of the focus room environment every day.

AN EXTREME ENVIRONMENT

If setting up a playroom or focus room for your child, including all of the guidelines and recommendations in this chapter, feels extreme to you, I want you to know that I agree with you. The

Son-Rise Program playroom *is* extreme. Your child has autism. Extreme is called for. The focus room is an extreme *temporary* environment designed to get extreme *permanent* results. If that is something you want, then taking the steps outlined in this chapter is worth considering.

ACTIVITY TIME!

As a way to get yourself started, take some time to fill out Table 12.

Five Things You Can Do To Optimize Your Child's Immediate Environment
1)
2)
3)
4)
5)

Table 12

ONLINE RESOURCES

For more in-depth help with the principles and techniques of this chapter, please go to www.autismbreakthrough.com/chapter13. Delve in!

STARTING POINT

Before you set up any kind of official playroom or focus room, you can take some very basic steps in your living room, your child's bedroom, or another room in the house where you will be with your child today. First, clear away any items on the floor, countertops, and tabletops. Close any open doors in this room as well. Unplug any appliances (other than the lights, of course!). Bring in three nonelectronic toys or games that you think your child likes or might like, such as a set of stuffed animals (counts as one item), a ball, a musical instrument—or, if she is more sophisticated, a card game, a board game, or paper and markers (counts as one item). Now you have a temporary focus room! Spend thirty minutes in this room with your child today and focus on enjoying this time with her.

FOURTEEN

Tantrums and Other Challenging Behaviors: How Changing Your Reactions Changes Everything

I'm sure your child doesn't have any behaviors that you find challenging, right? Okay, dumb question. If your child is a human being, then he does things that you, at times, find tough to deal with. That's all right. You're in good company, and so is your child.

What may surprise you is the outsized role you have in your child's tantrums (crying, hitting, biting, etc.) and other related behaviors. In fact, chances are extremely high that you are unwittingly teaching your child to do *more* of the very behaviors you most want him to cease.

How in the world could that be possible?

AN ANALOGY

Have you ever spent a significant amount of time in a foreign country where English was not spoken? On the other hand, have you ever spent time in a country where English is not the first language spoken but everyone can still speak English fluently?

Allow me, if you will, to walk you briefly through two of my foreign escapades. You may recall from Chapter 1 that I spent some time living in Stockholm, Sweden.

Now, the Swedes speak Swedish, of course. But they also speak superb English, and many of them enjoy practicing their English on native English-speakers. During the year that I lived in Stockholm, I took Swedish language classes five days a week. On top of that, I'm pretty good at languages, so I fully expected to be fluent by the end of the year.

I was utterly mistaken.

Swedish, as a language, is not particularly difficult. However, what I noticed, when I was out on the town in Stockholm, is that I would stop someone to ask for directions. I would begin speaking in Swedish, but as soon as I found myself stumbling the tiniest bit, I would fall back on my English. The moment I did so, whomever I was speaking to would respond to me in crystal clear English. It was awesome!

The only problem was, since this was a regular occurrence, I found that, by the end of the year, I was very un-fluent in Swedish. How come? As long as I knew that people understood English, it didn't matter how much Swedish I took or how many times my teacher told me to "Tala Svenska, du skit!" (That is: "Speak Swedish," followed by an expletive that I decline to translate.) I would fall back on my old language, never fully making the transition to the new one.

However, I also spent some time in Spain, where most people did not speak English. If I wanted to find a toilet I really, really had to ask in Spanish. Even though I had taken Spanish in high school, I was nevertheless shocked at how quickly I picked the language up in Spain. The key was: Spanish was the only language that anyone understood. Communicating in Spanish was the only way for me to get anything across to anyone. So, Spanish it was, and pronto.

TANTRUMS: THE OLD PARADIGM

The analogy above illustrates a concept that applies very powerfully to your child. Most of the time, when a child on the autism spectrum tantrums, hits, screams, cries, etc., parents take one of two roads. Option one: They get angry and reactive, scolding their child. Option two (most common): They try to "fix the problem." They ask, "What is it, sweetie-pie?" and then proceed to dash around frantically, trying to figure out what their child wants so they can give it to her—so that the tantrum will stop.

The driving, overriding question in most parents' minds is: How do I stop this tantrum? I call this question "the indentured-servitude question" because, once you ask it—congratulations! You are now a servant to your child's tantrum. You will do whatever it takes to bring that tantrum to a blessed end. Both types of reactions outlined above (option one and option two) fall under the heading of "big reactions." Big reactions are emotional, fast, animated, loud (usually), and action-packed.

The reason for these big reactions is that most parents see the tantrum as a kind of alarm system. When it goes off, they are immediately on high alert. They want to find and fix the emergency. What's more, there is usually a direct emotional connection between their child's tantrum and their own discomfort. They feel instantly agitated (which doesn't help their child to calm down).

This is not difficult to understand. Most parents feel agitated because they see the tantrum as something wrong, and every minute that the tantrum continues is a signal that they are not being a good mom or dad. After all, "good" mothers and fathers solve their children's problems and stop the tantrum, right?

But, wait! I haven't got to the best part yet!

Not only are you now an indentured servant, but you will, for sure, get more and more tantrums from your child. Why? Take a look at Figure 2, on the following page, which shows what most of us do when confronted with a challenging behavior— and how this affects our children's behavior over time.

As we can see, a big reaction from a parent leads to more challenging behavior from the child. And each time a parent (or teacher, therapist, family member, etc.) reacts this way, the

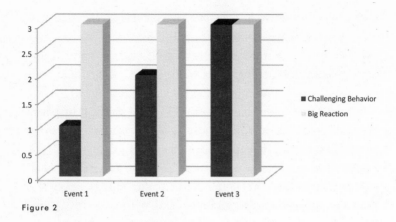

Figure 2

challenging behavior grows successively more frequent, more extreme, and longer in duration.

Furthermore, the term "challenging behavior" doesn't just refer to tantrums. It also refers to instances where your child does something such as pulling a painting off the wall, speaking loudly, being disruptive in a public place, breaking a household item, running into the street, or using profanity.

What happens when our child behaves in one of these challenging ways? In most cases, we light up like a Christmas tree. For instance, if our child pulls a painting off the wall, we might sprint over to where our child is (with a shocked or exasperated expression on our face) and exclaim, "Honey, what did you do?! You're not supposed to touch that!" For some of us, we may feel a bit guilty for reacting and say, "I know you didn't mean to. Let's take you into the other room." By this time, though, it's too late. We've already given a big reaction, and thus lived out the above graph.

Whether it is a tantrum or something else, the results of that graph are the same: *more* challenging behavior.

I'll explain why this is the case in a moment, but first let's explore a brand-new paradigm.

TANTRUMS AS COMMUNICATION

Here's the new paradigm: When your child is tantruming, hitting, crying, pinching, screaming, etc., he is trying to communicate! Terrific! You *want* him to communicate!

There's just one problem: Your child is speaking to you in Swedish! Speaking in Swedish is much more communicative than not speaking at all, but the downside of this—from your child's point of view—is that no one around here understands Swedish.

Your child can't go into a shop, scream, and get a packet of sweets. No one will know what he wants.

So it is important to understand that when your child is doing anything that resembles a tantrum, it's not an alarm bell. It's not a statement about you as a parent. It's just an attempt to communicate. (This is why we don't join in with tantrums. Joining is what we do when a child is exclusive and disconnected. A tantrum is the opposite. A tantruming child is specifically endeavoring to communicate with us, not to disconnect.)

Using this paradigm, let's return to the graph above. Why would your big response encourage your child to do more of the challenging behavior over time?

Two reasons: First, recall from Chapter 11 that big reactions lead to repeat actions. This serves your child when it applies to big celebrations—the type of big reaction discussed in that chapter. When you celebrate your child looking at you, you get more looks. But it doesn't serve your child (or you) when your big reaction acts as a highlighter for exactly what you don't want.

Remember that your child lives in a world in which he often feels no control or predictability. He is therefore always on the lookout for predictability and control. If you light up like a Christmas tree every time he does behavior X, he will do it more, if only to restore that predictability and control.

The second reason your big response results in more challenging behavior is that *your reaction tells your child that you understand Swedish*—especially if you are running around trying to "fix" things. Your child is no dummy. Why on earth would he work his tail off trying to speak in full sentences when he could just scream and be understood (at least generally)? Why should he do the heavy lifting required to formulate words when a tantrum sends everyone scurrying?

But wait! I *still* haven't got to the best part!

Not only are you now an indentured servant who is teaching your child to increase his or her challenging behaviors because you understand Swedish, but you have also helped to decrease your child's useful, productive communication.

Let's explore why this is.

Let's take another look at Figure 2.

Okay. Now what happens when your child engages in a sweet, communicative behavior? If you're like most people, you deem this a nonemergency, and you don't fall all over yourself trying to respond.

Suppose that you are making dinner and your child comes up to you and quietly says a word or two. Or gently tugs on your sleeve. If you're right in the middle of cooking, you probably say something like, "I hear you, sweetie. I'll be there in just a few minutes. I just need to finish dinner."

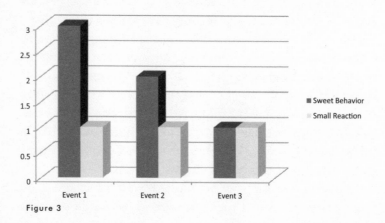

Figure 3

The results of that scenario are depicted in Figure 3.

Ah, but how do we react when we are making dinner and our child starts screaming? Dinner can wait—we have a crisis on our hands! Aaaaand we're back to Figure 2.

What does your child take from all of this? Any intelligent child would surmise the following: communicating sweetly gets me the slowest, most mellow, least urgent response, and screaming get me a fast, big, urgent response. When your child really wants to communicate something important, which method is he going to use?

All right, so now that we know this, what's the way out?

TURNING THE TABLES

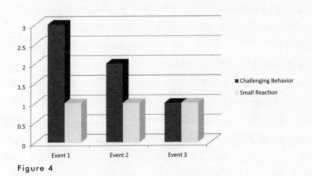

Figure 4

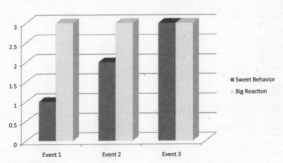

Figure 5

Take a gander at Figures 4 and 5. Do you see? You can turn the tables by reversing your reactions. When your child yells, cries, tantrums, whatever, you want your response to be slow and flat. (This is one of the very few times when I would advocate *not* using the three Es.) I'm not saying to ignore your child—or to be punitive and say something like, "Listen, buddy, I'm not going to help you when you whine and carry on." This isn't about punishing or "teaching her a lesson."

I'm talking about communicating to your child that you understand English, but you don't understand Swedish. The next time she tantrums, you want to immediately relax. Instead of asking yourself the indentured-servitude question ("How do I stop this tantrum?"), ask yourself this: "How can I help my child communicate more effectively?"

If you ask that question, you can't go wrong.

Remind yourself that your job as a parent is not to stop the tantrum, it's to help your child communicate. In the short term, that may mean that the tantrum goes on for *longer*.

One the other side of the equation, it is absolutely essential that you show your child that you really, really understand English. When your child behaves in a way that is sweet or communicative (using words, tugging gently at your sleeve, taking your hand, using a nice tone of voice, etc.), your mission in life is to respond quickly, urgently, and enthusiastically. The running-around-like-a-chicken-with-its-head-cut-off that used to happen during a tantrum—that's what needs to happen here instead.

To recap:

Tantrums, crying, screaming, hitting, biting, pinching → slow, flat, mellow.

Sweet, communicative behavior → fast, big, urgent, excited.

So, what do you actually do? Let's outline that in the context of a specific child so you can really see how it works.

The Story of Michelle

I was working with Michelle at an outreach I did some years ago, and she wanted one of her toys from the shelf. (You may recall from Chapter 4 that an outreach is when a Son-Rise Program teacher or child facilitator spends a couple of days in a family's house helping them implement their program.) I was more than happy to get it for her, and I had a good idea which one she wanted, but she was screaming a blue streak. ("Screaming a blue streak" is an expression I happily steal from William Hogan.)

Michelle was crying and yelling. One of her hands was pointing up at one of the shelves. The other was being ferociously bitten—by her. (Every time she jammed her hand in her mouth and bit down, she would look right at me.)

Knowing from her parents that this was a common response of Michelle's (she was very fluent in "Swedish"), I was quite glad that she was doing this with me. I thought to myself, *This is the perfect opportunity to help Michelle communicate more effectively!* (Sincerely, that's really what I thought. I know this may seem far-fetched to you, but we'll address how it can be totally doable for you in Chapter 17.)

I squatted down so that I wasn't standing over her. "Hey, Michelle, I really want to help you get what you want, but I can't understand you when you scream." I paused for a moment, then clapped my hand to my mouth. "Ooh, you know what? I can understand you when you use your words! Tell me what you want, and I'll *run* and get it!" I paused again, this time for a while.

Michelle screamed some more, bit her hand again, and threw something at me.

"Hmmm," I said, putting on my best "confused" look. "I don't know what that means." I very slowly wandered toward the shelves. Michelle continued screaming.

"Huh. I know you want something, but I can't understand screaming." I finally reached the shelves.

"I'm just not sure." Slowly, I reached up and plucked something down—a toy that I was fairly sure was *not* what she wanted.

I walked slowly back to her and handed the toy to her. "Is this the one you want?"

Michelle flung it across the room, continued screaming, and bit her hand again.

"Okay, so it's clearly not that one. Cool." I wandered back toward the shelf.

"I can't understand screaming, so I'm still not sure. If you use your words, Michelle, I'll know exactly what you want."

She continued screaming.

I picked another toy from the shelf—not what she wanted—made my way back to her, and said, "Is this the one you want?"

Michelle grabbed the toy and pitched it at the bowl of soup on the shelf. Missed.

I squatted down again so that I was at eye level. "I'll tell you what, Michelle. Since I can't understand you when you scream, I'm going to be over in that corner playing with some toys. If you want me, just use your words, and I will *run* and get you what you want so fast!"

I took some toys and went to the corner to play.

Michelle screamed for a while longer. Fifteen minutes passed.

Suddenly, from the other end of the room, I heard, barely audible: "Want doll."

I sprang up, bounded over to the shelf, grabbed the doll, ran over to her, and held it out to her. She snatched it.

"Hey, Michelle! You did it! Thank you so much for using your words! Now I can understand you!"

For the rest of my session with her, whenever she would so much as glance at the shelves, I would jump up and stand poised at the shelves, ready to follow her command, happy to show her how much she could get if she used her words.

She actually started to get a kick out this, ordering me to do various things, sometimes even laughing at my darting to and fro.

For the rest of my time in her home, she didn't tantrum at all. Her parents, who, of course, had been watching everything, were very excited because they saw a clear, effective way forward—and they took it.

GROWING UP TANTRUM-FREE

You can imagine what it was like growing up in my house. We all knew from the get-go that tantruming, screaming, crying, etc. was just never going to work with my parents.

I must admit that sometimes, as a little kid (post-autism), I found this annoying. But in the end, guess what? I didn't tantrum! Not as a kid, not as a teenager.

It's not that I never tried to cajole my parents into giving me something. It's just that I did it by talking and convincing, not by crying, whining, or complaining. And I certainly didn't always get what I wanted, but when I didn't, I still saw no point in flipping out about it because I knew that it wouldn't change anything anyway. (I will tell you that, one time, when I was little, after being turned down in my request for a family trek to get some ice cream, I went through the house, made all of the beds, vacuumed all the rooms, and then put up a sign for my parents to see, asking yet again. I got it!)

A NOTE ON THE WORD
"MANIPULATIVE"

I have, in the past, been asked whether the explanation of tantruming as something our children do in an attempt to communicate what they want means that our kids are being manipulative. To say that our children are being manipulative is to believe that our children are being insincere or deceptive in order to maneuver us to their ends. It has a somewhat sinister connotation.

When I say that your child is crying, yelling, screaming, hitting, biting, or pinching in order to communicate, I mean that quite literally. Your child may find communicating with words to be difficult, cumbersome, and, as we discussed earlier, not terribly useful in getting a fast response.

Your child is thus doing his level best to communicate. He's coming from a totally sincere place. Just because your child may be, for instance, using crying to *communicate* rather than because they are *upset* does not in any way impugn his motives.

Your child is doing the very best that he can to communicate in a topsy-turvy world. There is absolutely nothing wrong with that. "Manipulative" would be the very last word I would use to describe your child.

We help our children to communicate more effectively when we don't judge their current behaviors. In fact, you will find that following the guidelines in this chapter without any annoyance or judgment on your part will be enormously helpful in enabling your child to switch gears.

SENSORY OVERLOAD OR
PHYSICAL PAIN

It is possible that your child may be crying because she is in a state of sensory overload or because she is physically hurting (bumped her head, has a stomach ache, etc.).

If you clearly see that your child is hurt or hurting, of course you'll want to do what you can to help or soothe. James was prone to severe stomach aches, and there are many times when I or Charlotte would rub James's stomach as he was crying.

But even here, using our reactions to foster communication makes sense. Partly because, from the get-go, Charlotte used the "reactions" approach with James, he can now tell us what part of him is hurting. Don't you want your child to be able to communicate what is hurting? It will always be helpful to her if you give big and fast responses to language and slower, calmer responses to crying. Even if your child is hurting (or scared, etc.), wouldn't you want to send the message that it's okay—rather than sending the message that something scary and stressful is occurring (which is exactly the message we send when we react in a panic to crying)?

With respect to sensory overload, we have spent a great deal of time on this issue because of how important it is. The playroom or focus room described in Chapter 13 reduces meltdowns precisely because it eliminates sensory overload. Joining also helps in this regard. Keeping your child out of overstimulating situations will, without question, also reduce crying and meltdowns.

So, as much as possible, take your child out of overstimulating situations and environments, whether or not she is crying. If you see a sensory issue, such as a sound that's disturbing your child, and you can address it, then by all means do so, whether or not she is crying.

Here again, this chapter's principles apply. You want to communicate that nothing scary is happening, even when your child is overstimulated. And you want to show her that you understand English, not Swedish, precisely so that she can better communicate if something is overloading her.

In addition, letting your child work it out herself yields all kinds of benefits to her self-regulation and self-calming.

I certainly experienced this with James.

JAMES: MONTH ONE

Although James loved the ladies, he was very reactive to men. When I first began to work with him, he wasted no time in communicating this fact to me. I would enter his playroom, and the second he saw me, he would fall over like a toppling tree and start wailing and crying on the floor.

I had seen other people endeavor to talk to him and calm him down when he did this, and the result was always the same: the more they talked to him (regardless of what they said), the louder and more insistent his crying became. His agitation seemed to increase with each second that these people spent attending to him. Furthermore, if someone got too close to him during this period, he would push his chin into that person with quite a bit of force and sometimes dig his nails into the person's skin.

When he fell over and started crying as I entered his playroom, I honestly wasn't sure whether he was trying to communicate something (like maybe "Raun, get out!") or whether he was just overwhelmed and agitated because I was a man. Here's the thing: it didn't matter.

What I did was this: first, I would *very* briefly tell him, "Hey, bud, I'm going to be over in that corner when you want to play or use your words." Then I would go over to the corner and begin drawing something on the wall. (His playroom had special walls that you could draw on.)

Every time this occurred, I would feel genuinely relaxed, with zero urgency to stop James from crying. I knew that he needed to regulate himself, and I wanted to give him a chance to do that—without me judging him, pushing him, or placating him.

Another note: while I was drawing in the corner, I would deliberately position myself so that my side (profile) was toward him. Let me tell you why. I have found with many children—including James—that when they are in a tantrum or on a crying jag, if you sit (or stand) facing them, they can feel your attention and focus upon them, and they often become more agitated. On the other hand, you don't want to sit with your back to them because then you can't see them.

So I would sit facing the picture I was drawing (the hardest part of this whole endeavor, given the sad state of my drawing skills), and every so often I would give a quick sideways glance over at James to see what he was up to.

Before I tell you what happened, let me explain that I had seen James wail for *forty-five minutes to an hour* on a regular basis when certain people entered his playroom.

For the first month that I worked with him, James would fall to the ground and cry every single time I entered. I had never had a child cry like this more than once or twice when I entered, so I had to be very clear in my own mind that James was doing this for his own reasons (i.e., because I was a guy)—and not make it mean anything about me.

However, even though James did this for the first month, do you know how long he would cry after I entered each time? *Four minutes.* At most. Sometimes two. Out of a session that lasted between ninety minutes and three hours.

After a few minutes, James would stop crying, walk over to me, and spontaneously begin playing with me (wrestling, taking my hand, asking for something, falling into my lap and laughing).

At that point, I would immediately reciprocate, and that would set the stage for the rest of the session.

After that first month, James never again cried when I entered.

THE IMPORTANCE OF CONSISTENCY

This works only if done with total consistency. It *can't* not work because it plays to your child's intelligence *and* to your child's motivation to get what he wants.

For those who think you've implemented this strategy and believe it hasn't worked, I give you the following anecdote.

The Story of Hassan

We had a mom in the Start-Up course who had a son named Hassan who tantrumed a *lot*. This little guy really loved cookies (understandably). His mom would often let him eat cookies (a problem for separate reasons that we will go over in Chapter 16). However, there were certain times, such as just before bed, when Hassan's mom did not want to give him any cookies.

As she explained to us in class, oftentimes when she would refrain from giving Hassan his cookie, he would scream, cry, etc. When we explained the above principle, she immediately cut in, "Yes, I know, but that doesn't work with my son."

We had heard that response many, many times, so we asked her to take us through exactly what transpired the last time this situation popped up.

She recounted that the night before she flew to the ATCA for her Start-Up, she was getting Hassan ready for bed, and he said "I want cookie" (a phrase he knew quite well).

"And what did you do then?" the teacher asked.

"I told you," Hassan's mother said, "I told him that I was sorry, but that he couldn't have a cookie right before bed."

"Okay," the teacher replied, "and what did Hassan do then?"

Hassan's mom threw her hands up. "Well, that's when he started his routine. He began crying, saying, 'I want cookie!' over and over."

"All right," the teacher continued, "and what did you do then?"

"I told him that he could cry all he wanted, but that he wasn't going to get a cookie right before bed," Hassan's mother said in a tone that implied that she had just spoken the most obvious truth known to humankind.

The teacher followed up again. "And after you told Hassan that, what did he do then?"

"Oh, he really went for it then. He started screeching, rolling around on the floor, kicking his feet, and yelling "I want cookie!" over and over," Hassan's mom explained, looking exasperated.

"And what did you do at that point?" the teacher asked once more.

"Well, of course, this can go on all night, and I have to get him to sleep at some point, so, you know, eventually, after a long while, when there was no other alternative, I had to . . ." She mumbled the last few words of her sentence with her head down, so the teacher couldn't make it out.

"I couldn't make that last bit out," the teacher said gently. "What was it you said you had to do?"

"Give . . . him . . . the . . . cookie," Hassan's mom said hesitantly. She looked disheartened.

Allow me to chime in for a moment. I don't recommend showing your child that you understand Swedish by giving into the tantrum. However, I recommend even *less* the practice of holding out, holding out, holding out—and then giving in an hour later. Why? Because now you've just communicated the following to your child: if you want to get the cookie before bed, you need to speak Swedish (tantrum) *for an hour* before you get it.

Returning to our story, the teacher explained to Hassan's mother exactly what to do, and she went home and really did it. She made sure everyone else in the house did it. And she never wavered. She was slow, flat, and "confused" when Hassan tantrumed (and, of course, never ever gave him a cookie before bed), and she was fast and excited when her son communicated sweetly.

After being back for a couple of weeks, she told us that she was astounded by what she'd seen. The first few days, Hassan screamed, cried, and tantrumed even more than before. But after that, Hassan's mom said it was as if someone had flipped a switch. His tantruming went from several times a day to only once the entire past week. Hassan also became much more communicative, as he saw the power of using his words.

His mother told us that, although she certainly was happier and calmer, what was most exciting was to see that her son seemed so much happier and calmer, too.

One final note on this point. Once in a while, we'll get a parent who absolutely swears that he or she *never* gives his or her child the cookie, and yet the tantruming continues unabated. In response to this, I will, once again, quote my sister Bryn: "Then *someone's* giving your child the cookie."

If you are 100 percent sure that you never give in and never "understand Swedish," then the only other possibility is that someone else in your child's life is responding to crying, hitting, etc. There is no other way for the tantruming to continue. Your child is smart. There is simply no way that your child will, day in and day out, continue to use a mode of communication that never, ever works. It's just not possible.

NOT HITTING VERSUS BEING GENTLE

Don't think of a banana. Whatever you do, don't think of a ripe yellow banana. How'd you do? If you're like the rest of the world, you probably thought of a banana. Then, maybe you tried to imagine a piece of paper or a cloth or maybe just blackness covering the banana.

What does this prove? It illustrates something very important about the human mind: it cannot *not* think of something. If

I tell you *not* to think of a banana, this is impossible. What *is* possible is to *think of something else instead*—an orange, for instance.

Most of us say things to our children such as, "Don't hit," "Don't pinch," or "It's not nice to scratch your sister." For almost everyone, this seems like the most natural thing in the world.

The problem is that when we say "Don't hit," our children hear "Hit." When we say "Don't pinch," our children hear "Pinch." We are inadvertently taking the thing we don't want and making it bigger. We are focusing all of our children's attention on the behavior we *don't* want them to do.

Instead, let's focus on helping our children to *be gentle*. How often do we jump up and down and cheer when our children are gentle? We can show our children what being gentle looks like (touching a hand or shoulder gently). Even better, whenever our children do anything gently (touch our arm, take our hand), we want to make a *huge* deal out of it. Celebrate. Cheer. Clap. Sometimes, when a child who hits touches my arm gently, I run around the room rubbing my arm and exclaim, "Ooooh! That feels so awesome when you're gentle!"

In most cases, our children see us giving large reactions when they hit, pinch, or bite us—and very little, if any, reactions when they are gentle. We want to turn the tables in dramatic fashion!

Remember: our children can picture being gentle, but they cannot picture *not hitting*. Rather than thinking to ourselves, *I need to get my child to stop hitting*, we want to focus our energy and attention on *encouraging our children to be gentle*.

ACTIVITY TIME!

All you're going to do here is to compile a list of all of the behaviors and situations to react *less* to and all of those that you will react *more* to. This list—Table 13—will then serve as a very helpful guidepost going forward!

To React LESS To	To React MORE To

Table 13

ONLINE RESOURCES

For more in-depth help with the principles and techniques of this chapter, please go to www.autismbreakthrough.com/chapter14. Relax and relish!

STARTING POINT

This starting point has two separate parts.

Part 1

The very next time your child hits, cries, or tantrums, focus all of your attention on relaxing yourself. Take a few deep breaths. Remind yourself that what he's doing says nothing about you as a parent. He's just trying to communicate. Nothing terrible is happening.

Until you are relaxed, don't move (unless something unsafe is happening). When you are totally relaxed, say the following to your child: "I love you and want to help you, but I don't understand what you want." Then invite him to use his words to say what he wants. If your child does not yet have any language, invite him to point to what he wants.

If your child speaks or points (without screaming or hitting), then cheer him exuberantly and do your best to give your child what he wants.

Part 2

Find any excuse throughout the day to celebrate your child being gentle or communicating clearly. We're talking about *any* instance. It doesn't have to be right after a time when he was hitting or crying. Look for and notice any times when your child is gentle or communicating clearly, and cheer each instance with great gusto!

FIFTEEN

Asperger's Syndrome: Applying the Son-Rise Program Principles

AT THE AUTISM Treatment Center of America, we work with a large number of families who have children or adults with Asperger's syndrome or deemed "high functioning." All of the principles of The Son-Rise Program are just as effective (in some cases, more so!) with these unique individuals. In this chapter, we'll talk about how to apply these principles to your "extra-sophisticated" child.

I strongly recommend scanning back through each chapter before reading each section below. For instance, it will be of great help to you to scan back through Chapter 2 before reading the joining section below. Then, the suggestions below will be easier to understand and apply.

JOINING

When it comes to kids and adults with Asperger's syndrome, there are variations both in what we consider to be an ism and in how we join.

People with Asperger's syndrome will usually not engage in a traditional ism, such as hand-flapping, spinning, tearing off tiny strips of paper, etc. More often, they will either talk profusely about a particular subject (or set of subjects), or they will engage in a hobby in a very focused and intense manner. These are the two main types of behaviors that you want to think of as isms. When your child does either of these two things, you want to join like there's no tomorrow.

At the same time, the way you join with these behaviors will look different than joining a behavior that is less complex. We spoke earlier about how someone unfamiliar with the concept of joining could mistake, for instance, joining in with hand-flapping for copying, mimicking, mirroring, etc. Joining with your child with Asperger's syndrome, though, could never be mistaken for mimicking. With more sophisticated isms, you join by becoming an active participant in your child's interest.

Let's say your child loves trains. She talks about trains, reads about trains, and can name every type of train built within the last hundred years. What most often happens is that, at some point, everyone makes it very clear that they've really had enough of the train conversation and they want to move on. Parents (or teachers) will tell their child, "This isn't the time to talk about that," "Sam doesn't want to hear about that right now," "We've already talked about trains enough today, sweetie," or "Why don't you tell us about what you did with your dad yesterday."

Trying to move our children off their topic of choice ends up being very counterproductive, often resulting in their becoming more rigid about their subject, not less.

On the other hand, when it comes to the train conversation— and other similarly sophisticated isms—you do *not* want to simply copy whatever your child does (repeating everything she says, doing whatever she does). Instead, you want to join by becoming a fascinated student of your child's favorite subjects.

If your child likes to talk about (and read about, build, etc.) trains, your job is to become a train *freak*! If she wants to show you a picture of a train, look at the picture with great enthusiasm. When she talks about trains, listen intently. If she asks you a question about trains, answer it.

Answer as best you can, based on your own knowledge. If

this is the twelfth time you've been asked the exact same question, great! That means you probably know the answer, so go ahead and answer, even if that means giving the same answer you gave the first eleven times.

Take some time on your own and read up on trains. When your child next brings up the subject, you can contribute your train knowledge (only if your child gives you space to do so).

I'm just using trains as a simple example. Many variations are possible based on what your child actually does. If your child likes to build model airplanes, then go ahead and participate in this with her. If she does not want you to mess with what she's doing, get your own model airplane set and work on it in the same room as your child.

There are all kinds of ways that this type of joining can play out. I worked with a boy who loved post offices. He would put together envelopes and packages and then would want me to stamp them. So I joined him in that way, him putting together a package and me weighing and stamping it.

The key here is to look for an ism (an intense and rigid interest in a subject of conversation or hobby) and then join by participating as best you can (even if that means just listening intently).

MOTIVATION

There really is very little you need to do differently when applying the motivation principle to children or adults with Asperger's syndrome. As with any other child on the spectrum, you will want to observe your child and note what his interests and motivations are. In many cases, this will be very clear because your child will be talking quite often about whatever interests him. For example:

- Airplanes

- Characters from his favorite film

- Buildings

- A particular country

- Illnesses that people die from

You will want to begin with a game or activity (or conversation) centered around one of these motivations, such as:

- Talking about airplanes, reading about airplanes, etc.

- Pretend you are characters from your child's favorite movie

- Build models of your city's tallest buildings

- Take a pretend trip to your child's favorite country

- List illnesses, talk about differences between them, etc.

Once the game, activity, or conversation is under way, you can introduce a challenge or educational goal. Naturally, the goals or challenges that you choose may be fairly sophisticated. For instance:

- Focus on having a social conversation about what you each like to do.

- Set a goal of fifteen minutes of total flexibility, where you are seeking to inspire your child to play a game or have a conversation completely on your terms for that time.

- Work on your child asking you questions as a way to practice being interested in another person.

- Ask your child to teach you something—encouraging him to make sure you understand.

- Trade topics, where you talk about something your child loves for ten minutes, then something you love.

- Talk with your child about a subject he likes—say, spaceships—and eventually connect that topic to a social topic—such as, if you met an alien on another planet, how would you introduce yourself, what would you ask, etc. You could even role play, where you are the alien, or you could write an info sheet together, explaining everything your child would want the alien to know about him and about Earth.

- If your child loves trains, you might talk about different types of trains. You could then morph this into a conversation about who you'd want to take on the train with you, where you'd want to go with them, etc. You could even create an in-depth activity where he calls or talks to each one of his friends ("friends" could be people who work with him), finds out where each person would like to go and why, and makes a list of who would go where on what train. Later, you might even take a field trip to a train museum with some of your child's friends, with the understanding that it is his job to explain the trains to his friends and answer any questions they might have.

Take a look at this next story to see just how powerful the motivation principle is when it comes to children and adults with Asperger's syndrome.

The Story of Sandra

Sandra was a fifteen-year-old girl with Asperger's syndrome. While her verbal and academic skills were equal to those of you or me, she still had great difficulty with the simplest of social interactions. Her parents attended the Start-Up program, and right away they explained that, despite their daughter's advanced skills in many areas, she seemed unable to engage in basic, everyday conversations.

One of the chief goals that Sandra's parents had for her was to be able to have a conversation about what she—and the person with whom she was talking—liked to do on weekends. To these parents, who had been struggling with this for quite some time, this goal seemed to be a million miles away.

During the Start-Up course, we have special sessions just for parents of children diagnosed with Asperger's syndrome or deemed "high functioning." It was during one of these sessions that Sandra's parents brought up the difficulties they were having with their goal for Sandra.

Naturally, we began to explain the motivation principle to them, and we asked them to identify one of Sandra's interests. They both immediately chimed in with an answer—the *same* answer. Sandra liked daytime talk shows. But not just any daytime talk show. Sandra absolutely loved *The Jerry Springer Show*. Sandra did not simply enjoy *watching* Jerry Springer. She liked to *be* Jerry Springer.

Sandra would walk down the streets of her neighborhood, brandishing a short stick or a spoon (which she would use as her "microphone") and approach random people in the street, asking them questions such as: "So, Bob, why did you sleep with your wife's sister?"

Sandra's very straitlaced parents were horrified! They felt that this behavior was inappropriate and deeply embarrassing. They embarked on a full-fledged crusade to eliminate it.

Not surprisingly, the more they endeavored to clamp down on

Jerry Springer, the more rigid and controlling Sandra became about Jerry Springer—and conversations in general. By the time Sandra's parents had arrived at the Autism Treatment Center of America for their Start-Up program, the situation had escalated to the point where Sandra would *only* have conversations according to her own prescribed steps and rules. Only she could ask questions; others could not (because, of course, Jerry *asked* the questions; he didn't *answer* them!). Furthermore, all conversations had to follow the format of *The Jerry Springer Show*, with others giving only particular types of answers and discussing only specific types of subjects.

We explained to Sandra's parents that Jerry Springer wasn't the problem, he was the solution. *No, no,* they insisted, *trust us—Jerry Springer really is the problem!* We totally understood why they might see it this way, but we further clarified that Jerry Springer did not have to be the obstacle in Sandra's way. Rather, he could be her doorway out! *After all,* we continued, *you've already told us that you don't feel that the current way of addressing this with Sandra is working.*

They nodded, intrigued.

We helped them come up with a simple activity that they could do with Sandra when they returned home from the Start-Up course. And, indeed, the day after returning home, they made it happen.

They went into Sandra's room and set it up with a real microphone in the center (which Sandra had never had before!). Then they set up four chairs against one of the walls—one chair each for Sandra's mom, dad, aunt, and a family friend. (This, of course, was the Jerry Springer panel.)

When Sandra entered, she was ecstatic. This girl, who rarely expressed emotion and often had a flat facial expression, looked openly excited! She eagerly grabbed the microphone and began firing Jerry-Springer-esque questions at them. This time, though, whenever anyone was asked a question, they enthusiastically answered—no matter how outrageous the question.

As the "show" continued, Sandra's parents began to notice a change in Sandra's demeanor. She seemed not only happier, but more relaxed, less intense, less controlling, and more flexible. Sandra's father decided that it was time to try an experiment. So he asked Sandra a question. (Remember, asking Sandra a question was previously not allowed and would not result in getting an answer.) To everyone's surprise, Sandra answered her dad's question without the slightest fuss or hesitation. Her parents glanced at one another, doing their best to conceal their shock. A few minutes later, Sandra's mother tried asking her a question. Sandra answered it. A breakthrough!

As they all progressed further into the activity, Sandra's mom and dad found that they could push the envelope of the conversation more and more. They were slowly able to alter the entire direction of the conversation. An hour and a half later, the five of them (the four adults and Sandra) were all sitting around having a conversation about what each of them liked to do on the weekend and why. This was the exact goal that Sandra's parents had asked about during their Start-Up course!

SOCIALIZATION

As we've discussed, The Son-Rise Program Developmental Model runs a full five stages—from severely autistic all the way to socially successful and neurotypical. So of course it includes children and adults with Asperger's syndrome. Someone with Asperger's syndrome, for instance, might be at stage 2 in Fundamental 1, eye contact and nonverbal communication; stage 5 in Fundamental 2, verbal communication; stage 4 in Fundamental 3, interactive attention span; and stage 3 in Fundamental 4, flexibility.

You want to build forward from wherever your child is now.

Prioritizing social goals (rather than academic ones) is *crucially* important here. Many people with Asperger's are rock stars when it comes to academic subjects—at least the ones they like. And I'm not suggesting that you take what they love away from them or stop them from engaging with these subjects. What I am suggesting is that when you are with your child, focus especially on the social areas. Remember: if your child or adult has Asperger's or is high-functioning, *the entirety of what is holding her back is social in nature.*

Of course, you will want your approach to match your child's sophistication and maturity level. For instance, for eye contact, you may say something like, "Hey, bud, could you look at me when you say that?" Then, if your child looks, you might simply say, "Thanks, man," or "Awesome. That really helps me get what you're saying" (unlike with a younger, less sophisticated child, where we might jump up and down, shouting "Whoo-hoo! You are such a great looker!").

Eye contact and nonverbal communication is often an area that people with Asperger's really struggle with, so it is important to remain cognizant of this area even though your child may be very sophisticated in other areas. Most communication happens nonverbally. This means that no matter how advanced her language is, your child will be missing most communication unless you work on this.

You may think that your child is at stage 5 in verbal communication because she has a large vocabulary and perfect sentence structure. But your child may have difficulty talking about social things—what others think, how he feels, how you feel, joking, etc. This is why you want to relentlessly pursue this area when conversing with him (in a fun way!). Utilizing the motivation principle, you might begin with a subject that your child loves, and, as she becomes more relaxed and engaged, you might bridge that subject with a more social subject, as we already discussed. Another simple verbal strategy is, rather than peppering your child with questions all the time, sometimes it can be helpful to simply make a statement and see if she responds, such as, "I had so much fun with Kelly today!" or "I love having my friends over to hang out!"

When it comes to interactive attention span, again, you are still going to encourage your child to keep sticking with interactive, interpersonal activities (not video games!) for longer and longer periods of time. The strategies discussed in Chapter 8 work with all developmental levels.

Flexibility can often be a major issue for people with Asperger's syndrome. When playing a game or having a conversation, here are some examples of what you might say:

- "Wow, you sure explained how you built that train really fast! I've never built a model train before. Can you explain it more slowly and clearly so that I can understand how to build one?"

- "Oh, I had so much fun playing that game your way! Now let's try playing again, but this time with *my* rules!"

- "I know you love taking Seventh Avenue to the park. Thank you for describing it to me. What's a different route we could take to get there?"

Again, using the flexibility strategies is helpful regardless of your child's verbal sophistication. The "be silly," "get it 'wrong,'" and "role play" strategies from Chapter 9 are particularly useful.

The Story of Deshawn

Deshawn's mother could not understand why her son would ask her the same question over and over, even though he knew the answer. In fact, he *wanted* to hear the same answer. For instance, Deshawn might ask, "What time is lunch?" His mom would answer, "Twelve thirty," thinking, *He already knows this—why is he asking?* Then, Deshawn would ask again. His mom would answer again. And he would ask again. And she would answer again. After enough iterations of this scenario, Deshawn's mother's frustration would reach the point where she would either yell at him—telling him to "Stop asking, already!"—or just ignore him.

When she came to the ATCA for her Start-Up course, Deshawn's mom brought this issue up during the special question-and-answer session for parents of Asperger's and high-functioning children. As she related her recurring scenario—and her reaction to it—many parents nodded in agreement and understanding.

We explained that, first, Deshawn (and the other children and adults who do this) was not trying to be difficult or to annoy his mom. However, what he was doing *did* provide a fantastic opportunity to work on his flexibility—in a way that would be helpful to him and fun for his mother.

We told her to bring in the "be silly" and "get it 'wrong'" strategies. (We, of course, explained that this would only be useful if she actually felt relaxed and silly, not if she was tense and annoyed. The other parents nodded again, this time with guilty smiles on their faces.) We detailed very specifically how to do this.

At the end of the week, Deshawn's mother returned home excited to use her new Son-Rise Program techniques. When her son asked her what time lunch was, she answered him happily. When he asked again, she got silly.

"Lunch is at twelve thirty-two and fourteen seconds," she said with a smile. Her son looked startled. He asked her again.

"Lunch is at three little piggies o'clock." She put her hand over her mouth as she said this, looking at her son slyly. Deshawn stared at her. He asked her again.

"Lunch is at four in the morning. Oh, no! We'll have to eat in our sleep!" She looked at her son, throwing her arms up in an exaggerated manner. Deshawn blinked. Then he smiled.

"We can't do that," he said.

Deshawn and his mom then had a conversation about whether people could eat in their sleep and why people had lunch during the day.

Deshawn never asked what time lunch was again.

GIVING CONTROL

Many people with Asperger's syndrome can seem very controlling. Often, because those with Asperger's can be so verbal and sophisticated, we assume that they should "get" that they can't always have things their way. But it's not a question of "getting" it. It's a question of how in control of their environment they feel.

I'm not suggesting that you make your sixteen-year-old with Asperger's syndrome the boss of the house (or school). But there are a whole host of areas where you could give more control than you do. And there are almost certainly unnecessary control battles that occur in your home.

So step back and take an honest look at your child's day-to-day existence. Where can more control be given? Does it matter whether he sleeps on the floor instead of the bed? If he wants to wear clothes that don't match? If he prefers to eat his soup with a teaspoon? If he wants to sit in the back seat of the car even when the front seat is available? If he enjoys doing his work standing up? (I recently had a consultation with a very sweet mom who asked for my help in getting her son—who wanted to study an area of biology in college that had "low job growth"—to change his major! It will not shock you to learn that I suggested that we focus on helping him with his difficulty making friends and relating to people first!)

Also, ask yourself this: how often do you get so preoccupied with the "goal" that you compromise the interpersonal connection and interaction? Since social interaction is sometimes the only area where people with Asperger's syndrome are behind, this makes it all the more vital to prioritize the human interaction over any goal or task. For these children and adults, nothing on earth is more important for their development.

This might be a useful time to bring up a separate but related subject. I have met adults with Asperger's syndrome who tell me that they desperately want to be able to communicate and relate more with others and to operate more adeptly in the neurotypical world.

However, I have also met people with Asperger's who explain that they like and value who and how they are, and they don't want to change—and they don't want others to try to change them, either. I would never advocate trying to change these adults against their will. Like all of us, they have the right to be who they want to be and the desire to be respected and loved for who they are. Different does not equal worse. In fact, it often means talents and perspectives that are missing from the neurotypical community.

What I really appreciate about The Son-Rise Program is that using the principles we've been discussing is win-win when it comes to people with Asperger's syndrome, regardless of which of the above camps they might place themselves in. For those who want help overcoming their challenges and connecting with others, using these principles and techniques can really help them. For those who say that they don't want to be any different than they are, using these principles is the best way I can think of to respect them and to create the closest, most meaningful relationship possible with them. (And for those with Asperger's who are somewhat skeptical of "neurotypicals," experiencing someone helping them without disapproval, without pushing, and without saying that there is something wrong with them will often provide the crucial turning point for them.)

HELPING YOUR CHILD TO BE A GOOD TRYER

Celebrate your child's achievements, celebrate her attempts, and use the three Es—energy, excitement, and enthusiasm—but adapt all of this to your child. We've worked with kids with Asperger's syndrome who really enjoy it when we are loud, bouncy, and high-energy.

We've worked with just as many who really don't want us to jump around cheering them on; it's not "cool." No problem. In these cases, we calibrate our reactions to what resonates for them. For instance, I might give a thumbs-up and say calmly, "Dude, you rock. That was awesome." I might whisper "Nice job" while keeping my face very expressive. I might even fall out of my chair—and then explain that what they just did was so awesome that I couldn't keep my balance.

You could try various responses out. You could even ask your child what she would prefer. There isn't one right way to do it; just make it maximally digestible to your child.

Most important, you want to cultivate a feeling inside yourself of excitement and gratitude with regards to your child.

THE SON-RISE PROGRAM ABCS

You will want to continue to follow the ABC model with your child, but the specific red light signals are a little bit different. (The green lights are the same.)

Here is a red light list for a child with Asperger's syndrome:

- My child's eye contact plummets.

- My child is doing something that looks neurotypical, but he is excluding me from participating.

- My child seems rigid and controlling around the activity he's doing, the subject he's talking about, the arrangement of the room he's in, or the schedule for the day (or morning, afternoon, evening, etc.).

- My child responds when I speak to him, but he does so in a rigid or repetitive way.

- My child is saying no a lot.

- My child is talking about one of his favorite subjects in a rigid or repetitive way and does not seem amenable to any alteration in the conversation.

As you can see, unlike less verbal children whose red lights may include obvious repetitive behaviors (bouncing a ball, repeating the same word, stacking blocks, lining up objects, flapping hands, etc.), people with Asperger's syndrome often have more subtle red lights. You want to keep your eye out most especially for rigidity.

OPTIMIZING YOUR
CHILD'S ENVIRONMENT

If your child is, say, a sixteen-year-old with Asperger's syndrome, you may want to modify the focus room environment. (I wouldn't call it a playroom. Just stick with "focus room.") You will, of course, want much more sophisticated items in the room. Locking the door may not work, unless you get your child's permission. (This is actually doable. We've done it.)

I would still keep the electronics out of the room, even if it is just for the times when you two are working together. Keeping the room distraction-free and control-battle-free remains very important. Keeping all toys on a shelf usually isn't as important. (That's okay because you aren't working on language in the same way, anyway.)

In short, use common sense, but endeavor to preserve as many aspects of the focus room as possible. You can even feel free to explain to your child exactly what you're doing (for example, "For the next couple of hours, while you and I hang out, I'm going to clear out some things so we can both concentrate and not be distracted. Wanna help?")

DEALING WITH TANTRUMS AND
OTHER CHALLENGING BEHAVIORS

Some people with Asperger's syndrome tantrum the old-fashioned way (as do most neurotypical kids), and others tantrum not by kicking and screaming but by looking really angry, cursing, clenching their fists, calling their parents names, saying "I hate you," or finding the one thing to say that will push their parents' flip-out button.

In either case, it is important to hold fast to the principles from the previous chapter. Relax. Stay comfortable. Don't make your child's behavior mean anything about you. Ask, "How can I help my child to communicate more effectively?"—not "How do I stop this behavior?"

No matter how sophisticated, your child is still just trying to communicate what she wants as best she can.

The *only* difference here is that you can be more sophisticated in how you word your responses—both to tantrums (i.e., "Swedish," according to our analogy) and to sweet, communicative behavior (i.e., "English").

For instance, in response to "I hate you!" you can say, "That's okay, I love you. But saying that doesn't help me understand you, and I don't respond to that. If you want to ask me nicely, though, I am ready to get you what you want!" Or, if you cannot give your child what she wants, offer an alternative: "We can't do that now, but maybe later. You know what, though? We can do this other thing instead if you ask me nicely!"

You can also give your child a coping mechanism—a way to feel comfortable in the face of challenge. The best way to do this is to suggest a perspective; for example, if she says, "I'm very angry!" you can say, "It's okay to be angry, but you can also feel okay when you don't get what you want and find something else to be excited about," or "When I don't get what I want, I tell myself that it's okay, and I find something else fun to do."

If you feel that your child is experiencing sensory overload, you can say something such as, "If you're feeling a little overloaded, you don't have to get angry or push. You can just say, 'I'm overloaded' and leave the room," or "If you're feeling funny, try pushing your hands together as hard as you can for ten seconds. Let's try it!" (Then, you can do it together.)

When your child *does* communicate nicely, it is absolutely imperative that you thank her, cheer (in a way that she thinks is "cool"), and *immediately* do whatever you can to help her get what she wants. (Again, if it's not possible for that to happen, offer an alternative, and make it very clear that you are willing to move heaven and earth to help her.)

Remember: it is okay for your child to raise her voice, seem agitated, act out, etc. She is going to be okay. *Your* job is to help her so that she can find a way to cope and communicate differently.

Charlotte's son, James, doesn't have Asperger's syndrome, but one thing that Charlotte taught him, which is both very useful to him and very cute, is to say soothing things to himself. So, now, when James gets agitated, he says things like, "It's okay," and "No big deal." Saying these phrases out loud helps him to relax and self-regulate.

ONLINE RESOURCES

For more in-depth help with the principles and techniques of this chapter, please go to www.autismbreakthrough.com/chapter15. Have fun!

STARTING POINT

Become a student of one aspect of your child's world, and join him in it. If your child loves old-fashioned cars, read a book about old-fashioned cars, and talk about it with him. If your child likes telling people about space travel, enthusiastically listen when he's telling you about this subject. If your child loves sea creatures, get posters of sea animals, hang them up, and ask your child which ones are his favorites. Not only will your understanding of your child's world increase, but he will find it easier to connect with you—and to be more flexible!

SIXTEEN

The Recovery Mode: Addressing the Biology of Autism—Especially Diet

DISCLAIMER

I want to make sure that I am totally clear: nothing in this chapter should be construed as any kind of medical advice. This chapter is not intended to prevent, diagnose, treat, or cure any illness. I am not a medical doctor, nor do I play one on TV.

I have spoken at many autism conferences, listened to and conversed with many autism doctors, and seen many children respond to various biologically oriented interventions. In fact, quite a number of our families implement The Son-Rise Program alongside and in conjunction with biomedical and biological interventions.

AUTISM: THE BIOMEDICAL CONNECTION

We all know that autism is a neurological condition. But it is not *only* a neurological condition.

Many of our children face immunological and digestive challenges that are intimately connected with their social, relational, sensory, behavioral, and learning difficulties. At autism conferences nationwide, I've heard doctor after doctor discuss the biology of autism, particularly how many children on the spectrum have difficulty with digestion, with elimination, with fighting off pathogens, and with a host of other biological processes.

Some of you are already aware of this, and many more of you

may be reading this information for the first time. If this is the first (or second) time you are hearing this, you may be thinking that your child doesn't have these other challenges. You might be thinking that your child doesn't have food allergies, doesn't get sick often, and doesn't seem to have any physiological problems. And this may, indeed, be the case.

At the same time, with autism spectrum disorders, our kids' behaviors and overt difficulties can take up so much of our attention that many less obvious challenges can be hard to see. This is especially true if you've already been told by your doctor or others to focus exclusively on your child's behaviors (that is, your child's *symptoms*).

It is essential to understand, though, that your child's internal biological issues may be affecting her behaviors—possibly a great deal. The interaction between your child's physiology and her autism can be direct or indirect.

A direct interaction is when chemical reactions throughout your child's body are impairing or interfering with your child's developing brain. (I'll give you an example of how proteins in wheat and dairy can cause this in some children later in this chapter.)

An indirect interaction is when a physiological problem is giving your child a stomach ache, a headache, lethargy, etc. Think about how a severe headache affects your ability to work, converse, and interact. Imagine how an intense stomach ache, for instance, might impact your child as she is being asked to listen, look, interact, and learn new things.

So you can see why it might be important to look into your child's biology, if you haven't already done so.

One phenomenon that will become clear by the end of this chapter is that the principles of The Son-Rise Program and biological interventions (often called biomedical interventions or treatments in the autism community) affect one another. A child in The Son-Rise Program will often progress faster if she is responding well to biomedical treatments. Removing or lessening a child's physiological challenges can accelerate her Son-Rise Program.

It is equally true that, by shifting children from fight-or-flight survival mode to recovery mode, the principles of The Son-Rise Program can actually improve and enhance their bodies' capacity to respond favorably to biomedical interventions. More on this later.

CHOOSING THE RIGHT DOCTOR

I would strongly encourage you to see a doctor who specializes in autism, if you are not already doing so. Such a doctor can administer blood, urine, and other tests to get a better picture of your child's biological situation. He or she can then address problems with your child's digestive or immune system. These issues can be multifaceted, but they can also be as simple as a mineral deficiency.

Note: I have also worked with parents who have seen improvements in their children from seeing naturopaths, homeopaths, and other nonallopathic practitioners. Your child's situation may be quite complex, so it will always help to keep an open mind.

If you are going to take your child to an autism doctor, it is incredibly important to choose one who has vast experience with autism and knows what he or she is talking about. To my astonishment, I still hear from many parents who report that their GP makes statements such as, "Changing your child's diet is not going to have any effect whatsoever on his autism." (Other ill-informed statements of this nature include, "That rash covering your child's body is not related to your child's autism," and "Your child's constant diarrhea and constipation is just a phase. Nothing to do with your child's autism.")

Consider this: what we eat and drink affects our energy levels, our susceptibility to infections, our propensity for certain kinds of cancers, the onset of type 2 diabetes, the symptoms of Crohn's and celiac diseases, and the condition of our arteries and thus the likelihood that we will have a heart attack or stroke. Eating foods to which our body overreacts (if we have an allergy to peanuts, for example) can cause an immediate, and sometimes deadly, physiological response. Drinking a relatively small amount of alcohol impacts our brain function in short order. None of these facts are controversial. We know that what we consume affects us physiologically. So why is the fact that diet can affect the extrasensitive brains and bodies of children on the autism spectrum still in dispute?

I don't know a polite way to say this, so I'll just say it: any doctor who tells you that there is no way that what your child eats can have any impact on his autism does not really know or understand autism. In such cases, they are dispensing advice without knowledge, which is both unhelpful and potentially dangerous.

If your child has chicken pox, and you ask me for advice, I'm not going to give you any. You know why? Because I know nothing about chicken pox. Your GP may know a lot about fevers, strep throat, whooping cough, and hundreds of other conditions, but if he or she makes this kind of comment to you about dietary intervention, go elsewhere for your autism help. There are plenty of doctors out there who *do* know a lot about autism. I meet them all the time at conferences—and in the Start-Up course.

Charlotte's son, James, has many physiological challenges that directly affect his autism. One of his big issues is his inability to properly digest a vast array of foods. When James was much younger, Charlotte and her ex-husband went to a doctor because James had not had a poo in two weeks. He frequently held his stomach and screamed. The doctor said, "He's holding it in on purpose."

These types of statements represent such a profound lack of understanding of the biology of autism, it can seem a bit breathtaking. (In fact, once Charlotte—drastically—changed James's diet, he began pooing regularly and stopped holding his stomach and screaming. He also improved in a myriad of other ways.) My heart goes out to those of you who are still running into doctors who flatly deny the existence of occurrences that you can see with your own eyes. Trust me when I tell you, if you have a truly informed autism doctor, you won't have these types of experiences.

Another big factor to keep in mind when selecting an autism doctor is how long the doctor has been helping children with autism. You don't want your child being a guinea pig, even if the doctor has the very best of intentions. I recommend a minimum of five years' direct experience with autism. (Keep in mind that a doctor can take a three-day seminar and claim that he or she has been "trained" in autism treatment.)

Also, ask the doctor why he or she got into autism treatment. This question can often give you great insight into where the doctor is coming from. Because autism rates have been increasing so rapidly in recent years, some doctors have jumped on the band-wagon. On the other hand, there are an increasing number of wonderful doctors who are parents of children on the spectrum. They began focusing their medical expertise on autism to help their own children. I tend to trust these people the most, and I often find that, as autism parents themselves, they treat other parents with more respect.

THE DOCTOR CHECKLIST

When selecting an autism doctor, it is crucial to choose one who will support, not undermine, what you are doing to implement the principles of The Son-Rise Program. In this regard, here are ten questions I always recommend asking when choosing autism doctors.

1. Do they deeply and sincerely respect your role and your knowledge as the parent?

2. Do they see the value in building a bonded relationship with your child and in helping your child to connect with others? (It's okay if this isn't *your doctor's* focus, but they have to get why it's important.)

3. Do they seem interested in *your* emotional state?

4. Do they see your questions as inquiries and not challenges?

5. Are they gentle and relaxed with your child?

6. Do they value your child's emotional state—rather than seeing her as merely an immune system and digestive system to be fixed?

7. Do they value aspects of your child other than the areas they are treating directly?

8. Do they value other treatments (including interventions such as The Son-Rise Program) besides the ones they are providing?

9. Do they recognize that *how* an intervention is administered to your child can be as important as *what* intervention is administered?

10. Since any intervention only works if it can be administered, do they check in with you to find out how you are doing with delivering their treatment protocol?

THE IMPORTANCE OF YOUR CHILD'S DIET

What your child is eating might be having a huge effect on him. A child's behavior, level of interaction, frequency of isming, and his autism in general, can be greatly impacted one way or the other by diet. This is to say nothing about food's impact on his pooing, cravings, rashes, sleep, skin tone, autoimmunity, and sensory processing.

We will spend the bulk of this chapter discussing dietary intervention for two reasons. First, biologically speaking, it has the best chance to have the most immediate effect on your child's development. Second, dietary intervention is something that, like the rest of The Son-Rise Program, you can implement at home.

A great many children on the autism spectrum have food sensitivities. (I say "sensitivities" and not "allergies" because, often, these problems will not show up on a traditional allergy test, for reasons we will discuss in a moment.)

It will greatly help your child if you think about what he ingests in the following way: *to your child, food is either medicine or poison.*

Way back in 1974, long before our current understanding of the connection between autism and diet, my parents implemented dietary interventions with me. This was yet another arena in which my parents proved to be decades ahead of their time—so much so that even now I have trouble getting my head around just how far ahead of their time they really were.

They felt that I was being affected by what I ate, and they sought to remove any foods they could think of that might be hindering me. (In fact, as a way to make things simpler, improve everyone's health, and prevent accidental contaminations, they removed the offending foods from the diet of the whole family.)

First, they removed dairy. Interestingly, I was prone to chronic, sometimes life-threatening ear infections as a child. When my parents removed all dairy, my ear infections ceased.

Then, they went about removing sugar, artificial colors and flavors, red meat, and processed foods from my diet. They fed me only organic foods. (Remember that this was decades before every supermarket had an organic foods section.)

This dietary intervention was an important component of

what my parents did to help me. It accelerated the pace of my Son-Rise Program by removing biological obstacles so that the program could do its work. Fortunately or unfortunately, depending on how you look at it, I am now able to eat a completely regular diet—that is, the standard diabetes-, stroke-, cancer-, and heart attack-inducing American diet—without any deleterious effects. Ain't life grand?

At the Autism Treatment Center of America, these are the very first food items that we tell parents to begin looking at.

- Casein (a complex protein found in milk and milk products)

- Gluten (a complex protein found in wheat and many other grains—and also often added to non-glutinous foods such as crisps because it prevents them from sticking together)

- Caffeine

- Sugar

Let's look at these four items more closely.

GLUTEN AND CASEIN

The biological process I am about to describe has been outlined by many physicians in the autism field and explains why something as simple as eating wheat or dairy can affect brain function and brain development. (For the sake of brevity, I will not go into the biological processes behind why these foods can also cause diarrhea, constipation, and other nonbrain side effects.)

Some children on the spectrum are missing enzymes that break down the complex proteins gluten and casein. On top of that, these children have something that many doctors call leaky gut syndrome, which is when the walls of the small intestine (where most digestion takes place) are too permeable.

A simple way to think about what this means is to imagine that, for some children, the walls of the small intestine have little Swiss cheese–like holes. (The walls of the intestine are extremely important in keeping undigested or partially digested food from getting into the rest of the body.) Undigested or partially digested gluten and casein particles then enter the bloodstream through these "holes" in the small intestine.

These gluten and casein peptides circulate around the body and cross the blood-brain barrier. Once in the brain, they act as opiates, binding to the same receptors as morphine and heroin.

So, essentially, for many of our children, ingesting gluten or casein is like getting high on drugs. Moreover, when these foods are initially removed from a child with this issue, it is like suddenly removing drugs from a drug addict. At first, she ain't gonna thank you. She is powerfully addicted to these substances. Not only will a child going through the withdrawal process most likely have a very strong craving for gluten and casein; her body will go through all sorts of intense reactions—sometimes for as long as two weeks—from diarrhea and vomiting to tantrums and sleepless nights.

However, when it's over, what a beautiful day! We get reports of children making vastly more eye contact, sleeping regular hours, using more language, isming less, and overall, responding even more quickly to the principles of The Son-Rise Program.

It is absolutely critical, if you are going to remove gluten and casein from your child's diet, that you do it 100 percent; 99 percent is almost like not doing the diet at all.

You might be reading this and thinking, *There is no way I can do this because all my child eats is toasted cheese sandwiches and milk* (or some other wheat and dairy combination)! If so, I am extremely happy for you and your child! This is one of the surest signs that gluten and casein are a big problem for your child. Voluntarily eating a narrow list of foods like this is the behavior of an addict.

Why would I be happy about that? Because we tend to see that the kids who have this severe an addiction—this big an issue with gluten and casein—are the ones who respond most dramatically to the removal of those foods.

If you are feeling freaked out and intimidated by this revelation, hang on! I will shortly get to how to change your child's diet using the principles of The Son-Rise Program, and it doesn't have to be hard or scary.

CAFFEINE

Of course, we know that coffee has caffeine. (Decaf does, too. It just has less.) Caffeine is also found in colas and a host of other fizzy dinks. (There are a thousand things wrong with fizzy drinks from an autism point of view. Caffeine is but one.)

Remember, too, that caffeine is also present in chocolate. This is a big way that it enters the diets of our children. As I said earlier, I am a chocolate freak. So I deeply, passionately understand the desire for it.

The problem is: caffeine is a nerve stimulant. We don't want to be giving our children nerve stimulants. 'Nuff said.

SUGAR

Sugar is a tough one because it is added to almost everything. I'll tell you right now, you won't be able to remove all sugar from your child's diet. Luckily, this is okay, for two reasons. First, we need some sugar in our diets (though, ideally, it would be the naturally occurring type that is present in, say, an apple).

Second, the biological mechanism that makes sugar a problem for many of our children is totally different from the one that makes gluten and casein problematic. This means that, although you would need to reduce gluten and casein down to zero for that diet to have its intended effect, this is not the case for sugar. With sugar, the goal is just to get intake as low as possible.

The way that many autism doctors describe it, there are two biological issues happening with some children that make sugar a problem. The first is that some children on the spectrum secrete too much insulin in response to relatively small amounts of sugar. This causes blood sugar levels to crash, making them sluggish and irritable—and causing more sugar cravings. Then the child eats more sugar, blood sugar spikes, and, again, too much insulin is secreted, resulting in another crash and more cravings. We end up with a constant seesawing of blood sugar levels, which plays havoc with a sensitive child's brain and body.

According to the autism docs, the second, and most pernicious, biological challenge around sugar is that many children on the autism spectrum have candida yeast overgrowth. What this means is that, in some cases, children will have a higher than normal amount of yeast—a fungus—growing in their intestines. This can exacerbate the leaky gut problem outlined earlier and cause "brain fog"—which, for a child with autism, can be especially consequential.

And what does candida yeast live on? You guessed it: sugar!

In fact, there is some evidence to suggest that a big part of the powerful sugar cravings that some of our children experience is actually coming from the yeast itself. *The yeast* is craving the sugar, and as it begins to die off from lack of sugar, it gives the body an increased craving.

There are some autism doctors who prescribe antifungal medications for candida yeast overgrowth, but the first order of business is to simply reduce sugar intake, which, according to the professionals, reduces candida yeast levels.

If a child has high candida yeast levels, and sugar intake drops suddenly, this can cause what some call a "die-off." This term is used to describe the dying off of a lot of the candida yeast at once. When this fungus dies en masse, it is believed that the dying and breaking open of these organisms releases toxins into the body. This is used to explain why, at first, when some of these children have their sugar intake reduced, they can have symptoms such as nausea, vomiting, headaches, and low-grade fever for a few days.

I can tell you, from personal experience, that this phenomenon still appears to happen to me. I can eat whatever I want and be fine, but when I drastically cut down my sugar intake (as I do every time I want to drop a few pounds), I have two days of nausea, headaches, low-grade fever, swollen glands, and mild diarrhea. (I am fully aware that this may be more information than you wanted to know about me!) It is truly a delightful experience. However, afterward, my sugar cravings go way down, and so does any bloating I had. (Note: persistant bloating is another symptom of candida yeast overgrowth often cited by the professionals.)

DIETS TO LOOK INTO

There are a host of autism-friendly diets out there—and more and more foods available at the supermarket that are autism-safe. There are also a plethora of terrific books detailing these diets, so I won't seek to do that in a comprehensive way here. What I *will* do is give you three places to start.

The three diets below are my personal favorites. They are listed in order from least to most restrictive, and they build on one another. (This means that the second diet listed, for example, excludes the foods I mention *in addition to* gluten or casein.) If you decide to implement the gluten- and casein-free diet, and

it doesn't "work"—you don't see any difference in your child—
that does not necessarily mean that diet is not an issue for your
child. It might mean that *you haven't removed enough foods and
found the culprits yet.* This is the reason why many parents then
escalate to the next diet on the list.

I am not telling you to do these diets. Rather, I am advocating that you do some research and look into them.

1. The Gluten- and Casein-Free Diet (GFCF)

As we've already discussed, the gluten- and casein-free diet
involves the total removal of all foods containing gluten and
casein—milk products, wheat, and a myriad of other products with gluten in them. For most parents, this is the place
to begin. This diet is *much* easier now than it was years ago
because there are tons and tons of GFCF foods out there. Almost anything (milk, yogurt, bread, pasta, cookies, etc.) is
available in a GFCF version. Note: it is not recommended
that you simply replace milk products with loads of soy
products. Soy is highly allergenic and difficult to digest, and
some doctors and dieticians believe that it can mimic the
female hormone estrogen in the body.

2. The Specific Carbohydrate Diet (SCD)

Invented by Dr. Sidney V. Haas and popularized by Elaine
Gottschall, the specific carbohydrate diet is predicated on
the idea that, in some people, incomplete digestion of certain
complex carbohydrates and sugars results in the growth of
harmful bacteria in the gut—which then causes inflammation and autoimmune responses (where the immune system
attacks parts of the body). Many parents who found that their
kids did not respond strongly to the GFCF diet have reported
that their children have changed greatly with this diet. It has
many more guidelines than I can go into here, but a cornerstone of the diet involves removing potatoes, corn, and rice
(in addition to gluten and casein). If you are wondering what

there is left to eat, look up this diet. You'll be surprised! (Also, bear in mind that many cultures have existed over millennia without those three foods.) There is a diet similar to the specific carbohydrate diet called the gut and psychology syndrome (GAPS) diet, created by Dr Natasha Campbell-McBride.

3. The Body Ecology Diet (BED)

Invented by nutritionist Donna Gates, the body ecology diet has many similarities to the SCD, but it focuses more on achieving and maintaining a balance of gut flora (intestinal bacteria). There is a strong focus on reducing candida yeast overgrowth. Rather than focusing only on eliminating certain foods (sugar, grains, etc.), this diet puts a healthy emphasis on replenishing missing gut flora that are crucial to digestion by adding "cultured" foods such as fermented vegetables and young coconut kefir, a fermented drink. This diet could be considered the highest rung on the ladder in terms of strictness and comprehensiveness. A much smaller number of parents have their kids on this diet (which takes a lot of work), but many report significant improvement in their children after they've tried other diets.

Although it may seem that much of our dietary focus thus far has been aimed at removing substances, *adding* items can also make a difference. Sit down at any autism conference, and you will likely hear doctors discussing a variety of significant deficiencies that they see in children on the autism spectrum. Although all children are different, here are some items that are well worth exploring:

DIGESTIVE ENZYMES

In order to digest food, our bodies secrete a plethora of digestive enzymes. Without these enzymes, we could not digest anything. Since we require enzymes to extract nutrients from our food, food without enzymes is not food. For instance, the reason that wood is not food for us is because we lack their enzymes to break it down. If we were like termites and we had their enzymes to break down wood, it would be food to us. We might start the day with a sawdust sandwich! (Incidentally, we require (nondigestive) enzymes for almost every bodily function, such as fighting infections, temperature regulation, and even thinking.)

Some autism doctors feel that there is a great deal of evidence that many of our children lack the normal quantity and quality of digestive enzymes, resulting in compromised digestion. These doctors talk about the benefits of supplementation with enzymes to help these children digest and extract nutrients from their food, to ease bloating, constipation, diarrhea, and other digestive issues, and to aid the body in other areas such as immune system function. Enzymes are not drugs—or even vitamins; they are considered food products and are sold in health food shops.

A number of Son-Rise Program parents utilize enzymes and feel that they work synergistically with their program. Enzymedica, a company that focuses on making highly potent and very "clean" (i.e., without fillers) enzymes, feels so strongly about this synergy that, since 2009, it has paid for scores of parents to attend the Start-Up course at the Autism Treatment Center of America. Enzymedica helped to found the Autism Hope Alliance (AHA), a nonprofit organization that has also funded many parents' Start-Up course tuition.

As I mentioned earlier, James has a host of physiological challenges, from toxic levels of heavy metals to substantial digestive difficulties. He takes digestive enzymes and has been on all three of the above diets. He also gets mineral, essential fatty acid, and probiotic supplementation. (We'll discuss probiotics shortly.)

For James, enzymes have made a huge difference. He went from being a child with a constantly bloated stomach and dark circles underneath his eyes, who would often scream as he pressed on his stomach and oscillate between extreme constipation and diarrhea, to a kid with no bloating, no pain, no dark circles, and regular poos. As well, this regimen accelerated what was happening in his Son-Rise Program, with language improvements coming faster and big leaps in his interactive attention span.

PROBIOTICS

The term "probiotics" is the catch-all name for the beneficial microorganisms that we require for gut health. Like enzymes, these are also considered food products and are sold in health food shops and some pharmacies. If you've ever seen those yogurt commercials on TV advertising the benefits of their product for digestive health, that's because most yogurts contain probiotics. However, for our kids, yogurt is problematic because it is dairy (or soy). Also, a good probiotic capsule or powder that you would buy in a health food store contains far more probiotics than a serving of yogurt.

Again, I'm not telling you to go out tomorrow, buy a bottle of probiotics, and start feeding it to your child. What I recommend is to look into probiotics—and to ask your autism doctor about them.

VITAMINS AND MINERALS

I would certainly not recommend specific vitamins or minerals for your child, but I would strongly advocate that you have your child tested for large deficiencies. Many autism doctors talk about children they've treated with B12, magnesium and/or zinc deficiencies, for example. (As an interesting side note, a deficiency in zinc can make some vegetables taste bad and increase the desire for sugary foods.)

ESSENTIAL FATTY ACIDS

You may be familiar with all the recent research (outside autism circles) about omega-3 fats and essential fatty acids. It is increasingly understood that the right essential fatty acids provide us with all sorts of health benefits—for the heart, arteries, mood, digestive system, and brain.

Essential fatty acids are often recommended by autism doctors because, among other things, they are used to build and maintain the protective coating around brain and nerve cells. This coating is much like the rubber that coats electrical wires. Some doctors maintain that this can be highly beneficial to some children on the autism spectrum.

Essential fatty acids are sold in health food shops in liquid and capsule form. For now, just look into this. If you do decide to give them to your child, make absolutely sure that you conduct some research into specific products ahead of time. Simply feeding your child large amounts of fish oils, for example, can mean flooding his body with mercury and other toxins if you aren't careful.

USING THE SON-RISE PROGRAM TO CHANGE YOUR CHILD'S DIET

Even if you already knew everything I just explained about dietary intervention, this next section is going to change your life. Really! I find that even people who are very knowledgeable about autism and diet do not necessarily feel knowledgeable and confident about *how* to get their child to stop eating detrimental foods and start eating healthy ones.

So let us talk about the five Son-Rise Program feeding principles.

THE FIVE SON-RISE PROGRAM FEEDING PRINCIPLES

Control

Control is a core autism issue—and yet it is highly overlooked as related to feeding. Our children tend to be very controlling (for good reason, as we discussed in previous chapters). Remember, we want to always endeavor to see everything from our children's point of view. This absolutely includes food and feeding.

Ironically, many parents and caregivers get very controlling around feeding. We decide when our children will eat, what they will eat, how long they will eat for, and even *how* they will eat (at the table, with a fork, etc.).

If we want to change *what* our children eat, we have to give them control in every other area of eating. We need to take all of the pressure off. No more pushing our kids to eat. No more pressing our kids to eat at the table. Even, temporarily, no "lunchtime" versus "dinnertime." Offer the food at various times, and let them eat any time they want. Let them eat with any utensil that they want. Let them eat any place they want.

When you offer food, offer it in a gentle, relaxed, noncoercive, noncontrolling way. Present the food at a distance (rather than right in their face), and let your child come to *you* for it. As soon as your child even looks at the food, you might be tempted to thrust the food at her. It's easy to forget that when we grab a fork and jab it at a child's mouth, it can be startling to that child.

Take a buffet mentality with your child: "Grab anything you want."

Have plates of food around and accessible throughout the day. Touch the food. Fly toy airplanes around it. If your child doesn't want to actually eat it at this point, stay nonpushy about that, too. Also, do your best to avoid feeding your child when she is isming or giving you a strong red light.

Some children will only eat one item per plate; they'll eat peas and chicken, but not on the same plate. Allow this. Start to become aware of the temperature and consistency your child likes. Then adjust her meals accordingly. For now, cater the food to the way your child likes to eat it. (Remember, this does not mean that she gets to eat cookies and ice cream and cake. You're still choosing *what* is on offer for her to eat.)

Giving your child this kind of control over her food removes a big obstacle to her eating what you want her to eat. If your child does not feel that she has control, she will feel a strong desire to go against whatever dietary changes you are implementing.

Giving your child control in this area will also allow her to come to the food of her own volition, which is crucial for sustaining any restrictive diet.

Creativity

Actively seek new ways to present food in a fun way. Present food in a variety of ways. You can have toy cars carrying the food. You can be a witch presenting her magic brew. You can have the food take on personalities. Be a robot who needs the food as fuel, and invite your child to fuel up, too. Put a carrot in your mouth, and wiggle like a worm—and encourage your child to do the same. "Hide" the food, and then focus on finding and eating it.

When Charlotte was first endeavoring to get a reluctant James to eat broccoli, she dressed up as a giant stalk of broccoli and stomped into his playroom singing a broccoli song. He eventually got involved. They would sing the broccoli song and even talk to the real broccoli that Charlotte brought in with her. They did this for quite a while before the subject of actually *eating* the broccoli even came up. Now James eats broccoli regularly—and likes it. (He also happily eats carrots, spinach, kale, and every other healthy food.)

The first time I ever heard James say, "I want my algae," I almost fell out of my chair. Algae is exactly what it sounds like: the green stuff that grows on the bottom of lakes. James's algae is a cultivated version made into a green drink that James imbibes each day. If you ever tasted this drink, you would understand my awe that James would actually ask for it. It is truly a testament to Charlotte's effective use of all five of these feeding principles.

Relationship-building

This principle may appear unrelated to feeding, but it is essential. All of the joining, all of the celebrating, and all of the giving control really pays off here. If you have been building rapport with your child in these ways, he will trust you.

This trust will be the keystone to having food breakthroughs with your child. When your child trusts you, you have much more leeway to present and provide new foods to him. He will be open to what you have to offer.

Attitude

The attitude that you have around food and feeding is an absolutely vital component of any change in your child's diet. Parents, especially, tend to be tense about feeding their children on the spectrum, particularly if they have a child who is a picky eater. This brings a stress and agitation to feeding that will turn your child off at precisely the moment when you want her to be open.

When you are feeding your child, you are asking her to take

something outside herself into her body. That's a big request. It is so very important to have a calm, relaxed, and even excited attitude when dealing with anything food-related.

Really cultivate this attitude around your child's eating. Model eating foods with the three Es. You want your child's experience around food to be like slipping into a warm bath—relaxing, easy, comfortable, and deeply enjoyable. That's how you will get your child to want to jump into it.

Persistence

Okay. So, at the end of the day, changing your child's diet is all about who will persist longer. I know that you may feel that you've really tried to get your child to eat X or Y. But how many times did you try?

Successfully shifting what your child willingly eats is all about persevering. Staying the course. Refusing to get discouraged—even after many attempts. It will take a bit of time to train your child's palate to enjoy healthy foods. You are the key to your child having that time.

REMOVING PROBLEMATIC AND UNHEALTHY FOODS

Persistence applies to both sides of the food equation—to introducing new food *and* to removing unhealthy foods.

While introducing new foods can seem challenging because, ultimately, it is your child who will decide whether to eat them, removing foods should theoretically be far easier. Unless your child spends his days in environments where you are not present and have no say about the food given to him, you can remove any foods you like from the house and simply not provide them. In theory, your child does not get a choice.

From an emotional standpoint, however, removing foods is an entirely different matter. At the Autism Treatment Center of America, we see that removing foods can feel like Armageddon to many parents. There is often a huge amount of fear and anxiety around this issue, and I can understand why. A child who is not eating—while, at the same time, clamoring for food that we are not providing—touches on some very core parental beliefs and emotions. We see nourishment as one of our most basic jobs as parents. Feeding is often an expression of our love.

The first thing to understand is that, in our thirty years of experience, we have never seen a child starve himself to death when his diet was changed. We've certainly seen children go one day, two days, sometimes even three, but eventually these kids get hungry. As we've discussed, persistence is key.

I will say this: the kids who hold out the longest tend to be those determined souls who see cracks in their parents' armor. They see parents who look and feel guilty, who look and feel anxious, who have buckled many times in the past, who beg them to eat, who yell at them to eat, etc. In short, they believe—correctly, in most cases—that their parents are having such a hard time that they will cave after just a bit more waiting.

Children can usually outwait their parents. When Bryn is teaching parents in the Start-Up program, she astutely quotes the thought process of our kids this way: "I can *not* eat longer than you can *watch* me not eat." This factor alone elucidates why our attitude is so very important in this situation. If you believe that you are doing something mean or terrible to your child by removing harmful foods from his diet, then removing these foods will be very, very hard. You will feel guilty, anxious, and scared.

If, on the other hand, you believe that you are doing something very loving and very helpful to your child (which you are), then this process will feel very doable. You will feel comfortable, relaxed, and very clear about staying the course. Equally important, your child will then see that you are clear, comfortable, and free from any wavering, and, in most cases, will come around sooner. This is why, in the Start-Up course, we spend a great deal of time on your attitudes and emotions, not just on techniques.

I know that you may be thinking, "But my child *likes* those unhealthy foods." So, it's time to remind you of Bryn's quote: "Heroin addicts really like heroin. That doesn't mean it's good for them." (By the way, she speaks from personal experience. She and William put their daughter, Jade, on a special diet and stuck to it throughout her program.)

Your child may want "just a little piece of one cookie." If your child wanted to not wear a seatbelt "for just a little bit of the ride," or your child wanted to play with a sharp knife "for just a few minutes," or your child want to drink "just a bit" of liquid drain cleaner, I'm sure you wouldn't oblige. These are nonnegotiable issues.

You want to put your child's diet in the nonnegotiable category. This is your child's health and safety we're talking about. Make it nonnegotiable.

One final point—remember how, in Chapter 3, we talked about the problems with relying on rewards as the main driver of your child's behavior? I used an analogy about how many of us, when we were little, were trained to slog through the "gross" healthy food in order to get the "yummy" unhealthy dessert. In this case, there is no analogy; this *is* the actual situation.

Again, our beliefs about food are central. We think about and then present the least healthy foods as rewards—as "the good stuff." I've heard many, many parents make statements like, "Well, I don't want to deprive my child forever. When can my child get off this diet?" The beliefs hidden in these words will cripple your ability to help your child eat healthily. Why is not feeding your child foods that will harm him "depriving" him?

And the question of "when can my child get off this diet?" is worth examining closely. We are basically asking, "When is the soonest possible date when I can resume feeding my child poison—foods which will give my child heart disease, stroke, diabetes, premature aging, and cancer?" Why are we in such a rush to get these poisons back into our children's bodies?

FIGHT-OR-FLIGHT SURVIVAL MODE

Let's come full circle and return to the key component of your child's autism that I mentioned at the beginning of this chapter. There is a preponderance of evidence showing that the vast majority of children with autism are living in a near-perpetual fight-or-flight state. I first learned about this in detail from a discussion I had many years ago with Dr Scott Faber, who, at the time, was the Director of Developmental-Behavioral Pediatrics at Mercy Hospital in Pittsburgh (he is now with the Hospital at the Children's Institute), but it has since become a common understanding among many autism doctors. Why is this important?

When your body is in fight-or-flight, you are basically in immediate survival mode. These are some key biological processes of this state.

- Adrenaline (epinephrine) courses through your veins

- Your heart rate increases

- Blood vessels constrict (to prevent excessive bleeding)

- Blood flows away from your vital organs and into your arms and legs (to ready you for running or fighting)

- Lymphocytes from your immune system race toward your skin (in readiness for you being cut or bitten)

Also, of particular relevance to your child:

- Major, more vital areas of your immune system shut down—while other areas become hyperactive

- Your digestive system shuts down

- Physiological repair gets put on hold

- The brain gears up for quick, immediate, reflexive decision-making—rather than tasks such as learning and social interaction

- And, importantly, cortisol and corticotropin-releasing hormone levels skyrocket. Cortisol is the major long-acting stress hormone in your body. It is secreted by your adrenal glands. Corticotropin-releasing hormone (CRH) is a stress hormone released in the brain—but now found in other areas of the body in children with autism.

Now, let's take a look at what this means. The process outlined above is perfectly natural. It is a system that served our distant ancestors well. When a saber-toothed tiger is chasing you, the only thing that matters is getting away in one piece. In a few minutes, this kind of situation is over. You have either escaped or you were eaten. (What a happy thought!)

However, we are not designed to stew in this state indefinitely. Fight-or-flight survival mode works in a short burst. *Fight-or-flight survival mode for hours or days begins to cause detrimental breakdowns in the human body.*

Take this physiological situation and apply it to our children, and what do you get? Let's have another look at the last five bullet points above. Think about what happens if major areas of your child's immune system shut down, and she already has a compromised immune system (or if a child with an autoimmune disease keeps triggering immune system overreaction). Or if your child's digestive system shuts down, and she already has digestive issues. Or if you are administering biomedical interventions designed to help your child's digestive, immune, and other systems rebuild—and major physiological repair is on hold in her body.

Now also imagine trying to help your child to learn and interact socially when her brain is in this fight-or-flight state. Learning and social interaction are exceedingly difficult for our children when they are in this mode. Attention span is affected, interfering with learning, and the child is in a highly self-protective state, shutting down her ability to interact socially.

And then we have the cortisol issue.

THE PROBLEM WITH CORTISOL

During my conversation with Dr Scott Faber, he told me he found that children with autism often have chronically elevated stress hormone levels, particularly cortisol. This is a key sign of someone in fight-or-flight survival mode.

Dr Theoharis Theoharides, scientist, professor of internal medicine, and professor of pharmacology at Tufts Medical Center in Boston, has also found elevated levels of CRH in children on the spectrum. He has found it in areas of the body outside the brain (a fairly big deal, as it is thought to be released only by the hypothalamus inside the brain), and he believes it can exacerbate inflammation throughout the body, which is an issue that some of our children face. This presence of CRH is yet another sign of a body in fight-or flight mode.

I would add that, although I didn't know all of the biology surrounding this scenario, I didn't find this at all surprising when I heard it. If a child is in a constant state of sensory overload, surrounded by an environment that seems totally unpredictable, and then pushed and pulled in a myriad of directions against his will, the fight-or-flight response would seem the most likely result.

What is increasingly well understood is that chronically

elevated levels of cortisol cause the atrophy of cells in the hippocampus—and prevent the genesis of new hippocampal cells. The hippocampus is a small area near the center of the brain that is responsible for the formation of new memories, something of obvious and crucial importance to our children. Interestingly, the hippocampus is one of the first regions of the brain to suffer damage in people who have Alzheimer's disease. (See books such as *The End of Stress As We Know It*, by Ewan McGowan and *Social Intelligence*, by Daniel Goleman for more on stress, cortisol, and their effect on the hippocampus.)

These are the key points to take away from this discussion.

- We do not want our children to have chronically elevated levels of cortisol (or CRH).

- We do not want our children to be in a perpetual fight-or-flight state.

- We want to do whatever we can to enable our children to shift *out of* the fight-or-flight survival mode and *into* the recovery mode.

THE RECOVERY MODE

There is good news here. Everything described above is reversible. The most promising thing that Dr Faber discussed with me was why he felt The Son-Rise Program was so effective. He found that when the children with autism were joined, given control, handled with a nonjudgmental and welcoming attitude (all of which he termed "emotionally attuned intervention"), and placed in an environment that was not overstimulating, their stress hormone levels (adrenaline, cortisol) *dropped to normal ranges*.

I cannot tell you how excited I am about this. It explains an important aspect of why The Son-Rise Program works and gives us all a concrete way to help our children biologically, physiologically, neurologically, and developmentally.

You have the ability to powerfully impact the core biology of your child's autism. When your child shifts out of fight-or-flight survival mode and his stress hormones return to normal ranges, the door is open for breakthroughs on several fronts.

- Your child is relaxed and can think

- Your child's digestive system springs to life

- Your child's immune system is given its best chance to function optimally

- Your child's brain is in a nonthreatened state that allows for learning and social interaction

- When cortisol levels are not elevated, the process of hippocampal atrophy ceases and reverses itself, with cells growing and reproducing in the hippocampus again. (Remember, the hippocampus is crucial for learning, since it is the part of the brain responsible for the formation of new memories.)

- Your child's body can now engage in sustained physiological repair (SPR). This means that your child can make maximal use of his biomedical interventions. If your child is getting treatments designed to aid and rebuild his digestive, immune, neurological, and elimination systems, he needs a body that is actually going to respond, repair, and rebuild.

We call the state in which the above factors are present the recovery mode. Using The Son-Rise Program to enable your child to shift from fight-or-flight to recovery mode gives your child every chance to progress and grow.

It also provides your child with something most children on the spectrum lack: treatment synergy. Biomedical interventions can work more powerfully together with The Son-Rise Program than individually.

It is thus absolutely essential that we administer any biological interventions (diet, enzymes, biomedical treatments, etc.) in a manner that is relaxed, noncoercive, and fun. This must be done with our children's cooperation rather than their resistance. For this reason, utilizing The Son-Rise Program techniques outlined in this chapter (and others) is imperative. We want to do all that we can to shift our children from fight-or-flight survival mode to recovery mode. This is what really matters.

ACTIVITY TIME!

To begin, you will just do two simple things. First, decide on one food item that you can safely say is unhealthy for your child. This does not refer to an entire food group, such as dairy, but rather to a single food item, such as fizzy drinks, chocolate chip cookies, doughnuts, toasted cheese sandwiches, or pizza. Second, choose one food item that your child does not now eat which you will introduce, such as spinach, squash, or asparagus. Once you have decided, fill in Table 14.

One Food Item To Remove	One Food Item To Add

Table 14

ONLINE RESOURCES

For more in-depth help with the principles and techniques of this chapter, please go to www.autismbreakthrough.com/chapter16. Enjoy!

STARTING POINT

As a first step, let's just focus on removing that one food item on the left-hand side of Table 14. It is important not only to remove this item from your child's diet but to remove it from your house. If, for instance, you choose fizzy drinks, you will want to make your house fizzy drink-free. Look back over the five Son-Rise Program feeding principles and the section on removing problematic and unhealthy foods. Then, when you have one hundred percent conviction behind the need to remove this one food item, you're ready to go!

SEVENTEEN

Attitude: The Critical Element

THIS IS THE most important chapter of the entire book.

The subject of this chapter is, without question, *the* most overlooked area of autism treatment. Moreover, without this chapter, none of the other principles, techniques, and strategies of this book will work.

Did that get your attention?

WHY YOUR ATTITUDE IS THE CRITICAL ELEMENT

People like to learn hard skills. I don't mean hard as in "difficult." Rather, a hard skill is a skill that is physical and easily seen and measured. Joining, for instance, is a technique based on a hard skill. You can see if someone's joining a child. You can see if someone *isn't* joining.

Most parents, when I first speak with them, want to hear all about the hard skills and techniques of The Son-Rise Program. They want me to tell them about joining. They want to know how to use one of their child's interests in a skill-building game. They want to hear about the four fundamentals of socialization and how to teach them.

What they don't show as much interest in at first is learning about the importance of attitude and how to utilize it. Attitude is considered a "soft" skill. To many people, it feels mushy or touchy-feely. I cannot count the number of instances that I have heard a parent make this statement: "Look, I think The Son-Rise

Program will really help my child. I want to learn the techniques, such as joining. But, attitude? Attitude, shmattitude. I don't need to spend loads of time looking at my emotions and stuff like that. Just teach me the techniques."

In the same vein, I still occasionally hear the old and deeply misinformed critique: "The Son-Rise Program says that if you just love your child enough, your child will come out of his or her autism." This statement, at its core, is not a criticism of The Son-Rise Program—since we don't say or believe that—so much as it is a reflection of the far-reaching cultural bias against attitude as a relevant (and, in this case, crucial) component of treatment.

I see this bias all the time in the many psychiatrists, psychologists, psychotherapists, and others in the helping professions with whom we work. Many of these individuals experience sustained distress and discomfort routinely during their day, including while they are working with people. And yet they don't seem to view the dichotomy between the emotional well-being they endeavor to enable people to attain and their own lack of that well-being as particularly relevant. The idea that the attitude of the therapist bears no relationship to his or her ability to help people still reigns supreme. We believe that it's only knowledge and education that count. We remain married to the idea that, in the therapeutic and educational setting, the only thing that matters is *what* we do, rather than *how* we do it.

Even I, with a lifetime of evidence about the impact of attitude, briefly fell into this trap a couple of years ago; I'll tell you about it a little later.

The attitude of the person working with—or spending any time with—your child is of monumental importance for three primary reasons. Let's take them one at a time.

ATTITUDE HAS AN ENORMOUS IMPACT ON HOW RESPONSIVE OUR CHILDREN ARE

Children on the autism spectrum, as we've discussed before, are highly sensitive to their environment. They are easily overstimulated, they have difficulty processing incoming sensory input, they live in a world that seems haphazard and unpredictable to them, and, in many cases, they are in a continuous fight-or-flight state.

And, remember, autism is a social-relational disorder. Our children have difficulty leaving their own world and making interpersonal connections.

What do these factors mean when we put them all together? When our children are with someone who is uncomfortable or agitated, they perceive it as a threat. As a result, they either become more withdrawn or behave with more aggressiveness. These are both self-protection mechanisms.

When, on the other hand, our children are in the presence of someone who is relaxed, comfortable, welcoming, and truly nonjudgmental, they perceive this as safe and inviting. They respond more, engage more, display more flexibility, connect more, and, in most cases, shift out of fight-or-flight survival mode and into the recovery mode.

Thus, our attitude can provide the impetus for a challenged child to reach out to us, or it can act to drive that child away.

This is not some theory or idea. It is fact. We have seen this phenomenon play out with children for almost thirty years. We have seen children on the spectrum respond to attitude time and time again, moving away from those they perceive as agitated or uncomfortable and toward those they experience as comfortable, relaxed, and welcoming.

In truth, you have probably seen this many times as well. Have you ever noticed that your child will go to a particular therapy (say, occupational therapy or speech language therapy), and will respond quite powerfully to one therapist and not another? This is not a technique issue, since both therapists are doing the same type of therapy. Rather, your child's response is a function of the *attitude* of these two therapists. One of them has an attitude to which your child responds well, and the other doesn't.

An increasing body of research supports the attitude effect (see Appendix 1).

THE GIRL IN THE HOSPITAL

I want to share with you a brief but telling experience that my parents had when I was little. This occurred as they were waiting in a hospital lobby just prior to an important three-hour follow-up examination to be performed on me by the same team of neurologists, doctors, and associates as had performed a previous exam—with a very grim prognosis. Since the previous exam, I had made roughly 90 percent of what would become my full recovery—needless to say, a great surprise to the diagnosticians.

Here is their experience in that hospital lobby, taken directly my father's book, *Son-Rise: The Miracle Continues.*

> Samahria, Raun, and I sat together on the couch. A little girl and her mother came walking past. The child broke away from her mother's grasp and ran directly to Samahria, who smiled and opened her arms to her. The girl had teal blue eyes. Razor sharp! Samahria stroked the child's face gently and began talking to her in a whisper. The little girl just gazed into Samahria's eyes and then touched her head to Samahria's. They were like two old friends saying hello in the most intimate way. Finally, the child's mother came over. Without saying a word, she took the child's

hand and directed her toward the door. All this time, the little girl kept looking back at us.

Later, we inquired about this child. We were told that she was autistic and had always avoided human contact. Hmmm. Perhaps this little girl knew. Perhaps, when a loving and accepting attitude is expressed tangibly in a smile or in the gentle touch of a hand, the invitation might inspire even the most dysfunctional little person. Perhaps, in the face of such safety and encouragement, this child stretched herself beyond her normal limits.

THE AUTISM ONE / GENERATION RESCUE CONFERENCE

In 2011, we at the Autism Treatment Center of America had a powerful experience. I spoke at the Autism One / Generation Rescue conference in Chicago, Illinois, the largest and most broad conference of its kind at the time. (You may know Generation Rescue by its president, Jenny McCarthy.) I had spoken at this conference in previous years, but this year there was a fascinating twist. In a national survey conducted over a period of months by the conference, The Son-Rise Program had won the Best Autism Therapy award, and I had been awarded Best Presenter, which was a huge honor—but this wasn't the twist to which I refer.

For this conference, we had flown our entire team of child facilitators out to the conference to donate free child care to parents who attended the conference with their children on the autism spectrum. We were very excited, but, to be sure, this was also somewhat experimental. The Son-Rise Program is designed for a controlled, one-on-one, very personal environment, and this scenario would entail having two hotel rooms filled with special kids. Each room would have about twenty children and four or five adults.

We knew that, given these circumstances, we were not going

to be able to carefully implement each Son-Rise Program technique customized to each child, as we would normally do. Instead, our child facilitators decided to focus on the very basics. They would, above all, maintain a comfortable, welcoming, completely nonjudgmental attitude toward all of the children. Of course, in following what we all believed in, they would provide a safe and noncoercive environment. They would allow the children to do their isms. They would celebrate them and invite the kids to interact with them. But with a giant group of kids, even these basics had limits. In the end, we all knew that the one thing we could do with perfection no matter what was to maintain The Son-Rise Program attitude. And so that is what these wonderful child facilitators did.

Allow me to pause for a moment for a brief mea culpa. Although I was very excited about this whole endeavor, I was also a bit skeptical about it. How effective could we really be with just The Son-Rise Program attitude? In asking this question, I had fallen into that old cultural bias of valuing *what* we do over *how* we do it. In spite of all of my experience, I had, for a moment, fallen into the trap of failing to fully appreciate the paramount importance that attitude—yes, just attitude—has on treatment, and on our kids, especially. And I was quickly and vigorously disabused of my skepticism.

Over the three to four days the kids participated in our day care, some astonishing changes occurred. Parents would approach us, sometimes in tears, telling us stories about how different their children were in just a few days. They recounted events such as these.

- Jamie's parents told us that he was a very withdrawn child—except when a teacher at school would try to move him or get him to change what he was doing, at which point he would become aggressive. With us, he was extremely sweet, never once becoming aggressive in three days. Jamie would approach us and engage with us at times. His mother told us later that he was so much calmer after his time with us.

- Kaitlin cried the first whole day with us. She also scratched us and didn't want to participate in any way. Two days later, not only did she no longer cry, but she would come to us and insist on holding hands with us the entire time she was with us. She sang with us at times and at other times would continue to sing on her own.

- On the first day, Bianca would climb on everything and try to pull the other children's hair and push them. She would run from us and then look for a reaction. By the third day, she would come to us on her own for bounces, squeezes, and tons of celebrations. In the end, she was easily following directions (come eat your lunch, time to change your Pull-Up, etc.). She became incredibly loving and sweet, and she would watch the other kids, glance at their hair, and then *not* try to pull it. On her last day with us, she came through the door, calmly watched her mom and one of our child facilitators talk, waited until they were all done, *took the child facilitator's hand,* and then walked into the room with her.

- Kahanu's parents told us that his crying, which had been constant at home, decreased hugely after his time with us at the conference.

- Daniel, we were told, had "major separation issues." He had never before gone to a babysitter or to school without crying, tantruming, and becoming aggressive. His mother was used to holding him, both to restrain him from acting out on his teachers and babysitters and because he didn't want to be separated from her. Indeed, Daniel cried for most of his first day with us. On the second day (and every day thereafter), he pushed his parents out the door, saying "Bye-bye!" At the end of each day, he didn't want to leave. Throughout each day, he would smile, laugh, and participate with the other kids, occasionally interjecting, "Daniel's okay."

- Zach's parents came at the end of the day to pick him up and take him to a special "treat"—a trip to the museum that they had previously been looking forward to. Zach a high-functioning boy, explained to his parents that he didn't want to go—he wanted to stay with us. After his parents finally convinced him to go, Zach kept saying, as they were leaving, "But am I going to be able to come back? When can I come back?"

- A parent approached me at my conference booth and said, "After being with you guys, my son is so completely different than how he is every day when he comes home from school. I don't know if I can ever drop him back at school again."

- And many more instances of transformation, large and small: a little boy saying, "I love you" to us, a little girl's language increasing, a boy spontaneously sitting on his mother's lap for the first time, parents telling us that their children were suddenly calmer and happier, verbal children talking about their time with us for the rest of the night.

Keep in mind: this wasn't even from the full Son-Rise Program. This was just The Son-Rise Program *attitude*.

ATTITUDE DETERMINES OUR EFFECTIVENESS AT ENABLING OUR CHILDREN TO REACH NEW HEIGHTS

I know the walls of doubt and denial that you, as a parent, face from others about your child. I am aware of the avalanche of pessimistic messages that are communicated to you in a thousand different ways, subtle and unsubtle. And I am acutely cognizant of the undercurrent of social pressure that you may experience to "be realistic" about your child. To take some of that on yourself is totally understandable.

That is why it is so important for you and me to spend some time looking at the effect our attitudes have on how we are with our children—and how this affects their development. This is not in any way an indictment of those of us who struggle with feelings of anger, frustration, fear, sadness, pessimism, or hopelessness—and who buy into the barrage of predictions ladled out so copiously about our children.

On the contrary, this is our chance to use this knowledge to change our children's trajectories.

Believing that your child is capable of accomplishing things that she hasn't yet is *the* prerequisite to you making such leaps happen with your child. If we don't believe that our children are capable in these instances, several obstacles of our own making will appear.

- We won't encourage our children to acquire the new skill—certainly not with real sincerity or passion.

- We won't persevere in our attempts over time, which, for many of our children, is necessary for reaching the next level.

- We will communicate to our children, in a plethora of different ways, that we don't believe that they can do it; this discourages them from continuing to try.

- We won't see or recognize when our children actually begin to achieve the goal, sabotaging our ability to build on it in any way.

You may remember the discussion from Chapter 7 in which I recounted a phenomenon we've seen many times at The Son-Rise Program Intensive. (Recall that parents attend this program with their child.) There have been times, while watching one of our sessions with their children in which they spoke for the very first time, when the parents could neither see nor hear this momentous event. These parents, having been told so many times that their children cannot speak, internalized this prediction. And, having internalized it, they remained unable to hear when their children were contradicting the "fact" that they couldn't speak. There have been instances where we have had to play back video footage of a child speaking multiple times before the parents watching could see and hear their child speaking. Although this may sound extreme, smaller versions of this phenomenon happen all the time when we decide in advance what our children *can't* do.

Every single thing you do while you are with your child is determined by your attitude. Let's look back through The Son-Rise Program techniques for some examples:

Joining, at least in its true (and effective) form, comes directly from an attitude of nonjudgmental acceptance and genuine interest in our children's worlds. Let's say that you are lining up toy cars with your child. If you are simply copying your child, you will find joining to be only marginally effective.

Imagine instead that, while you are lining up the cars, you are feeling a sense of nonjudgmental acceptance of what your child is doing, curiosity about his world, and celebration of his uniqueness and ability to take care of himself. Now your joining is imbued with the characteristics that make it work. You are enjoying yourself, communicating love and warmth toward your child, and showing him that you are a safe and integral part of his world.

The *motivation principle* stems from a real excitement about our children's interests. To capitalize on our children's motivations, we need to, first, be interested in what those motivations are (so that we can watch for them). Then we need to engage in a game around one of the interests (say, submarines), which, if that game has any hope of enticing our children, must be created with full-throated enthusiasm.

We can only use *celebration* effectively if we are feeling sincere gratitude for and delight in something that our child has just done. Otherwise, it is simply a rote praise that will have no currency with our children (i.e., our children won't be moved by it to do more of what we are celebrating, thus negating its efficacy). We need the three Es—energy, excitement, and enthusiasm—to make it work. Also, we won't even notice what to celebrate if we aren't focusing on and feeling grateful for the wonderful things that our children are already doing.

When dealing with *tantrums and other challenging behaviors*, think about this: how can we stay truly nonreactive when our child is engaging in some challenging behavior unless we can honestly maintain a comfortable attitude? When our child scratches us and we light up like a Christmas tree (i.e., frown, scold, raise our voice, look agitated), this is because of our attitude—in this case, one of anger, frustration, or fear. When this happens, it isn't because we forget The Son-Rise Program technique that applies here (remaining calm, nonreactive, and playing "dumb"). It's because, *even though we know what to do, our attitude makes it impossible for us to do it.*

You can read this book and memorize all of the techniques

therein, but when you feel agitated or upset, you will not be able to effectively implement the principles you've just committed to memory. Our attitude affects everything we do. We cannot join with love and curiosity when we feel sad. We cannot celebrate with gratitude and excitement when we feel upset. We cannot stay relaxed and help our crying, scratching child to find a different way to communicate when we feel frustrated.

It's not that you have to be perfect and never get upset with your child again. It's just that, once you prioritize your attitude and begin to shift the ways you approach even some of the daily situations and challenges you face with your child, you clear the way for mammoth change to occur in how she relates to you. Each time you take even one event or behavior and approach it with The Son-Rise Program attitude, you maximize your power to be helpful to your child.

You already love your child more than anything. Now you can express your love in the way she can most understand.

ATTITUDE WILL DETERMINE WHETHER OR NOT WE WILL STAY MOTIVATED OVER TIME

This should come as no surprise to you, but it bears mentioning. If you are stressed out, burned out, bummed out, freaked out, or otherwise discouraged, disempowered, despondent, or demoralized, you will not stick with what you are doing. This is true if you are implementing The Son-Rise Program, but it is also true if you are implementing *any* program. For success, you must sustain your program (whatever program that is) *over time*. You will not be able to do this unless you can stay consistently motivated, upbeat, confident, and clearheaded.

Have you ever been at home with your child, when you could take some time to play with him, but you realize that you have a load of laundry to do? Do you ever see your child acting "autistic," and instead of spending some time with him, you put him in front of the TV for a while?

It's totally fine if you *have* done these things. Almost every parent I've worked with has. Many parents have difficulty enjoying their child on the spectrum, which affects the amount of time they spend with their child. And time is the one thing that is absolutely necessary for The Son-Rise Program to work.

When you are comfortable with your child, you will spend more time with your child—not because you think you're supposed to but because you *want* to. When you have real conviction behind what you are doing, you will stick to it. When you feel relaxed on a regular basis, you will *not* feel exhausted, and so you will have energy to give to your child. When you feel a sense of self-confidence with regard to your competence in helping your child, you will maintain the motivation and consistency over time that is critical for the principles of The Son-Rise Program to do its job.

One of the reasons why we spend so much time during the Start-Up program and the advanced programs working with parents on cultivating a comfortable, confident, relaxed, and hopeful attitude is that *nothing else will matter without it.*

BONUS REASON: YOUR PERSONAL RELATIONSHIP

For most of us, just navigating a marriage or similar long-term relationship can be hard enough. Couple that with raising a child—any child—and our lives can feel like a real challenge. That's *before* we have a child with autism.

When we *do* have a child on the spectrum, it can feel like an experience beyond the biggest challenge that we have ever imagined facing. Your child is different. She exhibits behaviors to which others respond with discomfort or confusion. The simplest daily tasks, like eating or taking a bath, are fraught with difficulty. Dire predictions are handed out like sweets. The most basic dreams that you and your partner had for your child seem dashed. You must choose from a confusing list of treatment options, or you're given only one option and told to be grateful that you have even that. Stress levels that may already be high often explode. For many, many couples, autism seems to push the relationship to the breaking point.

If there were things you could do to strengthen your relationship and increase the chances of it surviving autism, wouldn't you want to know what those things were? If you are still wondering if attitude is really important day-to-day in a relationship, ask yourself this. Have you ever noticed:

- How different you are with your significant other when you are stressed out about your child?

- How you feel about your significant other when he or she says something that you think means that he or she doesn't value you?

- How much harder it is for you to feel close to your significant other when you are feeling very critical of yourself?

These experiences are all about attitude. If you have a way to change your attitude, these experiences change.

I (and the other teachers at the Autism Treatment Center of America) have conducted a great many couples counseling sessions. This is one of the most satisfying aspects of my work. One of the most moving transformations I witness at the ATCA is seeing couples on the verge of dissolution learn to use their child's autism to grow closer and nurture a more caring, honest, and loving relationship.

For some of you, this may sound like a pipe dream, but it is not beyond the realm of possibility. The only way to turn the ship around, though, is to begin with attitude. You already know that how you are with your child (calm or frustrated, celebratory or annoyed, accepting or critical) affects every aspect of your relationship with him. In the same way, how you and your partner are attitudinally with one another affects every aspect of your partnership.

Even as you read this, you may be thinking that this sounds nice, but it's the *how* that eludes. Fair enough. We haven't yet discussed the *how* of attitudinal change, but we will. This chapter will give you some simple tools you can put to use immediately—with your child *and* your partner.

But, first, you have to be on board for the idea that *if* there were ways for you (and your partner) to face events with your child and each other in a more comfortable, clear, loving, and relaxed manner, it would be to your benefit—it would *matter*—for you to do so. So what do you say? Are you willing to prioritize attitude?

THE COMPONENTS OF THE SON-RISE PROGRAM ATTITUDE

The Son-Rise Program attitude can be summarized as follows: embracing *without judgment* where your child is today—while believing that she can go anywhere tomorrow. Of course, it goes deeper than this, but let's use the two halves of this concept as our jumping-off point.

"Embracing without judgment where your child is today" has profound meaning. It goes way beyond simply loving your child, which we all do. It means loving everything about your child, including the most autistic parts. It involves embracing your child's autism the way you embrace her brown eyes, curly hair, sweet smile, or any other aspect of who she is. It entails seeing your child ripping sheets of paper into tiny strips and falling in love with ripping paper. It means not labeling any of your child's behaviors as bad, wrong, or even inappropriate, which necessitates knowing that, right now, she is doing the very best that she can.

This essential ingredient of The Son-Rise Program attitude is what sets the stage for all relationship-building. We use the word "nonjudgmental," but we could also add the words "welcoming," "loving," "accepting," "caring," "at ease," "curious," and "delighting." You want to cultivate an attitude that involves sincerely cherishing every aspect of your child—especially those traits that make her different.

You may recall, in the first chapter of this book, that I quoted something from my father's book that he and my mom asked themselves upon receiving my diagnosis and the dark predictions that went with it: "Could we kiss the ground that the others had cursed?"

That's what The Son-Rise Program attitude is really about. Others may call your child's condition a tragedy. You don't have to. People might look upon your child with disapproving eyes. You can make your every gaze an embrace. You can kiss the ground that the others have cursed.

"Believing that your child can go *anywhere* tomorrow" is also very important. We can embody this part of the attitude with hope, optimism, anticipatory invitation, excitement, and, indeed, joyful silliness. It means seeing your child's abilities rather than focusing on supposed deficiencies. People will (with the best of intentions) try their best to convince you to be "realistic." They will urge you to "come to terms" with what you child cannot do.

When faced with such naysaying, it is all the more important to be *unrealistic*. This means cultivating a belief in what your child *can* do—unencumbered by the limited, pessimistic, stifling version of reality that others may espouse. After all, you are the parent. Your love is unrivaled, your experience is unmatchable, and your long-haul commitment is unparalleled. You do not have to apologize for believing in your child when no one else does. You don't have to feel embarrassed about seeing what no one else sees.

This vital piece of The Son-Rise Program attitude gives your child every chance to reach new heights. (It's not a guarantee, but it opens so many closed doors!) It allows you to have a child who has not yet spoken and say, "He just hasn't spoken yet, but he can absolutely do this." It enables you to know that what your child has done (or not done) up until now tells you *nothing* about what he can do in the future.

WHERE YOUR ATTITUDE COMES FROM—AND HOW TO SHIFT IT

I can understand how it might, at first, seem a bit pie-in-the-sky to read about the importance of cultivating a particular attitude when, in your day-to-day experience, that attitude may seem far off. You may feel as if events happen throughout your day, and you simply react to them as best you can. Some things happen that appear to brighten your day, while other, more challenging occurrences seem to make you upset. And when you experience a really massive event, such as having your child diagnosed with autism, it can certainly feel as if the event itself is *causing* your unhappiness.

This almost universally accepted model of the human psyche holds that the events and circumstances in our lives determine how we feel emotionally (happy, sad, excited, scared, content, angry). Our child ripping up the pages of a book *makes* us feel upset. Her tantrum *makes* us feel frustrated. A diagnostician telling us that our child will only improve slightly *makes* us feel devastated. On the other side of the equation, our child saying her first word *makes* us feel wonderful. A teacher telling us that our child has made progress *makes* us feel proud or hopeful.

There are two problems with this model, though. The first one is a flaw in logic: how do we explain two people responding in totally different ways to the same events? If events and circumstances really do *make* us feel the way we feel, then shouldn't everyone respond the same way to the same thing? How do we explain that one person feels devastated or worthless when he or she gets sacked, and someone else shrugs it off—or even feels excited about the prospect of moving on? How is it that some lottery winners say that winning was the best thing that ever happened to them and others maintain that it was the worst? Since everyone responds differently to the same events—and *we* respond differently to a particular event on different days, there must be something else besides the event that is determining how we feel.

The second problem is a practical one: this model makes us out to be victims. We don't determine how we feel; events outside us do. If only my child would communicate more, progress faster, not be autistic, not behave that way, etc., *then* I could feel good (comfortable, relaxed, hopeful, etc.).

Given this culturally reinforced paradigm, no one on earth could fault you for feeling distraught, upset, scared, angry, frustrated, or despondent about the challenges that your child—and, thus, you—face. Many of us feel like we are locked in a nonstop battle to get our children to behave a certain way or reach particular benchmarks just so that we can sleep at night. I can understand that. We want to be good parents. And we want our children to have fulfilling lives.

The problem is that when we need our children to be a certain way, it does a lot more than just make us miserable. It also greatly hinders our ability to help our children. Why? Because, as we've been discussing, we are different with our children—and they respond differently to us—depending on our attitude. In fact, if we need our children to behave a certain way or progress a particular amount in order for us to feel good, they will experience this need as a push. And if there is one thing we know about our children, it's that when they feel pushed, they dig their heels in (or push back).

So freeing ourselves from this prison is the very best thing we can do for ourselves and our children. The question is, how?

THE MISSING PIECE: BELIEFS

In reality, it is not the events and circumstances themselves that determine how we feel. It is, rather, our *beliefs*.

What, exactly, is a belief?

I like to think of beliefs as tinted sunglasses. You might have yellow lenses in yours, and, consequently, everything you see looks yellow. I might have green. Someone else might have blue. We might all insist that our color is the "real" color of things, but, in reality, we are all just gazing through our own lenses.

Because our human brains function as belief-making machines, we can never remove our sunglasses altogether. We are always believing *something*. What we *can* do, however, is to switch our lenses—as often as we like. If I feel that my green lenses aren't serving me (they are fueling my unhappiness or making me ineffective), then I can swap them for blue ones. If those don't work for me, I can replace them with red lenses. My vision will always be colored in some way by my lenses (beliefs), but I get to choose *how* they are colored. Are they rose-colored or mud brown?

So a belief is a conclusion that we draw about ourselves, other people, events, and the world around us in order to make sense of our environment and to take care of ourselves. In each particular situation, we hold a belief which acts as the lens through which we see that situation. Beliefs are perspectives, opinions, perceptions, biases, or preconceptions that provide our frame of reference for understanding what is happening.

Here are some examples of beliefs.

- My child will never change

- I did something wrong to bring about or contribute to my child's autism

- If I prioritize myself and what I want too much, I will become selfish and not be there for my child

- My child isn't capable of doing that (speaking, making friends, etc.).

Alternatively, we could believe this.

- My child is capable of profound growth and progress

- I didn't do anything "wrong" to cause my child's challenges, but I can be part of the solution

- If I take time to prioritize myself and what I want, this will leave me with more reserves, more health, and more focus to help my child

- My child is totally capable of doing that; he just hasn't done it *yet*.

The beliefs we hold determine every emotion we have, from joy to anger, from contentment to fear. It works like this.

- An event occurs in our lives (we are told that our child has autism)

- We filter the event through the belief we hold about it (my child is facing a lifetime of suffering and limited possibilities, this is my fault, etc.)

- We feel an emotion based upon our belief (sad, scared, angry, etc.).

Here are some more examples of our beliefs in action.

- A young boy with autism is lying on the floor and making loud noises in the middle of the supermarket, and his mom feels embarrassed as she sees the disapproving looks of others. The belief causing the embarrassment: If people are judging me, it means I'm doing something wrong as a parent.

- A mom feels proud and excited as she notices that her daughter is repetitively stacking blocks. The belief fueling the pride and excitement: My daughter knows exactly what to do to best take care of herself, and I can use her behavior as a way to connect with my daughter and know her world better.

- A dad feels frustrated as he sees his son with autism watch the same two minutes of a DVD over and over again. The belief fueling the frustration: This behavior means that my son is broken and incapable of change and growth.

- A little boy with autism says his first word, and his parents feel overjoyed. The belief fueling their joy: This is the first step to my child speaking fluently. More language is on the way.

- A mother of a five-year-old with autism feels angry and sad when she sees neurotypical kids. The belief causing the anger and sadness: My child can never turn out like those kids. Autism is bad. It's unfair that my child has autism while others don't.

WHERE DO WE GET OUR BELIEFS?

We are taught a great many of our beliefs from those around us. Throughout our lives, we are bombarded by a never-ending stream of beliefs by our parents, teachers, friends, strangers, the news, films, and television programmes. Most of the time, we are taught beliefs that fuel distress, fear, unhappiness, and ineffectiveness. We adopt and continue to hold such beliefs and the unhappiness they create as a strategy to take care of ourselves. We do, at times, adopt beliefs that lead to contentment, but our belief-adopting bias tends to lean toward "Oh, no!" rather than "Oh, yes!" perspectives. Some examples:

- A child who is told by her parents that she is irresponsible adopts this belief about herself and continues to hold on to it as an adult.

- A husband adopts the belief promoted to him by his father that he must financially provide for his new wife in order to be a good husband.

- A schoolchild is told by his teacher that he is not good at maths. He adopts this belief and retains it for decades. (This could work in the reverse direction as well: A college-aged woman adopts the belief promoted to her by her writing professor that she is a good writer.)

- A man is told by a news anchorperson that his favorite candidate has little chance of winning the election. He adopts this belief and does not vote for that candidate. (And, thus, a self-fulfilling prophesy is created.)

In some cases, we develop beliefs ourselves through our experiences. For example:

- A man who is mugged on a city street at night concludes that cities are dangerous and avoids metropolitan areas.

- A elderly man is repeatedly treated in a dismissive manner by people around him, and he concludes that his advancing age makes him less important.

- A middle-aged woman who has been through two divorces creates the belief that she can never find true love.

- A visitor to France is shouted at by someone in French on three different occasions. He creates the belief that the French are rude. (This could operate in the opposite direction, too: A visitor to Italy is treated sweetly by several Italian people and concludes that Italians are nice people.)

How does this relate to you as the parent of a child with autism? Think of how you felt when your child was first diagnosed—or when you first realized that something was very different about her. Did you feel scared? Angry? Sad? Did you feel like there was a bowling ball in your stomach or a hand around your throat?

For most of us, the second someone gives our child a diagnosis, they accompany that diagnosis with a stream of beliefs about what this diagnosis means about our child—and about us. We are told that our child will not be able to do what other kids can do. We are told that autism is a lifelong condition. We are given a myriad of details about what the next thirty years of our child's life will supposedly be like. And we are told of the many limitations that we ostensibly have as parents, such as a lack of the "proper" training/education or being "too emotional/too involved." Most important, we are told these things—these *beliefs*—as if they are facts.

In many cases we adopt these beliefs without ever really examining or considering them as optional perspectives. And who could blame us? We are surrounded by advocates and proponents of these beliefs and biases. We are immersed in these beliefs at a time when we are least equipped to be discerning. Our child is given a life sentence. We are inundated with pronouncements. We feel a sense of desperation—we know that our child is facing profound challenges, but we don't know what to do to help her.

In the face of this, we don't realize that we get to decide if we want to take on the beliefs we are presented with or not.

As time goes on, we pick up more beliefs (or create them on our own), most of them disempowering and unhappiness-producing. Then, when we're confronted with day-to-day experiences with our child, we face a never-ending torrent of triggers. He pinches or bites. She doesn't speak. He faces criticism from others. *We* face criticism from others. She engages in unusual repetitive behaviors. He doesn't appear to return our affection. She is rigid about how events must transpire.

But, remember: these triggers are only triggers because we're holding beliefs that make these events feel terrible. If, for example, we saw our child's pinching or biting as a temporary instance of our child's most sincere attempt to take care of himself instead of meaning that he will never change or doesn't love us, it would feel very different than it does.

Lest this picture appear gloomy, let us explore the most important part of this whole equation.

THE GOOD NEWS: BELIEFS ARE CHANGEABLE

Since beliefs are learned, we can unlearn them. And since our beliefs fuel our emotions about an event, changing them completely changes how we feel, even when there is no change in the event itself.

We work with many parents who change fundamental

unhappiness-producing beliefs about themselves and their children, often in just the five days of the Start-Up course. They go from seeing their child's autism as a nightmare to seeing the most profound beauty in their child's uniqueness. They shift from seeing themselves as ill-equipped to concluding that they have everything they need to make a profound and lasting impact on their child's trajectory. They change from thinking that their child is capable of only small and slow change to believing that their child is capable of vast and sweeping growth. These transformations are only possible because beliefs are changeable.

Understanding how beliefs work shifts us out of the victim position and into the driver's seat. One of the strongest ways to keep yourself in this driver's seat is to say to yourself, next time you are unhappy or upset: "I'm feeling upset not because of what's *happening* but because of what I'm *believing* about what's happening."

Okay, so if beliefs are changeable, how do we change them? First, we have to uncover them. And if you've never done this before, it can seem tricky at first. That's why we teach parents (and others) to use a special questioning process called the Option Process Dialogue to uncover and then change beliefs, preconceptions, and biases which might be getting in their way—particularly when it comes to maintaining The Son-Rise Program attitude so crucial for helping their child.

Explaining this entire process would entail a book by itself. (In fact, there is such a book. If you would like to learn the fundamentals of the Option Process Dialogue in detail, you can read *PowerDialogues*, by Barry Neil Kaufman.) What we can do here is give you some starting questions that will be enormously helpful to you if you use them regularly. I would recommend that you practice asking yourself these questions each time you find yourself feeling unhappy, upset, annoyed, or frustrated. This can include issues and events not related to your child because, as you get better at uncovering and changing beliefs, you will find that you will get more and more adept at feeling comfortable and maintaining The Son-Rise Program attitude in situations that *do* involve your child.

Okay. Ready?

THREE QUESTIONS TO ASK YOURSELF

1. What am I believing (i.e., telling myself) that is fueling my unhappiness (frustration, fear, sadness, anger, etc.)?

2. Why am I believing/telling myself this?

3. What could I believe instead, and how will believing this help me or my child? (Shortcut question: How can I see this situation as good—or at least okay?)

Wait! Hold on! Before you start using these questions, take a look at the following lists of common parental beliefs. Looking over these lists carefully will make it much easier for you to answer the three questions above. These lists are also essential for completing the vitally important Activity Time! section at the end of this chapter.

TOP SEVEN DISEMPOWERING, UNHAPPINESS-PRODUCING PARENTAL BELIEFS

1. My child's autism is a tragedy, and I cannot possibly feel okay about it.

2. My child's condition is static and unchangeable. (What my child has done in the past tells me a lot about what she is capable of accomplishing in the future.)

3. My child knows that she is not supposed to behave this way. She is doing this just to drive me crazy.

4. I just can't handle this.

5. This situation is going to ruin my marriage.

6. My unhappiness about my child's condition is a sign of how much I care and how much I love her.

7. I have to get other people to agree with me, understand me, or support me in order to feel okay.

TOP SEVEN EMPOWERING, HAPPINESS-PRODUCING PARENTAL BELIEFS

1. I love my child and can enjoy and see the beauty in my child exactly as he is—with all his differences.

2. My child is capable of limitless change and growth. (What my child has been able or unable to do in the past tells me absolutely *nothing* about what he is capable of accomplishing in the future.)

3. My child is behaving this way because it is the only way he knows how to take care of himself. He is doing the best he can.

4. I can absolutely handle this.

5. I can use this challenge to meaningfully enhance, improve, and deepen my marriage.

6. My unhappiness doesn't have to be the measurement of how much I care. I can express my caring through my love and effort.

7. I don't need others to understand, agree with, or support me in order to feel okay. I just need conviction behind what I'm doing.

To get more help with belief and attitudinal change, I strongly recommend reading the book *Happiness Is a Choice* by Barry Neil Kaufman. It is a clear and very easy-to-read book with specifics about how to make far-reaching attitudinal changes in ways that feel easy and doable. Of particular interest are the six shortcuts to happiness. These are simple steps you can take to cut through the craziness and get yourself into a comfortable and relaxed state of mind quickly.

ACTIVITY TIME!

For this section, you will want to choose an issue or area of emotional discomfort or unhappiness that you have concerning your child or your relationship to her. You can choose an issue that you feel unhappy about right now or one that comes up regularly, such as feeling sad about your child's autism, fearful about her future, or worried that you don't have what it takes to help her. Alternatively, you can choose a specific event or occurrence where you got upset, such as a time when you got frustrated about how your child was behaving or an incident where you felt embarrassed in public with her.

Once you've chosen your issue, take a look at Table 15. Now you can plug your event or issue into this table. Then continue to fill out the table from there. When filling out the final two boxes, it will help you enormously to take another look at the seven disempowering and empowering beliefs listed earlier. You can choose your beliefs from these lists or come up with your own beliefs to write down.

When you are filling out that final box, take a few moments

to really consider what alternative belief you want to focus on adopting because it will serve as your ultimate attitudinal goal. Allow it to be your guide, your North Star. Your mission in life, at this point, is to adopt this belief.

Most important: don't be hard on yourself if you don't just drop everything and adopt the alternative belief you've chosen. It will take some time. You've had years to cement your unhappiness-producing beliefs. The most essential step is to start the ball rolling. Tape the alternative belief onto your bathroom mirror, write down a list of evidence supporting this belief, have your partner or a friend remind you about it, write down how adopting this new belief will help you help your child—or do all of the above. But above all, be easy with yourself. That you are even doing this at all is a statement of love for your child and will make a meaningful difference for both of you.

Event or Circumstance	
How You Feel/Felt	
Belief Fueling This Emotion	
Alternate Belief to Adopt	

Table 15

ONLINE RESOURCES

For more in-depth help with the principles and techniques of this chapter, please go to www.autismbreakthrough.com/chapter17. Enjoy this final chapter's online assistance!

STARTING POINT

For starters, choose one aspect of your child's condition or behavior that you tend to judge or with which you have a hard time. Now, try asking yourself the three questions we discussed earlier. Here they are again for your convenience:

1. What am I believing (telling myself) that is fueling my unhappiness (frustration, fear, sadness, anger, etc.)?

2. Why am I believing/telling myself this?

3. What could I believe instead, and how will believing this help me or my child? (Shortcut question: How can I see this situation as good—or at least okay?)

Next, spend a few minutes thinking about one dream you have for your child that you might have begun to suppress or keep to yourself because you were concerned that people would think it was unrealistic. Now just sit with this dream for a moment. If you feel any part of you internally apologizing for having this dream, just let it go. You are allowed to dream for your child. You are allowed to want more for your child. And you are allowed to give your child every chance to reach new horizons.

A FINAL WORD FROM ME TO YOU

We have taken quite a journey together, you and I. I have put my mind and soul into these pages with the hope that they will find their way into your heart. More than anything, I want these ideas, principles, and strategies to be useful to you and to your wonderful, special, and unique child.

Please, please, do not hold yourself up to some impossible standard of perfection. You're a human being who loves your child. That's enough. As you endeavor to implement the tools and techniques in this book, be gentle with yourself. If you don't utilize these strategies every single second, that's okay. If you feel discouraged or down or afraid sometimes, that's okay, too. Just pick yourself up, dust yourself off, and get back on the horse.

And, whatever you do, don't believe anyone who tells you that your child's future has been written—whether your child is three or thirty-three.

The Story of Jarir

A few years ago, the mother of a thirty-three-year-old man with autism named Jarir came to the Autism Treatment Center of America from the United Kingdom for the Start-Up program. At the time, her son was being cared for in an institution, where he had spent much of his life.

Jarir spent most of his time isming, had minimal eye contact, communicated mainly using single words (though he could sometimes use two words together), and spoke mostly in response to requests rather than spontaneously and unprompted. He preferred being alone and showed very little interest in the activities of others, often rejecting attempts to engage him.

The Start-Up program was transformative for Jarir's mom, giving her new hope and specific strategies to help her son. Upon her return to the UK, she removed Jarir from the institution, took him home, and implemented a Son-Rise Program with him.

Over the next eighteen months, Jarir underwent a spectacular metamorphosis, isming only 10 to 20 percent of the time; his eye contact increased to a neurotypical level and his speech surged forward so that his average sentence length was five to six words, with some as long as ten words. Moreover, his communication was often spontaneous and self-generated rather than only in response to others' requests. And Jarir became a man who *wanted* others around him, joining in and enjoying the activities of others the vast majority of the time.

IT'S NEVER TOO LATE

Jarir's story is a testament to his mom's dedication, to the power of the strategies detailed in this book, and, most of all, to the capacity of Jarir—and all of our children—to change and grow in dramatic fashion, at any age, regardless of the circumstances preceding that transformation.

There are no permanent roadblocks for our children. There is no point of no return. The brain remains plastic throughout our children's entire lives. (This is why a man in his seventies can have a stroke, lose his speech capabilities, and then relearn to speak.) So don't let anyone convince you that it's too late, that it's time to give up, that what your child *has not done* is any indicator of what your child *cannot do*.

When it's late at night, and you're feeling all alone, please know that there is a team of us on a mountainside in a small town in the US who are rooting for you, cheering for you, and believing that you can help your child reach the stars.

Recommended Reading
and Viewing

I strongly recommend that you check out these books and DVDs.

- *Breakthrough Strategies for Autism Spectrum Disorders* by Raun K. Kaufman (DVD)
- *Inspiring Journeys of Son-Rise Program Families* (Free DVD)
- *Autism Solutions* (Free DVD)
- *Son-Rise: A Miracle of Love* (NBC-TV movie, available on Amazon .com)
- Three books by Barry Neil Kaufman: *Son-Rise: The Miracle Continues, A Miracle to Believe In,* and *Happiness Is a Choice*

Go to my website at www.autismbreakthrough.com for help applying the principles and techniques in this book, including webcasts, articles, interviews, and some awe-inspiring recovery videos—including some touching interviews with the recovered kids themselves.

Contact the Autism Treatment Center of America for a twenty-five-minute call with one of our Son-Rise Program Advisors at no charge to get your questions answered, inquire about financial aid, or register to attend a Start-Up program.

As a non-profit, charitable organization giving financial assistance to families seeking to come to the ATCA to learn to use the principles on this book, we welcome and deeply appreciate donations, which are one hundred percent tax deductible for US taxpayers.

This is how to reach us:

Autism Treatment Center of America
2080 South Undermountain Road
Sheffield, MA 01257
www.autismtreatment.org
sonrise@autismtreatment.org
1-800-714-2779
1-413-229-2100

EMPIRICAL RESEARCH SUPPORTING
THE SON-RISE PROGRAM

This appendix is all about the science. I've included it for two reasons: so the very scientific-minded parents and professionals among you can see exactly how the existing literature and research support the principles of The Son-Rise Program; and so you can provide this information to skeptical professionals, schools, etc., whom you are endeavoring to get on board with the ideas in this book and with funding your Son-Rise Program.

First, here is a link to a study in the *Journal of Communication Disorders* demonstrating the effectiveness and efficacy of The Son-Rise Program. This journal is published by Elsevier, one of the world's leading providers of science and health information, serving more than 30 million scientists, students, and health professionals worldwide. The peer-reviewed study ("Promoting Child-Initiated Social-Communication in Children with Autism: Son-Rise Program Intervention Effects"), conducted by Northwestern University in the U.S. and Lancaster University in the UK, showed significant improvements in the social skills and engagement of children who received The Son-Rise Program treatment compared to a control group of children who did not. Especially remarkable is that, even though this study was conducted over a five-day period, the children receiving The Son-Rise Program showed quantifiable results. So if someone asks you whether The Son-Rise Program is an evidence-based program supported by scientific, peer-reviewed research, you can answer with an emphatic, "Yes" and cite the study below!

http://www.sciencedirect.com/science/article/pii/S0021992413000518

Second, the following academic paper compiles an array of published studies that support the principles and techniques of The Son-Rise Program detailed in this book. As an academic, research-oriented paper, it makes for very dense technical reading—*much* less easy to read and to digest than the book itself. I hope that this paper is both informative and extremely useful to you! (You can download copies of it at www.autism breakthrough.com/appendix1.)

* * *

Since autism was first outlined (Kanner, 1943), an agreed-upon defini-tion of autism has been reached and standardized diagnostic methods produced. To date, however, no clear etiology has been established, and proposed treatments vary widely. Research has uncovered enough about autism's underlying neuro and cognitive psychology to allow us to out-line treatment implications to benefit those families seeking help now who are unwilling to wait for the elusive ultimate answer.

The Autism Treatment Center of America has been using The Son-Rise Program (SRP) with families since 1983 in order to fulfill this need. The SRP was developed by parents experimenting with ways to reach their severely autistic child (Kaufman, 1976). Science at this time offered no guidance on facilitating the social development of children with au-tism. Since their son emerged from autism after three and a half years of intensive work, the Kaufmans have offered SRP to families internation-ally. To date, no rigorous longitudinal testing of the efficacy of SRP has been performed yet it can be seen that the key principles of this ap-proach draw support from the current research literature. This paper will discuss some key principles of SRP in the context of current re-search in autism to create a platform for quantitative investigation.

PRINCIPLE: CREATE AN OPTIMAL PHYSICAL LEARNING ENVIRONMENT

Hyperarousal to sensory input among those with autism (Belmonte and Yurgelan-Todd, 2003; Hirstein et al., 2001; Tordjman et al., 1997) ac-companied by an impairment to choose between competing stimuli is widely observed. EEG studies involving tasks requiring people with au-tism to selectively attend to relevant stimuli and ignore irrelevant stim-uli have shown either an abnormal heightened P1 evoked potential to the relevant stimuli or an abnormally generalized response to irrelevant stimuli (Townsend and Courchesne, 1994).

Additionally, the N2 to novel stimuli is heightened in children with autism, even when these stimuli are irrelevant to the task (Kemner et al., 1994). Similar results have been seen using auditory stimuli (Kemner et al., 1995). This supports behavioral observations that children with autism can either be overly focused on one aspect of a task or greatly distracted by stimuli irrelevant or peripheral to the task. During tasks requiring shifts of attention between hemifields, those with autism have been shown to exhibit both hemispheres activating indiscriminately instead of the usual hemispheric-specific patterns of activation (Belmonte, 2000).

Physiological measures suggest that perceptual filtering in autism occurs in an all-or-nothing manner with little specificity in selecting the location of the stimulus, for the behavioral-relevance of the stimulus or even the sensory modality in which the stimulus occurs (Belmonte, 2000). It has been suggested that this tendency for hyperarousal to sensory input must result from some pervasive underlying abnormality in neural processing rather than one specific brain locus (Belmonte et al., 2004; Johnson et al., 2002; Akshoomoff et al., 2002). Some authors suggest this neuronal dysfunction to be low signal-to-noise ratio developing from abnormal neural connectivity (Bauman and Kemper, 1994; Raymond et al., 1996; Casanova and Buxhoeveden, 2002; Belmonte et al., 2004).

The result of this type of processing is that all stimuli are given equal priority by the autistic brain causing an overwhelming flood of sensory information to be handled. The typical brain is able to identify and ignore irrelevant stimuli and focus valuable attention on that which is task-relevant creating a much more efficient processing system. The autistic brain, on the other hand, takes it all in and then must actively discard irrelevant information at a later processing stage causing, in effect, a processing bottleneck (Belmonte, 2004). Functional neuroimaging studies show that the brains of those with autism tend to show increased activation in areas that rely on primary sensory processing and decreased activity in areas typically supporting higher-order processing (Ring et al., 1999; Critchley et al., 2000; Schultz et al., 2000; Pierce et al., 2001; Baron-Cohen et al., 1999; Castelii et al., 2002).

It has been proposed that this low-level processing disruption underlies the higher-level abnormalities exhibited in autism (Belmonte, 2004) and that the widely observed symptomology of autism (including issues of Theory of Mind and executive function) is an emergent property of abnormal neural growth (Akshoomoff, 2002). There is molecular evidence that this abnormality is present at birth (Nelson et al., 2001) even though obvious behavioral symptoms often do not typically arise until 18–24 months. A child born reliant on this over-aroused, underselective sensory processing is open to a flood of stimuli that is thought to overload the newly emerging higher-order cognitive processes (Belmonte and Yurgelun-Todd, 2003). When faced with this processing constraint, the developing and plastic brain is forced to re-organize to accommodate that constraint (Johnson et al., 2002). This is manifested in the abnormal organization of the autistic brain as described above and the cognitive style characteristic of autism that relies heavily on lower-order, local feature processing at the expense of higher-order, global information processing known as weak central coherence (Happe, 1999; Frith and Happe, 1994).

Central coherence describes the ability to process incoming information in context, pulling information together for higher-level meaning, often at the expense of memory for detail (Happe, 1999). Weak central coherence then is the tendency of those with autism to rely on local feature processing (the details) rather than taking in the global nature of the situation. Kanner (1943) saw, as a universal feature of autism, the "inability to experience wholes without full attention to the constituent parts." It is this cognitive style that makes people with autism superior at resisting visual illusions (Happe, 1999), have a higher occurrence of absolute pitch (Heaton et al., 1998), excel at the Embedded Figures Task (Shah and Frith, 1983; Jolliffe and Baron-Cohen, 1997) and possess the ability to copy "impossible" figures (Mottron et al., 2000).

These neurophysiological and neuroanatomical studies paint a picture of the world occupied by those with autism as chaotic, overwhelming and filled with "noise." Coupled with this is an internal environment of hyperarousal (Hirstein, 2001; Cohen and Johnson, 1977; Hutt and Hutt, 1979; Hutt et al., 1965; Kootz and Cohen, 1981; Kootz et al., 1982). This is corroborated by autobiographical reports from some people with autism (Bluestone, 2002; Williams, 1994; Gillingham, 1995; Jones et al., 2003). Considering this fragmented, chaotic and overwhelming world implies then that a child's external environment is a key and primary factor to be considered when designing a treatment program for children with autism. Physical environments with higher amounts of sensory stimulation (e.g bright visual displays, background noise, etc.) will add to the "noise" in an already overloaded sensory system, making any new learning extremely challenging. While there is acknowledgment that children with special needs do require specifically designed environments (Carbone, 2001; Reiber and McLaughlin, 2004; Schilling and Schwartz, 2004), the extent to which rooms can be tailored to meet the needs of these children is highly constrained by a typical classroom setting, mainly due to the presence of other children and the subsequent size of the room—even something as ubiquitous as fluorescent lighting has been shown to affect the behavior of children with autism (Colman et al., 1976). These environmental considerations are often overlooked and their importance underestimated.

The SRP bypasses the constraint of the classroom by employing a room (usually in the child's home) that is specifically designed to lower sensory stimulation. Only neutral colors are used and distracting patterns or highly contrasting colors are avoided. There are no distracting visual displays or noises and only incandescent or natural lighting is employed. All toys and objects are kept off the floor on wall-mounted shelves to provide a distraction-free floor area for play. Most importantly, play sessions in the playroom usually include one adult and one child. This means that the child does not have to try and filter out the noise and movement of other children but deals only with a predictable adult whom s/he trusts. The SRP holds that these simple measures aid in soothing the autistic child's over-active nervous system by making the world digestible and manageable. There is evidence for a sub-set of children with autism who do not exhibit an overactive autonomic system but instead display unusually low levels of arousal (Hirstein et al., 2001). These are the children who tend to engage in "extreme" activities (e.g., climbing very high, constantly moving, etc.) in order to "kick-start" their arousal levels. The SRP playroom provides a safe and contained environment in which to do these activities, many of which are not feasible in a typical classroom.

It can be seen that this treatment principle of SRP is supported by the current neuroanatomical and physiological data. Direct investigation of the effects on children with autism of the SRP playroom in contrast with traditional classrooms has not yet been undertaken. Children in home-based Son-Rise Programs often instigate going into the playroom, will play in there even when they are alone and talk about how much they enjoy their special room. There is much anecdotal evidence supporting this claim but to date, no study has looked at either qualitative measures of children's perceptions of their playrooms or quantitative physiological measures of nervous system activity of children with autism in these environments.

PRINCIPLE: CREATE AN OPTIMAL SOCIAL LEARNING ENVIRONMENT

This weak central coherence processing style may then impede the development of joint attention and shared affect in children with autism (Klin et al., 1992; Rogers and Pennington, 1991). These are two fundamental components of social interaction in which accurate response to stimuli depends crucially on social context. This explains why social situations are incredibly challenging for those with autism and why even high-functioning adults who score well on explicit measures of social reasoning fail to translate this to their everyday social interactions (Klin et al., 2000).

A precursor to joint attention and shared affect is social orienting—
that a child will spontaneously, or upon request, direct attention to another person. Children with autism show social orienting impairments
early in life by preferentially orienting to nonsocial over social stimuli.
Osterling et al. (2002) found 1-year-olds, who were later diagnosed with
ASD, looked at people and oriented to their own name less frequently
than children without a subsequent diagnosis. Lack of interest in faces at
6 months (Maestro et al., 2002) and lack of orientation to the human
voice at 24 months (Lord, 1995) have both been shown to be robust pre-
dictors of later ASD diagnosis. Dawson et al. (2004) found that autistic
children tended not to respond to a variety of stimuli more often than
typical or developmentally delayed children, but that the effect was more
severe in response to social stimuli. Numerous studies have shown deficits in basic visual processing of faces in autism that were not paralleled
by failures in developmentally equivalent nonsocial processing tasks
(Langdell, 1978; Hobson et al.; 1988; Klin et al., 1999; Boucher and Lewis,
1992; Weeks and Hobson, 1987). Children with autism have been similarly shown not to respond as typical children do to the human voice
(Klin, 1991, 1992; Osterling and Dawson, 1994; Werner et al., 2000).

When children and adults do orient to social stimuli they have been
seen to process the information differently than their typically developing counterparts. Typically developing children show a differentiated
brain event-related potential when viewing familiar and unfamiliar
faces; children with autism do not show this effect (Dawson et al., 1994).
Klin et al. (2003) found that autistic adults viewing a naturalistic social
scene focus twice as much on the mouth region of faces than controls
and 2.5 times less frequently on the eye regions than controls. Preferential looking at eyes rather than mouths has been shown in typically developing infants as young as three months (Haith et al., 1979). Typical
children will show large skin conductance responses when looking at a
person who looks back and much lower responses when looking at neutral objects. Children with autism have been found to show no difference in skin conductance response whether they are looking at a person
or looking at a cup (Hirstein et al., 2001).

These basic processing differences then translate into higher order
reasoning and attribution-making tasks. When viewing an animation
of geometric shapes acting like humans, typical viewers recognize the
social nature of these interactions and provide narratives describing relationships portrayed by the shapes and attributions of mental states.
Viewers with autism tended to use physical explanations of the movement of the shapes (e.g., "because it's heavy") even though these individuals had all earlier passed explicit social reasoning tasks (Heider and
Simmel, 1994).

It is not clear why children with autism avoid social stimuli. It may be due to a general impairment in attentional functioning (Bryson et al., 1994). Others believe that the rapid shifting in attention required to process social stimuli is to blame (Courchesne et al., 1995). An additional suggestion holds that children with autism avoid social stimuli because they are complex, variable and unpredictable and are thus difficult to process (Dawson, 1991; Dawson and Lewy, 1989; Gergely and Watson, 1999).

The autistic bias towards nonsocial stimuli is well documented in psychology and serves as illustration for the autobiographical descriptions offered by writers with autism (Williams, 1994; Grandin, 1986). This body of evidence shows how children with autism selectively attend to nonsocial aspects of their environment—seemingly to take care of their over-active perceptual systems—and in so doing, deprive themselves of learning about the social world from an early age. Klin points out that "to impose social meaning on an array of visual stimuli is an adaptive reaction displayed by typical children, from infancy onwards, at an ever increasing level of complexity. This spontaneous skill is cultivated in countless hours of recurrent social engagement." (Klin et al., 2003, p. 356). It is widely accepted that typically developing children develop through reciprocal social interactions that involve the child's active participation (Stern, 1977; Bronfenbrenner, 1979; Piaget, 1963; Vygotsky, 1978; Bandura, 1986; Brunner, 1977; Wertsch, 1985). These theories view developmental learning to be dependent upon children's *voluntary involvement in social interaction*, not upon the specific activity or information to which children are exposed (Kim and Mahoney, 2004). It is becoming more widely recognized that this principle holds true for children with autism (Greenspan and Wieder, 1998; MacDonald, 2004; Williams, 1988; Koegel et al., 2001) as theorists and therapists begin to develop treatment approaches that recognize the importance of voluntary social orienting and joint attention in the way SRP does.

It seems that due to their perceptual processing challenges, children with autism are selectively avoiding this social education which negates the learning of "pivotal developmental behaviors" (i.e., attention, persistence, interest, initiation, cooperation, joint attention and affect) (Koegel, Koegel, and Carter, 1999). This lack of development subsequently impacts all further learning. The development of the joint attention skill is considered essential to language, cognitive and social development in all children (Tomasello, 1995). The more time a child spends engaged with a significant adult, the more that child will learn. Children with autism who demonstrate greater skill with joint attention have been seen to reach greater levels of language development (Mundy et al., 1990; Sigman and Ruskin, 1997; Dawson et al., 2004). Individual differences in social orienting also predict the degree to which children with autism process nonverbal affective information (Dissanayake et al., 1996) crucial to comprehending any social situation. A 25-year follow-up of a group of 91 individuals originally showing serious social or mental challenges showed that the best predictor of outcome was social impairment—those who were socially impaired, particularly those in the aloof category, showed a poorer outcome (Beadle-Brown, Murphy, and Wing, 2005).

The implications for treatment are clear—to provide an environment that consistently and intensively favors social information and endeavors to increase the salience of the social world for children with autism. Theoretically, the SRP fulfills the treatment implications drawn from this body of work. The SRP suggests that through hours of immersion in this type of social environment, children with autism (a) increase their frequency of spontaneous social orienting, (b) maintain joint attention for longer and longer durations, and (c) intentionally initiate social interactions more frequently. Rigorous, empirical testing must be performed to substantiate these anecdotal observations.

This treatment implication then raises the question of *how* to provide an environment that consistently and intensively favors social information and endeavors to increase the salience of the social world for children with autism. The SRP proposes a unique method, some key principles of which will be outlined below in the context of current research.

A CHILD-CENTERED APPROACH MAKES SOCIAL INTERACTION MOTIVATING

Facilitators and parents employing the SRP make social interaction their primary focus when working one-on-one with a child with autism, recognizing that social avoidance is the crux of the autistic challenge. There are two ways in which a child-centered approach makes social interaction motivating.

Follow the Child: Start with the Child's Motivation

The SRP works with objects and activities for which the child is internally motivated. This play-based approach starts with the child's area of motivation (e.g., jumping on a trampoline). The adult joins in with this area of play until the child spontaneously socially orients to the adult (e.g., makes eye contact, physical contact or a vocalization attempt). This spontaneous expression of social interest from the child is then responded to by the adult in a manner designed to be motivating to the child (based on the individual child's interests and previous response patterns), for example, jumping on the trampoline while pretending to be a monkey. Any subsequent responses by the adult to the child's expressions of interest are similarly fine-tuned to be motivating to the child. Thus ensues a cycle of reciprocal social exchange within the area of the child's motivation. The SRP proposes that this approach raises the salience level of social interaction by tying the child's internal motivations to social interaction.

Autistic children can become very focused on their particular areas of motivation, often to the point of being termed "obsessional" or "perseverative." Many traditional approaches have tried to steer children away from their areas of motivation in an attempt to broaden the child's range of interest. The SRP instead recognizes these interests as doorways into that child's world, a means of forming a connection to become the foundation for more spontaneous and flexible social exchange. Support for this perspective comes from Koegel, Dyer, and Bell (1987) who found a negative correlation between social avoidance and child-preferred activities in autistic children. That is, when prompted to engage in activities the children had already demonstrated an interest in, children were much less socially avoidant than when prompted to engage in activities chosen by the adult.

Baker, Koegel, and Koegel (1998) further underlined the effectiveness of the child-centered approach with autistic children in a group setting. They took the obsessional interests of a group of children with autism (e.g., U.S. geography) and made them into common games that could be played by the autistic child and his/her peer group (e.g., tag game on a giant map of the U.S.). From very low levels of social interaction in the baseline condition, the percentage of social interactions increased dramatically during the intervention period and continued to be high at a 2-month follow-up. These increases in social play interactions continued even in the absence of the adult who had done the initial prompting. Furthermore, the autistic children began to engage more in other nonobsession-themed games after the intervention. Baker et al. (1989) conclude that "the obsessional themes of children with autism, which are typically viewed as problematic, can be transformed successfully into common games to increase positive social play interactions" (p. 306–307).

The parents of the autistic children involved in this study reported either no increase, or a decrease, in the child's engagement in the target obsessional theme at home, after the initiation of the obsessional themed games. This finding is consistent with Charlop et al. (1990) who used obsessional themes as reinforcers for children to complete other tasks and found no increase in the children's use of these particular obsessional themes. The SRP similarly maintains that using a child's obsessional theme or topics of perseveration as a platform for social interaction does not encourage further perseveration but instead helps transform perseverative, rigid play or conversation into socially appropriate, flexible, reciprocal interaction, because it makes social interaction more motivating than previously. Again, direct empirical observation is required to assess these observations.

Give Control: Be Responsive and Sensitive to the Child

The second crucial factor in facilitating the emergence of a genuine and spontaneous interest in the social world is giving control or employing a responsive style of interaction (Beckwith and Cohen, 1992). The SRP is child-centered. This means (a) the topic of play is derived from the child's individual interests, and (b) the child actively chooses when to begin and end that interaction. This is critical and the juncture at which traditional approaches to special education tend to differ. Trivette (2003) defined this responsive style of interaction as involving two important components. First, the adult responds only to the child's production of a behavior. This means that the adult responds only after the child makes a physical gesture (e.g., waves, smiles, touches), a vocal sound (e.g., a coo, a word) or an action (e.g., throws a ball, picks up toy). Second, the adult's response to this action is sensitive, that is, appropriate in its level of intensity. A sensitive response is one in which the intensity level matches the child's developmental level and mood. For example, if the child is crying, the adult may offer a soothing song; if the child is excited and laughing, the adult might offer a swing in the air (Trivette, 2003).

In a meta-analysis of 13 studies looking at the effects of this style of interaction, Trivette (2003) concluded "that a responsive caregiver style of interaction positively influences the cognitive development of children with, or at risk for, developmental disabilities" and also "has a positive influence on the social-emotional development of these children" (Trivette, 2003, p. 5). All 13 studies meeting inclusion criteria for this meta-analysis (1,336 children in total) showed the same result—that adult responsiveness substantially helped these children's cognitive and social-emotional development.

Subsequent research has continued to support this finding (Mahoney and Perales, 2003; Mahoney and Perales, 2005) and found that responsive interactive style also has positive outcomes on language development (MacDonald, 1989; Manolson et al., 1995). In a long-term study, Siller and Sigman (2002) found that the more mothers of children with autism engaged in responsive interaction with their children, the higher the levels of communication functioning their children attained at 1, 10, and 12 years of age. Mahoney et al. (1998) reported that in a large scale, multi-site early intervention research project (Infant Health and Development Program, 1990), maternal responsiveness accounted for six times more of the variance in the developmental functioning of low birth-weight children than did the children's participation in an intensive (25 hour per week) high-quality school program. Investigating responsive teaching is especially important in the light of findings that mothers of developmentally delayed children tend to be more directive (not responsive) when interacting with their children (Spiker et al., 2002).

Lewis and Goldberg (1969) suggest that this responsive style of interaction has such a positive effect on children's development because it facilitates the child's feelings of control and self-efficacy. This contributes to the child's sense of competence and so increases the likelihood of the child engaging in subsequent interactions and learning situations. Mahoney and Perales (2003) propose that a responsive style of interaction enhances social behaviors that may be the same as the pivotal response behaviors seen to enhance the efficacy of discrete trial training interventions (Koegel et al., 1999). Pivotal behaviors "are the processes children employ to learn and practice new behaviors during spontaneous interactions. Following this line of reasoning, it seems possible that as parents engage in higher levels of responsive interaction with their children, they are actually encouraging children to learn and use pivotal developmental behaviors, which are the processes enabling them to acquire untrained socioemotional competencies" (Mahoney and Percales, 2003, p. 84). This would explain why studies using interventions focusing on these pivotal developmental behaviors show children learning skills that they then generalize to other learning situations (Koegel, Koegel, and Carter, 1998; Kaiser, Carter, and Koegel, 2003).

The SRP employs, exclusively, a responsive style of interaction that they call "giving control." Under the SRP, each time a child makes spontaneous social contact, the adult responds in a "sensitive" manner as described above; additionally, when a child disengages from social contact, the adult responds by respectfully withdrawing and waiting for a social cue from the child before pursuing any further interactions. Each time this happens, the child learns that s/he has control over her/his social environment. Considerable research shows that children develop to the degree that they have control over their behavior and their effects on the environment (MacDonald, 2004). A child inhabiting the fragmented, unpredictable, chaotic perceptual world described above, who is also extremely challenged by communicating his/her wants, and whose autonomic system appears to be out of control, does not have a sense of being in control of the world or even of his/her body in the way a typically developing child does (Bluestone, 2004). Thus, the importance of providing a social environment maximizing the child's sense of control can be seen.

That children with autism do not have a sense of control in the world could explain why they seek out patterns—meaning, predictability and order in a chaotic world. Baron-Cohen (2004) found the content of rituals and topics of perseveration (of higher-functioning children and adults with autism and Asperger's Syndrome) is not random, but tends to cluster in the domain of systems (including technical, natural and abstract systems). These systems are underlain with rules and regularities more easily grasped by the autistic mind (Baron-Cohen, 2004). The social world is not an organized system regulated by fixed rules but rather a fluid, ever-changing bombardment of sensory input. If the autistic child is to feel comfortable in the social world, then the social world must be made as controllable as possible to encourage the autistic child to participate. This is exactly what is done by the SRP. So when a child in an SRP playroom disengages from the social interaction, the facilitator respects this and allows the child to disengage, does not keep pursuing the interaction as recommended in other relationship-based approaches (Greenspan and Wieder, 1998) and waits for the child to re-engage before continuing to build social interaction. When consistently immersed in a social environment of this nature, SRP proposes the child learns that he has control over the previously uncontrollable social world. This puts the child in the driver's seat and shows him that he can indeed effectively elicit a response from another when he chooses; this sense of control forms a foundation for reciprocal interaction (Dawson and Galpert, 1990). Koegel, Koegel, and McNerney (2001) review data suggesting that "when children with autism are motivated to initiate complex social interactions, it may reverse a cycle of impairment, resulting in exceptionally favorable intervention outcomes" (p. 19).

A POSITIVE ATTITUDE FACILITATES DEEPER SOCIAL CONNECTION

According to the SRP, the next vital factor in facilitating the emergence of a genuine and spontaneous interest in the social world is the use of a positive attitude. A positive attitude is one of acceptance of the child, appreciation and enjoyment of the child and the animated expression of such. The SRP stands alone in its assertion of the critical importance of a positive attitude. There are two fundamental reasons for this emphasis.

Acceptance Promotes Responsiveness

The SRP suggests that only an attitude of acceptance and appreciation of a child will allow parents to maintain consistently a responsive style of interaction. Acceptance is defined as nonjudgment, i.e., not labeling the child, or his/her condition, with any value-judgments (good/bad, right/wrong). The SRP does not view this type of acceptance as a passive resignation to the child's condition but instead as the first step to actively encouraging the child to develop. Professionals teaching the SRP consistently observe that when a parent lacks acceptance (as defined here), they instead label the child as "wrong" in some way ("needs fixing," "abnormal," "defective," etc.). The SRP holds that a parent with that perspective will find it very challenging to be responsive, that is, not to be directive, not to "teach" something to his/her child, even when the parent cognitively understands the importance of being responsive and giving the child control. The cognitive architecture behind a responsive style of interaction has yet to be addressed in the literature and points to another avenue of research crucial for training parents to run home-based interventions.

This importance of a positive attitude is empirically supported by the work of Gerald Mahoney and colleges using the Maternal Behavior Rating Scale (MBRS; Mahoney, 1992). The MBRS has been used in a variety of studies to assess the link between parents' interactional styles and the development of their children. It has 12 items assessing four dimensions of interactive style: responsiveness, affect, achievement orientation and directiveness. Use of the MBRS has been instrumental in highlighting the importance of caregiver responsiveness in children's development. These studies additionally show the "affect" dimension is similarly correlated with increases in various developmental performance outcomes.

In the MBRS, the affect dimension is composed of five measures: Acceptance, Enjoyment, Expressiveness, Inventiveness and Warmth. Mahoney and Perales (2005) found both responsiveness and affect to be significantly related to increases in children's levels of language development, social competence, joint attention and self-regulation. Kim and Mahoney (2004) again found maternal responsiveness and affect to be significantly correlated with the child's level of engagement, with maternal responsiveness accounting for 33 percent of the variance and affect accounting for 30 percent of the variance. This research still requires replication with larger and more diverse samples; nonetheless, the emerging direction of this new field of research is in line with the observations of the SRP—a positive attitude goes hand in hand with responsiveness in facilitating development in children with developmental disabilities.

Appreciation Encourages Engagement.

The other key component of a positive attitude in the SRP is a genuine appreciation and enjoyment of the child; this builds on the foundation of acceptance. The SRP advocates the use of animated expressions of appreciation, enjoyment and delight in the child. The SRP proposes that this will encourage a greater frequency of social orientation, extend periods of joint attention and increase child affect and motivation level within a social interaction. This, it is suggested, leads to more and longer periods of social interaction that result in the child learning more new behaviors and skills.

Typically developing children who naturally orient to social stimuli and engage in joint attention with adults experience the displays of positive affect that typically accompany these periods of joint attention (Kasari et al., 1990). Shared affective experience serves to motivate the typically developing child to attend to and engage in joint attention with adults (Dawson et al., 2004; Trevarthan and Aitken, 2001). These experiences then facilitate the child's development into a social "expert" as s/he attends to more and more initiations from adults and remains engaged in these interactions for longer and longer. Typical development revolves around mutual affective exchanges that both the child and adult find rewarding (Mundy et al., 1992). This process goes awry in children with autism for two reasons that interact to create a negative feedback loop. First, the child with autism engages in joint attention less frequently and for shorter periods than the typically developing child (Dawson et al., 2004), so has less opportunity to experience the positive affect associated with this social engagement. Dawson and Lewy (1989) suggest that this is because the affect-laden social interaction may be too over-stimulating for the autistic child due to the unpredictable and complex nature of these stimuli. Second, it appears that children with autism are less likely to display positive affect when engaged in joint attention (e.g., smile while making eye contact) (Kasari et al., 1999) and are much less likely to smile in response to their mother's smile than typical children (Dawson et al., 1990). The result is that mothers of autistic children are less likely to respond to their children's smiles than mothers of typical children (Dawson et al., 2004), probably because the children's smiles were not viewed as communicative as they were not accompanied by eye contact. Thus, from an early age, children with autism seem not to experience the delight and joy typical children are bathed in from birth that motivates them to keep moving towards deeper and deeper connections with other people. When this process is disrupted in otherwise typically developing children, for example when the mother suffers post-natal depression and does not engage as much in these affective exchanges, there can be serious effects for that child's development (Goldsmith and Rogoff, 1997).

The implication for treatment from this research again is clear: to redress this imbalance—to link joint attention to positive affect and motivate children to move towards more frequent and longer periods of joint attention in the way a typical child does. This is what the SRP claims to do. Whenever a child in an SRP playroom makes social contact (eye contact, language attempts or physical communication), he is greeted with a celebration: a visual and auditory display of positive affect and an expression of joy and delight from the adult to the child's initiation of joint attention. This is fine-tuned to the individual child's particular sensory requirement to maintain its function as a motivator and not allow it to become over-stimulating for the child.

The affect dimension of the MBRS (Mahoney, 1992) has five items, four of which—acceptance, enjoyment, expressiveness and warmth—involve directly, animatedly expressing positive affect and attitude to the child. It is this dimension (along with responsiveness) that has been closely linked to promoting child engagement and cognitive and language development. The fifth item on the MBRS affect dimension is inventiveness—the number of different approaches the adult uses, his/her ability to find different games and activities to interest the child, different ways of using toys and inventing games with and without toys. This is also an important part of the SRP. Once a child is engaged in a social interaction, the adult's intention is then to maintain that interaction for as long as the child will allow. Expressing positive affect is one way that those trained in the SRP maintain interactions; the second is through inventiveness or creativity. Decades of training people to use the SRP leads their trainers to assert that a positive attitude underlies the ability to be creative in the ways described on the MBRS. The logic is that when one is truly enjoying an interaction, one is more inclined to think of ways to add to the interaction to maintain it, whereas when one is not enjoying an interaction, one tends to be thinking of ways to end it. Again, the cognitive architecture underlying "inventiveness" warrants empirical investigation as an avenue for increasing the efficacy of professional and parental training.

The SRP suggests that the principles of taking a child-centered approach and having a positive attitude, when used in an optimally designed physical environment, have the effect of encouraging children with autism and other developmental delays to engage more in social interaction. This has the effect of helping these children be more motivated to initiate and engage in social interaction and grow stronger in pivotal developmental behaviors which pave the way for learning new skills and information. Longitudinal studies involving children actively engaged in home-based SRPs are needed to investigate these observations more fully.

The SRP asserts (as do other proponents of home-based programs; e.g., Lovaas, 1973) that this approach must be applied intensively and consistently over time for maximum efficacy. A 30-minute session twice a week will not retrain a brain that for years has skewed itself away from the social world. Children in the SRP typically spend from 15 to 50 hours a week in the playroom being responded to in this way. Facilitators and parents are trained to be exceptionally observant and attentive to the child to maximize the number of spontaneous social orienting events that are responded to in this way.

JOINING EXCLUSIVE AND REPETITIVE BEHAVIORS PROMOTES SOCIAL INTERACTION

This core principle of the SRP extends the principles of child-centeredness and responsiveness and takes them from a position radically different from that of any other treatment approach known by this author. A key behavioral symptom of autism, not yet addressed by this paper, is the engagement in stereotypical, repetitive movements or activities. Traditionally, the approach to these behaviors has been to attempt to eliminate them, the rationale behind this being the more "normal" the child looks, the more likely s/he is to be accepted by peers, and thus increase the likelihood of successful social experience. This perspective, however, seems to have negated attempts to understand the function of these behaviors, and this aspect of autism has received much less scientific scrutiny than any other (Turner, 1999). This perspective goes against the principle of acceptance and enjoyment of the child that has proved to be so fruitful.

The research that does exist in the domain of stereotypical and repetitive behaviors suggests that these repetitious behaviors are helpful to the child and are not, in fact, random byproducts of the disorder that serve no function (as has been suggested; e.g., Lewis et al., 1987). Repetition is a natural part of any child's development; Piaget (1952) noted that typically developing infants will repeat activities that affect the environment in ways that inspire their interest. Thelen (1979) found that typically developing infants show a variety of rhythmic and pronounced stereotypic behaviors, each with a characteristic age of onset, peak performance and decline. These behaviors appear to mark unmistakable phases in the stages of neuromuscular development. Children seem to move through these behaviors until they have gained a full sense of mastery over their muscles and, presumably, until they can predict the effects of their own movements on the environment. Militerni et al. (2002) looked at repetitive behaviors in two age groups of children with autism. They found that the younger children (age 2–4 years) exhibited motor and sensory repetitive behaviors while those in the higher age group (7–11 years) had more complex repetitive behaviors. Similarly, those children with estimated higher IQs also showed more complex repetitive behaviors. Militerni et al. (2002) suggest that these repetitive behaviors may be equivalent to the motor and cognitive behaviors seen in typical development.

Needless to say, in children with autism and related disorders, these behaviors are much more pronounced, more intense and engage more of the child's attention than in typically developing children. Hirstein et al. (2001) suggest that children with autism may employ repetitive behaviors in an attempt to control an autonomic system that fails to govern itself. Hirstein et al. (2001) measured skin conductance responses (SCR) in normal and autistic children in a variety of situations. They found that the SCRs of children with autism started rising at the beginning of the experiment and continued to rise, whereas the typically developing children's SCR returned to normal baseline level with the progression of the experiment. It appeared that the children with autism were not able to bring their SCR levels down once they had started to rise. Attempts at interaction with people exacerbated SCR levels. The researchers found, however, that the children with autism could bring down the SCR levels by plunging their hands into a container of dry beans. Similarly, sucking sweets, being wrapped in a heavy blanket and receiving deep pressure helped the children with autism lower their SCR levels. They also discovered that a subset of children with autism was characterized by a flat level of SCR that was only increased by extreme behaviors (e.g., self-injury, climbing, etc.).

Hirstein et al. (2001) additionally found that interruption of these self-stimulatory and calming activities by other people "often produced extremely large responses with agitated behavior following immediately"

(p. 1885). They go on to suggest that "the resistance to change one sees in autistic children may be caused by or exacerbated by bursts of sympathetic activity, which the child actively tries to avoid or dampen down" (Hirstein et al., 2001, p.1886). Hirstein et al. (2001) suggest that the autonomic nervous system of the autistic child is on constant alert; every incoming stimulus is tagged as relevant and so the child acts to shut the system down (conversely in the subset of children with low autonomic activity, it seems that nothing is tagged as relevant and extreme behaviors are engaged in to produce a sense of relevance). This is consistent with the research on perceptual filtering challenges in those with autism cited above. It has been suggested that the amygdala-limbic system may be involved, as this system typically is responsible for attaching a sense of value to incoming perceptual stimuli and is found to be abnormal in those with autism (Schultz, 2005; Critchley et al., 2000; Pelphrey et al., 2004; Akshoomoff et al., 2002; Baron-Cohen et al., 2000).

This work indicates that the repetitive, self-stimulatory behaviors of children with autism are not random or functionless but actually help the child to regulate his own autonomic system in a quest for homeostasis (Nijhof et al., 1998). Autobiographical reports from adults with autism again support the idea that repetitive behaviors serve to calm and soothe (Bluestone, 2004). Judith Bluestone likens these activities to meditation—turning off parts of the mind or body by intensely focusing on one thing—and points out that meditation has been accepted by the Western medical establishment for over 30 years as one of the best ways to reduce stress and increase mental organization (Bluestone, 2004). Willemsen-Swinkels et al. (1998) found that autistic children who were negatively excited showed a slower heart rate after they began engaging in a repetitive activity. Hirstein et al. (2001) predict that if children are prevented from engaging in these calming activities, one would expect to see signs of chronically high sympathetic activity. The biochemical consequences of this are elevated levels of cortisol and adrenaline. These hormones interfere with the ability to concentrate, learn and remember and increase vulnerability to viruses, over-reactivity to medications, and heightened sensitivities to certain foods or food additives (Bluestone, 2004), all of which are commonly observed in children with autism.

From a treatment standpoint, this research points to the need for a new perspective on repetitive behaviors. Rather than seeing these behaviors as something holding the child back from social acceptance and thus to be eliminated, this new perspective sees repetitive behaviors as useful to the child—something to be worked with rather than fought against. The SRP sees repetitive behaviors as functional and an avenue for building rapport which will form the basis of more expansive social interaction. Rather than trying to eliminate repetitive behaviors from the autistic child's repertoire to make the child more socially acceptable, the SRP facilitator starts with acceptance of the child—a deep, genuine appreciation for that child and holding the perspective that all his/her behaviors are attempts to take care of him-/herself. This attitude allows the SRP facilitator to a) not attempt to stop the child when he is engaging in repetitive, self-stimulatory behaviors, but wait for the child to spontaneously engage in social interaction and b) physically demonstrate this acceptance by joining in with the repetitive activity. This, the SRP suggests, is a more powerful way of communicating to the child that s/he is accepted and appreciated than a solely verbal communication and of demonstrating to the child that s/he has control over the interaction. This is a radical departure from more traditional approaches to autism, but is one that has been shown to be effective in helping children with autism to engage in social interaction more and, seemingly paradoxically, to spend less and less time engaging in repetitive, self-stimulatory behaviors.

Numerous studies have found that imitative play facilitates social responsiveness in children with autism; that is, joining in with their self-stimulatory, repetitious behaviors encourages children to engage more in social interaction. Dawson and Adams (1984) found that autistic children who had a low level of imitative ability were more socially responsive, showed more eye contact and played with toys in a less perseverative manner when the experimenter imitated the child instead of modeling other either familiar or unfamiliar actions. A similar study found that children with autism would look at the experimenter more frequently and for longer periods when the experimenter imitated the child's play (Tiegerman and Primavera, 1984). Dawson and Galpert (1990) took this line of investigation even further. They asked mothers to imitate their child's play for 20 minutes each day for two weeks. At the pre-intervention assessment, they found, as predicted by the earlier research, that autistic children's gaze at their mother's face was longer, and their toy play more creative, during imitative play sessions as compared to free play sessions. After only two weeks of this intervention (20 minutes a day), the post-intervention assessment found significant cumulative increases in duration of gaze at the mother's face and of creative toy play. Parents of children using the SRP are instructed to engage in imitative play ("joining") whenever their child is playing in an exclusive or repetitive way.

Another study experimenting with imitating autistic children split children into two groups; those of one group spent time with an adult who imitated their play, while members of the other group spent time with an adult who simply tried to play with the child on three separate occasions. In the second session, children in the imitation group spent a greater proportion of time than the other children showing distal social behaviors towards the adult—looking, vocalizing, smiling and engaging in reciprocal play. In the third session, children in the imitation group spent a greater proportion of time than the other children showing proximal social behaviors towards the adult—being close to the adult, sitting next to the adult and touching the adult (Field et al., 2001).

These results, that imitative play increases social responsiveness and joint attention, should not be surprising to those who study the development of typical infants and children. Parents of typically developing infants commonly imitate their infants' expressions, often in an exaggerated way (Malatesta and Izard, 1984; Papousek and Papousek, 1977; Trevarthen and Aitken, 2001). In fact, infants of 3 and 5 months old have been seen to prefer interaction with people who have been responsive to them in the past and avoid interaction with those who were unresponsive or whose responses were not congruent with the infant (Bigelow and Birch, 1999). This imitation forms the basis of communication and further growth by promoting a sense of shared mutuality, an experience of congruence by both partners that is mutually motivating (Nadel et al., 1999; Uzgiris, 1981; Panksepp et al., 1994). This normal interplay of nonverbal imitation between mother and infant is widely documented to be essential to promoting the child's neurological, cognitive, social and emotional growth (see Trevarthen and Aitken, 2001). Studies with typically developing (Rollins and Snow, 1998) and autistic children (Mundy et al., 1990; Rollins, 1999) suggest that emotional engagement and joint attention are more critical to language development than is instrumental use of language. Emotional engagement and joint attention are increased by imitative play. Trevarthen and Aitken state, "Imitative responses are found to be attractive to autistic children and can act as a bridge to collaborative play or communication, and improve the child's access to language (Dawson and Galpert,1990; Nadel, 1992; Nadel and Peze, 1993; Tiegerman and Primavera, 1982, 1984)" (Trevarthen and Aitken, 2001, p. 32). Siegel (2001) states simply that "Children need such joining experiences because they provide the emotional nourishment that developing minds require" (p. 78).

Studies with typical adults indicate that this intuitive use of imitation continues into adulthood, maintaining its function of building rapport between two people. Chartrand and Bargh (1999) found that participants mimicked, nonverbally, by a confederate in a variety of situations reported liking that confederate more than confederates who did not mimic them. Those who were mimicked also described the interaction as more smooth and harmonious. Similarly, Bernieri (1988) found a strong relationship between reported rapport and degree of reported movement synchrony. When looking at nonconscious mimicry, Larkin and Chartrand (2003) found that in situations where participants had either a conscious or nonconscious desire to affiliate with their experimental partner, they were more likely to nonverbally mimic that person than when they had no desire to affiliate with that person. It seems that mimicry can build rapport between adults. It has been suggested that this behavior evolved from initially having survival value (learning new skills) into a form of social glue that holds relationships together and allows access to a particular group (Larkin et al., 2003).

Imitation helps build rapport between typical adults, typical infants or children and their caregivers and between adults and autistic children. Dawson and Galpert (1990) postulate that imitative play works so well for autistic children because it puts the child in control (one of the fundamental principles of the SRP). This gives the child a predictable and salient response to his actions. "This strategy maximizes the possibility that the child will learn to expect and effectively elicit a response from another person, in this way providing a foundation for reciprocal social interaction" (Dawson and Galpert, 1990, p. 152). Additionally, imitative play is sensitive to the child's optimal range of sensory stimulation; the child can adjust the amount of sensory stimulation by adjusting his or her own actions creating an easy, controllable and predictable form of social interaction that is more digestible for the autistic child. Field (1977, 1979; cited in Dawson and Galpert, 1990) studied the effects of maternal imitation with pre-term infants who showed high levels of gaze aversion, negative affect and elevated tonic heart rates. When mothers imitated their infants' behavior, the infants became more attentive than when mothers spontaneously interacted with their infants. Decreases in tonic heart rate were recorded during imitative play. Applying this research to the autistic population by examining physiological measures during imitative play has yet to be done.

Dawson and Galpert (1990) conclude that "imitative play may be used to provide a foundation for establishing social interest and interactive play. This foundation can then be built upon by using other, more sophisticated, interactive strategies and games" (p. 161). This is exactly how imitative play, or "joining," is used by the SRP. Children are "joined" or imitated while they are playing in a self-stimulatory and exclusive way because the SRP recognizes the curative, calming and organizing nature of this self-stimulatory play. Through joining the child rapport is created and a social bridge is built. A relationship of trust is formed as the child learns that s/he is in control of the interaction and can initiate and end it at will, without the need for language. It follows then that children will start to initiate social contact more and more when immersed in this environment. This will open up increasing opportunities to build on this connection in a manner motivating to that child (as described above) and thus increase the frequency and duration of joint attention that leads to the child's neurological, cognitive, social and emotional development. Observational analysis of parents and SRP facilitators working with autistic children is required to fully understand the subtle variables involved in this type of interaction.

The technique of joining builds on the principle of being responsive. In Trivette's (2003) definition of the responsive style of interaction, an appropriate response is one that matches the child's developmental level and mood. The SRP adds a further requirement—that the adult's response be sensitive to the child's level of exclusivity, exclusivity indicating the child's *level of motivation for social interaction*. The SRP maintains that all children, regardless of diagnosis, have the capacity to move along an exclusive-interactive continuum. At the exclusive end of this continuum the child is not motivated for social interaction, and is absorbed in his own world; this state is usually accompanied by repetitive behaviors and activities or perseveration on repetitive topics. At the interactive end of the continuum, the child is motivated for interaction with another person and shows interest by maintaining joint attention, displaying positive affect and participating in an interactive and fluid activity or conversation. Observing the child's level of motivation for interaction, or degree of exclusivity, is the first vital step in the SRP to responding in a manner that will facilitate (a) the maximum amount of responsiveness from the child and (b) the maximal degree of new learning.

When the child is exclusive (not motivated for social interaction), the SRP holds that the most effective response is to join with the child's behavior. This type of response allows the child to use their repetitive activity to gain control of their autonomic system and facilitates more spontaneous social orienting from the child. As the child's level of motivation for social interaction increases, s/he will start to spontaneously orient to the adult more (e.g., by making eye contact, attempting verbal or nonverbal communications or making physical contact). The SRP-trained facilitator will begin to respond to these behaviors in the manner described by Trivette (2003)—by offering an activity they believe the child will find enjoyable. As the child's level of motivation for social interaction increases, the frequency and duration of the child's spontaneous social orientations will increase, as will their displayed positive affect. Once the child has reached a level of motivation for social interaction characterized by frequent or sustained eye contact, positive affect and nonverbal or verbal attempts to re-initiate the activity, the SRP-trained facilitator will move into a style of interaction that combines responding to the child to maintain the level of motivation, and requesting the child to participate in new ways (e.g., use more or clearer language, use more eye contact, be more flexible, use academic or friendship skills, etc.). The Son-Rise Program Social Developmental Model (Hogan and Hogan, 2004) provides guidelines indicating which skill to focus on depending on the child's developmental level. Once the child is motivated for social interaction and for the particular activity on offer, s/he will make attempts at the new skill in order to maintain the interaction. When the child's level of motivation changes, the facilitator will be responsive to this, observe where the child is on the exclusivity-interactive continuum, and respond accordingly.

It is through this subtle dance between maintaining a responsive interactive style, giving control, and excitedly requesting new skill use that the SRP claims to be able to facilitate extraordinary development in children with severe developmental disorders, as documented in the case studies by the founders (Kaufman, 1981, 1994). To the knowledge of this author, there is no research to date investigating the efficacy of changing one's responsive style based on the child's level of motivation for social interaction or an empirical investigation of the concept of an interactive-exclusive continuum. This is a gap in the literature that demands attention and could create a deeper understanding of children with autism and the most effective way to facilitate social interaction with this population.

CONCLUSION

A wealth of research spanning half a century has painted a clearer picture of the disorder first outlined by Kanner in 1943. This has helped us gain a deeper understanding of the physiology, neurology and cognitive psychology of those with autism and allows us to see some clear implications for treatment. The SRP developed over the past thirty years via a different route—from two parents' desire to reach their autistic child. Through their intensive experimentation, observation and deep longing to connect with their son, they developed a treatment approach that can now be seen to be supported by the more recent scientific literature. These two pathways—to essentially the same solution—have remained separate as the SRP has not been subjected to rigorous scientific study by independent researchers until very recently. The current work shows that the principles of SRP are solidly grounded in accepted theories of child development and supported by empirical study of the individual principles, although no study has yet addressed SRP in its entirety. The sheer number of families who have chosen to use SRP (over 8,000 to date) is testament to the fact that parents are looking for something other than what is offered by traditional approaches to autism. Approaches such as the SRP thus warrant more empirical investigation.

The SRP is parent-led; that is, parents are empowered to act as facilitators, trainers and managers of their home-based programs. In the eyes of the SRP, training parents to implement therapy with their children is more effective than relying on schools or specific professionals to implement therapies because, as discussed above, the intensity of the approach is essential. A parent trained in the SRP is able to implement the principles and techniques inside and outside the playroom, intensifying the child's immersion in a responsive, socially enhancing environment. Again, the literature supports the efficacy of home-based programs. One study assessing the relative efficacy of behavioral programs with autistic children compared residential, out-patient and home-based programs. They found that only the home-based group showed significant improvements on the behavioral observation measures (Sherman et al., 1987). Another study matched children receiving home-based behavioral treatments with those receiving conventional school-based and brief one-on-one interventions. Children receiving home-based treatments had significantly higher post-intervention IQs than their school-based counterparts; significant reductions in symptom severity were also found (Sheinkopf and Siegel, 1998).

More recent research has looked at changing the conventional discrete-trial format of traditional behaviorist approaches, to make them more adaptable to the home environment and thus more in line with the responsive nature of the SRP. Delprato (2001) reviewed eight studies looking at normalized behavioral language interventions, defined as consisting of loosely structured sessions of indirect teaching with everyday situations, child initiation, natural reinforcers and liberal criteria for reinforcer presentation. In all eight studies with children with autism, this method of language training was found to be significantly more effective than discrete-trial training. Kaiser and Hancock (2003) similarly found that teaching parents to implement naturalistic language intervention strategies at home can be highly effective. Furthermore, in the two studies in the Delprato (2001) review looking at parental affect, the normalized treatment yielded more positive affect than the discrete-trial training. In a study of families using The Son-Rise Program in their homes, Williams (2004) found that the families felt generally more positive since implementing the SRP and reported that interaction among the whole family had also improved.

The current literature supports an intervention for children with autism that emphasizes a specifically designed physical environment, with a focus on enhancing social relationships, having a positive attitude and joining a child's repetitive behaviors. The SRP focuses on precisely these principles.

REFERENCES

Akshoomoff, N., Pierce, K., and Courchesne, E. (2002). The neurobio-logical basis of autism from a developmental perspective. *Developmental Psychopathology,* 14, 613–634.

Alegria, J., and Noirot, E. (1978). Neonate orientation behavior towards human voice. *International Journal of Behavioral Development,* 1(4), 291–312.

American Psychiatric Association (1994). *Diagnostic and Statistical Manual of Mental Disorders (DSM-IV).* 4th ed. Washington, DC: APA.

Baker, M. J., Koegel, R. L., and Koegel, L. K. (1998). Increasing the social behavior of young children with autism using their obses-sive behaviors. *Journal of the Association of Peoples with Severe Handicaps,* 23(4), 300–308.

Bandura, A. (1986) *Social Foundations of Thought and Action.* Engle-wood Cliffs, NJ: Prentice Hall.

Baron-Cohen, S. (2004.) The cognitive neuroscience of autism. *Journal of Neurology, Neurosurgery and Psychiatry,* 75, 945–948.

Baron-Cohen, S., Ring, H. A., Bullmore, E. T., Wheelwright, S., Ashwin, C., and Williams, S. C. R. (2000) The amygdala theory of au-tism. *Neuroscience and Biobehavioral Reviews,* 24, 355–364.

Baron-Cohen, S., Ring, H. A., Wheelwright, S., Bullmore, E. T., Bram-mer, M. J., Simmons A. et al. (1999). Social intelligence in the normal and autistic brain: An fMRI study. *European Journal of Neuroscience,* 11(6), 1891–1898.

Bauman, M. L., and Kemper, T. L. (1994). Neuroanatomic observations of the brain in autism. In M. L. Bauman and T. L. Kemper (Eds.), *The Neurobiology of Autism.* Baltimore: Johns Hop-kins University Press.

Beadle-Brown, J., Murphy, G., and Wing, L. (2005). Long-term outcome for people with severe intellectual disabilities: Impact of social impairment. *American Journal of Mental Retarda-tion,* 110(1), 1–12.

Beckwith, L., and Cohen, S. E. (1992). Maternal responsiveness with preterm infants and later competency. In M. H. Bornstein (Ed.), *Maternal Responsiveness: Characteristics and Conse-quences. New Directions for Child Development,* 43, 75–87.

Belmonte, M. K., (2000.) Abnormal attention in autism shown by steady-state visual evoked potentials. *Autism*, 4, 269–285.

Belmonte, M. K., Cook, E. H., Anderson, G. M., Rubenstein, J. L. R., Greenough, W. T., Beckel-Mitchener, A. et al. (2004). Autism as a disorder of neural information processing: directions for research and targets for therapy. *Molecular Psychiatry*, 9(7), 646–663.

Belmonte, M. K., and Yurgelan-Todd, D. K. (2003). Functional anatomy of impaired selective attention and compensatory processing in autism. *Cognitive Brain Research*, 17, 651–664.

Bernieri, F. J. (1988). Coordinated movement and rapport in teacher-student interactions. *Journal of Nonverbal Behavior*; 12(2), 120–138.

Bigelow, A. E., and Birch, S. A. J. (1999). The effects of contingency in previous interactions on infants' preference for social partners. *Infant Behavior and Development*, 22(3), 367–382.

Bluestone, J. (2004) *The Fabric of Autism: Weaving the Threads into a Cogent Theory*. Seattle: The Handle Institute.

Boucher, J., and Lewis, V. (1992). Unfamiliar face recognition in relatively able autistic children. *Journal of Child Psychology and Psychiatry*, 33, 843–859.

Bronfenbrenner, U. (1979). *The Ecology of Human Development*. Cambridge, MA: Harvard University Press.

Brunner, J. (1977). Early social interaction and language acquisition. In: H. R. Schaffer (Ed.), *Studies in Mother-Infant Interaction*. New York: Academic Press.

Bryson, S. E., Wainwright-Sharp, J. A., and Smith, I. M. (1990). Autism: A developmental spatial neglect syndrome. In: J. Enns (Ed.), *The Development of Attention: Research and Theory* (pp. 405–427). North Holland: Elsevier.

Casanova, M. F., and Buxhoeveden, D. P. (2002). Minicolumnar pathology in autism. *Neurology*, 58, 428–432.

Carbone, E. (2001). Arranging the classroom with an eye (and ear) to students with ADHA. *Teaching Exceptional Children*, 34(2), 72–81.

Castelii, F., Frith, C., Happe, F., and Frith, U. (2002). Autism, Asperger syndrome and brain mechanisms for the attribution of mental states to animated figures. *Brain*, 125, 1839–1849.

Charlop, M .H., Kurtz, P. F., and Casey, F. G. (1990). Using aberrant be-
    haviors as reinforcers for autistic children. *Journal of Ap-
    plied Behavior Analysis*, 23, 163–181.

Chartrand, T. L., and Bargh, J. A. (1999). The chameleon effect: The
    perception-behavior link and social interaction. *Journal of
    Personality and Social Psychology*, 76, 893–910.

Cohen, D. J., and Johnson, W. T. (1977). Cardiovascular correlates of at-
    tention in normal and psychiatrically disturbed children.
    Archives of General Psychiatry, 34, 561–567.

Colman, R. S., Frankel, F., Rivito, E., and Freeman, B. J. (1976). The ef-
    fects of fluorescent and incandescent illumination upon re-
    petitive behaviors in autistic children. *Journal of Autism
    and Developmental Disorders*, 6(2), 157–162.

Courchesne, E., Chisum, H., and Townsend, J. (1995). Neural activity-
    dependent brain changes in development: Implications
    for psychopathology. *Development and Psychopathology*, 6,
    697–722.

Critchley, H. D., Daly, E. M., Bullmore, E. T., Williams, S. C. R., van
    Amelsvoort, T., Robertson, D. M. et al. (2000). The func-
    tional neuroanatomy of social behavior: changes in cerebral
    blood flow when people with autistic disorder process facial
    expressions. *Brain*, 123, 2203–2212.

Dawson G. (1991). A psychobiological perspective on the early socio-
    emotional development of children with autism. In: S. Toth
    and D. Cicchetti (Eds.), *Rochester Symposium on Develop-
    mental Psychopathology* (Vol. 3, pp. 207–234). Mahwah, NJ:
    Erlbaum.

Dawson, G., and Adams, A. (1984). Imitation and social responsiveness
    in autistic children. *Journal of Abnormal Child Psychology*,
    12(2), 209–226.

Dawson, G., and Galpert, L. (1990). Mothers' use of imitative play for fa-
    cilitating social responsiveness and toy play in young autis-
    tic children. *Development and Psychopathology*, 2, 151–162.

Dawson, G., and Lewy, A. (1989), Arousal, attention and the socio-
    emotional impairments of individuals with autism. In:
    G. Dawson (Ed.), *Autism, Nature, Diagnosis and Treatment*
    (pp. 49–74). New York: Guilford.

Dawson, G., Toth, K., Abbott, R., Osterling, J., Munson, J., Estes, A. et al.
    (2004). Early social attention impairments in autism: Social

orienting, joint attention, and attention to distress. *Developmental Psychology*, 40(2), 271–283.

Dawson, G., Webb, S. J., Carver, L., Panagiotides, H., and McPartland, J. (2004). Young children with autism show atypical brain responses to fearful versus neutral expressions of emotion. *Developmental Science*, 7(3), 340–359.

Delprato, D. J. (2001). Comparisons of discrete-trial and normalized behavioral language interventions for young children. *Journal of Autism and Developmental Disorders*, 31(3), 315–325.

Dissanayake, C., Sigman, M., and Kasari, C. (1996). Long-term stability of individual differences in the emotional responsiveness of children with autism. *Journal of Child Psychology and Psychiatry*, 36, 1–8.

Eimas, P., Siqueland, E., Jusczyk, P., and Vigorito, J. (1971). Speech perception in infants. *Science*, 171, 303–306.

Field, T., Field, T., Sanders, C., and Nadel, J. (2001). Children with autism display more social behaviors after repeated imitation sessions. *Autism*, 5(3), 317–323.

Frith, U., and Happe, F. (1994). Language and communication in autistic disorders. *Philosophical Transactions: Biological Sciences*, 346(1315), 97–104.

Gerland, G. (1997). *A Real Person: Life on the Outside* (trans. J. Tate), London: Souvenir Press.

Gergely, G., and Watson, J. S. (1999). Early socio-emotional development: Contingency perception and the social bio-feedback model In: P. Rochat (Ed.), *Early Social Cognition: Understanding Others in the First Months of Life* (pp. 1001–1136). Mahwah, NJ: Erlbaum.

Gillingham, G. (1995) *Autism: Handle with Care.* London: Future Horizons.

Goren, C. C., Sarty, M., and Wu, P. Y. (1975). Visual following and pattern discrimination of face-like stimuli by newborn infants. *Pediatrics*, 56(4), 544–549.

Goldsmith, D. F., and Rogoff, B. (1997). Mothers' and toddlers' coordinated joint focus of attention: Variations with maternal dysphoric symptoms. *Developmental Psychology*, 33, 113–119.

Grandin, T. (1986). *Emergence: Labeled autistic.* Novato, CA: Arena Press.

Greenspan, S. I., and Wieder, S. (1998). *The Child with Special Needs: Encouraging Intellectual and Emotional Growth*. Cambridge, MA: Perseus Publishing.

Haith, M. M., Bergman, T., and Moore, M. J. (1979). Eye contact and face scanning in early infancy. *Science*, 198, 853–855.

Happe, F. (1999). Autism: cognitive deficit or cognitive style? *Trends in Cognitive Neurosciences*, 3(6), 216–222.

Heider, F., and Simmel, M. (1994). An experimental study of apparent behavior. *American Journal of Psychology*, 57, 243–259.

Hirstein, W., Iverson, P., and Ramachandran, V. S. (2001). Autonomic responses of autistic children in response to people and objects. *Proceedings of the Royal Society of London B*, 268, 1883–1888.

Hobson, R. P., Ouston, J., and Lee, A. (1988) What's in a face? The case of autism. *British Journal of Psychology*, 79, 441–453.

Hogan, B., and Hogan, W. (2004). *The Son-Rise Program Social Developmental Model*. Sheffield, MA: Autism Treatment Center of America (available from the authors).

Hutt, C., and Hutt, S. J. (1970.) Stereotypies and their relation to arousal: A study of autistic children. In: C. Hutt and Hutt S. J. (Eds.), *Behavior Studies in Psychiatry* (pp. 175–204). New York: Pergammon Press.

Hutt, C., Hutt, S. J., Lee, D., and Ounsted, C. (1964). Arousal and childhood autism. *Nature*, 28(204), 908–909.

Infant Health and Development Program (1990), Enhancing the outcomes of low birthweight, premature infants: A multi-site randomized trial. *Journal of the American Medical Association*, 263, 3035–3042.

Johnson, M. H., Halit, H., Grice, S. J., and Karmiloff-Smith, A. (2002). Neuroimaging of typical and atypical development: A perspective from multiple levels of analysis. *Developmental Psychopathology*, 41, 521–536.

Jolliffe, T., and Baron-Cohen, S. (1997). Are people with autism and Asperger syndrome faster than normal on the Embedded Figures Test? *Journal of Child Psychology and Psychiatry*, 38, 527–534.

Jones, R. S. P., Quigney, C., and Huws, J. C. (2003). First-hand accounts of sensory perceptual experiences in autism: A qualitative analysis. *Journal of Intellectual and Developmental Disability*, 28(2), 112–121.

Kaiser, A. P., and Hancock, T. B. (2003). Teaching parents new skills to support their young children's development. *Infants and Young Children*, 16(1), 9–21.

Kaiser, L. K., Carter, C. M., and Koegel, R. L. (2003). Teaching children with autism self-initiations as a pivotal response. *Topics in Language Disorders*, 23(2), 134–145.

Kanner, L. (1943). Autistic disturbances of affective content. *Nervous Child*, 2, 217–225.

Kasari, C., Sigman, M., Mundy, P., and Yirmiya, N. (1990). Affective sharing in the context of joint attention interactions of normal, autistic and mentally retarded children. *Journal of Autism and Developmental Disorders*, 20, 87–100.

Kaufman, B. N. (1976). *Son-Rise*. New York: Harper-Collins.

Kaufman, B. N. (1981). *A Miracle to Believe In*. New York: Ballantine Books.

Kaufman, B. N. (1994). *Son-Rise: The Miracle Continues*. Tiburon, CA: H. J. Kramer Inc.

Kemner, C., Verbaten, M. N., Cuperus, J. M., et al. (1995). Auditory event-related brain potentials in autistic children and three different control groups. *Biological Psychiatry*, 38, 150–65.

Kemner, C., Verbaten, M. N., Cuperus, J. M., Camfferman, G., and van Engeland, H. (1994). Visual and somatosensory event-related brain potentials in autistic children and three different control groups. *EEG Clinical Neurophysiology*, 4, 269–285.

Kim, J., and Mahoney, G. (2004). The effects of mother's style of interaction on children's engagement: Implications for using responsive interventions with parents. *Topics in Early Childhood Special Education*, 24(1), 31–38.

Klin, A. (1991). Young autistic children's listening preferences in regard to speech: A possible characterization of the symptom of social withdrawal. *Journal of Autism and Developmental Disorders*, 21, 29–42.

Klin A. (1992). Listening preferences in regard to speech in four children with developmental disabilities. *Journal of Child Psychology and Psychiatry*, 33, 763–769.

Klin, A., Jones, W., Schultz, R., and Volkmar, F. (2003). The enactive mind, or from actions to cognition: lessons from Autism. *Phil. Trans. R. Soc. Lond. B*, 358, 345–360.

Klin, A., Sparrow, S. S., de Bildt, A., Cicchetti, D. V. Cohen, D. J., and Volkmar, F. R. (1999). A normed study of face recognition in autism and related disorders. *Journal of Autism and Developmental Disorders*, 29, 497–507.

Klin A., Volkmar F. R., and Sparrow, S. S. (1992). Autistic social dysfunction: some limitations of the theory of mind hypothesis. *Journal of Child Psychology and Psychiatry*, 33, 861–876.

Koegel, R. L., Dyer, K., and Bell, L. K. (1987) The influence of child-preferred activities on autistic children's social behavior. *Journal of Applied Behavior Analysis*; 20(3): 243–252.

Koegel, R. L., Koegel, L. K., and Carter, C. M. (1998). Pivotal responses and the natural language teaching paradigm. *Seminars in Speech and Language*, 19(4), 355–371.

Koegel, R. L., Koegel, L. K., and Carter, C. M. (1999.) Pivotal teaching interactions for children with autism. *School Psychology Review*, 28, 576–594.

Koegel, R. L., Koegel, L. K., and McNerney, E. K. (2001). Pivotal areas in intervention for autism. *Journal of Clinical Child Psychology*, 30(1), 19–32.

Koegel, L. K., Koegel, R. L., Shosan, Y., and McNerny, E. (1999). Pivotal Response Intervention II: Preliminary long-term outcome data. *Journal of the Associations for Persons with Severe Handicaps*, 24(3), 186–198.

Kootz, J. P., and Cohen, D. J. (1981). Modulation of sensory intake in autistic children: cardiovascular and behavioral indices. *Journal of the American Academy of Child Psychiatry*, 20(4), 692–701.

Kootz, J. P., Marinelli, B., and Cohen, D. J. (1982). Modulation of response to environmental stimulation in autistic children. *Journal of Autism and Developmental Disorders*, 12(2), 185–193.

Langdell, T. (1978) Recognition of faces: An approach to the study of autism. *Journal of Child Psychology and Psychiatry*, 19(3), 255–268.

Larkin, J. L., and Chartrand, T. L. (2003). Using nonconscious behavioral mimicry to create affiliation and rapport. *Psychological Science*, 14(4), 334–339.

Larkin, J. L., Jefferis, V. E., Cheng, C. M., and Chartrand, T. L. (2003). The chameleon effect as social glue: Evidence for the evolutionary significance of nonconscious mimicry. *Journal of Nonverbal Behavior*, 27(3), 145–162.

Lewis, M. H., Baumeister, A. A., and Mailman, R. B. (1987). A neurobiological alternative to the perceptual reinforcement hypothesis of stereotyped behavior: A commentary on "Self-stimulatory behavior and perceptual reinforcement." *Journal of Applied Behavioral Analysis*, 20(3), 253–258.

Lewis, M., and Goldberg, S. (1969). Perceptual-cognitive development in infancy: A generalized expectancy model as a function of the mother-infant interaction. *Merrill-Palmer Quarterly*, 15, 81–100.

Lord, C. (1995) Follow-up of two-year-olds referred for possible autism. *Journal of Child Psychology and Psychiatry*, 36(8): 1365–1382.

Lovaas, O. I., Koegal, R. L., Simmons, J. Q., and Long, J. S. (1973). Some generalizations and follow-up measures on autistic children in behavior therapy. *Journal of Applied Behavior Analysis*, 6, 131–166.

MacDonald, J. D. (1989.) *Becoming partners with children: From play to conversation*. San Antonio, TX: Special Press.

MacDonald, J. (2004). *Communicating Partners*. London: Jessica Kingsley Publishers.

Maestro, S., Muratori, F., Cavallaro, M. C., Pei, F., Stern, D., Golse, B., and Palacio Espas, F. (2002). Attentional skills during the first 6 months of age in autism spectrum disorder. *Journal of the American Academy of Child and Adolescent Psychiatry*, 41(10), 1239–1245.

Mahoney, G. (1992). *The Maternal Behavior Rating Scale—Revised*. Cleveland. OH: Case Western Reserve University (available from the author).

Mahoney, G., Boyce, G., Fewell, R., Spiker, D., and Wheeden, C. A. (1998). The relationship of parent-child interaction to the effectiveness of early intervention services for at-risk children and children with disabilities. *Topics in Early Childhood Special Education*, 18, 5–17.

Mahoney, G., and Perales, F. (2003). Using relationship-focused intervention to enhance the socio-emotional functioning of young children with autism spectrum disorders. *Topics in Early Childhood Special Education*, 23, 74–86.

Mahoney, G., and Perales, F. (2005). Relationship-focused early intervention with children with pervasive developmental disorders and other disabilities: A comparative study. *Developmental and Behavioral Pediatrics*; 26(2), 77–85.

Malatesta, C., and Izard, C. (1984). The ontogenesis of human social signals: From biological imperative to symbol utilization. In: N. Fox and R. Davidson (Eds.), *The Psychobiology of Affective Disturbance* (pp.106–216). Hillsdale, NJ: Erlbaum.

Manolson, A. (1995). *You Make a Difference in Helping Your Child Learn*. Toronto: Hanen Centre.

Militerni, R., Bravaccio, C., Falco, C., Fico, C., and Palerno, M. T. (2002). Repetitive behaviors in autistic disorder. *European Child and Adolescent Psychiatry*, 11(5), 210–218.

Mills, M., and Melhuish, E. (1974). Recognition of mother's voice in early infancy. *Nature*, 252, 123–124.

Mottron, L., Belleville, S., and Menard, E. (2000). Local bias in autistic subjects as evidenced by graphic tasks: Perceptual hierarchization or working memory deficit? *Journal of Child Psychology and Psychiatry*, 40(5), 743–755.

Mundy, P., Sigman, M., and Kasari, C. (1990). A longitudinal study of joint attention and language development in autistic children. *Journal of Autism and Developmental Disorders*, 20, 115–128.

Mundy, P., Sigman, M., Kasari, C. (1992). Joint attention, affective sharing and infant intersubjectivity. *Infant Behavior and Development*, 15, 377–381.

Nadel, J. (1992). Imitation et communication chez l'enfant autiste et le jeune enfant prélangagier. In: J. Hochman and P. Ferrari (Eds.), *Imitation et Identification chez l'Enfant Autiste* (pp. 1–5). Paris: Bayard.

Nadel, J., Guerini, C., Peze, A., and Rivet, C. (1999). The evolving nature of imitation as a format for communication. In: Nadel, J., and Butterworth, G. (Eds), *Imitation in Infancy* (pp. 209–234). Cambridge: Cambridge University Press.

Nadel, J., and Peze, A. (1993). Immediate imitation as a basis for primary communication in toddlers and autistic children. In: J. Nadel and L. Camiono (Eds.), *New Perspectives in Early Communicative Development* (pp. 139–156). London: Routledge.

Nelson, K. B., Grether, J. K., Croen, L. A., Dambrosia, J. M., Dickens, B. F., Jelliffe, I. L. et al. (2001). Neuropeptides and neurotrophins in neonatal blood of children with autism or mental retardation. *Annals of Neurology,* 46, 597–606.

Nijhof, G., Joha, D., and Pekelharing, H. (1998). Aspects of stereotypic behavior among autistic persons: A study of the literature. *British Journal of Developmental Disorders,* 44(1), 3–13.

Osterling, J., and Dawson, G. (1994). Early recognition of children with autism: A study of first birthday party home videotapes. *Journal of Autism and Developmental Disorders,* 24, 247–257.

Osterling, J., Dawson, G., and Munson, J. (2002). Early recognition of one year old infants with autism spectrum disorders versus mental retardation: A study of first birthday party home videotapes. *Development of Psychopathology,* 14, 239–252.

Panksepp, J., Nelson, E., and Siviy, S. (1994). Brain opioids and mother-infant social motivation. *Acta Paediatrica Suppliment,* 397, 40–46.

Papousek, H., and Papousek, M. (1977). Mothering and cognitive head-start: Psychobiological considerations. In: H. R. Schaffer (Ed.), *Studies in Mother-Infant Interaction: The Loch Lomand Symposium* (pp. 63–85). London: Academic Press.

Pelphrey, K. A., Sasson, N., Reznick, S., Paul, G., Goldman, B. D., and Piven, J, (2004). Visual scanning of faces in autism. *Journal of Autism and Developmental Disorders,* 32 (4), 249–261.

Piaget, J. (1952). *The Origins of Intelligence in Children.* New York: International Universities Press.

Piaget, J. (1963). *The Psychology of Intelligence.* Totowa, NJ: Littlefield, Adams.

Pierce, K., Muller, R-A., Ambrose, J., Allen, G., and Courchesne, E. (2001). Face processing occurs outside the fusiform "face area" in autism: Evidence from functional MRI. *Brain,* 124, 2059–2073.

Raymond, G. V., Vauman, M. L., and Kemper, T. L. (1996), Hippocampus in autism: A Golgi analysis. *Acta Neuropathologica,* 91, 117–119.

Reiber, C., and McLaughlin, T. F. (2004), Classroom interventions: Methods to improve academic performance and classroom behavior for students with attention-deficit/hyperactivity disorder. *International Journal of Special Education*, 19(1), 1–13.

Ring, H., Baron-Cohen, S., Wheelwright, S., Williams, S., Brammer, M., Andrew, C. et al. (1999). Cerebral correlates of preserved cognitive skills in autism: A functional MRI study of Embedded Figures Task performance. *Brain*, 122, 1305–1315.

Rogers, S. J., and Pennington, B. F. (1991). A theoretical approach to the deficits in infantile autism. *Developmental Psychopathology*, 3, 137–162.

Rollins, P. R. (1999). Early pragmatic accomplishments and vocabulary development in preschool children with autism. *American Journal of Speech Language Pathology*, 8, 181–190.

Rollins, P. R., and Snow, C. E. (1998), Shared attention and grammatical development in typical children and children with autism. *Journal of Child Language*, 25, 653–673.

Schilling, D. L., and Schwartz, I. S. (2004). Alternative seating for young children with autism spectrum disorder: Effects on classroom behavior. *Journal of Autism and Developmental Disorders*, 34(4), 423–432.

Schultz, R. T. (2005). Developmental deficits in social perception in autism: The role of the amygdala and fusiform face area. *International Journal of Developmental Neuroscience*, 23, 125–141.

Schultz, R. T., Romanski, L., and Tsatsanis, K. (2000). Neurofunctional models of autistic disorder and Asperger's syndrome: clues from neuroimaging. In: A. Klin, F. R. Volkmar, and Sparrow, S. S. (Eds.), *Asperger's Syndrome* (pp. 179–209). Plenum Press: New York.

Shah, A., and Frith, U. (1983). An islet of ability in autism: A research note. *Journal of Child Psychology and Psychiatry*, 24, 613–20.

Sheinkopf, S. J., and Siegel, B. (1998), Home-base behavioral treatment of young children with autism. *Journal of Autism and Developmental Disorders*, 28(1), 15–23.

Sherman, J., Barker, P., Lorimer, P., Swinson, R., and Factor, D. C. (1987). Treatment of autistic children: Relative effectiveness of residential, out-patient and home-based interventions. *Child Psychiatry and Human Development*, 19(2), 109–125.

Siegel, D. J. (2001). Toward an interpersonal neurobiology of the developing mind: Attachment relationships, "mindsight" and neural integration. *Infant Mental Health*, 22 (1–2), 67–94.

Sigman, M., and Ruskin, E. (1997). Joint attention in relation to language acquisition and social skills in children with autism. Paper presented at the Society for Research in Child Development. Washington, DC. Cited in: Mundy, P., and Markus, J. (1997). On the nature of communication and language impairment in autism. *Mental Retardation and Developmental Disabilities Research Reviews*, 3(4), 343–349.

Siller, M., and Sigman, M. (2002). The behaviors of parents of children with autism predict the subsequent development of their children's communication. *Journal of Autism and Developmental Disorders*, 32 (2), 77–89.

Simion, F., Valenza, E., Umilta, C., and Dalla Barba, B. (1998). Preferential orienting to faces in newborns: A temporal-nasal asymmetry. *Journal of Experimental Psychology Human Perception and Performance*, 24(5), 1399–1405.

Spiker, D., Boyce, G. C., and Boyce, L. K. (2002). Parent-child interactions when young children have disabilities. *International Review of Research in Mental Retardation*, 25, 35–70.

Stern, D. N. (1977). *The first relationship: Infant and mother.* Cambridge MA: Harvard University Press.

Thelen, E. (1979). Rhythmical stereotypies in normal human infants. *Animal Behavior*, 27, 699–715.

Tiegerman, E., and Primavera, L. H. (1982). Object manipulation: An interactional strategy with autistic children. *Journal of Autism and Developmental Disorders*, 11(4), 427–438.

Tiegerman, E., and Primavera, L. H. (1984). Imitating the autistic child: Facilitating communicative gaze behavior. *Journal of Autism and Developmental Disorders*, 14(1): 27–38.

Tomasello, M. (1995). Joint attention as social cognition. In: C. Moore and P. Dunham (Eds.), *Joint Attention: Its Origins and Role in Development* (pp. 103–130). NJ: Hillsdale, Erlbaum.

Tordjman, S., Anderson, G. M., McBride, P. A., Hertzig, M. E., Snow, M. E., Hall, L. M. et al. (1997). Plasma beta-endorphin, adrenocorticotropin hormone, and cortisol in autism. *Journal of Child Psychology and Psychiatry*, 38(6), 705–15.

Townsend, J., and Courchesne, E. (1994). Parietal damage and narrow "spot-light" spatial attention. *Journal of Cognitive Neuroscience*, 6, 220–232.

Trevarthan, C., and Aitken, K. (2001). Infant intersubjectivity: Research, theory and clinical applications. *Journal of Child Psychology*, 42(1), 3–48.

Trivette, C. M. (2003). Influence of caregiver responsiveness on the development of young children with or at risk for developmental disabilities. *Bridges*, 1(3), 1–13.

Turner, M. (1999). Repetitive behavior in autism: A review of psychological research. *Journal of Child Psychology and Psychiatry and Allied Disciplines*, 40, 839–849.

Uzgiris, I .C. (1981). Two functions of imitation during infancy. *International Journal of Behavioral Development*, 4, 1–12.

Vygotsky, L. S. (1978). *Mind in Society: The Development of Higher Psychological Processes* (Trans. and Eds. M. Cole, V. John-Steiner, S. Scribner, and E. Soubourne). Cambridge, MA: Harvard University Press.

Weeks, S., and Hobson, R. (1987). The salience of facial expressions for autistic children. *Journal of Child Psychology and Psychiatry*, 28, 137–151.

Werner, E., Dawson, G., Osterling, J., and Dinno, H. (2000). Recognition of autism spectrum disorder before one year of age: A retrospective study based on home videotapes. *Journal of Autism and Developmental Disorders*, 30, 157–162.

Wertsch, J. (1985). *Culture, Communication and Cognition: Vygotskian Perspectives*. Cambridge: Cambridge University Press.

Willemsen-Swinkels, S., Buitelaar, J. K., Dekker, M., and van Engeland, H. (1998). Subtyping stereotypic behavior in children: The association between stereotypic behavior, mood and heart rate. *Journal of Autism and Developmental Disorders*, 28(6), 547–557.

Williams, D. (1988). *Autism and Sensing*. London: Jessica Kingsley Publishers.

Williams, D. (1994). *Nobody Nowhere*. New York: Perennial.

Williams, K. (2004). The Son-Rise Program Intervention for Autism: An Investigation into Prerequisites for Evaluation and Family Experiences. PhD Summary, University of Edinburgh, UK.

APPENDIX 2

COMPARISON OF APPLIED BEHAVIOR ANALYSIS AND THE SON-RISE PROGRAM

This appendix is designed to provide you with a summary of the differences between The Son-Rise Program (SRP) and applied behavioral analysis (ABA). The two methodologies fall on opposite ends of the autism treatment spectrum, with ABA at the behavioral end and SRP at the social-relational end.

The appendix includes:

- A table listing some key differences
- A more in-depth discussion of these differences
- Links to ten "commercials" that playfully and humorously pinpoint these key differences—filmed in the style of the famous Mac versus PC television commercials
- A link to a ninety-minute webcast where I discuss these differences in detail

I understand that some of these items may be controversial. An ABA practitioner may see the distinctions between the two methodologies differently than I do. And not all ABA practitioners—or versions of ABA—are the same. However, all versions of applied behavior analysis (the middle word is "behavior," after all) rest upon the same fundamental concept (changing behavior through reinforcers) and question (how to eliminate behaviors we don't want and promote behaviors we do want). As well, we at the Autism Treatment Center of America—and I personally—have received many glowing written responses from ABA practitioners expressing excitement, delight, and great respect for the principles and techniques of The Son-Rise Program. Many have said that their exposure to these principles has permanently and completely altered their way of seeing and treating children on the autism spectrum.

Wherever you stand, I hope that you find the items useful and thought-provoking.

APPLIED BEHAVIOR ANALYSIS VS.
THE SON-RISE PROGRAM

Applied Behavior Analysis	Son-Rise Program
Understanding of Autism	
Sees autism as a **behavioral disorder**, with behaviors to be either extinguished or reinforced	Sees autism as a **social interactivity disorder**, where the central deficit is relating to other people
The child needs **structure** and must learn to sit appropriately, follow a schedule, and comply with requests	Helping the child to be **flexible and spontaneous** enables him/her to handle change and enjoy human interaction
Area of Focus	
Changing the behavior of the child	**Creating a relationship** with the child
Seeks to **"extinguish"** the child's repetitive "stimming" **behavior**	Uses **"joining"** technique to participate in the child's repetitive **behavior**
Method of Teaching New Skills	
Repetition: Uses discrete trials or similar method to prompt the child to perform a behavior (followed by a reward) over and over again until the child has demonstrated mastery	**Motivation:** Builds the child's own interests into every game or activity so that the child is excited, "comes back for more," generalizes skills, and relates naturally rather than robotically
Areas of Learning	
Often focuses on **academic skills**	Always teaches **socialization** first
Sees academic areas such as maths as an excellent way to help the child **compensate** for lack of social skills	Seeks to help the child **overcome** social skills deficits

Role of the Parents	
Professionals are the major players, with parents having a more observational role	**Parents are given the most central role** because their love, dedication, and experience with their child is unmatched

Facilitator's Attitude	
Sees attitude as largely irrelevant, with effective application of behavior-shaping techniques being what matters	**Sees attitude as vitally important**, since having a nonjudgmental and welcoming attitude determines whether the child feels safe and relaxed enough to interact and learn

UNDERSTANDING OF AUTISM

ABA treats autism as a behavioral disorder, with behaviors to be either extinguished or promoted. This means that repetitive, exclusive "stimming" behaviors common to children with autism are not permitted during learning sessions, "correct" behaviors are rewarded, sometimes with food, and new skills and behaviors are taught through structured repetition sometimes referred to as "discreet trials."

The Son-Rise Program sees autism as a social relational disorder. The central deficit of children on the autism spectrum is that they have difficulty connecting with and relating to other people. Almost all other difficulties spring from this primary challenge. Therefore, we do not seek to "correct" so-called inappropriate behaviors in the absence of a deeply bonded relationship. Rather, we endeavor to build a relationship with each child—a relationship that is the platform for all future education and development. We then help our children learn to connect and build relationships with others and to genuinely enjoy such interaction. All skills we teach are addressed within the context of our focus on human interaction.

We also believe that each child has a reason for every behavior they perform. Rather than forcing children to conform to a world they do not yet understand, we enter their world first. We seek to understand so that we can be most effective in helping the child. In The Son-Rise Program, the children show us the way in, and then we show them the way out.

Area of Focus

The focal points of each program are based upon how we see autism. In simple terms, ABA focuses on changing behavior; The Son-Rise Program focuses on creating a relationship.

An ABA facilitator might punish, reprimand, or attempt to discourage or redirect a repetitive or aggressive behavior. Compliance is seen as very important. Of course, there are a range of ABA-type programs and facilitators out there. Some using strong punishments of behaviors and others using much gentler forms of discouragement, but the overall focus is the same: behavior change and compliance with the requests of the facilitator. New behaviors and skills are often taught using a system based upon repetition and rewards sometimes called discreet trials, which will be discussed in more detail below.

In The Son-Rise Program, we consistently seek to built rapport and relationships with our children. One critical way in which we do this is called *joining*. Instead of prohibiting or discouraging repetitive, "autistic" behavior, we actually *participate* in these activities with the child. Far from reinforcing "autistic" behaviors (a concern voiced by some), we have seen, with thousands of children from around the world, the exact opposite. When children are joined, they tend to look at us more, pay more attention to us, and include us more in their activity. We see such children "stimming" less and interacting more. After all, we are building a stronger and stronger bond with the child, and at the same time, by showing genuine interest and participation in what is important to the child, we are actually teaching the very interpersonal skills that many of our children lack. When we have the child's willing engagement, we then use a variety of motivational and educational techniques to promote learning and skill acquisition.

Repetition vs. Motivation

With ABA, when attempting to teach a particular behavior or skill (such as getting dressed, to use a simple example), discreet trials are often used. With this methodology, a child might be told (or made) to sit in a chair. The facilitator would then say "coat on" and endeavor to train the child to put his coat on, doing this over and over again until the child has "mastered" the skill. Each time the child gets it right, he would get praise, a piece of food, or some other reward. While this approach can definitely succeed at getting some children to perform particular activities or skills, a common complaint we hear from parents is that, although their children perform the prescribed activity, they tend to do so in a manner that appears robotic and preprogrammed, rather than displaying any kind of spontaneity or enthusiasm. A second difficulty that we see is that many children, after participating in this program over a period of time, learn to loathe what they are being trained to do and can become aggressive and rebellious. A third drawback is that children get much of their training free of context (learning, for instance, to put their coats on when told rather than when it is cold out), often resulting in them learning compliance rather than the real skill (thus lacking the ability to generalize the skill).

In The Son-Rise Program, we want each child to "come back for more." This means that we want the child's willing engagement over time, so that we can teach them all that they need to learn and so that they value and enjoy interaction. We also see the importance of children being able to generalize learned skills to other areas, so that they don't need prompts, rewards, or our presence to act on what they've learned. Therefore, we do not want to continually repeat commands when the child, in all likelihood, does not understand *why* she is being asked to do this.

Consistently, we have found that motivation works faster and more powerfully and promotes greater generalization than repetition does. If a child likes a particular toy or physical movement or numbers, then we use this motivation as a teaching tool by combining it with an educational goal. For instance, if a child likes Thomas the Tank Engine and one of our educational goals is toilet training, we would construct a game that centered around Thomas and involved using the toilet. In this way, we create a desire to learn and use a skill (going to the toilet), and we keep the interaction with the child alive and well (and fun). An additional benefit of this approach is that it does not tend to produce a robotic, preprogrammed response because children get genuinely excited about the learning process. For this reason (as well as because of joining and the attitudinal component, described below), we also do not see children becoming aggressive or rebellious from participating in The Son-Rise Program.

Structure vs. Spontaneity

In ABA, a high premium is placed on structure. It is important for children to sit still in a seat and perform activities in a prescribed, regulated fashion. The thought behind this is that children on the autism spectrum need this kind of structure. Also, if they are to ever participate in school, they must learn to sit appropriately, obey a schedule, and comply with requests from the teacher.

In The Son-Rise Program, we see it differently. If children are to be successful in school and in life, what is most important for them to learn is to interact with others, make their own decisions, and be *flexible* (something which many children with autism have difficulty with). Because of this, we spend our time engaging in interactive games (when we aren't joining). In addition to teaching interaction and socialization, these games challenge children to be more flexible (rather than needing things to go a particular way) and to use their imagination to come up with different ideas and directions on the fly. We also keep the games fun, so that our children see that participating in our world (versus staying in their own) is both enjoyable and useful, rather than rigid and demanding.

Academic vs. Social Development

ABA practitioners tend to focus heavily on academic skills such as reading, writing, and math (in addition to verbal communication and basic "appropriate" behavior). We in The Son-Rise Program would certainly agree that such skills are important. However, if choosing between helping a child to be great at maths and or to be great at making friends, we choose the latter every time. In actual fact, academic and social skills are not mutually exclusive, and there are many instances where we do teach reading, writing, and maths. When we do, though, it is always in the context of an activity that teaches socialization first. If our children can learn to enjoy people, make friends, laugh at a funny joke, socialize, etc. (which many of our children do), then they have achieved what, for most of us, makes life most meaningful.

The Role of the Parents

ABA has many dedicated practitioners who often work with children in their own homes. The way the programs generally work, though, is that parents tend to be in a more observational role in their programs. The professionals are seen, in most cases, as the major players in the program, with parents watching on the side so that the practitioners can do their jobs.

We in The Son-Rise Program have seen nothing that matches the motivation, love, dedication, and lifelong commitment possessed by parents for their special children. Furthermore, no one has the kind of long-term, day-to-day experience *with their own particular child* that parents possess. Without question, professionals and other family members can be critically important. At the same time, because of their unique position in their child's world, parents can positively affect their child's life in a way no one else can. Therefore, not only do we acknowledge parents as the child's most important resource, but we seek to empower them to the child's advantage. This is why we teach them how to design, implement, and take a central role in their children's programs.

The Facilitator's Attitude

ABA focuses heavily on *what* the facilitator does. The Son-Rise Program not only focuses on what the facilitator does, but also on *how* the facilitator does it. We address and provide training in an area that we see as the most overlooked factor of autism treatment: the attitude of the facilitator. We see a nonjudgmental and optimistic attitude as crucial to effective child facilitation. What does this mean? First, it means that we don't label our children's repetitive and ritualistic behaviors as inappropriate, wrong, or bad. This principle is every bit as practical as it is idealistic. We see time and again that children with autism tend to move away from people they perceive as uncomfortable or judging and toward people they see as comfortable, easy, fun, safe, and nonjudgmental. Thus, we can use our attitude to become an interaction magnet.

As well, having a sincere sense of optimism—really believing in the child with which one is working—is key to helping that child to break through barriers that previously seemed insurmountable. We do not put limits on any child ahead of time, we do not believe that hope can ever be "false," and we believe in the potential of every child, regardless of age or diagnosis.

Moreover, we believe in the parents who work tirelessly to reach their children. That is why we spend a significant percentage of our time and effort providing parents with attitudinal training. We help them to create and sustain a nonjudgmental, optimistic, and hopeful attitude with their children. In this way, they can maximize their children's progress while finding peace with their children's diagnosis.

TEN HUMOROUS ABA VERSUS THE SON-RISE PROGRAM "COMMERCIALS"

On my website, at www.autismbreakthrough.com/appendix2, are links to ten sixty-second videos that playfully pinpoint the key differences between ABA and The Son-Rise Program. (That's me playing The Son-Rise Program!) These "commercials," which pay homage to the famous Mac versus PC ads, created quite stir when they were first released. I hope you enjoy them.

WEBCAST DISCUSSING DIFFERENCES BETWEEN ABA AND THE SON-RISE PROGRAM

At www.autismbreakthrough.com/appendix2 readers will find a 90-minute webcast, in which I discuss, in great detail, what The Son-Rise Program does differently than ABA and why.

TEN HOLIDAY HICCUPS AND HOW TO AVOID THEM

Ah, the holidays. Special meals. Special family gatherings. And, of course, our special children! Oftentimes, we just barrel through the holidays, hoping for the best but not taking the time and focus to make sure this celebratory time really feels like a celebration for us and for our children on the autism spectrum. Most of us find ourselves unwitting participants in at least one of the ten holiday hiccups.

We know we're in a hiccup when our special child is having more meltdowns . . . when our extended family members appear at a loss . . . or when we, ourselves, feel stressed out or burned out.

We may blame the hectic holidays, but, in reality, it's not the holidays causing the difficulty; it's the pitfalls we accidentally step into. This is great news because it means that our challenges are preventable!

Take a look below at the ten holiday hiccups and how to prevent them. You'll be thanking yourself from now till New Year's!

1. Stopping your child from isming ("stimming")
Given the commotion and changes in routine of the holidays, this is the most important time for our children to be allowed to self-regulate and cope with their environment. We know that isming is crucially important to our children and their nervous systems. Ideally, of course, we would join our children in their isms. But even during the times over the holidays when we aren't able to do this, we can still let our children do their thing. When we do this, everybody wins!

2. Feeding your child "crash and burn" foods
Yes, it's the holidays. Sugary, wheat-filled, dairy-crazy foods abound. It can be tempting to allow our children to partake in this glorious cornucopia. We might think it will be easier to just let them have it this once. Let me assure you: it will not be easier! There are a host of foods that we *know* are not going to be processed well by our children. Yes, the first few minutes of allowing them to eat whatever is around might seem easier. But a few minutes later . . . it's crash-and-burn time. The meltdowns, overeating, challenging behavior, and diarrhea that will result are truly not worth it. Taking the forethought to either keep these foods away from our children or, better yet, not have them around at all will make the whole holiday experience a million times easier.

3. Surprising your child

Sometimes, we can be so busy planning and getting ready for a holiday outing (e.g., going to Grandma's) or project (e.g., putting up the Christmas tree) that we forget to notify a crucial participant: our special child. Although our intention is not to surprise our children, this is often what happens when we depart on an outing or embark on a project without explaining everything that will happen to our children in advance. Even for our nonverbal children, explaining ahead of time what will happen and why it will be fun for them will go a long way toward minimizing tantrums and maximizing cooperation.

4. Leaving no way out

It is very common to go to someone else's house for a holiday celebration. Usually, we just take our child and hope for the best, thinking that we don't have a lot of control over the matter. But we do! We can designate, in advance, a calm room or space where our child can go to decompress once they begin to be overwhelmed by all the commotion and sensory input that comprise most celebrations. Every so often, it can really help to take our child to this room and spend some time alone with her.

5. Focusing on stopping challenging behaviors

Most of us dread our children behaving in a challenging way. We worry about it, we look for it, and we try to stop it as soon as it happens. Ironically, this puts all the focus on what we *don't* want from our children. If we don't want our children to hit, for instance, focusing on "not hitting" can actually create more hitting. Instead, we can celebrate our children every time they do something we do want. If we have a child who sometimes hits, it can make a huge difference to actively look for any time our child is at all gentle—and then cheer wildly!

6. Giving an over-stimulating present

Sure, we derive great joy from the experience of giving presents for our children. But when it comes to our special children, we want to be especially cognizant of what type of present we give. If we give a present with flashing lights and loud beeps, we're asking for challenging behavior later. Let's take some time to sincerely consider whether the gift we are about to give is going to contribute to the overstimulation of our children with sensitive sensory systems.

7. Leaving our children out of the giving process

We always consider our special child when purchasing gifts. But do we think of our special child as a potential *giver* of gifts? Thinking of other people—what they want, what we could do for them—is an essential element of the socialization that we want our children to learn. The holidays provide the perfect opportunity for this! We can schedule sessions with our special child in advance where we help them create something for one or more of the people in his or her life. (These gifts and activities can range from very simple to more complex, depending on our particular child's level of development.) Then, on the day of gift-giving, we can invite our special child to present (as best he can) any gifts that he has made.

8. Expecting your family to "get it"

Many of us may, at times, feel frustrated with members of our extended family for not being more understanding and responsive when it comes to our special child. But remember, if our extended family members don't live with our child, they won't "get it." When taking our special children on visits to extended family for holiday visits, we can send e-mails to them explaining what they can do to make the visit comfortable for us and our child. We can take this opportunity to explain why sudden loud noises might be problematic, or tell everyone the answer our child likes to hear when she asks the same question over and over. This way, we stack the deck in our child's favor.

9. Thinking that activities need to happen outside your home

We know that children on the autism spectrum will always do better when they are not overstimulated by the many sights, sounds, smells, and unpredictable events of the outside world. So we can create experiences in our homes that we would normally go out for. For instance, instead of going to an evening parade with a festival of lights, we can put Christmas or Hanukkah lights around the house, turn off all the lights, and play holiday music at a gentle volume. Some of us might be concerned about depriving our children of fun holiday experiences, but keep in mind that when our children can't digest the experience, they're not having the fun experience we want for them, anyway. That's why, if we can create a digestible version of the outing at home, our children can really take in and enjoy the experience. Thus, we are actually giving our children *more*, not less.

10. Seeing the wrapping instead of the gift

So often, we get caught up in the trappings of the holidays—the tree, the presents, the outings that have to go exactly as planned. It's okay to arrange fun things, but remember that these are only trimmings. They aren't the gift, they're just the wrapping. The gift is our special child. The gift is sharing sweetness with the people we love. Instead of using the holidays as a planning fest, we can use it to see the beauty in our child's uniqueness, to celebrate what our child can do, and to feel and encourage compassion for our child's very different way of experiencing the world.

HELPFUL ORGANIZATIONS

Autism Hope Alliance (AHA): www.autismhopealliance.org

United States Autism & Asperger's Association (USAAA): www.usautism.org

Alert Program®: www.alertprogram.com

American Medical Autism Board (AMAB): www.american medicalautismboard.com

The Listening Program®/Advanced Brain Technologies: www.thelisteningprogram.com

NAA (National Autism Association): www.nationalautism association.org

Talk About Curing Autism (TACA): www.tacanow.org

Medical Academy of Pediatric Special Needs (MAPS): www.medmaps.org

Autism One: www.autismone.org

Generation Rescue: www.generationrescue.org

ACKNOWLEDGMENTS

So many people helped me with this book, and I am so grateful!

For giving me integral, astute, and crucial feedback on ways to make the book better, I thank my sister Bryn, my brother-in-law William, my mom, and, most especially, my dad, who put an enormous amount of time, love, and thought into his detailed thoughts on each and every chapter. And a huge thanks to Bryn again for being my first Son-Rise Program teacher professionally and to my dad for teaching me the ins and outs of facilitating groups, which is now a huge part of my life. And, once again, a deep and abiding gratitude to both of my parents, who not only recovered me from severe autism but have been there for me in a thousand different ways big and small, supporting me and believing in me for my entire life.

A thanks and a cheer for all of the families—talked about and not talked about in the book—who are as much my teachers as my students, allowing me to be part of their wondrous journeys and showing me, in countless ways, what real love looks like.

A jumping-up-and-down thanks to the dedicated, creative, passionate, playful, totally sincere staff of the Autism Treatment Center of America, who love and care for our families like no one else in the world and are the most incredible people to work with!

My most sincere and warm appreciation to Stephanie Tade, the most awesome agent in the universe! With boundless thanks for loving, believing in, and truly "getting" the book from the very beginning—and working tirelessly to get it out to the world.

Gargantuan thanks to Nichole Argyres, my editor from heaven at St. Martin's Press, a very sharp, thoughtful, intelligent, caring, *very* patient, and wonderfully kind woman who made the book better and worked with me in such a sweet way. And a shout-out to Laura Chasen for her gracious help as well!

For publishing, supporting, and championing this book—and for backing it with a spectacular team—I give my heartfelt thanks to St. Martin's Press.

And how could I leave out Mr. Steve Small, my sixth grade English teacher and all-around terrific guy, who first stoked my huge love of writing (and has been a fantastic and caring teacher to my niece!) through kindness, excitement, smarts, support (giving me my first writing award!), and absolute fun. This book started with you!

About the Author

As the former CEO of the Autism Treatment Center of America, Raun K. Kaufman conducts lectures and seminars worldwide. In addition to his work with families and professionals over the past fifteen years, Kaufman brings a distinctive qualification to the realm of autism treatment—his own personal history. As a child, he was diagnosed with severe autism and recommended for lifelong institutionalization. Instead, his parents developed The Son-Rise Program, which enabled their son to completely recover from his autism with no trace of his former condition. His story was recounted in the best-selling book *Son-Rise: The Miracle Continues* and the award-winning NBC-TV movie, *Son-Rise: A Miracle of Love*. Now an international speaker, author, teacher, and graduate of Brown University with a degree in Biomedical Ethics, Kaufman has completed lecture tours in the United States, the United Kingdom, Ireland, the Netherlands, Sweden, Norway, Poland, Spain, and Portugal. He has written articles featured in journals such as *Good Autism Practice* and *The Autism File* and books such as *Silver Linings* and *Cutting-Edge Therapies for Autism 2010–2011*, and he has been interviewed by media such as National Public Radio, BBC Television, Fox News Channel, the London Telegraph, and *People* magazine. Kaufman was the recipient of the Best Presenter award at the national Autism One conference, given to the winner of their nationwide survey. He is currently the Director of Global Education for the Autism Treatment Center of America and serves on the advisory boards of the United States Autism and Asperger's Association (USAAA) and the Autism Hope Alliance (AHA). He cohosts the radio show *Raun and Kristin: Bringing Hope into Your Home* on Autism Approved Radio.

Contact Information
www.autismbreakthrough.com
www.raunkkaufman.com
Autism Treatment Center of America
2080 South Undermountain Road
Sheffield, MA 01257
www.autismtreatment.org
sonrise@autismtreatment.org
1-800-714-2779
1-413-229-2100